THE ROUGH GUIDE TO
BERLIN

ROUGH
GUIDES

This eleventh edition updated by
Paul Sullivan

Contents

OPPOSITE DECKCHAIRS ON THE RIVER SPREE **PREVIOUS PAGE** MEMORIAL TO THE MURDERED JEWS OF EUROPE

Introduction to
Berlin

With its notoriously hedonistic nightlife, tumultuous history and easy-going, cosmopolitan vibe, Berlin is indisputably one of Europe's most compelling cities. Add a generous feeling of physical space (thanks to a rare combination of large-scale urban planning and a relatively low population of just 3.6 million), a cutting-edge cultural scene and the emergence of a buzzy start-up culture, and it's easy to see why so many people are not just visiting the freewheeling German capital but moving here in droves.

Indeed, Berlin's **transformation** since the fall of its notoriously divisive Wall has been nothing short of extraordinary, and its 1989 rebirth is key to understanding the city's youthful vitality. The first wave of post-*Wende* ("turning-point") settlers – artists, squatters, musicians, DJs – set the edgy, alternative tone that still drives the city, despite encroaching gentrification and commercialization. Cheaper than London, liberal, multicultural and still very much at the heart of the European Union, Berlin today has grown into one of Europe's prime destinations for hip young things and entrepreneurial types alike.

Beneath the future-oriented, upbeat veneer, however, remain the poignant **scars** of the turbulent twentieth century, and its onslaught of war, partition and totalitarianism. A wealth of museums and memorials confront the past unflinchingly, commemorating and meticulously documenting the methodologies and crimes of successive authoritarian regimes, though a certain stream of nostalgia still lingers for the lighter aspects of the GDR, which remains vivid in the memories of many older Berliners.

This traumatic history has also taken its toll on the city visually. Not only was much of Berlin, once the grand capital of imperial Prussia, reduced to rubble at the end of World War II but many ugly and uninspired new buildings were thrown up afterwards. Following a second spate of frenetic construction in the immediate wake of the *Wende*, when a host of high-profile architects were commissioned to create an aesthetic suitable for the born-again capital, the city now presents a somewhat chaotic **architectural jigsaw**. It might not always be easy on the eye, but the urban cityscape seems to suit Berlin's slightly dishevelled nature,

ABOVE BERLIN CITYSCAPE AT DUSK

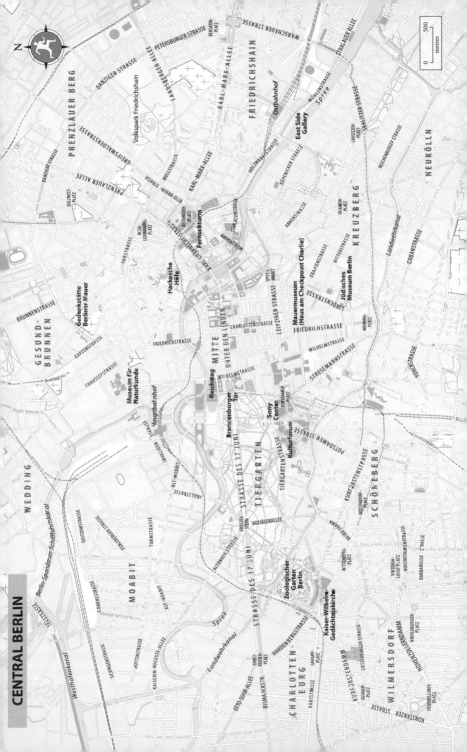

CENTRAL BERLIN

N

0   500
metres

Berlin-Spandauer-Schifffahrtskanal

Westhafenkanal

SECTSTRASSE

WEDDING

GESUND-
BRUNNEN

BRUNNENSTRASSE

DANZIGER STRASSE

PRENZLAUER BERG

PRENZLAUER ALLEE

GREIFSWALDERSTRASSE

KOLLWITZ-
PLATZ

Volkspark Friedrichshain

PETERSBURGER STRASSE

LANDSBERGER ALLEE

KARL-MARX-ALLEE

FRIEDRICHSHAIN

WARSCHAUER STRASSE

BERSEN-
PLATZ

Ostbahnhof

Spree

East Side
Gallery

NEUKÖLLN

STRALAUER ALLEE

KREUZBERG

MOABIT

Gedenkstätte
Berliner Mauer

Hackesche
Höfe

Fernsehturm

ALEXANDER-
PLATZ

KARL-LIEBKNECHT-STRASSE

SPITTEL-
MARKT

Museum für
Naturkunde

Hauptbahnhof

Reichstag

Brandenburger
Tor

MITTE

UNTER DEN LINDEN

FRIEDRICHSTRASSE

CHARLOTTENSTRASSE

LEIPZIGER STRASSE

WILHELMSTRASSE

Mauermuseum
(Haus am Checkpoint Charlie)

Jüdisches
Museum Berlin

FRIEDRICHSTRASSE

ORANIEN-
PLATZ

STRESEMANNSTRASSE

Sony
Center

POTSDAMER
PLATZ

Kulturforum

TIERGARTEN

STRASSE DES 17 JUNI

GROSSER
STERN

HOFJÄGERALLEE

POTSDAMER STRASSE

KURFÜRSTENSTRASSE

SCHÖNEBERG

Zoologischer
Garten
Berlin

Kaiser-Wilhelm-
Gedächtniskirche

WITTENBERG-
PLATZ

WILMERSDORF

CHARLOTTEN-
BURG

HARDENBERGSTRASSE

KURFÜRSTENDAMM

KONSTANZER STRASSE

Spree

Landwehrkanal

Landwehrkanal

with an unconventional charm all its own – and the overall effect is softened by the many parks, gardens and playgrounds that help make it such an appealing place to live.

Perhaps more than anywhere else in Europe, Berlin is a city – seemingly in a perpetual state of transformation – that repays repeated visits. Whether you're drawn by its world-class museums, endlessly absorbing history or frenetic, 24-hour nightlife, visit now and you'll be hooked forever.

What to see

The central **Mitte** district, cut off from the West for almost thirty years during the years of division, is Berlin's main sightseeing and shopping hub. Most visitors begin their exploration on the city's premier boulevard **Unter den Linden**, starting at the most famous landmark, the **Brandenburger Tor**, then moving over to the adjacent seat of Germany's parliament, the **Reichstag**, perhaps the greatest symbol of the nation's reunification. At its eastern end Unter den Linden is lined by stately Neoclassical buildings and terminates on the shores of **Museum Island**, home to some of Berlin's leading museums, but its natural extension on the other side of the island is **Karl-Liebknecht-Strasse**, which leads to a distinctively GDR-era part of the city around **Alexanderplatz**, one of Berlin's principal commercial and transport hubs. Northwest from here, the **Spandauer Vorstadt** was once the heart of the city's Jewish community, and has some fascinating reminders of those days, though today it's best known for the restaurants, bars, boutiques and nightlife around the Hackescher Markt.

Back at the Brandenburger Tor, a walk south along the edge of the sprawling **Tiergarten** park – past a trio of memorials to victims of Nazi crimes – takes you to the modern **Potsdamer Platz**, a bustling entertainment quarter that stands on what was once a barren field straddling the death-strip of the Berlin Wall. Huddled beside Potsdamer Platz is the **Kulturforum**, an agglomeration of cultural institutions that includes several high-profile art museums. Also fringing the park are Berlin's diplomatic and government quarters, where you'll find some of the city's most innovative post-*Wende* architecture, including the formidable **Hauptbahnhof**. The western end of the Tiergarten is given over to a zoo, which also gives its name to the main transport hub at this end of town. This is the gateway to **City West**, the old centre of West Berlin, and best known for its shopping boulevards, particularly the upmarket **Kurfürstendamm**.

Schöneberg, **Kreuzberg** and **Neukölln**, the three key residential districts immediately south of the centre, are home – along with

OFFBEAT BERLIN

Tempelhofer Feld Go cycling, skating or kite landboarding in Europe's biggest park, a former Nazi airport. See p.125

Street art Learn to graffiti with Alternative Berlin, then find your own bit of wall to practise on. See box, p.127

Badeschiff Cool off on a summer's day with a dip in the Badeschiff, a pool made from a converted barge, bobbing above the inky River Spree. See box, p.250

Go-karting Career around the streets in a go-kart. See p.24

Mauerpark Rummage for vintage clothes and the occasional item of GDR memorabilia at this Sunday flea market. See box, p.143

OPPOSITE FROM TOP SCHLOSS CHARLOTTENBURG; HAMBURGER BAHNHOF; OLYMPIASTADION

BERLIN'S MARVELLOUS MUSEUMS

Berlin boasts that it's Europe's only city with more museums than rainy days (some 180 and 106 respectively), which is great news weather-wise, but also means that all but the most committed museum nuts are spoiled for choice.

Most collections are expertly presented in striking buildings and nowhere is this more true than on **Museum Island** (see p.54), location of the city's headline acts. Here Middle Eastern antiquities and, to a lesser extent, German art and sculpture, are the main draws, while the latter also form the kernel of collections at Berlin's other main central museum agglomeration: the **Kulturforum** (see p.94). This is known for its medieval and early modern paintings and decorative art; the greatest concentration of twentieth-century art lies in the museums around **Schloss Charlottenburg** (see p.161) outside the city centre. In addition, the vast collection in the airy old warehouses of the **Hamburger Bahnhof** is an essential first stop for lovers of contemporary art – before embarking on an exploration of some of Berlin's 440 or so private galleries (see p.231).

Perhaps unsurprisingly, many of Berlin's most compelling museums are concerned with its astonishing **history** (see box, p.281). If weighty topics don't appeal, then Berlin's generic museums are a good bet, especially for **kids**: the Natural History Museum (see p.86) is famous for dinosaur skeletons; while the technology (see p.124) and communication (see p.122) museums are both engaging push-button places. Unsuitable for kids, but entertaining for the rest of us, are the **photography** museum (see p.109) devoted to Helmut Newton's nude photos and the **gay** museum (see p.253) which evokes the city's debauched 1920s. But for something truly offbeat, the dusty old exhibits of the freakish **Medical History Museum** (see p.106) are hard to beat.

Friedrichshain to the east – to much of Berlin's most vibrant nightlife. The relatively smart Schöneberg is the city's LGBT centre, while Kreuzberg and Friedrichshain, which straddle opposite sides of the Spree, have maintained a grungy and edgy ambience despite the inevitable onward march of gentrification.

Friedrichshain also offers some unusual architectural leftovers from the Eastern Bloc of the 1950s, while to the north yuppified **Prenzlauer Berg** is one of the few places in which the atmosphere of prewar Berlin has been preserved – complete with cobbled streets and ornate facades. North of Prenzlauer Berg is the sleepy, attractive district of **Pankow**, while to the west lies ever up and coming **Wedding**, with its large immigrant population and pockets of underground culture and nightlife.

ABOVE EGYPTIAN GALLERY IN THE NEUES MUSEUM **OPPOSITE** TIERGARTEN

Berlin's **eastern suburbs** are typified by a sprawl of prewar tenements punctuated by high-rise developments and heavy industry, though the lakes, woodland and small towns and villages dotted around **Köpenick** offer a bucolic break from the city. The leafy **western suburbs** are even more renowned for their woodland (the **Grunewald**) and lakes (the **Havel**), with more besides: attractions include the Baroque **Schloss Charlottenburg**, with its adjacent art museums; the impressive 1930s **Olympic Stadium**; and the medieval town of **Spandau**. Further out, foremost among possible **day-trips** are **Potsdam**, location of Frederick the Great's **Sanssouci** palace, and the former concentration camp of **Sachsenhausen**, north of Berlin in Oranienburg.

When to go

Lying in the heart of Europe, Berlin's **climate** is continental, with temperatures varying from sticky July highs of around 30ºC to January lows as bitingly cold as -18ºC. April is the earliest in the year you should go for decent weather: any earlier and you'll need winter clothing, earmuffs and a decent pair of waterproof shoes; that said, the city (especially the eastern part) has a particular poignancy when it snows. The best time to visit is in May; June and July can be wearingly hot, though the famed Berlin air (*Berliner Luft* – there's a song about its vitality) keeps things bearable.

AVERAGE MONTHLY TEMPERATURES AND RAINFALL

	Jan	Feb	Mar	Apr	May	Jun	Jul	Aug	Sep	Oct	Nov	Dec
BERLIN												
Max/min (ºC)	9/ 12	11/-12	17/-7	22/-2	28/2	30/6	32/9	31/8	28/4	21/-1	13/-4	10/-9
Max/min (ºF)	48/10	52/10	63/19	72/28	82/36	86/43	90/48	88/46	82/39	70/30	55/25	50/16
Rainfall (mm)	43	38	38	43	56	71	53	66	46	36	51	56

things not to miss

It's not possible to see everything that Berlin has to offer on a short trip – and we don't suggest you try. What follows is a subjective selection of the city's highlights, ranging from high-octane nightlife to lip-smacking local cuisine and outstanding architecture. All highlights are colour-coded by chapter and have a page reference to take you straight into the Guide, where you can find out more.

1 FERNSEHTURM
Page 61
Love or loathe its concrete curves, this incongruous Eastern Bloc relic has the best views over the city.

2 EAST SIDE GALLERY
Page 133
The Berlin Wall was always famous for its graffiti, and now, on the longest remaining stretch, vivid murals record its demise.

3 BERLINER WEISSE
Box, page 218
Few would argue that this brew is one of the world's best, but since you order it in either green or red it must be one of the most unusual.

4 THE REICHSTAG
Page 37
Perhaps Germany's most famous landmark, this muscular Neoclassical building now has a magnificent glass cupola you can walk round for free – though be sure to book in advance.

8

9

10

11 NIGHTLIFE
Page 216

You can party all night in Berlin's bewildering array of bars and clubs; world-famous *Berghain* has been called the best club on the planet.

12 WEEKEND BRUNCH
Box, page 202

Weekend brunch buffets are Berlin's best hangover cure.

13 TIERGARTEN
Page 102

Full of attractive lakes and wooded nooks, and just steps away from many headline attractions.

14 SONY CENTER
Page 89

Spectacular corporate architecture along the former Wall death strip.

15 MUSEUM ISLAND
Page 54

This cluster of world-class museums includes the exquisite Neues Museum, with its Ancient Egyptian treasures.

16 KADEWE
Page 112

A gigantic, classy department store with an excellent gourmet food court.

17 JÜDISCHES MUSEUM
Page 119

The stunning Libeskind-designed building is a worthy home for this affecting museum.

11

12

13

Itineraries

Berlin is a sprawling city, with several main drags and no defined centre. These itineraries – three day-long options and one all-nighter – will help you make the most of the place, and are easily followed with the help of a public transport *Tageskarte* (day ticket), plus some single tickets for the night-owl tour.

IMPERIAL BERLIN

Brandenburger Tor Berlin's foremost landmark and one of its biggest tourist attractions. A must for first-time visitors. **See p.35**

Reichstag and Holocaust memorials Climb the dome of this historic building for great city views. Then pay your respects at the four thought-provoking memorials nearby. **See p.37, p.38 & p.95**

Lunch Reserve in advance and enjoy a gourmet lunch with a view at *Käfer Dachgarten* in the Reichstag (see p.198); opt for classic Austrian dishes at old-fashioned *Café Einstein* (see p.205); or for budget options try sushi at *Ishin* (see p.198) or head for one of the many handy places in and around Potsdamer Platz (see p.202).

Gendarmenmarkt and Unter den Linden Walk off your lunch by wandering the length of Unter den Linden, with side trips to the elegant plazas of Gendarmenmarkt (see p.47) and Bebelplatz (see p.42). Stop en route at the Berlin Story shop (see p.239) to browse its selection of books about the city.

Boat trip For a change of pace and a different angle, take a boat trip along the River Spree from the quays beside Museum Island. **See box, pp.24–25**

Hackesche Höfe Finish the day with a wander around these pleasant urban courtyards and surrounding streets, filled with restaurants and bars. **See p.72**

GDR BERLIN

Gedenkstätte Berliner Mauer The Wall memorial on Bernauer Strasse has fascinating, and free, indoor and outdoor exhibitions. **See p.86**

Tränenpalast Discover what division really meant to the city at this former pedestrian border crossing. **See p.83**

DDR Museum Get hands on with GDR culture at this fun interactive museum. Nearby, on the edge of the Marx-Engels-Forum, monuments to these two icons of communism offer a fascinating glimpse into East German ideology. **See p.65**

Fernsehturm Gawp at the bleak GDR architecture of Alexanderplatz before taking a trip up the Fernsehturm for tremendous views over the city. **See p.61**

Karl-Marx-Allee Take in the vast dimensions of this communist boulevard where monumentalist, wedding-cake style architecture produced "palaces for workers, not American egg-boxes!" and admire the original Kino International, as featured in the film *Good Bye Lenin!* **See p.134**

Coffee Grab coffee and cake (or ice cream) at *Café Sybille*, which also hosts a small but informative exhibition about Karl-Marx-Allee. **See p.211**

East Side Gallery Finish up at the largest remaining section of the Berlin Wall, one of the world's largest open-air galleries , which now has a related museum. **See p.133**

ABOVE THE REICHSTAG AT NIGHT **OPPOSITE** CRUISE BOATS ON THE RIVER SPREE

Sleep For a complete *Ostalgie* experience (see box, p.65), book a night at the GDR-themed *Ostel* in Friedrichshain, which is also well placed for the neighbourhood's nightlife. **See p.195**

BUDGET BERLIN

Breakfast Start the day at *Morgenrot*, a bohemian café in Prenzlauer Berg where you pay according to your income. **See p.212**

Bus it Hop on the underground for a couple of stops to Alexanderplatz then take bus #100 or #200 in a loop for a free sightseeing tour of some of the city's main sights. **See box, pp.24–25**

Kaiser-Wilhelm-Gedächtniskirche On the #100 and #200 bus routes and close to Zoo Station, this dramatically shattered memorial church has a small exhibition on Berlin at the end of World War II. **See p.112**

Daimler Contemporary Stop off at Potsdamer Platz for free contemporary art. **See p.93**

Lunch *Joseph Roth Diele*, a charming restaurant nearby dedicated to the cult Austrian writer, offers excellent lunch deals. **See p.206**

Topographie des Terrors Built on the grounds of the former SS Headquarters, this memorial of Gestapo horrors will leave you reeling. **See p.122**

Holocaust memorials If you have time and energy, explore the moving Holocaust memorials, a short walk away. **See p.38 & p.95**

Evening drinks End your day at *Weinerei Forum*, a low-key hangout where you pay what you feel is fair for the wine. **See p.219**

NIGHT-OWL BERLIN

Dine in Spandauer Vorstadt Get your night started with dinner around Oranienburger Strasse, for example at *Amrit* or the *Schwarzwaldstuben*. **See p.201**

The Reichstag Either walk along the river or hop on the S-Bahn for one stop to Brandenburger Tor for a late tour of Germany's parliament building. Take time to check out the incredible sunset and night views over central Berlin. Book ahead. **See p.37**

Potsdamer Platz The roof of the Sony Center includes an impressive light show best enjoyed from the cafés and bars in its atrium. **See p.89**

East Side Gallery Take bus #200, #M48 or the underground to Alexanderplatz, admire the Fernsehturm (see p.61), then take the S-Bahn to Ostbahnhof to walk southeast along the length of the East Side Gallery. **See p.133**

Eastern Kreuzberg Take the underground one stop, or cross the Spree on the Oberbaumbrücke. Grab a burger at *Burgermeister* (see p.209) before exploring the neighbourhood's countless bars and legendary clubs, like *SO36* and *Kuter Blau* (see p.227 & p.228).

Kumpelnest 3000 When the clocks hit 5am, join sundry night-owls at this trashy but cool late-night haunt; five stops on the elevated subway line through Kreuzberg (night buses run when the underground stops). **See p.226**

S-BAHN POTSDAMER PLATZ

Basics

Getting there

The quickest and generally cheapest way of reaching Berlin from the UK and Ireland is by air, a journey of around ninety minutes. It is, however, possible to travel by train or by car via a ferry. Direct flights link Berlin to New York, Miami and Los Angeles, which can also prove useful routes for visitors from Australia and New Zealand, though changing flights at a major European hub such as London, Amsterdam or Frankfurt – the only option for South African travellers – will probably be less expensive.

Airfares vary considerably according to the season, with the highest around June to August; fares drop during the "shoulder" seasons – April and May, September and October – and you'll get the best prices during the low season, November to March (excluding Christmas and New Year when prices are hiked up and seats are at a premium). Flying at weekends will also usually raise the price of a return fare.

Flights from the UK and Ireland

Direct scheduled flights to Berlin are available from London airports with British Airways, easyJet, Eurowings, Lufthansa, Norwegian and Ryanair. Other UK airports with direct flights to Berlin include Birmingham (Air Berlin, Lufthansa, Norwegian, Eurowings); Bristol, Edinburgh, Glasgow, Liverpool, Newcastle and Manchester (easyJet, Eurowings); Leeds (Jet2); and Nottingham (Ryanair). In Ireland both Ryanair and Aer Lingus offer direct flights from Dublin.

The published return fare of the national airlines can cost as much as £300, but in reality booking at least a couple of weeks in advance can easily halve this amount. Prices with the budget airlines such as easyJet and Ryanair can start as low as £40 for a return, but you'll often need to book at least a month ahead to secure this and extra fees may

apply, from checking in bags to failing to print out your own boarding pass.

Flights from the US and Canada

There are several daily scheduled flights from North America to Berlin, with a choice of carriers and destinations. United Airlines, Lufthansa, American Airlines and Air Berlin fly direct from New York; Air Berlin also offers direct flights from Chicago, Miami and Los Angeles. If you are starting your journey from elsewhere in the US, you may well find a cheaper and better connection via a major European hub. Canadians will also end up flying via a major European hub and are unlikely to make any real savings by flying to the US first.

The lowest discounted scheduled return fares you're likely to get in low/high season flying midweek are US$750/$1000 from New York, Boston or Washington DC; US$670/$1200 from Chicago; US$600/$1400 from Los Angeles or Seattle, and US$600/$1100 from San Francisco. Canadians have fewer direct-flight options than Americans. The widest selections are out of Toronto and Montreal, with low/high-season fares to Berlin from around Can$600/$1000; from Vancouver expect to pay from Can$1000/$1400.

Flights from Australia, New Zealand and South Africa

There are no direct flights to Berlin from Australia, New Zealand or South Africa; most airlines use Amsterdam, Frankfurt, London or Paris as their European gateway. All involve either a transfer or overnight stop en route in the airline's hub city: bargain on flying times from the Antipodes of around 24 hours via Asia and around thirty hours via the US; from South Africa the shortest flight times, including transfer, are around 17 hours.

Flights to Europe are generally cheaper via Asia than the US, and typical low season/high-season economy fares from Sydney, Australia start at

A BETTER KIND OF TRAVEL

At Rough Guides we are passionately committed to travel. We believe it helps us understand the world we live in and the people we share it with – and of course tourism is vital to many developing economies. But the scale of modern tourism has also damaged some places irreparably, and climate change is accelerated by most forms of transport, especially flying. All Rough Guides' flights are carbon-offset, and every year we donate money to a variety of environmental charities.

around Aus$1200/$1800. Low season/high-season scheduled fares from Auckland start at around NZ$1600/$2000. From South Africa you'll pay between ZAR6500 and ZAR8000, depending on the season.

Trains

Travelling to Berlin **by train** costs more and takes far longer than flying, but is fairly hassle-free and many – not least anxious flyers – find it a more pleasant experience. By far the **fastest** and most popular train route to Berlin begins with **Eurostar** (Ⓦeurostar.com) from London St Pancras to Paris Gare du Nord (3hr), with a change of stations to Paris Gare de l'Est for the onward overnight train to Berlin (10hr). Return tickets for the complete journey begin at around £140, depending on your seating, when you travel and how far in advance you book. You can also get through-ticketing – including the London Underground journey to St Pancras International – from regional mainline stations in Britain.

Rail passes

You can buy a **rail pass** for the entire German rail network from Deutsche Bahn (Ⓦbahn.com). InterRail (Ⓦraileurope.co.uk) and Eurail passes (Ⓦeurail.com) – the latter for non-European residents only – include other European countries.

Buses

Travelling to Berlin by **bus** won't bring any major savings over the cheapest airfares, and the journey will be long and uncomfortable, interrupted every three to four hours by stops at motorway service stations. The one advantage is that you can buy an open return at no extra cost.

Services are run by **Eurolines** (Ⓦeurolines.com) from Victoria Coach Station in London. There are one – and sometimes two – buses daily to Berlin; the journey takes around twenty hours and costs around £120 return, though regular promotions and discounts for those under 26 can cut the cost up to 20 percent. Starting your journey outside London can add considerably to the time, but little to the cost – the complete journey time from Edinburgh is 37 hours, but tickets start from £120. If you are travelling elsewhere in Europe you might consider buying a **Eurolines Pass**. **Busabout**, meanwhile, runs guided bus tours of Europe for young people and offers a hop-on, hop-off bus pass (Ⓦbusabout.com).

Airlines, agents and operators

AIRLINES

Aer Lingus Ⓦ aerlingus.com
Air Berlin Ⓦ airberlin.com
Air Canada Ⓦ aircanada.com
Air France Ⓦ airfrance.com
Air New Zealand Ⓦ airnewzealand.com
British Airways Ⓦ ba.com
Cathay Pacific Ⓦ cathaypacific.com
Delta Ⓦ delta.com
easyJet Ⓦ easyjet.com
Eurowings Ⓦ eurowings.com
Jet2 Ⓦ jet2.com
KLM Ⓦ klm.com
LOT (Polish Airlines) Ⓦ lot.com
Lufthansa Ⓦ lufthansa.com
Norwegian Ⓦ norwegian.com
Qantas Airways Ⓦ qantas.com.au
Ryanair Ⓦ ryanair.com
SAS (Scandinavian Airlines) Ⓦ flysas.com
South African Airways Ⓦ flysaa.com
Swiss Ⓦ swiss.com
United Airlines Ⓦ united.com

AGENTS AND OPERATORS

Martin Randall Travel UK ☎ 020 8742 3355, Ⓦ martinrandall .com. Small-group cultural tours, usually accompanied by lecturers: an eight-day Berlin, Potsdam, Dresden package costs around £2840.

North South Travel UK ☎ 01245 608 291, Ⓦ northsouthtravel .co.uk. Friendly, competitive travel agency, offering discounted fares worldwide. Profits are used to support projects in the developing world, especially the promotion of sustainable tourism.

STA Travel UK ☎ 0333 321 0099, US ☎ 1800 781 4040, Australia ☎ 134 782, New Zealand ☎ 0800 474 400, South Africa ☎ 0861 781 781; Ⓦ statravel.co.uk. Worldwide specialists in independent travel; also student IDs, travel insurance, car rental, rail passes, and more. Good discounts for students and under-26s.

Trailfinders UK ☎ 020 7368 1200, Ireland ☎ 021 464 8800; Ⓦ trailfinders.com. One of the best-informed and most efficient agents for independent travellers.

Travel CUTS Canada ☎ 1800 667 2887, US ☎ 1800 592 2887; Ⓦ travelcuts.com. Canadian youth and student travel firm.

USIT Ireland ☎ 01 602 1906, Ⓦ usit.ie. Ireland's main student and youth travel specialists.

Arrival

All points of arrival lie within easy reach of the city centre via inexpensive and efficient public transport; the farthest of the city's two airports is just 25 minutes by train from Berlin's city-centre Haupt-

bahnhof, which is also where trains from all over Europe converge. Some trains also stop at other major stations such as Bahnhof Zoo, Alexanderplatz and the Ostbahnhof, which may be more convenient for your destination.

Public transport **tickets** are valid for the entire system of trams, buses and suburban and underground trains. If you plan to use public transport throughout your stay, then it's worth getting a ticket that covers several days (see p.23). All tickets can be validated to cover your journey from the airport and are available from ticket machines at all points of arrival. In addition, a handful of upmarket hotels offer courtesy **shuttles**.

By plane

Until the much delayed and anticipated completion of **Berlin Brandenburg Airport (BER)** – originally scheduled to open in 2010 and now not expected to be ready until 2018 at the earliest, though likely to take longer – Berlin's air traffic (W berlin-airport.de) will continue to be shared between the **Schönefeld** airport, which lies on an adjacent site, and **Tegel** airport, around 10km northwest of Alexanderplatz.

Tegel

Many flights still arrive at the small and manageable **Tegel Airport (TXL)**, where you'll find shops, currency exchange, left luggage facilities and several car rental companies on the land side. (When flying out, note that once past security it's another story, with only the most rudimentary services.)

Several buses head from Tegel into the city. The **TXL JetExpressBus** (daily 5am–11.30pm, every 15–20min) heads to Hauptbahnhof (28min) and Alexanderplatz (40min). The **#X9 JetExpress Bus** (Mon–Fri 4.50am–11pm, every 5–10min; Sat & Sun 5.20am–12.30am, every 10min) goes to Bahnhof Zoo (20min), while bus **#109** heads to S-Bahn Charlottenburg and **#128** to U-Bahn Osloer Strasse.

If you intend to buy a Berlin WelcomeCard, City Tour Card or simply a weekly **ticket** (see p.23), do this from the ticket machine just outside the terminal – the bus driver can only sell single (€2.70) and day tickets (€7 for zones A and B; Tegel is in zone B). **Taxis** cover the distance in half the time (depending on the traffic) and cost about €25.

Schönefeld

Schönefeld Airport (SXF), 20km southeast of Alexanderplatz, mostly serves budget airlines and holiday charters, and will eventually (perhaps) be consumed by Berlin Brandenburg Airport, which lies alongside it. The train station is a five-minute walk from the terminal; from here you can get the Airport Express **train** (daily 5am–midnight), which takes 30 minutes to reach the Hauptbahnhof, or the **S-Bahn** (4.30am–11pm), which takes about 40 minutes but may be more convenient as it has more stops; the same BVG zone ABC ticket (single €3.30; day pass €7.60) is valid on either service (see p.22). Long queues at the ticket machines in the underground passageway can usually be avoided by buying tickets from identical machines on the platform. A **taxi** into the town centre from Schönefeld costs around €40–45, depending on the specific destination.

By train

Trains from European destinations generally head straight to the swanky **Hauptbahnhof**, which has late-opening shops and all the facilities you would expect from a major train station. The station is also a stop on the major S-Bahn line, and on the U-Bahn network. Your train ticket may well include use of zones A and B of the city's public transport system (see p.22) at the end of your journey; if you're not sure, check with the conductor or at the ticket office.

By bus

Most international **buses** and those from other German cities stop at the **Zentraler Omnibus-bahnhof** or **ZOB** (Central Bus Station; W zob-berlin .de; map p.162), Masurenallee, Charlottenburg, west of the centre, near the Funkturm. Several city buses, including the **#M49** service to the centre, and the U-Bahn from U-Kaiserdamm, link it to the Ku'damm area, a journey of about fifteen minutes. The bus station has an information booth, a taxi stand and a couple of snack places.

By car

Getting into Berlin **by car** is relatively easy as Germany's famed autobahns (*Autobahnen*) pass reasonably close to the city centre. It may, however, be a long trip – the autobahns are very congested and delays are the norm. From the west you're most likely to approach on autobahn A2, which will turn into A10 (the ring-road around Berlin), from which you turn off onto A115, a highway that eases you onto Kaiserdamm on the western side of the city, from where it is just fifteen minutes to Zoo station.

From the south you'll approach on autobahn A9, but the route once you hit the A10 is the same. Drivers coming from the Hamburg area will approach from the north on M24, which also turns into A10, but this time you take the A111 into the Charlottenburg district of Berlin.

City transport

Berlin's public transport network is well integrated, efficient and inexpensive. The cornerstone of the system is the web of fast suburban (S-Bahn) and underground (U-Bahn) trains, which are supplemented on the streets by buses and trams. All are run by the BVG, whose network looks complicated at first glance but quickly becomes easy to navigate.

On board, illuminated signs and announcements ensure it's easy to find the right stop. **Tickets** are available from machines at stations and on trams, or from bus drivers – but in all cases be sure to validate them by punching them in a red or yellow machine when you travel. Apart from their colour the machines are identical, serve exactly the same function and are strategically placed by the entrance of every bus, tram or platform. Failure to punch your ticket will result in spot fines.

Public transport

The **U-Bahn** subway is clean, punctual and rarely crowded. Running both under- and overground, it covers much of the centre and stretches into the suburbs: trains run from 4am to around 12.30am, and all night on Friday and Saturday. Once they have closed down for the night their routes are usually covered by night buses – denoted by a number with the prefix "N".

The **S-Bahn** system is a separate network of suburban trains, which runs largely overground. It's better for covering long distances fast and effectively, and complements the U-Bahn in the city centre. It runs until 1.30am on week nights and all night on Friday and Saturday.

You never have to wait long for a **bus** in the city and the network covers most gaps in the U-Bahn system, with buses converging on Zoo Station and Alexanderplatz. Buses #100 and #200, between the two, are particularly good for sightseeing. **Night buses** mostly run every half-hour and routes often differ from daytime ones.

Berlin's quiet and comfortable **trams** operate for the most part in the eastern section of the city, where the network has survived from prewar days.

MetroBuses and **MetroTrams**, their numbers preceded by the letter M, are the core services, running particularly frequently and all night. There are also twelve **ExpressBus** services, most usefully those between Tegel airport and the city centre (see p.21).

Information and maps

For more **information** about Berlin's public transport system, call **BVG** (Berliner Verkehrsbetriebe) or check their website (☏ 194 49, 🖥 bvg.de) which has complete listings and timetables for the U- and S-Bahn systems, plus bus, tram and ferry routes; the BVG FahrInfo Plus **app** is also very useful. There are also transport information offices at Zoo Station, the Hauptbahnhof, Friedrichstrasse and Alexanderplatz, where you can also buy a complete and highly detailed guide to services, and even souvenirs of the network.

Kiosks on the platforms at most U-Bahn stations also provide simple free **maps** of the U- and S-Bahn, trams and some bus services.

Tickets

The same **tickets are valid** for all BVG services, allowing transfers between different modes of transport as well as all other public transport services within the VBB (Verkehrsverbund Berlin-Brandenburg) system, which includes buses and trams in Potsdam, Oranienburg and even Regional Express trains (marked "RE" when operating within the city limits). Tickets can be bought from the machines on U- and S-Bahn station platforms. These take €5, €10 and €20 notes and all but the smallest coins, give change and have a basic explanation of the ticketing system in English. Plain-clothes inspectors frequently cruise the lines, meting out on-the-spot **fines** of €60 for anyone without a correct ticket or pass that has been validated by a red or yellow machine (see above). You can also buy tickets, including day tickets, directly from the driver on a bus (change given); if you have a ticket already, show it to the driver as you board.

The transport network is divided into three **zones** – A, B and C. Zone A covers the inner city, as bordered by the Ringbahn; zone B ends at the city limits, with Potsdam, Oranienburg, Schönefeld airport and the rest of Brandenburg in zone C. Basic **single tickets** (**Einzeltickets**) for zone AB cost €2.70, while an ABC zone single ticket costs €3.30 (there are no tickets covering just zone A). All tickets are valid for two hours, enabling you to split a single

TRANSPORT AND DISCOUNT CARDS

As an alternative to buying transport-only tickets, you might consider picking up either the **Berlin WelcomeCard** (ⓦ visitberlin.de/en/welcomecard) or the slightly cheaper **City Tour Card** (ⓦ citytourcard.com). As well as covering your transport, both cards also give concessionary rates at a host of attractions and discounts at participating tour companies, restaurants and theatres; the main difference between the two is their partners, so check to see which are more appealing. Both cards are available for periods of 48 hours, 72 hours, four, five and six days. The City Tour Card starts at €17.50 for 48 hours in zone AB and ranges up to €43.50 for a six-day ABC pass. The Berlin WelcomeCard starts at €19.50 for 48 hours in zone AB, up to €45.50 for a six-day ABC pass. A 72-hour **Museum Island** (*Museumsinsel*) version of the WelcomeCard is also available, covering all the Museum Island museums (see p.54), and costs €42 (for zone AB) and €44 (ABC). Note that a separate Museum Island pass which excludes transport is also available (see box, p.28).

journey as often as you like, but can't be used for a return journey. A **Kurzstrecke**, or **short-trip ticket**, costs €1.70 and allows you to travel up to three train or six bus stops (no return journeys or transfers).

Buying a **day ticket (Tageskarte)**, valid from the moment you buy it until 3am the next morning, may work out cheaper: a zone AB *Tageskarte* costs €7, and for ABC it's €7.60. If you plan to use the network a lot you might also check out the excellent-value **seven-day ticket (Sieben-Tage-Karte)**, which costs €30 for zone AB and €37.20 for zone ABC.

A small **group ticket (Kleingruppenkarte)** is available for a whole day's travel for up to five people; it costs €17.30 for zone AB and €17.80 for zone ABC.

Another ticket of relevance is the **Fahrrad** ticket, which enables you to wheel a bike onto U- and S-Bahn services. It costs €2.50 for a single journey in zone ABC or an ABC day ticket - but note that it only covers the bike and you'll need to buy the appropriate pass for yourself, too.

If you're in Berlin for longer than a couple of weeks, consider buying a **monthly ticket (Monatskarte)**; various types are available and explained in full in English via the information buttons on dispensing machines.

By car

Though there's practically no need for a **car** within the city, you might want one to tour outside Berlin. The most important **rules** to bear in mind when driving are simple: drive on the right, main roads have a yellow diamond indicating priority; and unless otherwise indicated, traffic coming from the right normally has right of way. Trams also always have the right of way, which frequently catches out unwary visiting drivers who are prone to cutting in front of trams at junctions - a frightening and potentially lethal error. Also, when trams halt at

designated stops, it's forbidden to overtake until the tram starts moving, to allow passengers time to cross the road and board.

Thanks to widespread car ownership and extensive road construction projects, Berlin suffers **traffic snarl-ups** that can compete with the worst any European city has to offer. Rush-hour jams start at around 5pm and are particularly bad on Friday afternoons when you shouldn't be surprised if a journey takes three or four times as long as you expect.

Finding **parking spaces** in central Berlin can be tricky and you'll almost certainly have to pay. Meters, identifiable by their tall grey rectangular solar-power umbrellas, generally charge €1-3/30min. You're supposed to move after an hour, and stiff fines are handed out to cars parked for longer than that or without tickets. Parking garages generally charge around €2/hr and allow you to stay for several hours.

Central Berlin has been designated an **Umweltzone** - a green zone, announced by a sign with the word printed on it - in which all cars must display an emission badge (*Umwelt Plakette*; ⓦ umwelt -plakette.de). These can be purchased online in advance (€30) or bought for around €15 from any of the many garages in Germany that offer TÜV auto-testing (the German equivalent of an MOT) - look for the TÜV logo - as well as at many petrol stations. The badges work by using a traffic-light system - currently all vehicles with amber and red badges are banned in central Berlin; check the website to find out for details of each category. Fines for having the wrong badge or none at all are currently €80. All rental cars will have badges fitted.

Car, scooter and go-kart rental

All the major **car rental** agencies are represented in Berlin. Some have booths at the airports and most have pick-up points in the centre, too. You should be able to get something for around €30 a day though watch out for hidden costs such as limited mileage. Most rental places do good-value Friday afternoon to Monday morning deals. If you are willing to call to book, you may find better deals with **local operators** – Robben & Wientjes (⦿robben-wientjes. de), say, which offers cars from €18/day (for a mileage of less than 100km) and has branches at Prinzenstr. 90–91, Kreuzberg (☎030 61 67 70; ⦿Moritzplatz); Lahnstr. 36–40, Neukölln (☎030 683 770; ⦿/⦿Neukölln) and Prenzlauer Allee 96, Prenzlauer Berg (☎030 42 10 36; ⦿Prenzlauer Allee).

You could also zip around on a **scooter** with a company such as Rent A Scooter, Friedrichstr. 210, Kreuzberg (from €6/hr; ☎030 24 03 78 65, ⦿renta scooter-berlin.de; ⦿Kochstrasse), or for a more expensive but far more unusual experience, go for a street-legal **go-kart** with Kart 4 You (☎07723 91 45 60, ⦿kart4you.de); three hours will cost €49 (€59 at weekends).

Taxis

Berlin's cream-coloured **taxis** are plentiful, cruising the city day and night and congregating at useful locations. They're always metered: the basic fare is €3.90, then it's €2/km for the first 7km, and thereafter €1.50/km. Fares rise slightly between 11pm and 6am and all day Sunday. Short trips, known as *Kurzstrecke*, can be paid on a flat rate of €5 for up to 2km or five minutes, though this only works when you hail a moving cab, and you must request it on getting into the taxi. Taxi **firms** include: City Funk (☎030 21 02 02, ⦿cityfunk.de) and Funk Taxi Berlin (☎030 26 10 26, ⦿funk-taxi-berlin.de).

Cycling

An extensive network of bike paths makes **cycling** around Berlin quick and convenient. You can also take your bike on the U- and S-Bahn: useful if you wish to explore the countryside and lakes of the Grunewald. To take your bike on a train you'll need to buy a **Fahrrad ticket** (see p.23) for the underground system, available for short journeys, single journeys, day tickets or monthly tickets. There are also a number of cycling **tours** of the city (see box, pp.24–25). You can also download .gpx files of interesting **routes** on to your mobile for free at ⦿bit.ly /berlinbicycleroutes.

One good investment if you're going to explore

SIGHTSEEING TOURS

Fierce competition between several English-language companies means that the standard of **walking tours** is very high in Berlin. Most operators offer four-hour city tours for around €14, usually with the option of more specialized jaunts – Third Reich sites, Cold War Berlin, Jewish life, Potsdam and Sachsenhausen and the like – and there are several companies offering tours with an alternative edge. **Bike tours** are a great way of exploring the sprawling city centre itself; if that sounds too much like hard work, consider hiring a **velotaxi rickshaw** and driver, which are easy to find at the Brandenburger Tor and other key points (see below).

Bus tours abound, though you may find that buying a day ticket and hopping on and off the #100 (between Zoo Station and Alexanderplatz) and #200 (between Zoo and Prenzlauer Berg) services with a guidebook is more flexible (and certainly cheaper). Most bus tours depart from the Kurfürstendamm between Breitscheidplatz and Knesebeckstrasse, making the rounds several times every day, though schedules are curtailed in the winter.

Boats cruise Berlin's numerous city-centre canals and suburban lakes regularly throughout the summer and companies offer a variety of short jaunts and day-trips to the Wannsee or Potsdam. In most cases you can just turn up at quayside stops and buy a ticket on the spot; all city centre companies have central stops around the Spreeinsel. Several smaller companies run tours around the Havel lake by the Grunewald, which include trips to Potsdam, and tours of the waterways around Köpenick – find details at the Reederverband der Berliner Personenschiffahrt (⦿reederverband-berlin.de), the organization for operators of passenger boats in Berlin.

WALKING TOURS

Alternative Berlin Tours ☎0162 819 82 64, ⦿alternativeberlin .com. Tours of the graffiti art and squats of Berlin's underbelly.

Insider Tour Berlin ☎030 692 31 49, ⦿insiderberlintours .com. Reputable outfit for city tours.

Original Berlin Walks ☎030 301 91 94, ⦿berlinwalks.com. Walking tours of the main areas.

Sandeman's New Europe Tours ☎030 51 05 00 30, ⦿neweuropetours.eu. The city centre tour offered here is free, but generous tips are expected.

Slow Travel Berlin ☎0171 122 59 73, ⦿slowtravelberlin.com. Tours of residential districts plus culturally themed walks (literature, art, music, film).

the city by bike is the **cycle route map** published by the **German bicycle club** ADFC (☎ 030 448 47 24, ⓦ adfc-berlin.de) available from most city bookshops. The ADFC also has listings of bike rental and bike shops, with current rates and contact details.

Bike rental

Bike **rentals** are available at dozens of outlets, including many convenience stores, around Berlin, with rates around €15/day and €50/week. The nearest to your accommodation will probably be the most useful; otherwise one good company is **Fahrradstation** (ⓦ fahrradstation.com; Mon–Sat, check website for times), with six branches in central Berlin: Leipziger Str. 56, Mitte (☎ 030 66 64 91 80; ⓤ Hausvogteiplatz, map p.36); Dorotheenstr. 95, Mitte (☎ 030 28 38 48 48; ⓤ/Ⓢ Friedrichstrasse; map p.36); Auguststr. 29a, Mitte (☎ 030 22 50 80 70; ⓤ Rosenthaler Platz; map pp.70–71); Bergmannstr. 9, Kreuzberg (☎ 030 215 15 66; ⓤ Gneisenaustrasse; map p.118); Kollwitzstr. 77, Prenzlauer Berg (☎ 030 93 95 81 30; ⓤ Eberswalder Strasse; map p.136); and Goethestr. 46, Charlottenburg (☎ 030 93 95 27 57; ⓤ Wilmersdorfer Strasse; map p.162). There's also a seventh in Potsdam (see p.183).

TOP 5 BIKE RIDES
The Grunewald See p.168
The Müggelsee See p.157
Potsdam See p.175 & p.183
Tempelhofer Feld See p.125
Tiergarten See p.89 & p.102

In addition, the railway company Deutsche Bahn (DB) offers the **Call a Bike** scheme that involves its own fleet of rental bikes within zone A of the city, parked on street corners and at major points like the Brandenburger Tor and Potsdamer Platz. These silver-and-red, full-suspension bicycles can be rented at any time of day for €1/30min or €15 for 24hr (with a €3 registration fee); there are also longer-term options. To use one you first need to register a credit card by phone, on the web (☎ 0700 05 22 55 22, ⓦ callabike-interaktiv.de) or via the Call A Bike app, and your account will automatically be debited. once you've registered, you'll just need to quote the individual number on the side of the bike and you'll receive an electronic code to open the lock. To drop it off you can leave it on any street corner then get a code to lock the bike and leave its location.

CYCLING TOURS

Fat Tire Bike Tours ☎ 030 24 04 79 91, ⓦ fattirebiketours .com/berlin. This reputable specialist charges €28 for a guided 4hr pedal around central Berlin astride a beach-cruiser bike.

BUS AND VELOTAXI TOURS

Bex Sightseeing ☎ 030 880 41 90, ⓦ bex.de. A basic 2hr city bus tour costs about €20.

Tempelhofer Reisen ☎ 030 752 30 61, ⓦ tempelhofer.de. Hop-on hop-off service looping around central Berlin. City tour €19.

Velotaxi Tours ☎ 0178 800 00 41, ⓦ velotaxi.de. Tours, with a driver and guide, start at €24 for two people for 30min.

Zille Bus Tour ☎ 030 25 62 55 74, ⓦ bit.ly/ZilleBusTour. Nostalgic tours, using buses decorated in the style of the "Golden Twenties" originals that operated in the city between 1916 to 1928 – they even come with a driver in period uniform. Adults €5/40min; children up to 6 free. Tickets can be bought on the bus and at underground ticket machines. Departs from the Brandenburger Tor. April–Oct.

BOAT TOURS

Berlin Wassertaxi ☎ 030 65 88 02 03, ⓦ berliner-wassertaxi.de. One-hour tours (€14) through the historic centre and government quarter.

Reederei Riedel ☎ 030 67 96 14 70, ⓦ reederei-riedel.de. Several day-trips on the River Spree, taking in the Reichstag and the Landwehrkanal. Its Stadtkernfahrt (City Tour €13) lasts around an hour, or you can join the 3hr Brückenfahrt (Bridge Tour €22), which runs a large loop around all of central Berlin, at a number of points around the

city. The same company also runs a trip out to Müggelsee in the east (3hr; €17), and on other lakes surrounding Berlin. March to mid-Dec.

Reederei Bruno Winkler ☎ 030 349 95 95, ⓦ reedereiwinkler .de. Reliable boat tours.

Stern und Kreis Schiffahrt ☎ 030 526 36 00, ⓦ sternundkreis.de. Tours around the Havel lake, with trips to Potsdam, and of the waterways around Köpenick and to Schloss Charlottenburg starting from Treptower Park.

QUIRKY AND SPECIALIST TOURS

Air Service Berlin ☎ 030 53 21 53 21, ⓦ air-service-berlin.de. Splash the cash on a 20min helicopter flight over Berlin for €199 or take to the skies (150m high) in a tethered "Hi Flyer" hot-air balloon (€19.90 per person for 15min).

Berlin Music Tours ☎ 030 30 87 56 33, ⓦ musictours-berlin .com. Follow the musical trails of David Bowie, Iggy Pop, Depeche Mode, U2, Rammstein and more.

Berliner Unterwelten Tour the city's underground spaces, most notably the flak tower and bunkers around Gesundbrunnen (see p.147).

Original Berlin Tours ☎ 0157 838 93416, ⓦ woriginalberlin tours.com. Pub crawls and tours that take in Teufelsberg and Sachsenhausen as well as a popular night tour.

Trabi Safari ☎ 030 30 20 10 30, ⓦ trabi-safari.de. Unique tours that explore the city in a Trabant, the cute 26-horsepower fibreglass car of the GDR. You are shown how to operate the machine before setting off on a self-driven 90min tour in their fleet of colourful open-top cars. Daily day and night, starting at €45 per person (up to four in a car). Great recorded commentary.

The media

English is the second language in Berlin, so you won't have a problem finding a good range of English-language newspapers and magazines and – with a little searching – programmes on the TV and radio. You will also find a number of good listings magazines (see p.33) for what's-on information.

Newspapers

The best place to look for **British and US newspapers** is at the newsagents in the main train stations: Hauptbahnhof, Bahnhof Zoo, Alexanderplatz, Friedrichstrasse and the Ostbahnhof.

Berlin has four **local newspapers**. The *Berliner Morgenpost* (W morgenpost.de) is a staid, conservative publication, and *B.Z.* (W bz-berlin.de) is a trashy tabloid. *Berliner Kurier* (W berliner-kurier.de) is another tabloid – less trashy but otherwise similar. The other main local paper is the *Berliner Zeitung* (W berliner-zeitung.de), originally an East Berlin publication, which covers international news as well as local stories. Of the **national** dailies, the two bestsellers are the centre-left *Süddeutsche Zeitung* (W sueddeutsche.de) and the centre-right *Frankfurter Allgemeine Zeitung* (W faz.net), along with the liberal Berlin-based *Tagesspiegel* (W tagesspiegel.de) and the left-of-centre *Tageszeitung*, known as *taz* (W taz.de) – not so hot on solid news, but with good in-depth articles on politics and the environment, and an extensive Berlin listings section on Friday. It has the added advantage of being a relatively easy read for non-native German speakers. The centre-left Hamburg-based *Die Zeit* (W zeit.de) appears every Thursday.

Television

Germany has **two national public TV channels** – ARD (W ard.de) and ZDF (W zdf.de) – which somewhat approximate BBC channels or a downmarket PBS; Berlin also has a regional public channel, RBB (W rbb-online.de). Otherwise major commercial channels dominate, foremost among them Sat 1 (W sat1.de), RTL (W rtl.de) and VOX (W vox.de). All channels seem to exist on a forced diet of US reruns clumsily dubbed into German. With cable TV, available in larger hotels, you'll be able to pick up the locally available **cable channels** (more than twenty of them, including MTV and BBC World).

Radio

Berlin's radio output is reasonable, and you can find good things on the dial. The only **English-speaking radio** stations are the BBC World Service (W bbc.co.uk/worldserviceradio) and NPR Berlin (W nprberlin.de), with non-commercial news, talk and entertainment programmes. For **talk** radio in German try sophisticated Radio Eins (W radioeins .de). The best **local music** stations, depending on your taste, are Fritz Radio (W fritz.de), with some decent dance and hip-hop, and Star FM (W starfm berlin.radio.net), with its diet of American rock. For indie music try Flux FM (W fluxfm.de). Best of the classical music stations is Klassik Radio (W klassikradio.de); Jazz Radio (W jazzradio.net) offers jazz and blues.

Festivals

Berlin's festivals are, in the main, cultural affairs, with music, art and the theatre particularly well represented. Among the other events Volksfeste – small, local street festivals – are held in most districts between July and September and worth looking out if you're on a quest for open-air music, beer and *Wurst*.

We've included a selection of the best festivals below; for others, check the Visit Berlin website (W visitberlin.de) and listings websites and magazines (see p.33).

A festival calendar

JANUARY

Mercedes-Benz Fashion Week Berlin W berlin.mbfashionweek .com. Mid-Jan. First of two annual instalments of this major fashion show. See box, p.232.

Grüne Woche W gruenewoche.de. Late Jan. Berlin's annual agricultural show, held in the Messegelände, with food goodies to sample from all over the world.

Sechstagerennen W sechstagerennen-berlin.de. Late Jan. A Berlin tradition since the 1920s, this six-day nonstop cycle race takes place in the Velodrom, Paul-Heyse-Str., Prenzlauer Berg.

Lange Nacht der Museen W lange-nacht-der-museen.de. Late Jan. Many of Berlin's museums extend their hours – most until midnight – with surprisingly sociable results.

FEBRUARY AND MARCH

Berlinale W berlinale.de. Early to mid-Feb. The third largest film festival in the world. See box, p.237.

Impro ⓦ improfestival.de. Late March. Running since 2001 (though taking a break in 2017), this ten-day event is the biggest improvisational theatre festival in Europe.

APRIL AND MAY

Fesstage ⓦ staatsoper-berlin.de. Early to mid-April. International opera stars and the Staatskapelle Berlin (orchestra of the Staatsoper; see p.233) come together for a celebration of classical music.

A MAZE ⓦ amaze-indieconnect.de. Late April. Gaming festival that brings together fans and creators of indie games for three days of workshops, lectures, exhibitions and awards.

Gallery Weekend Berlin ⓦ gallery-weekend-berlin.de. Late April/early May. Over fifty galleries and small venues dedicated to art and design open for one weekend to present exclusive exhibitions and contemporary international art.

My Fest ⓦ myfest36.de. May 1. Open-air festival in Kreuzberg, with music and cultural events and a lot of food stalls (especially around Kottbusser Tor). Note that May Day demonstrations in the evening in the same area have a tendency to turn ugly, though the daytime is safe and fun.

Theatertreffen Berlin Early to mid-May. Large, mainly German-speaking theatre event held in various theatres, which tends towards the experimental. Check ⓦ berlinerfestspiele.de for details.

Karneval der Kulturen ⓦ karneval-berlin.de. Mid-May. Colourful weekend street festival held since 1996, with four music stages featuring acts from around the world, plus food and handmade arts and crafts. The high point is a street parade with around 4700 participants from eighty nations.

JUNE

Fête de la Musique ⓦ lafetedelamusique.com. Late June. Bands from all over Europe and beyond come to play in bars, clubs and other venues around the city as part of an ambitious event across 540 cities the world over.

Christopher Street Day ⓦ csd-berlin.de. Late June (usually). Parade with lots of floats, music and costumed dancers celebrating gay pride at the end of the week-long Berlin Pride Festival. Draws around 700,000 people. See box, p.254.

Deutsches-Französisches Volksfest ⓦ volksfest-berlin.de. Mid-/late June to mid-/late July. Mini-fair with food and music and a reconstruction of a different French town each year.

Projekt Galerie ⓦ projektgalerie.net. Late June/early July. Regular summer event spanning fashion, art and music.

JULY

Mercedes-Benz Fashion Week Berlin ⓦ berlin.mbfashionweek .com. Late June/early July. Big fashion show with local and international designers.

Classic Open Air ⓦ classicopenair.de. July. The Gendarmenmarkt makes the perfect setting for this five-day series of popular outdoor classical concerts. Previous events have included the Royal Philharmonic Orchestra London performing the complete James Bond title themes and The Scorpions performing with the Deutsches Filmorchester Babelsberg.

Tech Open Air ⓦ toa.berlin. Mid-July. The city's major technology and start-up related event, started in 2012 and is growing each year.

AUGUST

Beer Festival Berlin ⓦ bierfestival-berlin.de. Early Aug. The self-proclaimed Longest Beer Garden in the World is a gathering of over 300 breweries and 800,000 people along the Karl-Marx-Allee.

Tanz im August ⓦ tanzimaugust.de. Mid-Aug to early Sept. Around three weeks of dance performances featuring companies and artists from all over the world.

Lange Nacht der Museen ⓦ lange-nacht-der-museen.de. Late Aug. More than one hundred of Berlin's museums stay open until at least midnight and put on various special events in a repeat of the January event (see opposite).

Pop Kultur ⓦ pop-kultur.berlin. Late Aug/early Sept. Progressive event in Neukölln with live concerts, performances, talks and more.

SEPTEMBER

Bread & Butter ⓦ breadandbutter.com. Early Sept. The city's most prestigious winter fashion event. See box, p.232.

Lollapalooza Berlin ⓦ lollapaloozade.com. Early Sept. Big pop and alt music festival held in Treptower Park.

International Literature Festival ⓦ literaturfestival.com. Early to mid-Sept. Berlin's biggest literary event celebrates "diversity in the age of globalization" and features an eclectic and international selection of poets, short story writers and novelists over nine days.

Musikfest Berlin Early to mid-Sept. Series of events that brings together orchestras, composers, soloists and vocal ensembles from around the world. See ⓦ berlinerfestspiele.de for details.

Fest an der Panke Mid-Sept. Pankow Volksfest that's often among the city's best.

Berlin Art Week ⓦ berlinartweek.de. Mid- to late Sept. Big contemporary art event. See box, p.232.

Berliner Liste ⓦ berliner-liste.org. Mid-Sept. Locally focused art event held at around the same time as Berlin Art Week and Art Berlin Contemporary (see box, p.232).

Berlin Marathon ⓦ bmw-berlin-marathon.com. Late Sept. With around 40,000 participants from well over a hundred countries and the most marathon world records (for men and women) set here, this is one of the largest and most popular road races in the world. The route starts in the Tiergarten, looping around to Friedrichshain and Dahlem before finishing near the Brandenburger Tor. Closing date for entries is in October the previous year.

OCTOBER AND NOVEMBER

Tag der Deutschen Einheit Oct 3. The "day of German unity" is celebrated with gusto, beer, sausages and music at the Brandenburger Tor.

Festival of Lights ⓦ festival-of-lights.de. Mid-Oct. Every autumn, Berlin's famous sights – including the Brandenburger Tor, the Fernsehturm, Berliner Dom and more – are transformed into a sea of colour and light. The nightly light show (over ten days or so) comes with art and cultural events around the topic of light.

JazzFest Berlin Late Oct/early Nov. Running since the 1960s, with a varied programme attracting big names at venues throughout the city, Berlin's JazzFest is traditional and progressive in equal parts, focusing on big bands and large ensembles. See ⓦ berlinerfestspiele .de for details.

International Short Film Festival 🖰 interfilm.de. Mid-Nov.
Week-long festival, founded in 1982, that showcases numerous
competitions across all genres, as well as workshops, discussions and
parties.

DECEMBER

Christmas markets Dec. Folksy Christmas markets – with roasted
almonds, mulled wine and local handicrafts – dot the city. The most
significant are on Breitscheidplatz and Alexanderplatz, but the
prettiest are around the Staatsoper at Unter den Linden, on the
Gendarmenmarkt where evening performances add to the
atmosphere, at Schloss Charlottenburg, and outside the city in
Spandau's old town.

Silvester Dec 31. Germany's largest open-air New Year's Eve party takes
place along the Str. des 17 Juni, between the Brandenburg Gate and the
Siegessäule, to the sound of fireworks and pop music. Street stalls sell
sparkling wine.

Travel essentials

Addresses

In Berlin the **street name** is always written before
the number and all addresses are suffixed by a five-
figure postcode. Street **numbers** don't always run
odd–even on opposite sides of the street – often
they go up one side and down the other. Strasse
(street) is commonly abbreviated to Str., and often
joined on to the end of the previous word. Other
terms include Weg (path), Ufer (river bank), Platz
(square) and Allee (avenue).

Berlin **apartment blocks** are often built around
courtyards with several entrances and staircases:
the Vorderhaus, abbreviated as VH in addresses, is as
the name suggests, the front building; the Garten-

**TOP 10 FREE (OR ALMOST
FREE) BERLIN EXPERIENCES**
Gedenkstätte Berliner Mauer See p.86
Cycling the Tiergarten See p.102
East Side Gallery See p.133
Flea market browsing See p.246
Holocaust memorials See p.38 & p.95
Picnicking in Sanssouci See p.178
The Reichstag See p.37
Sachsenhausen See p.184
**Sightseeing from buses #100
and #200** See box pp.24–25
Tränenpalast See p.83

---

haus (GH; garden house) and the Hinterhof (HH;
back house) are at the rear of the building. EG
means the ground floor, 1 OG means the first floor,
and so on. Dachwohnung means the "flat under the
roof" – in other words, the attic.

Costs

By the standards of most European capitals, **prices**
in Berlin are reasonable and well short of the
excesses of Paris and London, even though the
quality of what's on offer can easily compete.
Nevertheless, for anyone heading out to Berlin's
famous nightspots or shopping at its designer
stores, visiting the city can become expensive.

Assuming you intend to eat and drink in moder-
ately priced places and use public transport
sparingly, the **minimum** you could comfortably get
by on – after accommodation costs, which start at
about €65 for a basic double room in the centre in
high season – is around €30 (around £26/US$33) a
day. For this you would get a basic breakfast (€5), a
sandwich (€3), an evening meal (€10), two beers
(€6) and one underground ticket (€3), though this
budget would limit you to visiting free museums
and making your own entertainment. A more
realistic figure, if you want to see as much of the
city as possible (and party at night), would be about
twice that amount.

Crime and personal safety

Crime in Berlin is very modest in comparison with
other European cities of equal size, and if tourists
encounter it at all it will most likely be **petty crime**
such as pickpocketing or bag-snatching in one of
the main shopping precincts.

As far as **personal safety** is concerned, most
parts of the city centre are safe enough. Use

**MUSEUM PASSES AND
DISCOUNTS**
While the Berlin WelcomeCard and City
Tour Card (see box, p.23), provide useful
discounts for museum visits on top of
access to the public transport system,
buying a **Museum Pass Berlin**
(🖰 visitberlin.de/en/museum-pass-
berlin) is an even more effective way to
cut costs, particularly if you're keen to
visit several. The three-day ticket costs
€24 and covers some fifty Berlin
museums, including all the state
collection. It's sold at all participating
museums, as well as at the Visit Berlin
information centres (see p.33).

common sense, but bear in mind that even the supposedly "rougher" neighbourhoods feel more dangerous than they actually are; Kreuzberg's U-Bahn Kottbusser Tor and its immediate environs, for example, might look alarming when compared to the rest of the system, but wouldn't stand out in many other European cities. The situation out In the suburbs (such as Marzahn, Lichtenberg and even parts of Neukölln) is a little trickier, with immigrant gangs flexing their muscles here and there, and neo-Nazi thugs an occasional issue in the east.

If you do have something stolen (or simply lose something), or suffer an attack you'll need to register the details and obtain an official statement (*Anzeige*) at the local police station: a straightforward, but inevitably bureaucratic and time-consuming process. Note the crime report number – or, better still, get a copy of the statement itself – for your insurance company.

The two offences you might unwittingly commit concern **identity papers** and **jaywalking**. By law you need to carry proof of your identity at all times. A driver's licence or ID card is fine, but a passport is best. It's essential that you carry all your documentation when driving – failure to do so may result in an on-the-spot fine. Jaywalking is also illegal and you can be fined if caught.

Culture and etiquette

Berliners are traditionally quite a gruff lot who don't suffer fools gladly, though much of this attitude is laced with a sardonic wit known as **Berliner Schnauze** – literally "Berlin snout". Learn to take all this in your stride: it's nothing personal, just an everyday way of dealing with urban living.

Another defining attribute for Berliners is their Prussian sense of orderliness and respect for rules and authority. **Jaywalkers** (see above) will more frequently be reprimanded by bystanders – "what if a child saw you?" – than by the police.

Thankfully, despite all this, Berlin is a famously **tolerant** place. This tolerance comes in part from the city's appeal to unconventional Germans who relocate from elsewhere in the country and partly from its large immigrant population. Staggering around in the small hours, drinking in the street, or being openly gay will neither raise an eyebrow nor turn a head. This open-mindedness also extends to a tolerance for **smoking** that is far higher than elsewhere in Western Europe – with many bars frequently ignoring bans (see box, p.33).

Electricity

Supply runs at 220–240V, 50Hz AC; sockets generally require a two-pin **plug** with rounded prongs. Visitors from the UK will need an **adaptor**, and those from North America may need a transformer, though most portable electrical equipment – like phones, tablets and laptops – are designed to accommodate a range of voltages.

Entry requirements

EU citizens can enter Germany on a valid passport or national identity card for an indefinite period; whether the situation changes for British citizens in the wake of the Brexit vote remains to be seen. US, Canadian, Australian and New Zealand citizens do not need a **visa** to enter Germany, and are allowed a stay of ninety days within any six-month period. South Africans need to apply for a visa, from the German Embassy in Pretoria (see below), which will cost around €60, plus a processing fee of ZAR380. Visa requirements vary for nationals of other countries; contact your local German embassy or consulate for information.

In order to extend a stay once in the country you must contact the nearest **Bürgeramt** (Citizens' Office) to register your address, and then make an email appointment with the Ausländerbehörde (Alien Authority), Friedrich-Krause-Ufer 24; ⑩ Amrumer Strasse (Ⓔ abh@labo.berlin.de). Full guidance is provided at ⑩ berlin.de, though all the relevant info is in German only.

GERMAN EMBASSIES ABROAD

Australia ⑩ canberra.diplo.de.
Canada ⑩ ottawa.diplo.de.
Ireland ⑩ dublin.diplo.de.
New Zealand ⑩ wellington.diplo.de.
South Africa ⑩ pretoria.diplo.de.
UK ⑩ london.diplo.de.
US ⑩ germany.info.

EMBASSIES AND CONSULATES IN BERLIN

Australia Wallstr. 76–79 ☎ 030 880 08 80, ⑩ germany.embassy .gov.au; map p.60.
Canada Leipziger Platz 17 ☎ 030 20 31 20, ⑩ canadainternational.gc.ca; map pp.90–91.
Ireland Jägerstr. 51 ☎ 030 22 07 20, ⑩ embassyofireland.de; map p.36.
New Zealand Friedrichstr. 60 ☎ 030 20 62 10, ⑩ nzembassy.com; map p.36.

EMERGENCY NUMBERS

Fire and ambulance ❶ 112
Police ❶ 110

South Africa Tiergartenstr. 18 ❶ 030 22 07 30, ⓦ suedafrika.org; map pp.90–91.

UK Wilhelmstr. 70–71 ❶ 030 20 45 70, ⓦ britischebotschaft.de; map p.36.

US Pariser Platz 2 & Clayallee 170 ❶ 030 830 50, ⓦ germany .usembassy.gov; map p.36.

Health

As a member of the European Economic Area (EEA), which includes all countries of the EU, Germany has free reciprocal health agreements with other EEA member states, whose citizens can apply – well in advance of their trip – for a free **European Health Insurance Card** (EHIC). The card will allow you to receive free or cut-rate treatment, but does not extend to repatriation. Without it, EEA citizens will have to pay in full for all medical treatment, which starts at about €30 for a visit to the doctor. At the time of writing, British citizens were still covered by the EHIC scheme, but in the wake of 2016's Brexit vote you should check the situation (ⓦ ehic.org.uk) before you travel. **Non-EEA residents** should check the level of cover that they might have from existing insurance policies, but in almost all cases are advised to take out travel insurance (see box below). If you need to make an insurance policy claim for health costs, be sure to keep all receipts relating to treatment.

If you need immediate medical attention, head for the 24-hour emergency room of a major **hospital**, such as the Charité, Charitéplatz 1, Mitte (❶ 030 450 53 10 00, ⓦ charite.de; ❶/❸ Hauptbahnhof). For **dental emergencies** one good clinic is the English-speaking Zahnärztlicher Notdienst (❶ 030 89 00 43 33, ⓦ kzv.de). In an **emergency**, phone ❶ 112 for an ambulance (*Krankenwagen*).

If you need a **doctor**, phone Arzt Besuche Berlin (❶ 030 89 00 91 00, ⓦ www.arztbesucheberlin .com; calls cost €0.14/min), an English-language service featuring practitioners who will discuss your symptoms and can refer you to or send an English-speaking doctor. A visit will cost €120–180 but can almost always be claimed back via health insurance.

To get a **prescription** filled, go to a **pharmacy** (*Apotheke*), signalled by an illuminated green cross. Pharmacists are well trained and generally speak English. There's a 24-hour pharmacy in the Hauptbahnhof, otherwise, outside normal hours (usually 8.30am–6.30pm), there will be a notice on the door of any pharmacy indicating the nearest one that's open. After hours you'll be served through a small hatch in the door, so don't be put off if it looks as though a place is closed.

Insurance

Though Berlin is a relatively safe city and healthcare privileges (see above) or your private medical plan may apply in Germany, an **insurance policy** is a wise precaution to cover against theft, loss and various other travel mishaps (see box below).

Internet

Berlin is very internet-savvy and online access is excellent. Virtually all hostels and hotels, a growing number of cafés, and all the main train stations have **wi-fi** hot spots (locally referred to as WLAN) – and there's a free one in the Sony Center). Access to terminals in internet cafés averages at about €2/30min.

Laundry

All large hotels generally provide a laundry service – but at a cost. **Launderettes** scattered throughout the city are generally cheaper, with an average load

---

ROUGH GUIDES TRAVEL INSURANCE

Rough Guides has teamed up with WorldNomads.com to offer great **travel insurance** deals. Policies are available to residents of more than 150 countries, with cover for a wide range of adventure sports, 24hr emergency assistance, high levels of medical and evacuation cover and a stream of travel safety information. Roughguides.com users can take advantage of their policies online 24/7, from anywhere in the world – even if you're already travelling. And since plans often change when you're on the road, you can extend your policy and even claim online. Roughguides.com users who buy travel insurance with WorldNomads.com can also leave a positive footprint and donate to a community development project. For more information, go to ⓦ roughguides.com/travel-insurance.

costing around €5 to wash and dry. Hours tend to be daily 7am–10pm.

Left luggage

There are **24-hour lockers** at both Tegel and Schöne-feld airports as well as at the Hauptbahnhof, Alexan-derplatz, Ostbahnhof, Ostkreuz, Friedrichstrasse, Potsdamer Platz, Gesundbrunnen, Zoologischer Garten, Südkreuz and Spandau train stations and the ZOB bus station. The Hauptbahnhof also has a left-luggage office. Charges for lockers range around €4–6/day, but note too that most **hotels and hostels** will hold guest baggage for the day free of charge.

Living in Berlin

A politicized, happening city with a dynamic arts scene and tolerant attitudes, Berlin is a magnet for young people from Germany and all over Europe, and has a large English-speaking community.

Numerous **job agencies** offer both temporary and permanent work – usually secretarial – but you'll obviously be expected to have a good command of German. Useful internet sources include ⓦ stepstone.de, ⓦ mamas.de, ⓦ jobs.de, ⓦ jobnet.de and ⓦ monster.de.

Work permits (*Arbeitserlaubnis*) aren't required for EU nationals working in Germany – whether, post-Brexit, the situation remains the same for British nationals remains to be seen – though everyone else will need one, and theoretically should not even look for a job without one. Applying for a long-term permit is to enter a world of complicated and tedious bureaucracy, and it's essential to seek advice from someone with experi-ence in the whole process, especially when completing official forms. The best official place for advice is the **Auswärtiges Amt** (German Federal Foreign Office; ⓦ auswaertiges-amt.de), whose website has the latest information – in English.

For non-EU nationals – North Americans, Austral-asians and everybody else – the best advice for finding work (legally) is to approach the German embassy or consulate in your own country (see p.29). Citizens of Australia, New Zealand and Canada aged between 18 and 30 can apply for a working holiday visa, enabling legal work in Germany for 90 days in a twelve-month period: contact German embassies for details.

For long-term **accommodation**, while newspapers advertise apartments and rooms, it's much quicker and less traumatic to sign on at one of the several **Mitwohnzentralen** – accommodation agencies that specialize in long-term sublets in apartments, such as ⓦ immobilienscout24.de, ⓦ immonet.de, ⓦ immowelt .de or ⓦ wg-gesucht.de (for flat shares). Anyone who wants to stay in Germany for longer than three months – including EU citizens – must first **register** their residence (*Anmeldung*) at a **Bürgeramt** (Citizens' Office; see p.29). The form for this requires a signature from your landlord.

Lost property

The **police lost and found** department (*Zentrales Fundbüro*) is at Platz der Luftbrücke 6, Tempelhof (Mon, Tues & Fri 9am–2pm, Thurs 1–6pm; ☎ 030 75 60 31 01; ⓤ Platz der Luftbrücke). For items lost on **public transport**, contact the BVG Fundbüro, Potsdamer Str. 182, Schöneberg (Mon–Thurs 9am–6pm, Fri 9am–2pm; ☎ 030 194 49; ⓤ Kleist-park). **Tegel** airport's lost property department can be contacted on ☎ 030 41 01 23 15; Schönefeld airport's is on ☎ 030 34 39 75 33.

Money and banks

Germany uses the **euro** as its currency, which is split into 100 cents. At the time of writing, the **exchange rate** was approximately €1.13 to the pound, €0.89 to the US dollar and €0.67 to the Australian dollar. For the latest rates, go to ⓦ xe.com.

Banks are plentiful, and their hours usually Monday to Friday from 8.30am to 5pm with later opening two days a week until 6pm. For currency exchange, the **Wechselstuben** (bureaux de change) at the main train stations and airports offer better rates than the banks and are open outside normal banking hours – usually daily 8am–8pm. If you do use a bank to change money it may be worth shopping around (including a branch of Sparkasse or one of the savings banks) as the rates of exchange and commission vary. The latter tends to be a flat rate, meaning that small-scale transac-tions should be avoided whenever possible.

The use of **debit and credit cards** is not as widespread as in the UK or North America, and cash is still the currency of choice, particularly in bars and restaurants. However, major credit and debit cards are good in department stores, mid- to up-market restaurants, and an increasing number of shops and petrol stations.

ATMs are plentiful: debit cards usually carry lower fees for withdrawing cash than credit cards, which carry a minimum fee, often around €2.50, and charge two to four percent of the withdrawal as commission; note, however, that your home bank will almost certainly levy a commission for use of the debit card abroad.

Opening hours and public holidays

Opening hours are provided throughout the Guide. On **public holidays** they generally follow Sunday hours: most shops will be closed and museums and other attractions will follow their Sunday schedules. Public holidays fall on January 1, Good Friday, Easter Monday, May 1, Ascension Day (forty days after Easter), Whitsun, October 3 (Day of German Unity), and December 25 & 26. In addition, October 31 (Reformation Day) is a public holiday in Brandenburg, and is likely to be adopted as a holiday in Berlin from 2017 onwards.

Phones

To **call Berlin from abroad**, dial the **international code** for Germany (☎ 49), followed by the city code (☎ 30) and then the number. **Mobiles** from the UK, Ireland, Australia, New Zealand and South Africa should work in Germany. There's a cap on mobile phone charges within Europe, so EU residents can use their own phones within all EU countries for the same price as at home – post-Brexit, this may or may not apply to British citizens: check with your phone company first. Some North American **cellphones** may not work in Europe, though if your smartphone is unlocked, you can use it with a local SIM card in Germany. Many service providers, including those in the United States offer call and data packages that can be used abroad at little or no extra charge.

If you are in Germany for a while, consider buying a local **SIM card** for your mobile phone. These tend to cost around €10–15 and are best bought through a phone shop. Top-up cards can be bought in supermarkets, kiosks and phone shops and even in BVG ticket vending machines.

Post

Post offices of **Deutsche Post** (Ⓦ deutschepost.de) and their unmissable bright yellow postboxes pep up the streetscape. One of Central Berlin's most conveniently situated **post offices** (*Postämt*), with the longest hours, is at Bahnhof Friedrichstrasse (under the arches at Georgenstr. 14–18; Mon–Fri 6am–10pm, Sat & Sun 8am–10pm). Other offices (generally Mon–Fri 9am–6pm, Sat 9am–1pm), often have separate parcel offices (marked *Pakete*) a block or so away, and you can also buy stamps from the small yellow machines next to some postboxes and at some newsagents.

When posting a letter, make sure you distinguish between the slots marked for various postal codes. Boxes marked with a red circle indicate collections late in the day and on Sunday. Mail to the UK usually takes three days; to North America one week; and to Australasia two weeks. A postcard or letter under 50g costs €0.85 to send worldwide.

Time

Germany is one hour ahead of UTC (GMT), six hours ahead of US Eastern Standard Time and nine ahead of US Pacific Standard Time.

Tipping

Service is, as a rule, included in the bill. **Rounding up** a café, restaurant or taxi bill to the next euro or so is acceptable in most cases, though when you run up a particularly large tab you will probably want to add some more.

Tourist information

Before you set off for Berlin, explore the **German National Tourist Board** website (Ⓦ germany .travel), and that of the **city tourist office** (Ⓦ visit berlin.de), which is more detailed, has a helpful

---

CALLING HOME FROM GERMANY

To make an international call, dial the international access code, then the country code, before the rest of the number. Note that the initial zero is omitted from the area code when dialling the UK, Ireland, Australia and New Zealand from abroad.

Australia international access code + 61
New Zealand international access code + 64
UK international access code + 44
US and Canada international access code + 1
Ireland international access code + 353
South Africa international access code + 27

WILL BERLINERS BUTT OUT?

With one-third of Berliners smoking, and typically puffing on their first cigarette aged 13, Germany's smoking ban, introduced after much deliberation in 2008, was always going to prove hard to enforce. As things stand, smoking is **banned** on **public transport** and to all intents and purposes **public buildings**. It's also banned from most **hotels** and **restaurants**, though some have separate smoking rooms, and local **bars** smaller than 75 square metres which don't serve food are also exempt. So too are **clubs**, though there is technically a ban on lighting-up on the dancefloor. Many other places have elected to continue to allow smoking, by declaring themselves a **Raucherclub** (smokers' club) with a sign in the window: an illegal compromise, but one police seem happy to tolerate.

accommodation service and maintains an excellent events section detailing most mainstream cultural happenings in the city. They run five **tourist information centres** (see below), with one more planned at the ZOB bus station, plus a call centre (Mon–Fri 9am–7pm, Sat 10am–6pm, Sun 10am–2pm; ☎030 25 00 23 33), that provides information as well as accommodation bookings. They also produce a handy map (€1).

Berlin has two essential **listings magazines** – *Tip* (ⓦtip-berlin.de) and *Zitty* (ⓦzitty.de) – which come out on alternate weeks. *Zitty* is marginally the better of the two, with day-by-day details of gigs, concerts, events, TV and radio, theatre and film, alongside intelligent articles on politics, style and the Berlin in-crowd, and useful classified ads.

TOURIST OFFICES IN BERLIN

Brandenburg Gate Pariser Platz (south wing); ⓤ/Ⓢ Brandenburger Tor; map p.36. Daily: April–Oct 9.30am–7pm; Nov–March 9.30am–6pm.
Fernsehturm (TV Tower) Panoramastr. 1a; ⓤ/Ⓢ Alexanderplatz; map p.60. April–Oct daily 10am–6pm; Nov–March 10am–4pm.
Hauptbahnhof (ground floor/Europaplatz); ⓤ/Ⓢ Hauptbahnhof; map pp.90–91. Mon–Sat 10am–8pm.
Europa Center (ground floor); Tauentzienstr. 9; ⓤ Kurfürstendamm; map p.108. Mon–Sat 10am–8pm.
Tegel Aiport Terminal A /Gate 1. Daily 8am–9pm.

USEFUL WEBSITES

ⓦ **berlin.de** The city's official site, with loads of general information, plus the latest events.
ⓦ **berlin-online.de** An excellent, all-purpose source for news, business, politics, entertainment, restaurants, listings and the like.
ⓦ **exberliner.com** Website of the useful monthly English-language listings magazine, which caters to Berlin's expats.

ⓦ **iheartberlin.de** Online magazine run by a group of twenty-something creative types that provides a great feel for the aspects of the city they love.
ⓦ **slowtravelberlin.com** Articles suggesting ways to meander around the less explored parts of Berlin and beyond. They also run tours and publish Berlin-themed books.
ⓦ **stilinberlin.de** The go-to site for the latest tips on food and fashion.
ⓦ **thelocal.de** English-language news about Berlin online.
ⓦ **tip-berlin.de** See above.
ⓦ **zitty.de** See above.

Travellers with disabilities

Access and **facilities** for the disabled (*Behinderte*) are good in Berlin: most of the major museums, public buildings and the majority of the public transport system are wheelchair friendly, and an active disabled community is on hand for helpful advice.

A particularly good meeting place with lots of useful **information** is the *Hotel MIT-Mensch*, Ehrlichstr. 48 (☎030 509 69 30, ⓦmit-mensch.com; Ⓢ Karlshorst), which provides friendly lodging run by and for wheelchair users. For more formal and in-depth information check out **Mobidat** (ⓦmobidat.net), a Berlin activist group that campaigns for better access for people with disabilities. They have a wealth of information on wheelchair-accessible hotels and restaurants, city tours for disabled travellers and local transport services.

The **public transport** system is disabled-aware: all of the buses and the majority of its tram routes have ramps to allow access – look for a blue wheelchair symbol on the side of vehicles. Trains are generally easy to board, but getting onto the platforms less so – most but not all U- and S-Bahn stations are equipped with lifts. The official U- and S-Bahn map indicates which stations are wheelchair-accessible; for more information check with the BVG first (see p.22).

BRANDENBURGER TOR

Unter den Linden and around

The natural place to start exploring Berlin is at its most famous landmark, the Brandenburger Tor, or Brandenburg Gate. It lies at the head of its premier boulevard, Unter den Linden, and beside the iconic Reichstag, the German parliament. During the Berlin Wall years all three became rather forlorn symbols of malaise: the Gate sat in the no-man's-land of the Wall, Unten den Linden led nowhere and the Reichstag lay largely empty. But now, following reunification, regeneration and Berlin's reinvention as Germany's capital, they again provide a nucleus for a city that lacked a coherent centre for so long. Gratifyingly, you can do a walking tour of the entire district that's manageable in a day. It's worth starting early with a booking to view the Reichstag dome – or consider ending your day's exploration here: the building's open until midnight and Berlin's nocturnal cityscape is an attraction itself.

This important historical district was key in Berlin's eighteenth-century transformation from a relative backwater to the capital of Prussia, when it became one of Europe's biggest players. With Prussia's rise its architects were commissioned to create the trappings of a worthy *Weldstadt* ("world city"), with appropriately stately institutions built on and around Unter den Linden. Traditional **Baroque** and **Neoclassical** styles predominate, and there are no great flights of architectural fancy. These buildings were meant to project an image of solidity, permanence and power, a bricks-and-mortar expression of Prussia's newly powerful role in Europe. However, almost every one of these symbols of Prussian might was left gutted by the bombing and shelling of World War II. Paradoxically, it was the postwar communist regime that resurrected them from the wartime rubble to adorn the capital of the German Democratic Republic. The result was a pleasing re-creation of the old city, though one motive behind this **restoration** was to create a sense of historical continuity by tacitly linking the East German state with its Prussian forebear.

The restoration was so successful that looking at these magnificent eighteenth- and nineteenth-century buildings it's difficult to believe that as recently as the 1960s large patches of the centre lay in ruins. Like archeologists trying to picture a whole vase from a single fragment, the builders took a facade, or just a small fraction of one, and set about re-creating the whole. And even though much of what can be seen today is an imitation, it's often easy to suspend disbelief and imagine unbroken continuity – or at least would be, were it not for the ongoing U-Bahn works along most of the street, due to be completed in 2020 (see box, p.62).

Building works aside, the rejuvenation is at its most impressive on the **Gendarmenmarkt**, a square just south of Unter den Linden where, even in the 1980s, its twin Neoclassical churches – the **Französischer Dom** and **Deutscher Dom** – remained bombed-out shells. Equally splendid are the reconstructed grand buildings in and around **Bebelplatz**, which under the noble rulers of Prussia – the Hohenzollerns – became an impressive prelude to the awesome buildings of the Spreeinsel, which included their palace and Museum Island (see p.50). Just south of the **Reichstag** and the **Brandenburger Tor** is the largest of several **Holocaust memorials** that dot the eastern edge of the Tiergarten. Perversely it paves the way to the site of **Hitler's Bunker** – where the Führer committed suicide – sitting within Berlin's prewar **Regierungsviertel** or "government quarter" along **Wilhelmstrasse**, almost nothing of which is left today.

Brandenburger Tor

Pariser Platz • ⓤ/Ⓢ Brandenburger Tor

Heavily laden with meaning and historical association, the **Brandenburger Tor** (Brandenburg Gate) has come to mark the very centre of Berlin. Built as a city gate-cum-triumphal arch in 1791, it was designed by Carl Gotthard Langhans, a Prussian builder and architect who worked in the Weimar Classicist style, and modelled after the Propylaea, the entrance to the Acropolis in Athens. The Gate became, like the Reichstag later, a symbol of German solidarity, along with the monolithic Siegessäule, a column celebrating Prussian military victories that originally stood outside the Reichstag before being moved by the Nazis to its current Tiergarten location (see p.103). In 1806 Napoleon marched under the arch and took home with him the **Quadriga**, the horse-drawn chariot that tops the Gate. It was returned a few years later, and the revolutionaries of 1848 and 1918 met beneath it; later the Gate was a favoured rallying point for the Nazis' torchlit marches.

After the building of the Wall placed the Gate in the Eastern sector, nearby observation posts became the place for visiting politicians – John F. Kennedy included (see p.80) – to look over the Iron Curtain from the West in what became a handy photo opportunity; the view was apparently emotive enough to reduce Margaret Thatcher to tears. With the opening of a border crossing here just before Christmas

1

1989, the east–west axis of the city was symbolically re-created. The GDR authorities, who rebuilt the Quadriga following wartime damage, had removed the Prussian Iron Cross from the Goddess of Victory's laurel wreath, which topped her staff, on the grounds that it was "symbolic of Prussian-German militarism". When the border was reopened, the Iron Cross was replaced, which some, mindful of historical precedent, still viewed with a frisson of unease –now, however, it certainly seems harmless enough and is used as a popular backdrop for photos of posing tourists.

Pariser Platz

Ⓤ/Ⓢ Brandenburger Tor

The Brandenburger Tor looms over **Pariser Platz**, whose ornamental gardens have been restored to reproduce its prewar feel, if not exact look, since the square is now surrounded by a mix of modern and reconstructed buildings. Millions of euros have gone into this redevelopment, with some interesting results despite the stringent building guidelines: windows have to be vertical in format and facades only a maximum of 49 percent glass – the rest should be stone – though this rule was deliberately flouted by the **Akadamie der Künste**.

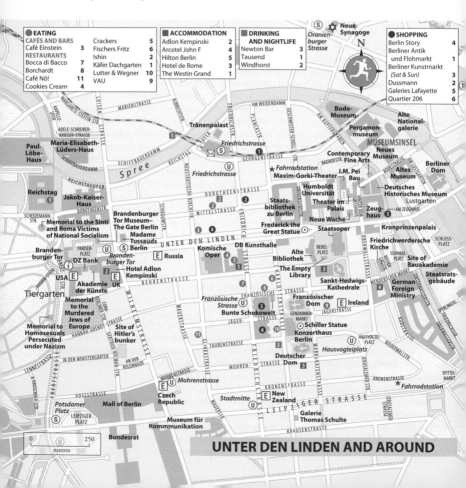

● EATING		■ ACCOMMODATION		■ DRINKING		● SHOPPING	
CAFÉS AND BARS	Crackers 5	Adlon Kempinski 2		**AND NIGHTLIFE**		Berlin Story 4	
Café Einstein 3	Fischers Fritz 6	Arcotel John F 4		Newton Bar 3		Berliner Antik	
RESTAURANTS	Ishin 2	Hilton Berlin 5		Tausend 1		und Flohmarkt 1	
Bocca di Bacco 7	Käfer Dachgarten 1	Hotel de Rome 3		Windhorst 2		Berliner Kunstmarkt	
Borchardt 8	Lutter & Wegner 10	The Westin Grand 1				(Sat & Sun) 3	
Café Nö! 11	VAU 9					Dussmann 2	
Cookies Cream 4						Galeries Lafayette 5	
						Quartier 206 6	

UNTER DEN LINDEN AND AROUND

Brandenburger Tor Museum – The Gate Berlin

Pariser Platz 4a • Daily 10am–6pm • €9 • ☎ 030 236 07 83 66, ⓦ brandenburggate-museum.com • ⓤ/Ⓢ Brandenburger Tor

Opened in 2016, the impressively multimedia-savvy **Brandenburger Tor Museum** offers a three-hundred year history of the city as witnessed via its iconic gate. Spread over two floors, the exhibition brings alive key events like the revolutions of 1848–49, the World Wars, the fall of the Wall, right up to the 2014 World Cup victory.

DZ Bank

Pariser Platz 3 • ⓤ/Ⓢ Brandenburger Tor

Described by Canadian-born architect Frank O. Gehry as the "best thing I've ever done", the **DZ Bank** is worth a second look, even if you can't do much more than crane your neck at its organic interiors from the lobby. While the building's plain exterior almost mockingly follows the exacting building codes – it's only just fifty percent stone, its windows only slightly taller than they are wide – inside, beyond the huge blocks of Portuguese marble in the entrance, thousands of individually formed metal panels give the conference rooms at its heart an aquatic, undulating curvaceousness. The structure is also unusual in that it moves from a height of five storeys at the front to ten at the rear. Though owned by a bank, the building is mostly used as offices and event space.

Akadamie der Künste

Pariser Platz 4 • Daily 10am–10pm • Prices depend on exhibition; usually around €5 • ☎ 030 20 05 /0 10 00, ⓦ adk.de • ⓤ/Ⓢ Brandenburger Tor

Standing shoulder to shoulder with the DZ Bank and every bit as eye-catching is the glassy **Akadamie der Künste** (Academy of Arts). The academy was originally founded in 1696, making it one of the oldest government-funded artist societies in the world. Its modern home somehow slithered around local building codes by ostensibly copying the design of the prewar building – though reconstructing it in glass and steel. Naturally a storm raged over how the building had been approved, but sensibly the courts upheld permission for it to stay. Inside you can see the last original structure from prewar Pariser Platz, tucked away at the back of building, and wander across sweeping concrete expanses for views of the Platz from the first floor. The building holds several temporary contemporary art exhibitions per year, and also includes a café.

Hotel Adlon Kempinski

Unter den Linden 77 • ☎ 020 22 61 11 11, ⓦ hotel-adlon.de • ⓤ/Ⓢ Brandenburger Tor

Standing on the southeast corner of the Platz, the **Hotel Adlon** (see p.187) is a 1990s reconstruction of one of Europe's grandest hotels – its legendary predecessor, host to luminaries from Charlie Chaplin to Lawrence of Arabia and Kaiser Wilhelm II (who supported its construction), was destroyed in the closing days of the war. Even if you can't afford a drink here, let alone a room, glance into the lobby, which evokes Berlin's eighteenth-century pomp as the cultural capital of Europe.

The Reichstag

Platz der Republik 1 • Daily 8am–midnight; last admission 10pm • Free; entry requires advance booking for a particular time slot (at least a few days in advance, especially in summer) or a restaurant reservation (see p.198) • Free guided tours (4 daily; 1hr 30min); additional tours on art and architecture and for families with kids aged 5–14 at weekends – see website for times and details • ☎ 030 22 73 21 52, ⓦ bundestag.de • ⓤ Bundestag

Directly behind the Brandenburger Tor a line of cobbles marks the course of the Berlin Wall where for 28 years it separated the Gate from the other great emblem of national unity, the **Reichstag**, which was restored as the seat of the Bundestag, Germany's parliament, in 1999. The imposing nineteenth-century Neoclassical Reichstag immediately impresses, its stolid, bombastic form wholly in keeping with its pivotal role in history. The building's main visitor attraction, however, is its giant glass **dome**,

1

THE REICHSTAG IN HISTORY

The current iteration of the **Reichstag**, an expanded version of its predecessor at Leipziger Strasse 3 (which today houses the Bundesrat, or Federal Council), was built between 1884 and 1894 using money gained from French war reparations after the Franco-Prussian War. In November 1918, Philipp Scheidemann, a leading politician within the Social Democratic Party (SPD), declared the founding of the German Republic from a window here, paving the way for the Weimar Republic. The Republic lasted just fourteen years until the Nazis claimed power in 1933, partly as a consequence of a Reichstag fire, seen across the world in flickering newsreels. Debate as to who actually started the fire continues to this day: in a show trial, an itinerant ex-communist Dutch bricklayer, **Marius van der Lubbe**, was successfully charged with arson and executed the following year, though it's more likely that the perpetrators were Nazi. What's beyond doubt is that the fire was used as an excuse to introduce an emergency decree, suspending civil rights and effectively instigating a dictatorship.

Equally famously, the Reichstag became a symbol of the Allied victory at the end of World War II, when soldiers raised the Soviet flag on its roof – even though heavy fighting still raged below. The building was left in tatters by the conflict, and only in 1971 was its reconstruction completed. In 1990 the government of a reunified Germany decided to move its parliament back, though that didn't happen until April 19, 1999, once all its interiors had been refashioned and the new cupola set atop the building. More than just a stunning new refurbishment, this became part of a huge drive to improve energy efficiency – the Reichstag is one of the most energy-efficient parliament buildings in the world, with all energy coming from renewables.

supported by a soaring mirrored column, which was designed by British architect Sir Norman Foster. A circular ramp spirals up through the interior to a **roof terrace** with stunning 360-degree views of the city. In the foreground the Regierungsviertel buildings (see p.104) and the massive Tiergarten dominate, but the Sony Center (see p.89), the Fernsehturm (see p.61) and the shimmering golden roof of the synagogue on Orianienburger Strasse (see p.77) are also obvious landmarks. If you haven't booked in advance, reserve a table at the *Käfer Dachgarten* restaurant (see p.198), which has fairly good views itself, but, crucially, also gives you access to the dome.

Having explored the Reichstag's interior, wander around the outside of the building and try to spot the scores of patched bullet holes around some of its windows, dating from the last days of the Battle of Berlin. At the back of the building, beside the River Spree and the nearest corner of the Tiergarten, there is also a poignant series of **plaques** and **crosses** with the names (where known) of those who died attempting to swim or climb the East German border here.

Pre-booked visitors can attend a free lecture in the visitors' gallery of the plenary chamber and watch a Bundestag debating session or, when parliament is not sitting, take a ninety-minute **tour** of the building, which discusses its architecture and various functions.

Memorial to the Sinti and Roma Victims of National Socialism

Simsonweg • ☎ 030 263 94 30, ⓦ stiftung-denkmal.de • ⓤ/Ⓢ Brandenburger Tor

The **Memorial to the Sinti and Roma Victims of National Socialism** (Denkmal für die im Nationalsozialismus ermordeten Sinti und Roma Europas) lies in the northeastern corner of the Tiergarten beside the Reichstag. Unveiled in 2012, a decade after its inception (and the most recent Holocaust monument until the memorial to euthanasia victims was erected in 2014; see p.95), it commemorates the half-million Roma and Sinti that died at the hands of the Nazis. Haunting violin music plays around a circular pond, surrounded by rough stone flags; at the centre is a rock upon which a single fresh flower is placed every day. According to Dani Karavan, the aptly named Israeli sculptor behind the project, this flower has supreme significance as the murdered Sinti and Roma lie in unmarked plots in huge cemeteries with only plants growing above them. The flower lies on a triangle, which represents the triangle the Nazis forced all gypsies to wear. Meanwhile the dark pond reflects the trees, the Reichstag and anyone who gazes into it – in that way the viewer becomes part of the memorial and part of the process of remembrance.

Memorial to the Murdered Jews of Europe

Cora-Berliner-Str. 1 • **Memorial** 24hr; free • Tours in English Sat 3pm; €3 • **Information centre** Tues–Sun: April–Sept 10am–8pm (last admission 7.15pm); Oct–March 10am–7pm (last admission 6.15pm) • Free; audio tours €4 • ☎ 030 26 39 43 36, ⓦ holocaustmahnmal.de • ⓤ/Ⓢ Brandenburger Tor

The block of land immediately south of the Brandenburger Tor and Pariser Platz is officially called the **Memorial to the Murdered Jews of Europe** (Denkmal für die ermordeten Juden Europas), and generally known as the **Holocaust Memorial**. Unveiled in 2006 after almost seventeen years of planning and controversy and six years of construction, the monument was the work of New York architect Peter Eisenman, who took inspiration from the densely clustered gravestones of Prague's Jewish graveyard. It involves 2711 dark grey oblong pillars (stele), evenly and tightly spaced but of varying heights, spread across an area the size of two football pitches. As there is no single entrance, visitors make their own way through the maze to the centre where the blocks are well above head height, tending to convey a sense of gloom, isolation and solitude, even though Eisenman insists his intent was to create a "place of hope". At night, the space is illuminated by 180 lights; a sombre yet stunning spectacle.

Undeniably powerful, the memorial has faced various criticisms: for being unnecessarily large in scale; for its use of prime real estate with little historical significance; and for its incredible costs (around €25 million) for a city with tight finances. Also highly contentious was the hiring of German company Degussa (now Evonik) to supply the anti-graffiti paint for the blocks, since they are a daughter company of IG Farben – the company that produced Zyklon B, the gas used in the Nazi gas chambers.

The underground **information centre**, in the southeast corner of the memorial, relates the life stories and plight of some Jewish victims of the Holocaust. Carefully researched and expertly presented, the small exhibition outlines the overall history of the Nazi hounding and extermination of Jews before moving on to the personal stories that lurk behind the monstrous statistics. Among them are notes left by those on their way to their death – including some thrown from the cattle wagons as they were transported to death camps. The **audio tour** is largely unnecessary, but does help flesh things out a little and acts as a donation to the foundation that built and runs the memorial.

Memorial to Homosexuals Persecuted under Nazism

Ebertstr. • ☎ 030 263 94 30, ⓦ stiftung-denkmal.de • ⓤ/Ⓢ Brandenburger Tor or ⓤ/Ⓢ Potsdamer Platz

Across the road from the Holocaust Memorial, the fringes of the Tiergarten hold one more concrete slab, the 4m-high cube dedicated as the Gay Holocaust Memorial. Officially called the **Memorial to Homosexuals Persecuted under Nazism** (Denkmal für die im Nationalsozialismus verfolgten Homosexuellen), it remembers the 54,000 people who were convicted of homosexual acts under the regime; an estimated eight thousand of these died in concentration camps. Inaugurated by Berlin's (gay) former mayor Klaus Wowereit in 2008, the monument mimics the stele commemorating Jewish victims, but also contains a window behind which plays a film of same-sex couples (alternating between men and women every year or so) kissing.

Hitler's bunker and around

Gertrud-Kolmar-Str. • ⓤ/Ⓢ Brandenburger Tor or ⓤ/Ⓢ Potsdamer Platz

It's only a minute's walk south of the Holocaust Memorial to its oddest possible bedfellow: the site of **Hitler's bunker** – of which nothing remains – where the Führer spent his last days, issuing meaningless orders as the Battle of Berlin raged above. Here

1

Hitler married Eva Braun and wrote his final testament: he personally was responsible for nothing; he had been betrayed by the German people, who had proved unequal to his leadership and deserved their fate. On April 30, 1945, he shot himself, and his body was hurriedly burned by loyal officers. A roadside sign at the end of the Ministergärten (see below) provides a plan of the bunker detailing its rooms and their functions. Though it's often assumed that the bunker was glamorously furnished, the diagram accurately reveals how spartan the facility was.

The sign also maps the astonishing number of other bunkers that were once in the vicinity, the largest one being under the **Neues Reichskanzlei** (New Reich Chancellery), the vast building designed by Albert Speer in 1938 as part of the Nazi remodelling of the government area around Wilhelmstrasse. This gigantic complex ran to the north of and almost the length of Vossstrasse. Today nothing remains, for even though the Chancellery building survived the war, it was torn down in a fit of revenge by the conquering Soviet army, who used its marble to fashion the memorial on Strasse des 17 Juni (see p.102) and the huge war memorial at the Soviet military cemetery in Treptower Park (see p.132).

In den Ministergärten

The lands immediately west of Hitler's bunker were, during the Wall years, part of the death strip separating East and West Berlin. On reunification it was decided to resuscitate this part of the Regierungsviertel by inviting the government ministries from Germany's sixteen states to build on a street named **In den Ministergärten** in their honour. However, only seven took up the offer – the rest chose to avoid the historically charged site – with all opting for similarly dynamic modern designs replete with imposing entrances, atria and exhibition spaces. For the most part, however, they simply house offices and ministerial accommodation.

Wilhelmstrasse

From 1871 to the end of the Third Reich, **Wilhelmstrasse** was Imperial Berlin's Whitehall and Downing Street rolled into one. Its many ministries and government buildings included the Chancellery and, after the Republic was established in 1918, the Presidential Palace. Today little remains, but trying to figure out what was where can be compelling, and information boards with photos and descriptions of the former buildings have helpfully been placed along the street. Most structures are fairly dull apartment buildings that once housed high-ranking East Germans; the only one that stands out is an apparent airport control tower that turns out to be the **Czech Embassy**. North of here, a road closure announces the presence of the **British Embassy**. This counter-terrorism measure allows you to properly appreciate the eye-pleasing, quirky building by Michael Wilford; its austere stone facade is broken up at the centre by a riot of shapes in cool grey and violent purple – playful elements thought to reflect the British sense of humour and style.

Unter den Linden and around

Berlin's grandest boulevard, **Unter den Linden**, runs east from the Brandenburger Tor towards the Spreeinsel and once formed the main east–west axis of Imperial Berlin. The street – "beneath the lime trees" – was named after the trees on its central island; the first saplings were planted by Friedrich Wilhelm, the Great Elector, during the seventeenth century to line the route from his palace to his hunting grounds in the Tiergarten (see p.102). The original trees were replaced by crude Nazi flagpoles during the 1930s, so the present generation dates from postwar planting.

Until 1989 the western end of Unter den Linden also marked the end of the road for East Berliners: a low barrier ran a hundred metres or so short of the Brandenburger Tor. From here it was possible to view the gate, beyond which the discreet presence of armed border guards and the sterile white concrete of the Wall signalled the frontier with West Berlin. This reduced Unter den Linden to little more than a grand blind alley, which – lined by infrequently visited embassies – gave it a strangely empty and largely decorative feel. Revitalization since 1989 has helped the boulevard reassume something of its old role and today it's busy and bustling, fringed by shops and cafés, though their presence is relatively muted.

Madame Tussauds Berlin

Unter den Linden 74 • Daily: June–Aug 9.30am–7.30pm (last entry 6.30pm); Sept–May 10am–7pm (last entry 6pm) • €14 booked online (children aged 3–14 €11), €23.50 on the day (kids €18.50); from €28 in combination with Berlin Dungeon (see p.64) • ☏ 0180 654 58 00, ⓦ madametussauds.com • ⓤ/Ⓢ Brandenburger Tor

The shiny faces and glassy eyes at **Madame Tussauds Berlin** belong mainly to German celebrities, though a clutch of Hollywood stars also get a look-in. Things kick off with Otto von Bismarck and Karl Marx, followed by Adolf Hitler sitting wild-eyed in a bunker, with Anne Frank and anti-Nazi campaigner Sophie Scholl close by to provide a kinder face for the era. Local political heroes and villains also make their appearances: John F. Kennedy; West German statesman Willy Brandt; East German leader Erich Honecker; Mikhail Gorbachev. All these waxworks feel pretty true to life; not so the laughably awkward renditions of Barack Obama and Angela Merkel. From the entertainment sections there's more local interest in the form of Marlene Dietrich and Bertolt Brecht, though it's the aggressive stance of former Germany goalkeeper Oliver Kahn that makes the greatest impression. A recently added *Star Wars* section offers extra interest for kids and adults alike; **book online** for sizeable discounts and time-slot tickets that will beat the queues.

Russian Embassy

Unter den Linden 63–65 • ⓤ/Ⓢ Brandenburger Tor

One of the first buildings you'll see as you head east from Pariser Platz is the massive **Russian Embassy**, rearing up on the right. Built in 1950 on the site of the prewar (originally Tsarist) embassy, it was the first postwar building to be erected on Unter den Linden and an example of the much maligned *Zuckerbäckerstil* or "wedding-cake style": a kind of blunted, monumental Classicism characteristic of Stalin-era Soviet architecture. Berlin has a number of such buildings, the most spectacular being along Karl-Marx-Allee (see p.134).

Friedrichstrasse

Halfway along Unter den Linden, you come to its most important intersection as it crosses the busy shopping street of **Friedrichstrasse**. Before the war this was one of the busiest crossroads in the city, with Friedrichstrasse a well-known prostitutes' haunt lined by cafés, bars and restaurants. Nazi puritanism dealt the first blow to this thriving *Vergnügungsviertel* (Pleasure Quarter), and the work was finished by Allied bombers, which effectively razed the street. Rebuilt considerably wider, what had once been a narrow, slightly claustrophobic street became a broad, desolate road. Since reunification, Friedrichstrasse has been extensively revamped. Bland modern edifices now house offices, malls and a series of fairly high-end boutiques that rub shoulders with more everyday shops, including several good bookshops.

Staatsbibliothek zu Berlin

Dorotheenstr. 27 • Mon–Fri 9am–9pm, Sat 9am–7pm; 90min tours Fri 5pm & first Sat in month 10.30am • Free, including tours • ☏ 030 26 60, ⓦ staatsbibliothek-berlin.de • ⓤ Französische Strasse or ⓤ/Ⓢ Friedrichstrasse

First the Prussian, then GDR state library, the **Staatsbibliothek zu Berlin** (State Library) is a typically grandiose edifice dating from the turn of the twentieth century, with a facade that was extensively patched up after wartime shrapnel damage. Now twinned with the Staatsbibliothek in the Kulturforum (see p.94), it is mainly the haunt of

1

Humboldt University students. Visitors who don't feel like delving into the volumes within can sit in the ivy-clad courtyard by the fountain. As you do so, admire a GDR-era sculpture showing a member of the proletariat apparently reading a didactic Brecht poem in relief on the other side of the fountain.

DB Kunsthalle
Unter den Linden 13–15 • Daily 10am–8pm • €4, free on Mon • ☎ 030 20 20 930, ⓦ deutsche-bank-kunsthalle.de • ⓤ Französische Strasse

Located on the ground floor of the Deutsche Bank – where it replaced the highly successful Deutsche Guggenheim – the **DB Kunsthalle** (DB Art Gallery) presents contemporary art from all corners of the globe (Asia, Africa, South America), running collaborations with local and international museums such as London's Tate Modern and the Jewish Museum in New York. The Kunsthalle's opening exhibition in 2013 was a retrospective of Pakistani artist Imran Qureshi, while others have included collaborations with the Zachęta gallery in Warsaw, and a retrospective of Indian painter Bhupen Khakhar. There are also weekly lunchtime lectures (Wed at 1pm), and free guided tours through the current exhibition followed by a vegan lunch (not free) based on fresh farm produce.

Bebelplatz and around
ⓤ Hausvogteiplatz

The imposing Neoclassical **Bebelplatz** marks the start of Berlin's eighteenth-century showpiece quarter, which stretches two blocks southwest from Unter den Linden to the Gendarmenmarkt (see p.47). Bebelplatz itself was conceived by Frederick the Great as both a tribute to ancient Rome and a monument to himself. He and the architect **Georg Wenzeslaus von Knobelsdorff** drew up plans for a space that would recall the great open squares of the Classical city and be known as Forum Fridericianum. It never quite fulfilled such lofty ambitions, although the architecture of many of the buildings – including the **Staatsoper**, the Law Faculty of **Humboldt Universität**, **Sankt-Hedwigs-Kathedrale** and the Dresdner Bank (now the swanky **Hotel de Rome**, whose interiors were used in the film *Run Lola Run*; see p.296) – did receive acclaim at the time. Their subsequent restorations today lend the square a fairly refined aura.

The Empty Library
Bebelplatz • ⓤ Hausvogteiplatz

At the windswept and otherwise featureless centre of Bebelplatz lies the **Empty Library**, a monument to the most infamous event to happen on the square. It was here that on May 10, 1933, the infamous **Büchverbrennung** took place, in front of the university, on what was then called Opernplatz. On the orders of Joseph Goebbels, Hitler's propaganda minister, twenty thousand books that conflicted with Nazi ideology went up in flames. Among them were the works of "un-German" authors like Erich Maria Remarque, Thomas and Heinrich Mann, Stefan Zweig and Erich Kästner, along with volumes by countless foreign writers, H.G. Wells and Ernest Hemingway among them. The most apt comment on this episode was made with unwitting foresight by the Jewish poet Heinrich Heine in the previous century: "Where they start by burning books, they'll end by burning people." The ingenious monument itself, by Micha Ullmann, is simply a room with empty shelves set in the ground under a pane of glass; it is at its most spectacular at night when a beam of light streams out.

Alte Bibliothek
Bebelplatz 1 • ⓤ Hausvogteiplatz

The **Alte Bibliothek** (Old Library), a former royal library, lines the western side of Bebelplatz with a curved Baroque facade that has given it the nickname *Die Kommode* ("the chest of drawers"). Built between 1775 and 1780, its design was based on that of the Michaelertrakt in Vienna's Hofburg, and, even though only the building's facade

OPPOSITE REICHSTAG DOME INTERIOR (P.37) >

1

survived the war, it has all been immaculately restored. Lenin spent some time here poring over dusty tomes prior to the Russian Revolution.

Frederick the Great statue

In the middle of Unter den Linden, just north of the Alte Bibliothek, is a nineteenth-century statue of **Frederick the Great** by Christian Rauch, showing Frederick astride a horse. Around the plinth, about a quarter of the size of the monarch, are representations of his generals, mostly on foot and conferring animatedly. After World War II, the statue of *Der alte Fritz*, as Frederick the Great is popularly known, was removed from Unter den Linden and only restored to its city-centre site in 1981 after a long exile in Potsdam.

Humboldt Universität

Unter den Linden 6 • Guided tours of the main building (1hr; €5; minimum two weeks advance notice) can be booked on ☎ 030 209 37 03 33 • ☎ 030 209 33 374, ⓦ hu-berlin.de • ⓤ/⑤ Friedrichstrasse

Over Unter den Linden from the Frederick statue but architecturally in tandem with the buildings around Bebelplatz, the restrained Neoclassical **Humboldt Universität** (Humboldt University) was built in 1748 as a palace for Frederick the Great's brother. In 1809 the philologist, writer and diplomat Wilhelm Humboldt founded a school here that was to become the University of Berlin; it was later renamed in his honour. Flanking the entrance gate are statues of Wilhelm and his brother Alexander, famous for their exploration of Central and South America. Wilhelm is contemplating the passing traffic, book in hand, and Alexander is sitting on a globe above a dedication to the "second discoverer of Cuba" from the University of Havana. Humboldt Universität alumni include Karl Marx, Friedrich Engels and Karl Liebknecht, the socialist leader and proclaimer of the first German Republic who was murdered in 1919 (see p.267). The philologists Jacob and Wilhelm Grimm (better known as the Brothers Grimm) and Albert Einstein are some of the best-known former members of staff.

Staatsoper

Unter den Linden 7 • ☎ 030 20 35 40, ⓦ staatsoper-berlin.de • ⓤ Hausvogteiplatz

Knobelsdorff's Neoclassical **Staatsoper** (State Opera House), on the east side of Bebelplatz, is among its plainer buildings, though it represented the pinnacle of the architect's career and was Berlin's first theatre. The building is best viewed from Unter den Linden, where an imposing portico marks the main entrance. Just under two centuries after its construction it became the first major building to fall victim to World War II bombing, on the night of April 9–10, 1941. The Nazis restored it for its bicentenary in 1943, but on February 3, 1945, it was gutted once again. Totally reconstructed after the war, the building has been undergoing extensive renovation since 2010 – during which period performances have been shifted to the Schiller Theater in west Berlin – and is set to reopen in autumn 2017.

Sankt-Hedwigs-Kathedrale

Hinter der Katholischen Kirche 3 • Mon–Wed 8am–2pm, Thurs 11.30am–5.30pm; closed Fri–Sun • Free • ☎ 030 20 348 10, ⓦ hedwigs-kathedrale.de • ⓤ Hausvogteiplatz

Just behind the Staatsoper is another Knobelsdorff creation, the stylistically incongruous **Sankt-Hedwigs-Kathedrale** (St Hedwig's Cathedral), which was built as a place of worship for the city's Catholic minority in 1747 and is still in use. According to popular legend it owes its circular shape and domed profile to Frederick the Great's demand that it be built in the form of an upturned teacup. Though the monarch did "advise" Knobelsdorff, in truth the building's shape was inspired by the Pantheon in Rome. The cathedral was reduced to a shell on March 2, 1943, and not reconstructed until 1963, a restoration that left it with a slightly altered dome and a modernized interior.

The vast **interior**, once you get past the hazy biblical reliefs of the entrance portico, is perhaps the most unusual aspect of the whole building. The most eye-catching feature is

the altar, which is bookended by dramatic columns and tall enough to span both levels of
the interior; the upper level is used on Sundays and special occasions, while the sunken
altar in the crypt, reached by a flight of broad stairs, is used for weekday masses. Additional
highlights worth looking out for are the wood, tin and copper pipes of the ethereal-
sounding organ above the entrance; the 1970s-style globe-lamps hanging from the ceiling;
and the crypt itself, with its eight grotto-like side chapels and near-abstract ink drawings.

Kronprinzenpalais

Unter den Linden 3 • ⑩ Hausvogteiplatz

The Baroque **Kronprinzenpalais** (Crown Prince's Palace) dates from 1663, but is really
defined by a 1732 facelift that gave it a more grandiose appearance to reflect its role as
a residence for Prussian princes. With the demise of the monarchy in 1918 it became a
national art gallery and a leading venue for modern art, though this lasted only fifteen
years until its closure by the Nazis, who declared the hundreds of Expressionist and
contemporary works housed within to be examples of *Entartete Kunst* or "degenerate
art". Most artworks were either sold off abroad or destroyed, though a number were
bought at knock-down prices by leading Nazis, Göring among them. Destroyed during
World War II, it was rebuilt in the 1960s, and since reunification has hosted a variety
of events and temporary exhibitions.

Deutsches Historisches Museum

Unter den Linden 2 • Daily 10am–6pm • €8 • ⑩ 030 20 30 44 44, ⑩ dhm.de • ⑤ Hackescher Markt

The **Deutsches Historisches Museum** (German Historical Museum) is spread across two
buildings: the Baroque **Zeughaus**, Unter den Linden's oldest building, and a modern
exhibition hall designed by Chinese-American architect **I.M. Pei**. Between them they
chart German history from the Dark Ages to the present via eight thousand or so
objects. You should allow at least two hours, and with only a relatively small proportion
of the exhibition in English, the **audio guide** is recommended. There's also a very
tasteful and little-known cinema (see p.257) and good restaurant, both entered from
the Spree side of the museum.

The Zeughaus

The museum's permanent exhibition is housed in the eighteenth-century **Zeughaus** (see
box below). Though slanted – understandably – towards military history, it does try to
show how big events or "epochs of change" have affected the masses. It's attractively set

---

THE ZEUGHAUS: A HISTORY

The sturdy old Prussian Arsenal, or **Zeughaus**, was built by the Brandenburg Elector Friedrich
III between 1695 and 1730. Many of its decorative elements are the work of Andreas Schlüter,
notably the walls of the **Schlüterhof**, the museum's inner courtyard, where reliefs depict the
contorted faces of dying warriors. There was much tumult at the Zeughaus on June 14, 1848,
when, during revolutionary upheavals, crowds of demonstrators stormed the building in
search for arms. No weapons were found but a number of citizens were killed, and the incident
gave the authorities an excuse to bring troops into the city and ban various newspapers and
democratic organizations.

Just over thirty years later the Zeughaus was turned into a Prussian army museum. During
the Nazi period it exhibited World War I propaganda – portraying the war as an undeserved
defeat and making much of the dishonest conduct of enemies during the peace treaties – and
hosted Heroes' Memorial Day speeches each March. At the 1943 event there was a failed
attempt on Hitler's life; the Führer changed his plans, giving the suicide bomber, Rudolf von
Gersdorff, just enough time to rush to the lavatory and defuse the bomb. Heavily damaged
during the war, the building became a museum of German history in 1952, at first offering a
communist perspective of events, and later, after reunification, a progressively more balanced,
Western view in the form of the Deutsches Historisches Museum.

1

out and deals cleverly with difficult or contentious areas – such as the rise of nationalism and concepts of German nationhood – by simply providing a balanced summary of the main facts and avoiding interpretation.

Highlights from the early collection include an extraordinary assemblage of **armour** from the old Zeughaus days – including a 15kg jousting helmet – and an impressive collection of early sixteenth-century **bibles**, some of the first books to be printed anywhere. But the most engrossing exhibits are of later periods, following the French Revolution, where the museum offers a balanced view of Prussia, attempting to explain how it slid from being one of the most progressive parts of Europe to one of its most militarized powers. On display are several **helmets** – gruesomely memorable for their bullet holes – of soldiers killed in action during World War I.

The exhibition goes on to examine Weimar Germany and the rise of philosophical extremes, particularly communism and fascism, with insightful displays of propagandist art and leaflets. The **Third Reich** is explored in every deplorable detail – including the depiction of the war in Russian, American and Nazi **propaganda films**, the last showing the launch of the *Blitzkrieg* in Poland and mocking Jewish captives in chain gangs. It also covers the GDR years, where the exhibition splits to tell the parallel stories of the two Germanys.

I.M. Pei Bau

The eye-catching swirling glass building behind the Zeughaus is the work of Chinese-American architect **I.M. Pei** – most famous for his glass pyramid at the entrance to the Louvre in Paris. Pei's hallmark geometric glass is here, too, with the resulting play of

---

KARL FRIEDRICH SCHINKEL (1781–1841)

Incredibly prolific, **Karl Friedrich Schinkel** was without doubt one of the most influential German architects of the nineteenth century: nearly every town in Brandenburg has a building in which he had some involvement. Schinkel's first-ever design, the small **Pomonatempel** in Potsdam, was completed while he was still a nineteen-year-old student in Berlin, though it was not till 1810, after a period working as a landscape artist and theatre-set designer, that he secured a job with the administration of Prussian buildings and begun submitting architectural designs for great public works.

In 1815 Schinkel was given a position in the new Public Works Department, and in the years up to 1830 designed some of his most renowned buildings. These included the Greek-style **Neue Wache** (see opposite), the elegant **Schauspielhaus** (see p.48) and the **Altes Museum** (see p.55) with its striking Doric columns – all of which served to symbolize the ever-expanding power of the Prussian capital. Later in his career Schinkel experimented with other architectural forms, a phase marked by the Romanesque **Schloss Charlottenhof** in Potsdam (see p.181) and the **Friedrichswerdersche Kirche**, a rather plain neo-Gothic affair inspired from churches he had seen on a visit to England in 1826.

THE BAUAKADEMIE

One of Schinkel's most interesting buildings was the **Bauakademie** (Building Academy), built in 1836 as an architectural school. Widely considered to be one of modern architecture's true ancestors, rejecting the Classicism around it in favour of brick exterior and terracotta ornamentation, the building spoke of industrialization and a changing view towards design and construction, and even at the time it was thought to be one of Schinkel's finest creations; he seemed to agree, moving in and occupying a top-floor apartment until his death in 1841. The Kaiser, however, hated it, referring to it as "the horrible red box that blots the view from the palace" (see box, p.52), and the GDR regime also had no time for it, demolishing it in 1962. There are, however, proposals to rebuild. As an advertisement and incentive, a corner section of the building has been reconstructed on its original site. The rest of the building has been recreated using scaffolding, wrapped in a canvas facade in an attempt to stimulate enthusiasm and raise funds for reconstruction. Detailed plans have been made for its future use, but despite rumours of an (anonymous) investor, no official announcements had been made at the time of writing.

1

light perhaps the most important factor in making the building work. Temporary exhibitions here usually delve into German social history from the last couple of centuries, and vary widely, though all have in common first-class displays and even-handedness in the treatment of often difficult subject matters.

Neue Wache

Unter den Linden 4 • Daily 10am–6pm • ⓤ Französische Strasse

Resembling a stylized Roman temple, Karl Friedrich Schinkel's most celebrated surviving creation, the Neoclassical **Neue Wache** (New Guardhouse), was built between 1816 and 1818 for the royal watch. It was converted in 1930–31 into a memorial to the military dead of World War I, a concept then extended under the GDR in 1957 to include those killed by Nazis: as a "Memorial to the Victims of Fascism and Militarism". Until 1990 one of East Berlin's most iconic ceremonies was played out in front of the Neue Wache – the goose-stepping ritual of the changing of the East German Nationale Volksarmee (NVA, or National People's Army) honour guard. These days the monument serves as the "National Memorial to the Victims of War and Tyranny": inside, a granite slab covers the tombs of an unknown soldier and an unknown concentration camp victim, at the head of which a statue depicts a mother clutching her dying son – a larger version of the famous *Mother with her Dead Son* sculpture by Käthe Kollwitz (see p.113).

Theater im Palais

Am Festungsgraben 1 • ⓣ 030 20 10 693, ⓦ theater-im-palais.de • ⓤ/ⓢ Friedrichstrasse

The grand-looking building behind the Neue Wache, the Palais am Festungsgraben (Palace on the Moat) has had a chequered career. Built during the eighteenth century as a palace for a royal gentleman of the bedchamber, it later served as a residence for Prussian finance ministers, and during GDR days as the Zentrale Haus der Deutsch-Sowjetischen Freundschaft (Central House of German–Soviet Friendship). Today it houses the **Theater im Palais** (see p.234). Next to the Palais, the **Maxim-Gorki-Theater** (see p.234) is a one-time singing academy converted into a theatre after World War II.

Gendarmenmarkt

ⓤ Französische Strasse

The immaculately restored **Gendarmenmarkt** is one of Berlin's architectural highlights – it's hard to imagine that all its buildings were almost obliterated during the war and that reconstruction was only completed in the 1980s. The Gendarmenmarkt's **origins** are prosaic. It was originally home to Berlin's main market until the Gendarme regiment set up their stables on the site in 1736 and gave the square its name. With the departure of the military, the Gendarmenmarkt was transformed at the behest of Frederick the Great, who ordered an architectural revamp of its two churches – the **Französischer Dom** and **Deutscher Dom** – in an attempt to mimic the Piazza del Popolo in Rome.

The surrounding grid-like streets are testament to the area's seventeenth-century origins, when this pattern of building was the norm, and when a number of city extensions took Berlin beyond its original walled core. Once known as Friedrichstadt, this area became a Huguenot stronghold thanks to Prussian guarantees of religious freedom and rights that attracted them in numbers.

Französischer Dom

Gendarmenmarkt 5 • **Church** Tues–Sun noon–5pm • Free • ⓦ franzoesische-friedrichstadtkirche.de • **Tower** Daily: Jan & Feb noon–5pm; early to mid-March 11am–6pm; mid- to late March 10.30am–6.30pm; April–Oct 10am–7pm (last entry 6pm) • €3.50 • ⓣ 03 02 29 17 60, ⓦ franzoesischer-dom.de • ⓤ Französische Strasse

Frederick the Great's Gendarmenmarkt revamp is at its most impressive and eye-catching in the **Französischer Dom** (French Cathedral), a colloquial name for what

1

is officially called the Französischen Friedrichstadtkirche (French Church in Friedrichstadt), at the northern end of the square. Built as a simple place of worship for the influential Huguenot community at the beginning of the eighteenth century, the building was transformed by the addition, eighty years later, of a Baroque tower, turning it into one of Berlin's most appealing churches. The **cathedral tower**'s bells ring out daily at noon, 3pm and 7pm, with bell-ringing concerts sometimes performed at other times – ask at the desk for details. You can climb up the tower via a longish spiral of steps to a platform with good views over the square – note that standing here when the bells ring will be a near-deafening experience.

The Dom tower is so striking that a lot of visitors don't actually notice the church proper, which is modest enough in appearance that it looks more like an ancillary building. The main entrance to the church is at the western end of the Dom, facing Charlottenstrasse. The church, reconsecrated in 1983 after years of restoration work, has a simple hall-like interior with few decorative features and only a plain table as an altar.

Hugenottenmuseum

Französischer Dom, Gendarmenmarkt 5 • Tues–Sat noon–5pm • €3.50 • ☎ 030 229 17 60, ⓦ hugenottenmuseum-berlin.de • ⓤ Französische Strasse

Inside the church at the base of the Dom tower is the entrance to the **Hugenottenmuseum**, detailing the history of the Huguenots in France and Brandenburg. Exhibits deal with the theological background of the Reformation in France, the Revocation of the Edict of Nantes leading to the flight of the Huguenots from their native country, their settlement in Berlin and the influence of the new arrivals on trade, science and literature. There is also a short section on the destruction and rebuilding of the Dom.

Deutscher Dom

Gendarmenmarkt 1–2 • Tues–Sun: May–Sept 10am–7pm; Oct–April 10am–6pm • Free; free English-language audio guides available at the front desk (ID required as deposit) • ☎ 030 22 73 043, ⓦ bundestag.de/deutscherdom • ⓤ Französische Strasse

At the southern end of the Gendarmenmarkt, the **Deutscher Dom** (German Cathedral), built in 1708 for the city's Lutheran community, is the stylistic twin of the Französischer Dom. It now hosts the fairly dull **"Wege-Irrwege-Umwege"** ("Way-wrong turns-detours") exhibition, which looks in detail at Germany's democratic history. A wander up through the Dom with its labyrinth of galleries is the highlight, and the reward for reaching the top is the chance to see a few scale models of some early Norman Foster designs for the reconstruction of the Reichstag (see p.37).

Konzerthaus Berlin

Gendarmenmarkt • Tours: 30min daily (free); 90min Sat 1pm (€3) • ☎ 030 203 09 23 33, ⓦ konzerthaus.de • ⓤ Hausvogteiplatz

Between the Gendarmenmarkt's two churches stands Schinkel's Neoclassical **Konzerthaus Berlin** (formerly called the Schauspielhaus), built between 1818 and 1821 on the site of Langhans' National Theatre, which burned down in 1817; Schinkel retained the theatre's original exterior walls and portico columns. A broad sweep of steps leads up to the main entrance and into the incredibly opulent interior, where chandeliers, marble, gilded plasterwork and pastel-hued wall paintings compete for attention. Gutted during a raid in 1943, the building suffered further damage during heavy fighting as the Russians attempted to root out SS troops who had dug in here. It reopened in October 1984 and during Christmas 1989, Leonard Bernstein conducted a performance of Beethoven's Ninth Symphony in the theatre to celebrate the *Wende*, with the word *Freiheit* ("Freedom") substituted for *Freude* ("Joy") in Schiller's choral finale.

Schiller statue

Gendarmenmarkt • ⓤ Hausvogteiplatz

The **statue of Schiller** outside the Konzerthaus was repositioned here in 1988, having been removed by the Nazis to make space for military parades more than fifty years earlier. It was returned to what was then East Berlin from the West in exchange for reliefs originally from the Pfaueninsel (see p.172) and a statue from a Tiergarten villa. Outside Germany, Friedrich Schiller (1759–1805) is best known for the *Ode to Joy* that provides the words to the final movements of Beethoven's Ninth Symphony, but in his homeland he is venerated as one of the greatest German poets and dramatists of Weimar Classicism. His works, from early *Sturm und Drang* dramas like *Die Räuber* ("The Thieves") to later historical plays like *Maria Stuart* (portraying the last days of Mary, Queen of Scots), were primarily concerned with freedom – political, moral and personal.

Bunte Schokowelt

Französische Str. 24 • Mon–Wed 10am–7pm, Thurs–Sat 10am–8pm, Sun 10am–6pm • Free • ❶ 030 20 09 50 80, ⓦ ritter-sport.de • ⓤ Französische Strasse

Despite being fairly barefaced corporate propaganda for German chocolatiers Ritter Sport, **Bunte Schokowelt** (Colourful Chocolate World) can be excused since the dozens of varieties of chocolate created by this family-run company are delicious. The key attraction here is that you can design your own chocolate bar and have it made on the spot; it takes about thirty minutes, during which time there's a little museum to browse – which includes a range of amusing Ritter Sport German TV ads from the 1950s onwards. There's also a pleasant café and many chocolatey bargains amid the extraordinary selection in the shop.

Jägerstrasse

ⓤ Französische Strasse

Leading west from the Gendarmenmarkt, **Jägerstrasse** was the site of particularly heavy fighting during the 1848 revolution, but is best known as the centre of Berlin's nineteenth-century **banking quarter**. It was from here that the Mendelssohn & Co., a huge Jewish concern founded by the sons of philosopher Moses Mendelssohn, bankrolled much of Berlin's industrial revolution: a plaque on the north side of the street, outside no. 51, tells the story.

German Foreign Ministry

Werdescher Markt 11 • ⓦ auswaertiges-amt.de • ⓤ Hausvogteiplatz

The **German Foreign Ministry** (Auswärtiges Amt der Bundesrepublik Deutschland) stands behind the Bauakademie (see box, p.46), beside the River Spree. The structure, though massive, projects an unassuming aspect by means of its plain glass facade, through which you can see a serene covered courtyard complete with trees and fountain. It illustrates one answer to a common problem facing architects for the German capital: how to create large and significant civic buildings while avoiding any hints of Nazi monumentalism. A good example of the latter, and now also occupied by the Foreign Office, lies directly behind: the immense and imposing former Reichsbank, built between 1934 and 1938. Having survived the war, it became the SED (Socialist Unity Party of Germany) headquarters and thus the nerve centre of the East German Communist party.

ISHTAR GATE, PERGAMONMUSEUM

Museum Island and around

The Museuminsel, or Museum Island, is home to some of the world's greatest museums and an absolute must for any visitor to Berlin. It occupies the Spreeinsel, the island in the River Spree that formed the core of the medieval twin town Berlin-Cölln (see p.261). From the fifteenth century onwards, due to its defensive position, the Spreeinsel became the site of the *Residenz* – the fortress-cum-palace and church of the ruling Hohenzollern family. The church – the Berliner Dom – still stands, as does the museum quarter built in the 1800s on the island's northern tip. There are five museums in total, each worthy of in-depth exploration: the Pergamonmuseum, with its jaw-dropping antiquities; the Altes Museum, and its superlative Greek vases; the Neues Museum, specializing in Ancient Egypt; the Altes Nationalgalerie, full of nineteenth-century European paintings; and the Bode-Museum, one of Europe's most important sculpture collections.

Schlossplatz and around

Just south of Museum Island lies the giant building site of **Schlossplatz**. Along with the **Berliner Dom**, the Schloss that once stood here (see box, p.52) formed the heart of the imperial *Residenz*. This began as a martial, fortified affair – as much for protection from the perennially rebellious Berliners as from outside enemies – but over the years domestic stability meant it could be reshaped on a more decorative basis. In a demonstrative break with Prussia's imperial past the GDR tore down the war-damaged palace to make way for a huge parade plaza and some of its most important civic buildings: the Palast der Republik (see box, p.52) and the **Staatsratsgebäude**. Then, in another demonstrative break, the postcommunist administration decided to tear down the former and rebuild the Schloss as the **Berlin Palace–Humboldt Forum** – an ongoing, and not uncontroversial project.

2

Berlin Palace–Humboldt Forum and Humboldt Box

Berlin Palace Humboldt Forum ⓦ sbs-humboldtforum.de • **Humboldt Box** Schlossplatz 5 • Daily: April–Nov 10am–7pm; Dec–March 10am–6pm • Free • ☎ 030 29 02 78 248, ⓦ humboldt-box.com • ⓢ Hackescher Markt

The reconstruction of the Hohenzollern royal palace is, along with the long-delayed Berlin Brandenburg Airport, one of the largest and most controversial building projects in the city. Following years of lengthy and divisive arguments between those for and against resurrecting the Prussian landmark – not least due to the hugely ambitious €670 million price tag for a notoriously debt-ridden city – plans were finally given the go-ahead in 2002. Dubbed the **Berlin Palace–Humboldt Forum**, the Schloss's new incarnation was well underway at the time of writing. Its design largely copies the eighteenth-century version's original dimensions and ornate facades – including Schlüter's famous open courtyard – though the eastern (Spree) side is strikingly modern. The interior, equally contemporary, will house a mix of cultural and scientific institutions, including two of the state museums in Dahlem, the Ethnologisches Museum and the Museum für Asiatische Kunst (see p.168).

Construction is unlikely to be complete before 2019 at the earliest, but in the meantime it's possible to visit the **Humboldt Box** – an incongruously angular and futuristic makeshift venue that offers a detailed history of the site, including a delightful scale model of Unter den Linden, Museum Island and the Schloss around 1900. A tremendous amount of work has gone into getting the historical details correct: even tiny statues have been reconstructed using aluminium foil. The exhibition also has some original palace stonework, detailed plans of the proposed reconstruction and a **café-restaurant** at the top, which offers great views over the building works and Museum Island.

Staatsratsgebäude

Schlossplatz 10 • ⓤ Hausvogteiplatz

When the Palast der Republik was pulled down, it left the one-time **Staatsratsgebäude**, or State Council building, as the only reminder of the GDR on

---

THE BRIDGES OF MUSEUM ISLAND

Unless you're hopping off bus #100 from Bahnhof Zoo or Alexanderplatz (alight at Schlossplatz) the most attractive way to get to Museum Island is from S-Bahn Hackescher Markt. From there walk west through the square, then through Monbijoupark to **Monbijoubrücke**, which crosses to the Bode-Museum, or duck under the railway arches and cross the Spree to the Alte Nationalgalerie on **Friedrichsbrücke**, another pedestrian bridge. Both bridges are replacements for ones destroyed by the German army during the Battle of Berlin – more interesting are a couple of the bridges that survived the war intact. Schinkel's **Schlossbrücke**, at the eastern end of Unter den Linden, is particularly impressive. It first opened on November 28, 1823 when not fully completed, lacking among other things a fixed balustrade: 22 people drowned when temporary wooden barriers collapsed. Eventually cast-iron balustrades were installed, featuring graceful dolphin, merman and sea-horse motifs designed by Schinkel. The **Jungfernbrücke**, meanwhile, a drawbridge tucked away behind the former Staatsratsgebäude, is Berlin's oldest surviving bridge, built in 1798.

Schlossplatz. A boxy 1960s building typical of East German state architecture, its facade is notable for the incorporation of a large section of the Schloss, including the balcony from which Karl Liebknecht proclaimed the German revolution in 1918 (see box below). The building is now the campus for the European School of Management and Technology.

Neuer Marstall

Schlossplatz 7 • ⑩ Klosterstrasse

2

The neo-Baroque **Neuer Marstall** (New Stables) was built at the turn of the twentieth century to house the hundreds of royal coaches and horses used to ferry the royal household around the city. During the 1918 November Revolution, it headquartered the revolutionary committee and sailors and Spartacists beat off government forces from within it. A pair of reliefs commemorate this deed of rebellious derring-do as well as Liebknecht's proclamation of the socialist republic. One shows Liebknecht apparently suspended above a cheering crowd of sailors and civilians, while the other, to the left of the entrance, has the head of Marx hovering over excited, purposeful-looking members of the proletariat.

FROM ROYAL SEAT TO COMMUNIST LANDMARK: THE OLD SCHLOSS AND THE PALAST DER REPUBLIK

Begun in 1443, the **Schloss** was home to the Hohenzollern family for nearly half a millennium. It was constantly extended and reshaped over the years; the first major overhaul came in the sixteenth century, which saw it transformed from a fortress into a Renaissance palace. Later the Schloss received a Baroque restyling, and subsequently virtually every German architect of note, including Schlüter, Schinkel and Schadow, was given the opportunity to add to it. For centuries it dominated the heart of Berlin, and until the 1930s no city-centre building was allowed to stand any higher.

On November 9, 1918, the end of the Hohenzollern era came when Karl Liebknecht proclaimed a "Free Socialist Republic" from one of the palace balconies, now preserved in the facade of the former Staatsrat building (see above), following the abdication of the Kaiser. Almost simultaneously, the Social Democrat Philipp Scheidemann announced a democratic German republic from the Reichstag; it was in fact the latter that prevailed, ushering in the pathologically unstable Weimar Republic of the 1920s.

After the war the Schloss, a symbol of the still recent imperial past, was an embarrassment to the GDR authorities, who dynamited its ruins in 1950, even though it was no more badly damaged than a number of other structures that were subsequently rebuilt.

THE PALAST DER REPUBLIK

It was no coincidence that the communist authorities chose the Imperial Schloss's former grounds as the site for the GDR's Volkskammer, or parliament. A piece of brutal 1970s modernism in glass and concrete, the huge, angular **Palast der Republik**, was completed in less than a thousand days, and became a source of great pride to Erich Honecker's regime. As well as the parliament, it also housed an entertainment complex: restaurants, cafés, a theatre and a bowling alley. It would host craft fairs, discos, folk nights and Christmas festivities, and going there on a day out – something that all East German children were entitled to do once they'd turned 14 – was considered by some a highlight of growing up.

While the exterior was notable for its bronze, reflective windows, the interior was at once a showcase of East German design and a masterpiece of tastelessness, the hundreds of lamps hanging from the ceiling of the main foyer giving rise to the nickname, *Erich's Lampenladen* – "Erich's lamp shop". Shortly before unification asbestos was discovered, and on October 3, 1990, the building closed for almost thirteen years while it was stripped out. With only the glass and a skeleton of steel beams left inside, the Palast briefly became a chic venue for exhibitions, concerts and installations (and even a nightclub on the fifteenth anniversary of the fall of the Wall) but in 2006, by order of the German Parliament, work started on its demolition.

Ribbeck-Haus

Breite Str. 35 • ⓾ Klosterstrasse

Dating from the seventeenth century, the delicately gabled, late-Renaissance **Ribbeck-Haus** is one of the city's oldest surviving buildings and now houses a branch of Berlin's public library. Although it has been modified several times throughout the centuries, it still serves as a good example of the wealthy and attractive townhouses that once lined this approach to the royal palace.

Berliner Dom

Am Lustgarten • Daily: April–Sept Mon–Sat 9am–8pm, Sun noon–8pm; Oct–March Mon–Sat 9am–7pm, Sun noon–7pm • €7, audio guide €3 • Guided tours can be booked on ☎ 030 202 69 119 • ⓦ berlinerdom.de • Ⓢ Hackescher Markt

2

A grand statement for the Protestant loyalties of the Hohenzollern family, the **Berliner Dom** (Berlin Cathedral) stands as a grand imperial symbol that managed to survive the GDR era. It was built at the start of the twentieth century – finished in 1905 – on the site of a more modest cathedral: fussily ornate with a huge dome flanked by four smaller ones, it was meant to resemble St Peter's in Rome, but comes across as a dowdy neo-Baroque imitation. The cathedral served the House of Hohenzollern as a family church until 1918, and its **vault** houses 94 sarcophagi containing the remains of various members of the line. The building was badly damaged in the war, but laborious reconstruction has created a simpler version of its prewar self, with various ornamental cupolas missing from the newly rounded-off domes.

The main entrance leads into the extravagantly overstated **Predigtkirche** (Sermon Church) the octagonal main body of the church. From the marbled pillars of the hall to the delicate plasterwork and gilt of the cupola, there's a sense that it's all meant to reflect Hohenzollern power rather than serve as a place of worship. As if to confirm this impression, six opulent Hohenzollern sarcophagi, including those of Great Elector Friedrich Wilhelm I, and his second wife, Dorothea – both designed by Schlüter – are housed in galleries at the northern and southern ends of the Predigtkirche. The spiritual underpinnings of the society they ruled are less ostentatiously represented by statues of Luther, Melanchthon, Calvin and Zwingli, along with four German princes, in the cornices above the pillars in the main hall.

In the south of the Predigtkirche is the restored **Tauf- und Traukirche**, a side chapel used for baptism and confirmation ceremonies. Ascend the 270 steps of the **outer walkway** around the dome for views of Museum Island and beyond.

Lustgarten

The **Lustgarten** (Pleasure Garden), the lively green expanse leading up to the Altes Museum on the northern side of the Schlossplatz, is a great spot for picnics or resting your feet between museum visits and so relaxed that it's hard to believe its history. Built as a military parade ground (and used by Wilhelm I and Napoleon), it later saw mass protests (a huge anti-Nazi demo here in 1933 prompted the banning of

demonstrations) and rallies (Hitler addressed up to a million people here). Bombed in the war and renamed Marx-Engels-Platz by the GDR, its current incarnation harks back to Peter Joseph Lenné's early nineteenth-century design with a central 13m-high fountain, as re-envisioned by German landscape architect Hans Loidl.

At the northern end of the Lustgarten, at the foot of the steps leading up to the Altes Museum, is a large **granite bowl** sculpture, carved from a huge glacier-deposited boulder found near Fürstenwalde, just outside Berlin, and brought here in 1828 to form part of the Altes Museum's rotunda. A mistake in Schinkel's plans meant that its 7m diameter made it too large, so, for want of a better plan, it was left here to become an unusual decorative feature.

Museum Island

The origins of **Museum Island** (Museumsinsel) as the location of Berlin's most important museums go back to 1810, when Friedrich Wilhelm III decided the city needed a museum to house his rather scant collection of royal treasures. He ordered the reclamation of a patch of Spree-side marsh and commissioned Schinkel to come up with a suitable building; thus was created the **Altes Museum**, at the head of the Lustgarten. Things really took off when German explorers and archeologists began plundering archeological sites in Egypt and Asia Minor. The booty brought back by the Egyptologist Carl Richard Lepsius in the 1840s formed the core of what was to become a huge collection, with the **Neues Museum** built to house it at the behest of Friedrich Wilhelm IV. Later that century the imperial haul was augmented by treasures brought from Turkey by Heinrich Schliemann, for which the vast **Pergamonmuseum**, opened in 1930, was constructed.

During World War II the contents of the museums were stashed away in bunkers and mine shafts, and in the confusion of 1945 and the immediate postwar years it proved difficult to recover the scattered works. Some had been destroyed, others ended up in museums in the Western sector and others disappeared to the East with the Red Army. Gradually, though, the various surviving pieces were tracked down and returned to Berlin – with the notable exception of **Priam's Treasure**, Schliemann's most famous find, which allegedly came from the ruins of the fabled city of Troy. This collection of nine thousand gold chains, elaborate silver pictures, gold coins and other amazing artefacts hit the front pages in 1993 when it finally resurfaced in Moscow, where it remains today.

Reunification brought together the impressive and long-divided collections of Museum Island, which is being completely **restored and partially remodelled** in an ambitious plan (ⓦmuseumsinsel-berlin.de), begun in 1999 and due for completion in 2017, which will include a new centralized visitor centre (with a café and shop) called the **James-Simon-Galerie**, and a so-called Archäologische Promenade (Archaeological Promenade) that will connect four of the museums to each other at basement level.

INFORMATION AND TOURS   MUSEUM ISLAND

Admission Individually Museum Island museums cost either €10 or €12. Better value is the Museum Pass Berlin (€24), valid for three days, which covers the permanent exhibitions in all the city's state museums, plus a selection of the city's private museums too (see box, p.28). Entry to the Museum Island museums is also included on the Berlin WelcomeCard and City Tour Card (see box, p.23). For regular visitors, it's also possible to purchase annual membership tickets, which start at €25

for year-long access to all of the main state museums during off-peak times. In all cases special exhibitions cost extra. Visitors to the busiest museums – the Neues Museum and the Pergamonmuseum – should purchase time-slot tickets in advance at ⓦsmb.museum.

Audio tours Most exhibits are in German only, but some collections do provide explanations and information sheets in English and most have excellent, multilingual audio tours included in the entrance price.

Altes Museum

Am Lustgarten • Tues, Wed & Fri–Sun 10am–6pm, Thurs 10am–8pm • €10 • ☎ 030 266 42 42 42, ⑩ smb.museum • ⑤ Hackescher Markt

At the head of the Lustgarten, the **Altes Museum** (Old Museum) is – along with the Konzerthaus Berlin (see p.233) – one of Berlin's most striking Neoclassical buildings and perhaps Schinkel's most impressive surviving work, with an 87m-high facade fronted by an eighteen-column Ionic colonnade. Opened as a home for the royal collection of paintings in 1830, it is now host to the **Antikensammlung** (Collection of Classical Antiquities): small sculpture and pottery from the city's famed Greek and Roman collections. Greek gods dominate the ground floor, with the upper floor containing a colossal range of Greek, Roman and Etruscan art – urns, shields, sarcophagi, friezes – all chronologically and thematically arranged. Many are small works that lack the power and drama of the huge pieces on view at the Pergamon, but can captivate nonetheless: *The Praying Boy*, a lithe and delicate bronze sculpture from Rhodes dating back to 300 BC, is the collection's pride and joy. Look, too, for the vase of Euphronios, decorated with an intimate painting of athletes in preparation – the series of Greek vases here is considered to be among the finest in the world.

Neues Museum

Bodestr. 1–3 • Daily 10am–6pm (Thurs till 8pm) • €12 • ☎ 030 266 42 42 42, ⑩ smh.museum • ⑤ Hackescher Markt

The **Neues Museum** (New Museum) opened in 1855 to house the imperial Egyptian Collection. Bombed out in the war, the building was slowly rebuilt and renovated under British architect David Chipperfield, who took great pains to preserve as many original features as possible, including fluted stone columns and battered faux-Egyptian ceiling frescoes. Entire wings had been destroyed in the war, including the central staircase, but rather than imitating every detail, plain concrete, bare brick and huge wooden rafters were used for repairs, creating both a sense of history and an effective contrast to the original sections. Eventually reopened in 2009, the building houses Berlin's Museum for Pre- and Early History, alongside its Egyptian treasures.

The most prized exhibit of the **Ägyptisches Museum und Papyussammlung** (Egyptian Museum and Papyrus Collection) is the 3300-year-old *Bust of Queen Nefertiti*, a treasure that has become a symbol for the city as a cultural capital. There's no questioning its beauty – the queen has perfect bone structure and gracefully sculpted lips – and the history of the piece is equally interesting. Created around 1350 BC, the bust probably never left the studio in Akhetatenin in which it was created, acting as a model for other portraits of the queen (its use as a model explains why the left eye was never drawn in). When the studio was deserted, the bust was left there, to be discovered some three thousand years later in 1912 and then officially unveiled in Berlin in 1924; this also marked the beginning of an ongoing diplomatic struggle by the Egyptian authorities to have it returned to Egypt. Elsewhere in the collection, atmospheric lighting is used to particularly good effect on the Expressionistic, almost Futurist, *Berlin Green Head* of the Ptolemaic period.

Another major collection within the building is the **Museum für Vor- und Frühgeschichte** (Museum for Pre- and Early History), which includes pieces from the Schliemann excavations of Troy. Though many pieces remain in Russia, carted away as spoils of war, some are represented here as replicas while delicate negotiations for their return continue. Highlights of the collection include the skull of the famous Le Moustier Neanderthal and the striking and mysterious Bronze Age *Berlin Gold Hat*, a long conical headdress made from thin gold leaf.

Alte Nationalgalerie

Bodestr. 1–3 • Tues, Wed & Fri–Sun 10am–6pm, Thurs 10am–8pm • €12 • ☎ 030 266 42 42 42, ⑩ smb.museum • ⑤ Hackescher Markt

Tucked just behind the Neues Museum is the **Alte Nationalgalerie** (Old National Gallery), a slightly exaggerated example of post-Schinkel Neoclassicism that contains the nineteenth-century section of Berlin's state art collection. The main body of the

2

museum, built in 1876, resembles a Corinthian temple and is fronted by an imposing equestrian statue of its royal patron, Friedrich Wilhelm IV.

Particularly noteworthy among the Alte Nationalgalerie's collection are several works of the "**German Romans**": mid-nineteenth-century artists like Anselm Feuerbach and Arnold Böcklin, who spent much of their working lives in Italy. Böcklin's eerie, dreamlike *Isle of the Dead* retains its power even today. A highlight of this school is the Casa Bartholdy **frescoes**: softly illuminated paintings by Peter Cornelius, Wilhelm Veit and others that illustrate the story of Joseph. The broad canvases of Adolph von Menzel strike a rather different note: though chiefly known during his lifetime for his detailed depictions of court life under Frederick the Great, it's his interpretations of Berlin on the verge of the industrial age, such as *The Iron Rolling Mill*, that make more interesting viewing today.

Other rooms contain important **Impressionist** works by Van Gogh, Degas, Monet and native son Max Liebermann, plus statues by Rodin. But it's on the top floor, in the **Galerie der Romantik**, with its collection of nineteenth-century paintings from the German Romantic, Classical and Biedermeier movements, that the collection is at its most powerful. The two central rooms here contain work by **Karl Friedrich Schinkel** and **Caspar David Friedrich**. Schinkel (see box, p.46) was the architect responsible for the Neoclassical design of the Altes Museum, and his paintings are meticulously drawn Gothic fantasies, often with sea settings. *Gothic Church on a Rock by the Sea* is the most moodily dramatic and didactic in purpose: the medieval knights in the foreground ride next to a prayer tablet – Schinkel believed that a rekindling of medieval piety would bring about the moral regeneration of the German nation. But more dramatic are the works of **Caspar David Friedrich**, all of which express a powerful elemental and religious approach to landscape.

Pergamonmuseum

Bodestr. 1–3 • Daily 10am–6pm (Thurs till 8pm) • €12 • ☎ 030 266 42 42 42, ⓦ smb.museum • Ⓢ Hackescher Markt

The **Pergamonmuseum** is accessible from Am Kupfergraben on the south bank of the River Spree. It's a massive three-winged structure, built in the early part of the twentieth century in the style of a Babylonian temple to house the treasure-trove of the German archeologists who were busy plundering the ancient world, packaging it up and sending it back to Berlin. The museum is chiefly famous for its outsized and genuinely jaw-dropping structures, though these are supplemented by a wealth of other artefacts.

The are three separate but overlapping collections, arguably the most important of which is the **Antikensammlung** (Collection of Classical Antiquities). While its most famous exhibit, the **Pergamon Altar** is not on display until 2019 (see box opposite), the section contains other spectacular pieces of Hellenistic and Classical architecture, including the two-storey **Market Gate** from the Turkish town of Miletus. Built by the Romans in 120 AD, the gate was destroyed by an earthquake just under a thousand years later and brought to Berlin in fragmentary form for reconstruction during the nineteenth century.

The **Vorderasiatisches Museum** (Museum of the Ancient Near East), also on the main floor, has some 270,000 items covering a time span of some six thousand years. Highlights includes the enormous **Ishtar Gate**, the **Processional Way** and the facade of the **Throne Room** from the ancient city of Babylon, all of which date from the reign of Nebuchadnezzar II in the sixth century BC. It's impossible not to be awed by the size and the remarkable state of preservation of the deep-blue enamelled bricks – but bear in mind that much of it is a mock-up, built around the original finds. Look out for the weird mythical creatures that adorn the Ishtar Gate.

Pride of place in the museum's **Museum für Islamische Kunst** (Museum for Islamic Art) goes to the relief-decorated stone facade of a Jordanian **Prince's Palace** at Mshatta, from 740 AD, presented to Kaiser Wilhelm II by the sultan of Turkey. Another highlight is the **Aleppo Room**, a reception chamber with carved wooden wall decorations, reassembled in Berlin after being removed from a merchant's house in present-day Syria.

THE RESTORATION OF THE PERGAMON ALTAR

One of the most famous exhibits not just in the Pergamon but across all Berlin's museums, the enormous **Pergamon Altar**, which measures over 35m wide and 33m deep, dates from 180–160 BCE and is regarded as a key masterpiece of Hellenistic art. Discovered at Bergama (western Turkey) by archeologist Carl Humann and brought to Berlin in 1903, the sculpture frieze is dedicated to Zeus and Athena and shows a tremendous battle between the Olympian gods and giants, with powerfully depicted figures writhing in a mass of sinew and muscle. While the main hall within which it sits is being comprehensively remodelled, the Pergamon Altar is **inaccessible until 2019**, though an elaborate 3D model can in the meantime be found at Ⓦ 3d.smb.museum/pergamonaltar.

2

Note that ongoing renovations to add a fourth wing to the museum mean that alternating parts of the museum will be closed until 2025–26: check the museum website before visiting for news of what's currently on show.

Bode-Museum

Am Kupfergraben • Tues, Wed & Fri–Sun 10am–6pm, Thurs 10am–8pm • €12 • ☎ 030 266 42 42 42, Ⓦ smb.museum • Ⓢ Hackescher Markt

The stocky, neo-Baroque **Bode-Museum** at the northern tip of Museum Island suffered such heavy damage in World War II that it was scheduled for demolition in the late 1940s, until Berliners protested in the streets.

Expensive renovation over the years has created impressive results: opulent entrances and stairways, a swish first-floor **café**, and, most importantly, a seamless backdrop for the **Skulpturensammlung**, one of Europe's most impressive sculpture collections. Wilhelm von Bode, the first director of the museum that now bears his name, would probably have approved: his ambition, to present a complete history of European sculpture and place in a proper context, led to his scouring Europe for items like fireplaces, frescoes and even whole ceilings for the museum. The present setup isn't quite as exhaustive, but despite wartime losses the collection represents a good tour of European sculpture between the third and nineteenth centuries. A particular strength is the early **Italian Renaissance** with pieces by Luca della Robbia, Donatello, Desiderio da Settignano, Francesco Laurana and Mino da Fiesole among the highlights. Also from Italy is the unusual attraction of the **Tiepolo-Kabinett**, a small white and pastel room rich in stucco ornamentation, with immaculate frescoes by Giovanni Battista Tiepolo that were originally created for a north Italian *palazzo* in 1759.

The **German collection** is equally authoritative, particularly in sections detailing the Middle Ages – including work by masters like the late fifteenth-century woodcarver Tilman Riemenschneider, along with Hans Multscher, Hans Brüggemann, Nicolaus Gerhaert van Leyden and Hans Leinberger. Equally significant, particularly in the local context, are sculptures of several proud and imposing Prussian generals by Andreas Schlüter, created for Wilhelmplatz – a square in Berlin's former government quarter (see p.40); the imposing statue of Friedrich Wilhelm I sitting astride a horse in the museum lobby is also his work.

Also in the building is the **Museum für Byzantinische Kunst** (Museum of Byzantine Art), said to be second only to that of Istanbul's archeological museum. It's particularly strong on early Christian religious items, and also features ornamental Roman sarcophagi and several intricate mosaics and ivory carvings. Finally, the museum is also home to a gigantic **Münzkabinett** (Numismatic collection) of around half a million coins. Though mainly appealing to those with a specialist interest, it's worth a quick look for its prize possessions, which include seventh-century coins that were among the first to have ever been minted.

The collection suffered greatly during the war, with many pieces in storage being irreparably damaged, such as the early sixteenth-century bust by Antonio della Porta, damaged by fire and now resembling a gruesomely disfigured figure or traumatized victim of war. It's displayed in the museum as a memorial to the others.

FERNSEHTURM AND WELTZEITUHR

Alexanderplatz and around

With the gigantic adjacent TV tower looming above all Berlin, dreary Alexanderplatz – an unmistakable product of the old East Germany – is easy to find. And as a major U-Bahn, S-Bahn and tram station it's also easy to get to. During East Berlin's forty-year existence, while Unter den Linden was allowed to represent the glories of past Berlin, Alexanderplatz and its environs were designed to represent the glories of a modern socialist capital. However, while the concrete gigantism of the GDR era don't date as well as the efforts of Schinkel and his contemporaries, Alexanderplatz should not merely be passed by. It's worth exploring not only the area's handful of historic buildings but also the East German creations that have their own place in Berlin's architectural chronology.

This is one part of town where there's little point in trying to spot prewar remains, as there's almost no trace of what stood here before 1945. Whole streets have vanished – the open area around the base of the TV tower, for example, used to be a dense network of inner-city streets – and today only a few survivors like the **Marienkirche** and **Rotes Rathaus** remain amid the modernity.

The nearby **Nikolaiviertel** is a pedestrian quarter that recreates a portion of Berlin's destroyed medieval heart, and is also home to the **Zille Museum**, which sketches out the life and work of cartoonist and satirist Heinrich Zille. The Nikolaiviertel backs onto an attractive stretch of the **River Spree** from where riverside paths join to form a loop, past a stretch of Berlin's medieval first wall (built to keep people out rather than in) and a couple of cultural sights, such as the **Märkisches Museum**, where you can brush up on some of the city's history.

Alexanderplatz

Though long an important business and traffic centre, today's **Alexanderplatz** – a sprawling, windswept, pedestrianized plaza surrounded by high-rises – is largely the product of a 1960s GDR vision of how the centre of a modern, socialist metropolis should look. In the eighteenth century routes to all parts of Germany radiated from here, and a cattle and wool market stood on the site. It acquired its present name after the Russian tsar Alexander I visited Berlin in 1805. Today, in addition to the S-Bahn line running overhead, three underground lines cross beneath the Platz, various bus routes converge on the area, and several tram lines course through it, making it one of central Berlin's busiest spots.

From the main doors at the southern end of the **train station** – which looks much the same as it did before the war despite being a 1960s rebuild – the route onto "Alex" leads through a gap between a couple of prewar survivors: the **Alexanderhaus** and the **Berolinahaus**, two buildings designed at the beginning of the 1930s by the architect and designer Peter Behrens, whose ideas influenced the founders of the Bauhaus movement. With their opaque glass towers beautifully lit at night, these are the only Alexanderplatz buildings not to have been destroyed in the war. The most intriguing communist-era landmark on the square is the **Weltzeituhr** ("World Clock") in front of the Alexanderhaus. Central Berlin's best-known rendezvous point, it tells the time in different cities throughout the world, and is a product of the same architectural school responsible for the Fernsehturm.

3

ALEXANDERPLATZ: A TURBULENT HISTORY

Alexanderplatz has figured prominently in city **upheavals** ever since revolutionaries (including writer Theodor Fontane) set up barricades here in 1848. In 1872 it was the site of a demonstration by an army of homeless women and children, and nearly half a century later, during the revolution of 1918, sailors occupied the Alexanderplatz police headquarters (a feared local landmark just southeast of the Platz – a plaque marks the spot) and freed the prisoners. Then in November 1989 it was the focal point of a million-strong demonstration and subsequent rallies when hundreds of thousands of people crammed into the square to hear opposition leaders speak.

Throughout its existence, the face of Alexanderplatz has undergone many **transformations**. A major reshaping at the end of the 1920s cleaned up what had become a rather sleazy corner of the city and turned it into one of its main shopping centres, with two expensive department stores in the vicinity: Hermann Tietz and Wertheim. Both were Jewish-owned until "Aryanized" by the Nazis. The Kaufhof department store facing the fountain was, as Centrum, one of the best-stocked shops in East Germany, though these days it's just another standard big store, now joined by several other chain stores and malls in and around the square.

In 2015, the city listed the communist-era buildings dotted around the square as historical monuments, scuppering an alternative plan to pull them down and replace them with new skyscrapers and more modern constructions. That said, some new towers are still being planned for the area, including a residential and commercial complex designed by Frank Gehry.

Loxx am Alex – Miniatur Welten Berlin

Grunerstr. 20 • Daily 10am–8pm • €12.90, under-14s €8, children below 1m free • ☏ 030 44 72 30 22, ⓦ loxx-Berlin.de •
Ⓤ/Ⓢ Alexanderplatz

Tucked away on the top floor of the Alexa Centre shopping mall, **Loxx am Alex – Miniatur Welten Berlin** (Miniature Worlds Berlin) may well be run by a fringe group of modelling enthusiasts, but it's certainly no small operation. Here a battery of forty computers and dozens of monitors equip a nerve centre that runs four hundred model trains and even a model airport: "night flights" occur every twenty minutes. The Berlin

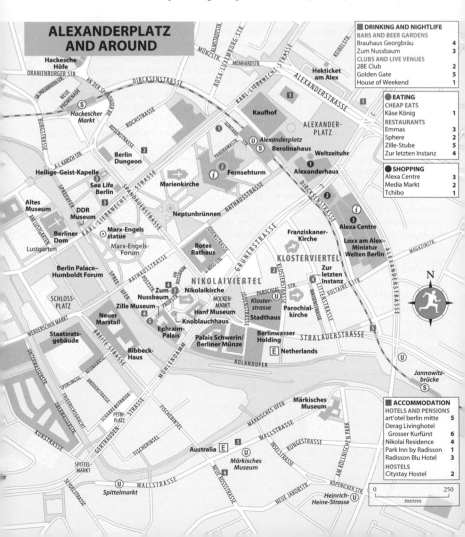

ALEXANDERPLATZ
AND AROUND

■ DRINKING AND NIGHTLIFE
BARS AND BEER GARDENS
Brauhaus Georgbräu — 4
Zum Nussbaum — 3
CLUBS AND LIVE VENUES
2BE Club — 2
Golden Gate — 5
House of Weekend — 1

■ EATING
CHEAP EATS
Käse König — 1
RESTAURANTS
Emmas — 3
Sphere — 2
Zille-Stube — 5
Zur letzten Instanz — 4

● SHOPPING
Alexa Centre — 3
Media Markt — 2
Tchibo — 1

■ ACCOMMODATION
HOTELS AND PENSIONS
art'otel berlin mitte — 5
Derag Livinghotel
  Grosser Kurfürst — 6
Nikolai Residence — 4
Park Inn by Radisson — 1
Radisson Blu Hotel — 3
HOSTELS
Citystay Hostel — 2

cityscape on display took 400,000 man hours to create; scores of Berlin landmarks have been faithfully reproduced on an exacting 1:87 scale, from a soaring Fernsehturm that's well above average human height down to mock-Byzantine enclosures of Berlin zoo and the *Plattenbau* high-rises of the GDR. Even with its creative geography it's a delight, especially for anyone who knows the city.

Fernsehturm

Panoramastr. 1a · Daily: March–Oct 9am–midnight; Nov–Feb 10am–midnight · April–Oct €14; Nov–March €13; reservations not required for the tower, but are advisable for the restaurant in high season – pre-booked Fast Track tickets (€19.50, or €13 early-bird or late-night options) enable you to dodge the queues, as do pre-booked restaurant tickets (from €19.50); check website for details · ☎ 030 24 75 75 875, Ⓦ tv-turm.de · Ⓤ/Ⓢ Alexanderplatz

Overshadowing every building in the vicinity, the gigantic **Fernsehturm**, or TV tower, looms over the eastern Berlin skyline like a displaced satellite on a huge factory chimney. The highest structure in Western Europe, the 368m-high transmitter was built during the isolationist 1960s, when the eastern part of the city was largely inaccessible to West Germans, and intended as a highly visible symbol of the permanence of East Berlin and the German Democratic Republic. Its construction was watched with dismay and derision by West Berliners (and many in the East), who were heartily amused on its completion by the fact that sunshine reflecting off the globe on the tower forms a cross visible even in western Berlin; they dubbed it the "pope's revenge", much to the reported chagrin of the old GDR authorities. Nevertheless, once it opened in 1969 the tower soon became a popular stop-off on the East Berlin tourist circuit.

Having outlasted the regime that conceived it, the Fernsehturm has now become part of the scenery, and though few would champion it on the grounds of architectural merit, it does have a certain retro appeal. As well as being an unmissable orientation point, the tower also provides a tremendous **view** (up to 80km on a rare clear day) from the observation platform, reached by a very fast lift. Above the platform is *Sphere*, a restaurant whose key selling point is that it revolves on its own axis once an hour (see p.199). The tower receives around a million visitors a year and the queues can be long whatever the weather; if time is short, consider investing in a Fast Track ticket (see above).

Marienkirche

Karl-Liebknecht-Str. 8 · Daily: Jan–March 10am–6pm, April–Dec 10am–8pm (no visits during services) · Free · Ⓦ marienkirche-berlin.de · Ⓤ/Ⓢ Alexanderplatz

Once hemmed in by buildings, but now standing oddly alone in the shadow of the huge Fernsehturm, the **Marienkirche** (St Mary's Church) is Berlin's oldest parish church. The Gothic stone-and-brick nave dates back to about 1270, but the tower is more recent, having been added in 1466, with the verdigris-coated upper section tacked on towards the end of the eighteenth century by Carl Gotthard Langhans, designer of the Brandenburg Gate. This uncontrived combination of architectural styles somehow makes the Marienkirche one of Berlin's most appealing churches, its simplicity a reminder of the city's village origins.

The **interior** is an excellent place to escape the increasingly frenetic street life of the area and listen to an organ recital (free on Thurs & Fri at 1.30pm). Near the main entrance at the western end of the church is a small cross erected by the citizens of Berlin and Cölln as penance to the pope, after a mob immolated a papal representative on a nearby marketplace. There are five holes in the cross and, so the story goes, medieval convicted criminals wishing to prove their innocence could do so by inserting the fingers of one hand into the holes simultaneously – not too many escaped

3

punishment, though, as the feat is almost an anatomical impossibility. Just inside the entrance, look out for the 22m-high *Totentanz* (*Dance of Death*) frieze, dating from the fifteenth century. It's very faded, but accompanied by a representation of how it once looked, with Death shown as a shroud-clad mummy popping up between people from all levels of society.

The vaulted nave is plain and white but enlivened by some opulent decorative touches. Foremost among these is Andreas Schlüter's magnificent **pulpit**, its canopy adorned with cherubs and backed by a cloud from which gilded sunrays radiate. Complementing this are the white marble altar with a huge triptych altarpiece and the eighteenth-century organ, a riot of gilded filigree and yet more cherubs, topped by a sunburst.

Neptunbrunnen

The centrepiece of the large square just southwest of the TV tower is the **Neptunbrunnen** (Neptune Fountain), an extravagantly imaginative fountain incorporating a statue of a trident-wielding Neptune sitting on a shell. A serpent, seal and alligator spray the god of the sea with water, and he is supported by strange fish and eel-draped aquatic centaurs with webbed feet instead of hooves. Around the rim of the fountain sit four female courtiers, symbolizing what were at the time the four most important German rivers: the Rhine, the Vistula, the Oder and the Elbe. The statue was built in 1891 and was originally on Schlossplatz.

Rotes Rathaus

Rathausstr. 15 • Mon–Fri 9am–6pm • Free • ☏ 030 90 260 • ⓤ Klosterstrasse

A rare survivor of Hohenzollern-era Berlin, the **Rotes Rathaus** (Red Town Hall) is so called because of the colour of its bricks rather than its politics. It has a solid angularity that contrasts sharply with the finicky grandeur of contemporaries like the Dom, perhaps because it's a symbol of the civic rather than Imperial Berlin of the time – a city in the throes of rapid commercial expansion and industrial growth. The building has lost some of its impact now that it's been hemmed in by new structures, but it remains a grandiose, almost Venetian-looking edifice; look out for the intricate bas-relief in terracotta, illustrating episodes from the history of Berlin, that runs around the building at first-floor level. The Rathaus was badly knocked around in 1945, but made a good comeback following restoration during the 1950s. During GDR days it was headquarters of the East Berlin city administration, and since 1991 has housed the united city's administration. Inside, a grand stairwell leads to a coat-of-arms hall with a few exhibits on the city, including some engaging

---

THE U5 EXTENSION AND THE MARX-ENGELS-FORUM

The huge building works in front of the Rotes Rathaus and extending all the way along Unter den Linden are part of a mighty project to extend the **U5** underground line across the heart of Berlin between Alexanderplatz and the Hauptbahnhof, with three new stations – Berliner Rathaus, Museuminsel and Unter den Linden – and a connection with the U55 at Brandenburger Tor. Completion is planned for 2020, but in the meantime viewing platforms allow passers-by to inspect progress. Much of the work is taking place on the **Marx-Engels-Forum**, a severe plaza just west of the Rathaus. It's dedicated to the two revolutionary thinkers Karl Marx and Friedrich Engels and their landmark commemorative bronze – about five times their former real sizes. The statues are currently located at the edge of the plaza, close to Karl-Liebknecht-Strasse, but will eventually be moved to their central pride of place again.

FROM TOP DDR MUSEUM (P.65); NIKOLAIVIERTEL (P.66) >

aerial photos. The building also has a **cafeteria** offering low-price lunches – accessed via a door on the east side.

The reconstruction of the Rathaus and thousands of other Berlin buildings is largely due to the *Trümmerfrauen* or "rubble women", who set to work in 1945 clearing up the 100 million tons of rubble created by wartime bombing and shelling. Their deeds are commemorated by the **statue** of a robust-looking woman facing the eastern entrance to the Rathaus on Rathausstrasse. Women of all ages carried out the bulk of the early rebuilding work, since most of Berlin's adult male population was dead, disabled or being held in POW camps by the Allies. Despite this, the male contribution to the work is also marked by a statue of a man looking wistfully towards his *Trümmerfrau* counterpart from the western end of the Rathaus.

Sea Life Berlin

Spandauer Str. 3 · Daily 10am–7pm, last admission 6pm · €19.95, children aged 3–14 €16.50, discounts and ticket combo deals (with Madame Tussauds Berlin) available online · ☎ 0180 666 690 101, ⓦ visitsealife.com · Ⓢ Hackescher Markt

The large, modern colossus that overlooks the Marx-Engels-Forum from the north, and incorporates the *Radisson Blu* hotel (see p.188), is a touristy mall that contains **Sea Life Berlin**, an overtly commercial aquarium that displays the fairly dreary aquatic life of the region's rivers and the North Atlantic. But at least the species here, highlights of which include sea horses, jellyfish, small sharks and manta rays, are elegantly displayed, particularly in the **AquaDom**, a gigantic tubular tank, located in the lobby of the *Radisson Blu* hotel, which you can rise through on a leisurely elevator (included in all Sea Life tickets).

Berlin Dungeon

Spandauer Str. 2 · Daily 10am–7pm, last admission 6pm · from €11.50 booked online (kids aged 10–14 from €9.50); €23 on the door (kids €18.50); ticket combo deals with Madame Tussauds Berlin (see p.41), Sea Life Berlin (see above) and Legoland Discovery Centre Berlin (see p.93) are available; children under 8 are not allowed (10 is the recommended minimum age) · Tours (1hr) in German and English daily; times change seasonally – check website · ☎ 01806 25 55 44, ⓦ thedungeons.com/berlin · Ⓢ Hackescher Markt

For a populist history of some of the city's gorier moments, visit the **Berlin Dungeon**. Tours take in theatre sets of several Berlin eras while costumed actors try to scare and amuse with tales of torture, serial killings, plagues and the like. Crucially the material comes to an end with the 1920s, when, of course much of the real horror started, making the attraction seriously flaccid in a city where a former concentration camp is only a suburban train ride away. That said, the recent addition of a free-fall tower, **Exitus**, adds an extra adventure thrill.

Heilige-Geist-Kapelle

Spandauer Str. 1; entrance in the Wirtschaftswissenschaftlichen Fakultät (Economics Faculty) of Humboldt University · Thurs noon–1pm · Ⓢ Hackescher Markt

The red-brick Gothic **Heilige-Geist-Kapelle** (Holy Ghost Chapel) is one of Berlin's oldest surviving buildings. A remnant of the fourteenth century, it's now quaintly incongruous, dwarfed by a larger, newer building (part of Humboldt University) that was grafted onto it at the start of the twentieth century. The original interior has not survived, but it's a miracle that the chapel is still standing at all: it has endured the huge city fire of 1380, an enormously destructive explosion of a nearby gunpowder magazine in 1720, and, above all, wartime bombing. The space is now mostly used for private events, though the medieval roof of the chapel can be viewed from the second floor of the Economics Faculty building staircase.

DDR Museum

Karl-Liebknecht-Str. 1 • Mon–Fri & Sun 10am–8pm, Sat 10am–10pm • €9.50, online from €7.50 • ☎ 030 847 12 37 31, ⓦ ddr-museum.de • Ⓢ Hackescher Markt

On the banks of the Spree, opposite the Berliner Dom, the popular **DDR Museum** is an homage to *Ostalgie* (see box below). Using hands-on displays to reminisce on life in the GDR, it offers memories of the school system, pioneer camps and the razzmatazz with which the feats of model workers were celebrated. Less impressive were the GDR's awkward attempts to rival Western fashions, as its collection of polyester clothing and

OSTALGIE

In the years following the fall of the Wall, a sense of **Ostalgie** – nostalgia for the East (or rather *Nostalgie* for the *Osten*) – began to emerge in certain quarters of the old East Germany. The sentiment originated with those for whom memories of the collapsed country remained vivid, though this nostalgia for the iconography of communist East Germany also proved immensely popular with visitors, spawning a mini-industry in Berlin which still shows no sign of abating.

The meaning of *Ostalgie* is a little nebulous. What started as a melancholic craving for the securities of life in a communist state by the 16 million East Germans thrust into the turbulent and uncertain world of capitalism became an expression of both discontent and identity. It was a protest at the quick eradication of a unique East German culture and its absorption into the West – a process that implied that all things Western were superior, and tended to mock everything from the East as laughably backward. *Ostalgie* became a way of affirming that some aspects of the GDR were worth celebrating, and that – despite the many shortcomings of the state – it had also produced rewarding moments.

Around the turn of the millennium, *Ostalgie* began to shift away from serious political debate towards the kind of kitschy, innocent nostalgia, beautifully evoked in the hugely successful tragicomic film *Good Bye Lenin!* (2003). Visiting Berlin today you'll come across a number of cult GDR icons, including the chubby, cheerful **Ampelmann** from East German pedestrian crossings and the cute fibreglass **Trabant** car. There's even been a revival of utilitarian GDR products, including foods, household products and cosmetics made by companies that went out of business when Western goods flooded the market. Some pop up in grocery stores and corner shops, but the entire range is most easily found online; try Ossiversand (ⓦ ossiversand .de). Most of Berlin's *Ostalgie* shops concentrate on souvenirs, particularly the Ampelmann stores (see p.247) or Mondos Arts (online only, ⓦ ost-shop.de).

Most agree that *Ostalgie* is just a good laugh, but the sentiment has its critics. Some warn of the dangers of posthumously glorifying any aspect of a totalitarian dictatorship and glossing over a dreadful chapter of Germany's history. Among them is Berlin's former mayor Klaus Wowereit, who bluntly warned of the "need to be careful that the GDR does not achieve cult status". Certainly, cheerful as the Ampelmann and Trabi may be, and as refreshing as cravings for simple pleasures and a frugal existence may seem, a balanced view of East Germany is essential. Some counterbalance came from the film *Das Leben der Anderen* (*The Lives of Others*), winner of the 2006 best foreign film Oscar, which reminded Germany and the world of the oppression, censorship, secret police and intimidation that underpinned life in communist Europe. More recently, within the framework of a spy drama, the gripping TV series *Deutschland 83* (2015) captured the paranoia of the mid-1980s and the outrageous invasion of the state into ordinary lives.

OSTALGIE HOTSPOTS

Drive a Trabi Unleash your inner Ossi behind the wheel of the two-stroke chariot and decide for yourself if this old East German workhorse deserves its cult status. See box, pp.24–25.
Ampelmann Galerie, Hackeshen Höfe You can buy a whole host of Ampelmann-branded items at its flagship store (one of several), from deck chairs and diaries to T-shirts and toys – and even a bicycle helmet. See p.247.
DDR Museum Explore daily life in old East Germany. See above.
Osseria Dine on East German fare like *Eisbein* (pickled ham hock) and schnitzel in this GDR-themed restaurant. See p.213.
Verkehrsberuhigte Ost-Zone (VEBOZ) This bar is decked out in GDR memorabilia. See p.219.
Ostel Nod off at the orange-and-brown-furnished *Ostel* lodging. See p.195.

3

bleached jeans shows. Small wonder, perhaps, that one big GDR passion was nudism – as one very revealing display explains – which was considered as healthy as the many sports that the state unceasingly supported. The section devoted to travel is particularly good, and includes the chance to sit behind the wheel of a Trabi, and enjoy a driving simulation experience through the streets of the former East; for journeys further afield you can consult an Eastern Bloc road atlas, which clearly defines where the freedom of the open road ends.

The museum's highlight is the chance to mooch around a tiny reconstructed GDR apartment, ablaze with retro browns and oranges, where you can nose through cupboards and cosy up on a sofa to watch speeches by Erich Honecker: "*Vorwärts immer, rückwärts nimmer*" ("always forwards, never backwards"). Many of the remaining areas of the museum are gloomy but important, since they tackle the dark sides of the GDR era – such as censorship and repression – and help round off this snapshot of East German life.

3

Nikolaiviertel

Just southwest of the expansive open spaces that surround the Fernsehturm lie the compact network of streets of the **Nikolaiviertel**. This old district was razed overnight on June 16, 1944 but rebuilt by the GDR authorities in the early 1980s in an attempt to recreate some of Berlin's **medieval** core. One or two original buildings aside, the Nikolaiviertel consists partly of exact replicas of historic Berlin edifices and partly of stylized buildings not based on anything in particular, but with a vaguely "old Berlin" feel. Sometimes it doesn't quite come off, and in places the use of typical East German *Plattenbau* construction techniques, with prefabricated pillars and gables, isn't too convincing, but all in all the Nikolaiviertel represents a radical and welcome architectural departure from the usual East German response of levelling an area and erecting enormous concrete edifices.

Unfortunately, the district has never really taken seed, and has the somewhat sterile air of a living history museum, attracting only tourists and those Berliners who work in the restaurants and *Gaststätten* (which, in keeping with their surroundings, tend to specialize in heavy traditional German food). Some of the most attractive **houses** – mostly pastel-facaded townhouses four or five storeys high – are around the **Nikolaikirche**, along Propststrasse, and on the southern side of Nikolaikirchplatz, behind the church itself, where they are particularly convincing. To compare these with an original head to the **Knoblauchhaus** on Poststrasse.

Nikolaikirche

Nikolaikirchplatz • Daily 10am–6pm • €5, free on first Wed every month • ☎ 030 24 00 21 62, ⊛ stadtmuseum.de • ⓤ Klosterstrasse

The centrepiece of the Nikolaiviertel is the thirteenth-century Gothic **Nikolaikirche** (St Nicholas' Church). The twin-towered church is one of the city's oldest, and it was from here on November 21, 1539, that news of the Reformation was proclaimed to Berlin's citizens. The distinctive needle-like spires date from a nineteenth-century restoration, or rather their design does – the building was thoroughly wrecked during the war, as extensive patches of lighter, obviously modern masonry betray. An unusual feature of its **interior** is the bright colouring of the vault ribbings: the orange, purple, green and other vivid lines look like a 1960s Pop Art addition, but actually follow a medieval pattern discovered by a 1980s restorer. A **museum** inside the church traces the building's history.

Propstrasse

Propststrasse runs past the side of Nikolaikirche all the way down to the River Spree and ends in a rather clichéd statue of St George and the Dragon. Along it are a couple of places associated with **Heinrich Zille** – the Berlin artist who produced earthy satirical drawings of Berlin life around the turn of the twentieth century. One of his favourite watering holes – along with another Berlin artist Otto Nagel – was the sixteenth-century **Zum Nussbaum** pub (see p.218), though in those days it stood on the opposite side of the Spree on the Spreeinsel where it was destroyed by wartime bombing. The replica is a faithful copy, right down to the walnut tree in the tiny garden. Many of Zille's drawings of early twentieth-century proletarian life were based on stories overheard in this pub.

Zille Museum

Propststr. 11 • Mon–Sat 11am–6pm, Sun 1–6pm • €6 • ☎ 030 24 63 25 00, ⓦ zillemuseum-berlin.de • Ⓤ Klosterstrasse

The excellent little **Zille Museum** provides a fine insight into the artist's life and attitude. It makes no allowances for non-German speakers but if you know a little of Zille's background, it's easy enough to enjoy the three rooms and short film about him, and appreciate his economical, humorous and vivid portrayals of squalid working-class life.

Knoblauchhaus

Poststr. 23 • Tues–Sun 10am–6pm • Free • ☎ 030 24 00 21 62, ⓦ stadtmuseum.de • Ⓤ Klosterstrasse

The southern end of Poststrasse features the **Knoblauchhaus**, a Neoclassical townhouse built in 1759 and a rare survivor of the war. It was home to the patrician Knoblauch family, who played an important role in the commercial and cultural life of eighteenth- and nineteenth-century Berlin, and now contains an exhibition (with nothing in English) about their activities. The house's **interior**, with its grand-bourgeois furnishings, gives a good impression of upper-middle-class life in Hohenzollern-era Berlin.

Ephraim-Palais

Poststr. 16 • Tues & Thurs–Sun 10am–6pm, Wed noon–8pm • €6; free on first Wed of month • ☎ 030 24 00 21 62, ⓦ stadtmuseum.de • Ⓤ Klosterstrasse

With its elegantly curving Rococo facade, Tuscan columns, wrought-iron balconies, oval staircase and ornate ceiling crafted by Schlüter, the **Ephraim-Palais** is exquisite. This relic of Berlin bourgeois high life, a rebuilt merchant's mansion, now houses a museum of Berlin-related art from the seventeenth to the beginning of the nineteenth centuries, changing special exhibitions giving a good impression of the city in its glory days. The Ephraim-Palais was built in 1762 by Veitel Heine Ephraim, court jeweller and mint master to Frederick the Great, and all-round wheeler-dealer. He owed his lavish lifestyle primarily to the fact that – on Frederick's orders – he steadily reduced the silver content of the Prussian *thaler*. This earned a great deal of money for Frederick and Ephraim himself but ruined the purchasing power of the currency.

Hanf Museum

Mühlendamm 5 • Tues–Fri 10am–8pm, Sat & Sun noon–8pm • €4.50 • ☎ 030 242 48 27, ⓦ hanfmuseum.de • Ⓤ Klosterstrasse

The **Hanf Museum** is 250 square metres of space devoted exclusively to the agricultural, manufacturing, industrial and legal aspects of hemp – a plant most commonly associated with marijuana. While slightly dingy, the museum isn't just for the stoners: the aim is to give a broader overview of this fascinating botanical treasure and its myriad applications, from textile and paper to medicine and cosmetics. Texts are in German only.

Molkenmarkt

Ⓤ Klosterstrasse

The busy but soulless square just east of the Nikolaiviertel, the **Molkenmarkt** (Whey Market), is one of Berlin's oldest public spaces. On its eastern side, Jüdenstrasse – "Jews' Street" was Berlin's original Jewish ghetto, until they were driven out of Brandenburg in 1573. When allowed back into Berlin in 1671 they mainly settled near today's Hackescher Markt (see p.72). Glowering over the road, the large domed **Stadthaus** is reminiscent of the Französischer Dom (see p.47) but dates from as recently as 1911, a relic of the days when the area served as the administrative district of Wilhelmine

Berlin. Also on the Molkenmarkt is the smooth zinc-clad **Berlinwasser Holding** building, with its fiercely angular arches and windows, which belongs to the local water company. The work of highly acclaimed local architect Christoph Langhof, it cleverly plays on the **Palais Schwerin**, the traditional building next door – one of two pompous buildings that make up the **Berliner Münze** (Berlin Mint), whose most impressive feature is a replica of a frieze depicting coining techniques by Gottfried Schadow, designer of the Brandenburger Tor Quadriga.

Plans are underway to redevelop the Molkenmarkt and Klosterviertel (see below) into a more lively commercial and cultural district, so don't be surprised to find the area something of a building site.

Klosterviertel and around

East of the Molkenmarkt, the **Klosterviertel** (Monastery Quarter) features several minor points of interest. Lying near the junction of Klosterstrasse and Parochialstrasse, the **Parochialkirche** is a sixteenth-century Baroque church with a bare brick interior (a legacy of the usual wartime gutting), which provides a venue for changing but often low-key art exhibitions (free). Parochialstrasse itself had a brief moment of importance when the building at **Parochialstrasse 1** hosted the first meeting of Berlin's post-Nazi town council, headed by future SED chief Walter Ulbricht, even as fighting still raged a little to the west. Ulbricht and his comrades had been specially flown in from Soviet exile to sow the seeds of a communist civil administration, and they moved in here, having been unable to set up shop in the still-burning Rotes Rathaus.

The northern end of Klosterstrasse is worth a quick look for the gutted thirteenth-century **Franziskaner-Klosterkirche** (Franciscan Cloister Church), which gives the area its name. The church was destroyed by a landmine in 1945 and left a ruin by GDR authorities as a warning against war and fascism. Another ruin from Berlin's history is behind it on Littenstrasse where a fragment of **Stadtmauer**, the original thirteenth-century Berlin wall, survives. Behind it is the atmospheric old **Zur letzten Instanz**, Berlin's oldest pub (see p.199).

Märkisches Museum

Am Köllnischen Park 5 · Tues–Sun 10am–6pm · €5, free on first Wed every month · ☎ 030 24 00 21 62, ⓦ stadtmuseum.de ·
Ⓜ Märkisches Museum

Occupying a building that resembles a red-brick neo-Gothic cathedral, the **Märkisches Museum** feels somewhat dated in its treatment of Berlin and Brandenburg's history. Small rooms are crammed with paintings, gadgets and glass vitrines, and the text is in German only. The displays, which predate reunification, are also episodic: eighteenth- and nineteenth-century culture is definitely the museum's forte. One of the first rooms deals with Berlin's late nineteenth-century role as a centre of **barrel organ** production, an industry established by Italian immigrants. Many of these music-makers are on display, as well as their increasingly large and more intricate progeny. Organ-grinding performances are given every Sunday at 3pm.

Other rooms are divided into sections of the city – Unter den Linden, Friedrichstrasse and so on. Among them is the **Gottische Kapelle**, a room resembling a small chapel and filled with wonderful pieces of medieval sacred art from (usually) unknown local artisans. More secular is the room devoted to the "Panorama", a huge arcade-like machine, built over a hundred years ago: as you peer through the eyepiece, a huge drum rotates to show you dozens of fascinating **3D photographs** of 1890s Berlin.

Less rewarding are the early history displays, from prehistoric pottery pieces to copies of royal proclamations from Friedrich Wilhelm, the Great Elector. A marvellous bronze statue of Bismarck dressed as a blacksmith manfully forging German unity is a highlight, and there are seven original sections of the Berlin Wall.

GEDENKSTÄTTE BERLINER MAUER (BERLIN WALL MEMORIAL)

The Spandauer Vorstadt

The Spandauer Vorstadt (Spandau suburb), the crescent-shaped area running north of the River Spree between Friedrichstrasse and Alexanderplatz, is the heart of Mitte and serves today as Berlin's primary "downtown". Before the war this was the city's prewar Jewish quarter – by the start of the twentieth century the district had become the cultural and spiritual centre of a well-established, wealthy and influential Jewish community. Things changed dramatically under the Nazis, but after the *Wende* the Spandauer Vorstadt underwent a dramatic revival. Squatters and artists were the first pioneers; restoration projects soon followed, renovating the backstreets to usher in a tide of bars, boutiques, cafés and restaurants. Following two decades of commercialization, the area now boasts a booming (if fairly touristy) shopping, dining and nightlife scene, all easily navigable on foot.

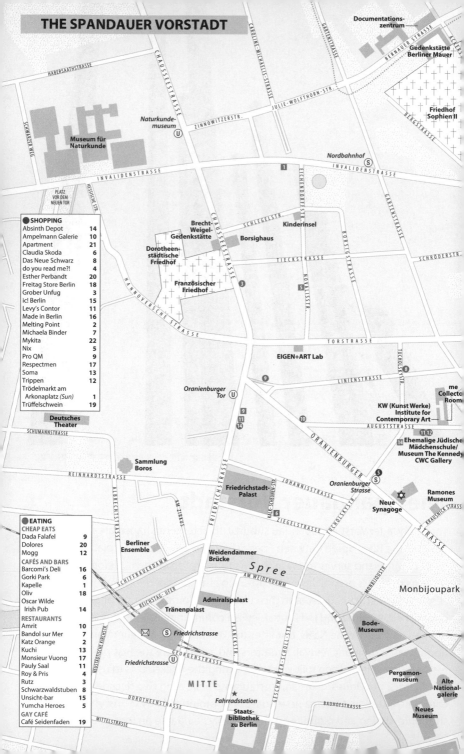

THE SPANDAUER VORSTADT

Documentations-
zentrum

Gedenkstätte
Berliner Mauer

Friedhof
Sophien II

Naturkunde-
museum

Museum für
Naturkunde

Nordbahnhof

PLATZ
VOR DEM
NEUEN TOR

Brecht-
Weigel-
Gedenkstätte

Kinderinsel

Borsighaus

Dorotheen-
städtische
Friedhof

Französischer
Friedhof

EIGEN+ART Lab

Deutsches
Theater

Oranienburger
Tor

me
Collecto
Room

KW (Kunst Werke)
Institute for
Contemporary Art

Ehemalige Jüdische
Mädchenschule/
Museum The Kennedy
CWC Gallery

Sammlung
Boros

Friedrichstadt-
Palast

Oranienburger
Strasse

Neue
Synagoge

Ramones
Museum

Berliner
Ensemble

Weidendammer
Brücke

Spree

Monbijoupark

Admiralspalast

Bode-
Museum

Tränenpalast

Friedrichstrasse

Friedrichstrasse

Pergamon-
museum

Alte
National-
galerie

MITTE

Fahrradstation

Staats-
bibliothek
zu Berlin

Neues
Museum

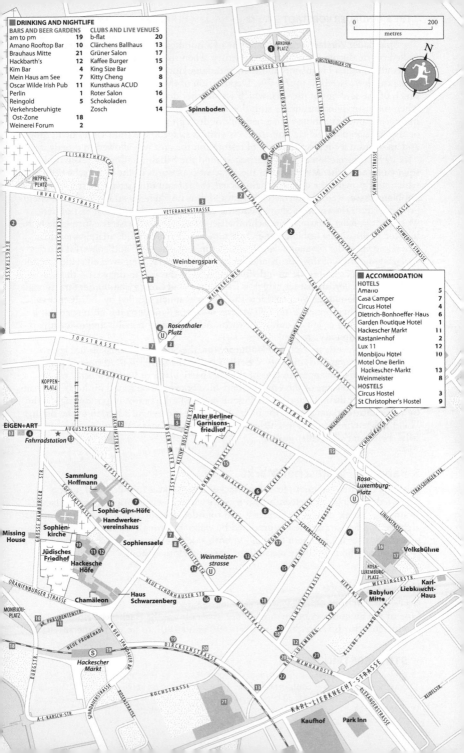

DRINKING AND NIGHTLIFE

BARS AND BEER GARDENS
am to pm	19
Amano Rooftop Bar	10
Brauhaus Mitte	21
Hackbarth's	12
Kim Bar	4
Mein Haus am See	7
Oscar Wilde Irish Pub	11
Perlin	1
Reingold	5
Verkehrsberuhigte Ost-Zone	18
Weinerei Forum	2

CLUBS AND LIVE VENUES
b-flat	20
Clärchens Ballhaus	13
Grüner Salon	17
Kaffee Burger	15
King Size Bar	9
Kitty Cheng	8
Kunsthaus ACUD	3
Roter Salon	16
Schokoladen	6
Zosch	14

ACCOMMODATION

HOTELS
Amano	5
Casa Camper	7
Circus Hotel	4
Dietrich-Bonhoeffer-Haus	6
Garden Boutique Hotel	1
Hackescher Markt	11
Kastanienhof	2
Lux 11	12
Monbijou Hotel	10
Motel One Berlin Hackescher-Markt	13
Weinmeister	8

HOSTELS
Circus Hostel	3
St Christopher's Hostel	9

The **Spandauer Vorstadt** originated as one of a number of suburbs just beyond Berlin's walled centre during the seventeenth century, when the population swelled firstly with persecuted French Huguenots and then with large numbers of persecuted Eastern European Jews (see box, pp.78–79). Deportation of the Jews under the Nazis took much of the soul out of the area, which was further decimated during the GDR era when most surviving businesses shut down. From the 1950s until the *Wende* the quarter became little more than a network of decrepit prewar streets punctuated by the occasional slab of GDR-era housing. Few visitors strayed here from Unter den Linden, and apart from a couple of pockets of restoration the area was allowed to quietly decay.

Its 1990s resurrection began in earnest around the S-Bahn station and convivial square of **Hackescher Markt**, and in the adjacent courtyards of the **Hackesche Höfe** which now provide the district's main focus. The surrounding streets, particularly **Sophienstrasse**, were also attractively restored, but nowhere was the injection of energy greater than in the youthful shops peddling cool clothes and shoes just east of here, where Rosenthaler Strasse, Neue Schönhauser Strasse and Münzstrasse form a de facto hub for Berlin's indie **fashion scene**. This zone bleeds into a residential district that, when known as the **Scheunenviertel**, was Berlin's most squalid and colourful district – Nazi demolition of this unruly and heavily Jewish enclave removed all evidence of it, however. The Nazis also left an indelible imprint on the area to the west – the heart of Berlin's prewar **Jewish district**, which is focused around **Grosse Hamburger Strasse** and the busy **Oranienburger Strasse**. Here the past is as much recalled by the absence of landmarks as their presence, though at least the **Neue Synagoge** has been restored, if only as a museum of Jewish culture. Nearby, **Auguststrasse** remains a significant part of Berlin's contemporary art scene.

At its western end, around **Oranienburger Tor**, the Spandauer Vorstadt has less to offer, though it was once the hub of Berlin's industrial revolution. Almost all points of interest around here appeal to fans of **theatre**, particularly of **Bertolt Brecht**, whose house, grave and some of the venues where he worked can be found in the area. Finally, just beyond the district's northern fringes is one of Berlin's most important sights: the **Gedenkstätte Berliner Mauer**, the only place in the city where a section of the Berlin Wall has been preserved in its entirety – complete with border defences and a "death strip" between two parallel walls.

S-Bahnhof Hackescher Markt

Running the entire southern length of **Hackescher Markt** is its **S-Bahnhof**, now a protected building. A nineteenth-century construction whose original red-tile facade retains the mosaic decorative elements and rounded windows typical of the period, its architectural features are best appreciated by walking through the station itself and taking a look at the northern facade. On both sides the renovated arches under the S-Bahn tracks house touristy restaurants, bars and clothes shops.

Hackesche Höfe

Rosenthaler Str. 40–41 • ☎ 030 28 09 80 10, ⓦ hackesche-hoefe.com • Ⓢ Hackescher Markt

One of the main draws of the Spandauer Vorstadt are the **Hackesche Höfe**, a series of nine courtyards (*Höfe*) built between 1905 and 1907 to house businesses, flats

---

STOLPERSTEINE

Look at the ground around the entrances to some Hackesche Höfe and you'll see brass-plated cobblestones known as **Stolpersteine**, or "stumbling-blocks" (ⓦ stolperstein.com). These are some of the nine thousand laid into footpaths around Germany as a memorial to the victims of Nazi persecution: each carries a name, birth date and their fate.

and places of entertainment. Restored to their Art Deco glory in the 1990s, the courtyards bustle with crowds visiting the cafés, stores, galleries and cultural spaces within. The first courtyard, decorated with blue mosaic tiles, is home to the Chamäleon (see p.236), at the forefront of the revival of the city's interwar cabaret tradition.

Though thoroughly beautified today, these courtyards preserve a layout that was common in this district and much of prewar Berlin, where daily life was played out in a labyrinth of *Hinterhöfe* – courtyards that were hidden from the shops and offices on the main road. Within the *Hinterhöfe* were a warren of workshops – with housing above and behind – that together produced a microcosm of the city, with rich and poor, housing and commerce crammed together for better or worse, creating the squalid turn-of-the-twentieth-century urban culture that was most famously satirized by Heinrich Zille (see p.66).

Haus Schwarzenberg

Rosenthaler Str. 39 • ☎ 030 30 87 25 73, ⓦ haus-schwarzenberg.org • Ⓢ Hackescher Markt

Haus Schwarzenberg is the unapologetically grungy sidekick of the gentrified Hackesche Höfe, just a couple of doors away. It has only been minimally refurbished and at least part of its allure is provided by its atmospherically crumbling and graffitied facades around a central courtyard. It harbours a number of low-key cafés, bars, shops and galleries (street-art lovers will want to visit Neurotitan Gallery; ⓦ neurotitan.de), as well as – right at the back of the courtyard – the idiosyncratic **Monsterkabinett**, an underground network of monster sculptures built by local artists (Thurs 6–10pm, Fri & Sat 4–10pm; €8; guided tours only; ☎ 01521 259 86 87, ⓦ monsterkabinett.de). In addition, there's a trio of small **museums** relating to **Jewish life**.

Gedenkstätte Stille Helden

Daily 10am–8pm • Free • ☎ 030 27 59 68 65, ⓦ gedenkstaette-stille-helden.de • Ⓢ Hackescher Markt

Spreading over a couple of rooms above the hubbub of the Hackescher Markt, the **Gedenkstätte Stille Helden** (Memorial to the Silent Heroes) remembers Germans who tried to save Jewish lives by risking their own. The museum's high-tech interactive format uses photographs, documents and oral testimonies to uncover the faces and stories of those who worked in isolation and lived with a daily fear of discovery to uphold moral values and undermine Nazi racial decrees. The heroic successes and even the tragic failures help restore your faith in human nature in this era. If all this piques your interest, be sure to investigate the overlapping content of the more studied Gedenkstätte Deutscher Widerstand (see p.100), in the diplomatic district.

Museum Blindenwerkstatt Otto Weidt

Daily 10am–8pm • Free • ☎ 030 28 59 94 07, ⓦ museum-blindenwerkstatt.de • Ⓢ Hackescher Markt

The **Museum Blindenwerkstatt Otto Weidt** (Museum of Otto Weidt's Workshop for the Blind) occupies the former rooms of a broom and brush factory run by one Otto Weidt, whose employees were mostly deaf, blind and Jewish. Luckily the factory was considered important to the war effort, so for a long time Weidt was able to protect his workers from deportation to concentration camps. But in the 1940s, as pressure grew, he resorted to producing false papers, bribing the Gestapo and providing food and even hiding places to keep them alive, all at considerable personal risk. One small room, whose doorway was hidden by a cupboard, was the refuge for a family of four until their secret was discovered and they were deported and murdered in Auschwitz. The exhibition has relics of the wartime factory – brushes, photos and letters from the workers – in English as well as German.

Anne Frank Center

Tues–Sun 10am–6pm • €5 (children under 10 free) • ☏ 030 288 86 56 00, ⓦ annefrank.de • Ⓢ Hackescher Markt

Across the courtyard from the Museum Blindenwerkstatt Otto Weidt, the **Anne Frank Center** tells the world-famous story of the bright, popular, middle-class Jewish girl who died in Bergen-Belsen, leaving behind poignant diaries of Nazi persecution. The familiarity of the tale allows the exhibition to take only a relatively superficial look at it, starting with the background to the persecution – including diagrammatic representations of the 1935 Nuremberg laws, which delineated in pointless and obsessive detail whether marriage between people is admissible based on the amount of Jewishness of a great-grandparent – before sketching out the basics of Anne's life, wonderfully photographed by her father Otto. Anne had no connection with Berlin, and the centre, partner to the Anne Frank House in Amsterdam, simply chose this site for its location in the middle of Berlin's prewar Jewish quarter. Nonetheless her story is woven into the local context in a large section of the museum that shows video interviews with Berlin teenagers, from ethnic minorities about the age Anne was when she died, as they relate their aspirations and experiences.

Scheunenviertel

Ⓤ Rosenthaler Platz or Ⓢ/Ⓤ Alexanderplatz

Northeast of the Hackesche Höfe is the **Scheunenviertel** ("barn quarter"), now a fairly unremarkable residential area enclosed between Rosenthaler Strasse and Alexanderplatz. Despite today's appearance, its history is a fairly lively one, Founded in 1672, following a decree that flammable hay could no longer be stored within the city limits, Scheunenviertel was originally a base for Berlin's poorest peasants; in later years it attracted impoverished political and religious refugees from all over Europe, with its heyday coming towards the end of the nineteenth century when it became a magnet for Jewish migrants from eastern Europe and Russia (see pp.78–79). The neighbourhood's melting-pot atmosphere made it an ideal refuge for those at odds with the Prussian and later the Imperial German establishment, making it a notorious centre of revolutionary activity. By the early twentieth century the Scheunenviertel had become an infamous slum, rife with deprivation and petty crime. In the 1930s it became a regular battleground for the street gangs of the left and right, while artists and writers – including Bertolt Brecht, Alfred Döblin, Marlene Dietrich and actor Gustav Gründgens – were attracted to the area, quick to create their own bohemian enclave. The Nazis put a stop to much of the activity by pulling chunks of the Scheunenviertel down, ostensibly to make way for a U-Bahn station. At the same time they played on the district's unsavoury reputation by extending the term Scheunenviertel to include the affluent and bourgeois Jewish areas around the Oranienburger Strasse – an attempt to tar all Jews with the same brush.

Alter Berliner Garnisonsfriedhof

Kleine Rosenthaler Str. 3 • **Cemetery** Daily: April–Sept 7am–7pm; Oct–March 8am–4pm **Exhibition** April–Sept Sat & Sun 10am–4pm; Oct–March Sun noon–3pm • Free • ⓦ garnisonfriedhofberlin.de • Ⓤ Rosenthaler Platz

Dating from the eighteenth century, the leafy **Alter Berliner Garnisonsfriedhof** (Old Garrison Cemetery) is full of rusting cast-iron crosses with near-obliterated inscriptions commemorating officers and men of the Prussian army. Also here is the rather grander tomb of Adolph von Lützow, a general who found fame during the Napoleonic Wars, contrasting sharply with the overgrown wooden crosses commemorating victims of the Battle of Berlin, hidden away in a far corner. Information is available from the administration offices near the entrance, which also house a small permanent **exhibition** as well as supplementary changing ones.

Rosa-Luxemburg-Platz and around

Ⓤ Rosa-Luxembourg-Platz

At the heart of the Scheunenviertel district is **Rosa-Luxemburg-Platz**. The most prominent landmark here is the **Volksbühne** theatre, built in 1913 with money raised by public subscription. Under the directorship of the ubiquitous Max Reinhardt, it became Berlin's people's theatre and, daringly for that time, put on plays by Hauptmann, Strindberg and Ibsen. Erwin Piscator continued the revolutionary tradition from 1924 to 1927, and immediately after the war in September 1945 a production of Lessing's plea for tolerance, *Nathan the Wise*, was put on here. The venue was officially reopened in 1954; it became – and remains – one of the capital's best theatres (see p.234).

Nearby, at Weydingerstrasse 14 and Kleine Alexanderstrasse 28, is the **Karl-Liebknecht-Haus**, the former KPD central committee headquarters, which also housed the editorial offices of the communist newspaper *Rote Fahne* ("Red Flag"). From the late 1920s onwards this was an important centre of resistance to the increasingly powerful Nazis: 100,000 pro-communist workers demonstrated here on January 25, 1933, just days before Hitler came to power. After the Reichstag fire in February 1933 the KPD was broken up and its headquarters ransacked.

Sophienstrasse

Sophienstrasse, first settled at the end of the seventeenth century, was once the Spandauer Vorstadt's main street. Extensively restored in the 1980s, it's now the best-looking street in the Hackescher Markt district and features a mix of retailers and arts workshops. In places, however, the restoration is only skin-deep and the pastel frontages of the old apartment houses conceal run-down, crumbling courtyards.

4

Sammlung Hoffmann

Sophie-Gips Höfe, Sophienstr. 21 • Sat 11am–4pm; closed Aug • Tours every 30min (1hr 30min; pre-booking required; English tours available) • €10 • ☎ 030 28 49 91 20, ⓦ sammlung-hoffmann.de • Ⓢ Hackescher Markt or Ⓤ Weinmeisterstrasse

A doorway on Sophienstrasse leads to the **Sophie-Gips Höfe**, a renovated retail and office complex where large outdoor works of art announce the presence of **Sammlung Hoffmann**. Started by avid collectors Erika and Rolf Hoffmann, this private contemporary art museum includes painting, sculpture, photography and video, and spreads over two light-filled floors. Organized subjectively – there are no names or curatorial texts – its theme changes each year, but the exhibition always features internationally renowned names such as Jean-Michel Basquiat, Felix Gonzalez-Torres and Bruce Nauman. Entry is by tour only, which offers a pleasantly interactive and informative way of experiencing such major works.

Handwerkervereinshaus

Sophienstr. 18 • Ⓢ Hackescher Markt

The vaguely Gothic-looking **Handwerkervereinshaus** (Craftmen's Club House) used to be the headquarters of the old craftsmen's guild. Until the founding of the German Social Democrat Party (SPD), this had been the main focus of the Berlin workers' movement, and continued to play an important role as a frequent venue for political meetings, including, on November 14, 1918, the first public gathering of the Spartakusbund (Spartacus League), the breakaway anti-war faction of the SPD that later evolved into the KPD (Communist Party of Germany). Since 1996 the block has housed the **Sophiensäle**, a venue for contemporary theatre, dance and theatre (see p.236).

Sophienkirche

Sophienstr. 22 • May–Sept Wed 3–6pm, Sat 3–5pm • ☎ 030 308 79 20 • Ⓢ Hackescher Markt

The **Sophienkirche**, built in 1712, is one of the city's finest Baroque churches, and the only central Berlin church to survive the war more or less undamaged. Its clear, simple lines come as a welcome change after the monumental Neoclassicism and fussy Gothic revivalism of so much of Berlin's architecture. The church's 70m-high tiered tower, added during the 1730s, is one of the area's most prominent landmarks. Built on ground gifted by the Jewish community to the Protestant community, who at the time were slightly financially embarrassed, the church itself was paid for by Princess Sophia Louise, third wife of Friedrich I, in order to provide a parish church for the neighbourhood. The **interior**, in washed-out shades of green and grey, is simple but pleasing; the one note of aesthetic exuberance is a pulpit with a crown-like canopy, set on a spiral pillar, which makes it look exactly like a chalice.

Grosse Hamburger Strasse

Ⓢ Hackescher Markt

Grosse Hamburger Strasse is dotted with several poignant reminders of the area's Jewish past. It's home to Berlin's oldest **Jewish cemetery**, established in 1672, and the first **Jewish old people's home** to be founded in the city. The Nazis used the building as a detention centre for Jews, and 55,000 people were held here before being deported to the camps. A memorial tablet, on which pebbles have been placed as a mark of respect (following the Jewish practice for grave-site visits), and a sculpted group of haggard-looking figures representing deportees, mark the spot where the home stood. The grassed-over open space behind is the site of the cemetery itself. In 1943 the Gestapo smashed most of the headstones and dug up the remains of those buried here, using gravestones to shore up a trench they had excavated through the site. A few cracked headstones with Hebrew inscriptions line the graveyard walls. The only freestanding monument was erected after the war to commemorate Moses Mendelssohn, the philosopher and German Enlightenment figure. Also adorned with pebbles, it's on the spot where he is thought to have been buried, with an inscription in German on one side and in Hebrew on the other.

Just to the north of the cemetery at **Grosse Hamburger Strasse 27** is a former Jewish boys' school, now a Jewish secondary school for both sexes. On the facade a plaque pays homage to Mendelssohn, who was a founder of Berlin's first Jewish school here in 1778, and who, until 1938, was commemorated by a bust in the garden.

On the other side of the street, the **Missing House** is a unique and effective monument to the wartime destruction of Berlin. A gap in the tenements marks where house number 15–16 stood until destroyed by a direct hit during an air raid. In the autumn of 1990 the French artist Christian Boltanski put plaques on the side walls of the surviving buildings on either side as part of an installation, recalling the names, dates and professions of the former inhabitants of the vanished house.

Oranienburger Strasse and around

Oranienburger Strasse, the centre of Berlin's affluent prewar Jewish community, still bears some reminders from this time. During its spell in East Berlin it was one of the city centre's more desolate streets, but after 1989 it became an atmospheric bar-crawling strip, and is now principally known for its restaurants and stylish watering holes, which attract locals and tourists in equal numbers. After dark, prostitutes openly solicit along much of the road; their presence alongside gawping visitors is a little reminiscent of Amsterdam's red-light district.

Monbijouplatz

Ⓢ Hackescher Markt

Sedate **Monbijouplatz**, at the eastern end of Oranienburger Strasse, is of interest for a couple of modern buildings, at numbers 3 and 5, designed by innovative local architects Grüntuch Ernst. Though radically different, the two buildings share a harmony in their geometric facades and attention to detail, such as in the intricacy of the small mosaic tiles on the detailing between the vertical bands at number 5, and in the play of light and shadow allowed by the aluminium louvres on the balconies of number 3.

Monbijoupark
🟢 Oranienburger Strasse

Sitting next to Monbijouplatz, **Monbijoupark** was once the grounds of a Rococo royal palace, reduced to rubble by the war and, like so many Hohenzollern relics, never rebuilt. The park makes an unexpected and shady refuge and is a good place to picnic or lie out with a book. The pleasant promenade that separates it from the Spree leads to a footbridge to Museum Island (see box, p.51).

Ramones Museum
Krausnickstr. 23 · Daily 10am–10pm · €4.50 (concerts vary but mostly free) · ☎ 030 75 52 88 89, 🌐 ramonesmuseum.com · 🟢 Oranienburger Strasse

Berlin's own shrine to the American proto-punks, the **Ramones Museum** began life as a modest affair in Kreuzberg in 2005 but has now expanded to more than three hundred items of memorabilia – an eclectic assortment, ranging from childhood photos of the group to gig set lists and flyers. The museum also hosts film screenings, the occasional acoustic show and special events.

Neue Synagoge
Oranienburger Str. near the corner of Krausnickstr. · April–Sept Mon–Fri 10am–6pm, Sun 10am–7pm; Oct–March Mon–Thurs & Sun 10am–6pm, Fri 10am–3pm · Museum €5 (special exhibitions are subject to an additional fee), dome (April–Sept only) €3 · ☎ 030 88 02 83 00, 🌐 cjudaicum.de · 🟢 Oranienburger Strasse

During the initial waves of Jewish immigration from the seventeenth century onwards the area around Oranienburger Strasse was a densely populated and desperately poor ghetto, but by the nineteenth century Berlin's Jews had achieved a high degree of prosperity and assimilation. This was reflected in the building of the grand **Neue Synagoge** (New Synagogue), to a design by Eduard Knoblauch. The synagogue was inaugurated in the presence of Bismarck in 1866, a gesture of official recognition that, coming at a time when Jews in Russia were still enduring officially sanctioned pogroms, must have made many feel that their position in German society was finally secure. The acceptance that they had enjoyed in Wilhelmine Germany contributed to the sense of disbelief many Jews felt at the rise of Nazism during the 1920s and 1930s.

The Neue Synagoge was built in mock-Moorish style, with a bulbous gilt and turquoise dome. It was Berlin's central synagogue for more than sixty years, serving also as a venue for concerts, including one in 1930 by Albert Einstein in his lesser-known role as a violinist. A Jewish museum was opened next door on January 24, 1933, just six days before the Nazi takeover. Neither museum nor synagogue survived the Third Reich. Both were damaged on *Kristallnacht* (see p.271), though the synagogue wasn't actually destroyed thanks to the intervention of the local police chief who chased off SA arsonists and called the fire brigade to extinguish the flames. It remained in use as a place of worship until 1940 when it was handed over to the Wehrmacht, who used it as a warehouse until it was gutted by bombs on the night of November 22, 1943.

After the war the synagogue remained a ruin, and in 1958 the main hall, which was thought to be on the verge of collapse, was demolished, leaving only the building's facade and entrance rooms intact. For many years these stood here largely overlooked, a plaque on the shattered frontage exhorting the few passers-by to *Vergesst es nie* – "Never forget". The Jewish community pressed for what was left to be turned into a museum, but the authorities did not respond until 1988, when it was decided to resurrect the shell as a "centre for the promotion and preservation of Jewish culture".

A new plaque was affixed to the building amid much official pomp on November 9, 1988, the fiftieth anniversary of *Kristallnacht*, and work began on restoring the facade and reconstructing the gilded dome, which, visible from far and wide, has once again

BERLIN'S JEWS

Jews have been part of Berlin's make-up since the earliest days of the twin towns of Berlin-Cölln. As elsewhere in Europe, their history has been studded by episodic persecution, though nothing comes close to their ruthless extermination by the Third Reich. Nevertheless, the Jewish community also has a history of determinedly and repeatedly rising to prominence against the odds: punching well above its weight in the city's prewar entrepreneurial and cultural scene and again today with the city's Jewish population increasing steadily over the past two decades.

EARLY SETTLERS AND THE FIRST POGROMS

Berlin's earliest Jewish settlers gravitated to a tight-knit area around today's Jüdenstrasse (see p.67) where, banned from most other trades, they successfully traded and lent money and slowly built a community. But in difficult times – of economic hardship or epidemics – they frequently became scapegoats. Bouts of persecution included during the plague of 1349; 1446, when they were driven from the city; and the **witch hunts** of 1510 when fifty Jews were tortured to death or burnt at the stake, with the rest again barred from the city. Though readmitted thirty years later, they found themselves barred once again in 1573 following a spate of pogroms after Joachim II was murdered and his much-disliked Jewish finance minister was accused of the crime.

Jews were permitted to return to Berlin in 1671, following the expulsion of several rich families from Vienna and given the economic woes of Brandenburg which, in the wake of the detrimental Thirty Years' War, sought powerful people to help with its rebuilding. Despite suffering personal restrictions and extra taxes, the Jewish population grew, so that by 1700 the city had 117 Jewish families, and in 1712 its **first synagogue** was built near today's Rosenstrasse.

EQUALITY AND PROMINENCE

The numbers of Jews in the Spandauer Vorstadt and particularly in the **Scheunenviertel** slum was greatly bolstered by a 1737 order that all Berlin's non-home-owning Jews must move there and that Jews could only enter the city through its northern gates. From that point on, and particularly in the nineteenth century, the area became a refuge for Jews fleeing pogroms in eastern Europe and Russia.

A big part of Berlin's draw was the loosening of Prussia's restrictions and the growing equality of its Jewish population, relative to the rest of Europe. By 1869 German Jews had full rights, and within years Jews rose to prominence in government, one influential group, dubbed the "*Kaiserjuden*", becoming close advisors to the Kaiser. By the 1920s Jewish department stores, such as **Wertheim**, had become part of the landscape and Jews were also highly active in the cultural and intellectual scenes with the likes of scientist **Albert Einstein**, physician **Magnus Hirschfeld**, theatre directors **Bertolt Brecht** and **Max Reinhardt** and writers and theorists like **Walter Benjamin** all contributing to the dynamism of Weimar culture.

THE RISE OF THE NAZIS: PERSECUTION AND EMIGRATION

By 1933, when the **Nazis** assumed power and state-backed persecution started, there were 160,564 Jews in Berlin: around four percent of the population and one third of those in the German Reich. The process of persecution began with an SA-enforced boycott of Jewish shops, businesses and medical and legal practices on April 1 of that year; many of the wealthiest Jews left the same year, as a series of laws banning them from public office, the civil service, journalism, farming, teaching, broadcasting and acting were introduced. Then in September 1935 the **Nuremberg laws** effectively deprived Jews of their German citizenship, by introducing apartheid-like classifications of "racial purity". There was a brief respite in 1936 when Berlin hosted the Olympic Games and the Nazis, wishing to show an acceptable face to the outside world, eased up on overt anti-Semitism, but by the following year large-scale expropriation of Jewish businesses began. Jews who could see the writing on the wall, and had money, escaped while they could (even though other European countries, the US and Palestine all restricted Jewish immigration), but the majority stayed put, hoping things would improve, or simply because they couldn't afford to emigrate.

KRISTALLNACHT, WAR AND THE FIRST DEPORTATIONS

After the violent escalation of Nazi anti-Semitism of **Kristallnacht** – the night of November 9, 1938 – Jews' already beleaguered position became intolerable. "Crystal Night" – named for the shattered glass from the attacks on Jewish shops and institutions – resulted in the deaths of at least 36 Berlin Jews, many beaten on the streets while passers by looked on, along with the destruction of 23 of the city's 29 synagogues and wrecking of hundreds of shops and businesses. Afterwards the Nazi government fined the German-Jewish community one billion marks – ostensibly to pay for the damage – and then forcibly "Aryanized" all remaining Jewish businesses, effectively excluding Jews from economic life. With the **outbreak of war** in September 1939, Jews were forced to observe a night-time curfew and forbidden to own radios. Forced transportation of Jews to the East (mainly occupied Poland) began in February 1940, and September 1941 saw the introduction of a law requiring Jews to wear the yellow Star of David, heralding the beginning of **mass deportations**.

THE FINAL SOLUTION

In January 1942, the **Wannsee Conference**, held in a western suburb of Berlin (see p.171), discussed the *Endlösung* or "Final Solution" to the "Jewish Question", drawing up plans for the removal of all Jews to the East and, implicitly, their extermination (see box, p.273). As the **Final Solution** began to be put into effect, daily life for Berlin's Jews grew ever more unbearable: in April they were banned from public transport, and in September their food rations were reduced. By the beginning of 1943 the only Jews remaining legally in Berlin were highly skilled workers in the city's armaments factories, and in February deportation orders began to be enforced for this group too. Most Berlin Jews were sent to Theresienstadt and Auschwitz concentration camps, and only a handful survived the war. By the end of the war the combined effects of emigration and genocide had reduced Berlin's Jewish population by around 96 percent to about 6500; around 1400 had survived as "U-boats", hidden by gentile families at great personal risk, and the rest had somehow managed to evade the final round-ups in precariously legal conditions, usually by having irreplaceable skills vital to the war effort, or by being married to non-Jews.

JEWS IN POSTWAR GERMANY

Since the war Berlin's Jewish population has steadily increased to between 35,000 and 45,000, with an influx in recent decades from the countries of the former Soviet Union, as well as from Israel – making it by far the largest such community in Germany and one of the world's fastest-growing. With the renovation of the **Neue Synagoge** – one of eight in the city – as a cultural centre and the opening of several Jewish cafés, Oranienburger Strasse has regained a little of its pre-Nazi identity, yet some Jews complain that the tourist interest in this area and their community has led to a theme-park-like faux celebration of Jewish life. Jewish insignias have begun to appear where there was never a link, and restaurants and cultural events pop up simply to provide visitors with stereotypes – local toyshops even sell *menorah*, the Jewish candelabra. They also argue that although sympathy and interest in sites associated with Jewish culture and persecution is welcome, if their reason is to understand the Holocaust rather than simply indulge a ghoulish interest, then the focus should be on the perpetrators, not the victims.

Despite the lure of Berlin and Germany in general for many Jewish migrants, anti-Semitism has definitely not gone away. In 2015, a report by the EU's Agency for Fundamental Rights found that anti-Semitic crimes throughout Germany had risen to a five-year high, a trend backed up by the Berlin-based Department for Research and Information on Anti-Semitism, which reported an increase in anti-Semitic incidents of 34 percent in 2015 against the previous year. On the other hand, for most Berlin remains a tolerant and exciting place to live, with plenty of opportunities – a key aspect of its appeal to all comers.

JEWISH TOURS

Milk and Honey Tours ☏ 030 61 62 57 61, ⌨ milkandhoneytours.com. This operator, which specializes in tours of Jewish Europe, offers a variety of first-class guided tours of Jewish Berlin, either on foot and public transport or in a private vehicle. They can also take you to further-flung sites of Jewish interest, including concentration camp memorial sites.

become a Berlin landmark. In 1995, the building was reopened as a museum and cultural centre, officially called **Neue Synagoge Berlin – Centrum Judaicum**. Inside are two permanent exhibitions, one on the history of the synagogue itself and another on the Jewish life and culture that was once found in the area. You'll have to pass through airport-style security to get in – a sad reflection of the continuing threat to Jewish institutions from terrorist attack.

Auguststrasse

Auguststrasse was the epicentre of the 1990s Berlin art scene, and though it has long since lost much of its original edge, it still features workspaces and commercial galleries (see p.82 & p.231). The breathtaking transformation of the street from decrepit inner-city district to thriving arts scene began in 1989 and was given legitimacy in June 1992 when city authorities stumped up enviable financial support for the "37 Rooms Exhibition", during which the whole of Auguststrasse was turned into a giant gallery. Since then the street's galleries continue to attract artists and their interesting and controversial work from all over the world.

Ehemalige Jüdische Mädchenschule

Auguststr. 11–13 • Ⓦ maedchenschule.org • Ⓢ Oranienburger Strasse

Built on the late 1920s as one of the last major Jewish structures in the city before the Nazis took power, the corridors of the business-like dark-brick **Ehemalige Jüdische Mädchenschule** (Former Jewish Girls' School) were pounded by some thousand Jewish schoolgirls, most of whom were later deported or murdered in concentration camps. In recent years the building has been refurbished, partly in tribute to the building's poignant history and partly to create a ritzy hangout for the city's art-and-culture cognoscenti. As well as three floors for contemporary art, including the CWC Gallery (a branch of Camera Work; see p.231), you'll find upscale restaurant, *Pauly Saal* (see p.201); *Mogg*, a Jewish deli serving some of the best pastrami sandwiches in town (see p.199); and, slightly incongruously, Berlin's John F. Kennedy museum.

Museum The Kennedys

Auguststr. 11–13 • Tues–Fri 10am–6pm, Sat & Sun 11am–6pm • €7 • ☎ 030 20 65 35 70, Ⓦ thekennedys.de • Ⓢ Oranienburger Strasse

Inspired by the US president's 1963 visit to Berlin – then the front line of the Cold War – **Museum The Kennedys** is now a much broader homage to JFK. Kennedy understood, as no other politician before him, the power of photos and then television – partly thanks to his former-photojournalist wife Jackie. As Norman Mailer put it: "America's politics … (became) … America's favorite movie, America's first soap opera, America's bestseller." Evidence of this carefully orchestrated media campaign (which included a ban on photos showing Kennedy wearing glasses) and resultant cult of personality abounds in the museum's three hundred **photos** and magazine covers. The dozens of other 1960s relics include JFK's old ties, cufflinks, phonebook and some preserved presidential doodles – twirling shapes casually interspersed with words like Cuba, Berlin, Eastern Europe – as well as the crocodile-skin briefcase that accompanied him on his fateful trip to Dallas. Also here is a brilliant **photomosaic** of Kennedy by American artist Robert Silvers who invented the technique: it uses hundreds of pictures from his life to build a mask.

The real highlights of the museum, however, are exhibits relating to JFK's eight-hour **Berlin visit** on June 26, 1963. The Berlin Wall had been built just two years earlier, so the city's emotions ran high, and there's wonderful footage here of ecstatic crowds – people breaking free of security cordons to shake hands with the passing president. Kennedy's city parade included a stop at the viewing platform in front of the Brandenburg Gate – draped for the occasion by the Russians in enormous red flags and

OPPOSITE HACKESCHE HÖFE (P.72) >

communist placards – before he retreated to Schöneberg to deliver his impassioned "Berliner" speech (see p.116). The day proved so emotional that at the end of it JFK commented to his aides "we'll never have another day like this one as long as we live".

me Collectors Room

Auguststr. 68 • Tues–Sun noon–6pm • €6 • ☎ 030 86 00 85 10, ⓦ me-berlin.com • Ⓢ Oranienburger Strasse

The **me Collectors Room** was conceived and built by chemist and endocrinologist Thomas Olbricht to showcase his private art collection – which happens to be among the most comprehensive in Europe, including works by John Currin, Franz Gertsch, Marlene Dumas and Gerhard Richter – via a series of alternating exhibitions. The "me" here is not misplaced egotism but an acronym for "moving energies": the collection spans painting, sculpture, photography, installation and new media works from the early sixteenth century to the present day. The permanent Wunderkammer section rekindles the tradition, popular during the Renaissance period, of bringing together eccentric curiosities and "wonders" from around the world. A spacious **café** serves coffee and snacks (Tues–Sun 11am–6pm).

KW Institute for Contemporary Art

Auguststr. 69 • Daily except Tues 11am–7pm (Thurs till 9pm) • €8 • ☎ 030 243 45 90, ⓦ kw-berlin.de • Ⓢ Oranienburger Strasse

The **KW (Kunst-Werke) Institute for Contemporary Art** was one of the prime movers in the post-*Wende* transformation of Auguststrasse. Once a nineteenth-century margarine factory, KW was turned into a dedicated art space by Klaus Biesenbach and a group of fellow art-lovers in the early 1990s. The elegant facade leads into a lovely, tree-filled courtyard and a building complex that includes the glass-walled *Café Bravo*, designed by American artist Dan Graham, and a 400-square-metre exhibition hall in the rear wing, designed by Berlin architect Hans Düttman. The institute mainly exhibits cutting-edge international works from both up-and-coming and major names such as Doug Aitken, Dinos and Jake Chapman and Paul Pfeiffer. KW also runs the immensely popular **Berlin Biennale** (see box, p.232).

The theatre district

There's not all that much to see in Mitte's **theatre district**, which gathers around the section of Friedrichstrasse north of the river, though you can't fail to notice the giant **Friedrichstadt-Palast**, a clumsy GDR-era Jugendstil pastiche that rears up just south of U-Bahn Oranienburger Tor. This is the place to come if you're into big, splashy, scantily clad revues. Equally hard to miss, a block to the west, is **Sammlung Boros**, a five-floor concrete World War II bunker that has been converted into one of the city's most unique art spaces (see p.233).

Most impressive among the more highbrow theatres dotted about is the elegant **Deutsches Theater**, at Schumannstrasse 13, founded in 1883 (see p.234). Max Reinhardt became its director in 1905, thereafter dominating the theatre scene for nearly three decades. In 1922 a young and unknown Marlene Dietrich made her stage debut here, and a couple of years later Bertolt Brecht (see box, p.86) arrived from Munich to begin his energetic conquest of Berlin's theatre world; his **Berliner Ensemble**, just south of the Deutsches Theater, is still in operation too.

The best of the district's theatres are reviewed in our chapter on the Arts (see p.234).

Berliner Ensemble

Bertolt-Brecht-Platz 1 • Box office Mon–Fri 8am–6pm, Sat & Sun 11am–6pm • ☎ 030 28 40 81 55, ⓦ berliner-ensemble.de • ⓤ/Ⓢ Friedrichstrasse

The austere exterior of the early 1890s **Berliner Ensemble**, tucked away on Bertolt-Brecht-Platz, hides a rewarding and opulent neo-Baroque interior. This is where, on

August 31, 1928, the world premiere of **Bertolt Brecht**'s *Dreigroschenoper* ("The Threepenny Opera") was staged, the first of 250 consecutive performances in a ritualistic tribute to one of the few world-famous writers East Germany could later claim as its own: after exile in America during the Nazi era, Brecht returned in 1949 with his wife, Helene Weigel, to take over direction of the theatre, marking his return by painting a still-visible red cross through the coat of arms on the royal box. During box office times you can view the foyer, but the rest of the theatre is only open to the public during shows (see p.234), which still include regular performances of Brecht's works.

Admiralspalast

Friedrichstr. 101 • ⓤ/ⓢ Friedrichstrasse

Across the Spree on Weidendammer Brücke towards Bahnhof Friedrichstrasse, the Jugendstil **Admiralspalast** was built as a variety theatre in 1910. Its partly gilded facade, fluted columns and bas-reliefs come as a surprise amid the predominantly concrete architecture of the area. As one of the few buildings in these parts to have survived bombing, it became an important political meeting hall in the immediate postwar years and on April 22 and 23, 1946, was the venue for the forced union of the social democratic SPD with the prewar Communist party, the KPD. This resulted in the birth of the SED (Sozialistische Einheitspartei Deutschlands), the GDR Communist Party that controlled the country until 1990. The building puts on a wide range of shows (see p.234).

4

Bahnhof Friedrichstrasse

Georgenstr. 14/17 • ⓢ Friedrichstrasse

Now a grubby edifice, with its mediocre shopping arcade and budget restaurants, before the *Wende* **Bahnhof Friedrichstrasse** was a train station of real consequence as the main border crossing point for western visitors to East Berlin, and probably the most heavily guarded station in Europe. There was a regular flow of mainline and S-Bahn traffic between Friedrichstrasse and West Berlin – except during the Berlin Blockade of 1948–49 (see box, p.126) – but until late 1989 the East German government did all it could to keep its own citizens from joining it. A tangle of checkpoints, guard posts and customs controls and, more discreetly, armed guards separated westbound platforms from the rest of the station.

Tränenpalast

Reichstagufer 17 • Tues–Fri 9am–7pm, Sat & Sun 10am–6pm • Free • ☎ 030 46 77 77 90, ⓦ hdg.de/berlin • ⓢ Friedrichstrasse

One structure that really stood out in the Friedrichstrasse border complex was its departure hall, a glass-and-concrete construction between the Bahnhof and the River Spree. Grimly nicknamed the **Tränenpalast** or "Palace of Tears" by Berliners, this was the scene of many a poignant farewell as people took leave of relatives, friends and lovers here. Until 1990 an estimated eight million travellers a year – visitors and tourists and occasionally East German citizens with exit visas – queued inside to get through passport and customs controls before travelling by U- or S-Bahn to West Berlin or beyond to West Germany.

A glut of reminders from the era survive in an engaging **museum**, which explores the consequences and daily restrictions of the German division right up to reunification. There are plenty of original artefacts, documents, photographs and old newsreels and many exhibits devoted to personal stories. Taking all this in, it's easy to overlook the loveless character of the building and imagine for a moment the contrastingly deep and varied emotions it's witnessed.

Chausseestrasse

Chausseestrasse was, during the nineteenth century, the location of one of Berlin's densest concentrations of heavy industry. Development began here during the 1820s with the establishment of a steam-engine factory and iron foundry and in 1837 August Borsig built his first factory – by the 1870s his successors were churning out hundreds of steam engines and railway locomotives each year.

Other industrial concerns were also drawn to the area, earning it the nickname *Feuerland* – "Fireland". However, by the end of the century most had outgrown their roots and relocated en masse to the edges of the rapidly expanding city. A reminder of the past, and of Borsig's local influence, is the **Borsighaus** at Chausseestrasse 9. Once the central administration block of the Borsig factories, this sandstone building, its facade richly decorated with bronze figures, looks like a displaced country residence.

Dorotheenstädtische Friedhof

Daily: March–Oct 8am–8pm; Nov–Feb 8am–5pm • Free • ⓤ Oranienburger Tor or ⓤ Naturkunde Museum

At the **Dorotheenstädtische Friedhof** (Dorotheenstadt Cemetery), eastern Berlin's VIP cemetery, you'll find the graves of luminaries including: Bertolt Brecht and Helene Weigel; architect Karl Friedrich Schinkel, his last resting place topped by an appropriately florid monument; John Heartfield, Dada luminary and interwar

---

4

THE BERLIN WALL

After the war, Berlin was split among Britain, France, the US and USSR, as Stalin, Roosevelt and Churchill had agreed at the Yalta Conference in February 1945. Each sector was administered by the relevant country, and was supposed to exist peacefully with its neighbours under a unified city council. But, almost from the outset, antagonism between the Soviet and other sectors was high. Just three years after the war ended, the Soviet forces closed down the land access corridors to the city from the Western zones in what became known as the **Berlin Blockade**: it was successfully overcome by a massive **airlift** of food and supplies that lasted nearly a year (see box, p.126). This, followed by the 1953 uprising (see box, p.121), large-scale cross-border emigration (between 1949 and 1961, the year the Wall was built, over three million East Germans – almost a fifth of the population – fled to the Federal Republic) and innumerable "incidents", led to the building of what the GDR called an "an antifascist protection barrier".

The Wall was erected overnight on **August 13, 1961** when, at 2am, forty thousand East German soldiers, policemen and Workers' Militia went into action closing U- and S-Bahn lines and stringing barbed wire across streets leading into West Berlin to cordon off the Soviet sector. The Wall followed its boundaries implacably, cutting through houses, across squares and rivers with its own cool illogicality. Many Berliners were evicted from their homes, while others had their doors and windows blocked by bales of barbed wire. Suddenly the British, American and French sectors of the city were corralled some 200km inside the GDR, yet though they reinforced patrols, the Allies did nothing to prevent the sealing of the border.

Despite earlier rumours, most people in West and East Berlin were taken by surprise. Those who lived far from the border area only learned of its closure when they found all routes to West Berlin blocked. Crowds gathered and extra border guards were sent to prevent trouble. There was little most people could do other than accept this latest development, though some – including a few border guards – managed to find loopholes in the new barrier and flee west. But within a few days, building workers were reinforcing the barbed wire and makeshift barricades with bricks and mortar. As an additional measure, West Berliners were no longer allowed to cross the border into East Berlin. From 1961 onwards the GDR strengthened the Wall making it an almost impenetrable barrier – two walls separated by a *Sperrgebiet* (forbidden zone), dotted with watchtowers and patrolled by soldiers and dogs. It was also known as the *Todesstreifen* (**death strip**) as border troops, known as Grepos, were under instructions to shoot anyone attempting to scale the Wall, and to shoot accurately: any guard suspected of deliberately missing was court-martialled, and his family could expect severe harassment from the authorities. Over the years, over two hundred people were **killed** endeavouring to cross the Wall.

photomontage exponent, under a headstone decorated with a runic H; philosopher Georg Hegel, whose ideas influenced Marx; author Heinrich Mann; former president Johannes Rau; and journalist Günter Gaus. A plan detailing who lies where is located beside the cemetery administration offices (on the right at the end of the entrance alley).

Next to the Dorotheenstädtische Friedhof is the **Französischer Friedhof** (French Cemetery; entrance on Chausseestrasse and closer to Oranienburger Tor), originally built to serve Berlin's Huguenot community.

Brecht-Weigel-Gedenkstätte

Chausseestr. 125 • Guided tours: Tues every 30min 10am–3.30pm, Wed & Fri every 30min 10–11.30am, Thurs every 30min 10–11.30am & 5–6.30pm, Sat every 30min 10am–noon & 1–3.30pm, Sun hourly 11am–6pm • €3 • ☎ 030 200 57 18 44, ⓦ adk.de/de/archiv/gedenkstaetten/ • ⓤ Oranienburger Tor or ⓤ Naturkunde Museum

The **Brecht-Weigel-Gedenkstätte** (Brecht-Weigel Memorial) preserves the final home and workplace of the playwright, poet and theatre director Bertolt Brecht and his wife, actress and Berliner Ensemble theatre manager Helene Weigel. Guided tours take in the seven simply furnished rooms – an absolute must for Brecht fans, but not so fascinating if you're only casually acquainted with his works. Access is by guided tour only.

Initial **escape** attempts were straightforward, and often successful – hollowing out furniture, ramming checkpoint barriers and simple disguise brought many people over. However, the authorities quickly rose to the challenge, and would-be escapees were forced to become more resourceful, digging tunnels and constructing gliders, one-man submarines and hot-air balloons. By the time the Wall came down, every escape method conceivable seemed to have been used – even down to passing through Checkpoint Charlie in the stomach of a pantomime cow – and those desperate to get out of the GDR preferred the long wait and complications of applying to leave officially to the risk of being gunned down by a border guard.

An oddity of the Wall was that it was built a few metres inside GDR territory; the West Berlin authorities therefore had little control over the **graffiti** that covered it. The Wall was an ever-changing mixture of colours and slogans, with occasional bursts of bitterness: "My friends are dying behind you"; humour: "Why not jump over and join the Party?"; and stupidity: "We shoulda nuked 'em in 45".

Late in 1989 the East German government, spurred by Gorbachev's *glasnost* and confronted by a tense domestic climate, realized it could keep the impossible stable no longer. To an initially disbelieving and then jubilant Europe, travel restrictions for GDR citizens were lifted on **November 9, 1989** – effectively, the Wall had ceased to matter, and pictures of Berliners, East and West, hacking away at the detested symbol filled newspapers and TV bulletins around the world. Within days, enterprising characters were renting out hammers and chisels so that souvenir hunters could take home their own chip of the Wall.

Today, especially in the city centre, it's barely possible to tell exactly where the Wall ran: odd juxtapositions of dereliction against modernity, and the occasional unexpected swathe of the erstwhile "death strip", are in most cases all that's left of one of the most hated borders the world has ever known. The simple row of **cobbles** that has been placed along much of the former course of the Wall acts as a necessary reminder. Few significant stretches remain; the sections devoted to the East Side Gallery (see p.133) and the Gedenkstätte Berliner Mauer (see p.86) are the most notable exceptions.

One sad postscript to the story of the Wall hit the headlines in spring 1992. Two former **border guards** were tried for the murder of Chris Gueffroy, shot dead while illegally trying to cross the border at Neukölln in February 1989. Under the GDR government the guards had been treated to a meal by their superiors and given extra holiday for their patriotic actions; under the new regime, they received sentences for murder – while those ultimately responsible, the former leaders of the GDR, largely avoided punishment.

4

4

BERTOLT BRECHT

Bertolt Brecht (1898–1956) is widely regarded as one of the leading German dramatists of the twentieth century. Born in Augsburg, the son of a paper-mill manager, he went on to study medicine, mainly to avoid full military service in World War I. Working as an army medical orderly in 1918, his experiences helped shape his passionate anti-militarism. Soon he drifted away from medicine onto the fringes of the theatrical world, eventually winding up as a playwright in residence at Munich's Kammerspiele in 1921.

It wasn't until the 1928 premiere of the *Dreigroschenoper* – "**The Threepenny Opera**" – co-written with the composer Kurt Weill, that Brecht's real breakthrough came. This marked the beginning of a new phase in Brecht's work. A couple of years earlier he had embraced Marxism, an ideological step that had a profound effect on his literary output, leading him to espouse a didactic, "epic" form of theatre. The aim was to provoke the audience, perhaps even move them to revolutionary activity. To this end he developed the technique of **Verfremdung** ("alienation") to create a sense of distance between spectators and the action unfolding before them. By using effects such as obviously fake scenery, monotone lighting and jarring music to expose the sham sentimentality of love songs, he hoped to constantly remind the audience that what they were doing was watching a play – in order to make them judge, rather than be drawn into, the action on stage. The result was a series of works that were pretty heavy-going.

In 1933, unsurprisingly, Brecht went into self-imposed exile, eventually ending up in the States. His years away from Germany were among his most productive. The political message was still very much present in his work, but somehow the dynamic and lyrical force of his writing meant that it was often largely lost on his audience. Returning to Europe, he finally settled in East Berlin in 1949, after a brief period in Switzerland. His decision to try his luck in the Soviet-dominated Eastern sector of Germany was influenced by the offer to take over at the Theater am Schiffbauerdamm, where the *Dreigroschenoper* had been premiered more than twenty years earlier. However, before heading east, Brecht first took the precaution of gaining Austrian citizenship and lodging the copyright of his works with a West German publisher. The remainder of Brecht's life was largely devoted to running what is now known as the Berliner Ensemble (see p.82) and facing up to his own tensions with the fledgling GDR.

Museum für Naturkunde

Invalidenstr. 43 • Tues–Fri 9.30am–6pm, Sat & Sun 10am–6pm • €8, under-16s €5 • ☎ 030 20 93 85 91, ⓦ naturkundemuseum-berlin .de • ⓤ Naturkundemuseum

One of the world's largest natural history museums, the **Museum für Naturkunde**'s origins go back to 1716, though the present building and the nucleus of the collection date from the 1880s. As well as the skeletons of a brachiosaurus and a Tyrannosaurus rex (part of the exhibition "Tristan – Berlin bares teeth", which runs until 2019), visitors can see the taxidermied remains of famous Berlin polar bear Knut, who died in 2011. There are also some entertaining rooms devoted to the evolution of vertebrates and the ape family, and an interesting, if slightly ghoulish, section on how the numerous other stuffed animals were "prepared for exhibition". The museum also boasts a vast mineralogy collection, including a number of meteorites.

Gedenkstätte Berliner Mauer

Bernauer Str. 111–119 • Open-air memorial daily 8am–10pm; Visitor Centre and Documentation Centre Tues–Sun 10am–6pm • Free; downloadable mobile tour guides also available from the website in English (free) • ☎ 030 467 98 66 66, ⓦ berliner-mauer-gedenkstaette.de • Ⓢ Nordbahnhof or ⓤ Bernauer Strasse

A short walk north of S-Bahn Nordhof is the first of several buildings dedicated to the **Gedenkstätte Berliner Mauer** (Berlin Wall Memorial), the most moving of the city's Wall memorials and the only one where it's still possible to gain a true sense of how it divided the city. Bernauer Strasse was literally bisected by the Wall; before the Wall was built you could enter or exit the Soviet Zone just by going through the door of one of the buildings, which is why, on August 13, 1961, some citizens, who woke up to find themselves on the wrong side of the newly established "national border", leapt out of windows to get to the West. Over the years, the facades of these buildings were cemented up and incorporated into the partition itself, until they were knocked down and replaced by the Wall proper in 1979.

This official city memorial stretches 1.4km along Bernauer Strasse: steel poles mark out the original route of the west-facing Wall, around which are an impressive collection of information boards and large-scale photographs relating the stories of the years of division, focusing specifically on those who met their end here as well as those who survived. Indeed, many of the Wall's most famous escapes occurred here: from the 57 people who fled to the West though Tunnel 57 over two nights in October 1964 to 19-year-old East German border guard Conrad Schumann, who famously leapt over barbed wire during the Wall's construction and was spirited away to safety by Western officials. Further along the route are the **Chapel of Reconciliation**, a modern, circular church built to replace the original that the GDR blew up in 1985 as it was deemed an "obstruction" – prayer services for the victims of the Berlin Wall are held in the chapel on weekdays at noon – and the **Window of Remembrance** memorial, which pays poignant tribute to the 136 individuals who lost their lives to the Wall with individual photos and relevant personal data. A short **section of the Wall** as it once was – both walls and a death strip between – remain preserved at the corner of Bernauer Strasse and Ackerstrasse.

Renovated for the 25th anniversary of the *Mauerfall* in 2014, the **Wall Documentation Centre** at Bernauer Strasse 111 keeps the broader story of the Wall alive via a multimedia exhibition that draws on photos, sound recordings, objects and information terminals – there's also a useful **viewing tower** that you can climb to contemplate the barrier and the way in which it once divided the city.

The memorial's main **Visitor Centre**, which contains a comprehensive bookshop, can be found opposite S-Bahn Nordbahnhof, while inside the station is an exhibition relating to the era's so-called "**ghost stations**" – underground train stations (Nordbahnhof included) that were sealed off and heavily guarded to allow trains to cross the divided city while preventing passengers from escaping.

SONY CENTER

Potsdamer Platz and Tiergarten

A huge swathe of peaceful green parkland, smack in the middle of Berlin, the Tiergarten stretches west from the Brandenburger Tor and Reichstag, its beautifully landscaped meadows, gardens and woodlands a welcome antidote to the bustle of the city. The park and its immediate surroundings form a sub-district of the city's central Mitte district, and its southeastern edge, once occupied by the Berlin Wall, has flourished in recent decades. Huge building projects have mushroomed here, many reclaiming death-strip lands in prime locations at the centre of a unified city. The most obvious of these is the one-time hub of Potsdamer Platz, which has been transformed from a Cold War wasteland into the city's most impressive ensemble of skyscrapers and hosts several interesting museums whose themes vary from German film to espionage.

5

Adjacent to Potsdamer Platz is the **Kulturforum**, Berlin's second great collection of museums and cultural institutions, highlights of which include the **Gemäldegalerie**, with its internationally renowned collection of European art, and the applied arts of the **Kunstgewerbemuseum**. A third world-class museum, the Neue Nationalgalerie, is closed until 2020 for refurbishment, though other smaller institutions, such as the **Musikinstrumenten-Museum**, are fun to explore.

To the west of the Kulturforum is a **diplomatic district**, where the Bendlerblock, site of several July Bomb Plot executions, houses the interesting **Gedenkstätte Deutscher Widerstand**, a museum of German resistance against the Nazis. Further west, one architecturally impressive embassy flanks another as far as the **Bauhaus-Archiv**, a homage to that influential art and design movement. This is as good a place as any to begin an exploration of the **Tiergarten** itself. Walk or cycle west to a couple of beer gardens or take a bus a couple of quick stops north to the park's proud centrepiece: the **Siegessäule**, a huge column that celebrates Prussian military victories and delivers fine views over the park and the city.

The northeastern corner of the Tiergarten, above the Reichstag, is occupied by Berlin's modern-day **Regierungsviertel** (Government Quarter), where a string of modernist government buildings constructed in the 1990s cling to a bend in the River Spree known as the **Spreebogen**. Surveying all this is the monumental glass-and-steel **Hauptbahnhof**, Berlin's huge and modern main train station. It occupies a rather desolate, still underdeveloped patch of town, though nearby is the **Hamburger Bahnhof**, a top-notch contemporary art museum.

GETTING AROUND | POTSDAMER PLATZ AND TIERGARTEN

By train The Hauptbahnhof and Potsdamer Platz, with its U- and S-Bahn station, are the main transport hubs for the Tiergarten district.

By bus The extremely frequent #100 and #200 buses between Bahnhof Zoo and Alexanderplatz are the best options for getting around the area. The #200 stops at the Kulturforum, while #100 stops at all the major points in the Tiergarten.

By bike The most flexible way to explore the Tiergarten, particularly the park itself, is by bike, with Call a Bike (see p.25) in invariably good supply at Potsdamer Platz.

Potsdamer Platz and around

Pulverized during the war, then forced into hibernation by the Berlin Wall, the busy junction of **Potsdamer Platz** has now fully re-emerged following 25 years of frantic building as a temple of commercialism. The Platz is worth visiting for its **modern architecture** alone, and for the museums on and around it. These include the excellent **Museum für Film und Fernsehen**, which will appeal to anyone with even a passing interest in German cinema, the **Daimler Contemporary** gallery for modern art buffs and, for kids and rainy days, the **Legoland Discovery Centre Berlin**.

Sony Center

Potsdamer Platz • ⓦ sonycenter.de • ⓤ/ⓢ Potsdamer Platz

Designed by Helmut Jahn, the striking, eco-friendly **Sony Center** occupies several glass-sheathed buildings grouped around a capacious, circular courtyard. Its rotunda, topped by a conical glass roof, is easily the most impressive showpiece in the area, open to the elements but at the same time providing a remove from the surrounding urban racket. The centre houses shops for everything from cosmetics and jewellery to, of course, Sony electronics, as well as many cafés, bars and restaurants. Berliners have adopted the courtyard as a place to congregate for public events.

POTSDAMER PLATZ AND TIERGARTEN

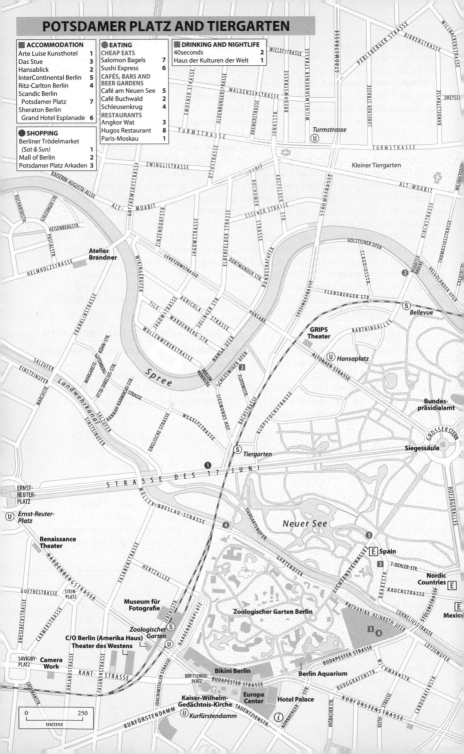

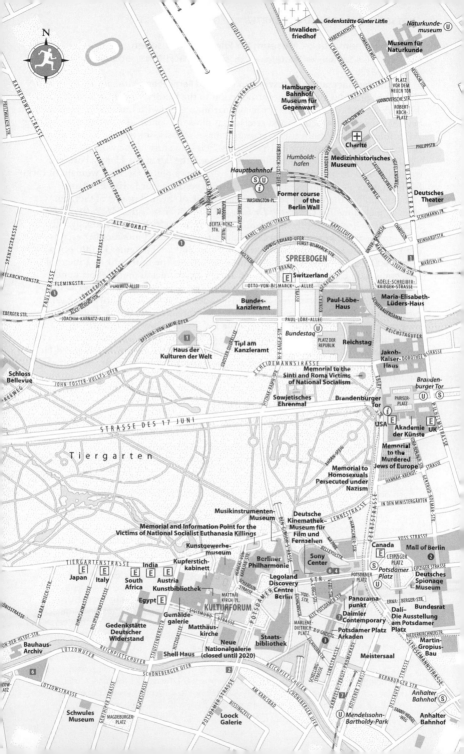

5

Deutsche Kinemathek – Museum für Film und Fernsehen

Potsdamer Str. 2 • Tues–Sun 10am–6pm, Thurs till 8pm • €7, free Thurs 4–8pm • ☎ 030 300 90 30, ⓦ deutsche-kinemathek.de • ⓤ/ⓢ Potsdamer Platz

The **Deutsche Kinemathek – Museum für Film und Fernsehen** (Museum for Film and Television) provides an excellent introduction to the history of German cinema and TV, with an audio guide that is especially useful to those with limited German. Using a bevy of clips, reconstructions and artefacts, it plots the course of German film-making via various technical innovations, stars and major releases, starting with clips from Berlin's first public screening in 1895 (see p.293) – the first in the world – and highlighting early **pioneers** and film stars. Among the latter was Henny Porten, a sturdy blonde often portrayed in 1920s Germany as an ideal German woman, but who fell from grace under the Nazis when she refused to leave her Jewish husband.

The turmoil of the **Weimar years** produced some of the highpoints of German cinema, including *The Cabinet of Dr Caligari* (1920), Fritz Lang's *Metropolis* (1927) and *The Blue Angel* (1930), which launched **Marlene Dietrich** internationally. The museum is particularly strong on Dietrich, since it inherited much of her estate on her death in 1992 – and quite a haul it was too: over 3000 documents, 15,000 photos and some 3000 items of clothing stuffed into sixty valises. The museum's treatment of the **Nazi era** is both clever and circumspect. There's slender detail on the most famous film-maker of the time **Leni Riefenstahl**, known for her magnificent portrayal of the 1936 Olympics in *Olympia*, but infamous for her willingness to glorify the Nazis in **propaganda** films like *Triumph of the Will*. The museum plays this and other propaganda films, including the deplorable *Jud Süss*, a tale of a dishonest Jew, on TV sets in unmarked drawers that line the walls of the room; you'll probably need to try a few drawers to find them. Propaganda was obviously a part of the Nazi era, but far more popular, particularly during the war, were **escapist** films – Hitler himself was a big fan of Mickey Mouse.

POTSDAMER PLATZ REGENERATED

Said to have been the busiest square in prewar Europe, **Potsdamer Platz** was once a vibrant area, surrounded by stores, bars and clubs. The war left it severely battered, though it regained some of its vitality in the chaotic years immediately following as a black-market centre at the junction of the Soviet, American and British sectors. Later, West Berliners watched from their side of the dividing line as the Soviets put down the East Berlin uprising of 1953.

The Cold War was then played out here in words, with the Western authorities relaying their version of the news to East Berliners by means of an electronic newsboard – countered by an Eastern billboard exhorting West Berliners to shop in cheap East Berlin stores. This ended with the coming of the Wall, which finally put a physical seal on the ideological division of Potsdamer Platz. On the Eastern side all the buildings (which were mostly war-vintage wrecks) were razed to give the GDR's border guards a clear field of fire, while in the West only a couple of battered survivors, including the hulk of the fine old *Hotel Esplanade*, were left as a reminder of the way things used to be.

The dismantling of the Wall produced one of Europe's most valuable lots, a huge empty site in the middle of the city. It was no surprise, therefore, that – despite earlier plans for a more flexible use – in the end huge multinational corporations won out, purchasing the land and creating equally huge sprawling **commercial complexes**. Building this mini-city from scratch represented a feat of engineering. An entire power, water and sewage infrastructure was created; subway tunnels drilled and new S- and U-Bahn stations built; the surviving Haus Huth, a landmark building, was picked up and trundled to another spot (see opposite); and the remaining interior portions of the *Hotel Esplanade* were incorporated into a new restaurant.

Now, after years of construction work, Potsdamer Platz is – future projects notwithstanding – complete. Dominated by the offices and apartments of the rich, it's the most muscular display of multinational power in the city – and so not to everyone's taste – but probably exactly what Berlin needed to compete as a global metropolis.

5

Postwar cinema receives less attention, but includes some fascinating material on the output of East Germany's state-controlled DEFA and West Germany's Neuer Deutscher Film (New German Cinema), an arty reaction against Hollywood-style entertainment movies. **Television** fans will enjoy the video retrospective in which thousands of images from German television are simultaneously shown on a big screen. There's also a formidable back catalogue of TV programmes accessible in viewing booths and the museum also hosts **temporary exhibitions** on the history of both film and television.

Legoland Discovery Centre Berlin

Potsdamer Str. 4 • Mon–Sat 10am–7pm • Online tickets (children and adults) from €11; on the door €18; under-3s free • 𝕋 030 301 04 00, ⓦ legolanddiscoverycentre.de • ⓤ/Ⓢ Potsdamer Platz

The **Legoland Discovery Centre Berlin** obviously exists mainly to promote a product, but few kids leave disappointed. Its five million bricks are aimed largely at 3- to 10-year-olds and there's a 4D cinema, castle, dragon rides and a workshop in which to go brick-crazy – the few small freebies go down very well. A couple of things will entertain adults too – particularly MiniLand, a plastic mini-brick reproduction of Berlin's main landmark buildings. Earmark at least a couple of hours.

Panoramapunkt

Potsdamer Platz • Daily: April–Oct 10am–8pm; Nov– March 10am–6pm • €6.50 • 𝕋 030 25 93 70 80, ⓦ panoramapunkt.de • ⓤ/Ⓢ Potsdamer Platz

Soar above Potsdamer Platz in Europe's fastest, stomach-churning elevator to arrive at **Panoramapunkt**, the top floor of the complex's largest skyscraper. The views are among the city's best – which you'd expect given the immense height and ideal central location – and the exposed outdoor viewing deck provides an immediacy that you won't find at the Fernsehturm, the other main contender. There's also an exhibition on the history of the area and a café with an outdoor terrace.

Daimler Contemporary

Alte Potsdamer Str. 5 • Daily 11am–6pm • Free • 𝕋 030 25 94 14 20, ⓦ art.daimler.com • ⓤ/Ⓢ Potsdamer Platz

Occupying the elaborately renovated Haus Huth, the sole surviving prewar building on Potsdamer Platz, the **Daimler Contemporary** was set up as an exhibition space for the Daimler Art Collection in 1998. Particularly strong on twentieth-century German art, supplemented by international artists such as Andy Warhol and Jeff Koons, the impressive collection encompasses approximately 1800 pieces, showcased in regular rotating exhibitions. Much of the collection and most of the exhibitions are challenging and abstract in nature; check website for details of what's on.

Meistersaal

Köthener Str. 38 • Regular tours organized by Berlin Music Tours (see box, pp.24–25) • ⓦ meistersaal-berlin.de • ⓤ/Ⓢ Potsdamer Platz

A five-minute walk south of Potsdamer Platz is the **Meistersaal**, a former chamber music hall that became a West Berlin recording studio for record label Hansa. For many years an almost neighbourless building set among overgrown fields, rubble and skeletal ruins – and of course with a grand view of the Berlin Wall – it became known as "Hansa by the Wall". Its cheap prices – around a tenth of London's Abbey Road in the 1970s and 1980s – and top-notch acoustics inspired scores of musicians – most famously David Bowie (see box, p.115), U2, Iggy Pop, Nick Cave and Depeche Mode. The Meistersaal is still used for recordings today and also serves as an event location, though is accessible on organized tours.

Leipziger Platz

Created by Berlin's expansion in the early 1700s, the civilized and beautiful **Leipziger Platz** was once almost as busy as Potsdamer Platz, thanks to the presence of shops including

5

Alfred Messel's **Wertheim** department store. What little of the square that hadn't been destroyed by the war was levelled in 1961 for the death strip of the Berlin Wall, leaving behind just an octagonal footprint as a reminder. The Platz is dominated by a series of dreary seven-floor office blocks in monotonous light colours, though the addition of a new 270-store shopping mall – the imaginatively titled Mall of Berlin (see p.242) – in 2014, and new **Deutsches Spionagemuseum**, as well as the adjacent **Dalí exhibition**, provide some interest.

Deutsches Spionagemuseum

Leipziger Platz 9 • Daily 10am–8pm • €12, children €8; guided tours almost hourly (depending on availability) • ☎ 030 20 62 03 54, ⓦ deutsches-spionagemuseum.de • Ⓤ/Ⓢ Potsdamer Platz

The **Deutsches Spionagemuseum** (German Spy Museum), the city's newest major museum, traces the history of espionage in a large modern space situated just a few metres from where the Berlin Wall once ran (there's a display piece on the lawn outside). The thousand-plus exhibits on display track the development of global spy culture from Ancient Egypt right up to the present day, with a specially impressive section on Berlin during the Cold War. There's a fair amount of text (in German and English) but it's regularly punctuated by and supplemented with interactive installations – including screens that offer real-time insights into modern hacking and encryption techniques – and display cases with abundant fascinating World War II and GDR-era equipment; among the highlights you'll find weapons disguised as umbrellas, smoking pipes and walking sticks, an original Enigma machine, some impossibly tiny spy cameras and a whole section devoted to James Bond and other movie spies. There's even a room where you can try out some laser parkour.

Dalí – Die Austelling am Potsdamer Platz

Leipziger Platz 7 • Mon–Sat noon–8pm, Sun 10am–8pm • €12.50 • ☎ 0700 32 54 23 75 46, ⓦ daliberlin.de • Ⓤ/Ⓢ Potsdamer Platz

Though Salvador Dalí had no real links with Germany or Berlin (apart, perhaps, from dying the year the Wall fell, in 1989), **Dalí – Die Austellung am Potsdamer Platz** is among the world's best exhibitions of the Surrealist maestro's work. On view are more than four hundred eccentric pieces by the versatile Catalan, including paintings, sketches, books, films, sculptures, coins and even 3D installations.

Kulturforum

The **Kulturforum** offers a mixture of museums and cultural spaces that could easily fill a day of exploring. Many of the buildings were designed in the 1960s – most by modernist architect Hans Scharoun, a disciple of Bruno Taut (see p.139), with the exception of Mies van der Rohe's impressive Neue Nationalgalerie. Attractions are individually ticketed, though all the Kulturforum museums currently open are also covered by the three-day Museum Pass Berlin (see box, p.28).

Staatsbibliothek

Potsdamer Str. 33 • Mon–Fri 9am–9pm, Sat 10am–7pm • Free • ☎ 030 26 60, ⓦ staatsbibliothek-berlin.de • Ⓤ/Ⓢ Potsdamer Platz

As you walk west from Potsdamer Platz, the first building on your left is the **Staatsbibliothek** (State Library), which has more than three and a half million books, occasional exhibitions, a small concert hall, a reasonable café and a wide selection of British newspapers. The final building to be designed by Hans Scharoun, the *Staabi* is the most popular of his works among his fans; it was used as an important backdrop in Wim Wenders' poetic film elegy to the city, *Wings of Desire*.

Berliner Philharmonie

Herbert-von-Karajan-Str. 1 • Tours (in German and English) daily 1.30pm; €5 • ☎ 030 25 48 80, ⓦ berliner-philharmoniker.de • Ⓤ/Ⓢ Potsdamer Platz

At the northeast corner of the Kulturforum, the honey-coloured **Berliner Philharmonie** is home to the Berlin Philharmonic orchestra, considered by many to be the world's best. Conducting here is a huge privilege, and to be the resident conductor – a post occupied by Austrian supremo **Herbert von Karajan** (1908–89) from 1956 until his death – the ultimate accolade, since it's the members of the orchestra themselves that vote for this. Looking at the gaudy gold-clad 1960s building, designed by Hans Scharoun, and bearing in mind von Karajan's famously short temper with artists and rigid discipline that alienated many who worked under him – yet proved fabulously successful in the field of popularizing classical music – it's easy to see why Berliners nicknamed it "Karajan's circus". However, Scharoun's complicated floor plan around the orchestra offers top-notch acoustics and views, regardless of your seat.

Obviously the best way to see the venue is to attend a performance (see p.233), but **tours** are also run, and if you can't get a ticket you can watch live streams of performances on Ⓦdigitalconcerthall.com. The orchestra's current principal conductor is **Sir Simon Rattle**, former director of the City of Birmingham Symphony Orchestra, though his last season will be 2017/2018. After a gap, Russian-Austrian **Kirill Petrenko** is scheduled to take over during the 2019–2020 season.

Memorial and Information Point for the Victims of National Socialist Euthanasia Killings

Tiergartenstr. 4 • ☎ 030 263 94 30, Ⓦ t4-denkmal.de • Ⓤ/Ⓢ Potsdamer Platz

The most recently completed of Berlin's Holocaust memorials (see p.38), just north of the Berliner Philharmonie on the edge of the Tiergarten, opened in 2014 on the site of the administrative headquarters of the Nazis' "T4" operation, which initiated, coordinated and carried out the mass murder of patients from clinics and care homes in the Third Reich in 1940–41. Around 300,000 people died as a result of the operation and related killings, which was halted following growing criticism from the general population and several high profile members of the church. The **Memorial and Information Point for the Victims of National Socialist Euthanasia Killings** (Gedenk- und Informationsort für die Opfer der nationalsozialistischen "Euthanasie" Morde) consists of a 24-metre-long wall of light blue glass set into a grey concrete surface that gently slopes towards the centre, plus an outdoor exhibition that provides a history of the euthanasia killings, and their legacy up to the present day.

Musikinstrumenten-Museum

Tiergartenstr. 1 (visitor's entrance on Ben-Gurion-Str.) • Tues, Wed & Fri 9am–5pm, Thurs 9am–8pm, Sat & Sun 10am–5pm • €6 • ☎ 030 25 48 81 56, Ⓦ sim.spk-berlin.de • Ⓤ/Ⓢ Potsdamer Platz

The **Musikinstrumenten-Museum** embraces Germany's glorious musical history, with over three thousand instruments from the sixteenth to the twenty-first centuries, making it one of the country's largest collections. Many are on permanent display here, including a rare Stradivarius violin, flutes played by Frederick the Great to entertain his guests, a glass harmonica invented by Benjamin Franklin and – the flamboyant centrepiece – a massive Mighty Wurlitzer theatre organ once owned by the Siemens family, which is demonstrated every Saturday at noon. The museum also veers into modern and electronic music with electric guitars, mixing stations and other

CLOSED FOR RENOVATION: THE NEUE NATIONALGALERIE

By far the Kulturforum's finest building – architecturally speaking – is the **Neue Nationalgalerie** (New National Gallery). A black-rimmed glass box, with a ceiling that seems almost suspended above the ground, it was designed by Mies van der Rohe in 1965, and has a clarity of line and detail with all the intelligent simplicity of the Parthenon. The building closed in 2015 for a comprehensive renovation and is scheduled to reopen in 2019/2020, at which point its many twentieth-century artistic highlights – including works by the Brücke group and international Cubist heavyweights like Braque and Picasso – will be once again on display. For updates, check Ⓦsmb.museum.

5

experimental instruments, including the Mixtur-Trautonium on which composer Oskar Sala created sound effects for Hitchcock's film *The Birds*.

Kunstgewerbemuseum

Matthäikirchplatz • Tues–Sun 10am–6pm • €8 • ☎ 030 26 64 24 242, ⓦ smb.museum • Ⓤ/Ⓢ Potsdamer Platz

Across the road from the Philharmonie is the **Kunstgewerbemuseum** (Museum of Applied Arts) with its encyclopedic, but seldom dull, collection of European arts and crafts. Reopened in 2014 following a fairly major structural overhaul, the museum provides a systematic overview of the key achievements of European design. Renaissance, Baroque and Rococo highlights include municipal silver from the former Hanseatic town of Lüneburg and the treasures from the Stiftskirche in Enger (in North Rhine-Westphalia), while furniture figures prominently among the Jugendstil and Art Deco objects. Newer displays include a Fashion Gallery, which houses around 130 costumes representing 150 years of fashion history (including the creations of Paul Poiret and Christian Dior), a solid assembly of Bauhaus furniture and a display on the evolution of product design. Yet more interior design pieces from the sixteenth to eighteenth centuries can be found in the museum's picturesque second venue, the Schloss Köpenick (see p.156).

Gemäldegalerie

Matthäikirchplatz 4/6 • Tues, Wed & Fri 10am–6pm, Thurs 10am–8pm, Sat & Sun 11am–6pm • €10 • ☎ 030 26 62 951, ⓦ smb.museum • Ⓤ/Ⓢ Potsdamer Platz

The jewel of the Kulturforum, the **Gemäldegalerie** (Picture Gallery) holds a stupendous collection of early European paintings. Almost nine hundred are on display, arranged in chronological order, and subdivided by region.

German work from the Middle Ages and Renaissance includes the large *Wurzach Altar* of 1437, made in the workshop of the great Ulm sculptor Hans Multscher; its figures' exaggerated gestures and facial distortions make it an ancient precursor of Expressionism. Otherwise some of the best works here are by Albrecht Altdorfer, one of the first fully realized German landscape painters, and Holbein the Younger, represented by several superbly observed portraits. Notable among the many examples of Cranach are his tongue-in-cheek *The Fountain of Youth*, and his free reinterpretation of Bosch's famous triptych *The Garden of Earthly Delights*.

Religious subjects receive a lighter treatment in the **Netherlandish section**, featuring fifteenth- and sixteenth-century work. Jan van Eyck's beautifully lit *Madonna in the Church* is crammed with architectural detail and has the Virgin lifted in the perspective for gentle emphasis. Sixteenth-century works include those of Bruegel the Elder, whose *Netherlandish Proverbs* is an amusing, if hard-to-grasp, illustration of more than a hundred proverbs including "armed to the teeth", "banging a head against a brick wall" and "casting pearls before swine".

The later **Dutch and Flemish collections**, with their large Van Dyck portraits, light-bathed Vermeer paintings and fleshy Rubens canvases, are another high point. The highlights are several paintings by **Rembrandt**: though *The Man in the Golden Helmet* has been proved to be the work of his studio rather than the artist himself, this does little to detract from the portrait's elegance and power.

Finally, the **Italian section**, spanning the years from the Renaissance to the eighteenth century, is particularly strong on works from the Florentine Renaissance, including, most importantly, two paintings by Botticelli: *Madonna with Saints* and *Mary with the Child and Singing Angels*.

Kupferstichkabinett

Matthäikirchplatz • Tues–Fri 10am–6pm, Sat & Sun 11am–6pm • €6 • ☎ 030 26 64 242, ⓦ smb.museum • Ⓤ/Ⓢ Potsdamer Platz

Sharing its main entrance with the Gemäldegalerie, the **Kupferstichkabinett** (literally, Engraving Cabinet) holds a vast collection of mostly European prints, drawings and

5

engravings from medieval and Renaissance times up to the present, with artists such as Sandro Botticelli, Albrecht Dürer, Rembrandt, Adolph von Menzel, Pablo Picasso and Andy Warhol represented. Due to the size and sensitivity of the collection (being largely on paper), there's no permanent display – visitors must check for special exhibitions, or request to see specific artworks via the study room.

Kunstbibliothek

Matthäikirchplatz 6 • Tues, Wed & Fri 10am–6pm, Thurs 10am–8pm, Sat & Sun 11am–6pm • €6 • ☎ 030 26 64 24 242, ⓦ smb.museum • ⓤ/Ⓢ Potsdamer Platz

With 350,000 volumes and more than 1300 international periodicals, the **Kunstbibliothek** (Art Library), next to the Gemäldegalerie, is a gigantic resource for

---

ANTI-NAZI RESISTANCE AND THE JULY BOMB PLOT

Anti-Nazi resistance in Germany was less overt than in occupied Europe, but existed throughout the war, particularly in Berlin, where a group of **KPD-run communist cells** operated a clandestine information network and organized acts of resistance and sabotage. But the odds against them were overwhelming, and most groups perished. More successful for a while was the **Rote Kapelle** (Red Orchestra), headed by Harro Schulze-Boysen, an aristocrat who worked in the Air Ministry, with agents in most of the military offices who supplied information to the Soviet Union. The **Kreisau Circle**, a resistance group led by Count Helmut von Moltke, and the groups around Carl Goerdeler (former mayor of Leipzig) and General Beck (ex-chief of staff) talked about overthrowing the Nazis and opening negotiations with the western Allies. However, the most effective resistance came from within the military. There had been attempts on Hitler's life since 1942, but it wasn't until late 1943 and early 1944 that enough high-ranking officers had become convinced defeat was inevitable, and a wide network of conspirators established.

A PLOT IS HATCHED

The **July Bomb Plot** that took place in the summer of 1944 at Hitler's HQ in occupied Poland, the "Wolf's Lair" in Rastenburg, was the assassination attempt that came closest to success. The plot was led by the one-armed **Count Claus Schenk von Stauffenberg**, an aristocratic officer and member of the General Staff, with the support of several high-ranking members of the German army. Sickened by atrocities on the eastern front, and rapidly realizing that the Wehrmacht was fighting a war that could not be won, Stauffenberg and his fellow conspirators decided to kill the Führer, seize control of army headquarters on Bendlerstrasse and sue for peace with the Allies. Germany was on the precipice of total destruction; only such a desperate act, reasoned the plotters, could save the Fatherland.

On July 20, Stauffenberg was summoned to the Wolf's Lair to brief Hitler on troop movements on the eastern front. In his briefcase was a small bomb, packed with high explosive: once triggered, it would explode in under ten minutes. As Stauffenberg approached the specially built conference hut, he triggered the device. He then positioned the briefcase under the table, leaning it against one of the table's stout legs less than 2m away from the Führer. Five minutes before the bomb exploded, the Count quietly slipped unnoticed from the room. One of the officers, Colonel Brandt, then moved closer to the table to get a better look at the campaign maps and, finding the briefcase in the way of his feet under the table, picked it up and moved it to the other side of the table leg. This put the very solid support of the table leg between the briefcase and Hitler.

A PLAN IS FOILED

At 12.42pm the bomb went off. Stauffenberg, watching the hut from a few hundred metres away, was shocked by the force of the explosion; he didn't doubt that the Führer, along with everyone else in the room, was dead, and hurried off to a waiting plane to make his way to Berlin to join the other conspirators. Meanwhile, back in the wreckage of the conference hut, Hitler and the survivors staggered out into the daylight. Four people were killed, including Colonel Brandt, who had unwittingly saved the Führer's life. Hitler himself, despite being badly shaken, suffered no more than a perforated eardrum and minor injuries. After being attended to, he prepared himself for a meeting with Mussolini later that afternoon.

those with an interest in art, photography and graphic design. The library also has its own galleries for temporary exhibitions, which are almost always worth at least a quick look.

5

Matthäuskirche

Matthäikirchplatz 1 • Tues–Sun noon–6pm • Free • ☎ 030 262 1202, ⓦ stiftung-stmatthaeus.de • ⓤ/ⓢ Potsdamer Platz

The clear odd man out in the Kulturforum is the brick neo-Romanesque **Matthäuskirche** (Matthias Church), built between 1844 and 1846 and the only survivor of the war in the area. It now houses temporary exhibitions and you can climb the tower for aerial views of the other, far more modern and angular, Kulturforum buildings.

It quickly became apparent what had happened, and the hunt for Stauffenberg was on. Hitler issued orders to the SS in Berlin to summarily execute anyone who was slightly suspect, and dispatched Himmler to the city to quell the rebellion. Back in the military Supreme Command headquarters in Bendlerstrasse, the conspiracy was in chaos. Word reached Stauffenberg and the two main army conspirators, Generals Beck and Witzleben, that the Führer was still alive. They had already lost essential hours by failing to issue the carefully planned order to mobilize their sympathizers in Berlin and elsewhere, and had even failed to carry out the obvious precaution of severing all communications out of the city. Goebbels succeeded in telephoning Hitler, who spoke directly to the arrest team, ordering them to obey his propaganda minister. Then Goebbels set to work contacting SS and Gestapo units, and reminding army garrisons of their oath of loyalty to the Führer. After a few hours of tragicomic scenes as the conspirators tried to persuade high-ranking officials to join them, the Bendlerstrasse HQ was surrounded by Wehrmacht troops, and it was announced that the Führer would broadcast to the nation later that evening. The attempted coup was over. At 9pm, Hitler broadcast on national radio, saying he would "settle accounts the way we National Socialists are accustomed to settle them".

HITLER'S FURY

The conspirators were gathered together, given paper to write farewell messages to their wives, taken to the courtyard of the HQ (a memorial stands on the spot) and, under the orders of one General Fromm, shot by firing squad. Stauffenberg's last words were "Long live our sacred Germany!" Fromm had known about the plot almost from the beginning, but had refused to join it. By executing the leaders he hoped to save his own skin – and, it must be added, save them from the torturers of the SS.

Hitler's revenge on the conspirators was severe even by the ruthless standards of the Third Reich. All the colleagues, friends and immediate relatives of Stauffenberg and the other conspirators were rounded up, tortured and taken before the "People's Court" – the building where the court convened, the Kammergericht, still stands (see p.115) – where they were humiliated and given more or less automatic death sentences, most of which were brutally carried out at **Plötzensee Prison** (see p.165). Many of those executed knew nothing of the plot and were found guilty merely by association. As the blood lust grew, the Nazi party used the plot as a pretext for settling old scores, and eradicated anyone who had the slightest hint of anything less than total dedication to the Führer. General Fromm himself was among those tried, found guilty of cowardice and shot by firing squad. Those whose names were blurted out under torture were quickly arrested, the most notable being Field Marshal Rommel, who, because of his popularity, was given the choice of a trial in the so-called People's Court or suicide and a state funeral. He chose suicide, but other high-ranking conspirators were forced before the court for a public show trial. All were sentenced to death by the Nazi judge Ronald Freisler and hanged on meat-hooks at Plötzensee Prison, their death agonies being filmed for Hitler's private delectation.

The July Bomb Plot resulted in the deaths of around 150 people, including some of Germany's most brilliant military thinkers and almost all of those who would have been best qualified to run the postwar German government. (Freisler himself was killed by an American bomb.) Within six months the country lay in ruins as the Allies advanced; had events at Rastenburg been only a little different, the entire course of the war – and European history – would have been altered incalculably.

5

The diplomatic district

Immediately west of the Kulturforum is an area once filled by ostentatious residences: fine villas with long, narrow gardens overlooking the Tiergarten, before the Nazis forcibly acquired them to generate a **diplomatic district**, with many of the best plots going to close allies like Japan, Italy and Spain. The war saw most of the district destroyed, and while the West German government was in Bonn, few countries made much of their plots. But after the government moved back in Berlin many re-established their presence here, in preference to their East Berlin embassies, producing another of Berlin's stimulating showcases of modern architecture. It's best admired by walking along Tiergartenstrasse – which conveniently lines the way to the **Bauhaus-Archiv**.

Gedenkstätte Deutscher Widerstand

Stauffenbergstr. 13–14 • Mon–Wed & Fri 9am–6pm, Thurs 9am–8pm, Sat & Sun 10am–6pm • Free • ⓦ gdw-berlin.de •
⓪/Ⓢ Potsdamer or #200 to Tiergartenstrasse

Along the eastern edge of the diplomatic district is Stauffenbergstrasse, which takes its name from Count Claus Schenk von Stauffenberg, one of the instigators of the July Bomb Plot aginst Hitler (see box, pp.98–99). Here stands the **Bendlerblock**, once the home to the German Army headquarters – where Stauffenberg was chief of staff – and now the German Defence Ministry.

The floors where Stauffenberg worked are occupied by the absorbing exhibition **Gedenkstätte Deutscher Widerstand** (Memorial to German Resistance), a huge collection of photos and documents covering the many and wide-ranging groups who actively opposed the Third Reich – an eclectic mix that included communists, Jews, Quakers and aristocrats. Much of the exhibition is in German, though the free English audio tour (ID required as deposit) gives a good taste by covering the highlights in around forty minutes. The memorial courtyard, meanwhile, is dedicated to the conspiring German army officers who were killed after the assassination attempt.

Shell-Haus

Reichpietschufer 60 • Bus #200 to Tiergartenstrasse

At the southern end of Stauffenbergstrasse, beside the Landwehrkanal, the **Shell-Haus** – also called the BEWAG (Berlin Electric Company) building – is one of Berlin's few great modernist buildings to largely survive World War II intact. Designed by Emil Fahrenkamp in 1931, the office building's tiered levels and undulating facade were an attempt to reproduce elements of the adjacent canal and became a leading piece of modernist architecture.

The embassies

The **diplomatic district** begins at the northern end of Stauffenbergstrasse, site of the dignified **Egyptian Embassy**, with its polished stonework and detailed engravings, and the flamboyant **Austrian Embassy**, the work of Viennese architect Hans Hollein. West along Tiergartenstrasse, the bulky building hewn from rough-cut red sandstone is the **Indian Embassy**, a clever design that attempts to symbolize India's complexities in architectural terms. The entrance is through a gap in a cylinder that starts a contrast of void and solid that continues throughout the building, though the public can only get a closer look during rare exhibitions (check ⓦindianembassy.de for details).

Further west down Tiergartenstrasse are the two unmistakable Nazi-era edifices of Germany's closest prewar allies. The **Japanese** completed their embassy in 1942 as many other buildings in Berlin started to collapse in bombing raids. Though it has been restored and remodelled since reunification, the architects carefully respected the original design, preserving stone cladding and only removing some ornamentation – replacing it with sleek lines that tend to add to the monumentalism. The **Italian Embassy** has a similar look, as does the beautifully restored **Spanish Embassy**, a fifteen-minute walk west on the corner of Lichtensteinallee and Thomas-Dehler-Strasse. Providing a sharp contrast are the bold bright lines of the area's most exciting modernist buildings in between the two on Klingelhöferstrasse.

Nordic Embassies

Rauchstr. 1 • **Felleshus** Mon–Fri 10am–7pm, Sat & Sun 11am–4pm **Canteen** Mon–Fri 10–11.30am & 1–4pm • ☎ 030 50 500, ⓦ nordicembassies.org • ⓤ Wittenbergplatz, or bus #100 or #200

Just off Klingelhöferstrasse, in the stunning **Nordic Embassies** complex, offices for Denmark, Sweden, Finland, Iceland and Norway each occupy a separate building but share an outer skin of pre-oxidized copper panels that playfully reflect changes in light or weather – it looks particularly stunning when floodlit at night. Though each country employed different architects, all feature stone and timber designs with a light, simple elegance. The compound includes the **Felleshus** ("House for Everyone"), where exhibitions and events are put on, and a **canteen** where visitors can enjoy herring, meatballs and other Nordic specialities.

Mexican Embassy

Klingelhöferstr. 3 • **Exhibitions** Mon–Fri 9am–5pm • ☎ 030 269 3230, ⓦ embamex2.sre.gob.mx/alemania • ⓜ Wittenbergplatz or bus #100 or #200

The avant-garde **Mexican Embassy**, next door to the Nordic Embassies, is another tribute to the simplicity and beauty of modernism, and like its neighbour is floodlit after dark to tremendous effect. Its main features are slanting supports that create a vertical blind effect and a massive concrete-and-marble entranceway. The public exhibition area in the atrium is an homage to a Maya observatory, the first cylindrical construction in the Americas.

Bauhaus-Archiv

Klingelhöferstr. 14 • Daily except Tues 10am–5pm • Mon, Sat & Sun €8, Wed–Fri €7 (includes audio tour) • ☎ 030 25 40 020, ⓦ bauhaus.de • ⓤ Nollendorfplatz or bus #100 to Lützowplatz

Germany's Bauhaus design school may have only lasted from 1919 to 1933, when it was closed down by the Nazis but it went on to became one of the twentieth century's

---

BAUHAUS

Bauhaus, whose literal meaning is "building-house", has become a generic term for the aesthetically functional design style that grew out of the art and design philosophy developed at the Dessau school, in Saxony-Anhalt. The origins of the movement lie in the Novembergruppe, a grouping of artists founded in 1918 by the Expressionist painter Max Pechstein with the aim of utilizing art for revolutionary purposes. Members included Bertolt Brecht and Kurt Weill, Emil Nolde, Eric Mendelssohn and the architect **Walter Gropius**. In 1919 Gropius was invited by the new republican government to oversee the amalgamation of the School of Arts and Crafts and the Academy of Fine Arts in Weimar into the **Staatliche Bauhaus Weimar**. It was hoped that this new institution would break down the barriers between art and craft, creating a new form of applied art. It attracted more than two hundred students who studied typography, furniture design, ceramics and wood-, glass- and metalworking under exponents like Paul Klee, Wassily Kandinsky and László Moholy-Nagy.

By the end of the 1920s, the staff and students of the Bauhaus school had become increasingly embroiled in the political battles of the time, and throughout the early 1930s Nazi members of Dessau town council called for an end to its subsidies. Their efforts finally succeeded in the summer of 1932, forcing the school to close down and relocate to the more liberal atmosphere of Berlin, where they set up in a disused telephone factory in Birkbuschstrasse in the Steglitz district. However, after the Nazis came to power, police harassment reached such a pitch that on July 20, 1933, director **Ludwig Mies van der Rohe** took the decision to shut up shop for good. He and many of his staff and students subsequently went into exile in the United States.

5

most influential movements (see box, p.101). Founded by Walter Gropius, the movement explored the links between fine art and craftsmanship and – a bit later – art and mass production. The **Bauhaus-Archiv**, housed in a distinctive building designed by Gropius himself (though only completed in 1979), is the best place to explore the breadth and depth of Bauhaus's expansive activities. Here are Marcel Breuer's seminal chair (still, with minor variations, in production today), armchairs and desks from Mies van der Rohe, paintings from Itten, Schlemmer, Feininger, Albers and Klee…even dapper wallpaper and beautiful chess sets. The archive next door holds the largest Bauhaus resource in the world, while the museum shop stocks an impressive range of high-quality reproductions, and there's an adjoining café.

Tiergarten

Ⓢ Tiergarten – though the park is best accessed by bus #100, which cuts through it on its way between Bahnhof Zoo and Alexanderplatz

The **Tiergarten** is a restful expanse of woodland and lakes that was originally designed as a hunting ground under Elector Friedrich III. Largely destroyed during the 1945 Battle of Berlin, after the war the park was used as farmland, chiefly to grow potatoes for starving citizens; since then the replanting has been so successful that these days it's hard to tell it's not original.

The best way to appreciate the park is on foot or by bike, though the quickest way through is on the #100 bus. At the very least, try wandering along the **Landwehrkanal**, an inland waterway off the River Spree that separates the park from the zoo. It's an easy hour's walk between **Corneliusbrücke** (Cornelius Bridge) – just up Corneliusstrasse from the Bauhaus-Archiv (see p.101) – and Bahnhof Zoo, via the popular *Schleusenkrug* beer garden (see p.202). At Corneliusbrücke a small, odd sculpture commemorates the radical leader **Rosa Luxemburg**. In 1918, along with fellow revolutionary Karl Liebknecht, she reacted against the newly formed Weimar Republic and especially the terms of the Treaty of Versailles, declaring a new Socialist Republic in Berlin along the lines of Soviet Russia (she had played an important part in the abortive 1905 revolution). The pair were kidnapped by members of the elite First Cavalry Guards: Liebknecht was gunned down while "attempting to escape", and Luxemburg was knocked unconscious and shot, her body dumped in the Landwehrkanal.

Just north of the Landwehrkanal, and deeper inside the park, a pretty little group of ponds makes up the grand-sounding **Neuer See** (New Lake). There's a popular (summer-only) beer garden and (year-round) restaurant here, the *Café am Neuen See* (see p.202), and it's possible to rent **boats** by the hour.

Strasse des 17 Juni

The broad, straight **Strasse des 17 Juni** cuts through the Tiergarten, passing the Siegessäule (see opposite), to form the continuation of Unter den Linden beyond the Brandenburg Gate (see p.35). Originally named Charlottenburger Chaussee, it was also once known as the East–West Axis and was a favourite strip for Nazi processions. Indeed, Hitler had the stretch from the Brandenburg Gate to Theodor-Heuss-Platz – formerly Adolf-Hitler-Platz, 7km west – widened in order to accommodate these mass displays of military might and Nazi power; on his birthday in 1938, forty thousand men and six hundred tanks took four hours to parade past the Führer. Later, in the final days of the war, Charlottenburger Chaussee became a makeshift runway for aeroplanes ferrying Nazi notables to and from the besieged capital. Its current name commemorates the day in 1953 when workers in the East rose in revolt against the occupying Soviet powers (see box, p.121), though it later became better known as the main venue for the hedonistic Love Parade. Nowadays, though it's an ordinarily busy thoroughfare by day, by night prostitutes line its western end and the Siegessäule becomes a prime gay cruising spot. Come any big sporting event, however, like a football World Cup – which prompts the construction of a *Fanmeile* ("fan-mile") – or an annual festivity such as the Berlin Pride (see box, p.254), this stretch of road really comes alive.

Siegessäule

Grosser Stern 1 • April–Oct Mon–Fri 9.30am–6.30pm, Sat & Sun 9.30am–7pm; Nov–March daily 10am–5.30pm • €3 • ⑪ Hansaplatz or bus #100

In the midst of the park and approached by four great boulevards stands the **Siegessäule**, a column celebrating Prussia's military victories (chiefly that over France in 1871). It was shifted from in front of the Reichstag to this spot on Hitler's orders in 1938, part of a grand design for Berlin as capital of the Third Reich; with the same forethought Hitler had the monument raised another level to commemorate the victories to come in what became World War II. Though the boulevard approaches exaggerate its size, it's still an eye-catching monument: 67m high and topped with a gilded winged *Goddess of Victory* that symbolically faces France. The summit offers a good view of the surrounding area, but climbing the 285 steps to the top is no mean feat. Have a look, too, at the mosaics at the column's base, which show the unification of the German peoples and incidents from the Franco-Prussian War. The four bronze reliefs beside them on the four sides depict the main wars and the victorious marching of the troops into Berlin; these were removed after 1945 and taken to Paris, only to be returned when it was felt that the lust for war spoils had subsided.

Dotted around the Siegessäule are **statues** of other German notables, the most imposing being that of Bismarck, the "Iron Chancellor", under whom the country was united in the late nineteenth century. He's surrounded by figures symbolizing his achievements.

Schloss Bellevue

Spreeweg 1 • ⑪ Hansaplatz or bus #100

An eighteenth-century building that was once a guesthouse for the Third Reich, **Schloss Bellevue** (Bellevue Palace) is today the Berlin official residence of the Federal President. The house is closed to the public but you might also catch a glimpse of the **Bundespräsidialamt** – a polished granite oval of presidential administrative offices that plays with the reflections of surrounding trees.

Haus der Kulturen der Welt

John-Foster-Dulles-Allee 10 • Exhibitions daily except Tues 11am–7pm; free entry Mon • ☎ 030 39 78 70, ⓦ hkw.de • ⑪ Bundestag

The eye-catching oyster-shaped building squatting amid the greenery of John-Foster-Dulles-Allee is the **Haus der Kulturen der Welt** (House of Cultures of the World), an exhibition centre with a focus on international contemporary art and culture, and auditorium for performances of music and theatre. It was originally built in 1957 as the Kongresshalle, whose ambition couldn't be matched by the technology of the era: its roof collapsed in 1980, killing one person. It was rebuilt in 1987 with modifications as Haus der Kulturen der Welt, then still at the border between West and East, and modernized again in 2016.

Sowjetisches Ehrenmal

North side of Str. des 17 Juni • ⑪ / Ⓢ Brandenburger Tor

Built symbolically close to the Brandenburg Gate and the Reichstag, the **Sowjetisches Ehrenmal** (Soviet War Memorial) commemorates the Red Army troops who died in the Battle of Berlin. Crafted from the marble of Hitler's destroyed Berlin headquarters, the Reich Chancellery, it's flanked by two tanks that were supposedly the first to reach the city.

Spreebogen

The sharpest bend in central Berlin's River Spree, known as the **Spreebogen**, runs through one of Berlin's newest and quietest city quarters just northwest of the Reichstag

5

(see p.37). Here the German government has built a **Regierungsviertel**, or government quarter; it's also the location of Berlin's new space-age **Hauptbahnhof** train station. But a lot is still missing on a human scale, with visitors left to potter across huge empty plazas in front of giant buildings. The only exception to this is alongside the Spree where a new hangout of sorts is emerging as deck chairs colonize its banks and bars and cafés do a brisk trade, making it a pleasant place to while away an hour or two in the summer as boats cruise by. A good way to see much of this area is on a boat cruise; these leave regularly from various points including the Spreeinsel (see box, pp.24–25).

Before the war this part of town was known as the **Alsenviertel**, an area of luxurious apartments that overlooked Königsplatz (now Platz der Republik) and a much shorter Siegessäule, which stood midway between the Reichstag and the Kroll Opera House, until it was moved to its present position (see p.103) to make way for the planned *Volkshalle* ("People's Hall"). This giant structure, loosely based on Rome's Pantheon, was to be the centrepiece of Hitler and Speer's World Capital Germania, with an unfeasibly large cupola that would have been impossible to build with the technology of the time. In reality, the war gutted and largely levelled the area, its proximity to the East Berlin border deterring any redevelopment. West Berliners would come here to barbecue or learn to drive in empty lots, while boats from the East – mainly Polish freighters delivering coal to West Berlin's power stations – sailed through the only river checkpoint; all were meticulously scanned underwater for possible escapees.

Regierungsviertel

New and strikingly well-designed modern buildings form Berlin's **Regierungsviertel**, a district built largely in the 1990s to give the Federal Government a home. Here structures straddle the Spree, symbolically linking East and West. They're also connected to one another, underlining the correlation of government, and are designed to be accessible and transparent, as a metaphor for the need for openness of government. These design concepts are best appreciated, in the first instance, by getting an overview from the top of the Reichstag (see p.37).

Jakob-Kaiser-Haus

Dorotheenstr. 100/101 • ⓤ Bundestag or ⓤ Brandenburger Tor

The Regierungsviertel's biggest but least attention-grabbing building is administrative **Jakob-Kaiser-Haus**, immediately east of the Reichstag, whose 1750 offices make it one of Europe's largest office blocks. However, despite its size, it avoids becoming too monstrous or monotonous by following Berlin's traditional courtyard principle – almost creating a neighbourhood – and by integrating well into its surroundings.

Paul-Löbe-Haus and Maria-Elisabeth-Lüders-Haus

Platz der Republik 1 • ⓤ Bundestag

The offices and conference rooms of the **Paul-Löbe-Haus** and **Maria-Elisabeth-Lüders-Haus** lie just north of the Reichstag and west and east of the Spree respectively. Symbolically joined to one another via a footbridge across the river and over the former East–West border, both were designed by Stefan Braunfels and completed in 2001. Of note are the large windows that form part of the buildings' energy-efficient heating system by collecting heat – along with the roof – while interior ceilings double as cooling mechanisms.

Bundeskanzleramt

Willy-Brandt-Str. • ⓤ Bundestag

With its comb-like layout, the Paul-Löbe-Haus plays on design themes in the imposing **Bundeskanzleramt** (Federal Chancellery), opposite. A pet project of Helmut Kohl, it was cleverly designed by Axel Schultes and Charlotte Frank to contain subtle references to Le Corbusier and Luis Kahn in the studied detailing and structure. The centrepiece is a nine-storey white cube – earning the building

5

the nickname "the washing machine" – which contains the chancellor's offices. Originally the building was to be connected with Paul-Löbe-Haus, to reinforce the symbolic relationship between chancellor, administration and parliament, but the project ran short of money; today the only connections are those running underground between the Reichstag and Paul-Löbe-Haus. The Bundeskanzleramt is best appreciated from the northern banks of the Spree.

Swiss Embassy

Otto-von-Bismarck-Allee 4a • Mon–Fri 9am–noon • ☎ 030 390 40 00 • ⓤ Bundestag

The **Swiss Embassy**, just northeast of the Bundeskanzleramt, was one of the few Neoclassical buildings to survive the war intact. Its 2001 extension, spurred on by the German government's move back to Berlin, caused some outrage, though experts judge the two buildings to be a clever play of opposites – not even the floor levels are aligned – and praise the careful exterior concreting, done in one pour so that no shuttering or expansion joints are visible.

Hauptbahnhof

ⓤ/Ⓢ Hauptbahnhof

A superlative piece of architecture in both look and scale, the landmark glass-and-steel five-level **Hauptbahnhof** (Central Station) opened in time for the 2006 football World Cup. The Hamburg-based architects Meinhard von Gerkan and Volkin Marg produced a striking but functional station – Europe's largest ever – that handles around 350,000 travellers and 1800 trains per day. Yet it remains an oddity thanks to the sterile surroundings, which – despite the construction of hotels – are devoid of graffiti, grit and other seedy signatures common to Europe's major train stations.

Like London, Berlin historically had a ring of terminus stations, but as early as the 1930s plans were being drawn up to transform that impractical ring into a cross. After reunification, the opportunity was seized, and this central station at the crossing point of the two main west–east and north–south lines was planned. This was the one-time location of the old Lehrter Bahnhof, which operated from 1871 to 1952 before it was left to rot alongside Berlin's Cold War dividing line. Its replacement is now hailed as a symbolic central point of Europe, with trains running through between Rome and Copenhagen, Moscow and Paris.

Inside, the building works well. Always quick with a nickname, Berliners soon christened it the "glass cathedral", and the basic principles of Gothic-style construction really are in evidence: supports and weights; the space's upward thrust; braces resembling Gothic clustered piers; and a series of "vaults". Though to a casual observer it may seem more like an airy shopping mall crisscrossed by trains, the main hall, with its many-layered staircase systems, elevator tubes, skylights and aperture windows, is also said to be a formal analogy to the feverish spatial fantasies of the Italian Baroque.

Hamburger Bahnhof/Museum für Gegenwart

Invalidenstr. 50–51 • Tues, Wed & Fri 10am–6pm, Thurs 10am–8pm, Sat & Sun 11am–6pm • €14 • ☎ 030 39 78 341, ⓦ hamburgerbahnhof.de • ⓤ/Ⓢ Hauptbahnhof

Occupying a capacious and architecturally interesting space – formerly the **Hamburger Bahnhof**, one of the city's first terminal stations – the **Museum für Gegenwart** (Museum for Contemporary Art) is one of the city's major art venues. Its permanent collection focuses on the principal movements of the late twentieth century up to the present day, with an emphasis on video and film and the expansive Joseph Beuys archive, to which the entire west wing is dedicated. The museum's Marx Collection has works by Anselm Kiefer and Andy Warhol, while Friedrich Christian Flic's collection – donated in 2004 – added 166 works by artists like John Cage, Bruce Nauman and Wolfgang Tillmans.

5

Alongside rotating showcases from these permanent collections, the museum hosts temporary exhibitions by international artists usually at the forefront of their respective fields. There's a good bookstore and a café-restaurant on the premises, and look out too for the calendar of concerts, lectures and artist appearances.

Invalidenfriedhof and around

Scharnhorststr. 9 • ⓦ foerderverein-invalidenfriedhof.de • ⓤ Schwarzkopfstrasse or bus #120

On the opposite bank of the Humboldthafen canal from the Hamburger Bahnhof, there's the opportunity for a pleasant offbeat walk along a towpath to the **Invalidenfriedhof** (Invalids' Cemetery), a one-time important Prussian military cemetery. The earliest graves date from the mid-eighteenth century, but the most impressive belong to prominent Prussian figures, like Count Tauentzien and generals Winterfeldt and Scharnhorst. These all remained largely undisturbed until the building of the Berlin Wall, when parish boundaries dictated that the death strip would surround the graves. Some of the graveyard was levelled and given over to access tracks, which remain, but a good number of memorials – all those here today – were preserved and provided a surreal and macabre touch to the death strip.

This section of the Berlin Wall was also famed for another depressing reason; it was here that Günter Litfin, the first victim of the Wall, was shot and killed on August 24, 1961, as he attempted to swim across the canal. An information board commemorates the event, and around the corner, at the **Gedenkstätte Günter Litfin**, Kielerstr. 2 (see map pp.308–309) you can find a memorial inside an original GDR watchtower, which was set up – and is still maintained – by his brother.

Medizinhistorisches Museum

Charitéplatz 1 • Tues, Thurs, Fri & Sun 10am–5pm, Wed & Sat 10am–7pm • €7; no children under 12, and under-16s need to be accompanied by an adult • ☎ 030 450 536 156, ⓦ bmm-charite.de • ⓤ/Ⓢ Hauptbahnhof

Medical textbook horrors come alive at the old-fashioned **Medizinhistorisches Museum** (Medical History Museum), where two floors of a working hospital are lined with exhibits that trace three hundred years of medical history. These include progressive innovations as well as the sometimes ghoulish mistakes and assorted macabre ephemera, such as a smoker's tarred lungs, an alcoholic's fatty liver and a collection of deformed foetuses and babies. Note that there are no English-language texts.

MUSEUM FÜR FOTOGRAFIE

City West and Schöneberg

Lying immediately southwest of the Tiergarten, City West was once West Berlin's downtown but has now reverted to its prewar role as the city's prime high-end shopping area. It's focused on the famed Kurfürstendamm (or Ku'damm) and the adjoining Tauentzienstrasse, where the opening of swanky new hotels and designer malls indicate the area's ongoing refurbishment, though enough showcase Cold War-era building projects remain to give the place a distinctive feel. City West largely covers the most central portion of the immense, moneyed, white and rather sedate Charlottenburg-Wilmersdorf district, but on its eastern fringes it also spreads into Schöneberg, to the southeast, where Nollendorfplatz forms the gateway to Berlin's long-standing and world-famous gay village.

The most popular City West attraction is without doubt the well-run **Zoologischer Garten Berlin**, along with the next door **Aquarium Berlin**, but the most eye-catching is the huge **Kaiser-Wilhelm-Gedächtniskirche**, one of the neighbourhood's very few remaining prewar buildings, whose iconic semi-ruined church tower now serves as a memorial. An easy walk from both are a smattering of good **museums and galleries** worth going out of your way for: particularly those devoted to fashion photographer Helmut Newton and anti-war artist Käthe Kollwitz, plus the C/O Berlin photo gallery and a lively multimedia museum on Berlin's history. The **Schöneberg** neighbourhood,

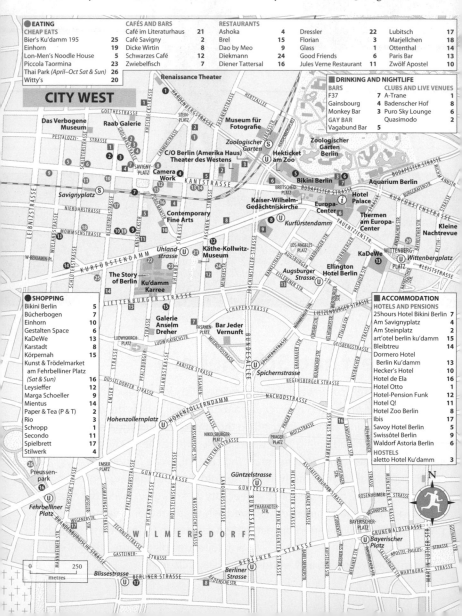

EATING

CHEAP EATS

Bier's Ku'damm 195	25
Einhorn	19
Lon-Men's Noodle House	5
Piccola Taormina	23
Thai Park (April–Oct Sat & Sun)	26
Witty's	20

CAFÉS AND BARS

Café im Literaturhaus	21
Café Savigny	2
Dicke Wirtin	8
Schwarzes Café	12
Zwiebelfisch	7

RESTAURANTS

Ashoka	4	Dressler	22	Lubitsch	17
Brel	15	Florian	3	Marjellchen	18
Dao by Meo	9	Glass	1	Ottenthal	14
Diekmann	24	Good Friends	6	Paris Bar	13
Diener Tattersal	16	Jules Verne Restaurant	11	Zwölf Apostel	10

CITY WEST

DRINKING AND NIGHTLIFE

BARS

F37	7
Gainsbourg	4
Monkey Bar	3

GAY BAR

Vagabund Bar	5

CLUBS AND LIVE VENUES

A-Trane	1
Badenscher Hof	8
Puro Sky Lounge	6
Quasimodo	2

SHOPPING

Bikini Berlin	5
Bücherbogen	7
Einhorn	10
Gestalten Space	6
KaDeWe	13
Karstadt	8
Körpernah	15
Kunst & Trödelmarket am Fehrbelliner Platz (Sat & Sun)	16
Leysieffer	12
Marga Schoeller	9
Mientus	14
Paper & Tea (P & T)	3
Rio	3
Schropp	1
Secondo	11
Spielbrett	17
Stilwerk	4

ACCOMMODATION

HOTELS AND PENSIONS

25hours Hotel Bikini Berlin	7
Am Savignyplatz	4
Am Steinplatz	2
art'otel berlin ku'damm	15
Bleibtreu	14
Dormero Hotel Berlin Ku'damm	13
Hecker's Hotel	10
Hotel de Ela	16
Hotel Otto	1
Hotel-Pension Funk	12
Hotel Q!	11
Hotel Zoo Berlin	8
Ibis	17
Savoy Hotel Berlin	5
Swissôtel Berlin	9
Waldorf Astoria Berlin	6

HOSTELS

aletto Hotel Ku'damm	3

0   250
metres

N

in contrast, has more in the way of atmosphere than actual sights, though its city hall witnessed John F. Kennedy's famous "Ich bin ein Berliner" speech.

ARRIVAL AND GETTING AROUND   CITY WEST AND SCHÖNEBERG

By train Bahnhof Zoo is the main transport hub in this part of Berlin, from where buses radiate to all the sights in the west.

Getting around City West is fairly easily explored on foot, as is much of Schöneberg, where most points of interest are an easy walk from Nollendorfplatz. However, Rathaus Schöneberg is best reached by U-Bahn or bus #M46 from Bahnhof Zoo.

6

City West

Long before the term **City West** was coined for the old centre of West Berlin, its main role was as a shopping district, particularly along **Kurfürstendamm** (universally called **Ku'damm**). Even in the grim first few years after the war, a few retailers managed to struggle on here, but it was with the coming of the Berlin Wall that the area got a real boost. With Berlin's true centre snatched away by the GDR, this area quickly became an awkward surrogate. Large amounts of modern building work aimed to transform City West into the heart of a great late twentieth-century metropolis, but the work was largely in vain. Once the Wall came down the city hastily shifted back to its previous centre, abandoning West Berlin's old centre to years in the doldrums. In recent years, however, its iconic avenues have been reborn, home to couture stores and high-street shops, as well as some plush new hotels, and many of the streets that run between Ku'damm and Kantstrasse, to the north, have charm of their own, with a wealth of independent cafés, bars, restaurants and boutiques.

Bahnhof Zoo

Squeezed between a couple of scruffy shopping precincts, **Bahnhof Zoo** has long been the district's shabby main transport hub. In the 1980s it was the notorious haunt of heroin dealers and child prostitutes, as depicted in the famous film, *Christiane F. – Wir Kinder von Bahnhof Zoo* (see p.296). Despite being cleaned up significantly post-reunification, it still maintains a fairly gloomy, gritty atmosphere, though plans are underway to revamp the station – along with the surrounding area – with some glossy new shops and restaurants.

Museum für Fotografie

Jebenesstr. 2 • Tues, Wed & Fri 10am–6pm, Thurs 10am–8pm, Sat & Sun 11am–6pm • €10 • ☎ 030 266 42 42 42, ⓦ smb.museum • ⓤ/ⓢ Zoologischer Garten

Behind Bahnhof Zoo, and best reached through its back door, is another of Berlin's excellent municipal museums, the **Museum für Fotografie**. The home of the **Helmut Newton Foundation**, it features works both by this world-famous photographer as well as changing exhibitions of works from the Kunstbibliothek's collection displayed on the building's top floor.

The collection, Newton's gift to his home city shortly before his untimely death in 2004, occupies the first two floors. The ground floor is a museum to the man himself, including a reconstruction of his quirky Monaco office and his oversized made-to-measure beach buggy, complete with monogram on the steering wheel – no doubt perfect for cruising around Monte Carlo. Most interesting among the rest of the memorabilia is his camera collection, which spans several decades. On the first floor, Newton's work is shown in regularly changing exhibitions, displaying his unique and heavily stylized portrait, glamour and nude photography, his celebrity portraiture and penchant for Amazonian women. Some of the most intriguing pieces are from his personal collection of unpublished photos. Both Newton and his wife (who worked under the pseudonym Alice Springs) seem always to have had cameras to hand to chart every aspect of their life together and obsess over each other's naked forms. The images from Newton's deathbed are particularly stark.

6

C/O Berlin
Amerika Haus, Hardenbergstr. 22–24 • Daily 11am–8pm • €10 • ☎ 030 28 44 41 60, ⓦ co-berlin.org • ⓤ/Ⓢ Zoologischer Garten

Since its foundation back in 2000, **C/O Berlin** has hosted some of the city's best photography exhibitions, with shows featuring international heavyweights such as Martin Parr, Annie Leibovitz, René Burri and Karl Lagerfeld. Previously occupying a gorgeous post office in Mitte, it moved to West Berlin's Amerika Haus in 2014, where it has continued hosting big-name retrospectives like Sebastião Salgado as well as continued promotion of young and new international talents.

While you're in the neighbourhood, you should also make sure to stop by Camera Work, another excellent gallery around the corner on Kantstrasse (see p.231).

Zoologischer Garten Berlin
Hardenbergplatz 8 • Daily: March & Oct 9am–6pm; April–Sept 9am–6.30pm; Nov–Feb 9am–4.30pm; check online for exact dates and times • €14.50, children aged 4–15 €7.50; combined ticket with aquarium €20/€10 • ☎ 030 51 53 10, ⓦ zoo-berlin.de • ⓤ/Ⓢ Zoologischer Garten

Step out east through the main entrance of Zoo Station and you're in a maelstrom of bright lights, traffic and high-rise buildings, but walk over the area occupied by the bus station to the other side of the plaza and you'll find yourself at the gates of the **Zoologischer Garten Berlin** (Berlin Zoo), which contains a zoo and aquarium (see below). Laid out in 1844 on the basis of Friedrich Wilhelm IV's private zoo from Pfaueninsel (see p.172), this survived the destruction of World War II, and subsequent pressure from a local starving populace, to become one of Europe's most important zoos, with more than 1500 species represented. It's pleasantly landscaped, with reasonably large compounds for the animals, peaceful nooks for quietly observing animal behaviour, and lots of benches that make it ideal for picnicking.

Highlights include a large glass-sided **hippo pool** and the **Nachttierhaus**, an underground nocturnal environment whose principal attraction is the bat cave, though an ongoing €60 million renovation project – scheduled to end in 2035 – is adding various new elements. Recent additions have included a revamped **bird house**, with more space and enhanced natural light, and a new **petting zoo** in 2016. Since the demise of **Knut**, the adorable polar bear cub who quickly gained worldwide attention before his untimely death in 2011, the zoo's most famous denizen has been **Fatou**, the world's second oldest known female gorilla, who will turn 60 in 2017. Fatou's pre-eminence may be under threat, however – at the time of writing, talks were underway with the Chinese government to import a new pair of **pandas**, with plans for a new enclosure in 2017.

Aquarium Berlin
Budapester Str. 32 • Daily 9am–6pm • €14.50, children aged 4–15 €7.50; combined ticket with zoo €20/€10 • ☎ 030 25 40 10, ⓦ aquarium-berlin.de • ⓤ/Ⓢ Zoologischer Garten

Situated next to the zoo, the impressive **Aquarium Berlin** lives up to its international reputation with more species than any other in the world. Built in 1913, it's retained its old-fashioned appearance, albeit incorporating modern elements, and now houses over fourteen thousand creatures on three floors. The large, humid crocodile hall is the most memorable section, though also check out the new glass-roofed "Hippoquarium". Despite the attractive price of the **combined day ticket**, trying to get around both the zoo and aquarium in a day can be quite a rush.

Breitscheidplatz
ⓤ Kurfürstendamm

A short two-block walk east of Bahnhof Zoo, the angular concrete **Breitscheidplatz** is a magnet for vendors, caricaturists and street musicians, and often hosts fairs and festivals, including a large Christmas market. On its eastern edge is the rather generic

KAISER-WILHELM-GEDÄCHTNISKIRCHE (P.112) >

6

Europa Center shopping mall, which was built in the 1960s as a capitalist symbol for West Berlin, topped by a huge, rotating Mercedes-Benz symbol. An intriguing sculpture entitled *Flow of Time*, an alternative clock consisting of an elaborate series of liquid-filled glass pipes, does, however, deserve some attention down in the lobby, and over the road the swanky new Bikini Berlin concept mall (see p.242), which occupies the 1950s Bikini-Haus, and hip *25hours* (see p.190) hotel have given a more contemporary slant to the square.

Kaiser-Wilhelm-Gedächtniskirche

Breitscheidplatz • Daily 9am–7pm; guided tours daily except Sun hourly 12.15–3.15pm; Mon, Fri & Sat also 10.15am & 11am • Free • ☎ 030 218 50 23, ⓦ gedaechtniskirche-berlin.de • ⓤ Kurfürstendamm

The focal point of Breitscheidplatz is the ruined **Kaiser-Wilhelm-Gedächtniskirche** (Kaiser Wilhelm Memorial Church), one of Berlin's great landmarks. Built at the end of the nineteenth century by architect Franz Schwechten, it was destroyed by British bombing in November 1943 and left as a reminder. The haunting skeleton is a strangely effective memorial, the crumbling tower providing a hint of the old city. You can go inside what remains of the nave: a small exhibit shows wartime destruction and a "before and after" model of the city centre. Adjacent, a modern **chapel** contains a sad charcoal sketch by Kurt Reubers, *Stalingrad Madonna*, dedicated to those who died – on both sides – during the Battle of Stalingrad. The blue-glass campanile on the opposite side of the ruined church to the chapel has gained the nicknames the "Lipstick" or the "Soul-Silo" because of its tubular shape; in its base is a shop selling fair-trade goods.

KaDeWe and around

Tauentzienstr. 21 • ☎ 030 212 10, ⓦ kadewe-berlin.de • ⓤ Wittenbergplatz

At the eastern end of Tauentzienstrasse, the rather bland continuation of Ku'damm east of the Kaiser-Wilhelm-Gedächtniskirche, is the largest department store in Europe, **KaDeWe** (see p.242). An abbreviation of Kaufhaus Des Westens ("Department Store of the West"), it opened in 1907 and quickly became a temple of luxury in a rapidly modernizing city. Decades later the Nazis seized it from its Jewish owners, and in 1943 an American fighter plane crashed into it, igniting a fire that gutted the building. Almost 180,000 Berliners attended its reopening in 1950, and during the Cold War it became a symbol of West Berlin's capitalist prosperity. It averages up to fifty thousand visitors per day, many of whom head to the superb sixth-floor **food hall** with its mouthwatering snacks. The department store is scheduled for a major design overhaul by Dutch architect Rem Koolhaas's OMA firm, which will add a new glass rooftop extension, new escalators and sculptural staircases in a series of stages expected to be completed in 2020.

Outside KaDeWe, **Wittenbergplatz U-Bahn station** has been likeably restored to its prewar condition both inside (1920s kitsch) and out (Neoclassical pavilion). Near the entrance, a tall sign reminds passers-by of the wartime concentration camps: it states that the German people must never be allowed to forget the atrocities that were carried out there, and lists the names of some of the camps. It's an odd memorial, neither terribly poignant nor at a significant site, and one that goes largely unnoticed by shoppers.

Käthe-Kollwitz-Museum

Fasanenstr. 24 • Daily 11am–6pm • €6 • ☎ 030 882 52 10, ⓦ kaethe-kollwitz.de • ⓤ Uhlandstrasse

The **Käthe-Kollwitz-Museum**, just south of the Ku'damm, is devoted to the work of Kollwitz, who created some of the most moving works of the first half of the twentieth century. Born in 1867, the artist lived almost all her life in Prenzlauer Berg (see p.142), where her work developed a socially aware, generally left-wing perspective. Following the death of her son in World War I, her woodcuts, lithographs and prints became explicitly pacifist, often dwelling on the theme of mother and child. Her sculptures, too, often deal with this subject: two of her bronzes, *Tower of Women* and the pietà *Mother with Dead Son*, can be seen here. When her grandson was killed in World War II her work became even sadder and more poignant. As she was a staunch pacifist and committed socialist, the Nazis watched her carefully and forced her resignation from a prestigious post at the Faculty of Arts, while at the same time using some of her work for their own propaganda purposes. She died in 1945, shortly before the end of the war.

The Story of Berlin

Kurfürstendamm 207–208 • Daily 10am–8pm, last admission 6pm • €12 ; kids aged 6–16 €5 • ☎ 030 88 72 01 00, ⓦ story-of-berlin.de • ⓤ Uhlandstrasse

The Story of Berlin is an excellent multimedia exhibition and an ideal first step in unravelling Berlin's history, with each section extensively labelled in English. Tucked away in the back of a mall, the museum uses its odd layout to its advantage. On the way round you'll be confronted with life-size dioramas, film clips, noises, flashing lights, smoke and smells, which illustrate the trawl through the highs and lows of the city's turbulent past. The end result will entertain all ages and will take at least two hours to complete, not including the additional bonus: a taste of the Cold War given on the frequent guided tours of the 1970s Allied-built nuclear bunker below the mall. It's still functional, with space for 3592 people to shelter in the first two weeks after a nuclear attack. If you've run out of time or energy having visited the museum, you can use your ticket to return another day to view the bunker.

Schöneberg

Once a separate entity, **Schöneberg** was swallowed up by Greater Berlin as the city expanded in the late eighteenth and nineteenth centuries. Blown to pieces during the war, it's now a mostly middle-class residential area. The gateway to the district is **Nollendorfplatz**, a long-standing centre in the city's LGBT community. Schöneberg's main drag, Potsdamer Strasse, runs a block or so east of here, past **Heinrich-von-Kleist-Park**, around which are some reminders of a fascinating and moving past. On the southern fringes of the district lies **Rathaus Schöneberg**, where on June 26, 1963 John F. Kennedy made his "Berliner" speech.

GAY BERLIN IN THE WEIMAR AND NAZI YEARS

Even by contemporary standards, Weimar Berlin's gay scene in the 1920s and early 1930s was prodigious: there were around forty gay bars on and near **Nollendorfplatz** alone, and gay life in the city was open, fashionable and well organized, with its own newspapers, community associations and art. The city's theatres were filled with plays exploring gay themes, homosexuality in the Prussian army was little short of institutionalized, and gay bars, nightclubs and brothels proudly advertised their attractions – there were even gay working men's clubs. All this happened at a time when the rest of Europe was smothered under a welter of homophobia and repression.

Under the Third Reich, however, homosexuality was quickly and brutally outlawed: gays and lesbians were rounded up and taken to concentration camps, branded for their "perversion" by being forced to wear pink or black triangles. (The black triangle represented "antisocial" offenders: in an attempt to ignore the existence of lesbianism, lesbians were arrested on pretexts such as swearing at the Führer's name.) As homosexuality was, at the time, still illegal in Allied countries, no Nazis were tried for crimes against gays or lesbians at Nuremberg. A red granite **plaque** in the shape of a triangle at Nollendorfplatz U-Bahn station commemorates the gay men and women who were murdered for their sexuality – a local echo of the larger memorial found at the edge of the Tiergarten (see p.39).

Cabaret Berlin ☎ 0151 25 22 03 42, ⓦ cabaret-berlin.com. Well-informed 75min English-language walking tours around Berlin's gay village with emphasis on places relating to Christopher Isherwood. Sat 11am; €15.

Nollendorfplatz

ⓊNollendorfplatz

The busy road and rail intersection of **Nollendorfplatz** throbs by night as western Berlin's main gay hub, but by day holds few specific attractions. Even so, it's worth doing a lap of the block on the south side of the square, east of the proto-Deco **Neues Schauspielhaus** (New Theatre), and down Massenstrasse and on to Nollendorfstrasse. Here, at no. 17, stands the building in which the writer **Christopher Isherwood** lived during his years in the prewar city, a time elegantly recounted in his famous collection of stories *Goodbye to Berlin* (see p.291):

From my window, the deep solemn massive street. Cellar shops where lamps burn all day, under the shadow of top-heavy balconied facades, dirty plaster frontages embossed with scroll work and heraldic devices. The whole district is like this: street leading into street of houses like shabby monumental safes crammed with the tarnished valuables and secondhand furniture of a bankrupt middle class.

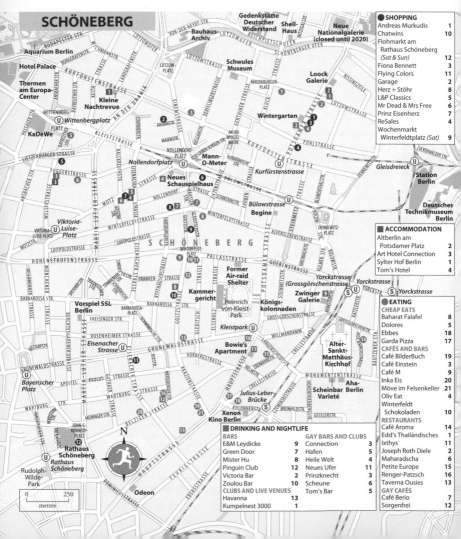

Schöneberg has since been reborn as a fancy, even chic, neighbourhood; latter-day Isherwood wannabes hang out in Neukölln.

Heinrich-von-Kleist-Park and around
① Kleistpark

On Pallasstrasse, east of Winterfeldtplatz, you'll spot a huge and undistinguished apartment building straddling the road and backing onto the northern edge of the **Heinrich-von-Kleist-Park**. On the south side of the street a huge concrete cube forms the base of the structure; this began life as one of Berlin's **air-raid shelters** in case of Allied raids. After the war the tower proved impervious to demolition attempts, and the lower levels were used by NATO troops to store food and provisions in case of a Soviet invasion. Ironically, in the post-Cold War years, supplies reaching the end of their shelf life were sold off – usually on the cheap to Russia. On the northern side of the street the apartment building rests on land that until 1973 accommodated the **Sportpalast**, a sports centre that became the main venue for Nazi rallies in the 1930s. Hitler delivered some of his most famous speeches here – witness those old newsreels showing him working himself up into an oratorical fever. It was also where Goebbels asked the German people if they wanted "total war" – at which they jubilantly applauded.

At its eastern end, Pallasstrasse finishes at Potsdamer Strasse, a couple of minutes' walk south down which brings you to the **Königskolonnaden** – a colonnade from 1780 that originally stood on Alexanderplatz – which on a misty morning makes this stretch of road look a little Parisian.

Kammergericht
Elssholzstr. 30–33 • **①** Kleistpark

On the western side of the Kleistpark looms the sturdy **Kammergericht** (Supreme Court of Justice). During the war, Nazi show trials took place, as did the "People's Court" under the infamous Judge Freisler following the July Bomb Plot (see box, pp.98–99), both preludes to the inevitable executions, which often took place in Plötzensee Prison (see p.165). Freisler met his unlamented end here in the final weeks of the war: on his way from the courtroom a bomb from an American aircraft fell on the building, dislodging a beam that crushed his skull. After the war the building was taken over by the Allied Control Council and the Quadripartite Agreement (see p.281) was signed here in 1971. After a spell in Charlottenburg, the court moved back into the building in 1997.

BOWIE'S BERLIN

In August 2016, seven months after his death, the city of Berlin placed a bone china memorial plaque to **David Bowie** outside his former apartment at Hauptstrasse 155 in Schöneberg. Arriving in the summer of 1976 along with his protégé Iggy Pop, ostensibly in order to escape a spiralling drug habit in Los Angeles, Bowie stayed until 1978, hanging out at cult hotspots like *Dschungel* (now the *Ellington Hotel Berlin*), *Paris Bar* (see p.205) and *SO36* (see p.227), visiting West Berlin's museums and galleries and crossing the border now and again to explore life in the former East. As well as co-producing two Iggy albums – *The Idiot* (1976) and *Lust for Life* (1977), Bowie produced three raw and expressionistic albums of his own – 1977's *Low*, followed a year later by *Heroes*, and then by *Lodger* (1979), aka the "Berlin Trilogy" – alongside co-producer Tony Visconti and occasional collaborator Brian Eno. Though recorded in various locations, one of the venues consistently used for these records was Berlin's Hansa Studios, housed in the Meistersaal (see p.93), some of whose rooms can today be visited as part of a music tour. Bowie moved to New York in 1978, later recalling:

I had not intended to leave Berlin, I just drifted away. Maybe I was getting better. It was an irreplaceable, unmissable experience and probably the happiest time in my life up until that point.

Alter-Sankt-Matthäus-Kirchhof

Grossgörschenstr. • ⓊYorckstrasse or ⓈYorckstrasse (Grossgörschenstrasse)

The **Alter-Sankt-Matthäus-Kirchhof** (Old St Matthew's Churchyard) contains the graves of the Brothers Grimm, united in death as they were in copyright. The bodies of Stauffenberg and his co-conspirators were also buried here following the July Bomb Plot, only to be exhumed a few days later and burned by Nazi thugs.

6

Rathaus Schöneberg

John-F-Kennedy-Platz • **Exhibition** Daily except Fri 10am–6pm • Free **Tower** April–Sept daily 10am–4pm • Free • ⓊRathaus Schöneberg

Schöneberg's most famous attraction is the **Rathaus Schöneberg**. Built just before World War I, the city hall became the seat of the West Berlin parliament and senate after the last war, and it was outside here in 1963 that **John F. Kennedy** made his celebrated speech on the Cold War, just a few months after the Cuban Missile Crisis:

There are many people in the world who really don't understand, or say they don't, what is the great issue between the free world and the Communist world. Let them come to Berlin. There are some who say that Communism is the wave of the future. Let them come to Berlin. And there are some who say in Europe and elsewhere we can work with the Communists. Let them come to Berlin. And there are even a few who say it is true that Communism is an evil system, but it permits us to make economic progress. Lässt sie nach Berlin kommen. Let them come to Berlin ... All free men, wherever they may live, are citizens of Berlin, and, therefore, as a free man, I take pride in the words "Ich bin ein Berliner".

Rousing stuff. But what the president hadn't realized as he read from his phonetically written text was that what he had said could also mean "I am a doughnut", since *Berliner* is a name for jam doughnuts – though not in Berlin, where it is usually known as a *Pfannkuchen*. The urban myth that peals of laughter greeted this embarrassing error only developed years later. People did laugh at the time, after applauding, but because the president thanked his interpreter, who had simply repeated his quote, for translating his German. Five months later, the day after Kennedy was assassinated, the square in front of the Rathaus was given his name – a move apparently instigated by the city's students, among whom the president was highly popular.

One of the rooms in the Rathaus features a permanent **exhibition**, Wir Waren Nachbarn ("We Were Neighbours"), relating to prewar Jewish life in the area, and you can climb the **Rathaus tower** and see the replica **liberty bell** donated to the city by the US in 1950.

Kreuzberg-Friedrichshain, Neukölln and around

The mainly residential borough of Kreuzberg-Friedrichshain, south and east of Mitte, was formed in 2001 by joining two distinct and traditionally very separate districts that until 1989 were even on opposing sides of the Berlin Wall. Given Kreuzberg's own internal differences, the borough can be divided into three. Most visited by tourists is middle-class western Kreuzberg, the northern part of which is home to several of the city's key attractions, including the sobering Jüdisches Museum (Jewish Museum), the modern and multifaceted Berlinische Galerie, and the world's most famous Cold War border crossing, Checkpoint Charlie. Eastern Kreuzberg, meanwhile, is its scruffier cousin – a magnet for anarchists, gays, Turkish immigrants and, these days, hipsters, drawn to some of the city's best nightlife.

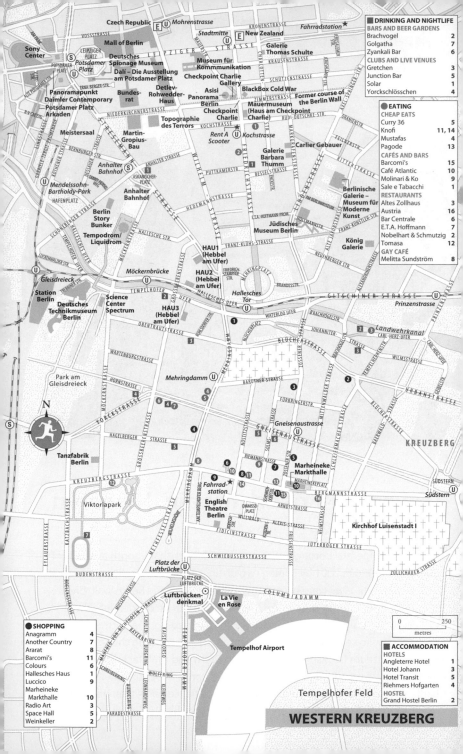

WESTERN KREUZBERG

To the north of eastern Kreuzberg, **Friedrichshain** is an old East Berlin neighbourhood with a feel somewhere between the two, with hip warehouse clubs rubbing shoulders with ever-gentrifying residential streets. Just south of Kreuzberg lie several adjacent districts which hold the odd attraction. Gritty **Neukölln** has, over the last few years, established itself to be as vibrant as eastern Kreuzberg with its fair share of underground galleries and nightlife spaces. **Tempelhof** and **Treptow**, meanwhile, are interesting for two huge and impressive monuments to crumbled regimes: the Nazi-built former Tempelhof Airport, and Treptow Park's immense Soviet Memorial.

GETTING AROUND　　　　KREUZBERG-FRIEDRICHSHAIN, NEUKÖLLN AND AROUND

Western Kreuzberg The main sights are all within walking distance of the U6 U-Bahn line, which runs south from Friedrichstrasse in Mitte. If you're feeling energetic, you could easily walk between them all in a day, in which case you might start by taking bus #248 from Alexanderplatz to the Jüdisches Museum and set off from there.

Eastern Kreuzberg and Treptower Kottbusser Tor, Moritzplatz or Schlesisches Tor U-Bahn stations are the best way in, after which it's mostly a matter of walking around

– though the Treptower Park's Soviet Memorial is a bus ride from the latter station.

Friedrichshain The rapid U5 U-Bahn line travels beneath Karl-Marx-Allee from Alexanderplatz, from where the S-Bahn also leaves for the Ostbahnhof, Warschauer Strasse and Ostkreuz.

Neukölln Neukölln's sights are within easy reach of one another on foot or via the speedy U8 underground line, which ends at one of the district's main hubs, Hermannplatz.

Western Kreuzberg

When, in the 1830s, Berlin's industries started recruiting peasants from the outlying countryside to work in their factories and machine shops, it was to the small village of **Kreuzberg** that many came. They ended up living in low-rent buildings thrown up by speculators, making Kreuzberg a solidly working-class area and, in time, a suburb of Greater Berlin. Siemens, the electrical engineering giant, began life in a western Kreuzberg courtyard. In the 1930s local trade unionists and workers fought street battles with the Nazis, and during the war it was one of the very few areas to avoid total destruction, and among the quickest to revive in the 1950s.

The nondescript modern city blocks just south of Mitte are atypical, displaying almost no evidence of Kreuzberg's countercultural roots or its preserved nineteenth-century past. Nonetheless, this part of the district is worth investigating for its **museums** and its most famous sight, **Checkpoint Charlie**. Farther south, western Kreuzberg offers a fairly upscale array of restaurants, bars, cafés and shops, as well as the popular **Viktoriapark**.

Jüdisches Museum Berlin

Lindenstr. 9–14 • Mon 10am–10pm, Tues–Sun 10am–8pm • €8 • ☎ 030 25 99 33 00, ⓦ jmberlin.de • ⓤ Hallesches Tor

A phenomenal silver fortress in the midst of residential streets once levelled by wartime bombing, the **Jüdisches Museum Berlin** (Jewish Museum Berlin) is one of Berlin's most exciting pieces of architecture. Uncomfortable angles and severe lines create a disturbed and uneasy space that mirrors the difficult story portrayed inside: that of the history and culture of German Jewry.

The extraordinary **building** is by Daniel Libeskind. The ground plan is in the form of a compressed lightning bolt (often interpreted as a deconstructed Star of David, though this was not Libeskind's intention), while the structure itself is sheathed in polished metallic facing, with windows – or, rather, thin angular slits – that trace geometric patterns on the exterior. There's no front door and entry is through an underground tunnel connected to the **Kollegienhaus** – the Baroque building next door that serves as an annexe to the museum and is used for temporary exhibitions.

The **interior** is just as unusual, manifesting Libeskind's ideas about symbolic architecture, while retaining a sculptural symmetry: a "void" – an empty and inaccessible diagonal shaft – cuts through the structure, while three long intersecting corridors, each representing an element of Jewish experience, divide the space at

basement level. At the foot of the basement stairs the "axis of exile" leads outside to a garden of pillars; the "axis of the Holocaust" crosses it, connecting with the Holocaust Tower, dimly lit and, again, completely empty; and the "axis of continuity" follows, leading to a trudge up several flights of stairs to the permanent exhibition space. Part way up the stairs, the first floor contains the **Memory Void**, an eerie space filled with the sounds of clanking as visitors walk across a space scattered with piles of thousands of grimacing iron masks; a powerful reminder of the Holocaust.

The **permanent exhibition** begins on the top floor and focuses, in a broadly chronological way, on pre-1900 German-Jewish history before moving to the second floor to deal with the painful twentieth century, and ending with the present day. Note, though, that planned renovations at the end of 2017 will change the current layout.

In 2012, the museum opened the **W. Michael Blumenthal Akademie** in an equally eye-catching building across the road. Also designed by Libeskind, it's formed from three inclined cubes that surround a central "Diaspora Garden" and features meeting rooms, event spaces and a library, all dedicated to education and research relating to Jewish history and culture.

Berlinische Galerie – Museum für Moderne Kunst

Alte Jakobstr. 124–128 • Daily except Tues 10am–6pm • €8, €4 on 1st Mon of the month; prices vary during special exhibitions • ☎ 030 78 90 26 00, ⓦ berlinischegalerie.de • ⓤ Hallesches Tor

Behind the Jüdisches Museum lie the vast airy halls of a former warehouse that have been renovated to house the **Berlinische Galerie – Museum für Moderne Kunst** (Museum of Modern Art). Some of Berlin's darkest and most tortured pieces of art are displayed here as part of a permanent collection, mostly dating from the twentieth century, when movements such as Secessionism, Dadaism and the New Objectivity called Berlin home. All challenged the accepted art world and the establishment, and reflected Europe's troubled times; consequently much of the collection is unsettling. Specific artworks are rotated fairly regularly, but celebrated local artists to look for include Lesser Ury, whose moody, often rain-filled paintings evoke a distinctively nocturnal atmosphere, and Dadaists George Grosz and Otto Dix, whose bold and controversial works often exposed the darker and more hypocritical aspects of the post-World War 1 period. Traumatized by the war, Dix used dry-point technique to produce ghastly caricatures of mutilated war veterans playing cards, while Grosz was known for juxtaposing prostitutes next to oleaginous bankers. As well as paintings, the gallery shows photographs from the same period, from the likes of Heinrich Zille (see p.66) and Arno Fischer, and also covers architecture, urban design and graphic art. There are also regular lectures, workshops, readings and other events, and the café is a pleasant spot for lunch.

Checkpoint Charlie and around

One of the most famous names associated with the Wall and Cold War-era Berlin, the Allied military post known as **Checkpoint Charlie** marked the border between East and West Berlin and was the main gateway between the two Berlins for most non-Germans. With its dramatic "YOU ARE NOW LEAVING THE AMERICAN SECTOR" signs and unsmiling border guards, it became the archetypal movie-style Iron Curtain crossing. In the Cold War years it was the scene of repeated border incidents, including a standoff between American and Soviet forces in October 1961, which culminated in tanks from both sides growling at each other for a few days.

The site of the border crossing itself is barely recognizable now. Removed in July 1990, the original border post is in the AlliiertenMuseum (see p.170), and a **replica** now marks the original site. Around it are modern offices, retail complexes and a few tacky souvenir shops, though a couple of newer museums have spring up in recent years providing more historical context. On Zimmerstrasse, diagonally across from the Mauermuseum (see opposite), there's also the **Checkpoint Charlie Gallery**, an interesting outdoor exhibition on the Berlin Wall that includes info boards and many large-format photos.

Mauermuseum – Haus am Checkpoint Charlie

Friedrichstr. 43–45 • Daily 9am–10pm • €12.50 • ☎ 030 25 37 250, ⓦ mauermuseum.de • ⓤ Kochstrasse

For tangible evidence of the trauma of the Wall, head for the **Mauermuseum** (Wall Museum), also known as the **Haus am Checkpoint Charlie**. Here you can see photos of escape tunnels and some of the modes of transport, often hand-built – from aircrafts to converted cars and even a hot-air balloon – by which people attempted, succeeded, and sometimes tragically failed, to break through the border. Films document the stories of some of the people murdered by the East German border guards, and there's a section on human rights behind the Iron Curtain. Overall, though, the huge collection is somewhat jumbled and rambling, and not quite the harrowing experience that some visitors expect. Related exhibits focus on the concept of freedom and non-violent struggles in general, while showcasing artefacts such as the typewriter used to type Charter 77, the civil rights document drawn up in communist Czechoslovakia, and Mahatma Gandhi's diary.

BlackBox Cold War – Exhibition at Checkpoint Charlie

Friedrichstr. 47 • Daily 10am–6pm • €5 • ☎ 030 21 63 571, ⓦ www. bfgg.de/en/centre-of-cold-war.html • ⓤ Kochstrasse

The recently established **BlackBox Cold War** museum offers a potted history of the Cold War in a neat, organized and neutral way that's at odds with the chaotic (and decidedly non-neutral) Mauermuseum across the street. Drawing on interesting artefacts, such as hand grenades used in training exercises for schoolchildren, plus large-format photos and interactive media stations, the 200-square-metre space also examines the ongoing effects of those years on today's geopolitics.

7

THE UPRISING OF JUNE 1953

On June 16 and 17, 1953, Leipziger Strasse was the focal point of a **nationwide uprising** against the GDR's communist government. General dissatisfaction with economic and political conditions in eastern Berlin came to a head when building workers (the traditional proletarian heroes of GDR mythology) went on strike, protesting against longer hours without increased pay. The first to protest were workers from the prestigious Stalinallee project, who downed tools to march on the city centre, joined by other workers and passers-by. At Strausberger Platz they swept aside Volkspolizei units and headed for Unter den Linden. From here, the now roughly eight-thousand-strong **demonstration** marched to the Haus der Ministerien – then the seat of the GDR government – and demanded to speak to GDR President Otto Grotewohl and SED General Secretary Walter Ulbricht. Eventually three lesser ministers were sent out to address the demonstrators. Clearly alarmed at the scale of the demonstration, they promised to try and get the work hours decreased. But by now the crowd wanted more, and began calling for political freedom. After declaring a **general strike** for the next day, the protesters returned to Stalinallee, tearing down SED placards on the way. Grotewohl's announcement rescinding the new working conditions later that day failed to halt the strike, news of which had been broadcast across the GDR by Western radio stations. About 300,000 workers in 250 towns joined in, and East Berlin came to a standstill as a crowd of 100,000 people marched towards the House of Ministries once again. Clashes with the police followed as demonstrators attacked SED party offices and state food stores. The GDR authorities proved unequal to the situation, leading the city's Soviet military commandant to declare a state of emergency.

When **Soviet tanks** appeared on Leipziger Strasse, they found their route blocked by a vast crowd that refused to budge. After loudspeaker warnings that martial law had been declared, the first shots rang out, leaving youths to confront the T-34s with bricks and bottles. **Street fighting** raged throughout East Berlin for the rest of the day, and it wasn't until nightfall that the Soviets reasserted control. At least 267 demonstrators, 116 policemen and eighteen Soviet soldiers were killed, and some 92 civilians (including a West Berliner just passing through) were summarily shot after the **suppression of the uprising**. Some fourteen death sentences and innumerable prison terms followed, and eighteen Soviet soldiers were executed for "moral capitulation to the demonstrators".

Asisi Panorama Berlin

Friedrichstr. 205 • Daily 10am–6pm (last entry 5.30pm) • €10 • ☎ 03 41 35 55 340, ⓦ asisi.de • ⓤ Kochstrasse

Artist Yadegar Asisi specializes in painting giant, detailed and often very realistic panoramas. The **Asisi Panorama Berlin** depicts a normal (fictional) day in the 1980s, when the Wall was still up. On one side is edgy, alternative eastern Kreuzberg, with its punks and squats; on the other the eerily quiet, desolate Mitte district, all death strips and border fortifications with the TV tower looming in the distance. Accompanied by sound effects and a soundtrack by film composer Eric Babak, it's an absorbing and sobering experience, and is complemented by a photo exhibition in the foyer.

Museum für Kommunikation

Leipziger Str. 16 • Tues 9am–8pm, Wed–Fri 9am–5pm, Sat & Sun 10am–6pm • €4, under-18s free • ☎ 030 202 940, ⓦ museumsstiftung.de • ⓤ Stadtmitte

The former Imperial postal ministry, on the high-rise-lined arterial road of Leipziger Strasse, is now home to the **Museum für Kommunikation**. The museum traces its roots back to the world's first postal museum, which opened in Berlin in 1872 and moved into this Baroque palace in 1898. When the building was damaged in the war the collection was dispersed, and only reopened in its historic home in 2000. There's a lot more here than just stamps; highlights include early examples of wax seals, postcards and stamps (such as the famous Blue Mauritius), telephones, radios, film, telegraphs and computers. Much is displayed with kids in mind, though the frequently excellent temporary exhibitions are often more adult-minded, overlapping as they sometimes do with contemporary art.

Detlev-Rohwedder-Haus – Former Luftfahrtministerium

Wilhelmstr. 97 • ⓤ /ⓢ Potsdamer Platz

The city block west of the Museum für Kommunikation is marked out by the fortress-like **Detlev-Rohwedder-Haus**, originally Hermann Göring's **Luftfahrtministerium** (Air Ministry). A rare relic of the Nazi past, it has survived very much intact and once formed the southern end of the former Third Reich government quarter along Wilhelmstrasse (see p.40). Göring promised Berliners that not a single bomb would fall on the city during the war; if this were to happen, the Reichsmarschall said, he would change his name to Meyer – a common Jewish surname. Ironically, the air ministry was one of the few buildings to emerge more or less unscathed from the bombing and Red Army shelling. After the establishment of the GDR it became the SED regime's **Haus der Ministerien** (House of Ministries), and was the target of a mass demonstration on June 16, 1953 (see box, p.121). There's a historical irony of sorts in the fact that the building became, for a number of years after reunification, the headquarters of the Treuhandanstalt, the agency responsible for the privatization of the former GDR's economy. It now houses the Federal Finance Ministry, but the 18m mural on the Leipzigerstrasse side, created by German painter Max Lingner (along with fourteen artisans) between 1950 and 1952, provides a reminder of its socialist past.

Topographie des Terrors

Niederkirchnerstr. 8 • Daily 10am–8pm (outside areas until dusk) • Free • ☎ 030 25 45 09 50, ⓦ topographie.de • ⓤ /ⓢ Potsdamer Platz

Lurking behind central Berlin's most substantial but dilapidated stretch of Wall is a city block that between 1933 and 1945 headquartered the Reich security services, including the Gestapo and SS. Some ruined foundations remain, but the flawlessly sleek and silvery piece of memorial-chic architecture in the middle houses the **Topographie des Terrors** (Topography of Terror), Germany's most significant museum on the perpetrators of Nazi terror. Inside, this dreadful history is retold on numerous information panels (in both English and German) which include many reproduced black-and-white photos of Nazis and their forlorn victims at a range of miserable events – book burnings, public humiliations, the destruction of Jewish property and

synagogues, the rounding-up of Jews and others to be murdered in concentration camps. It's all sadly familiar, but what many don't realize, and the exhibition goes out of its way to show, is that many of the perpetrators were never brought to justice.

Meanwhile, in the Reich Security ruins outside, more info panels provide a potted history of the Third Reich in Berlin and reveal gruesome insights: the ground beneath the exhibition once held the cellars where prisoners were interrogated and tortured.

Martin-Gropius-Bau

Niederkirchnerstr. 7 • Daily except Tues 10am–7pm • Prices vary; around €10 • ☎ 030 25 48 60, ⓦ gropiusbau.de • ⓤ/Ⓢ Potsdamer Platz

The magnificently restored building beside the Topographie des Terrors is the **Martin-Gropius-Bau**, built between 1877 and 1881 by Martin Gropius, a pupil of Schinkel and the uncle of Bauhaus guru Walter (see box, p.101). Until its destruction in the war the Gropius-Bau was home of a museum of applied art, but rebuilt and refurbished, it now houses changing exhibitions of contemporary art, photography and historical archeology.

Anhalter Bahnhof

The **Anhalter Bahnhof** is a sad reminder of a misguided civic act that some would term vandalism. Completed in 1870, this train station was once one of Europe's greatest, forming Berlin's gateway to the south. During the Holocaust it was one of the three stations used to deport Jews to Theresienstadt (Terezín), and from there to the death camps. Nearly ten thousand Jews were deported from here, usually in groups of fifty to a hundred, with the last train leaving on March 27, 1945. The station received only mild damage during World War II, which left it roofless but otherwise mostly intact. Despite attempts to preserve it, it was blown up in 1952 – someone had put in a good offer for the bricks. Now just a fragment of the facade stands, hinting at past glories. The patch of land that the station once covered is today a park, and includes the **Tempodrom**, a tent-shaped arts and music venue.

Berlin Story Bunker

Schöneberger Str. 23a • Tues–Fri 10am–7pm, Sat & Sun noon–8pm • €9.50 • ☎ 030 26 55 55 46, ⓦ berlinstory-bunker.de • Ⓢ Anhalter Bahnhof or ⓤ Mendelssohn-Bartholdy-Park

One of a handful of Nazi buildings left in the city, the blunt and featureless former bunker just southwest of the old Anhalter Bahnhof was built during the war by the Reichsbahn for travellers using the station. Today it hosts three museums over five floors: the **Berlin Story Museum**, which re-creates a variety of scenes from 800 years of Berlin history (including a replica of the bunker room where Hitler committed suicide); the **Medizin in alten Zeiten** section, showcasing a fairly gruesome selection of old medical and torture equipment; and the top-floor **Gruselkabinett** (Chamber of Horrors), which includes professional "ghosts" that jump out at you – certainly not a place for young children (or faint-hearted adults).

Deutsches Technikmuseum Berlin

Trebbiner Str. 9 • Tues–Fri 9am–5.30pm, Sat & Sun 10am–6pm • €8, children aged 6–14 €4; under-6s free • ☎ 030 90 25 40, ⓦ sdtb.de • ⓤ Möckernbrücke

Opened in 1983 in the former goods depot of the Anhalter Bahnhof, the **Deutsches Technikmuseum Berlin** presents a comprehensive – some might say overwhelming – overview of technology created in Germany. There's a strong emphasis on rail, with trains from 1835 to the present day, but there are also maritime and aviation halls and exhibits on technology from the industrial revolution to the computer and space age, and on the development of the pharmaceutical and chemical industry and its impact on everyday life. Newer exhibitions on the history of road transport (with high-wheel bicycles and horse-drawn carriages) and the internet are on show in the nearby **Ladestrasse complex** (Möckernstr. 26). Next door, the **Science Center Spectrum** features around 150 hands-on interactive exhibits, in contrast to the life-sized reproductions and actual machines of the main museum.

Bergmannstrasse and around
Ⓤ Gneisenaustrasse

At the end of the nineteenth century, many buildings around **Bergmannstrasse** housed working-class families. Those that survived the war were painstakingly restored, and the area is now thoroughly gentrified, though with a laidback bohemian feel. Bergmannstrasse is certainly a pleasant place to live, lined with cafés, bistros and *Trödelläden* (junk and antique shops), and boasting the **Marheineke Markthalle**, a varied and – these days – fairly trendy indoor food market (see p.244).

Chamissoplatz, just south of Bergmannstrasse, is worth a look for its well-preserved, balconied nineteenth-century houses and, a block south, its water tower. On Saturdays, a charming farmers' market selling largely regional products takes place on the square, which also boasts one of Berlin's few remaining Wilhelmine *pissoirs*: ornate public toilets, characteristically dark green in colour, erected in an early attempt at sanitation. This one has been recently renovated, and is open to the public (men only).

Viktoriapark
Accessible from Kreuzbergstr., Dudenstr., Katzbachstr. and Methfesselstr. • Ⓤ Platz der Luftbrücke, Ⓤ Mehringdamm or Ⓤ Yorckstrasse

Draped across the slopes of a hill, **Viktoriapark** is one of the city's most likeable parks, a relaxed ramble of trees and green space run through by a pretty brook. Here you'll find the *Golgatha* beer garden (see p.220), packed on summer evenings; Germany's northernmost vineyard; and, atop the hill, the **Cross** (more a Neoclassical spire) from which Kreuzberg gets its name, designed by Schinkel to commemorate the Napoleonic Wars. The view is good, too.

Tempelhofer Feld
Accessible from Columbiadamm Tempelhofer Damm and Oderstr. • **Park** Dawn to dusk • Ⓦ gruen-berlin.de • **Airport tours** Wed & Fri–Sun 1.30pm (2hr; in English and German) • €15 • ☎ 030 20 03 74 41, Ⓦ thf-berlin.de • Ⓤ Platz der Luftbrücke

Technically continental Europe's largest park, **Tempelhofer Feld** (Tempelhof Field) occupies the flatlands of what was once **Tempelhof Airport**, one of the best surviving examples of Nazi architecture. The airport opened in 1923 and became Germany's largest; the current complex dates to 1936–41. After the war it was used for visiting dignitaries and the military, and a light load of small carrier flights, until it finally closed in 2008. In 2010 the airport's vast expanse was turned over to the public as a giant recreational space and now offers designated barbecue and picnic areas, urban gardens, skateboarding and sports areas, plus regular events – and has quickly become one of the city's most beloved outdoor landmarks. A public referendum in 2014 voted against plans to build private residences on the park, and more recently part of the sprawling, historically listed airport building has been used to provide shelter for the city's influx of refugees. To explore the airport's main building, which includes underground tunnels and bunkers, the original check-in hall and basketball courts used by the American military after World War II, you'll need to take an official **tour**.

To the north of the airport buildings, on the Platz der Luftbrücke, is the **Luftbrückendenkmal**, a memorial to the Allied airmen and crew who died during the airlifts that helped defeat the Berlin Blockade of 1948–49 (see box, p.126). The memorial represents the three air corridors used, and forms half of a bridge: the other half, "joined by air", is in Frankfurt.

Eastern Kreuzberg

Eastern Kreuzberg was one of the few areas to avoid total destruction during the war, and among the quickest to revive in the 1950s. Things changed when the Wall was built in 1961, however: with the neighbourhood severed from its natural hinterland in the East, families moved out, houses were boarded up and the area started dying. But at the same

THE BERLIN BLOCKADE (1948–49)

The **Berlin Blockade** was the result of an escalation in tensions between East and West in the late 1940s. These came to a head when the Western zone introduced the Deutschmark as currency in June 1948; the Soviets demanded that their own Ostmark be accepted as Berlin's currency, a move that was rejected by the city's parliament. Moscow's answer to this was an attempt to bring West Berlin to its knees by severing all road and rail links to the Western zones and cutting off the power provided by plants on the Eastern side.

With only one month's food and ten days' coal supply left in the city, the British and Americans realized that they had to support West Berlin, but were unwilling to use military force to push their way in overland. After some consideration it was decided to try and supply the city by air: the Soviets, it was gambled, would not dare risk an international incident – possibly even war – by shooting down Western aircraft. However, there were serious doubts as to whether it was possible to sustain two million people by an airlift. The only previous attempt on a comparable scale – maintaining the German Sixth Army at Stalingrad – had been an utter failure. Berlin's needs were calculated at 4000 tons of supplies per day, yet the available aircraft could carry fewer than 500 tons.

Nevertheless the airlift began on June 26, 1948. At its height nine months later, it had become an around-the-clock precision operation with planes landing or taking off every thirty seconds, bringing 8000 tons of supplies to the city each day. Winter was exceptionally tough. Power cuts and severe food rationing reduced living standards to the level of the immediate postwar period. The Russians made supplies available in the eastern half of the city, but relatively few West Berliners – in a spirited show of defiance – chose to take advantage of them.

The Soviets called off the Blockade in May 1949, but they had been defeated in more ways than one. Though it had cost the lives of 78 airmen and crew and millions of dollars, the airlift thwarted Stalin's attempt to expel the Allies from West Berlin. Moreover for the occupying British and Americans the propaganda value was enormous: aircrews who a few years previously had been dropping bombs on the city now provided its lifeline. Photographs of the "candy bomber" – a USAF captain who dropped chocolate bars and sweets from his plane on small parachutes for the city's children – went around the world. No longer were the occupiers seen as enemies, but rather as allies against the Soviet threat.

time, by providing Berlin's cheapest rents it attracted waves of **immigrant workers** from southern Europe – particularly Turkey – who brought their families and customs. Here too, came the radicals, students and dropouts of the 1968 generation – coming to Berlin because of its national service loophole, and to Kreuzberg for its vast number of abandoned buildings in which to **squat**. It was here that the youth of the Federal Republic came to get involved in alternative politics, making it the place to hang out and hit raucous and avant-garde nightspots. Since the Wall came down the atmosphere has become more apolitical – even if the annual May Day demonstration still traditionally turns into a riot between police and anarchists, extreme-leftists and anti-capitalists. Meanwhile, Turks and other immigrants still thrive and gentrification continues to take hold.

Eastern Kreuzberg's four U-Bahn stops – three on the U1 (whose tracks actually run on elevated tracks in these parts) and one, Moritzplatz, on the U8, provide focal points. On the U1, **Kottbusser Tor** leads to the most overtly Turkish area, with a smattering of alternative businesses and several clubs. U-Bahn **Görlitzer Bahnhof** is much more the hub for "alternative" Kreuzberg. It lies between Wiener Strasse and its northwestern continuation Oranienstrasse, which together form eastern Kreuzberg's bohemian main drag, lined with restaurants, bike shops, café-bars, galleries and alternative boutiques. The next stop east is U-Bahn **Schlesisches Tor**, which leads to an area known as the **Wrangelkiez**, another popular eating and nightlife district. This neighbourhood remains fairly gritty, especially around **Görlitzer Park**, the haunt of itinerant punks and drug pushers, and where several muggings have been reported. U-Bahn Schlesisches Tor is also a handy place to get a bus to the Soviet Memorial in Treptower Park (see p.132). Finally, the area around U-Bahn **Moritzplatz** has developed significantly in recent years, and offers everything from urban gardens and clubs to design stores.

STREET ART: BERLIN'S BLIGHT OR BOUNTY?

Ever since the Wall provided the world's most famous canvas for **graffiti**, this form of self-expression has thrived in Berlin, with artists from all over Europe and North America joining the hundreds of local sprayers. It's everywhere – as the S-Bahn ride through central Berlin reveals – but the greatest concentrations are in central, lower-rent neighbourhoods where older tenements have survived. Kreuzberg is particularly well smothered, with thousands of tags and the occasional more complex piece on every accessible piece of wall – and a few near-inaccessible spots too.

An art form and a sign of a vibrant youth culture, perhaps, but certainly all this daubing costs Berlin around €8m per year to fix, triggering numerous campaigns against it, with some even involving nocturnal helicopter missions with infrared cameras. Polls suggest at least two-thirds of Berliners hate graffiti but many equally feel it is a valid aspect of the city's post-reunification identity.

Alternative Berlin ☎ 062 81 98 264, ⓦ alternative berlin.com. Tours of the more worthwhile pieces in the Spandauer Vorstadt and Kreuzberg; they even offer workshops where you can learn the ropes and get directions to free legal walls.

Overkillshop Köpenicker Str. 195a ☎ 030 61 07 66 33, ⓦ overkillshop.com; Ⓤ Schlesisches Tor. An impressive array of spray cans for sale; their professionalism makes it hard to believe the activity is mostly illegal. See p.239.

Kottbusser Tor and around

Catching U-Bahn line 1 (nicknamed the "Istanbul Express" along this stretch) to **Kottbusser Tor** is a good introduction to eastern Kreuzberg. The intersection around the U-Bahn has its own special feel – think an Istanbul market in an eastern-bloc housing development – and the area around the station is a scruffy, earthy shambles of Turkish street vendors and cafés, the air filled with the aromas of southeast European cooking. Things are at their liveliest on Tuesday and Friday afternoons at the colourful **Türkischer Markt** (Turkish Market), a ten-minute walk south along Kottbusser Strasse – over the **Landwehrkanal** and left down Maybachufer (see p.245). From here, the walk east along the leafy canal at the southern edge of the district passes along Berlin's most attractive stretches of water through a residential district: more reminiscent of Amsterdam than Berlin.

Museum der Dinge

Oranienstr. 25 • Mon & Thurs–Sun noon–7pm • €6 • ☎ 030 92 10 63 11, ⓦ museumderdinge.de • Ⓤ Kottbusser Tor

The delightful **Museum der Dinge** (Museum of Things) successfully presents an interesting array of mostly everyday items – housewares, furniture, knick-knacks and much more – from the nineteenth century to the present day. The range is startling and impressive, from Manoli ashtrays and Art Deco fondue sets to World War II memorabilia. It's a design-fiend's dream, exhibited in a modern, well-organized space on the third floor of a nineteenth-century factory building. A star attraction is the modular "Frankfurt Kitchen" designed by Viennese architect Margarete Schütte-Lihotzky in 1926 – the forerunner of today's fitted kitchen. The exhibition text is in English as well as German, and the institution doubles as the main archive and institution for the German Werkbund movement, a forerunner of Bauhaus.

Moritzplatz and around

Of all the parts of eastern Kreuzberg that have changed in the last few years, the area around **Moritzplatz** has seen the most development. For many decades a rather forlorn ensemble of uninspiring 1970s residential blocks, it has been transformed over the last few years by an influx of contemporary developments ranging from the urban garden of **Prinzessinnengarten** to the **Aufbau Haus** cultural complex, set inside a former piano factory, which encompasses a design and craft shop, alternative theatre space (TAK) and the royal-themed *Parker-Bowles* deli and *Prince Charles* nightclub (see p.227).

7

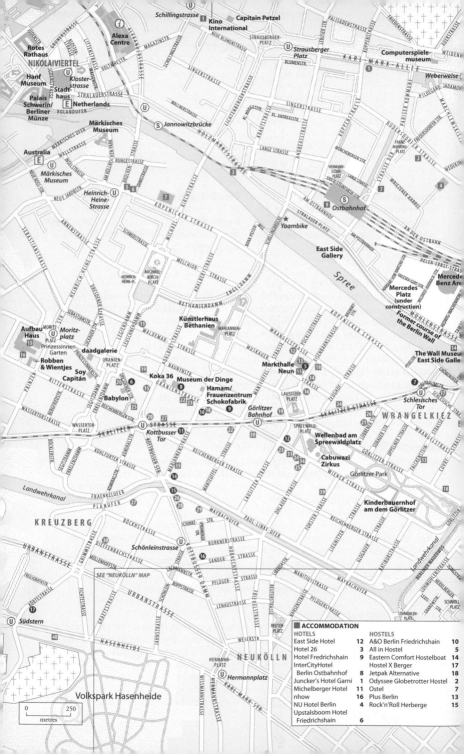

ACCOMMODATION

HOTELS

East Side Hotel	12
Hotel 26	3
Hotel Fredrichshain	9
InterCityHotel Berlin Ostbahnhof	8
Juncker's Hotel Garni	1
Michelberger Hotel	11
nhow	16
NU Hotel Berlin	4
Upstalsboom Hotel Friedrichshain	6

HOSTELS

A&O Berlin Friedrichshain	10
All in Hostel	5
Eastern Comfort Hostelboat	14
Hostel X Berger	17
Jetpak Alternative	18
Odysee Globetrotter Hostel	2
Ostel	7
Plus Berlin	13
Rock'n'Roll Herberge	15

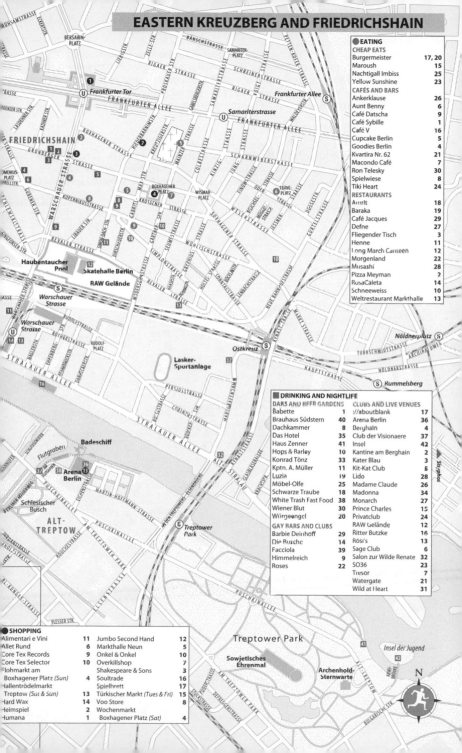

EASTERN KREUZBERG AND FRIEDRICHSHAIN

● EATING

CHEAP EATS
Burgermeister	17, 20
Maroush	15
Nachtigall Imbiss	25
Yellow Sunshine	23

CAFÉS AND BARS
Ankerklause	26
Aunt Benny	6
Café Datscha	9
Café Sybille	1
Café V	16
Cupcake Berlin	5
Goodies Berlin	4
Kvartira Nr. 62	21
Macondo Café	7
Ron Telesky	30
Spielwiese	8
Tiki Heart	24

RESTAURANTS
Amrit	18
Baraka	19
Café Jacques	29
Defne	27
Fliegender Tisch	3
Henne	11
Long March Canteen	12
Morgenland	22
Musashi	28
Pizza Meyman	2
RosaCaleta	14
Schneeweiss	10
Weltrestaurant Markthalle	13

■ DRINKING AND NIGHTLIFE

BARS AND BEER GARDENS
Babette	1
Brauhaus Südstern	40
Dachkammer	8
Das Hotel	35
Haus Zenner	41
Hops & Barley	10
Konrad Tönz	33
Kptn. A. Müller	11
Luzia	19
Möbel-Olfe	25
Schwarze Traube	18
White Trash Fast Food	38
Wiener Blut	30
Würgeengel	20

GAY BARS AND CLUBS
Barbie Deinhoff	29
Die Busche	14
Facciola	39
Himmelreich	9
Roses	22

CLUBS AND LIVE VENUES
://aboutblank	17
Arena Berlin	36
Berghain	4
Club der Visionaere	37
Insel	42
Kantine am Berghain	2
Kater Blau	3
Kit-Kat Club	5
Lido	28
Madame Claude	26
Madonna	34
Monarch	27
Prince Charles	15
Privatclub	24
RAW Gelände	12
Ritter Butzke	16
Rösi's	13
Sage Club	6
Salon zur Wilde Renate	32
SO36	23
Tresor	7
Watergate	21
Wild at Heart	31

● SHOPPING

Alimentari e Vini	11	Jumbo Second Hand	12
Allet Rund	6	Markthalle Neun	5
Core Tex Records		Onkel & Onkel	10
Core Tex Selector	10	Overkillshop	7
Flohmarkt am		Shakespeare & Sons	3
Boxhagener Platz (Sun)	4	Soultrade	16
Hallentrödelmarkt		Spielbrett	17
Treptow (Sat & Sun)	13	Türkischer Markt (Tues & Fri)	15
Hard Wax	14	Voo Store	8
Heimspiel	2	Wochenmarkt	
Humana	1	Boxhagener Platz (Sat)	4

Prinzessinnengarten

Prinzenstr. 35–38/Prinzessinnenstr. 15 • Daily 10am till late (weather dependent) • Ⓦ prinzessinnengarten.net • Ⓤ Moritzplatz

One of the first projects to transform the area, the now beloved **Prinzessinnengarten** was started in 2009 by a small collective of volunteers on an area of former wasteland. Today it features an organic café (from 11am), workshops on everything from beekeeping to gardening and other community events.

Neukölln

Much like Eastern Kreuzberg, **Neukölln** is a district dominated by Turkish, Arab and Kurdish immigrants; walking along its arterial roads **Karl-Marx-Strasse** and **Sonnenallee**, between budget department stores and Middle Eastern greengrocers,

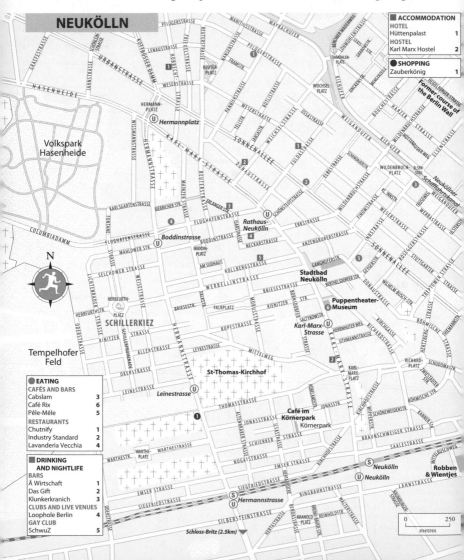

NEUKÖLLN

■ **ACCOMMODATION**
HOTEL	
Hüttenpalast	1
HOSTEL	
Karl Marx Hostel	2

● **SHOPPING**
Zauberkönig	1

● **EATING**
CAFÉS AND BARS	
Cabslam	3
Café Rix	6
Pêle-Mêle	5
RESTAURANTS	
Chutnify	1
Industry Standard	2
Lavanderia Vecchia	4

■ **DRINKING AND NIGHTLIFE**
BARS	
Ä Wirtschaft	1
Das Gift	2
Klunkerkranich	3
CLUBS AND LIVE VENUES	
Loophole Berlin	4
GAY CLUB	
SchwuZ	5

it's not hard to imagine yourself in the Istanbul suburbs. But as hip young bargain-seekers have moved in so parts of the area have grown increasingly gentrified, particularly the streets south of the Landwehrkanal (see p.127) between Kotbusser Damm and Pannierstrasse – which are often nicknamed **Kreuzkölln** – and the **Schillerkiez**, the streets east of Tempelhofer Park. Here, and along the district's "hip-strip", **Weserstrasse**, visitors can find a slew of shabby-chic cafés and late-night bars, underground galleries and boutiques, usually interspersed with casinos and budget ethnic restaurants.

Once upon a time Neukölln was Rixdorf, a tiny village outside Berlin studded with windmills and boasting fantastic views from its impressive hillsides; a few reminders of those times remain in the charming old heart of **Alt-Rixdorf**. In came the Industrial Revolution and away went the hills (used for buildings as the city expanded), and Rixdorf developed into a district of entertainment and revelry – so much so that it was renamed Neukölln in 1912 in an effort to change its riotous image. Farther south is the more residential district of Britz, whose chief focus of interest is the **Schloss-Britz**.

7

Volkspark Hasenheide

Entrances on Hasenheide, Columbiadamm and Karlsgartenstr. • Open access • ⓤ Hermannplatz

Originally used as a hunting ground for the Grand Elector in the seventeenth century, then as parade grounds for the Prussian military, the green expanse of the **Volkspark Hasenheide** in the heart of Neukölln is today the domain of local sun-worshippers and picnickers. The long rows of trees are reminders of the former shooting ranges but little else of the park's past remains; instead, the main draws are a popular petting zoo, restaurant and a (summer-only) open-air stage for music, films and theatre. A popular funfair is also held in the southern part of the park each May.

Puppentheater-Museum

Karl-Marx-Str. 135 • Mon–Fri 9am–3pm, Sun 11am–4pm • €4, children €3 • ☎ 030 687 81 32, ⓦ puppentheater-museum.de • ⓤ Karl-Marx-Strasse

The quirky **Puppentheater-Museum** houses a charming mix of glove and shadow puppets, vintage show posters and marionettes from all over the world, some from famous stage and puppet designers. What's on show changes each year and is supplemented by performances, temporary exhibitions and workshops. Guided tours, covering the history of puppetry and the theatre, are also available.

Alt-Rixdorf

ⓤ Karl-Marx-Strasse

The most obvious reminders of Neukölln's medieval origins lie between Karl-Marx-Strasse and Sonnenallee in the area known as **Alt-Rixdorf**. A wander around the cobbled streets – centred on historical **Richardplatz** – reveals a centuries-old blacksmith's business, attractive churches and the remains of the district's eighteenth-century Bohemian village – founded for Protestant refugees fleeing persecution – with its cute houses and attractive gardens.

Körnerpark

Schierker Str. 8 • Tues–Sun 10am–6pm • Free • ☎ 030 90 23 92 876, ⓦ körnerpark.de • ⓤ/Ⓢ Neukölln

Refined **Körnerpark** might not be the biggest park in Neukölln, but it is easily the prettiest – a stark contrast to the vast, featureless expanse of nearby Tempelhofer Park. With its manicured hedges, elegant promenades and marble fountains, it provides an ideal setting for wedding photos and summertime events such as galas, fairs and concerts. The attractive, ivy-covered **Orangerie** – unique among Berlin's parks – is a highlight, and contains the elegant covered *Café im Körnerpark* (till 8pm), which has a popular outdoor terrace in the warmer months.

Schloss-Britz

Alt-Britz 73 • Tues–Sun 11am–6pm • €3 • ☎ 030 60 97 92 30, ⓦ schlossbritz.de • ⓤ Parchimer Allee then a 10min walk or bus #M46 to Fulhamer Allee

Three stops south of U-Bahn Neukölln, in the former village – now a Neukölln district – of Britz, is the splendid manor house, **Schloss-Britz**. Built in the late eighteenth century and later redesigned, the house is now a museum offering architectural and aesthetic insights into the nineteenth-century *Gründerzeit* era. As well as a series of elaborately reconstructed rooms – including oak-panelled men's and ladies' meeting rooms and a striking, stucco-covered banqueting hall – there's a farmyard area and pleasant park.

Treptower Park

ⓢ Treptower Park/Plänterwald, or bus #265 from Schlesisches Tor

Now chiefly of interest for its large and sobering **Soviet Memorial** to troops killed in the Battle of Berlin, **Treptower Park** was originally built as a park for Berlin's nineteenth-century tenement-dwellers. By 1908 it had more than thirty dance halls and restaurants; later, during the interwar years, it became a well-known assembly point for revolutionary workers about to embark on demonstrations or go off to do battle with the Brownshirts.

Until the *Wende* most park visitors were either East Berliners out for a day at Spreepark, a (now defunct) GDR-era amusement park, or Soviet citizens arriving by the busload to pay their respects at the memorial. The pleasant harbour area close to the Treptower Park S-Bahn station is one attraction, but the main hub of activity is now on and around the Insel der Jugend, further south along the Spree.

The Sowjetisches Ehrenmal

At the heart of Treptower Park, the **Sowjetisches Ehrenmal** (Soviet Memorial) commemorates the Soviet Union's 305,000 estimated casualties during the Battle of Berlin in April and May 1945; five thousand of them were buried here. It's best approached from the arched entrance on the south side of Puschkinallee. A little way to the south of here is a sculpture of a grieving woman representing the Motherland, to the left of which a broad concourse slopes up towards a viewing point flanked by two vast triangles of red granite, fashioned from stone bought from Sweden by the Nazis to furnish Berlin with projected victory monuments. From the viewing point, a long sunken park of mass graves of the Red Army troops is lined by sculpted frescoes of stylized scenes from the Great Patriotic War and quotes from Stalin with German translations. These lead the way to the centrepiece: a vast symbolic statue and typical piece of Soviet gigantism, built using marble from Hitler's Chancellery. More than 11m high, and set on top of a hill modelled on a *kurgan* or traditional warrior's grave of the Don region, it shows an idealized Russian soldier clutching a saved child and resting his sword on a shattered swastika. Inside the plinth is a memorial crypt with a mosaic in true Socialist Realist style, showing Soviet citizens (soldiers, mother, worker, peasant and what looks like an old-age pensioner) honouring the dead.

The rest of the park

Archenhold Sternwarte Alt-Treptow 1 • Wed–Sun 2–4.30pm; tours Thurs 8pm, Sat & Sun 3pm; museum free, tours €6 • ☎ 030 536 06 37 19, ⓦ sdtb.de

The rest of the park conceals a couple of low-key attractions, including the **Karpfenteich**, a large carp pool just south of the memorial, and, a little to the east of here, the **Archenhold Sternwarte** (Archenold Observatory), which has the longest refracting telescope in the world; check the website for stargazing sessions. The park continues north of Puschkinallee, where you'll also find *Haus Zenner* (see p.220), a riverside *Gaststätte* whose origins go back to the eighteenth century.

East of here is the **Insel der Jugend** (Island of Youth), a small island in the Spree reached via the **Abteibrücke** (Abbey Bridge), an ornamental footbridge built by French prisoners of war in 1916. The island was originally the location of an abbey, but now the main attraction is the venue *Insel* (see p.227).

Returning across the bridge, you can walk northwest back to the S-Bahn station via a grass-lined boardwalk – rowing boat and paddleboat rental are available nearby (from €8/hr). At the northern tip of the boardwalk, you'll find a very tasty *Imbiss* stand serving fresh smoked fish. Southeast from the bridge lies the closed Spreepark but the surrounding **Plänterwald** woods, which cover a couple of square kilometres, are the main draw. You can also take a cruise around the surrounding waterways (see box, pp.24–25).

Friedrichshain

East of the Spree from Kreuzberg, the former East Berlin borough of **Friedrichshain** is overwhelmingly residential. Comprehensively destroyed during the war, it lost more than two-thirds of its buildings – as much as any Berlin district – and today is virtually all of GDR vintage. A magnet for lefties, anarchists and students, it has managed to resist the levels of gentrification borne by neighbouring Prenzlauer Berg thanks to an organized squatter scene, activist demos and the occasional car-burning frenzy; one such riot in July 2016, sparked by a squat eviction, injured over two hundred police and protestors. Even so, its defiantly unkempt environs have succumbed to an invasion of cafés and bars clustered on **Simon-Dach-Strasse** and around **Boxhagener Platz**, and construction is underway on the commercial **Mercedes-Platz** development opposite the East Side Gallery. Meanwhile, various clubs continue to inhabit old industrial buildings on the area's fringes.

The district gathers around two major arterial roads: **Warschauer Strasse**, which forms the link to Kreuzberg and **East Side Gallery**, Berlin's longest surviving stretch of Wall; and the grand **Karl-Marx-Allee**, connecting to Alexanderplatz and Mitte. Forming Friedrichshain's northwestern boundary is **Volkspark Friedrichshain**, one of the eastern city's oldest and nicest parks; it's best accessed from Prenzlauer Berg (see p.137).

Oberbaumbrücke

Ⓤ Warschauer Strasse

The handsome, neo-Gothic **Oberbaumbrücke** connects Friedrichshain with Kreuzberg, across the Spree. The double-decker bridge (and its name) dates back to the eighteenth century when it was originally constructed – from wood – and acted as a gateway to the city. A new version opened in 1896, designed by architect Otto Stahn. In 1945 the bridge was partly destroyed by the Wehrmacht to stop the Red Army crossing it, and afterwards ended up straddling the American and Soviet sectors. When the Berlin Wall went up in 1961 the bridge became part of East Berlin's border with West Berlin; when it fell in 1989, it was restored to its former appearance with a new steel middle section designed by Spanish architect Santiago Calatrava. Today the bridge stands as a symbol of unity between Friedrichshain and Kreuzberg (and is the site of a friendly "water battle" in summer). Look out for the neon *Stone Paper Scissors* installation by Thorsten Goldberg – a political statement about the apparent arbitrariness of decisions to grant immigration or asylum status.

East Side Gallery

Mühlenstr. • Ⓦ eastsidegallery-berlin.de • Ⓤ/Ⓢ Warschauer Strasse

Trailing the banks of the River Spree is the **East Side Gallery**, a 1.3km stretch of surviving Berlin Wall painted with political and satirical murals that is now one of the city's best-known landmarks. Originally painted just after the Wall fell the murals resonate with the attitude and aesthetics of the time: some are imaginative, some trite and some impenetrable, but one of the most telling – and often imitated – shows Brezhnev and Honecker locked in a passionate kiss, with the inscription, "God, help me survive this deadly love". Given their outdoor and exposed nature, all the paintings are subject to vandalism and decay; the original artists have been invited back to repaint their works a couple of times, most recently to mark the twentieth anniversary of the *Mauerfall* in 2009.

In 2012 the removal and auctioning-off of portions of the Wall – to enable the building of a luxury development – sparked outrage and protests, but the residences went ahead anyway, paving the way (symbolically) for a commercial overhaul of the adjacent area. Now renamed **Mercedes Platz** (Ⓦmercedes-platz.de), the development will expand on the existing **Mercedes-Benz Arena**, with a mix of bars, hotels, a large mall and bowling complex, and is scheduled to be completed in 2018.

The Wall Museum East Side Gallery

Mühlenstr. 78–80 • Daily 10am–7pm • €12.50 • ☏ 030 63 96 26 62, Ⓦ thewallmuseum.com • Ⓤ/Ⓢ Warschauer Strasse or Ⓤ Schlesisches Tor

Opened in 2016, the **Wall Museum East Side Gallery** is one of the city's newest museums – and yet another that tells the story of the Wall years. The bonus here is the location, right where the longest section of the wall still stands, as well as the highly multimedia nature of the presentations, which feature interactive displays, original newsreel footage and filmed interviews with former border guards. Texts are in English as well as German.

Warschauer Strasse and around

Ⓤ/Ⓢ Warschauer Strasse

Warschauer Strasse is Friedrichshain's main cross street. It's fairly dull, so tram #M10 is a welcome way to speed your journey – better still to peel off at the first opportunity down Revaler Strasse where graffiti paves the way to the sprawling **RAW Gelände** complex. A former train repair yard, the complex has been converted into a hub of alternative culture complete with indoor skate hall and climbing wall, several bars and clubs, including a street-art-themed beer garden (see p.228), and a surprisingly chic outdoor swimming pool (see p.250). Opposite lies the **Simon-Dach-Strasse**, at first glance an ordinary tree-lined residential street, but also the hub of the local nightlife scene with good cafés, restaurants and bars, many with outdoor seating. At its northern end Simon-Dach-Strasse joins Boxhagener Strasse: a block to the right lies the leafy **Boxhagener Platz**, which bustles with a popular food market on Saturdays (see p.245) and a flea market on Sundays (see p.246).

Karl-Marx-Allee

Ⓤ Frankfurter Tor, Ⓤ Weberweise or Ⓤ Strausberger Platz

A vast 1.9km boulevard lined with 1950s and 1960s communist housing developments, **Karl-Marx-Allee** (or Stalinallee, as it was known in the 1950s) is a mixed bag. The monumentalist *Zuckerbäckerstil* (wedding-cake style) towers that bookend the street at Frankfurter Tor and Strausberger Platz are architecturally impressive, and the apartments among the Eastern Bloc's finest. Yet, despite the wide pedestrian boulevards on each side, the street gets relatively little foot traffic, which gives it a bit of an eerie and empty feel and makes it traditionally quite difficult for businesses to survive here.

The best way to explore – despite the thundering traffic – is to walk (or bike) in either direction between Frankfurter Tor and Strausberger Platz, taking a break at **Café Sybille** at Karl-Marx-Allee 72 (see p.211), which has a good little exhibition on the history of the Stalinallee and the protests of 1953 (see box, p.121).

Computerspielemuseum

Karl-Marx-Allee 93a • Daily except Tues 10am–8pm • €8 • ☏ 030 60 98 85 77, Ⓦ computerspielemuseum.de • Ⓤ Weberweise

The **Computerspielemuseum** (Computer Games Museum), is a fun and highly interactive tribute to gaming. It features pretty much every kind of arcade machine and games console ever made, from the pioneering *Nimrod* (1951) and legendary *Pong* (1972), right up to more recent classics like *Tomb Raider*. There are plenty of opportunities to punch keyboards and waggle joysticks – and even get a jolly old electric shock via the two-player Pain Station.

KULTURBRAUEREI

Prenzlauer Berg and around

Northeast of Mitte, the district of Prenzlauer Berg was originally a densely populated working-class district. It was fought over street by street during the war, which meant that many of its hallmark turn-of-the-twentieth-century tenement blocks survived, along with its leafy cobbled streets. In the GDR days, this was a uniquely vibrant and exciting corner of East Berlin, home to artists and young people seeking an alternative lifestyle. After the *Wende*, the venerable atmosphere, central location and low rents quickly made this a lively and fashionable district. Merciless gentrification, with an influx of wealthy creative types and middle-class families, has dullened the ambience a little, though the area still retains a distinctive buzz, with lots of independent bars and cafés, boutiques and health-food stores, plus the buzzy Sunday flea market at the Mauerpark.

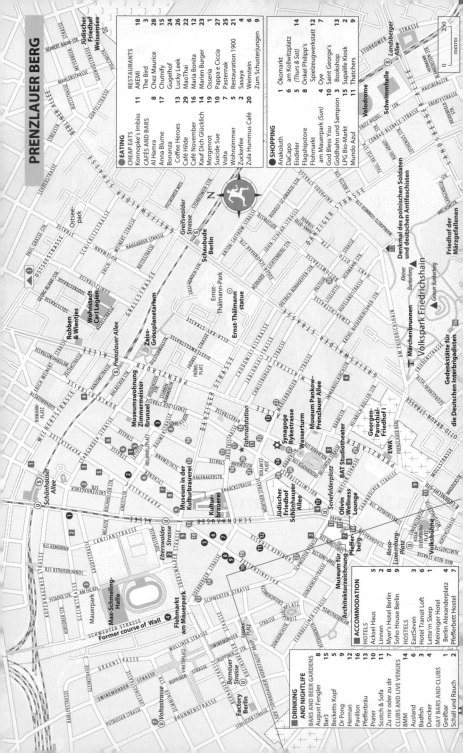

Prenzlauer Berg is strung out along several arterial roads that are well served by public transport from Alexanderplatz or Hackescher Markt. From Alexanderplatz, Otto-Braun-Strasse, which becomes Greifswalder Strasse heads northeast, passing close to **Volkspark Friedrichshain**, one of the city's best parks and final resting place for victims of the 1848 revolution. Further north, between Greifswalder Allee and **Prenzlauer Allee** are the GDR-era **Ernst-Thälmann-Park**, behind which lurk the **Zeiss Planetarium** and the modernist **Wohnstadt Carl Legien** housing estate, while to the northeast is the increasingly middle-class district of **Weissensee**, where you'll find the city's largest **Jewish cemetery**.

To the west of Prenzlauer Allee, another arterial road – **Schönhauser Allee** – runs close to the former East–West border and is the main route to some of Prenzlauer Berg's most gentrified streets. This is an area to explore on foot, taking in sights such as the **Kulturbrauerei** and **Kollwitzplatz**, which was once another important area for Jews, as a large nearby **cemetery** and a restored **synagogue** attest.

North of Prenzlauer Berg lies the district of **Pankow** (not to be confused with the larger borough of Pankow – Berlin's most populous – which also includes Prenzlauer Berg and Weissensee among its thirteen districts). Once home to much of the GDR's elite, Pankow offers a Baroque summer palace and pretty surrounding park, as well as a sedate, almost village-like atmosphere as it gives way to rural Brandenburg.

Just over the famous Bösebrücke, where the Bornholmer Strasse border crossing was first officially breached in November 1989, lies the former Western district of **Gesundbrunnen**, whose most obvious source of interest to visitors is its series of fascinating wartime and Cold War bunkers. Though now a separate locality, Gesundbrunnen was formerly part of **Wedding**, the district to its west. Known for their large immigrant populations and edgy charm, both Gesundbrunnen and Wedding are up-and-coming areas peppered with the kind of underground spaces that were once common in Prenzlauer Berg during the 1990s.

8

ARRIVAL AND GETTING AROUND PRENZLAUER BERG AND AROUND

Prenzlauer Berg The quickest way to get to Prenzlauer Berg is by public transport from Alexanderplatz. Tram #M4 travels up Greifswalder Strasse to Weissensee, the #M2 passes along Prenzlauer Allee, and the #M1 can be taken from Hackescher Markt, Oranienburg Strasse and other parts of Mitte up to Eberswalder Strasse and Schönhauser Allee. The U2 stops at Senefelder Platz and Eberswalder Strasse, both useful starting points to generally explore the district, and S-Bahn stations Prenzlauer Berg and Schönhauser Allee, both on the city's Ringbahn, are also

convenient for its northern sections.

Pankow Tram #M1 continues through Prenzlauer Berg to various parts of Pankow, including Ⓤ Pankow (where the U2 also terminates), the pleasant Bürgerpark and the Rathaus. Ⓢ Pankow is also on several lines: the S2, S8 and S9.

Wedding and Gesundbrunnen The U8 is the best underground line for Wedding, stopping at several key stations within the district including Bernauer Strasse on the former border, Pankstrasse and Osloer Strasse. On the S-Bahn, Gesundbrunnen and Wedding are the most useful stops.

Volkspark Friedrichshain

Am Friedrichshain 1; entrances also on Danziger Str. and Friedenstr. • Open 24hr, though some inside areas are closed after dark • Bus #100 or #200, or tram #M4

Just within the limits of the Friedrichshain district, **Volkspark Friedrichshain** is one of the city's oldest and largest parks. It's a sprawling place with lots of recreational possibilities and a wealth of impressive monuments. At its western entrance is the **Märchenbrunnen** (Fairytale Fountain), a neo-Baroque arcade and fountain with statues of characters from Brothers Grimm stories. Intended as a gift to tenement-dwelling workers, it was put up in 1913 at the instigation of Social Democratic members of the city council, in direct contravention of the Kaiser's wishes. A few hundred metres southeast stands the **Gedenkstätte für die Deutschen Interbrigadisten**, a monument to the German members of the International Brigades who fought against the fascists in the Spanish Civil War. Of the five thousand Germans (including many leading communists) who went to Spain, only two thousand returned.

The park's two main hills, **Grosser Bunkerberg** and **Kleiner Bunkerberg**, were created when a million cubic metres of rubble from bombed-out Berlin were dumped over the ruins of a flak gun and control tower respectively. In between the two is a small, tree-shaded lake, sport and recreation centre, plus giant outdoor chess sets. Set on a grassy slope a little to the east, the **Denkmal des polnischen Soldaten und deutschen Antifaschisten** commemorates the joint fight of the Polish army and German resistance against the Nazis. Given the feelings most Germans and Poles had for each other, the sentiments expressed seem rather unconvincing.

Friedhof der Märzgefallenen

Ernst-Zinne-Weg • Daily 10am–6pm (exhibition closed Wed) • Free • ☎ 030 21 47 27 23, ⓦ friedhof-der-maerzgefallenen.de

Just off Landsberger Allee, the **Friedhof der Märzgefallenen** is a monument to victims of an upheaval closer to home. This is where many of the 183 Berliners killed by the soldiers of Friedrich Wilhelm IV during the revolution of March 1848 were buried, their interment attended by eighty thousand of their fellow citizens. Only a few of the original gravestones survive, but the dead of 1848 have been joined by 33 of those killed in the November Revolution of 1918, commemorated by a statue of a *Rote Matrose* or "Red Sailor" at the cemetery entrance, reflecting the role played in the revolution by Imperial navy sailors. An **exhibition**, housed in a shipping container next to the cemetery, covers the history of the March Revolution, the development of the barricade battles and of the cemetery.

Georgen-Parochial-Friedhof I

Greifswalder Str. 229–234 • Times vary according to season, though usually 8am–dusk • ⓤ Rosa-Luxemburg-Platz or tram #M4

The **Georgen-Parochial-Friedhof I** is a venerable and overgrown affair dating back to the early nineteenth century, with some elaborate tombstones and vaults. Many of the memorials bear shrapnel and bullet scars, an indication of just how intense the fighting during the Battle for Berlin must have been; even the city's graveyards were fought for inch by inch.

Ernst-Thälmann-Park and around

Entrances on Danziger Str., Greifswalder Str. and Prenzlauer Allee • Open 24hr • ⑤ Greifswalder Strasse

The **Ernst-Thälmann-Park** is a prime example of former-GDR civic window-dressing. Here, a model housing development is set in and around a small park fronted by a gigantic marble sculpture of the head and clenched fist of Ernst Thälmann, the pre-1933 communist leader who was imprisoned and later murdered by the Nazis. Floodlit and guarded around the clock by police in pre-*Wende* days, his likeness is now usually daubed with graffiti, and the concrete terrace on which it stands is favoured by local skateboarders. About four thousand people, mostly from the ex-GDR elite, live here in high-rise buildings with restaurants, shops, nurseries, a youth theatre and a swimming pool all immediately at hand.

Zeiss-Grossplanetarium

Prenzlauer Allee 80 • Tues–Thurs 9am–6pm, Fri 9am–11pm, Sat & Sun 2–11pm; show times vary – call or check online • €8 • ☎ 030 421 84 50, ⓦ sdtb.de • ⑤ Prenzlauer Allee

A massive silver golf ball set back from bustling Prenzlauer Allee, the **Zeiss-Grossplanetarium** was, when it was built in 1987, one of Europe's largest and most modern stellar theatres, with its giant silver dome measuring 23m across. Reopened in 2016 following a renovation, its auditorium hosts entertaining and impressive astronomy-themed film and music programmes.

Wohnstadt Carl Legien

🚇 Prenzlauer Allee

Northeast of Prenzlauer Allee's distinctive, yellow-brick 1890s S-Bahn station – one of the best-looking in the city – is the **Wohnstadt Carl Legien** model housing development which was built during the Weimar era according to plans by renowned architect Bruno Taut. With his associate Franz Hillinger, Taut wanted to create mass housing that broke away from the city's tenement-house concept. Basing their design on work already done in the Netherlands, they diffused the angularity of their apartment blocks with corner windows and balconies, and left open areas between them to create cheerful, bright back yards.

Museumswohnung Zimmermeister Brunzel

Dunckerstr. 77 • Mon, Tues & Thurs–Sat 11am–4.30pm • €3 • ☎ 030 445 23 21, 🌐 ausstellung-dunckerstrasse.de • 🚇 Prenzlauer Allee

Though it sits today on a leafy, very middle-class street, the **Museumswohnung Zimmermeister Brunzel** (Museum Apartment of Master Carpenter Brunzel) was once one of hundreds of *Mietskasernen*, or tenement flats, that sprouted in districts like Prenzlauer Berg to house workers between the 1870s and 1890s. Virtually all followed standardized plans that were loosely based on the traditional Berlin courtyard layout of places like the Hackesche Höfe (see p.72). The smartest flats faced the street, while the dowdiest were tucked away on the top floors above the rear courtyard. All were pretty basic, with lavatories on the common landings. Much of this world was lost in the war and following generations of home improvements, but one apartment has been well preserved and reconstructed to help provide, along with the other two institutions of the Museum Pankow (see p.142 & p.144), a rare social history of Berlin.

Inhabited until the 1990s, this particular flat had seen few renovations, making it an ideal candidate for restoration and careful furnishing to re-create the past. Short **tours** – usually in German unless you request an English-speaking guide ahead of time reveal a kitchen with an ice-powered fridge; a muted brown decor that minimized the impact of singeing from gas-powered lanterns; and a cupboard above the front door designed as a bedroom for the maid. Wall displays, also in German (with some English translations here and there), explain how, despite the basic conditions, such apartments denoted a certain social standing, with only master craftsmen and the like able to afford them. Less skilled workers slept in poor houses or became *Trockenwohner*, temporary tenants who rented digs in new apartment blocks that were still too damp to be properly habitable; their presence literally helped the houses dry quicker, hence their nickname.

Jüdischer Friedhof Weissensee

Herbert-Baum-Str. 45 • April–Sept Mon–Thurs 7.30am–5pm, Fri 7.30am 2.30pm, Sun 8am–5pm; Oct–March Mon–Thurs 7.30am–4pm, Fri 7.30am–2.30pm, Sun 8am–4pm; male visitors should keep their heads covered, skullcaps loaned free at the cemetery office, to the right of the entrance • ☎ 030 92 53 330, 🌐 jewish-cemetery-weissensee.org • 🚇 Greifswalder Strasse or tram #M4 to Albertinenstr.

The **Jüdischer Friedhof Weissensee** (Jewish Cemetery Weissensee) opened in 1880 when the Schönhauser Allee cemetery (see p.140) had finally been filled, becoming Europe's largest Jewish cemetery – its 115,600 graves spreading over the equivalent of 86 football pitches. Immediately in front of the entrance, a poignant memorial "to our murdered brothers and sisters 1933–45" from Berlin's Jewish community takes the form of a circle of tablets bearing the names of all the large concentration camps. Beyond here are the cemetery administration buildings (where information is available), with the cemetery itself stretching back from the entrance for about 1km: row upon row of headstones, with the occasional extravagant family monument including some Art Nouveau graves and mausoleums designed by Ludwig Mies van der Rohe and Walter Gropius (for example, the grave of Albert Mendel). More moving are the four hundred urns containing the ashes of concentration camp victims (Lot G7), and the headstones on the hollow graves of those whose remains were never found or identified. A handful of well-tended postwar

8

graves near the administration buildings are, paradoxically, symbols of survival – witness to the fact that a few thousand Berlin Jews did escape the Holocaust and that the city still has a small Jewish community (see pp.78–79).

Senefelderplatz and around

Although it's not an official boundary, **Senefelderplatz** forms a natural segue between Mitte and Prenzlauer Berg, connecting with Rosa-Luxemburg-Platz to the south and Kollwitzstrasse and Schönhauser Allee to the north. Previously known as **Pfefferberg** (Pepper Hill) after the brewer Joseph Pfeffer, who founded the Pfefferbräu brewery nearby – the name is still in use, and applies to the complex occupying the old brewery site just below Senefelderplatz, which now features an arts centre, start-up offices and the *Pfefferbett Hostel* (see p.195) and *Pfefferbräu* brewery-restaurant (see p.223). The square was later renamed after the inventor of the lithographic process (Alois Senefelder), a statue of whom stands near the U-Bahn station with his name appearing on the base in mirror script, as though on a lithographic block.

Museum für Architekturzeichnung

Christinenstr. 18a • Mon–Fri 2–7pm, Sat & Sun 1–5pm • €5 • ☎ 030 43 73 90 90, ⓦ tchoban-foundation.de • ⓤ Senefelderplatz

Housed within the Pfefferbräu complex, the **Museum für Architecturzeichnung** (Museum of Architectural Drawing), as its name suggests, displays architectural plans and drawings from leading international architects of the twentieth and twenty-first centuries. These include Yakov Chernikhov, Mies van der Rohe, Aldo Rossi, Zaha Hadid, as well as its founder, Sergei Tchoban.

Jüdischer Friedhof Schönhauser Allee

Schönhauser Allee 22 • Mon–Thurs 8am–4pm, Fri 7.30am–1pm; male visitors should keep their heads covered, skullcaps loaned free at the entrance • ☎ 030 441 98 24, ⓦ jg-berlin.org • ⓤ Senefelderplatz

The **Jüdischer Friedhof Schönhauser Allee**, Prenzlauer Berg's Jewish cemetery, opened in 1827 when space ran out at the Grosse Hamburger Strasse cemetery (see p.76). Almost 22,000 people are buried here, including painter Max Liebermann, publisher Leopold Ullstein, composer Giacomo Meyerbeer and German-Jewish banker Joseph Mendelssohn (son of philosopher Moses Mendelssohn). But for most, this last resting place is an anonymous one: in 1943 many of the gravestones were smashed and a couple of years later the trees under which they had stood were used by the SS to hang deserters found hiding in the cemetery during the final days of the war; a memorial stone near the entrance reminds visitors of the event, by stating "You stand here in silence, but when you turn away do not remain silent". Those stones that could be restored are now housed in the cemetery's **lapidarium**.

Wasserturm

Knaackstr. 23 • Dates and times of tours are posted on the main door on the tower's southern side • ⓤ Senefelderplatz or tram #M2 to Knaackstr.

The handsome 30m-high cylindrical brick **Wasserturm** (water tower) was constructed in 1877 by the English Waterworks Company on the site of a pre-industrial windmill, and has become one of Prenzlauer Berg's best-known landmarks. During GDR times it was used to store canned fish but was later abandoned. Today the refurbished tower is home to much-coveted wedge-shaped apartments (formerly belonging to the tower's operators), while the underground reservoir space is home to sporadic art and music events, and is sometimes open for tours. It's surrounded by a small urban **park** with a landscaped garden, playground and table-tennis tables.

The tower lies close to the site of a (now torn-down) machine house that was infamous for Nazi atrocities. Once the party came to power the SA turned it into a torture chamber – the bodies of 28 of their victims were later found in the

underground pipe network. A **memorial stone** close to the site on Knaackstrasse commemorates them: "On this spot in 1933 decent German resistance fighters became the victims of fascist murderers. Honour the dead by striving for a peaceful world."

Museum Pankow – Prenzlauer Allee

Prenzlauer Allee 227–228 • Mon–Fri 9am–6pm • Free • ☎ 030 90 29 53 917, ⓦ berlin.de/museum-pankow/ • Ⓤ Senefelderplatz or on #M2 to Knaackstr.

Spread across the first floor of a yellow-brick former school on the Prenzlauer Allee side of the Wasserturm area, the largely overlooked **Museum Pankow – Prenzlauer Allee**, the principal of the three institutions that make up the Pankow Museum, documents the history of Prenzlauer Berg and its mainly poor working-class inhabitants from the nineteenth century to today. The permanent exhibition consists mainly of photos and text (German only) displayed along school-like corridors, though a couple of large rooms and a separate building across the courtyard are occasionally given over to more modern, multimedia exhibitions on local themes, such as the several Jewish schools that used to dot the district.

Synagoge Rykestrasse

Rykestr. 53 • Open for services only: Nov–March Fri 6pm; April–Oct Fri 7pm, Sat 9.30am • ☎ 030 88 02 81 24, ⓦ jg-berlin.org • Ⓤ Senefelderplatz

Built by Johann Hoeniger at the start of the twentieth century, the gorgeous Neoclassical **Synagoge Rykestrasse** (inaugurated in 1904) is one of Germany's oldest and biggest – and one of Berlin's loveliest – synagogues. The building survived *Kristallnacht* in 1938 as it was located between "Aryan" apartment buildings, although precious Torah scrolls were damaged and rabbis and congregation members were deported to Sachsenhausen. The synagogue was used as stables during the war, but was finally restored to its former glory by architects Ruth Golan and Kay Zareh in 2007, who used black-and-white photographs and a €6 million budget to lavishly re-create the remarkable original.

Kollwitzplatz and around

Ⓤ Senefelderplatz

A Prenzlauer Berg focal point, **Kollwitzplatz** is named after artist **Käthe Kollwitz**, of whom there's a large statue in the little park on the square. From 1891 to 1943 she lived on nearby Kollwitzstrasse (then Weissenburgerstrasse; a plaque marks the house at no. 56a), creating political and pacifist art that you can see in the Käthe Kollwitz Museum (see p.112). The square is also home to the well-regarded *Restauration 1900*, a restaurant established long before the Wall came down (see p.213).

The streets around Kollwitzplatz were among the first to be gentrified when the Wall fell in 1989 and today many of its yuppie pioneers have settled and had children, explaining the overwhelming presence of little ones in the district. It's a lovely place to come for a stroll – three playgrounds and a leafy park lie within the square and endless restaurants, cafés and smart boutiques are scattered around its perimeter. Saturdays are especially popular thanks to the extensive **farmers' market** that takes over a couple of blocks along Kollwitzstrasse, offering everything from organic meat and fish, fruit and veg, sweets and coffee and clothes (see p.245). A smaller (and less crowded) organic market also takes place on Thursdays.

Husemannstrasse and around

The street running north from Kollwitzplatz is **Husemannstrasse**, a nineteenth-century tenement street that was restored to its former glory in late-GDR days and turned into a kind of living museum in an attempt to recall the grandeur of old Berlin. After the *Wende*, restoration projects transformed the neighbouring streets too, covering raddled facades with fresh stucco and installing new wrought-iron balconies. A quiet stroll north on Husemannstrasse finds its abrupt end at the busy **Danziger Strasse**, where trams and traffic and a mix of cheap and trendy shops fight for space and attention.

Eberswalder Strasse and around

U-Bahn Eberswalder Strasse is Prenzlauer Berg's busiest hub; under the station and the elevated railway tracks along Schönhauser Allee lies the famous **sausage kiosk** *Konnopke's* (see p.211). North of the station, Schönhauser Allee assumes its true identity as Prenzlauer Berg's main drag, an old-fashioned shopping street that, thanks to its cobbles and narrow shop facades, still retains a vaguely prewar feel – an atmosphere also evoked by the area's principal focus, the **Kulturbrauerei** events centre, which fills the city block southeast of the U-Bahn station.

Crossing the main road south of the Kulturbrauerei leads to **Oderberger Strasse** and **Kastanienallee**, both of which have some of the best **cafés**, **bars** and **restaurants** in eastern Berlin. Keep your eyes open and you may spot one or two buildings whose facades have not been touched since the *Wende*, scarred with bullet and shell marks inflicted during the Battle of Berlin.

Kulturbrauerei

Schönhauser Allee 36; entrances on Sredzkistr. and Danziger Str. • ☎ 030 44 35 26 14, ⓦ kulturbrauerei-berlin.de •
ⓤ Eberswalder Strasse

The building complex now known as the **Kulturbrauerei** (literally, Culture Brewery) dates back originally to the middle of the 1800s, and was expanded for major local brewer Schultheiss in the 1890s. Its pseudo-Byzantine style was conceived by royal architect Franz Heinrich Schwechten, whose high-profile works include the Kaiser-Wilhelm-Gedächtniskirche in City West (see p.112). The main entrance, a narrow gateway on Danziger Strasse, quickly widens to reveal a spacious inner courtyard that often serves as a live-music venue, and is flanked by old workshops which house a theatre, exhibition spaces, a *Literaturhaus*, a few shops, clubs and bars and a mainstream cinema, as well as a small museum. The southern gateway of the brewery leaves the complex on Sredzkistrasse, near the bustle of Schönhauser Allee.

Museum in der Kulturbrauerei

Knaackstr. 97 • Tues–Sun 10am–6pm, Thurs 10am–8pm • Free • ☎ 030 46 77 77 911, ⓦ hdg.de • ⓤ Eberswalder Strasse

The small **Museum In der Kulturbrauerei** opened in 2013. Using its chosen theme of **Alltag in der DDR** ("Everyday Life in the GDR"), it traces the glaring, frightening and sometimes farcical differences between the official projection of life under the SED and the reality of the daily grind: objects include a Trabant with a bolted-on roof tent, and a comical, unusably narrow chair, constructed to make a satirical point about how all the best GDR products were exported.

SUNDAY IN THE MAUERPARK: FLEA MARKETS AND KARAOKE

One of Berlin's best-loved flea markets, **Mauerpark Flohmarkt** (Bernauer Str. 63;
☎ 029 77 24 86, ⓦ flohmarktimmauerpark.de; ⓤ Bernauer Strasse or ⓤ Eberswalder Strasse) is a city institution, popular every Sunday with hungover students, bargain-hunters, families and bemused-looking, shade-wearing clubbers who come to scan the food stalls, clothes shops and nostalgic junk that seems to extend forever. The selection is eclectic, to say the least: bikes (freshly stolen and resprayed), 1950s cutlery, faded jigsaws, new and vintage clothes, GDR memorabilia, banana telephones and record players, bibles and lots of vinyl and CDs. As with most flea markets, there's a good amount of junk among some genuine antiques. Adjacent to the market you'll find the actual **Mauerpark**, a strip of landscaped green that was once the site of a stretch of Berlin Wall and the associated death strip, loomed over by the Friedrich-Ludwig-Jahn-Sportpark and the Max-Schmeling-Halle. When the weather's warm check out the weekly **karaoke** session in the "bearpit", which attracts massive crowds on Sundays between 1.30pm and 5pm – officials have tried to stop it a few times, but public protest seems always to bring it back.

Pankow

From Prenzlauer Berg, Schönhauser Allee leads north to the district of **Pankow**, which during the GDR days was always much more than just another East Berlin suburb. For years Pankow's villas and well-maintained flats were home mainly to members of the upper reaches of East Berlin society: state-approved artists and writers, scientists, East Berlin resident diplomats and the *Parteibonzen* (party bigwigs) of the old regime. The name of the suburb was also appropriated by one of the ex-GDR's best-known rock bands, in a satirical dig at the social hierarchy of the workers' and peasants' state. Today, it's a pleasant enough district, alternating between fairly dull working-class and livelier middle-class areas, its predominantly traditional pubs and restaurants spiced up by the occasional trendy spot. The main drag is **Breite Strasse**, but more attractive (read: gentrified) are streets like Florastrasse, a couple of blocks to the south, and the belt of parks – the **Schlosspark**, **Bürgerpark** and **Volkspark Schönholzer Heide** – that lie to the north.

Breite Strasse

Ⓤ/Ⓢ Pankow

At the junction of Berliner Strasse and **Breite Strasse**, on a mid-road island that used to be the village green, is the **Alte Pfarrkirche**, Pankow's old parish church and oldest building. It dates back to the fifteenth century but was extensively restored in 1832, a project in which Schinkel had a hand, resulting in an unusual-looking neo-Gothic jumble. At the western end of Breite Strasse, at the end of the main strip of chain stores and boutiques, is the early twentieth-century neo-Baroque **Rathaus**, a red-brick affair of fanciful gables, towers and cupolas.

Museum Pankow – Heynstrasse 8

Heynstr. 8 • Tues, Thurs & Sun 10am–6pm • Free • ☎ 030 481 40 47, ⓦ berlin.de/museum-pankow/ • Ⓤ/Ⓢ Pankow

While Berlin's workers could hope to afford lodgings such as those at Museumswohnung Zimmermeister Brunzel (see p.139), the city's wealthy could aspire to apartments like **Heynstrasse 8**, beautifully preserved as a branch of **Museum Pankow**. Formerly the apartment of factory owner Fritz Heyn – who was important enough to have the street named after him – it is quite the bourgeois palace. Showy chandeliers preside over heavy furniture, while scores of decorative Prussian touches – eagles, prints of Bismarck – are all part of the rich over-decoration. None of this extends to the servants' quarters around the back, of course.

Schloss Schönhausen

Tschaikowskistr. 1 • **Palace** April–Oct Tues–Sun 10am–6pm; Nov–March (guided tours only in winter) Sat & Sun 10am–5pm • €6 **Garden** Daily 8am–sunset • Free • ☎ 0331 96 94 200, ⓦ spsg.de • Tram #M1 or bus #250 from Ⓢ Pankow

Lurking in the leafy grounds of the **Schlosspark**, north of Breite Strasse, is the **Schloss Schönhausen**, former home of Elisabeth Christine, the estranged wife of Frederick the Great. The Schloss was built at the beginning of the eighteenth century and given an extensive but run-of-the-mill face-lift in 1764. During GDR days it could only be admired from a distance, as it served first as official residence of President Wilhelm Pieck, from 1949 to 1960, and then as the old regime's most prestigious state guesthouse under Walter Ulbricht. Since then it has been revamped and reopened to visitors who can admire some of the original royal residence interiors, the offices of the GDR's president and the suites of its most honoured guests. The palace is also surrounded by a slightly dreary 1950s-era garden that you're free to wander around.

Volkspark Schönholzer Heide

Herman-Hesse-Str. • Ⓢ Schönholz

The heath-like **Volkspark Schönholzer Heide** is Pankow's most impressively wild park. In its southwest corner lies a humble **cemetery**, a burial ground for civilians who died in the final days of the Battle of Berlin. Most are women or children and for many the

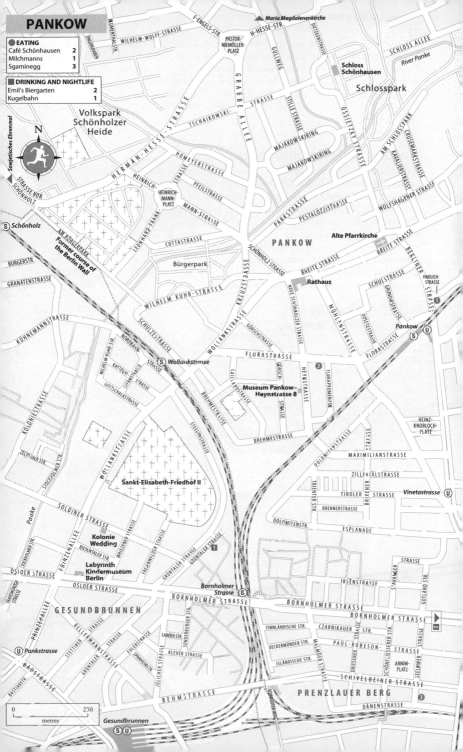

PANKOW

EATING
Café Schönhausen	2
Milchmanns	1
Sgaminegg	3

DRINKING AND NIGHTLIFE
| Emil's Biergarten | 2 |
| Kugelbahn | 1 |

Maria Magdalenenkirche

Schloss Schönhausen

River Panke

Schlosspark

Volkspark Schönholzer Heide

Sowjetisches Ehrenmal

N

STRASSE VOR SCHÖNHOLZ

PASTOR-NIEMÖLLER-PLATZ

BLUMENTHALSTR.

WILHELM-WOLFF-STRASSE

F-ENGELS-STR.

H-HESSE-STR.

ZINGERGRABEN

TSCHAIKOWSKISTRASSE

GRAEBE ALLEE

STILLESTRASSE

GUILWEG

DIETZGENSTRASSE

SCHLOSS ALLEE

AM SCHLOSSPARK

OSSIETZKY STRASSE

GRÜNMARKSTRASSE

KUHALESTRASSE

WOLFSHAGENER STRASSE

HERMAN–HESSE–STRASSE

ROMEYERSTRASSE

HEINRICH-STRASSE

HEINRICH-MANN-PLATZ

PFEILSTRASSE

MANN-STRASSE

LEONHARD-FRANK-STRASSE

MAJAKOWSKIRING

MAJAKOWSKIRING

PARKSTRASSE

PESTALOZZISTRASSE

PARKSTRASSE

PANKOW

Alte Pfarrkirche

BREITE STRASSE

BELLERMANNSTRASSE

AM BÜRGERPARK
Former course of the Berlin Wall

Schönholz

BURGERSTR.

GRANATENSTRASSE

KÜHNEMANNSTRASSE

COTTASTRASSE

Bürgerpark

WILHELM KÜHR-STRASSE

SCHULZESTRASSE

NORDBAHN

SCHÖNHOLZ STRASSE

KREUZSTRASSE

BREITE STRASSE

Rathaus

NEUE SCHÖNHOLZER STRASSE

SCHULSTRASSE

GÖRSCHSTRASSE

MÜHLENSTRASSE

DUSEESTRASSE

FLORASTRASSE

SCHULSTRASSE

BERLINER STRASSE

HADLICH-STRASSE

Pankow

Wollankstrasse

WOLLANKSTRASSE

WILHELM-KÜHR-STR.

KATTEGATSTRASSE

GOTSCHALKSTRASSE

STERNSTRASSE

FLURASTRASSE

GAILLAPPSTRASSE

Museum Pankow-Heynstrasse 8

BREHMESTRASSE

STEGMANNSTRASSE

GÖRSCH STRASSE

HEYNSTRASSE

FLORAPROMENADE

STRASSE

STRASSE

HEINZ-KNOBLOCH-PLATZ

KOLONIESTRASSE

ZECHLINER STR.

SPIEKERMANN STR.

WOLLANKSTRASSE

Sankt-Elisabeth-Friedhof II

BREHMESTRASSE

DOLOMITENSTRASSE

MAXIMILIANSTRASSE

ZILLERTHALSTRASSE

TRIENTER STR.

TIROLER STRASSE

BRIXENER STRASSE

Vinetastrasse

BRENNERSTRASSE

DOLOMITENSTR.

ESPLANADE

Paake

SOLDINER STRASSE

FRINZNALLEE

Kolonie Wedding

BIESENTALER STR.

WALTERSTALER STRASSE

FREIENWALDER STRASSE

GRÜNTALER STRASSE

GODINTALER STRASSE

STRASSE

STANGER

IBSENSTRASSE

STRASSE

GOTLAND STR.

OSLOER STRASSE

Labyrinth Kindermuseum Berlin

OSLOER STRASSE

GRÜNTALER STRASSE

Bornholmer Strasse

BORNHOLMER STRASSE

BORNHOLMER STRASSE

BORNHOLMER STRASSE

GESUNDBRUNNEN

TRAVEMÜNDER STR.

PRINZENALLEE

Pankstrasse

BADSTRASSE

BASTIANSTR.

STETTINER STRASSE

BELLERMANNSTRASSE

GRÜNTALERSTRASSE

SPANHEIMSTR.

EULERSTRASSE

JÜLICHER STRASSE

KLEVER STRASSE

LABÖER STR.

SONDERBURGER STR.

FINNLÄNDISCHE STR.

UECKERMÜNDER STR.

ISLÄNDISCHE STR.

CZARNIKAUER STR.

DRIESENER STRASSE

MALMÖER STR.

SCHÖNFLIESSER STR.

PAUL–ROBESON–STRASSE

ARNIM-PLATZ

SEELOWER STR.

BEHMSTRASSE

SCHIVELBEINER STRASSE

PRENZLAUER BERG

DÄNENSTRASSE

0 — 250
metres

Gesundbrunnen

dates of birth and death, and in some cases even names, are unknown, a stark reminder of the many untold stories that are lost in the dehumanizing chaos of war. In contrast is the grandeur of the huge **Sowjetisches Ehrenmal** (Soviet Memorial), at the northwestern edge of the park. Here dozens of communal graves contain the remains of 13,200 soldiers killed during the same battle. Military hierarchy is observed in death as in life, with officers occupying the central lower tiers and privates around the fringes of the grounds.

Wedding and Gesundbrunnen

With their long-standing immigrant population and increasing influx of creative expats, **Wedding** and **Gesundbrunnen** – two adjoining districts that lie west of Prenzlauer Berg (and form a northern extension of the borough of Mitte) – are generally regarded as outlier areas. Both areas have something of a frontier feel in places – there are still entire streets or blocks decorated with Turkish flags and dominated by Middle Eastern cafés – though as increasing numbers of European and North American expats move in for cheap rent and their keep-it-real, multicultural atmosphere, a low-key arts scene has developed that spans cultural complexes like the **Uferhallen** (Uferstr. 8; ⓦuferhallen.ag), home to Uferstudios (see p.237), several underground bars and clubs and the occasional trendy restaurant, and the

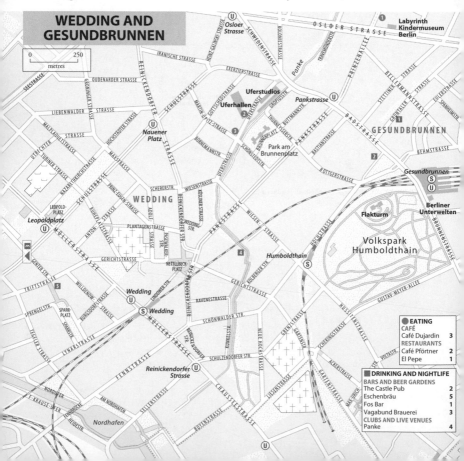

● EATING	
CAFÉ	
Café Dujardin	3
RESTAURANTS	
Café Pförtner	2
El Pepe	1

■ DRINKING AND NIGHTLIFE	
BARS AND BEER GARDENS	
The Castle Pub	2
Eschenbräu	5
Fos Bar	1
Vagabund Brauerei	3
CLUBS AND LIVE VENUES	
Panke	4

longer-established **Kolonie Wedding**. The area's other historic and recreational highlights include wartime **bunkers** and an indestructible **flak tower**, the pleasant Volkspark Humboldthain and – for families – the **Labyrinth Kindermuseum Berlin** (see p.257).

Kolonie Wedding

Soldiner Str. 92 • ☏ 030 49 91 46 50, ⓦ koloniewedding.de • Ⓢ Bornholmer Strasse

One of the area's most interesting artistic developments is **Kolonie Wedding**, a collaboration between the local district, housing company DEGEWO and local artists, which started way back in 2001. The collective operates a number of small galleries and nightlife spaces around the Soldiner Strasse area, putting on a steady stream of art shows, concerts, pop-up culinary, community events and more.

The Gesundbrunnen bunkers

Tours €11–14; times vary (see website for details) • Tickets available from the Berliner Unterwelten office in the southern entrance hall of ⓤ Gesundbrunnen from 10am on the day • ☏ 030 49 91 05 17, ⓦ berliner-unterwelten.de • ⓤ/Ⓢ Gesundbrunnen

Around U- and S-Bahn **Gesundbrunnen**, several underground passages and World War II **bunkers** are open for fascinating and unusual tours run by the non-profit Berliner Unterwelten. Those covered here are in **English**; tours in other languages are listed on the website.

Tour 1: Dark Worlds

Tour 1: Dark Worlds explores the large, well-preserved main Gesundbrunnen bunker, one of hundreds used towards the end of the war by Berliners waiting out the Allied bombing raids. It was here also where many women committed suicide rather than be raped by advancing Russians. As a valuable part of the U-Bahn network the Gesundbrunnen bunker was one of the few spared from destruction during Germany's demilitarization, and today its rooms and passages contain countless artefacts from the time. Among them are various items cleverly crafted from military waste immediately after the war: helmets became pots, gas masks became oil lamps and tyres were used to sole shoes. Equally interesting are the finds from the Nazi bunker beneath the Neues Reichskanzlei (see p.40), including paintings by SS artists and an Enigma machine. Other remnants unearthed from around town and displayed here come from the Battle of Berlin and include the contents of the pockets of two Volksturm recruits – a fifteen-year-old and a 69-year-old – killed in the fray. These items all come from modern-day excavations of Berlin, and weapons and bombs are still regularly found by building crews, sometimes with deadly consequences – as one display shows.

Tour 2: From the Flak Towers to Mountains of Debris

Tour 2: From the Flak Towers to Mountains of Debris goes into the Volkspark Humboldthain opposite the Gesundbrunnen station to explore two of the seven levels of the **Flakturm Humboldthain** anti-aircraft gun tower that proved too beefy for the Soviets to destroy. It is cold down there, even in summer, and you won't be welcome in flip-flops or sandals for safety reasons.

Tour 3: Subways and Bunkers in the Cold War

Tour 3: Subways and Bunkers in the Cold War investigates another World War II bunker, but also goes into Cold War-era tunnels and bunkers, including refuges – like that at Pankstrasse U-Bahn – that were equipped for West Berliners in case of a nuclear strike, and underground labyrinths that were blocked to prevent East Germans escaping to the West.

Tour M – Under the Berlin Wall

Tour M – Under the Berlin Wall explores tunnels dug under the Berlin Wall by would-be escapees and relates stories of success – three hundred people managed to escape the GDR in this way – and failure.

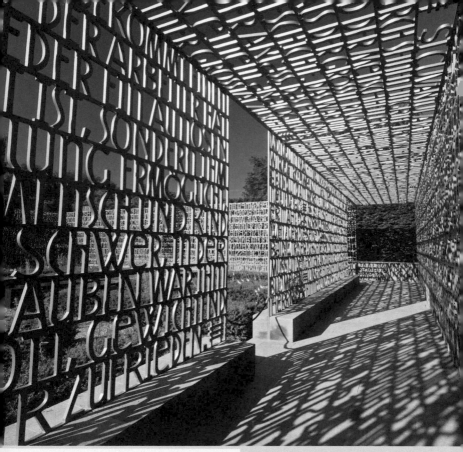

GÄRTEN DER WELT

The eastern suburbs

Berlin's eastern suburbs have inevitably changed significantly since reunification but they're still in many ways the best place to gain some insights into East Berlin, not least because of the masses of GDR-style *Plattenbauten* (high-rises) built during the 1960s and 1970s and still dwelt in by many East Berliners. Today the blocks are also home to a lot of the city's recent immigrants, too – as well as the longstanding Vietnamese community – and the socialist buildings are interspersed with incongruous post-Wall malls and other new developments, creating a more heterogeneous vibe. The southern fringes also feature some genuine rural breathers that offer a break from the city. All of the places described here are easily reached on public transport by S- or U-Bahn, though a slower tram or bus journey will allow you to get more of a feel for this part of the city.

9

The most important sights in this part of town relate to the GDR secret police, or Stasi, particularly the Stasi's prison, **Gedenkstätte Hohenschönhausen**, and their headquarters, now the **Stasi Museum Berlin**, in the borough of **Lichtenberg**; both are sombre places. The rewarding **Deutsch-Russisches Museum Berlin-Karlshorst**, in the same borough, concerns itself with twentieth-century German–Russian relations so is hardly uplifting either. Thankfully in the midst of them lies the more cheerful **Tierpark Berlin**, eastern Berlin's sprawling and pleasantly wooded zoo.

East of Lichtenberg is **Marzahn-Hellersdorf**, a late-1970s satellite town and perhaps Berlin's least obvious sightseeing destination. The borough's silo-like apartment blocks and soulless shopping precincts stretch out towards the edge of the city and its 1990s reputation was, if anything, even more foreboding than Lichtenberg's. But despite the monotonous and sometimes bleak feel of Marzahn-Hellersdorf (especially in winter), there is a small medieval village at its heart, the excellent Gärten der Welt, and a complete lack of pretension that's at odds with central Berlin's incessant hipster feel.

Probably the most pleasant day out in the eastern suburbs is **Köpenick**, in the far southeast, which has an attractive small-town feel and surprisingly unspoiled **lakes**, particularly the Grosser Müggelsee with its thick belt of surrounding woods.

Lichtenberg

East of Friedrichshain lies the traditionally working-class district of **Lichtenberg**, part prefabricated postwar mass dwellings and part traditional tenement blocks, with heavy concentrations of industry in the north and south. Until the mid-nineteenth century Lichtenberg was little more than a country town and popular Sunday outing destination for Berliners. With industrialization, however, the familiar Berlin tenements sprang up and the area's rustic past was soon forgotten. Hard hit by the collapse of the old order, its reputation for a hotbed of neo-Nazism is mostly – but not completely – exaggerated these days, as more immigrants and international students take advantage of the area's relatively cheap rents.

Gedenkstätte Hohenschönhausen

Genslerstr. 66 • Daily 9am–6pm • Free (including audio guide) • Tours (in English at 10.30am, 12.30pm & 2.30pm) €6 • ☎ 030 98 60 82 30, ⓦ stiftung-hsh.de • Tram #M5 from Hackescher Markt or bus #256 from ⓤ/Ⓢ Lichtenberg – get off either tram or bus at Freienwalder Str.; the entrance is at the end of the road

A potent antidote to *Ostalgie* – nostalgia for the GDR (see box, p.65) – is a visit to the grim former Stasi prison at **Gedenkstätte Hohenschönhausen** (Hohenschönhausen Memorial), which offers an insight into the fear and oppression upon which the regime was founded. Hohenschönhausen began life in 1945 as a **Soviet Special Camp**, with 4200 inmates penned in together in horrendous living conditions. By 1946 around a thousand had died. Officially most of these were interned because of suspected Nazi links, but in most cases there was no evidence. Underground torture chambers became vital for acquiring "confessions" that usually led to decades of forced labour – though ultimately almost all prisoners were declared innocent by the Russian authorities in the 1990s. In 1951 the Stasi (see box, p.151) inherited the facility and turned it into a **remand prison** that was quickly blotted from city maps. The smallest sign of resistance or opposition to the state, including comments written in personal letters – which were all routinely steamed open – would earn you a spell here. Typically, you'd be caught unawares on your way to work, bundled into a van, and then brought to the site.

The prison's permanent exhibition, **Inhaftiert in Hohenschönhausen** (Imprisoned in Hohenschönhausen), focuses on the experiences of political prisoners during their detention. It rotates about five hundred rare objects at a time (there are some 15,000 in the still-growing collection), including clothing and tools used by guards and prisoners,

9 banned publications, and one of the vans – famously disguised as a food delivery truck to remain clandestine – routinely used to pick up prisoners. In addition there are over three hundred historical photographs and interactive "media stations" offering interviews with former inmates, digitized historical sources (including internal Stasi publications) and touch-screen maps. One section addresses the lives of the Stasi prison staff and enquires about their motives.

Tours, meanwhile, led by former prisoners deliver an absorbing insight into the psychological rather than physical abuse that followed in the solitary world of padded cells, tiny exercise yards, endless corridors and interrogation rooms.

THE EASTERN SUBURBS

THE STASI

East Germany's infamous Staatssicherheitsdienst (State Security Service), or **Stasi**, kept tabs on everything in the GDR. It ensured the security of the country's borders, carried out surveillance on foreign diplomats, business people and journalists, and monitored domestic and foreign media. It was, however, in the surveillance of East Germany's own population that the organization truly excelled. Very little happened in the GDR without the Stasi knowing about it: files were kept on millions of innocent citizens and insidious operations were orchestrated against dissidents, real and imagined. By the time of the *Wende* the Stasi had a budget of £1 billion, 91,000 full-time employees and 180,000 informers within the East German population; figures brought into context by the more puny, albeit more ruthless, 7000-strong Nazi Gestapo.

At the beginning of 1991 former citizens of the GDR were given the right to see their Stasi files. Tens of thousands took the opportunity to find out what the organization had recorded about them, and, more importantly, who had provided the information; many a friendship and not a few marriages came to an end as a result. The process of unravelling truths from the archives also provided material for numerous stories, including Timothy Garton Ash's **book** *The File: A Personal History* (see p.290) and the **film** *Das Leben der Anderen* (*The Lives of Others*; see p.296). Not all documents survived, though; many were briskly shredded as the GDR regime collapsed, resulting in an unenviable task for one government organization who spent literally years piecing them together to bring people to justice, thankfully with some success.

Stasi Museum Berlin

Ruschestr. 103 • Mon–Fri 10am–6pm, Sat & Sun 11am–6pm; free guided tours in English every Sat & Sun at 3pm • €6 • ☎ 030 553 68 54, Ⓦ stasimuseum.de • Ⓤ Magdalenenstrasse

Haus 1, the main building in the huge former Stasi headquarters complex, is now the **Stasi Museum Berlin**, which uncovers the massive surveillance apparatus of the GDR's secret police. Walking along the bare, red-carpeted corridors and looking at the busts of Lenin and Felix Dzerzhinsky – founder of the Soviet Cheka, models for both the KGB and Stasi – it all seems part of a distant past, not an era that ended little more than a quarter of a century ago. But then the obsessively neat office and apartment of **Erich Mielke**, the Stasi head from 1957 to October 1989, makes it all the more immediate. Everything is more or less just as he left it: white and black telephones stand on the varnished wooden desk as though awaiting calls, and a room at the back – though technically off-limits – allows a peek into the private area he used when he stayed in the building overnight.

Overhauled in 2013 with new photos and information, the rest of the museum contains fascinating displays on the development and strategies of the institution. As well as the well-known main protagonists, there are profiles of clandestine collaborators, glass cabinets showing bugging devices and cameras – concealed in everything from watering cans, jackets and radios – as well as medals, uniforms and other associated paraphernalia. Infographics break up the texts (which are all in English as well as German), revealing aspects such as the number of Stasi agents that defected to the West and the impressive extent of the counterculture that existed in areas like Prenzlauer Berg. The campaign by East Germans against the regime, culminating in the huge protest rally at Alexanderplatz on November 4, 1989, is also the theme of an outdoor exhibition.

A small but cute café ensconced in one of the rooms sells coffee and soft drinks and a scale model in the foyer gives an overview of the immense size of the original complex – of which Haus 1 was only a part.

Alte Pfarrkirche Lichtenberg

Am Loeperplatz • ☎ 030 97 10 49 44, Ⓦ kirche-alt-lichtenberg.de • Ⓢ Frankfurter Allee, then a 10min walk or bus #M13

Just north of the rather sinister-looking Rathaus Lichtenberg is the improbably rustic **Alte Pfarrkirche** (Old Parish Church), a reminder of Lichtenberg's village origins. The stone walls date from the original thirteenth-century structure, but the rest is more modern, with the spire tacked on as recently as 1966.

9

Dong Xuan Center

Herzbergstr. 128–139 • Daily except Tues 10am–8pm • ☎ 030 55152038, ⓦ dongxuan-berlin.de • Ⓢ Landsberger Allee, then #M8 to Herzbergstr./Industriegebiet

The idiosyncratic **Dong Xuan Center**, opened in 2005, makes for a fascinating day-trip and insight into Berlin's Vietnamese community, with lots of food stalls and restaurants and plenty of opportunities for kitsch and cheap shopping. The several hangar-style buildings, located in an industrial no-man's-land, contain a slew of stores – retail and wholesale – that hawk everything from groceries to cut-price clothing and jewellery.

Gedenkstätte der Sozialisten

Gudrunstr. • 1km or so northeast of Ⓤ / Ⓢ Lichtenberg

Lichtenberg's **Zentralfriedhof Friedrichsfelde** (Friedrichsfelde Central Cemetery), also known as the **Gedenkstätte der Sozialisten** (Memorial to the Socialists), is perhaps only for die-hard fans of GDR relics. Its centrepiece is a 4m chunk of red porphyry bearing the inscription *Die Toten mahnen uns* – "The dead remind us" – commemorating the GDR's socialist hall of fame from Karl Liebknecht and Rosa Luxemburg onwards. A tablet bears a list of names that reads like the street directory of virtually any town in pre-*Wende* East Germany, recording the esoteric cult figures of the workers' and peasants' state in alphabetical order; until 1989 the East Berlin public were cajoled and coerced into attending 100,000-strong mass demonstrations here. The whole thing actually replaced a much more interesting Mies van der Rohe-designed memorial that stood here from 1926 until the Nazis destroyed it in 1935. Altogether more uncompromising, featuring a huge star and hammer and sickle, the original memorial caused problems for Mies van der Rohe when he came before Joseph McCarthy's House Un-American Activities Committee in 1951. The Gedenkstätte is also the burial place of Walter Ulbricht, the man who decided to build the Berlin Wall, and Wilhelm Pieck, the first president of the GDR.

Tierpark Berlin

Entrances on the eastern side of Am Tierpark • Daily: March & Oct 9am–6pm; April–Sept 9am–6.30pm; Nov–Feb 9am–4.30pm; check online for exact dates and times • €13, under-16s €6.50 • ☎ 030 51 53 10, ⓦ tierpark-berlin.de • Ⓤ Tierpark

Lichtenberg's sprawling zoo, **Tierpark Berlin**, ranks as one of the largest in Europe and a thorough exploration of its wooded grounds could easily absorb the better part of a day. Virtually every species imaginable, from alpaca to wisent (European bison), can be found here, including rare Przewalski horses, which have been bred here over the years, helping bring the breed back from the edge of extinction. The public animal feedings and skill-training presentations (with giraffes and polar bears) are popular, and both younger and older visitors alike might want to seek out Edgar, the park's baby elephant, born in 2016.

Schloss Friedrichsfelde

Daily: summer 10am–6pm; winter 10am–4.30pm • Free with zoo entrance • ☎ 030 51 53 14 07, ⓦ schloss-friedrichsfelde.de • Ⓤ Tierpark

Hidden away in the grounds of the zoo, just beyond an enclosure of lumbering pelicans, is **Schloss Friedrichsfelde**, a Baroque palace showcasing some fine eighteenth- and nineteenth-century decor and furnishings. The poet Theodor Fontane was exaggerating when he described it as the Schloss Charlottenburg of the East – though the ornamental grounds are pretty and the restored ballroom, which hosts concerts and other events, is quite striking.

Deutsch-Russisches Museum Berlin-Karlshorst

Zwieseler Str. 4 • Tues–Sun 10am–6pm • Free • ☎ 030 50 15 08 10, ⓦ museum-karlshorst.de • Ⓢ Karlshorst

For many years you were likely to hear as much Russian as German spoken in the sub-district of **Karlshorst** as the area was effectively a Russian quarter, thanks to the presence of large numbers of Soviet soldiers and their dependants. The Allied powers accepted the unconditional surrender of the German armed forces in a Wehrmacht engineers' school here on May 8, 1945, and went on to establish their Berlin headquarters nearby. For many years, Karlshorst was fenced off and under armed guard, out of bounds to ordinary East Germans. Later, they were allowed back in part, but the area retained an exclusive cachet, its villas housing the GDR elite – scientists and writers – or used as foreign embassy residences.

The Russians finally left Karlshorst in 1994, but a reminder of their presence endures as the **Deutsch-Russisches Museum Berlin-Karlshorst**, in the building where the German surrender was signed. When the GDR still existed, this museum was officially known as the "Soviet Military Museum of the Unconditional Surrender of Fascist Germany in the Great Patriotic War 1941–45", though it now conveys a self-consciously balanced view of the tumultuous German–Russian relations in the twentieth century.

Refurbished in 2014, the museum now has a pleasantly contemporary feel, the several darkened rooms surrounding the historic main hall tracing the mercurial and turbulent relationship between the two countries between 1914 and 1945. As well as poignant photos, relevant books and propaganda posters from both sides, the accompanying texts (in German, Russian and English) provide very good insight into the complicated nature of the major events during these eras, and displays showcase uniforms, medals and weapons. Highlights include a huge stained-glass depiction of the Hero of Treptow statue at Treptower Park's Soviet Memorial (see p.132), a 3D depiction of the capture of the Reichstag by Soviet troops (complete with battle sound effects), and a looped recording of the 1941 radio address by Molotov announcing the German invasion.

Marzahn-Hellersdorf

Like Lichtenberg, **Marzahn-Hellersdorf** earned itself a fairly rough reputation during the tough post-Wall years. Also like Lichtenberg, that reputation has endured somewhat, but is arguably less justified than ever, thanks to an influx of immigrants and students moving to the district in recent years. Marzahn was one of the GDR's model new towns of the late 1970s – part of Honecker's efforts to solve his country's endemic housing shortage by providing modern apartments in purpose-built blocks with shopping facilities and social amenities to hand. The result here was several kilometres of high-rise developments housing 250,000 people, where, like similar developments in the West, things never quite worked according to plan, with the usual problems surfacing.

Most people will see enough of the area by travelling to S-Bahn Springpfuhl and then taking tram #M8 past endless high-rises to **Alt-Marzahn**, the original, slightly quaint and now hugely incongruous district centre. Complete with a green, pub, cobbled streets, war memorial and parish church, something of a village past survives. Admittedly it's not a very pleasant past: from 1866 the fields of the area were used as *Rieselfelder*, designated for the disposal of Berlin's sewage. Marzahn acquired a **Dorfkirche** (village church) in neo-Gothic style a few years later, built by Schinkel's pupil Friedrich August Stüler.

From here you can wander to Landsberger Allee, to take in the immensity of all the high-rises and then bus to the **Gärten der Welt**, a large park with a collection of ornamental gardens. This bus goes on, though very indirectly, to the **Gründerzeitmuseum Mahlsdorf**, a museum that brings together a fine collection of late nineteenth-century furnishings from the beginning of the German Empire.

Gärten der Welt

Eisenacher Str. 99 • March & Oct 9am–6pm, April–Sept 9am–8pm • €5 • ☎ 030 700 90 66 99, ⓦ gruen-berlin.de • ⓜ Cottbusserplatz, then bus #195

Opened in 1987 as part of the city's 750th birthday celebrations, **Gärten der Welt** (Gardens of the World) forms an attractive oasis amid Marzahn's high-rises. The park is dotted with decorative features, pleasant nooks and playgrounds, but its star turns are

9

the trio of exotic gardens. The sprawling and ornate **Chinese Garden** is the biggest in Europe, with a restaurant, snack bar and a teahouse (see p.214), while the **Japanese Garden** is much more regimented, with water and rock features competing for space with shrubs and bonsai trees. The park also boasts several other themed gardens, including a **Balinese Garden** in a warm damp greenhouse where you'll find a traditional rural family home amid the ferns and orchids.

Gründerzeitmuseum Mahlsdorf

Hultschiner Damm 333, Mahlsdorf • Wed & Sun 10am–6pm; guided tours only – call ahead to arrange one in English • €4.50 • ☎ 030 567 83 29, Ⓦ gruenderzeitmuseum.de • Tram #62 to Alt-Mahlsdorf from Ⓢ Mahlsdorf

The suburb of **Mahlsdorf**, about 5km sou^t ast of Alt-Marzahn, is no cultural centre, but it does boast one of the city's most notable museums, the excellent **Gründerzeitmuseum Mahlsdorf**, a collection of furniture and household gear from 1880–1900, the period known as the *Gründerzeit* or "foundation time", when the newly united Germany was at its imperial peak. The museum's founder, the late transgender writer **Charlotte von Mahlsdorf** (born Lothar Berfelde), put the collection together during GDR days when such an undertaking was by no means an easy task, creating a representative *Gründerzeit* apartment by taking the complete contents of rooms and relocating them in this eighteenth-century manor house. Depending on your tastes the result is either exquisite or over the top, but either way the museum is fascinating and certainly worth the long haul out to the suburbs – don't miss the basement, filled with furnishings from the *Mulack-Ritze*, a famous early twentieth-century Berlin *Kneipe* that originally stood on Mulackstrasse in the Scheunenviertel.

Köpenick

A slow-moving little place on the banks of the River Spree near the southeast edge of Berlin, **Köpenick**, easily reached by S-Bahn from Alexanderplatz, is an ideal escape from the city centre and a convenient base for exploring Berlin's southeastern lakes, in particular the **Müggelsee**, with its appealing shoreline towns of Friedrichshagen and Rahnsdorf. Also easily accessible are the **Müggelberge**, Berlin's 150m-high "mountains".

Köpenick was a town in its own right during medieval times, and though it has since been swallowed up by Greater Berlin, it still retains a distinct identity. The presence of a number of major factories meant that it always had a reputation as a "red" town. In March 1920, during the Kapp Putsch attempt, workers from Köpenick took on and temporarily drove back army units who were marching on Berlin to support the coup. The army later returned, but its success was short-lived as the putsch foundered – thanks mainly to a highly effective general strike. This militancy continued into the Nazi era: on January 30, 1933, the day Hitler came to power, a red flag flew from the chimney of the brewery in the suburb of Friedrichshagen. This defiance was punished during the *Köpenicker Blutwoche* ("Köpenick Week of Blood") in June that year, during which the SA swooped on Social Democrats and communists. Five hundred people were imprisoned and 91 murdered.

Altstadt

Tram #62, #63 or #68 from Ⓢ Köpenick

To walk to Köpenick's old town from the S-Bahn station, follow Borgamannstrasse to Mandrellaplatz, location of Köpenick's **Amtsgericht** (district court), where victims of the *Köpenicker Blutwoche* were executed. From Mandrellaplatz, Puchanstrasse leads to Am Generalshof and **Platz des 23 April**, which commemorates the arrival in Köpenick of the Soviet army – liberators or conquerors, depending on your point of view. On the Platz a sculpted clenched fist atop a stone tablet honours those killed by the Nazis in 1933.

9

From Mandrellaplatz, the Dammbrücke (boats can be rented at the foot of the bridge for €7/hr) leads across the Spree into Köpenick's **Altstadt** (old town). Situated on an island between the Spree and Dahme rivers, the Altstadt's streets run more or less true to the medieval town plan and remain slightly down-at-heel – it's not hard to picture this area as it must have been a century or so ago. A number of typical nineteenth-century *Bürgerhäuser* with restored facades on **Grünstrasse** and **Böttcherstrasse** are worth a look, but the most prominent building is the early twentieth-century neo-Gothic **Rathaus** on Alt Köpenick, a typically over-the-top gabled affair with an imposing clock tower and a cellar restaurant (see p.214). A statue of **Wilhelm Voigt** at the entrance to the building commemorates the town's most famous incident (see box opposite).

Schloss Köpenick

Schlossinsel • April–Sept Tues–Sun 11am–6pm; Oct–March Thurs–Sun 11am–5pm • €6; €12 with the Kulturforum's Kunstgewerbemuseum • ☎ 030 226 29 02, ⓦ smb.museum • Ⓢ Spindlersfeld

At the southern end of the Altstadt a footbridge leads to the Schlossinsel, the island home of **Schloss Köpenick** (Köpenick Palace), the seventeenth-century fortified Baroque manor that houses treasures from the Kunstgewerbemuseum at the Kulturforum (see p.96). Showcasing a collection of Renaissance, Baroque and Rococo furnishings from the sixteenth to eighteenth centuries, it's perhaps less impressive than the Kulturforum museum, but the Schloss has the advantage of being able to display many pieces *in situ*.

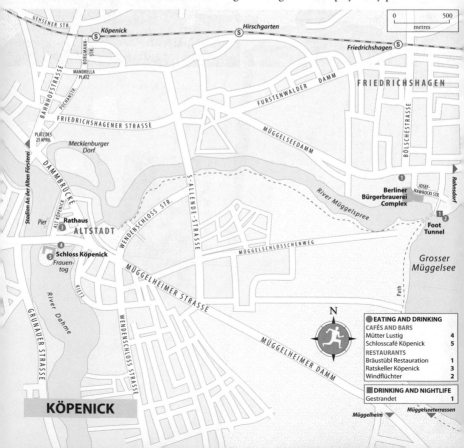

9

THE CAPTAIN OF KÖPENICK

On October 16, 1906, unemployed shoemaker **Wilhelm Voigt** disguised himself as an army officer, commandeered a troop of soldiers, marched them to Köpenick's Rathaus and requisitioned the contents of its safe. Having ordered his detachment to take Köpenick's mayor and book-keeper to the guardhouse in the city centre, he disappeared. The impostor was soon caught, but the story became an example of the Prussian propensity to blindly follow anyone wearing uniform. Later, playwright Carl Zuckmeyer turned the incident into a play, *Der Hauptmann von Köpenick* ("The Captain of Köpenick") and the robbery is now re-enacted every summer in the second half of June during the Köpenick summer festival.

A first-class audio tour, included in the admission price, greatly enhances a visit.

The exhibition begins with the Italian Renaissance, which sparked Europe-wide stylistic change and was quickly bolstered by the French, whose grand pieces of furniture inhabit the next room. These form a preamble to the German Renaissance, the museum's strong point, and on the first floor themes of love, marriage and fertility are intriguingly explored by arrangements of sturdy Teutonic furniture. After a brief foray into Dutch Baroque, the self-guided tour leads to a group of gigantic beer mugs, strongly underlining the Germanic nature of the collection, followed by a few Polish Renaissance pieces, which offer a distraction en route to the museum's most famous exhibit: the silver buffet from the Berliner Schloss – one of its few treasures to survive intact.

The second floor is replete with Chinese vases and commodes that seventeenth-century Dutch and British traders brought back from the Orient, which helped inspire the Rococo movement. Much of the sizeable collection belonged to Friedrich II, who was clearly a big fan of the style. The *pièce de résistance* – an excessively flamboyant porcelain lampshade – was one of a series that Friedrich liked to give as presents in an era when gifts like these would win friends and influence people.

Frauentog and around

Boats Mon–Fri noon–8pm, Sat & Sun 10am–8pm; from €11/hr

Just beside the Schloss Köpenick and its attendant Schlossplatz are views out over the **Frauentog**, a small bay where Köpenick's fishermen used to cast their nets; this becomes the Langer See further south. The sheltered bay is now home to the Solarbootpavillon, which rents out **solar-powered boats**. On the east side of the bay, just to the southeast of the Altstadt, is the **Kietz**, a cobbled street of fishing cottages dating back to the early thirteenth century. Renovation has brightened up the shutters and whitewashed facades of most of these cottages, making it a pleasant street for a stroll.

Grosser Müggelsee and around

A few kilometres east of Köpenick, the **Grosser Müggelsee** is one of Berlin's main lakes, with a couple of suburbs – **Friedrichshagen** and **Rahnsdorf** – with lovely, small-town atmospheres on its shores. The lake and the surrounding woods provide welcome relief from pounding Berlin's relentless urban streets, but beware – the Müggelsee area can get crowded at any time of year – in summer, people swarm here for sun and sailing, and in winter to go ice-skating.

Friedrichshagen

Ⓢ Friedrichshagen; from Köpenick take a Stern und Kreisschiffahrt boat (Ⓦ sternundkreis.de) from the quay opposite the Rathaus or tram #60 from Schlossplatz

Friedrichshagen was founded in 1753 as a settlement for Bohemian cotton spinners who, as a condition of their being allowed to live here, were legally required to plant mulberry trees to rear silkworms. Both trams and trains stop beside Friedrichshagen's main drag, **Bölschestrasse**, where a number of single-storey houses survive from the

9

original eighteenth-century settlement, dwarfed by later nineteenth-century blocks, and a few vestigial mulberry trees still cling to life at the roadside. About halfway down this otherwise attractive street the **Christophoruskirche**, a gloomy neo-Gothic church in red brick, puts a Lutheran damper on things.

To get away from it, make for the lake, along Josef-Nawrocki-Strasse, passing the extensive **Berliner Bürgerbrauerei** complex, the former brewery from whose chimney the red flag flew provocatively the day Hitler was sworn in as chancellor. Following the road around leads to a small park at the point where the Spree flows into the Grosser Müggelsee. You can follow a foot tunnel under the river, and, at the other side take a path that follows the lakeshore through the woods. Perfect for strolling, it leads all the way to the Müggelberge, 2km away (see below).

Rahnsdorf

Ⓢ Rahnsdorf or tram #61 from Friedrichshagen; take bus #161 from the S-Bahn to "Grünheider Weg", then follow the signs for Altes Fischerdorf, to reach Dorfstr.

Rahnsdorf is one of eastern Berlin's more delightful hidden corners, a sprawl of tree-shaded lakeside houses with an old fishing village at its core. Head for **Dorfstrasse**, a cobbled street at the southern end of the village, lined by fishermen's cottages and centred around a small parish church. The best way to explore Rahnsdorf is to simply wander the lakeside and soak up the atmosphere. Just off Fürstenwalder Damm, on the western edge of town, there's an FKK (*Freikörperkultur*) **nudist beach**.

The Müggelberge

Bus #X69 from Ⓢ Köpenick to bus stop "Rübezahl" or walk along a 2km lakeshore path from Friedrichshagen • **Lehrkabinett** Mon–Thurs & Sun 10am–4pm • ☎ 030 94 38 07 01 • **Müggelturm** Daily 10am–4pm • €2 • ☎ 030 94 38 07 01, ⓦ mueggelturm.berlin

The **Müggelberge** are a series of rolling forested hills overlooking the Grosser Müggelsee. From the bus stop a path leads south through the woods up to the summit. Around about the halfway mark is the **Teufelssee** (Devil's Lake), a small pool with a glass-smooth surface, from which various nature trails start. More information on these, and on the flora and fauna of the area, can be obtained at the nearby **Lehrkabinett** information centre. Pushing on and up through the woods leads to the **Müggelturm,** a functional-looking observation tower offering great views of the lake and woods, plus a snack shop. Both the Teufelssee and Müggelturm are accessible by foot along reasonably well-surfaced tracks from the main road.

STRANDBAD WANNSEE

The western suburbs

Berlin's smart, sleepy and wealthy western suburbs encompass a disparate group of attractions of cultural and historical interest, as well as the woodlands and lakes beyond them, where hikes through dense forests and swims from sandy beaches feel a world away – not just a half-dozen S-Bahn stops – from the city centre. The closest of the main attractions to the centre is Schloss Charlottenburg – Berlin's pocket Versailles – where opulent chambers, attractive gardens and excellent art museums can easily fill a day. Elsewhere, given the easy transport links, it's possible to have a good day out visiting the attractions of village-like Dahlem, going for a short hike in the Grunewald, and rounding things off with a visit to Spandau's citadel. Alternatively, you could take a private boat trip on the Havel (see box, pp.24–25).

To the north of the palace and museums of **Schloss Charlottenburg**, lies the depressing **Gedenkstätte Plötzensee**, Berlin's main Nazi torture site. Infinitely more pleasant is the wealthy, and properly suburban, residential **Westend** district west of the Schloss. Its significant reminders of prewar Berlin are much more upbeat, and include the Funkturm broadcasting tower and Olympic Stadium. South of here, in the Steglitz-Zehlendorf borough, are the world-class trio of museums in **Dahlem** – though only until sometime in 2017 when two of them will close and eventually move to the Berlin Palace–Humboldt Forum (see p.51).

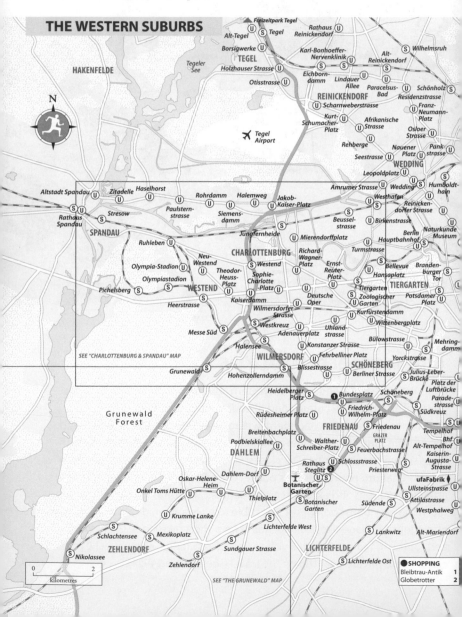

THE WESTERN SUBURBS

To the west lie other interesting museums, particularly the **AlliiertenMuseum**, where the original Checkpoint Charlie booth is kept, and the verdant woodlands of the **Grunewald**, which eventually reach the banks of the huge **Havel** lake. Here, the **Wannsee** bay is famed for its large sand beach as well as for being the location of the **Wannsee villa**, where a Nazi conference sealed the fate of millions of Jews. At the northern end of the Havel, where it joins the Spree, lies **Spandau**, where the small-town feel is enhanced by the presence of one of the world's best-preserved Renaissance forts.

ARRIVAL AND GETTING AROUND | THE WESTERN SUBURBS | 10

Thanks to the efficient U- and S-Bahn systems, it's possible to reach Berlin's western edges in 45min, but once there the main form of public transport is often the bus – the double-deckers are great for sightseeing.

The Westend The Westend is well served by trains, though buses rival them for speed and reveal a lot more of the city on the way. From Bahnhof Zoo #M49 heads to the Funkturm, then on to Theodor-Heuss-Platz before heading along Heerstrasse to S-Bahn Heerstrasse for the Georg-Kolbe-Museum, and on to the Flatowallee stop for the Olympic stadium. From there you have a choice of U- and S-Bahn stations to whizz you back into the centre.

The Wannsee Most destinations around the Wannsee are best reached by public transport from S-Bahn Wannsee, from where various buses radiate. The sole exception is the Strandbad Wannsee which is a 10min walk from S-Bahn Nikolassee, one stop earlier on the line from central Berlin. Cross the main road outside S-Bahn Wannsee and you're a couple of minutes' walk through a park away from regular ferries (which are part of the BVG public transport system and included in the price of a BVG day-ticket) to Alt-Kladow on the opposite side of the lake.

Spandau The hourly ferry across the Havel, linked with bus #X34 or #134 from Alt-Kladow, also makes a picturesque way of getting to Spandau.

Schloss Charlottenburg

Spandauer Damm 10–22 • Individual tickets are available for the various parts of the Schloss but the Charlottenburg + combined day-ticket (€12 + €2 online booking fee; includes timed visiting slot) provides the best value if you wish to see all ticketed sights • 📞 030 32 09 11, 🌐 spsg.de • 🚇 Richard-Wagner-Platz, bus #M45 from Bahnhof Zoo or by boat with Stern und Kreis Schifffahrt (see box, pp.24–25) from Jannowitzbrücke (1hr 15min) or Treptower Park (1hr 45min)

Commissioned as a country house by the future Queen Sophie Charlotte in 1695 (she also gave her name to the district), **Schloss Charlottenburg** (Charlottenburg Palace) was expanded and added to throughout the eighteenth and early nineteenth centuries to provide a summer residence for the Prussian kings; master builder Karl Friedrich Schinkel (see box, p.46) provided the final touches. It's just as well to remember, however, that much of the Schloss is in fact a fake: a reconstruction following wartime damage. Approaching the sandy elaborateness of the Schloss through the main courtyard, you're confronted with Andreas Schlüter's **statue** of Friedrich Wilhelm, the Great Elector, cast as a single piece in 1700. It's in superb condition, despite (or perhaps because of) spending the war years sunk at the bottom of the Tegeler See for safekeeping. Note that renovations of the palace are ongoing until November 2017, and until that time some parts are likely to be closed.

The Schloss

Tues–Sun: April–Oct 10am–6pm; Nov–March 10am–5pm • Guided tours (in German only), last tour 1hr before close; free English audio guides available • €10, or Charlottenburg + ticket (see above)

Immediately behind the statue of Friedrich Wilhelm is the entrance to the **Altes Schloss** (Old Palace), which includes the apartment of Friedrich Wilhelm IV and the Baroque rooms of Friedrich I and Sophie Charlotte, as well as other sumptuous chambers and bedrooms, all filled with gilt and carvings. Look out for the **porcelain room**, packed to the ceiling with china, and the **chapel**, which includes a portrait of Sophie Charlotte as the Virgin ascending to heaven. Parts of the Altes Schloss – including Friederich I's apartment and the porcelain room, will be closed for renovations until November 2017.

That the Schloss is largely a postwar reconstruction is most apparent in the Knobelsdorff designed **Neuer Flügel** (New Wing), to the right of the Schloss entrance as

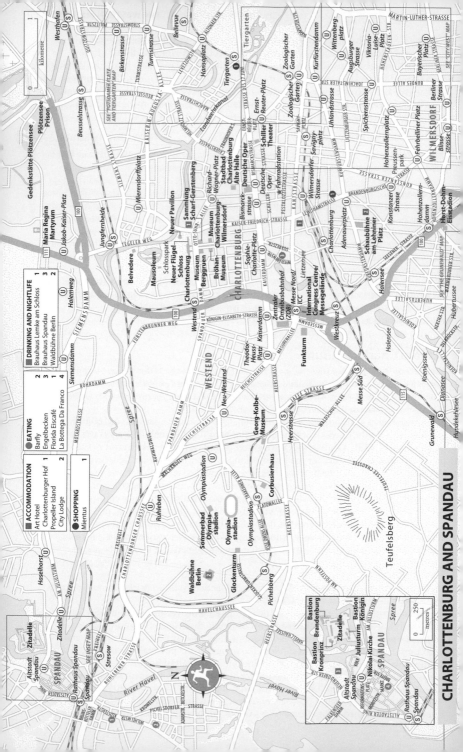

you face it; the upper rooms, such as the elegantly designed **Golden Gallery**, are too breathlessly perfect, the result of a recent intensive restoration. Better is the adjacent **White Hall**, whose eighteenth-century ceiling, made grungy by regular clouds of candle soot during festivities, was replaced at the end of the nineteenth century by a marble and gold confection with full electric illumination. Next door, the Concert Room contains a superb collection of works by **Watteau**, including one of his greatest paintings, *The Embarkation for Cythera*, a delicate Rococo frippery tinged with sympathy and sadness. Also here is his *The Shop Sign of Gersaint*, painted for an art dealer in 1720–21.

10

The Schlosspark
Daily 9am–dusk • Free; individual attractions charge a fee

Laid out in the French style in 1697, the **Schlosspark** (Palace Garden) was transformed into an English-style landscaped park in the early nineteenth century; after severe damage in the war, it was mostly restored to its Baroque form. Though it's possible to buy a map in the Schloss, it's easy enough to wander through the garden to the lake and the grounds behind, which do indeed have the feel of an English park.

The Neuer Pavillon
Tues–Sun: April–Oct 10am–6pm; Nov–March 10am–5pm • €4, or Charlottenburg + ticket (see p.161)

The first place to head before hitting the gardens proper is the **Neuer Pavillon** (New Pavilion, also called the Schinkel Pavillon), just to the east of the Schloss, which was designed by Schinkel (see box, p.46) for Friedrich Wilhelm III. The king preferred to live here, away from the excesses of the main building. Inside, furniture, decorative arts and paintings from the Romantic and Biedermeier periods are on display, including works by Carl Blechen, Schinkel and Eduard Gaertner.

The Belvedere
April–Oct Tues–Sun 10am–6pm • €4, or Charlottenburg + ticket (see p.161)

Within the gardens, on the north side of the lake, is the **Belvedere**, built as a teahouse in 1788 and today housing a collection of Berlin porcelain – tea and coffee sets, dinnerware services and decorative pieces. Much of the craftsmanship is extremely delicate, and pieces commemorating the fall of Napoleon or depicting scenes from the palace and gardens have a real sense of history about them.

Mausoleum
April–Oct Tues–Sun 10am–6pm • €2, or Charlottenburg + ticket (see p.161)

On the western side of the gardens, a long, tree-lined avenue leads to the hushed and shadowy **Mausoleum**, where Friedrich Wilhelm III is buried: his sarcophagus, carved with his image, makes him seem a good deal younger than his seventy years. Friedrich Wilhelm had commissioned the mausoleum to be built thirty years earlier for his wife, Queen Luise, whose own delicate sarcophagus apparently depicts her not dead but sleeping. Later burials here include Kaiser Wilhelm I, looking every inch a Prussian king.

Museums opposite the Schloss

Though you could happily spend a whole day wandering around the Schloss and its gardens, just across the way another group of excellent **museums** beckons. Any of these in themselves could easily take an afternoon of your time.

Sammlung Scharf-Gerstenberg
Schlossstr. 70 • Tues–Fri 10am–6pm, Sat & Sun 11am–6pm • €10 including Museum Berggruen, audio guide included • ☎ 030 266 42 42 42, ⓦ smb.museum • ⓤ Richard-Wagner-Platz or bus #M45 from Bahnhof Zoo

The two buildings at the head of Schlossstrasse together served the palace's Gardes du Corps regiment in the late nineteenth century. The building to the east, the former stables, now houses the **Sammlung Scharf-Gerstenberg** (Scharf-Gerstenberg Collection), the personal collection of Otto Gerstenberg, who made his fortune in the insurance industry of the early twentieth century and "liked looking at pictures", in the words of his grandson Dieter Scharf. Scharf expanded the collection (which was prodigious despite extensive losses in the war and its ransacking by Russians looking for war booty) and put it at Berlin's disposal. The collection suggests Gerstenberg had a penchant for the graphic arts and sculpture, particularly from the French Romantic and Surrealist schools; certainly the pictures Gerstenberg liked to look at tended to be unusual.

On show are the massive structures by Giovanni Battista Piranesi, some odd island-like forms by Victor Hugo and a woman copulating with a beast in Henri Rousseau's *Beauty and the Beast* – which apparently uses the depiction to play with notions of the active and the passive. Other oddities include Max Klinger's local roller-skating works, which were based on his dreams, and works from Wolfgang Paalen, who painted with candle soot, and Jean Dubuffet who used coal, cement and butterfly wings. You'll also see impressive pieces by Max Ernst, René Magritte, Salvador Dalí and Paul Klee, who contributed a bit of orderly Bauhaus structure – many more of his works can be enjoyed over the road at the Museum Berggruen (see below).

Museum Berggruen

Schlossstr. 1 • Tues–Fri 10am–6pm, Sat & Sun 11am–6pm • €10 including Sammlung Scharf-Gerstenberg, audio guide included • ☎ 030 266 42 42 42, ⓦ smb.museum • ⓤ Richard-Wagner-Platz, ⓤ Sophie-Charlotte-Platz or bus #M45 from Bahnhof Zoo

Opposite the Sammlung Scharf-Gerstenberg, the wonderful **Museum Berggruen** houses the collection of Heinz Berggruen, a young Jew forced to flee Berlin in 1936, who wound up as an art dealer in Paris – where he got to know Picasso and his circle – and assembled a collection of personal favourites. In the mid-1990s Berlin gave him this building to show off his revered compilation in a comfortable and uncrowded setting. There are over a hundred works by Picasso, including the richly textured Cubist *The Yellow Sweater* and large-scale *Reclining Nude*, while other highlights include a handful of Cézannes and Giacomettis and seventy or so works by Paul Klee, which span the interwar period.

Museum Charlottenburg-Wilmersdorf

Schlossstr. 55 • Tues–Fri 10am–5pm, Sat & Sun 11am–5pm • Free • ☎ 030 90 29 24 106, ⓦ villa-oppenheim-berlin.de • ⓤ Richard-Wagner-Platz or bus #M45 from Bahnhof Zoo

Set inside the elegant Villa Oppenheim, along the road from the Scharf-Gerstenberg collection, is the **Museum Charlottenburg-Wilmersdorf**. It charts the history and development of the two eponymous districts, with photos, objects and films, and also covers the history of the villa itself. There are also occasional temporary exhibitions.

Bröhan-Museum

Schlossstr. 1a • Tues–Sun 10am–6pm • €8 • ☎ 030 32 69 06 00, ⓦ www.broehan-museum.de • ⓤ Richard-Wagner-Platz, ⓤ Sophie-Charlotte-Platz or bus #M45 from Bahnhof Zoo

Just south of the Berggruen Collection, the compact and enjoyable **Bröhan-Museum** houses a fine selection of Art Nouveau, Art Deco, and Berlin Secession works, including applied art and design pieces such as ceramics and furniture. Their assembly was the passion of Karl Bröhan (1921–2000), who donated all the pieces he had amassed to the city to commemorate his sixtieth birthday. Spread across several rooms, what's on show changes every couple of years, but you'll see works by the likes of architects and designers such as Hector Guimard and Peter Behrens, and painters like Hans Baluschek and Lesser Ury.

Gedenkstätte Plötzensee and around

Hüttigpfad • Daily: March–Oct 9am–5pm; Nov–Feb 9am–4pm • Free • ☎ 030 26 99 50 00, ⓦ www.gedenkstaette-ploetzensee.de • Bus #123 from Hauptbahnhof to "Gedenkstätte Plötzensee", then walk back along the route and turn right on Hüttigpfad

One of Berlin's handful of surviving Third Reich buildings, the **Gedenkstätte Plötzensee** (Plötzensee Prison Memorial) sits in the northwest of the city centre, on the border of Charlottenburg and Wedding. Many of the former prison buildings where the Nazis brought dissidents and political opponents have been refurbished and repurposed as a juvenile detention centre, so the memorial consists of only those buildings where executions took place. Between 1933 and 1945 more than 2900 people were hanged or guillotined here and their relatives were sent a bill for the execution.

Today, the execution chamber has been restored to its wartime condition: on occasion, victims were hanged eight at a time, and the hanging beam, complete with hooks, still stands. Though decked with wreaths and flowers, the atmosphere in the chamber is chilling, and in a further reminder of Nazi atrocities an urn in the courtyard contains soil from each of the concentration camps. Perhaps more than at any other wartime site in Berlin, Plötzensee conveys most palpably the horror of senseless, brutal murder.

Maria Regina Martyrum

Heckerdamm 230 • ⓤ Jakob-Kaiser-Platz or four stops from the Gedenkstätte Plötzensee on the #123 bus

Completed in 1963, the **Maria Regina Martyrum** (Mary Queen of Martyrs) is a purposefully sombre memorial church dedicated to those who died under the Nazis. Its brutally plain exterior, surrounded by a wide courtyard whose walls are flanked by abstract *Stations of the Cross* modelled in bronze, fronts a plain concrete shoebox, adorned only with an abstract altarpiece that fills the entire eastern wall. It's a strikingly unusual design, and successfully avoids looking dated.

The Westend

In the late nineteenth century, mansions belonging to Berlin's wealthy bourgeoisie sprung up in northwestern Charlottenburg-Wilmersdorf, in an area that became known, inspired by London's West End, as the **Westend**.

Georg-Kolbe-Museum

Sensburger Allee 25 • Daily 10am–6pm • €7 • ☎ 030 304 21 44, ⓦ georg-kolbe-museum.de • ⓢ Heerstrasse or buses #M49 or #X34 from Bahnhof Zoo

The **Georg-Kolbe-Museum**, occupying the artist's former villa, displays many of his drawings and bronzes alongside galleries of modern and contemporary art. Though Kolbe never quite achieved the eminence of his contemporary Ernst Barlach, his vigorous, modern, simplified classical style had broad appeal and he became one of the most successful sculptors of the early twentieth century. His many admirers included Mies van der Rohe, who used a Kolbe sculpture – *Morgen* – in his Barcelona Pavilion.

Corbusierhaus

Flatowallee 16 • Free • ⓢ Olympiastadion or bus #M49 from Bahnhof Zoo to stop "Flatowallee"

The blocky **Corbusierhaus**, built by the French architect, Le Corbusier, for the 1957 International Building Exhibition, contains more than five hundred apartments and was heralded a modernist ideal living environment. A German-language exhibition (always open) on the ground floor tells its story and you can ride the lifts up to the shiny corridors on the top floor for views from the fire escapes.

10

Funkturm

Messedamm 22 • Mon 10am–8pm, Tues–Sun 10am–11pm • €5 • ☎ 030 30 38 19 05, ⓦ funkturm-messeberlin.de • Ⓢ Messe Nord/ICC or bus #M49 from Zoologischer Bahnhof to stop "Haus des Rundfunks"

The **Funkturm** (Radio Tower) was inaugurated in 1926 as a radio transmitter, though also served as a navigation aid for planes and from its inception as a tourist attraction; from 1929 until 1962 it was used for TV broadcasts, too. Today the Funkturm only serves police and taxi frequencies, but the mast remains popular with Berliners for the toe-curling views from its 126m-high **observation platform**. With the aluminium-clad monolith of the closed **Internationales Congress Centrum** (ICC) immediately below, the vista across deserted, overgrown S-Bahn tracks to the gleaming city in the distance is a mesmerizing sight at night.

Olympiastadion

Daily: April–July, Sept & Oct 9am–7pm; Aug 9am–8pm; Nov–March 10am–4pm • €7; check online for details of English-language tours (1hr; €11): there's usually one at noon and as many as 4 daily in summer; multimedia app guide €4 • ☎ 030 25 00 23 22, ⓦ olympiastadion-berlin.de • Ⓢ Olympiastadion, ⓤ Olympia-Stadion or bus #M49 from Bahnhof Zoo, stop "Flatowallee"

Built for the 1936 Games, the **Olympiastadion** (Olympic Stadium) is one of Berlin's few remaining fascist-era buildings, and remains very much in use, and even well looked after thanks to a major renovation for the 2006 football World Cup. Despite its history, the building is impressive, the huge Neoclassical space a deliberate rejection of the modernist architecture that began to be in vogue in the 1930s. Inside, its sheer size comes as a surprise, since the seating falls away below ground level to reveal a much deeper auditorium than you'd imagine. On the western side, where the Olympic flame was kept and where medal winners are listed on the walls, it's easy to see how this monumental architecture, and the massive sculptures dotting the grounds outside (some of which still stand) could inspire the crowds. During the Olympics, Berliners were kept up to date with commentary on the games, interspersed with stirring music, from hundreds of loudspeakers that ran all the way from Museum Island via Unter den Linden and the Brandenburg Gate, through the Tiergarten and out to the stadium. Standing here, looking back out to the city, you realize what an achievement this was.

As the home ground of **Hertha BSC**, Berlin's best football team, and a venue for major music gigs, the stadium is regularly closed for events so it's best to check online before trudging out. Tours take you behind the scenes, to the VIP areas, locker rooms and so on; the knowledgeable guides provide interesting anecdotes along the way.

Glockenturm

Am Glockenturm • Daily: April–Oct 9am–6pm • €4.50 • ☎ 030 305 81 23, ⓦ glockenturm.de • Ⓢ Pichelsberg or bus #M49 from Bahnhof Zoo, stop "Flatowallee"

Just a ten-minute walk from the Olympic Stadium, the **Glockenturm** (Bell Tower) towers above the spot where Hitler would enter the stadium each morning, state business permitting. Rebuilt after wartime damage, the building includes an exhibition about the history of the Olympic grounds here, while its tower offers stupendous views not only over the stadium but also north to the natural amphitheatre that forms the **Waldbühne**, an open-air concert site (see box, p.228), and south to the Teufelsberg and the beginnings of the Grunewald.

Teufelsberg

Tours (Fri, Sat & Sun 10am; €15) are run by Original Berlin Tours (see box, pp.24–25) • Ⓢ Heerstrasse, and then a 20min walk south down Teufelsseechaussee

A massive mound topped with an abandoned former US signals and radar base, built to listen in to eastern bloc radio signals, **Teufelsberg** (Devil's Mountain) has become something of a pilgrimage site for historians and urban explorers alike. The mountain itself is artificial: at the end of the war, the mass of debris that was once

Berlin was carted to several sites around the city, most of the work being carried out by women known as *Trümmerfrauen* – "rubble women". Beneath the poplars, maples and ski runs lies the old Berlin, about 25 million cubic metres of it, perhaps awaiting the attention of some future archeologist. Although the former listening station is officially sealed off and accessible only via guided tours, many still chance illegal entry. The hill itself is popular as a place for kite-flying, and, in winter, skiing and tobogganing.

10

Dahlem and around

The mostly residential suburb of **Dahlem**, southwest of central Berlin, has the feel of a neat village-like enclave a world away from the city centre. The main draws are the exotic artefacts in the excellent **Museen Dahlem** group, but you could also visit the **Domäne Dahlem**, a working pre-industrial farm-cum-museum; the nearby **Dorfkirche St.-Annen**, a pretty brick church that dates back to 1220 (open sporadic weekdays; call ☎030 83 13 813 or check ⓦkg-dahlem.de), which boasts a Baroque pulpit and gallery and a carved wooden altar; and the city's impressive **Botanischer Garten**. You should, too, investigate the good **beer gardens** of the area (see p.224) – popular with forest walkers and students from the nearby Free University.

Museen Dahlem

The **Museen Dahlem** incorporates the **Ethnologisches Museum** and the **Museum für Asiatische Kunst** – both of which will be closed in late 2017, and eventually moved to the Berlin Palace–Humboldt Forum (see p.51) when the latter opens – and, a block in the opposite direction from the underground station, the **Museum Europäischer Kulturen**.

Ethnologisches Museum

Lansstr. 8 • Tues–Fri 10am–5pm, Sat & Sun 11am–6pm • €8 • ☎ 030 830 14 38 or ☎ 030 266 42 42 42, ⓦ smb.museum • ⓤ Dahlem-Dorf

The **Ethnologisches Museum** (Museum of Ethnology) imaginatively displays just a small portion of one of the world's most extensive ethnological collections, detailing the varying cultures of dozens of civilizations and ethnic groups, each with their own traditions, religious beliefs and artistic forms. Note that major elements of the exhibition have already been packed away in preparation for the move to the new Schloss – at the time of writing, the stunning South America, North America and South Seas sections had already been closed, with the rest of the exhibits due to be put in storage throughout 2017.

Museum für Asiatische Kunst

Lansstr. 8 • Tues–Fri 10am–5pm, Sat & Sun 11am–6pm • €8 • ☎ 030 266 42 42 42, ⓦ smb.museum • ⓤ Dahlem-Dorf

The exceptional **Museum für Asiatische Kunst** (Asian Art Museum) is split into two sections – one dealing with the Indian subcontinent and one devoted to the Far East. The former includes an assortment of intricate bronze, wood or jade religious sculptures, many of which come from the Buddhist temples and monasteries along the northern Silk Route. Religious art naturally comprises the great bulk of the collection but there's also an intriguing series of miniature paintings covering secular subjects, such as court scenes and nature studies, and displaying a certain informality and playfulness. The Far East section includes an impressive Chinese calligraphy collection but many of the best exhibits are Japanese, including woodcuts, a stunning seventeenth-century gold-and-lacquer throne inlaid with mother-of-pearl, and a tearoom. As with the Ethnological Museum, the museum exhibits are being packed away bit by bit in advance of the eventual move to Museum Island.

Museum Europäischer Kulturen

Im Winkel 6, a short signposted walk down Archivstr. directly opposite Ⓤ Dahlem-Dorf • Tues–Fri 10am–6pm, Sat & Sun 11am–6pm • €8 •
☎ 030 266 42 68 02 or ☎ 030 266 42 42 42, ⓦ smb.museum • Ⓤ Dahlem-Dorf

The one museum that will remain in Dahlem after 2017 is the **Museum Europäischer Kulturen** (Museum of European Cultures), which uses its extraordinary 275,000-item collection of handicrafts, paintings, prints and the like to put together changing exhibitions on subjects such as religious practices, modernization and commerce in various European regions. It's strong on German culture, with lots from France and Russia too.

10

Domäne Dahlem

Königin-Luise-Str. 49, just west of and over the road from Ⓤ Dahlem-Dorf • Daily 8am–7pm; museum Tues–Sun 10am–5pm • €4 (free for under-18s) • ☎ 030 666 30 00, ⓦ domaene-dahlem.de • Ⓤ Dahlem-Dorf

Domäne Dahlem, a working farm and handicrafts centre attempts to show off the lifestyle and skills of the pre-industrial age. The old estate house has a few odds and ends, most intriguing of which are the thirteenth-century swastikas, but the collection of agricultural instruments in an outbuilding is more comprehensive. Elsewhere there are ponies, turkeys, pigs, sheep and cows in the grounds, and demonstrations of woodcarving, wool- and cotton-spinning and various other farm crafts. At weekends some of the old agricultural machinery is fired up and the animals are paraded, and the complex also now features the Culinarium: a kid-friendly, interactive cultural history of food – from farm to fork – complete with locally produced goods to buy.

The Botanischer Garten and Botanisches Museum

Königin-Luise-Str. 6–8 • **Gardens** Daily 9am–dusk, greenhouse closes 30min before garden • €6 • **Museum** Daily 10am–6pm; included in Botanical Gardens entry, or €2.50 • ☎ 030 83 85 01 00, ⓦ bgbm.org • Ⓢ Botanischer Garten, Ⓤ/Ⓢ Rathaus Steglitz, bus #X83 from Dahlem or bus #M48 from Alexanderplatz

Founded as an extension to the royal palace's kitchen garden by the Elector of Brandenburg in 1679 and moved to Dahlem in the early twentieth century, the city's splendorous **Botanischer Garten** (Botanical Garden) today hosts some 20,000 species of plants across 43 hectares, making it one of the largest and most diverse of its kind in the world. The sixteen greenhouses (*Gewächshäuser*) house plants from an array of climatic zones ranging from desert and rainforest, and there's an area where visitors with disabilities can explore plants via smell and touch. The attached **museum** contains a section on preserved fossils and looks at the world of plants in terms of psychoactives.

Zehlendorf and the Grunewald

The **Grunewald** is made up of around 32 square kilometres of mixed woodland. Though more than two-thirds were cut down in the postwar years for badly needed fuel, the subsequent replanting replaced pine and birch with oak and made it more attractive and popular with Berliners for its clean air and walks.

The eastern edge of the Grunewald, where the wealthy suburb of **Zehlendorf** begins, is dotted with a series of modest but unusual **museums** that can be combined with time spent hiking in the forest to make a well-rounded day out. These include the **Brücke Museum**, which showcases German Expressionism, the **Jagdschloss Grunewald** with its small collection of old masters, the **Alliierten-Museum**, which has important relics of Cold War Berlin, and the **Museumsdorf Düppel**, which re-creates medieval village life.

GRUNEWALD HIKES

The Jagdschloss is a good starting point for **hikes** into the Grunewald: a 45 minute ramble along the eastern side of the Grunewaldsee brings you to S-Bahn Grunewald; or you can walk south to U-Bahn Krumme Lanke in about an hour, crossing Hutten Weg and then Onkel-Tom-Strasse to walk around the shores of Krumme Lanke lake.

10

Brücke Museum

Bussardsteig 9 • Daily except Tues 11am–5pm • €5 • ☎ 030 83 12 029, Ⓦ bruecke-museum.de • Ⓤ Fehrbeliner Platz or
Ⓢ Hohenzollerndamm then bus #115 (direction Neuruppiner Strasse) to "Pücklerstrasse" stop

The **Brücke Museum** displays German Expressionist works by the group known as *Die Brücke* ("The Bridge"), active in Dresden and Berlin from 1905 to 1913, and who were banned by the Nazis. The big names are Kirchner, Heckel and Schmidt-Rottluff, who painted Expressionist cityscapes – using rich colours and playful perspectives – and who had a great influence on later artists. Many of their works were destroyed during the war, making this collection all the more interesting. Exhibitions change regularly, but tend to include early and later works from the movement.

Jagdschloss Grunewald

Hüttenweg 10 • March, Nov & Dec Sat & Sun 10am–4pm; April–Oct Tues–Sun 10am–6pm • €6 • ☎ 030 813 35 97, Ⓦ spsg.de •
Ⓤ Dahlem-Dorf, then bus #X83 to "Clayallee"

Within the depths of the Grunewald is the **Jagdschloss Grunewald**, a royal hunting lodge built in the sixteenth century and enlarged by Friedrichs I and II. Today it's a museum housing old furniture and Dutch and German paintings, including works by Cranach the Elder and Rubens. There's also a small hunting museum in the outbuildings. However, walking around the adjacent lake, the **Grunewaldsee**, may prove more stimulating than the collections (see box, p.169).

Alliierten-Museum

Clayallee 135 • Tues–Sun 10am–6pm • Free • ☎ 030 818 19 90, Ⓦ www.alliiertenmuseum.de • Ⓤ Oskar-Helene-Heim, then bus #115 to "Alliierten-museum" stop

Berlin's **Alliierten-Museum** (Allied Museum), as the name suggests, gives the Western powers' perspective on the Cold War in Berlin – everyday life in the respective French, British and American communities as well as the broader contexts and coverage of the

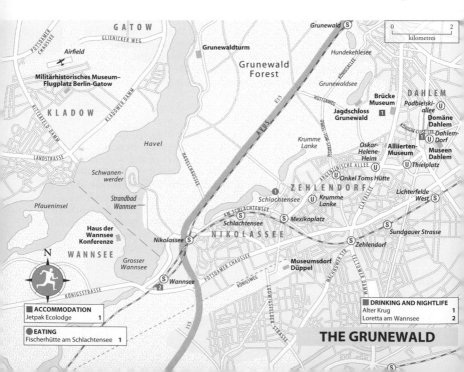

major events. Though a somewhat turgid exhibition at times, it's well presented, with highlights including the original Checkpoint Charlie guard cabin, an aeroplane used in the airlift during the Berlin Blockade (see box, p.126) in the outside courtyard, and a reconstruction of the famous spy tunnel used in Operation Gold, the largest CIA/MI6 operation of the era.

Museumsdorf Düppel

Clauertstr. 11 • Easter–Oct Sat & Sun 10am–6pm • €3.50, children under 12 free • ☎ 030 802 66 71, ⓦ dueppel.de • ⓢ Zehlendorf then bus #115 to "Ludwigsfelderstrasse" stop

With its dozen thatched buildings built on the site of a twelfth-century settlement, the reconstructed medieval country village, **Museumsdorf Düppel** (Düppel Museum Village), in the far southwest of the city, gives an impression of what things might have looked like hereabouts 800 years ago. Traditional local breeds of sheep are reared and old strains of rye grown, and you can see demonstrations of handicrafts and farming techniques from the Middle Ages. Afterwards you can explore the lovely surrounding Düppel Forest.

Wannsee

Of the many lakes that dot the Grunewald, the best known is the **Wannsee**. The main attraction here, on the lake's eastern side, is the **Strandbad Wannsee**, Europe's largest lido, which gets packed as soon as the sun comes out. From here it's easy to wander into the forest and to smaller, less-populated beaches along the lakeside road **Havelchaussee**. The main tourist destination around the Wannsee is, however, the **Wannsee villa**. Nearby, the infinitely more pleasant **Pfaueninsel**, once a royal island playground, is now a bucolic park roamed by peacocks.

Strandbad Wannsee

Wannseebadeweg 25 • April–Sept daily 10am–6pm, with varying but extended hours (usually until 8 or 9pm) June–Aug • €5.50 • ⓦ www.berlinerbaeder.de • ⓢ Wannsee/Nikolassee

Just a twenty-minute train ride from the city centre, **Strandbad Wannsee**'s impressive 1.3km-long (and 80m-wide) sweep of sandy beach has long been a venerable summer destination for Berliners (see p.250). Having undergone a €12.5 million refurbishment for its centenary celebrations a decade ago, it attracts up to 230,000 visitors per year and has been designated a cultural heritage site, though in essence has changed little in character since Heinrich Zille sketched the working classes at play here in the late nineteenth century.

Along the Havelchaussee

From ⓢ Wannsee/Nikolassee, bus #218 runs all the way along the Havelchaussee

If the Strandbad Wannsee is too commercial for you, head north along the shore, following the **Havelchaussee**, which runs past 6km of quiet, sandy coves. This area is also good for a spot of **hiking** – both along the lakeshore and inland into the forest. One possible start or terminus of a hike, 4km north of the Strandbad, is the **Grunewaldturm** (daily 10am–10pm; €3), a 55m-high observation tower right next to the Havel lake. Built at the end of the nineteenth century as a memorial to Kaiser Wilhelm I, it has a smart restaurant and fine views out across the lakes.

Haus der Wannsee Konferenze

Am Grossen Wannsee 56–58 • Daily 10am–6pm • Public tours every Sat & Sun 4pm & 5pm (German only) • Free; audio guide €3 • ☎ 030 80 50 010, ⓦ ghwk.de • #114 bus from ⓢ Wannsee to "Haus der Wannsee-Konferenz"

While not the most enjoyable of sights, one place that should on no account be missed on a trip to the Wannsee is the **Haus der Wannsee Konferenze** (House of the Wannsee Conference), the villa overlooking the Wannsee, where, on January 20, 1942, the fate of European Jewry was determined (see box, p.273). The deeply moving exhibition here shows the entire process of the Holocaust, from segregation and persecution to the deportation and eventual murder of the Jews from Germany, its allies and all the lands the Third Reich conquered. Many of the photographs and accounts are horrific, and the events they describe seem part of a world far removed from this quiet locale – which, in many ways, underlines the tragedy. Particularly disturbing is the photograph of four generations of women – babe-in-arms, young mother, grandmother and ancient great-grandmother – moments before their execution on a sand dune in Latvia.

The room where the conference took place remains as it was, with documents from the meeting on the table and photographs of participants around the walls; biographies show that many lived to a comfortable old age. Even 75 years after the event, to stand in the room where a decision was formalized to coldly and systematically annihilate a race sends shivers down the spine.

Pfaueninsel

Nikolskoer Weg • **Schloss** April–Oct Tues–Sun 10am–5.30pm • €6 (guided tours only) • ☎ 030 805 86 831, Ⓦ spsg.de • Ⓢ Wannsee, then bus #218, then a passenger ferry (daily: March & Oct 9am–6pm; April & Sept 9am–7pm; May–Aug 9am–8pm; Nov–Feb 10am–4pm; €4)

Designed as a royal fantasy getaway on one of the largest of the Havel islands, the **Pfaueninsel** (Peacock Island) is now a nature reserve with a flock of peacocks stalking around its landscaped park. No cars are allowed on the island (nor are dogs, ghetto-blasters or smoking). Attractions include a mini-**Schloss**, built by Friedrich Wilhelm II for his mistress and containing a small **museum**. Most enjoyable, though, are the gardens, landscaped by Peter Lenné, the original designer of the Tiergarten.

Militärhistorisches Museum – Flugplatz Berlin-Gatow

Am Flugplatz Gatow 33 • Tues–Sun 10am–6pm • Free • ☎ 030 36 87 26 01, Ⓦ mhm-gatow.de • Ⓢ Spandau, then bus #135 to "Luftwaffenmuseum" stop, 1.5km from the entrance

The giant **Militärhistorisches Museum – Flugplatz Berlin-Gatow** (Military History Museum – Berlin-Gatow Airfield) records more than a hundred years of air force history across several hangars on Berlin's Gatow airfield. This was one landing place for the "raisin bombers" breaking the Berlin Blockade (see box, p.126), and also where the RAF was stationed in the days of West Berlin; the exhibition itself leaves no aileron or propeller unturned in its examination of the German military's aeronautical past. There are dozens of planes to view, from Red Baron-era World War I aircraft to Cold War-era fighter jets from both sides of the Iron Curtain. Though most information is in German, enthusiasts could easily spend the best part of a day here; the café is very basic, however, and it's a long way to come, on infrequent buses – bring supplies.

RUDOLF HESS (1894–1987)

Devoted to Hitler from the moment he first heard him speak at a rally in 1920, **Rudolf Hess** marched in the Munich Beer Hall *putsch* of 1923 and was subsequently imprisoned with Hitler in Landsberg jail, where he took the dictation of *Mein Kampf*. For a time he was the **deputy leader** of the Nazi party, second only to the Führer himself. An experienced World War I airman, he flew himself to Scotland in 1941, ostensibly in an attempt to sue for peace with King George VI and ally Great Britain with Germany against the Soviet Union. It remains unclear whether he did this with Hitler's blessing, but there is evidence to suggest that the Führer knew of Hess's plans. Either way, he was immediately arrested and Churchill refused to meet him; he was held until sentenced to life imprisonment at the Nuremberg trials. He finally committed suicide in 1987 in his Spandau jail – the only inmate in a jail designed for six hundred – hanging himself on a short piece of lamp flex, aged 93.

Spandau

Spandau, situated on the confluence of the Spree and Havel rivers, about 10km northwest of its centre, is Berlin's oldest suburb. Granted a town charter in 1232, it escaped the worst of the wartime bombing, preserving a couple of old village-like streets – at their best during the Christmas market – and an ancient moated fort, the **Zitadelle**. Though the word Spandau immediately brings to mind its jail's most famous – indeed, in later years, only – prisoner, **Rudolf Hess** (see box opposite), there's little connection between Hess and Spandau itself. The jail, 4km away from the centre, was demolished after his death to make way for a supermarket for the British armed forces; the space is now occupied by a branch of the Kaufland hypermarket chain.

10

Spandau Altstadt

Ⓢ Spandau or Ⓤ Altstadt Spandau

In comparison to its Zitadelle, Spandau's **Altstadt**, or old town, is of minor interest. It begins just to the northeast of the Rathaus and is at its best around the medieval **Nikolai Kirche** (St Nicholas Church); the **Reformationsplatz** (with a good *Konditorei*), where playful sculptures adorn the modern marketplace; and in the restored street called **Kolk**. Also here is the **Brauhaus Spandau**, a nineteenth-century brewery that produces beer to a medieval recipe (see p.224).

Zitadelle

Am Juliusturm 64 • Daily 10am–5pm • €4.50 • ☏ 030 354 94 40, ⓦ zitadelle-spandau.de • Ⓤ Zitadelle, or a 10min walk through the Altstadt from Ⓢ Spandau where the #134 from Alt-Kladow stops

The postcard-pretty **Zitadelle** (Citadel), just northeast over the Havel from the Altstadt, was established in the twelfth century to defend the town. Its moat and russet walls were built during the Renaissance by an Italian architect and it's an interesting place to explore, if not totally engrossing, with a small local history museum with temporary exhibitions, a pricey restaurant and the thirteenth-century **Juliusturm** (Julius Tower), from which there's a good view over the ramshackle Zitadelle interior and the countryside.

SCHLOSS SANSSOUCI

Out of the city

When Berlin's city fringes don't seem like breather enough from its bustle, a day-trip into its sleepy Brandenburg hinterland (ⓦbrandenburg-tourism.com) might be just the thing. This federal state is replete with gentle scenery, a patchwork of beech forests, heaths and fields of dazzling rapeseed and sunflowers, all sewn together by a multitude of rivers, lakes and waterways. Thanks to Berlin's superb transport network, the key towns of Potsdam and Oranienburg are easy and economical day-trips. And since the S-Bahn network allows you to transport a bike, you should seriously consider bringing one along, or renting one. Potsdam's parks are particularly ideal for a day's gentle exploration on two wheels coupled with a picnic. But should you wish to explore the state more widely by car, you're sure to find cruising the flat tree-lined avenues that typify Brandenburg's minor roads a pleasure.

Many of Brandenburg's headline attractions are southwest of Berlin in **Potsdam**, a town whose size is effectively doubled by surrounding landscaped gardens dotted with royal piles and follies, which include Frederick the Great's famous Schloss, **Sanssouci**. Meanwhile, just north beyond Berlin's fringes, the town of Oranienburg is far less attractive, but equally absorbing as the site of former concentration camp, **Sachsenhausen**. For something completely different, the **Tropical Islands complex**, to the south of Berlin, offers a fun day out where you can enjoy the waters and beaches of warmer climes.

Potsdam

For most visitors **POTSDAM** means **Sanssouci**, Frederick the Great's splendid landscaped park of architectural treasures that once completed Berlin as the grand Prussian capital. However, Potsdam's origins date back to the tenth-century Slavonic settlement Poztupimi, and predate Berlin by a couple of hundred years. The castle built here in 1160 marked the first step in the town's gradual transformation from sleepy fishing backwater to **royal residence** and **garrison town**, a role it enjoyed under the Hohenzollerns until the abdication of Kaiser Wilhelm II in 1918.

World War II left Potsdam badly damaged: on April 14, 1945, a bombing raid killed four thousand people, destroyed many fine Baroque buildings and reduced its centre to ruins. Less than four months later – on August 2 – the victorious Allies converged on Potsdam's **Schloss Cecilienhof** to hammer out the details of a division of Germany and Europe. Potsdam itself ended up in the Soviet zone, where modern "socialist" building programmes steadily erased many architectural memories of the town's uncomfortably prosperous imperial past. Yet it's this past that has given us its most popular sights – not just at Sanssouci but across the Havel in **Babelsberg**, the site of the most important film studio in German film history.

The town itself has a few well-preserved quarters, though in truth its attractions are scant in comparison with what awaits in Park Sanssouci. Its main drag is **Friedrich-Ebert-Strasse**, and **Brandenburger Strasse** is the pedestrianized main shopping street.

Alter Markt

North from the train station, beyond Lange Brücke, is the **Alter Markt**, the fringe of Potsdam's town centre, which is framed by the arresting outlines of the unmistakably GDR-era *Mercure Hotel* and the stately domed **Nikolaikirche**. It was here that the town's earliest fortifications were built and where the medieval village flourished.

Landtag Brandenburg

Am Alten Markt 1 · Mon–Fri 8am–6pm · ☎ 0331 96 60, ⓦ landtag.brandenburg.de

The Alter Markt is best known as the former site of the Stadtschloss, a Baroque residence built by the Great Elector between 1662 and 1669. World War II (specifically the night of April 14/15, 1945) reduced it to a bare, roofless shell, and the GDR demolished what remained in 1960 – around eighty percent of the building – to remove the last vestiges of Potsdam's grandest imperial buildings. Today, Brandenburg's parliament building, the **Landtag**, copies the footprint of the old Schloss and incorporates many of its elements into its design: not least the reconstruction of the

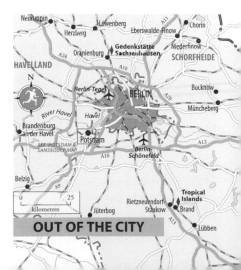

OUT OF THE CITY

11

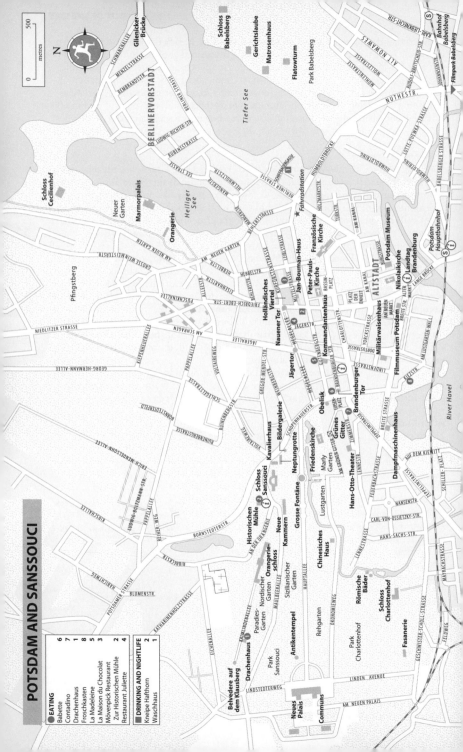

POTSDAM AND SANSSOUCI

EATING

Babette	6
Contadino	7
Drachenhaus	1
Froschkasten	8
La Madeleine	5
La Maison du Chocolat	3
Mövenpick Restaurant	2
Zur Historischen Mühle	2
Restaurant Juliette	4

DRINKING AND NIGHTLIFE

Kneipe Hafthorn	2
Waschhaus	1

gate to the palace forecourt, the domed Fortunaportal, which completes the re-creation of three domed structures that traditionally dominated the square.

The Nikolaikirche

Am Alten Markt • **Church** Mon–Sat 10am–6pm, Sun 11.30am–6pm • **Viewing platform** Open till 5pm; €5 • ⓦ nikolai-potsdam.de

The elegant, Schinkel-designed Neoclassical **Nikolaikirche** (St Nicholas' Church) is the most significant of the Alter Markt's three domes. There's not much to look at inside, but the 42-metre-high viewing platform offers great views over Potsdam.

Potsdam Museum

Am Alten Markt 9 • Tues, Wed & Fri 10am–5pm, Thurs 10am–7pm, Sat & Sun 10am–6pm • €5 • ☎ 0331 289 68 68, ⓦ potsdam-museum.de

The third of the Alter Markt's domes belongs to Potsdam's former Rathaus, which was built in the mid-eighteenth century in Classical Palladian style, and now contains the **Potsdam Museum**, with a permanent exhibition that explores the town's development and history, plus temporary exhibitions. The obelisk in front, designed by Knobelsdorff, originally bore four reliefs depicting the Great Elector and his successors. When re-erected during the 1970s these were replaced with reliefs of the architects who shaped much of Potsdam: Schinkel, Knobelsdorff, Carl Philipp Christian von Gontard and Friedrich Ludwig Persius.

11

Filmmuseum Potsdam

Breite Str. 1a • Tues–Sun 10am–6pm • €5 • ☎ 0331 271 81 12, ⓦ filmmuseum-potsdam.de

The squat but elegant **Marstall** is Potsdam's oldest town-centre survivor. Built as an orangery towards the end of the seventeenth century and converted into stables by that scourge of frivolity, Friedrich Wilhelm I, the building owes its current appearance to Knobelsdorff, who extended and prettified it during the eighteenth century. Today it houses the **Filmmuseum Potsdam**, which draws on material from Babelsberg's movie studios nearby (UFA, DEFA, Studio Babelsberg; see p.182) to present both a technical and artistic history of German film from 1895 to the present day, with some particularly fascinating material concerning the immediate postwar period. The museum **cinema** is the best in Potsdam and there's also a good **café**-restaurant.

Just behind the Marstall, **Am Neuen Markt** leads to a few handsome and now very rare vestiges of old Potsdam, including some improbably grand eighteenth-century coaching stables with an entrance in the form of a triumphal arch.

Altstadt

North beyond Alter Markt, **Friedrich-Ebert-Strasse** passes into an area once occupied by Potsdam's **Altstadt** before it was fairly comprehensively destroyed in the war. Luckily, a couple of residential districts survived substantially intact and slowly emerge along the north end of Friedrich-Ebert-Strasse.

Bassinplatz

A block east of Friedrich-Ebert-Strasse, **Bassinplatz** is a grand plaza and park that's disfigured by a huge modern bus station, but dominated by the nineteenth-century **Peter-Pauls-Kirche**, a replica of the campanile of San Zeno Maggiore in Verona. At the southeastern corner of the square lies the **Französische Kirche**, completed according to plans by Knobelsdorff in 1753 in imitation of the Pantheon in Rome, a recurring theme in German architecture of the period.

Holländisches Viertel

ⓦ hollaendisches-viertel.net

The appealing **Holländisches Viertel**, or Dutch quarter, consists of around 150 gabled, red-brick houses built in the classic Dutch style, with shuttered windows and slanted roofs, which were put up by Dutch builders for immigrants from the Netherlands who were invited to work in Potsdam by Friedrich Wilhelm I. The quarter has seen periods of dereliction since, but recent restoration and gentrification has produced a small colony of trendy shops and cafés. At Mittelstr. 8, the **Jan Bouman Haus** preserves a typical house of the era (Mon–Fri 1–6pm, Sat & Sun 11am–6pm; ☎0331 28 03 773, Ⓦjan-bouman-haus.de; €2).

Brandenburger Strasse

Brandenburger Strasse, today's main shopping street, is the Altstadt's key cross street, leading west to Park Sanssouci and forming the backbone of a **Baroque quarter** – built between 1732 and 1742 on the orders of Friedrich Wilhelm I for tradespeople as Potsdam rapidly expanded. The triumphal **Brandenburger Tor** marks its western end, built by Gontard in 1733 with a playfulness lacking in its Berlin namesake. The Grünes Gitter park entrance lies just beyond the northwestern corner of the adjacent Luisenplatz.

Gedenkstätte Lindenstrasse

Lindenstr. 54–55 • Tues–Sun 10am–6pm • €1.50; €3 with tour • Ⓦ gedenkstaette-lindenstrasse.de

The Dutch-style Kommandantenhaus has uncomfortable associations. From 1933 until the *Wende* it served as a court and prison for political persecution known as the *Lindenhotel*. It now houses the **Gedenkstätte Lindenstrasse** (Lindenstrasse Memorial), where you can view the chilling cells and an exhibition details the building's use, which included spells as a Nazi prison and "hereditary-health court", where decisions about compulsory sterilization were made; as a secret police detention centre during Soviet occupation; and as the East German secret police headquarters for the Potsdam region.

Park Sanssouci

Stretching west out of Potsdam's town centre, **Park Sanssouci** was built for Frederick the Great as a retreat after he decided in 1744 that he needed a residence where he could live "without cares" – *sans souci* in the French spoken at court. The task was entrusted to architect Georg von Knobelsdorff, who had already proved himself on other projects in Potsdam and Berlin. **Schloss Sanssouci**, on a hill overlooking the town, took three years to complete, while the extensive parklands were laid out over the following five years. As a finishing touch Frederick ordered the construction of the **Neues Palais** at the western end of the park, to mark the end of the Seven Years' War. Numerous additions over the following hundred and fifty years or so included the **Orangerie**. The park is most beautiful in spring, when the trees are in leaf and the flowers in bloom, and least crowded on weekdays.

INFORMATION AND TICKETS   PARK SANSSOUCI

Information There are two main visitor centres (☎0331 969 42 00) for the park: one is by the Historische Mühle (Tues–Sun: April–Oct 8.30am–5.30pm; Nov–March 8.30am–4.30pm; see 000); the other is by the Neues Palais (daily except Tues: April–Oct 9am–6pm; Nov–March 9am–6pm). For more information, see Ⓦ spsg.de.

Tickets Individual tickets are available for all ticketed sights, and can only be purchased at palace entrances. If you plan to visit several buildings, however, consider a combination ticket: a Sanssouci + ticket, available at the palace and Potsdam visitor centres (€19), or online (€21, including a timed entry slot for Sanssouci) allows entry to all park buildings. Potsdam Family Tickets, valid for two adults and up to four children, are also available, though only at the visitor centres (€49 with palace entry, €25 without). Entrance to the park itself is free, although a €2 donation is suggested.

Friedenskirche

Am Grünen Gitter 3 • Mid-March to April Mon–Sat 11am–5pm, Sun noon–5pm; May to mid-Oct Mon–Sat 10am–6pm, Sun noon–6pm; mid-Oct to mid-March Sat 11am–4pm, Sun 12.30pm–4pm • Free • Ⓦ spsg.de

Immediately north of the Grünes Gitter (Green Grid) entrance lies the 1850 Italianate **Friedenskirche** (Church of Peace), designed by Persius for Friedrich Wilhelm IV. With its 39m-high campanile and lakeside setting, it conjures up the southern European atmosphere that Friedrich Wilhelm strove for by using the San Clemente basilica in Rome as a model, and with the design centred on the magnificent Byzantine apse mosaic from San Cipriano in Murano. Adjoining the church, the domed Hohenzollern mausoleum contains the tombs of Friedrich Wilhelm IV and his wife Elizabeth, and Friedrich III and his wife Victoria.

The garden to the west is the **Marly-Garten**, once the kitchen garden of Friedrich I, who named it, with intentional irony, after Louis XIV's sumptuous Marly park.

The approach to the Schloss

To approach Schloss Sanssouci as Frederick the Great might have done, make for the eighteenth-century **obelisk** on Schopenhauerstrasse. Beyond, Hauptallee runs through the ornate Knobelsdorff-designed **Obelisk-Portal** – two clusters of pillars flanked by the goddesses Flora and Pomona – to the **Grosse Fontäne**, the largest of the park's many fountains, around which stand a host of Classical statues, notably Venus and Mercury. The approach to the Schloss itself leads up through terraced ranks of vines that are among the northernmost in Germany.

Schloss Sanssouci

Maulbeerallee • Tues–Sun: April–Oct 10am–6pm; Nov–March 10am–5pm; book online in advance or arrive early as demand is high (tickets go on sale at 10am) • €12 (includes audio guide), or Sanssouci + ticket (see opposite) • ⓦ spsg.de

The highlight of any trip to Potsdam, **Schloss Sanssouci** (Sanssouci Palace) is a surprisingly modest one-storey Baroque affair, topped by an oxidized green dome and ornamental statues, looking out over the vine terraces towards the high-rises of central Potsdam. Frederick had definite ideas about what he wanted and worked closely with Knobelsdorff on the palace design, which was to be a place where the king, who had no great love for his capital, Berlin, or his wife Elizabeth Christine, could escape both.

Once **inside**, you'll find a frenzy of Rococo in the twelve rooms where Frederick lived and entertained his guests – a process that usually entailed quarrelling with them. The most eye-catching rooms are the opulent **Marmorsaal** (Marble Hall) and the **Konzertzimmer** (Concert Room), where the flute-playing king forced eminent musicians to play his own works on concert evenings. Frederick's favourite haunt was the **Bibliothek** (Library) where, surrounded by two thousand volumes – mainly French translations of classics and a sprinkling of contemporary French writings – he could oversee work on his tomb. One of Frederick's most celebrated house guests was **Voltaire**, who lived here from 1750 to 1753, acting as a kind of private tutor to the king, finally leaving when he'd had enough of Frederick's behaviour, damning the king's intellect with faint praise and accusing him of treating "the whole world as slaves". In revenge Frederick had Voltaire's former room decorated with carvings of apes and parrots.

Bildergalerie

Im Park Sanssouci 4 • Mid-May to Oct Tues–Sun 10am–6pm • €6, or Sanssouci + ticket (see opposite) • ⓦ spsg.de

East of Schloss Sanssouci, overlooking the ornamental Holländischer Garten (Dutch Garden), is the restrained Baroque **Bildergalerie** (Picture Gallery), which, it's claimed, was the first building in Europe built specifically as a museum. Unfortunately, wartime destruction and looting scattered the contents, but the new collection includes Caravaggio's wonderful *Incredulity of St Thomas* and several works by Rubens and Van Dyck.

Neue Kammern

April–Oct Tues–Sun 10am–5pm • €4 with tour, €3 without, or Sanssouci + ticket (see opposite) • ⓦ spsg.de

West of the Schloss, from a point near the Cleopatra statue, steps lead down to the **Neue Kammern** (New Chambers), the architectural twin of the Bildergalerie, originally

11

an orangery and later a guesthouse. Today it showcases several ostentatiously decorated banquet rooms and suites, as well as the **Jaspissaal** (Jasper Room) which is peppered with ancient busts and lined with jasper.

Sizilianischer Garten and Nordischer Garten
Maulbeerallee

Immediately west of the Neue Kammern is the prim **Sizilianischer Garten** (Sicilian Garden), crammed with subtropical plants and complementing the **Nordischer Garten** (Nordic Garden), another ornamental garden just to the north. The latter's most interesting feature is the strange-looking **Felsentor** (Rock Gate), a gateway fashioned out of uncut stones and topped by a lumpen-looking eagle with outstretched wings.

Historische Mühle
Maulbeerallee 5

Frederick was prepared to go to some lengths to achieve the desired carefree rural ambience for Sanssouci and retained an old wooden windmill as an ornament just north of the Neue Kammern. Four years after his death, this was replaced by a rustic-looking stone construction, the **Historische Mühle** (Historic Mill), now a restaurant (see p.184).

Orangerieschloss
An der Orangerie 3–5 • April Sat & Sun 10am–6pm; May–Oct Tues–Sun 10am–6pm • €4, or Sanssouci + ticket (see p.178) • Ⓦ spsg.de

With its belvedere towers, the Italianate Renaissance-style **Orangerieschoss** (Orangery Palace) is one of the most visually impressive buildings in the Sanssouci park. A series of terraces with curved retaining walls sporting waterspouts in the shape of lions' heads leads up to the sandy-coloured building, whose slightly down-at-heel appearance adds character. It was built at the behest of Friedrich IV and, like the Friedenskirche (see p.178), inspired by architecture seen on his Italian travels. The facade is lined with allegorical statues set in niches, such as "Industry" who holds a cogwheel.

The western wing of the building is still used as a refuge for tropical plants in winter, and during the summer – after mid-2018 when it reopens after refurbishment – it will be possible to ascend the western tower for views of the Neues Palais and vistas of Potsdam's high-rises. The palace also houses a gallery, the **Raffaelsaal** (Raphael Hall), with copies of paintings looted by Napoleon.

The Belvedere auf dem Klausberg and Drachenshaus

From the western wing of the Orangerie, the arrow-straight Krimlindenallee, lined with lime trees, leads towards a Rococo **Belvedere auf dem Klausberg**, the last building to be built under Frederick the Great. It was the only building in the whole of Sanssouci park to suffer serious war damage, but has now been restored to its former glory. A couple of hundred metres short of the Belvedere, a path off to the left leads to the **Drachenhaus** (Dragon House), a one-time vintner's house built in the style of a Chinese pagoda for the small vineyard nearby. There's a café inside (see p.184).

Antikentempel

The **Antikentempel** (Antique Temple) was built in 1768 to house part of Frederick the Great's art collection. This domed rotunda is now the last resting place of a number of Hohenzollerns, including the Empress Auguste Victoria, and Hermine, whom Wilhelm II married in exile, and who became known as the "last Empress".

Neues Palais
Am Neuen Palais • Daily except Tues: April–Oct 10am–6pm; Nov–March 10am–5pm • €8, or Sanssouci + ticket (see p.178) • Ⓦ spsg.de

Rising through the trees at the western end of Park Sanssoucci, the **Neues Palais** (New Palace) is another massive Rococo extravaganza from Frederick the Great's time, built between 1763 and 1769 to reaffirm Prussian might after the Seven Years' War. At the centre of the palace is a huge green-weathered dome, topped by a crown, while the edges of the roof around the entire building are adorned by lines of Classical figures, mass-produced by a team of sculptors.

The main entrance is in the western facade, and once inside, you'll find the interior predictably opulent, particularly as you enter the vast and startling **Grottensaal** (Grotto Hall) on the ground floor, which is decorated entirely with shells and semiprecious stones to form images of lizards and dragons. The equally huge **Marmorsaal** (Marble Hall) is the other highlight, with its beautiful floor of patterned marble slabs. The southern wing contains Frederick's apartments and theatre where he enjoyed Italian opera and French plays. The last imperial resident of the Neues Palais was Kaiser Wilhelm II, who packed sixty train carriages with the palace contents before fleeing with his family in November 1918, following the revolution and abdication.

Facing the Neues Palais entrance are the **Communs**, a couple of Rococo fantasies joined by a curved colonnade. They look grandiose, but their purpose was mundane: they housed the palace's serving and maintenance staff.

Rehgarten and Park Charlottenhof

From the Neues Palais, Ökonomieweg leads east between the **Rehgarten** (Deer Garden), the former court hunting ground – and still home to a few deer – and **Park Charlottenhof**, created by Friedrich Wilhelm III as a Christmas present for his son, and today one of Sanssouci's quieter corners.

Chinesisches Haus

Am Grünem Gitter • May–Oct Tues–Sun 10am–6pm • €3, or Sanssouci + ticket (see p.178) • W spsg.de

The slightly kitsch **Chinesisches Haus** (Chinese House) is a kind of Rococo pagoda that reflects the eighteenth-century fashion for Oriental architecture and arts. The highly decorative interior is worth a peek and houses a small museum of Chinese and Meissen porcelain, while outside are a series of eerily lifelike statues of Oriental figures.

Schloss Charlottenhof and Römische Bäder

Geschwister-Scholl-Str. 34a • Both sights May–Oct Tues–Sun 10am–6pm • Schloss €6, Bäder €5; Kombiticket €8; or Sanssouci + ticket (see p.178) • W spsg.de

The Roman-style **Schloss Charlottenhof** (Charlottenhof Palace) was designed by Schinkel and Persius for Friedrich IV. Though designated a palace, it is, in reality, little more than a glorified villa, but its interior, unlike most Sanssouci buildings, is original. The effect is impressive: the hallway is bathed in blue light filtered through coloured glass decorated with stars, a prelude to the **Kupferstichzimmer** (Print Room), whose walls are now covered in copies of Italian Renaissance paintings.

Across the lawns to the north a path leads over a bridge past a small farm building to the **Römische Bäder** (Roman Baths), built by Schinkel and Persius in convincing imitation of a Roman villa. The ensemble of buildings – which include a teahouse and garden house – are set around an attractive lake that was planned and built by celebrated architect Lenné.

Dichterhain and Fasanerie

Immediately east of Schloss Charlottenhof is the **Dichterhain** (Poets' Grove), an open space dotted with busts of Goethe, Schiller and Herder, among others. West of here through the woods and across a racetrack-shaped clearing called the Hippodrom is the **Fasanerie**, another Italian-style edifice built between 1842 and 1844.

Neuer Garten

Free, suggested donation €2, or Sanssouci + ticket (see p.178)

Immediately northeast of Potsdam's centre lies the **Neuer Garten** (New Garden), a large park, commissioned by Friedrich Wilhelm II, that borders the Heiliger See. Designed as a modern version of the Baroque Sanssouci, it followed a more English-style design, with various additions over the centuries.

Marmorpalais

Im Neuen Garten 10 • May–Oct Tues–Sun 10am–6pm; Nov–March Sat & Sun 10am–4pm; April Sat & Sun 10am–6pm • €6, or Sanssouci + ticket (see p.178) • Ⓦ spsg.de

Built for Friedrich Wilhelm II, the Neoclassical **Marmorpalais** (Marble Palace) has been restored to an approximation of its original royal condition and its sumptuous rooms are on show. Friedrich Wilhelm II died a premature death here, allegedly as a consequence of his dissolute lifestyle.

Schloss Cecilienhof

Im Neuen Garten 11 • Tues–Sun: April–Oct 10am–6pm; Nov–March 10am–5pm • €6, or Sanssouci + ticket (see p.178) • Ⓦ spsg.de • Tram #92 or #96 to "Reiterweg/Alleestrasse" stop then change to bus #603 to Schloss Cecilienhof

In the grounds of the Neuer Garten, looking like a mock-Elizabethan mansion, is **Schloss Cecilienhof** (Cecilienhof Palace); the last palace to be commissioned by the Hohenzollerns, it was begun in 1913 and completed in 1917, the war evidently doing nothing to change the architectural style. Cecilienhof would only rate a passing mention were it not for the fact that the **Potsdam Conference** – confirming earlier decisions made at Yalta about the postwar European order – was held here from July 17 to August 2, 1945. The conference was heavily symbolic, providing a chance for Truman, Stalin and Churchill (replaced mid-conference by Clement Attlee) to show the world that they had truly won the war by meeting in the heart of the ruined Reich. As a result, the main attraction inside is the **Konferenzsaal** (Conference Chamber), where the Allies worked out details of the division of Europe. Everything has been left pretty much as it was in 1945, with the huge round table, specially made in Moscow for the conference, still in place. It's also possible to visit the delegates' workrooms, furnished in varying degrees of chintziness. Cecilienhof has been used as an expensive hotel and restaurant since 1960.

Babelsberg

Babelsberg, on the eastern bank of the Havel, was once a separate town but is now officially part of Potsdam. Lining the banks of the Tiefer See is **Park Babelsberg**, Potsdam's third great park complex, designed by Lenné, but not as popular. Tracks lead through the hilly, roughly wooded park to **Schloss Babelsberg** (closed for renovation; Ⓦ spsg.de), a neo-Gothic architectural extravaganza, built by Schinkel at the behest of Prince Wilhelm, brother of Friedrich Wilhelm IV, and inspired by Windsor Castle in England. But Babelsberg's real claim to fame is as the one-time heart of the German film industry. Founded in 1917, it was here that the **UFA film studios** rivalled Hollywood during the 1920s.

Filmpark Babelsberg

Grossbeerenstr. 200, Potsdam-Babelsberg • Late March to Oct daily 10am–6pm • €21, children aged 4–16 €14, audio guides €3 • ☎ 0331 721 27 55, Ⓦ filmpark.de • Buses #690 and #601 from Ⓢ Babelsberg

Today, the huge old UFA film studios complex – films produced here during its heyday included *Das Kabinett des Dr Caligari*, *Metropolis* and *Der Blaue Engel* (see p.293) – has reinvented itself as a theme park, **Filmpark Babelsberg**. Most of interest to those with a good knowledge of the German film industry, it allows visitors to roam sets from old films, witness stuntmen in action and marvel at the special effects. The audio guide provides extras insights into the Filmpark's history. There's also a 4D action cinema, and the park is especially good (if not better) for kids, who will enjoy the Jungle Playground and the Animal Farm.

ARRIVAL AND DEPARTURE POTSDAM

By train All services, including the S-Bahn from Berlin (around 30min) arrive at Potsdam's Hauptbahnhof. Potsdam's local bus and tram services are included in the BVG ticket (see p.22) that include zone C, so buying an ABC day-ticket is the most economical option for day-trips from Berlin.

GETTING AROUND

By bus and tram The city's main bus station lies beside the Hauptbahnhof, from where Verkehrsbetrieb Potsdam (ViP; w vip-potsdam.de) bus #X15 runs straight to Schloss Sanssouci. Take #X5 or bus #605 to "Neues Palais" to walk from the furthest reaches of the park via its attractions back to the Altstadt. Tram #92 heads from the Hauptbahnhof to the Altstadt, though it's more interesting to simply walk 10min via Lange Brücke and Alter Markt.

Bike rental Potsdam per Pedales at the train station (May–Sept daily 9.30am–8pm; T 0331 748 00 57, w potsdam-per-pedales.de) rents bikes (€11/day), as well as Potsdam audio guides (€6/day); also Fahrradstation (see p.23), Gutenbergstr. 52 (T 0331 280 38 16). However, you can only cycle on a single loop within the park and are not allowed to park your bike within it.

11

TROPICAL ISLANDS

An old hangar for zeppelins 60km south of Berlin now houses Tropical Islands (T 035 477 60 50 50, w tropical-islands.de), a landscaped water park, the size of nine football fields, containing pools, lagoons, water slides, waterfalls, whirlpools and saunas as well as a clutch of bars, restaurants and shops. The quality of the landscaping is first class, and the tropical shrubbery and birds that flit around its undergrowth get to luxuriate in the constant 26ºC temperature. A Disneyesque quality is added by interior buildings and monuments – like the Bali, Borneo, Thai and Samoan pavilions – and in 2016 a new outdoor section, Amazonia, was opened, offering yet more water activities. But what really sets the place apart is its laidback convenience: a wristband provided when you enter electronically tallies all purchases – you settle up on leaving – but best of all, the place is open 24hr throughout the year and allows you to **stay overnight**. Tents (€69/person) can be rented, but most people just crash on the beach with a mat and blanket, which costs an additional €34.60 per night on top of the one-off complex entry charge of €42 (or €49 with sauna complex). Tropical Islands lies off the A13 motorway from Berlin (exit Staakow), and near Brand Tropical Islands train station, where free shuttle buses to the complex meet every train between 5.30am and midnight. Trains leave from Berlin Hauptbahnhof, with the fastest taking fifty minutes.

11

INFORMATION

Tourist information There are tourist offices in the train station (April–Oct Mon–Sat 9.30am–8pm, Sun 10am–4pm; Nov–March Mon–Fri 9.30am–6pm, Sun 10am–4pm); on the ground floor of the Landtag in the Alter Markt (Mon–Sat 9.30am–7pm, Sun 10am–4pm); and at Brandenburger Str. 3, by Potsdam's own Brandenburger Tor (April–Oct Mon–Fri 9.30am–6pm, Sat & Sun 9.30am–4pm; Nov–March Mon–Fri 10am–6pm, Sat & Sun 9.30am–2pm; ☎0331 27 55 88 99, ⓦpotsdam -tourism.com).

EATING

IN TOWN

Babette Brandenburger Str. 71 ☎0331 29 16 48. Pleasant café with outdoor seating, in the shadow of the Brandenburger Tor, that's a good place to rest weary feet and have an indulgent *Torte* after trekking around Sanssouci Park. The large menu, available in English, features simple snacks (€7.50) and main meals (from €10) though the quality of both is fairly ordinary. Mon–Sat 9am till late, Sun 10am till late.

Contadino Luisenplatz 8 ☎0331 951 09 23. The casual surroundings overlooking the plaza and Brandenburger Tor make this mid-priced Italian restaurant a perfect place to eat before or after tackling Sanssouci. Along with pasta and pizza there's a wealth of good alternatives: chops, steaks and pan-fried Iberian and South American food. Some items and daily specials cost as little as €4. Daily noon–late.

Froschkasten Kiezstr. 4 ☎0331 29 13 15, ⓦfrosch kasten.de. Just outside the centre, this is one of the oldest and most authentic inns in Potsdam, and serves good, traditional German food, with several great fish dishes including a delicious grilled salmon fillet (€21). Mon–Sat noon–midnight, Sun noon–10pm.

La Madeleine Lindenstr. 9 ☎0331 270 54 00, ⓦcreperie-potsdam.de. Smart *crêperie* with a good selection of delicious French crêpes from €8 – the buckwheat versions are particularly good – such as the Nordic, with salmon and radish, or the ratatouille version. Daily noon–10pm.

La Maison du Chocolat Benkertstr. 20 ☎0331 237 07 30, ⓦschokoladenhaus-potsdam.de. Café-restaurant with outdoor seating on the pavements of the pretty Dutch quarter. Good spot for breakfast or regional and seasonal specialities (from around €9); but it's the rich, indulgent, and frankly unmissable, hot chocolates that really put the place on the map. Great cakes and good wines too. Cash only. Daily 10am–10pm.

★**Juliette** Jägerstr. 39 ☎0331 270 17 91, ⓦrestaurant-juliette.de. This cosy restaurant is among Potsdam's best, offering French flair (and wines) and an unpredictable range of dishes that might include the exotic likes of loach with couscous and avocado purée or steak with truffles and foie gras. Mains from €18, set menus from €52. Daily noon–3.30pm & 6–10pm.

PARK SANSSOUCI

Drachenhaus Maulbeerallee 4a ☎0331 505 38 08, ⓦdrachenhaus.de. Genteel little café in the grounds of Schloss Sanssouci, housed in a pagoda-style building once used by royal vintners. You can eat well here, with a choice of sturdy Brandenburg specialities or just a piece of *Torte*. March–Oct daily 11am–7pm; Nov–Feb Tues–Sun 11am–6pm.

Mövenpick Restaurant Zur Historischen Mühle Zur Historischen Mühle 2 ☎0331 281 493, ⓦmövenpick -restaurants.com. This spacious restaurant, conveniently located in the park grounds, offers a decent range of breakfasts, lunches and dinners. Dishes tend towards German cuisine but there are burgers and salads too, and the outdoor terrace and beer garden are a boon in warm weather. Mains from €14. Daily 8am–10pm.

DRINKING AND NIGHTLIFE

★**Hafthorn** Friedrich-Ebert-Str. 90 ☎0331 280 08 20, ⓦhafthorn.de. Hip and happening pub with snacks (€3–9) including superb burgers, *rösti* and potato pancakes. A fashionable but very mixed crowd packs the place out until late, even when there's no live music, and there's also a busy beer garden. Daily 6pm–midnight.

Waschhaus Schiffbauergasse 1 ☎0331 271 560, ⓦwaschhaus.de. Large cultural venue where there's always something going on. It lies just off Berliner Str. on the way into town from the Glienicker Brücke, and incorporates galleries, an open-air cinema (summer-only) beer garden, live music stages and Fabrik (☎0331 280 03 14, ⓦfabrikpotsdam.de), a theatre for contemporary dance and music.

Gedenkstätte and Museum Sachsenhausen

Str. der Nationen 22, Oranienburg • Daily: mid-March to mid-Oct 8.30am–6pm; mid-Oct to mid-March 8.30am–4.30pm (museums closed Mon in winter) • Free, audio tour €3, leaflet €0.50 • ☎033 01 20 00, ⓦstiftung-bg.de

The former concentration camp of Sachsenhausen on the fringes of the small town of Oranienburg, 35km north of Berlin, has been preserved as the unremittingly grim

Gedenkstätte Sachsenhausen (Sachsenhausen Memorial) as a reminder of the crimes of two of the last century's most powerful and terrible regimes. Established in 1936, this Nazi camp was a prototype upon which others were based. It was never designed for large-scale mass extermination; nonetheless tens of thousands of the 204,000 prisoners who passed through its gates never left, with death either from starvation, disease, forced labour or mistreatment, or as a result of the SS's programme of murder. In 1941, over ten thousand Soviet POWs were systematically executed, and at the end of the war thousands more were killed or lost their lives on death marches. After the war the Soviets used the core area as a prison.

At the entrance to the camp, its largest structure, the impossibly detailed **Neues Museum** (New Museum), charts the camp's origins in a defunct brewery in the centre of Oranienburg, which the local Nazis filled with many of their classmates, colleagues and neighbours. The camp proper begins under the main **watchtower** and beyond a gate adorned with the ominous sign *Arbeit macht frei* ("Work frees"), perimeter wall and former high-voltage fence – site of frequent inmate suicides. Many areas of the camp have been chillingly well preserved or reconstructed: a number of **barracks**, which house exhibitions explaining the history of the site and telling the stories of selected inmates; the camp **prison** – a prison within a prison – from which internees seldom returned; and the former **kitchen** where harrowing films show the camp on liberation. Just outside the perimeter lie pits where **executions** took place and bodies were incinerated.

At the northern tip of the camp an exhibition in a guard tower investigates what the local populace knew and thought of the camp, via video interviews, while the jumbled hall next door, the **Museum Sowjetisches Speziallager**, examines the postwar Soviet Special Camp (1945–50). Sixty thousand people were interned here over five years, including six thousand German officers transferred from Western Allied camps. By the time the camp closed in the spring of 1950, twelve thousand had died of malnutrition and disease.

ARRIVAL AND DEPARTURE GEDENKSTÄTTE AND MUSEUM SACHSENHAUSEN

By train Trains (hourly; 25min) from Berlin– Hauptbahnhof and Ⓢ Friedrichstrasse (frequent; 42min) travel to Oranienburg train station – if you don't fancy the signposted 20min walk, take buses #M804 and #M821 to the memorial (BVG day-tickets valid for whole journey) from just north of the square beside the station.

OSTEL

Accommodation

Berlin has an increasingly broad selection of hotels, pensions and hostels, along with a glut of private rooms and apartments for both long- and short-term rental. In typical Berlin fashion there is considerable overlap between all these categories, so even if you don't want to sleep in a dorm, for example, it's worth scanning our hostel listings for private single or double rooms. Prices tend to be good value, despite the city's enduring popularity: competition is extremely keen everywhere, which keeps things affordable, and even some smart hotels offer online deals that have been known to rival hostel rates.

ESSENTIALS

Booking If you can, try to book at least a couple of weeks in advance – or even further ahead during important festivals (see p.26) – to be assured of getting exactly what you want. The online reservation service of Visit Berlin (☎ 030 25 00 23 23, ⓦ visitberlin.de) is great for hotel and pension bookings, and has hostel beds too. There are also several websites where you can search and pay in advance for a dorm bed or private room in a hostel. These often take their commission from the hostels rather than the customer, so there is nothing extra to pay – you may even find that online deals beat what you'd be offered at a hostel reception. Check out ⓦ gomio.com, ⓦ hostelbookers.com, ⓦ hostelworld.com and ⓦ hostelz.com.

Rates The prices at the end of our hotel and pension reviews indicate the cost of the least expensive double room, midweek and in high season (May–Sept). Note that while rates at the less expensive hotels don't vary much across the week, many of the more upmarket hotels slash their rates at the weekend. These rates generally include free wi-fi and breakfast, though many hotels offer a choice of rates that are inclusive and exclusive of breakfast; where breakfast is excluded we have listed the price. For hostels, we quote prices for the cheapest dorm beds, singles and doubles in the same period, exclusive of breakfast.

City Tax Since the beginning of 2014, overnight stays have been subject to a City Tax that amounts to 5 percent of the room rate (excluding VAT). Most – but not all – establishments include it in their rates. The prices quoted below are usually inclusive of City Tax but some, especially hostels, will request it as an extra. Business travellers (who can prove as much) are exempt from the tax.

Minimum stays Wherever you stay minimum-stay requirements are unusual but not unheard of, particularly at busy times such as New Year.

HOTELS AND PENSIONS

Although traditional **pensions** – usually smaller and cheaper than a **hotel**, although the categories do overlap – are in decline, they still do exist, especially in City West. (Some may be called "Hotel-Pensions", which may be either or both, so don't take too much notice of the labels.) Note that **single rooms** are usually only a third cheaper than doubles. **Breakfast** is generally included in the room rate, but we have stated exceptions where they occur.

12

UNTER DEN LINDEN AND AROUND

★**Adlon Kempinski** Unter den Linden 77 ☎ 030 22 61 11 11, ⓦ hotel-adlon.de; ⓤ/Ⓢ Brandenburger Tor; map p.36. The jewel of Berlin's prewar luxury hotels was re-created in the 1990s in all its excessive splendour. Prices are fit for a Kaiser – you'll part with at least €26,000/night for the royal suite. Breakfast €26. **€265**

Arcotel John F Werderscher Markt 11 ☎ 030 405 04 60, ⓦ arcotelhotels.com; ⓤ Hausvogteiplatz; map p.36. Close to Gendarmenmarkt, this 190-room hotel is a slightly cheaper option than the neighbouring big guns but has all the facilities you'll need – gym, sauna, meeting rooms, restaurant and bar. Breakfast €22 **€142**

Hilton Berlin Mohrenstr. 30 ☎ 030 20 23 00, ⓦ hilton .com; ⓤ Stadtmitte; map p.36. Luxurious, expensive and not very different to any other Hilton hotel, apart from its fine view of the Gendarmenmarkt. Facilities include sauna, swimming pool and squash court. Wi-fi chargeable. **€107**

Hotel de Rome Behrenstr. 37 ☎ 030 460 60 90, ⓦ roccofortehotels.com; ⓤ Französische Strasse; map

WHERE TO STAY

With Berlin a city of distinct districts, deciding **where to stay** may be your most important choice. While the public transport network is excellent, staying in the area of town that suits you best will make your visit easier. **Mitte** is the most obvious choice, particularly if you're after a major hotel. Within this central district, the **Spandauer Vorstadt** around Oranienburger Strasse is best for smaller-scale or budget accommodation, with a good selection of hostels and boutique hotels which, as well as being within walking distance of many city-centre attractions, have good eating and nightlife options nearby. If you are going to be in Berlin a little longer than a weekend or prefer a quieter, less touristy and more residential neighbourhood, charming and upbeat **Prenzlauer Berg** is a good choice, as is **Schöneberg** – the latter particularly for gay travellers (see p.253). If you fancy some good clubbing, or just want to hang out in more alternative bars and cafés, try to lay your head in **Friedrichshain** or **eastern Kreuzberg**, where you'll find the most cutting-edge nightlife. The other major concentration of accommodation in the city is in **City West** – the old centre of West Berlin – where you'll find a good range of both affordable pensions and high-end five-stars, and plenty of options in between. It's a little away from Berlin's brightest lights, so nightlife is very thin, but the restaurant scene is generally top-notch here, as are transport links.

p.36. Occupying a nineteenth-century former Dresdner Bank building, this high-class hotel mixes history with a swanky interior, luxurious rooms, an expansive spa and rooftop terrace. **€295**

The Westin Grand Friedrichstr. 158–164 ☎030 202 70, ⓦwestin.com/berlin; ⓤFranzösische Strasse; map p.36. Fully living up to its name, this GDR-era hotel once served party bigwigs but was overhauled in the 1990s to provide oodles of traditional upmarket luxury with a refined Belle Époque interior and beautifully appointed rooms and suites. Wi-fi free in the lobby only. **€229**

ALEXANDERPLATZ AND AROUND

art'otel berlin mitte Wallstr. 70–73 ☎030 24 06 20, ⓦartotels.com; ⓤMärkisches Museum; map p.60. Smart, lively, quirky hotel – lots of contemporary and modern art, including an impressive range of Georg Baselitz paintings – in a quiet corner of Berlin, close to the U-Bahn. **€63**

Derag Livinghotel Grosser Kurfürst Neue Rossstr. 11–12 ☎030 24 60 00, ⓦderaghotels.de; ⓤMärkisches Museum; map p.60. Sleek hotel in a renovated early twentieth-century building, with straightforward, spotless rooms and apartments (minimum stay a week; €130/ night). There's a very decent restaurant too. Breakfast €18. **€84**

Nikolai Residence Am Nussbaum 5 ☎030 400 44 59 00, ⓦnikolai-residence.com; ⓤKlosterstrasse; map p.60. Cute and well-run three-star in the heart of the Nikolaiviertel. Decor is fairly modern and dotted with paintings and photos by German artists, and the 21 rooms are simple, reasonably stylish and comfortable. No breakfast served on premises. **€90**

Park Inn by Radisson Alexanderplatz ☎030 238 90, ⓦparkinn-berlin.com; ⓤ/Ⓢ Alexanderplatz; map p.60. Big, ugly block bang in the middle of things, with brilliant views over the city and hard to beat for convenience. Of the 1000 or so en-suite rooms, the business-class ones are a notch above the rest. Gym, sauna and a rooftop terrace. Wi-fi €9.90/day; breakfast €19. **€90**

Radisson Blu Hotel Karl-Liebknecht-Str. 3 ☎030 23 82 80, ⓦradissonblu.com/hotel-berlin; Ⓢ Hackescher Markt; map p.60. Impressive, central and modern hotel that offers rooms either with views over the Spree and the Dom, or facing inwards onto a vast aquarium of 2500 tropical fish in the lobby-cum-atrium, which is part of Sea Life Berlin (see p.64). Decent spa and restaurant. Breakfast €25. **€134**

12

LIVING LIKE A LOCAL: ROOMS AND APARTMENTS

Private room and apartment rentals are often a good-value choice for travellers to Berlin, and a plethora of options exist all over the city. The best apartments offer value for money, are well located – usually in the more popular areas such as Prenzlauer Berg, Mitte, Schöneberg and Kreuzberg – and some offer stylish or interesting decor. The typical charge for a private room is €30–40 per person per night, while for a whole apartment expect to pay around €80–100 per night. Though we list agencies that primarily specialize in short-term rentals – of up to about a month – below, longer-term lets are available too (see p.31). Note that in 2016 the city authorities banned short-term apartment rentals via **AirBnB**, **Wimdu** and other agencies without a permit, though in practice the law – which allows renting out less than 50 percent of an apartment's floor space (and thus means that room rentals are still permissible) will be hard to monitor. Note too that private rentals are subject to City Tax (see p.187), usually levied as a separate fee.

APARTMENT RENTAL AGENCIES

9flats ⓦ9flats.com. Berlin company that aims to help you find "affordable private accommodations, rented out by friendly locals all over the world".

Be My Guest ⓦbe-my-guest.com. A good spread of short-stay apartments, B&Bs and guest rooms for all budgets.

Bed & Breakfast in Berlin ☎030 44 05 05 82, ⓦbed-and-breakfast-berlin.de. Single and double rooms and apartments.

Bed & Breakfast Privatzimmervermittlung ⓦbed-and-breakfast.de. Part of a national chain, offering rooms ranging from the simple to the luxurious.

Brilliant Apartments ⓦbrilliant-apartments.de.

Specializes in apartments in the Prenzlauer Berg district.

Citybed ☎030 23 62 36 30, ⓦcitybed.de. Online accommodation booking, with prices starting at around €25 per person.

Ferienwohnung Berlin ⓦferienwohnungen-berlin.de. A wide range of rooms and apartments all over the city with a vast online booking engine.

Oh Berlin ⓦoh-berlin.com. Berlin apartments to suit all tastes and budgets.

Roomsurfer ⓦroomsurfer.com. The most casual and low-budget accommodation site: much like ⓦcouchsurfing.com, but with money changing hands.

Wimdu ⓦwimdu.com. Another big international database for apartments, holiday homes and B&Bs.

THE SPANDAUER VORSTADT

★Amano Auguststr. 43 ☎030 80 94 150, ⓦamanogroup.de; ⓤRosenthaler Platz; map pp.70–71. This well-located four-star has slick designer rooms and apartments (some rather small), a spacious lobby, lovely courtyard garden and rooftop terrace bar (see p.218) that's popular with locals. Reception rents out Xboxes and bikes. **€120**

Casa Camper Weinmeisterstr. 1 ☎030 20 00 34 10, ⓦcasacamper.com; ⓤWeinmeisterstrasse; map pp.70–71. Smart boutique hotel whose solid-wood interiors try to mirror a bit of Berlin's quirkiness. Around-the-clock snacks and drinks are on offer at the hotel restaurant, which has impressive rooftop views. Sauna and bike rental available. **€210**

★Circus Hotel Rosenthaler Str. 1 ☎030 20 00 39 39, ⓦcircus-berlin.de; ⓤRosenthaler Platz; map pp.70–71. Sixty smartly appointed rooms, a secluded, ivy-covered courtyard, and a rooftop with excellent views. The hotel restaurant, *Fabisch*, serves fresh regional cuisine with a twist, and there's a microbrewery across the road at the *Circus Hostel* (see p.194). Breakfast buffet €9. **€109**

Dietrich-Bonhoeffer-Haus Ziegelstr. 30 ☎030 28 46 70, ⓦhotel-dietrich-bonhoeffer.de; ⓢOranienburger Strasse; map pp.70–71. This small, church-affiliated three-star is where the first round of talks between the GDR regime and the opposition – which led to free elections and reunification – were held in December 1989. The airy en-suite rooms are simple, quiet and equipped with desks and TVs. **€109**

Garden Boutique Hotel Invalidenstr. 122 ☎030 28 44 55 77, ⓦhonigmond-berlin.de; ⓤNaturkundemuseum; map pp.70–71. A relative bargain in a charming 1845 building. The rooms are sparsely furnished, but their original wooden floors help generate an authentic elegance. Guests have access to the relaxing back garden. Breakfast €10. **€137**

Hackescher Markt Grosse Präsidentenstr. 8 ☎030 28 00 30, ⓦhotel-hackescher-markt.com; ⓢHackescher Markt; map pp.70–71. Refurbished in 2015, this hotel is located on a quiet side street but in the middle of the Hackescher Markt bar scene. Rooms are simple and functional but clean; those overlooking the courtyard are quieter. Breakfast €15. **€119**

Kastanienhof Kastanienallee 65–66 ☎030 44 30 50, ⓦkastanienhof.biz; ⓤSenefelderplatz; map pp.70–71. This slightly old-fashioned hotel in an elegant nineteenth-century tenement house has 44 rooms with decorative touches that nod to Berlin's fascinating history, including photos, illustrations and maps. There's also an in-house restaurant and bar, and it's in a great location for Prenzlauer Berg and Mitte nightlife. Breakfast €9. **€120**

Lux 11 Rosa-Luxemburg-Str. 11 ☎030 93 62 800, ⓦlux-eleven.com; ⓤWeinmeisterstrasse; map pp.70–71. This designer apartment-hotel, oozing style, has big,

TOP 5 BOUTIQUE HOTELS

Am Steinplatz See p.190
Amano See above
Arte Luise Kunsthotel See below
Casa Camper See above
Hotel Q! See p.191

comfy rooms (with kitchenettes and spacious, open bathrooms), a swanky neighbouring restaurant (*Prince*) and a design shop called Type Hype. Breakfast €18. **€109**

★Monbijou Hotel Monbijouplatz 1 ☎030 61 62 03 00, ⓦmonbijouhotel.com; ⓢHackescher Markt; map pp.70–71. Intimate boutique hotel with high-quality rooms furnished in vintage-luxe style. Amenities include a rooftop terrace, gym and a fantastic cocktail bar, and the pretty Monbijoupark is right over the road. **€130**

★Motel One Berlin Hackescher-Markt Dirckenstr. 36 ☎030 20 05 40 80, ⓦmotel-one.com; ⓤ/ⓢAlexanderplatz; map pp.70–71. *Motel One*'s stylish lobbies, flatscreen TVs and modular 70s furniture suggest far higher prices than its cheerfully straightforward en-suite rooms command. The location, a couple of minutes' walk from Alexanderplatz, makes it a downtown bargain; the chain has seven other locations in Berlin. Breakfast €9.50. **€72**

Weinmeister Weinmeisterstr. 2 ☎030 755 66 70, ⓦthe-weinmeister.com; ⓤWeinmeisterstrasse; map pp.70–71. Spacious and stylish rooms sporting large beds and funky designer furnishings. There's a spa and beauty salon on site, and guests can make free use of a nearby health club. **€139**

POTSDAMER PLATZ AND TIERGARTEN

★Arte Luise Kunsthotel Luisenstr. 19 ☎030 28 44 80, ⓦluise-berlin.com; ⓤ/ⓢFriedrichstrasse; map pp.90–91. Each of the 52 rooms here is an eccentric, and impressive, work of art: one comes with bananas all over the walls and hot-pink velvet bedding, while another is *Alice in Wonderland*-themed with oversized furniture. The elegant rooms at the front tend to suffer from train noise (earplugs provided) but the quieter rooms at the back are a bit blander. Not all are en suite. Breakfast €11. **€53**

★Das Stue Drakestr. 1 ☎030 311 72 20, ⓦdas-stue.com; ⓤ/ⓢZoologischer Garten, then a 15min walk or bus #200; map pp.90–91. Lodge in luxury at the severely stylish prewar Danish embassy, where views of the Zoo's antelopes and ostriches from the elegant 1920s-themed bar add to the charm. Rooms have smart modern furnishings and detailing and share a small pool, spa and first-class restaurant. Has its own private entrance to the Zoo. **€240**

Hansablick Flotowstr. 6 ☎030 390 48 00, ⓦhotel-hansablick.de; ⓢTiergarten; map pp.90–91. Riverside

12

hotel a short hop from the Tiergarten whose rooms sport cheerful multicoloured furnishings, art by the likes of Otmar Alt and Heinrich Zille, and all the usual mod cons. Breakfast €6.50. **€89**

InterContinental Berlin Budapester Str. 2 ☎ 030 260 20, ⓦ berlin.intercontinental.com; ①/Ⓢ Zoologischer Garten; map pp.90–91. Modern luxury for high-powered business people close to the Zoo and Ku'damm. Amenities include a fully equipped fitness centre, sauna and pool. Basic wi-fi free, otherwise chargeable. Breakfast €30. **€250**

Ritz-Carlton Berlin Potsdamer Platz 3 ☎ 030 33 77 77, ⓦ ritzcarlton.com; ①/Ⓢ Potsdamer Platz; map pp.90–91. Distinctive skyscraper hotel with 303 rooms (some with views of Potsdamer Platz and the Tiergarten) sporting cherry wood closets and watercolours. Amenities include a glamorous wellness area, a great brasserie, lounges and *Fragrances*, the world's first cocktail bar inspired by high-end perfumes. Wi-fi free in public spaces only. **€215**

★**Scandic Berlin Potsdamer Platz** Gabriele-Tergit-Promenade 19 ☎ 030 700 77 90, ⓦ scandichotels.com; ① Mendelssohn-Bartholdy-Park; map pp.90–91. Smart yet informal homage to Scandinavian design, part of the international hotel chain, in a no-man's-land south of Potsdamer Platz that's surprisingly close to much greenery and very handy for the U-Bahn. Floors and rooms are successfully themed by season, and the chain's eco-friendly policies are much in evidence: no disposable sachets; local ingredients – even down to the breakfast honey, from rooftop hives – in the restaurant; and bikes available to rent. On-site gym and bar. Breakfast €12. **€82**

Sheraton Berlin Grand Hotel Esplanade Lützowufer 15 ☎ 030 25 47 80, ⓦ esplanade.de/en; ① Nollendorfplatz; map pp.90–91. Sleek top-class hotel close to the Tiergarten with good facilities (including sauna, pool, fitness centre and spa), a flashy New York-style cocktail bar and three restaurants. Breakfast €22. **€99**

CITY WEST

★**25hours Hotel Bikini Berlin** Budapester Str. 40 ☎ 030 12 02 210, ⓦ 25hours-hotels.com; ①/Ⓢ Zoologischer Garten; map p.108. The hotel that put some much-needed hip back into City West when it opened in 2014 is still impressing the punters with its self-consciously urban-chic design, comfortable rooms and great location right next to the Zoo. As well as a very good Middle-East-meets-Mediterranean restaurant (*Neni*) and a rooftop bar (*Monkey Bar*; see p.219) it offers Minis (yes, really) and stylish bike rental for free. Breakfast €19. **€95**

Am Savignyplatz Kantstr. 22 ☎ 030 50 18 17 36, ⓦ am-savignyplatz-hotel.de; Ⓢ Savignyplatz; map p.108. Housed in a beautiful old building that has been thoroughly modernized, the *Am Savignyplatz* is surprisingly stylish – its eleven rooms are spacious and modern, and one of them even has a small garden. **€69**

Am Steinplatz Steinplatz 4 ☎ 030 554 44 40, ⓦ hotelsteinplatz.com; ①/Ⓢ Zoologischer Garten; map p.108. Sumptuous boutique hotel set inside a heritage-listed building that was once the haunt of the more well-heeled and intellectual Weimar set. Rooms are richly appointed with a mix of vintage and modern furnishings and there's a top-notch restaurant and classy bar with craft beer and occasional DJs. Breakfast €25–€35. **€190**

art'otel berlin ku'damm Lietzenburger Str. 85 ☎ 030 88 77 770, ⓦ artotels.com; ① Uhlandstrasse; map p.108. Sleek hotel, one for Andy Warhol fans, with more than two hundred of his originals scattered about the place. His style extends to the staff uniforms and the furniture: white leather beds and purple chairs. **€76**

Bleibtreu Bleibtreustr. 31 ☎ 030 88 47 40, ⓦ bleibtreu .com; ① Uhlandstrasse; map p.108. With an interior designed by Herbert Jacob Weinand and eco-minded furnishings handcrafted in Germany and Italy, this unique and discreet hotel has bright white rooms, a café and florist. **€110**

Dormero Hotel Berlin Ku'damm Eislebener Str. 14 ☎ 030 2140 50, ⓦ dormero.de; ① Augsburger Strasse; map p.108. A mixture of modern Bauhaus and romantic intimacy, this beautiful hotel offers impeccable service, superlative (if expensive) Scandinavian dining in the Michelin-starred *Die Quadriga* restaurant and a light-filled lounge area that spills out onto an outdoor patio in summer. Breakfast €22. **€130**

Hecker's Hotel Grolmanstr. 35 ☎ 030 88 900, ⓦ heckers-hotel.de; ① Uhlandstrasse; map p.108. Swanky boutique hotel near the Savignyplatz restaurants. Rooms include three luxurious themed suites (Bauhaus, Tuscany and Colonial), starting at €290/night. Breakfast €16. **€95**

Hotel de Ela Landshuter Str. 1 ☎ 030 23 63 39 60, ⓦ hotel-de-ela.de; ① Viktoria-Luise-Platz; map p.108. Twenty-first-century design in a nineteenth-century Victorian building: family-friendly *de Ela* has large, comfortable rooms with a classic feel at very decent rates. Breakfast €7.95. **€40**

Hotel Otto Knesebeckstr. 10 ☎ 030 54 71 00 80, ⓦ hotelotto.com; ① Ernst-Reuter-Platz; map p.108. *Otto* eschews the traditional for a cheery, modern experience that's all blues, magentas and greens. The 46 rooms are chic and individually designed and the organic breakfast – served on the rooftop terrace – is a great touch too. Breakfast €18 for adults (teens €9, under-13s free). **€120**

★**Hotel-Pension Funk** Fasanenstr. 69 ☎ 030 882 71 93, ⓦ hotel-pensionfunk.de; ① Uhlandstrasse; map p.108. Interesting re-creation of a prewar flat, with furnishings from the 1920s and 1930s, when Danish silent-movie star Asta Nielsen lived here. Given this, its location, and the breakfast buffet (included), it's a bargain. The cheapest rooms share bathrooms. **€89**

Hotel Q! Knesebeckstr. 67 ☎030 810 06 60, ⓦhotel-q.com; ⓤUhlandstrasse; map p.108. Very swanky, even for über-cool Berlin: all Bauhaus-inspired elegance and quirks (bathtubs in bedframes), plus chocolate massages, great buffet breakfasts (though these cost extra) and a Thai kitchen, and affable staff. Breakfast from €9.50. **€100**

★ **Hotel Zoo Berlin** Kurfürstendamm 25 ☎030 88 43 70, ⓦhotelzoo.de; ⓤKurfürstendamm; map p.108. This historic hotel reopened to great fanfare in 2014, its 144 rooms sumptuously appointed with tasteful fashion photographs and high-quality wooden floors and furnishings. There's a restaurant and lounge, and two sixth-floor penthouse suites if you feel like splashing. **€180**

★ **Savoy Hotel Berlin** Fasanenstr. 9–10 ☎030 31 10 30, ⓦhotel-savoy.com; ⓤ/ⓢZoologischer Garten; map p.108. Luxury hotel whose traditional, old-world atmosphere has been happily married with some Cuban decorative flair – there's even a cigar shop in the lobby. Breakfast €20. **€110**

Swissôtel Berlin Augsburger Str. 44 ☎030 22 01 00, ⓦswissotel.com; ⓤKurfürstendamm; map p.108. Smart 316-room international chain hotel in an extraordinary building amid the bright lights of the Ku'damm. Vertical louvres bristle around the exterior, and the interior is equally impressive thanks to a bright and welcoming glass-roofed lobby and a restaurant with superb views of Berlin's main shopping strip. Eco-friendly credentials, bar/lounge, sauna and fitness facilities. **€120**

Waldorf Astoria Berlin Hardenbergstr. 28 ☎030 81 40 00, ⓦwaldorfastoriaberlin.com; ⓤ/ⓢZoologischer Garten; map p.108. This classy, towering five-star – nicknamed the *Zoofenster* ("zoo window") for its views over the adjacent Berlin Zoo and buzzy surrounding area – has sumptuous rooms, impeccable service and Michelin-starred cuisine. It also houses Germany's only Guerlain spa. Wi-fi €25/day. **€250**

SCHÖNEBERG

Altberlin am Potsdamer Platz Potsdamer Str. 67 ☎030 26 06 70, ⓦaltberlin-hotel.de; ⓤKurfürstenstrasse; map p.114. Large pension-style hotel in a turn-of-the-twentieth-century, Wilhelminian-era hotel with old-world decor in its "grandma"-style rooms and long-forgotten Berlin specialities served at the restaurant. Large buffet breakfast included. **€120**

Sylter Hof Berlin Kurfürstenstr. 116 ☎030 212 00, ⓦsylterhof-berlin.de; ⓤWittenbergplatz; map p.114. Well-appointed eighteen-storey hotel just behind Wittenbergplatz and the Ku'damm. The rooms and suites are smart and spacious, and most – along with public areas – have been recently renovated. Breakfast €11. **€80**

TOP 5 STEP BACK IN TIME

Altberlin am Potsdamer Platz
  See above
Garden Boutique Hotel See p.189
Hotel-Pension Funk See opposite
Riehmers Hofgarten See below
Savoy Hotel Berlin See above

WESTERN KREUZBERG

Angleterre Hotel Friedrichstr. 31 ☎030 20 21 37 00, ⓦhotel-angleterre.de; ⓤKochstrasse; map p.118. The "England Hotel" has a restaurant and bar/lounge, 24hr room service and lots of charming old detailing, including restored murals, stuccoed ceilings, wood finishes and wall mirrors. Handy for Checkpoint Charlie and the Jewish Museum. Breakfast €15.90. **€189**

Hotel Johann Johanniterstr. 8 ☎030 22 50 740, ⓦhotel-johann-berlin.de; ⓤPrinzenstrasse; map p.118. In a good location for Bergmannstrasse and the Jewish Museum, the *Johann* a fairly nondescript but friendly hotel, with spacious rooms and a peaceful garden. Breakfast €8.50 **€84**

Hotel Transit Hagelberger Str. 53 ☎030 789 04 70, ⓦhotel-transit.de; ⓤMehringdamm; map p.118. Bright, breezy hotel in a former factory building with fifty spacious – if basic – rooms and an upbeat atmosphere. Breakfast is included and served until noon. Dorms (3–6 person) from **€25**, singles **€62**, twins **€72**

★ **Riehmers Hofgarten** Yorckstr. 83 ☎030 78 09 88 00, ⓦriehmers-hofgarten.com; ⓤMehringdamm; map p.118. There's a low-key, residential atmosphere at this hotel, which occupies a historic building. The 23 rooms (including one apartment) have a nineteenth-century feel and there's a delightful living room for relaxation. Breakfast €9. **€131**

NEUKÖLLN

Hüttenpalast Hobrechtstr. 65–66 ☎030 37 30 58 06, ⓦhuettenpalast.de; ⓤHermannplatz; map p.130. Satisfyingly eccentric place where you get to camp in vintage caravans or mountain huts inside a converted factory. All have been stylishly overhauled so you won't be roughing it. Pleasant garden, too, and a great café serving breakfast. Bathrooms are mostly shared though there are a few en-suite doubles. Breakfast €9.50. **€86**

FRIEDRICHSHAIN

East Side Hotel Mühlenstr. 6 ☎030 29 38 33, ⓦeastsidehotel.de; ⓤ/ⓢWarschauer Strasse; map pp.128–129. Small, laidback, modern hotel just over the Spree from Kreuzberg in southern Friedrichshain and overlooking the East Side Gallery. Exceptional service and a 24hr check-in, room service and café. Original artwork in the hotel includes quirky murals by Birgit

12

Kinder, who famously painted the Trabant at the East Side Gallery. **€62**

Hotel 26 Grünberger Str. 26 ☎030 297 77 80, ⓦhotel26.de; ⓞ/Ⓢ Frankfurter Tor; map pp.128–129. Set in a former factory, this basic but upbeat hotel is close to Friedrichshain's many bars and has clean and functional singles, doubles and suites as well as a friendly café. **€96**

Hotel Friedrichshain Warschauer Str. 57 ☎030 97 00 20 30, ⓦhotel-friedrichshain-berlin.de; ⓞ/Ⓢ Warschauer Strasse; map pp.128–129. Clean, modern hotel with uncluttered, fairly unexciting rooms. There's a small lounge area and bar on site, and the reasonable buffet breakfast costs €7. **€45**

★**InterCityHotel Berlin Ostbahnhof** Am Ostbahnhof 5 ☎030 29 36 80, ⓦintercityhotel.com; Ⓢ Ostbahnhof; map pp.128–129. Sleek, budget-conscious business hotel at the Ostbahnhof, very convenient for the S-Bahn and the Friedrichshain scene. Rooms are of the usual international business standard, and rates include a public transport pass (zones A, B & C) for the duration of your stay. **€62**

Juncker's Hotel Garni Grünberger Str. 21 ☎030 293 35 50, ⓦjunckershotel.de; ⓞ Frankfurter Tor; map pp.128–129. Small, family-run hotel with high-quality rooms and apartments (€65), friendly staff and a quiet atmosphere only occasionally interrupted by the hostel next door. Breakfast €8. **€59**

★**Michelberger Hotel** Warschauer Str. 39 ☎030 29 77 85 90, ⓦmichelbergerhotel.com; ⓞ/Ⓢ Warschauer Strasse; map pp.128–129. Modern, trendy and relaxed haunt with its cool warehouse-style interior provides anything but workaday accommodation. Apart from enjoying its self-conscious designer feel – exposed, distressed concrete pillars; lampshades made from book pages – you can also take advantage of its great bar, concerts in the courtyard and a decent restaurant. Excellent buffet breakfast (€16). **€80**

nhow Stralauer Allee 3 ☎030 290 29 90, ⓦnhow -hotels.com; ⓞ/Ⓢ Warschauer Strasse; map pp.128–129. This four-star concept hotel merges a music theme with designer hotel rooms. There's a restaurant, sauna and gym, and the majority of the rooms have great views over the river. Breakfast €24.90. **€110**

NU Hotel Berlin Gubener Str. 46 ☎030 68 81 12 20, ⓦnuhotel.de; ⓞ Frankfurter Tor; map pp.128–129. Close to the East Side Gallery and Mercedes-Benz Platz, this three-star hotel has 28 functional rooms, all with lots of natural light and decent amenities. **€71**

Upstalsboom Hotel Freidrichshain Gubener Str. 42 ☎030 29 37 50, ⓦhotelfriedrichshain-berlin.de; ⓞ/ Ⓢ Warschauer Strasse; map pp.128–129. This functional four-star has comfortable, colourful rooms and a couple of restaurants serving north German and international dishes, plus a fitness centre and roof terrace. **€110**

PRENZLAUER BERG

★**Acksel Haus** Belforter Str. 21 ☎030 44 33 76 33, ⓦackselhaus.de; ⓞ Senefelderplatz; map p.136. Small, offbeat hotel on an attractive residential street in the heart of the lively Prenzlauer Berg scene. Themed rooms (Rome, Picasso, Safari) come with access to the Mediterranean garden. **€130**

★**Linnen** Eberswalder Str. 35 ☎030 47 37 24 40, ⓦlinnenberlin.com, ⓞ Eberswalder Strasse; map p.136. This stylish boutique spot is tucked discreetly away inside a lovely nineteenth-century building and just 10min from the famous Mauerpark. Amenities are minimal but the staff are friendly, the rooms and apartments gorgeously appointed and there's an associated café next door that serves great breakfasts and lunches. **€90**

Myer's Hotel Berlin Metzer Str. 26 ☎030 44 01 40, ⓦmyershotel.de; ⓞ Senefelderplatz; map p.136. Set in a renovated nineteenth-century Neoclassical building, this tastefully done hotel has 51 rooms, arranged around a glass-roofed courtyard, in a range of shapes and sizes (some quite small); all pleasantly furnished. There's a lounge bar and garden, plus regular exhibitions and concerts, too. **€120**

Soho House Berlin Torstr. 1 ☎030 405 04 40, ⓦsohohouseberlin.com; ⓞ Rosa-Luxemburg-Platz; map p.136. Set in a restored Bauhaus building, this private member's club and hotel has 86 rooms and several newer apartments (€500) that range from tiny to huge and decadent. Decor is quirky and fun, hinting at the faded glamour of the late 1920s. There's also a lovely spa, gym, rooftop pool, restaurant, bars, screening room and a sprawling designer shop and café-restaurant next door. Cheap offers from €100 are sometimes available for smaller rooms. **€230**

THE WESTERN SUBURBS

Ibis Brandenburgische Str. 11, Wilmersdorf ☎030 86 20 20, ⓦibishotel.com; ⓞ Fehrbelliner Platz; map p.108. One of ten Berlin branches of the international chain. Rooms are small but inexpensive. **€55**

★**Propeller Island City Lodge** Albrecht-Achilles-Str. 58, Wilmersdorf ☎030 891 90 16, ⓦpropeller-island.de; ⓞ Adenauerplatz; map p.162. Entertainingly wacky hotel where the furnishings in every room have been handcrafted by the owner according to individual themes: check the website to choose from among the likes of the Space Cube, the Mirror Room, Electric Wallpaper or Upside Down. **€79**

12

HOSTELS

The standard of **independent hostels** in Berlin, with their stock of private rooms, is very good – in recent years they have swept aside many a pension with cheaper rooms, a communal atmosphere that seems to match Berlin's party spirit, and – in many cases – some serious contemporary style too. While traditional facilities, such as a laundry and kitchens, have become unusual, the nearest launderette or snack bar is never far away – and you'll almost certainly have free **wi-fi**. Dorm **rates** vary according to the number of people sharing: a twenty-bed dorm may cost around €10 per person, while five sharing a room might each pay double that. We quote the cheapest dorm rates available for each hostel, plus the cheapest rates for singles and doubles; for **booking** sites, see p.187. **Bedding** is provided in most places – though sometimes there's a one-off fee of around €3. Most hostels offer a simple buffet **breakfast** for around €6–7; at some places it is included in the rate – we've noted where in our reviews below.

ALEXANDERPLATZ AND AROUND

★**Citystay Hostel** Rosenstr. 16 ☎030 23 62 40 31, ⓦcitystay.de; ⓢHackescher Markt; map p.60. Berlin's best-located hostel for sightseeing – within walking distance of the S-Bahn, Hackescher Markt and Museum Island – is a large, well-run place spreading over several immaculate floors. It has a good selection of private rooms, some en suite, and pleasant communal areas including a leafy courtyard. Facilities include an all-night bar, home-made sandwiches and cakes, and it's also a hub for tours and bar crawls. Dorms €19, twins €55

THE SPANDAUER VORSTADT

★**Circus Hostel** Weinbergsweg 1a ☎030 20 00 39 39, ⓦcircus-berlin.de; ⓤRosenthaler Platz; map pp.70–71. Top-notch hostel in fantastic location, with friendly staff and good facilities. Rooms are full of colour, and facilities include a café on site as well as a bar and in-house microbrewery. Bicycles for rent, free walking tours, regular events, and even a museum dedicated to the Hoff. Dorms €19, singles €46, doubles €58

St Christopher's Hostel Rosa-Luxemburg-Str. 39–41 ☎030 81 45 39 60, ⓦst-christophers.co.uk; ⓤRosa-Luxemburg-Platz; map pp.70–71. Well-run branch of a European hostel chain. The large bar is perfect for partying all night, serving up tasty burgers, bar snacks and an entertainment programme that spans live music, comedy and other events. There's also billiards, and the staff and guests are a lively international mix of locals and expats. Rates include a basic breakfast. Dorms (some single-sex) €26, singles €55, doubles/twins €80

CITY WEST

aletto Hotel Ku'damm Hardenbergstr. 21 ☎030 21 41 00, ⓦaletto.de; ⓤ/ⓢZoologischer Garten; map p.108. This colourful and lively hostel has singles, doubles and dorms for up to eight people, plus table football, a large DVD library and a big garden with table tennis and kids' playground to keep guests entertained. Breakfast included. Dorms €19, singles €49, doubles €59

WESTERN KREUZBERG

★**Grand Hostel Berlin** Tempelhofer Ufer 14 ☎030 20 09 54 50, ⓦgrandhostel-berlin.de; ⓤMöckernbrücke; map p.118. Set inside a listed historic building near the Landwehrkanal, this award-winning hostel ups the ante in terms of elegance and space. There's a bar and library room on site, furnishings are design-savvy and the bright, stylish rooms and dorms don't have bunks. Linen costs €3.60. Dorms €12, singles €35, doubles €48

EASTERN KREUZBERG

Hostel X Berger Schlesische Str. 22 ☎030 91 51 51 31, ⓦhostelxberger.com; ⓤSchlesisches Tor; map pp.128–129. Dowdy, but clean and friendly hostel a hop, skip and a stagger from several of Berlin's best clubs. Common areas include a basic kitchen but little else. Dorms €12, singles €36, doubles €46

Jetpak Alternative Görlitzer Str. 38 ☎030 62 90 86 41, ⓦjetpak.de; ⓤSchlesisches Tor; map pp.128–129. This slick hostel offers a pretty stark contrast to Kreuzberg's gritty but happening Wrangelkiez neighbourhood. All rooms have high-end fittings such as underfloor heating in en-suite bathrooms. Other perks include a cheap bar, free on-street parking and a free buffet breakfast. Dorms €22

Rock'n'Roll Herberge Muskauer Str. 11 ☎030 61 62 36 00, ⓦrnrherberge.de; ⓤGörlitzer Bahnhof; map pp.128–129. Budget hangout with rooms designed by local artists, billiards and table football and vegan and non-vegan breakfasts and snacks. It's especially set up for musicians and music lovers – as the graffiti of Falco and Joe Strummer testify to. Breakfast included. Rooms for up to five people (not dorms) are available. Doubles €49

NEUKÖLLN

Karl Marx Hostel Karl-Marx-Str. 176 ☎030 68 97 49 47, ⓦkarlmarxhostel.com; ⓤKarl-Marx-Strasse; map p.130. Located in the hip "Kreuzkölln" area between Kreuzberg and Neukölln, this friendly and fun-loving hostel offers clean, smart rooms, a large garden area and an on-site cafe. Dorms €15, singles €50, doubles €69

FRIEDRICHSHAIN

A&O Berlin Friedrichshain Boxhagener Str. 73 ☎030 809 47 54 00, ⓦaohostels.com; ⓢOstkreuz; map pp.128–129. A good choice if you're travelling with kids,

12

with family rooms alongside the usual selection, plus a children's games room and a large garden – childcare is even offered at weekends. Dorms €15, singles €43, doubles €49, family rooms €96

All in Hostel Grünberger Str. 54 ☎030 288 76 83, ⓦall-in-hostel.com; ⓤFrankfurter Tor; map pp.128–129. Clean, modern and well-managed hostel just metres from the nocturnal goings-on of Simon-Dach-Str. All the usual facilities are offered, with breakfast included in rates. Though frequently beset by German school groups, it's a good choice for its hotel-standard private en-suite rooms and rock-bottom off-season prices. Dorms €10, singles €40, twins €80

Eastern Comfort Hostelboat Mühlenstr. 73 ☎030 66 76 38 06, ⓦeastern-comfort.com; ⓤ/ⓢWarschauer Strasse; map pp.128–129. Sleep swaying on the River Spree in a range of accommodation – from spacious doubles through shared cabin bunks to tents on deck. All cabins except dorms are en suite and the boat has a lounge. Highly unconventional, lots of fun, and close to many of Berlin's nightlife hotspots. Tents €15, bunks €16, doubles €50

Odyssee Globetrotter Hostel Grünberger Str. 23 ☎030 29 00 00 81, ⓦglobetrotterhostel.de; ⓤFrankfurter Tor; map pp.128–129. Imaginatively decorated and sociable hostel hard by the Friedrichshain scene and with a happening bar of its own. Dorms €17, singles €69, doubles €80

★ **Ostel** Wriezener Karree 5 ☎030 25 76 86 60, ⓦostel .eu; ⓢOstbahnhof; map pp.128–129. Step back into the 1970s amid a haze of browns and oranges at this GDR-themed budget hotel a short walk from the Ostbahnhof. The rendition is creepily accurate, but thankfully the whole thing's done with a sense of humour and just the thing for those needing an *Ostalgie* fix (see box, p.65). Some rooms share bathrooms; there's also a four-person apartment (€80/night). Singles €30, doubles €39

Plus Berlin Warschauer Platz 6 ☎030 311 69 88 20, ⓦplushostels.com; ⓤ/ⓢWarschauer Strasse; map pp.128–129. Upscale and vibrant backpacker located inside a striking red-brick building with stylish, high-ceilinged rooms, a lively bar and restaurant, large garden area, sauna and even a pool. Dorms from €8, doubles €120

PRENZLAUER BERG

EastSeven Schwedter Str. 7 ☎030 93 62 22 40, ⓦeastseven.de; ⓤSenefelderplatz; map p.136. Laid-back hostel located on the border of Mitte and Prenzlauer Berg. Rooms (singles, doubles/twins, dorms) and public areas are clean and functional, furnishings are decent quality and there's a lounge area with books and board

games. No stag or hen groups. Breakfast €3. Dorms €14, singles €35, doubles €68

Hotel Transit Loft Immanuelkirchstr. 14 ☎030 48 49 37 73, ⓦtransit-loft.de; ⓤSenefelderplatz or tram #M4 to Hufelandstr.; map p.136. Part budget hotel, part hostel, this modern hotel occupies a nineteenth-century, yellow-brick factory a 10min walk from Kollwitzplatz. The 47 rooms (singles and dorms included) are airy and well lit with basic furnishings and en-suite showers. The same owners run *Hotel Transit* in Kreuzberg (see p.191). Dorms (3–6-bed) €25, singles €62, twins €72

Lette'm Sleep Lettestr. 7 ☎030 44 73 36 23, ⓦlettemsleephostel.berlin; ⓤEberswalder Strasse; map p.136. Quirky hostel with clean and comfy, if basic, rooms, just steps away from the action in Prenzlauer Berg. Big plus points include the cosy living room, coffee and tea; DVD evenings; summer beer garden; and communal kitchen. Discounts for stays of three nights or more. Dorms €13, twins €49, apartments €69

Meininger Hotel Berlin Alexanderplatz Schönhauser Allee 19 ☎030 98 32 10 74, ⓦmeininger-hotels.com; ⓤSenefelderplatz; map p.136. Part hotel, part hostel, this smart, well-run and well-located 90-room (328 beds) place is part of an international chain – there are three others in Berlin alone. A little more sterile and less happening than many other hostels, but with a lounge, games room and café-bar nonetheless. Dorms €18, singles €40, doubles €51

Pfefferbett Hostel Christinenstr. 18–19 ☎030 93 93 58 58, ⓦpfefferbett.de; ⓤSenefelderplatz; map p.136. This welcoming, well set-up hostel has clean, smart rooms and dorms, a buzzy lobby and a lovely courtyard garden that doubles as the *Pfefferbräu* beer garden (see p.223). Bicycle rental (€12/day), free guided tours and laundry services available. Dorms from €12, doubles €32.50

THE WESTERN SUBURBS

★ **Jetpak Ecolodge** Pücklerstr. 54, Dahlem ☎030 832 250 11, ⓦjetpak.de; ⓤFehrbelliner Platz then bus #115 to Pücklerstrasse; map p.170. One-of-a-kind hostel with a laidback international vibe, in the woods on the southwestern edge of Berlin. The large communal spaces have plenty on offer, including free nightly big-screen movies and lots of indoor and outdoor games. Bring supplies, though, as there are no shops in the vicinity. Bike rental offered. Note some #115 buses don't go as far as Pücklerstrasse, but night buses from Zoo stop a 10min walk from the hostel. Dorms €16, twins €42, doubles €45

12

Eating

Berlin has all the gastronomic variety you'd expect from a major European capital, with virtually every imaginable cuisine represented: indeed, German cooking generally takes a back seat to Turkish, French, Italian, Indian and east and southeast Asian cuisines, to name just a few. Berliners tend to eat out regularly, so prices are fairly reasonable – a main dish typically costs around €10–16 – though you can easily triple this figure by dining at top-end places. In line with Berlin's rolling nightlife timetable, you can pretty much eat around the clock. Most restaurants happily serve until around 11pm, and even later it's not hard to find somewhere in most neighbourhoods.

13

Another common feature of Berlin's dining scene is how many places **morph** from one type of venue into another through the day. A good place to sip a morning coffee and read a paper may well become a restaurant later on, before bringing out the DJ decks until the wee small hours, then closing only to start the cycle again two or three hours later. Throughout the city the distinction between restaurants, cafés, bars and even clubs can be difficult to make. We have tried to classify venues by their primary purpose – focusing on establishments best known for their food in this chapter – but be aware that many of the places covered under "Drinking and nightlife" (see p.216) will be happy just to serve you a coffee, and some of the tastiest food you'll eat on your trip could well be in a bar or beer garden.

Berlin still has its share of traditional places, including male-oriented bare-bones **Kneipen** (pubs), which usually serve simple, hearty fare, as well as classic **cafés** specializing in coffee and rich mid-afternoon cakes. Meanwhile, the **Imbiss** (see box, p.204) or snack stand is even more ubiquitous in Berlin than elsewhere in Germany, and is bolstered by an increasing number of international **street-food**-style stalls and markets hawking everything from burgers and burritos to *bánh mì* and pierogi.

Despite the difficulties inherent in pinning establishments down by category, our **listings** are divided into **cheap eats** – mostly *Imbiss* places and affordable street food spots – **cafés and bars** that are good for casual dining and **restaurants** recommended for a full meal.

ESSENTIALS

Reservations For most restaurants and cafés reviewed below you can just walk in, though on weekend nights or at the most expensive places, booking is recommended.

Tipping A fifteen percent service charge is normally included in your bill by law, and so it's customary only to round up the nearest euro or two. Try to give the tip (cash is usually preferred) to the server when paying the bill if you can, rather than leaving it on the table.

UNTER DEN LINDEN AND AROUND

CAFÉS AND BARS

Café Einstein Unter den Linden 42 ☎030 204 36 32, ⓦeinstein-udl.com; ⓤ/ⓢBrandenburger Tor; map p.36. The younger sibling to the famous *Café Einstein* on Kurfürstenstrasse (see p.205) lacks its elder's panache, but it's popular with Berlin's cultural elite (and tourists), and serves excellent Austro-Hungarian specialities. Also handy for coffee and cake. Daily 7am–10pm.

RESTAURANTS

Bocca di Bacco Friedrichstr. 167 ☎030 20 67 28 28, ⓦboccadibacco.de; ⓤFranzösische Strasse; map p.36. *Bocca di Bacco* blends a down-to-earth atmosphere with high-quality cuisine that takes its inspiration from Tuscany and other parts of Italy. The menu includes pasta, game and fish and plenty of wonderful desserts. The three-course lunch is a pretty good deal at €19.50. Mon–Sat

---

EATING YOUR WAY AROUND BERLIN

You can find more or less every type of restaurant, café, bar and *Imbiss* in every Berlin district, but a few generalizations stand. Places around **Unter den Linden** and all the way to **Alexanderplatz** largely provide sightseers with coffee and big slabs of rich cake and traditional German meals, with the latter particularly well represented in the **Nikolaiviertel**, Berlin's old quarter. The **Spandauer Vorstadt**, particularly the stretch along Oranienburger Strasse, is far more eclectic and hip, but still caters primarily to visitors so standards tend to be lower and prices higher than further out of the centre. But it's still a good district for browsing if you're unsure what you're after.

Beyond Mitte, Savignyplatz (and the Ku'damm and Kantstrasse in general) in **City West** are busy and varied dining districts, and the area has a particular concentration of traditional coffee houses. **Schöneberg's** Winterfeldplatz is a popular gay centre and Bergmanstrasse in **western Kreuzberg** a relatively bohemian strip, while around **Friedrichshain's** Boxhagener Platz, **eastern Kreuzberg's** Oranienstrasse and Wrangelkiez, and Karl-Marx-Strasse, Sonnenallee and Rixdorf in **Neukölln**, a mix of budget, ethnic and hip places tend to dominate. Berlin's moneyed bohemian district, **Prenzlauer Berg**, is also a good foodie destination, with a great mix of cafés and smarter restaurants that tend to draw an older, less image-conscious crowd, while **Wedding** to the north mostly offers cheap Middle Eastern eateries with the occasional hip spot.

13

noon–midnight, Sun 6pm–midnight.

Borchardt Französischer Str. 47 ❶030 81 88 62 62, ⓦborchardt-restaurant.de; ❶Französische Strasse; map p.36. A re-creation of a nineteenth-century high society hangout, this upmarket spot has elegant marble columns, plush seating and an Art Nouveau mosaic discovered during renovations. The daily changing menu is good-quality French-German – the outsized *Wiener Schnitzel* is justly renowned – though if you're not a regular, service is likely to be offhand at best. Mains from €20. Popular with politicians, celebrities and tourists. Book ahead. Daily 11.30am–midnight.

★**Café Nö!** Glinkastr. 23 ❶030 201 08 71, ⓦcafe-noe .de; ❶Französische Strasse; map p.36. This wine bar-restaurant serves quality south German and Mediterranean food at very reasonable prices. The menu includes *Flammkuchen* (a type of thin-crust pizza, originally from Alsace) and the like, a huge mixed plate for two featuring almost everything on the menu is €28.50, and the wine list is vast enough for most tastes. Service is pleasant and not too formal. Mon–Fri noon–1am, kitchen till midnight.

Cookies Cream Behrenstr. 55 ❶030 27 49 29 40, ⓦcookiescream.de; ❶Französische Strasse; map p.36. Deliberately difficult to find (see website for creative directions – walk down the service road and past the dustbins of the *Westin Grand* off Behrenstr.) this stylish vegetarian restaurant, one of the best in the city, is worth seeking out. At €44 for a three-course menu and €25 for a main it's pricey, but the seasonal, inventive food is well worth it. Tues–Sat 7pm–midnight.

Crackers Friedrichstr. 158 ❶030 68 07 30 488, ⓦcrackersberlin.com; ❶Französische Strasse, map p.36.

This swish and spacious restaurant occupies what was once one of the city's funkiest clubs (*Cookies*). Downstairs from the equally clubby *Cookies Cream* (see above), it offers a European-nouveau menu of meat and fish, with some vegetarian options, a great cocktail bar and hip service. DJ dinner sets on Fri & Sat. Mains €16–33. Daily 7pm–midnight.

Fischers Fritz Regent Berlin, Charlottenstr. 49 ❶030 20 33 63 63, ⓦfischersfritz-berlin.de; ❶Französische Strasse; map p.36. *Fischers Fritz* is the domain of Christian Lohse, whose way with fish and seafood has earned him numerous accolades (including two Michelin stars). This is imaginative stuff, bursting with originality in terms of presentation, flavours and ideas. There's a price, naturally, namely €105 for three courses. Daily 6.30–10.30pm.

Ishin Mittelstr. 24 ❶030 20 67 48 29, ⓦishin.de; ❶/ ❸Friedrichstrasse; map p.36. There are six *Ishin* restaurants in Berlin. The interior of this central one is slightly functional but the decent, fresh sushi, good prices and quick service make it very popular, especially for lunch. There's a happy hour every day until 4pm (all day Wed & Sat), with €2–4 off sushi and full menus from €6.50. Plenty of veggie dishes and free green tea. Mon–Fri 11.30am–9.30pm, Sat noon–9.30pm.

★**Käfer Dachgarten** Platz der Republik 1 ❶030 22 62 990, ⓦen.feinkost-kaefer.de/berlin; ❶Bundestag; map p.36. Famous for its location on the roof of the Reichstag and its 180-degree view of eastern Berlin, this restaurant specializes in gourmet renditions of regional German dishes (mains €17.50–30). A reservation here also means you get to avoid the registration process through the Bundestag. Daily 9am–4.30pm & 6.30pm–midnight (last orders 9.15pm).

GERMAN CUISINE

To enjoy traditional **German cuisine**, it does help if you share the national penchant for heavy meat dishes accompanied by potatoes and fresh (or pickled) vegetables or salad. That said, in keeping with the general trend for seasonal, healthier dining and local produce, modern German cooking tends to pare down the heavier national recipes and use more imaginative sauces and alternative ingredients to keep things lighter and fresher.

The **pig** is the staple of the German menu – it's prepared in umpteen different ways, and just about every part gets eaten. Sausages are the country's most popular snack, while *Kassler Rippen* (smoked and pickled pork chops) and *Eisbein* (pickled ham hock) are Berlin favourites – although the fatty *Eisbein* tends to be more of a winter speciality. *Königsberger Klopse* (meat dumplings in a caper- and lemon-flavoured sauce) also appear on many menus.

Potatoes are used imaginatively, too: try *Kartoffelpuffer* (grated potato mixed with flour and eggs into a pancake) or *Pellkartoffeln mit Quark und Leinöl*, a combination of baked potatoes, low-fat cheese and linseed oil that's best digested with lashings of beer or schnapps. Other popular dishes include *Maultaschen*, the Swabian version of ravioli, which are usually larger and can be filled with meat and/or vegetables and herbs. And pizza aficionados will almost certainly enjoy *Flammkuchen*, which hails from the Alsace region (it's called *tarte flambée* in France) and consists of a thin, crusty base with toppings – crème fraiche, onions and lardons are traditional.

Surprisingly for a country known for its cakes, **desserts** in Berlin's German restaurants are an anticlimax. *Rote Grütze* (mixed soft berries eaten hot or cold with vanilla sauce) is one of the few distinctive dishes; if you have a sweet tooth, you may be best off heading for a café that serves one of the delicious cakes or *Torten* of which Germans are so fond.

Lutter & Wegner Charlottenstr. 56 ☎030 202 95 415, ⓦl-w-berlin.de; ⓤFranzösische Strasse; map p.36. This refined, airy Austro-German restaurant is the finest of the *Lutter & Wegner* mini empire. It was here the wine merchant started (in 1811) – there's a high-end wine store alongside. Prices are high (mains from €19.50) but that's what happens when the *New York Times* crowns your *Wiener Schnitzel* the best outside Vienna (though in truth the *Sauerbraten* is the real highlight). There's a cheaper bistro on site with a shorter menu and the same list of around 750 wines. Book ahead. Daily 11am–3am, kitchen till 1am.

VAU Jägerstr. 54–55 ☎030 202 97 30, ⓦvau-berlin.de; ⓤHausvogteiplatz; map p.36. Acclaimed (and expensive) restaurant run by chef Kolja Kleeberg – a famous TV chef who produces fantastic, modern takes on classic international cuisine, specializing in using ingredients from the Berlin area. The menu changes often, but expect to see intriguing combinations such as scallops, red beets, dove and polenta, or halibut, spiced tabbouleh, carrot and apple – with mains at around €35. The six-course "improvised" menu costs €140, three-course lunches are €45, and the wine list is superb. Reservations essential. Mon–Sat noon–2.30pm & 7–10.30pm.

ALEXANDERPLATZ AND AROUND

CHEAP EATS

Käse König Panoramastr. 1 ☎030 25 29 50 97, ⓦkaesekoenig.de; ⓤ/ⓢAlexanderplatz; map p.60. Join locals at this basic cafeteria serving simple, decent German and Central European food at low prices from a small daily menu – schnitzel or goulash with boiled potatoes, say, for around €8. Two branches share the same block; the larger is further from the bustle of the street and has more outdoor seating. Daily 9am–7pm.

RESTAURANTS

Emmas Heiligegeistkirchplatz 1 ☎030 24 63 17 32, ⓦemmas.berlin; ⓢHackescher Markt; map p.60. Smart bistro specializing in simple fresh German food of the meat and potatoes variety, but with the addition of more fresh veggies and modern twists to make things less stodgy. It's a particularly good choice for inexpensive lunches (€8.20), such as carrot and ginger soup followed by a rich goulash. Daily 11.30am–midnight.

Sphere Panoramastr. 1a ☎030 24 75 75 875, ⓦtv-turm.de; ⓤ/ⓢAlexanderplatz; map p.60. The revolving restaurant at the top of the TV tower (p.61) serves a reasonable enough menu of traditional Berlin/ Brandenburg and international dishes aimed squarely at tourists. You might have to pay upwards of €13 to access the restaurant and another €15 for a plate of ravioli, but where else can you get to see all of Berlin in half an

hour? Daily: March–Oct 9am–midnight; Nov–Feb 10am–midnight.

Zille-Stube Spreeufer 3 ☎030 242 52 47, ⓦzillestube -nikolaiviertel.de; ⓤKlosterstrasse; map p.60. Traditional German restaurant and homage to Berlin life – and to artist Heinrich Zille, who used to drink nearby at *Zum Nussbaum* (see p.218) and whose illustrations line the wood-clad walls. Particularly good on the menu of old Berlin favourites are the *Rinderrouladen* (beef stuffed with cabbage leaves and pickles; €14.90) and the *Rissole* (beans with bacon, baked onion rings and parsley potatoes; €10.50). Daily noon–9pm.

★ **Zur letzten Instanz** Waisenstr. 14–16 ☎030 242 55 28, ⓦzurletzteninstanz.com; ⓤKlosterstrasse; map p.60. Berlin's oldest *Kneipe*, with a wonderfully old-fashioned interior, including a classic tiled oven, and a great beer garden. The reasonably priced traditional dishes all have law-themed names, like *Zeugen-Aussage* ("eyewitness account") – a reminder of the days when people used to drop in on the way to the nearby courthouse. It's considered so authentically German that foreign heads of state are often brought here to dine. If the meaty dishes (€9–14) look too heavy, try the slightly lighter *Boulette*, Berlin's home-made mince-and-herb meatball, done here to perfection. Mon 5pm–1am, Tues–Sat noon–1am, Sun noon–11pm.

THE SPANDAUER VORSTADT

CHEAP EATS

Dada Falafel Linienstr. 132 ☎030 27 59 69 27, ⓦdadafalafel.de; ⓤOranienburger Tor; map pp.70–71. Tiny Middle Eastern *Imbiss* with sleek decor, some seating and excellent falafel and *shawarma* sandwiches – the best of a clutch of cheap and cheerful options at this end of Oranienburger Str. Mon–Thurs & Sun 10am–2am, Sat 10am–3pm.

Dolores Rosa-Luxemburg-Str. 7 ☎030 28 09 95 97, ⓦdolores-berlin.de; ⓤ/ⓢAlexanderplatz; map pp.70–71. As good a burrito as you'll find in Berlin, dished up in a

small, funky and generally overcrowded cafeteria at staggeringly low prices. You'll leave very full, only €4–6 poorer and maybe a bit bewildered by the à la carte menu system. There's another branch in Schöneberg (see p.205). Mon–Sat 11.30am–10pm, Sun 1–10pm.

Mogg Auguststr. 11–13 ☎030 330 06 07 70, ⓦmoggmogg.com; ⓢOranienburger Strasse; map pp.70–71. This breezy and chic deli, located inside the former Jewish Girls' School (see p.80) serves up delicious, Jewish-inspired food, including one of the best pastrami sandwiches in the city (€9.50/€13.50) and a range of

13

BERLIN OHNE SPECK – A GUIDE FOR VEGETARIANS

This may come as a surprise to those who associate the country with heavy meat dishes, but Germany has one of the largest non-meat-eating communities within the EU – around seven million at the last count, including around a million vegans. Pretty much every inner-city district in Berlin now has a **vegetarian and/or vegan café or restaurant** – and often several. And most cafés and all but the most traditional restaurants will usually serve at least one and usually several **veggie or vegan options**, which might span pasta and potato-based dishes, salads, soups and more – this applies to most buffet breakfasts and brunches, too. In addition, the city's cosmopolitan spread of cuisines means that there are plenty of Italian, Indian, Turkish or Mexican establishments you can choose from, which will usually yield some good meat-free options It's also increasingly common for menus to label items that are vegan, vegetarian and gluten-free, though this is far from ubiquitous – ask the waiting staff if you're unsure, and be wary of more traditional pubs and restaurants, which often use lard and beef stock liberally.

Berlin also has several **vegan supermarkets** and shops, including Veganz (stores in Kreuzberg, Friedrichshain and Prenzlauer Berg and; ⓦveganz.de) and Neukölln's Dr Pogo (Karl-Marx-Platz 24; ⓦveganladen-kollektiv.net).

USEFUL PHRASES

I am a vegetarian (feminine ending in parenthesis) Ich bin Vegetarier(in)
I don't eat meat or fish Ich esse keinen Fleisch oder Fisch
I don't want to eat bacon or meat stock Ich möchte keinen Speck oder Fleischbrühe essen
Has it got meat in it? Gibt's Fleisch drin?
Do you have anything without meat in it? Gibt's was ohne Fleisch?

TOP 10 FOR VEGANS AND VEGETARIANS

*Cookies Cream See p.198
Dada Falafel See p.199
Einhorn See p.203
*Goodies Berlin See p.211
†Lucky Leek See p.213

Monsieur Vuong See opposite
*Morgenrot See p.212
Pappa e Ciccia See p.213
†Pêle-Mêle See p.211
*Yellow Sunshine See p.209

* vegetarian only
† vegan only

---

delicious salads, lentil and hummus dishes (from €7). Mon–Fri 11am–10pm, Sat & Sun 10am–10pm.

CAFÉS AND BARS

Barcomi's Deli Sophienstr. 21 ☎030 28 59 83 63, ⓦbarcomis.de; ⓤWeinmeisterstrasse; map pp.70–71. Situated in a pleasant courtyard, accessible from both Sophienstrasse and Gipsstrasse, *Barcomi's* is a nice place to rest while gallery-hopping; it serves interesting soups and American-style baked goodies, as well as great breakfasts. Mon–Fri 8am–6pm, Sat 10am–6pm, Sun noon–6pm.

Gorki Park Weinbergsweg 25 ☎030 448 72 86, ⓦgorki-park.de; ⓤRosenthaler Platz; map pp.70–71. Tongue-in-cheek Soviet-themed café with 1970s Eastern Bloc-style furnishings and tasty and affordable Russian dishes like *blinis* and *pelmeni* (mains average €11). Mon–Fri 8am–1am, Sat & Sun 9am–1am.

Kapelle Zionskirchplatz 22–24 ☎030 44 34 13 00, ⓦcafe-kapelle.de; ⓤRosenthaler Platz; map pp.70–71. High ceilings and apricot walls in the shadow of the historic Zionskirche. A little off the beaten track but worth the detour – particularly if you're heading to the Arkonaplatz flea market. Breakfasts, snacks, cakes and Brazil-inspired fruit juices available. Daily 10am–late.

Oliv Münzstr. 8 ☎030 89 20 65 40, ⓦoliv-cafe.de; ⓤWeinmeisterstrasse; map pp.70–71. With a modern interior, great coffee and decent, unpretentious food (sandwiches, quiches, soups, cakes), this is a pleasant spot for breakfast or lunch, and very convenient for a respite from boutique shopping. A newer outpost can be found in Schöneberg (see p.206). Cash only. Mon–Fri 8.30am–7pm, Sat 9.30am–7pm, Sun 10am–6pm.

Oscar Wilde Irish Pub Friedrichstr. 112a ☎030 282 81 66, ⓦoscar-wilde-irish-pub.de; ⓤOranienburger Tor; map pp.70–71. Generic Irish bar and something of a social club for Berlin's English-speaking community. The all-day breakfasts (€7.40) are good if you're craving a fry-up, and the Irish stews (€6) aren't bad either. Mon–Thurs 4pm–2am, Fri & Sat noon–3am, Sun noon–midnight.

RESTAURANTS

Amrit Oranienburger Str. 45 ☎030 28 88 48 40, ⓦamrit.de; ⓤOranienburger Tor; map pp.70–71. A cut above most of Berlin's very average Indian restaurants, delivering quality ingredients and fresh spices at reasonable prices (mains €8–15, lunch specials from €4.90) in clean-cut contemporary surroundings. Lots of veggie choices. Mon–Thurs & Sun noon–1am, Fri & Sat noon until late.

Bandol sur Mer Torstr. 167 ☎030 67 30 20 51, ⓦbandolsurmer.de; ⓤRosenthaler Platz; map pp.70–71. A former kebab kiosk refurbished into a tiny but casually upmarket French restaurant that in 2015 gained a Michelin star. The menu, chalked up on the all-black walls, consists of fine French cuisine like snails, entrecôte and foie gras. There's not too much innovation for the price (mains around €18, five-course menus €82) but the food is consistently good. Thurs–Sun 6–11pm.

Katz Orange Bergstr. 22 ☎030 98 32 08 430, ⓦkatzorange.com; ⓢNordbahnhof; map pp.70–71. Tucked away in a restored nineteenth-century brewery, the chic and glamorous "Orange Cat" offers a pleasant blend of casual and fine dining with an international menu that spans salads and quality fish and meat dishes such as pulled ribs with soy sauce (€23) and Loch Duart salmon (€23). There's also a cocktail bar (till 3am) and a lovely courtyard terrace for warmer weather. Kitchen daily 6–11pm.

Kuchi Gipsstr. 3 ☎030 28 38 66 22, ⓦkuchi.de; ⓤRosenthaler Platz; map pp.70–71. *Kuchi* might not serve the best sushi in Berlin, but it's definitely the buzziest place to eat it, with a classy interior, hipster clientele and upbeat atmosphere. The menu ranges beyond sushi (nigiri from €4) to noodles and tempura. If it's full, try tiny *Cocolo* next door, which has hands down the best ramen in town. Mon–Sat noon–midnight, Sun 6pm–midnight.

★**Monsieur Vuong** Alte Schönhauser Str. 46 ☎030 99 29 69 24, ⓦmonsieurvuong.de; ⓤWeinmeisterstrasse; map pp.70–71. Snazzy Vietnamese place with delicious soups and noodle dishes (€8–11) from a tiny menu – look out also for the daily specials on the blackboard, which are available with organic tofu instead of meat. Bench seating means you'll sometimes have to squeeze together with other diners – expect queues at peak times. Don't miss the delicious jasmine and artichoke teas, or the zesty fruit smoothies. Daily noon–midnight.

Pauly Saal Auguststr. 11–13 ☎030 33 00 60 70, ⓦpaulysaal.com; ⓢOranienburger Strasse; map pp.70–71. The Michelin-starred *Pauly Saal* is located in a former school gymnasium and serves innovative and regionally inspired German dishes such as Pomeranian entrecôte and suckling pig from Brandenburg. As well as the smart main dining room, there's a pleasant courtyard garden and a nice bar (open until 2.30am). Four-course dinner menus from €76. Tues–Sat noon–2pm & 6–9.30pm.

Roy & Pris Weinbergsweg 8a ☎0176 22 01 82 45, ⓦroyandpris.de; ⓤRosenthaler Platz; map pp.70–71. With the same owners as neighbouring dumpling hotspot *Yumcha Heroes* (see below), this stylish eatery, fronted by a pleasant terrace, serves upmarket Chinese food that ranges from delicious dim sum to innovative salads and mains like Szechuan fillet of beef (€15) and tempura prawns (€13.50). Daily noon–midnight.

Rutz Chausseestr. 8 ☎030 24 62 87 60, ⓦrutz-restaurant.de; ⓤNaturkundemuseum; map pp.70–71. Michelin-starred cuisine on the first floor and more than 700 international wines offered in the ground-floor bar make this a *de rigueur* stop for foodies. It's expensive – multi-course menus €98–165 – but the *Weinbar* sells slightly cheaper (but still great) home-style dishes. Tues–Sat: wine bar 4–11pm; restaurant 6.30–10.30pm.

Schwarzwaldstuben Tucholskystr. 48 ☎030 28 09 80 84, ⓦschwarzwaldstuben-berlin.com; ⓢOranienburger Strasse; map pp.70–71. This Mitte mainstay doubles as a casual restaurant serving hearty Swabian food – think *Sauerkraut, Maultaschen* and *Flammkuchen* (from €7) – and a friendly bar in the evenings with decent German beers on draught. Cash only. Daily 9am–midnight.

Unsicht-bar Gormannstr. 14 ☎030 24 34 25 00, ⓦunsicht-bar-berlin.de; ⓤWeinmeisterstrasse; map pp.70–71. Hugely successful novelty restaurant where you eat in total darkness. First, pick from one of several three- or four-course fixed menus (€40–62), including a vegetarian option, then follow your blind or partially sighted waiter into the pitch black for your meal. The idea is that without your eyesight, your other senses will be heightened, but you're likely to make other discoveries, too, including how hard it is to judge the amount of food that's on your plate or fork, or even down your front. Wed, Thurs & Sun 6pm–midnight, Fri & Sat 5pm–midnight.

Yumcha Heroes Weinbergsweg 8 ☎030 76 21 30 35, ⓦyumchaheroes.de; ⓤRosenthaler Platz; map pp.70–71. With the same owners as nearby Portuguese café *Galao*, this is the place in Mitte for dumplings – steamed, baked or in a tasty broth. The food is handmade and MSG-free, cooked in an open kitchen and served in a small, but stylish interior. Two-course daily lunch menu €9.50. Daily noon–midnight.

TOP 5 SWEET TREATS

Anna Blume See p.212
Café BilderBuch See p.205
Café Buchwald See p.202
Café Einstein (Schöneberg) See p.205
Winterfeldt Schokoladen See p.206

13

BREAKFAST AND WEEKEND BRUNCH

Breakfast (*Frühstück*) will often be provided by your hotel (see p.187), but many cafés serve it throughout the day. Prices start around €4.50 for a basic bread, eggs and jam affair, rising to €18 for more exotic, champagne-swigging delights.

Typically, you'll be offered a small platter of **cold meats** (usually sausage-based) and **cheeses**, along with a selection of marmalades, jams and honey, and, occasionally, muesli or another cereal. You're also generally given a variety of **breads**, one of the most distinctive features of German cuisine. Both brown and white rolls are popular, often baked with caraway, coriander, poppy or sesame seeds. The rich-tasting black rye bread, known as *Pumpernickel*, is a particular favourite. Freshly brewed **coffee** is the normal accompaniment, though plain or herbal **tea** and **hot chocolate** are also common. A glass of orange **juice** is sometimes included as well.

Weekend brunch is a very popular affair (see box opposite), offering first-class people-watching and often excellent food – and proves particularly good value when offered as part of a **buffet**. Expect to pay €8–16 for unlimited food; drinks are paid for separately.

POTSDAMER PLATZ AND TIERGARTEN

CHEAP EATS

Salomon Bagels 1st floor, Potsdamer Platz Arkaden ☎030 25 29 76 26, ⓦsalomon-bagels.de; ⓤ/ⓢPotsdamer Platz; map pp.90–91. Good selection of bagels, sandwiches and desserts (including a tasty New York-style cheesecake), but as with all the cheap eating places in this mall – they're concentrated in the basement – the noise and bustle don't exactly create a relaxing atmosphere. The prices, however, are reasonable. Mon–Sat 9am–10pm, Sun 10am–8pm.

Sushi Express Potsdamer Platz 2 ☎030 26 55 80 55, ⓦsushi-express-berlin.de; ⓤ/ⓢPotsdamer Platz; map pp.90–91. Tricky to find – it's off the Sony Center courtyard on a passage to the S-Bahn – but worthwhile for a decent range of conveyor-belt sushi, especially when there are half-price offers (Mon–Fri 11.30am–9pm). Hot dishes and lunchboxes also available, though it's usually packed at lunchtimes. Main courses €5. Mon–Fri 11.30am–10pm, Sat noon–10pm, Sun 2–8pm.

CAFÉS, BARS AND BEER GARDENS

★**Café am Neuen See** Lichtensteinallee 2 ☎030 25 44 930, ⓦcafeamneuensee.de; ⓢTiergarten or bus #100 or #200 from Potsdamer Platz; map pp.90–91. A little piece of Bavaria in the middle of the Tiergarten, this beer garden is next to a picturesque lake where you can rent a rowing boat. The usual snacks – and superb pizzas (€9–15) – are served alongside frothing beer jugs, and there is also a very decent restaurant (with a summer terrace) open year-round. Daily 9am–late (beer garden May–Sept only).

Café Buchwald Bartningallee 29 ☎030 39 15 931, ⓦkonditorei-buchwald.de; ⓢBellevue; map pp.90–91. This old-fashioned *Konditorei* has been serving its famed *Baumkuchen,* a kind of layered cake, since 1852 (€3) and used to supply the royal court. A perfect break from a stroll around the Tiergarten. Mon–Sat 8am–6pm, Sun 9am–6pm.

Schleusenkrug Müller-Breslau-Str. ☎030 31 39 909, ⓦschleusenkrug.de; ⓤ/ⓢZoologischer Garten; map pp.90–91. Wedged between a canal lock, the Zoo and Tiergarten, this beer garden is a great spot to spend a last hour before hopping on a train at Zoo Bahnhof. Chairs are easy to move around for optimal sunning, and anything from the small daily menu (mains €8.50–14.50) is a safe bet. Inside, it's retro diner chic. Daily: March–Oct 10am until late (kitchen until 10pm); Nov–Feb 10am–6pm (restaurant only).

RESTAURANTS

Angkor Wat Paulstr. 22 ☎030 39 33 922, ⓦangkorwat .kambodschareise.de; ⓢBellevue; map pp.90–91. Excellent place, serving subtle variations on traditional Cambodian food at moderate prices (mains €10–15). The set meals (from €15.50) are a great way to sample a cross-section of delicious dishes, and the Cambodian "fondue" is great. Tues–Fri 6–11pm, Sat & Sun noon–11pm.

Hugos Restaurant Budapester Str. 2 ☎030 26 02 12 63, ⓦhugos-restaurant.de; ⓤWittenbergplatz; map pp.90–91. In a gorgeously appointed room at the top of the *InterContinental Berlin* hotel (see p.190), chef de cuisine Eberhard Lange creates New German-Mediterranean food that you can sample – for a price – while enjoying the restaurant's panoramic views (menus €70–130). Tues–Sat 6–10.30pm; closed mid-July to mid-Aug.

Paris-Moskau Alt-Moabit 141 ☎030 394 20 81, ⓦparis-moskau.de; ⓤ/ⓢHauptbahnhof; map pp.90–91. Housed in a nineteenth-century rail signalman's house (on the Paris to Moscow line), this French gourmet restaurant offers a curious mix of old Berlin and contemporary elegance and serves hearty dishes like deer and rabbit and vegetarian lasagne with beetroot and chestnuts (€16–26), all backed up by a great wine list. Popular with politicians and civil servants from the nearby government district, and elegant without being too snooty. Mon–Fri noon–3pm & 6–11pm, Sat & Sun 6pm–midnight.

CITY WEST

CHEAP EATS

Bier's Ku'damm 195 Kurfürstendamm 195 ☎030 88 18 942, ⓦbier-s.com/kudamm195; ⓞUhlandstrasse; map p.108. Neon-lit place famed for its *Currywurst* and its popularity with German politicians and celebrities (you can even get champagne), although its prices remain highly reasonable (from €2). Also serves meat skewers and meatballs. Mon–Thurs 11am–5am, Fri & Sat 11am–6am, Sun noon–5am.

Einhorn Mommsenstr. 2 ☎030 881 42 41, ⓦeinhornonline.de; ⓞUhlandstrasse; map p.108. Wholefood at its best, with a daily changing international menu – the mostly vegetarian dishes might include lentils with goat's cheese – and a fabulous lunch bar where food is priced by weight (€1.50/100g; normal prices €4.50–8.50). It's compact and usually crowded but the atmosphere remains friendly and relaxed. Mon–Fri 10am–5pm.

Lon-Men's Noodle House Kantstr. 33 ☎030 31 51 96 78; ⓢSavignyplatz; map p.108. A relaxed, tiny Taiwanese noodle shop run by friendly grandmas who make excellent dumplings and noodle soups (small and large portions available). Try the fried "Chinese Maultaschen" (€8–10)– and ask for the home-made noodles (not on the menu). Daily noon–11pm.

Piccola Taormina Uhlandstr. 29 ☎030 881 47 10, ⓦpiccola-taormina.net; ⓞUhlandstrasse; map p.108. Enduringly popular wafer-thin pizza specialist with a strange setup: order and pay at the bar, find a seat in the back room, listen out for a tannoy announcement; then head back to the bar to collect. It's all a bit chaotic and very Italian, but well worth it for the food – lasagne and pizzas from €5. Daily 11am–2am.

Witty's Wittenbergplatz 5 ☎030 21 19 496, ⓦwittys-berlin.de; ⓞWittenbergplatz; map p.108. One of the city's first and finest organic sausage stands, *Witty's* has customers lined up along the square for their *Currywurst* and crispy fries. Eat here, then cross the street for an exquisite chocolate or two from KaDeWe (see p.242). Mon–Sat 11am–10.30pm, Sun noon–9.30pm.

CAFÉS AND BARS

Café im Literaturhaus Fasanenstr. 23 ☎030 88 25 414, ⓦliteraturhaus-berlin.de; ⓞUhlandstrasse; map p.108. Every bit as classic and elegant as the name suggests. The spacious interior or beautiful summer garden are great spots for coffee and cake, lunch or dinner: the menu changes weekly (soup €6.50, mains €15.50–29.50) and has vegetarian and organic options. Breakfast until 2pm, lunch and dinner menus from 11.30am. Daily 9am–midnight.

Café Savigny Grolmanstr. 53 ☎030 44 70 83 86, ⓦcafesavigny.de/en/; ⓢSavignyplatz; map p.108. A small, classic spot that's been serving great breakfasts and coffee for more than a decade. Lunches start at €5.50 (soups) with a hearty Burgundy stew for €13.50. Service is good and it's also nice for an evening drink. Daily 9am–midnight.

Dicke Wirtin Carmerstr. 9 ☎030 312 49 52, ⓦdicke-wirtin.de; ⓢSavignyplatz; map p.108. Traditional Berlin *Kneipe*, here since the 1920s, but spruced up a little since to appeal to Berlin visitors who can pick from nine draught beers and a basic menu of snacks and soups (from €3). Daily 11am until late.

Schwarzes Café Kantstr. 148 ☎030 313 80 38, ⓦschwarzescafe-berlin.de; ⓢSavignyplatz; map p.108. The slightly ragged charm of the "Black Café" makes it feel like it would be better placed in the east. Downstairs is small and intimate, but upstairs the large, airy room has a relaxed, convivial vibe. Food is served 24hr, including breakfasts (from €5.80) – but it comes into its own as a night-owl place. Daily 24hr.

Zwiebelfisch Savignyplatz 7 ☎030 312 73 63, ⓦzwiebelfisch-berlin.de; ⓢSavignyplatz; map p.108. Corner bar and 1970s throwback for would-be arty and intellectual types. Jazz, earnest debate and good cheap grub (€8–12.50), including goulash and Swabian *Maultaschen*, served until 1am. Daily noon–6am.

RESTAURANTS

Ashoka Grolmanstr. 51 ☎030 31 01 58 06, ⓦmyashoka.de; ⓢSavignyplatz; map p.108. Ashok Sharma opened this restaurant in 1975 as he was missing the food from his home in Punjab. It offers well-priced, decent food (curries around €6.50–8.50) in a small *Imbiss*-style place. Vegetarian options and friendly staff. Daily 11am–midnight.

Brel Savignyplatz 1 ☎030 31 80 00 20, ⓦcafebrel .berlin; ⓢSavignyplatz; map p.108. This well-established bistro has a comfortable, friendly but sophisticated feel, with a long wooden bar, black-and-white photos and grand piano. It's matched by excellent

---

TOP 10 WEEKEND BRUNCH SPOTS

Anna Blume Prenzlauer Berg. See p.212
Cabslam Neukölln. See p.210
Café Aroma Schöneberg. See p.206
Café Datscha Friedrichshain. See p.211
Café Einstein Schöneberg. See p.205
Morgenland Eastern Kreuzberg.
   See p.210
Pappa e Ciccia Prenzlauer Berg. See p.213
Pasternak Prenzlauer Berg. See p.213
Schneeweiss Friedrichshain. See p.211
Zwölf Apostel City West. See p.205

13

French food (*bouillabaise* €12.50, rump steak and frites €24.50) and wines. Daily 10am till late.

Dao by Meo Kantstr. 133 ☎030 37 59 14 14, ⓦdao-restaurant.de; Ⓢ Savignyplatz; map p.108. Opened by a Berliner and his Thai wife Dao in the 1970s (and now run by Meo), this Thai spot serves tasty dishes that avoid unnatural products and brim with flavour. As well as tucking into authentic *pad Thai* (€9.50) and fish and duck dishes (up to €20), you can also take classes at Meo's cooking school. Daily noon–midnight.

Diekmann Meinekestr. 7 ☎030 883 33 21, ⓦdiekmann-restaurants.de; Ⓤ Kurfürstendamm; map p.108. Long-standing Berlin bistro, with French colonial touches in the decor and on the menu. The oft-changing mains (€21–23) are always fresh and reliable – the oysters are particularly good. Mon–Sat noon until late.

Diener Tattersall Grolmanstr. 47 ☎030 881 53 29, ⓦdiener-berlin.de; Ⓢ Savignyplatz; map p.108. This Berlin alehouse is a local institution – not only because it was opened in 1954 by former German heavyweight boxer Franz Diener, but also because it serves dishes like *Königsberger Klopse* (€10.50) and has an atmosphere as old-school as the menu. Daily 6pm till late.

Dressler Kurfürstendamm 207–208 ☎030 883 35 30, ⓦrestaurant-dressler.de; Ⓤ Uhlandstrasse; map p.108. German take on a French brasserie with an old-fashioned feel and an Art Nouveau interior – formal but friendly. The seasonal food is very good, and the small front bar is perfect for a quick coffee or lunch (three courses €13). Daily 8am–1am (kitchen till midnight).

Florian Grolmanstr. 52 ☎030 313 91 84, ⓦrestaurant-florian.de; Ⓢ Savignyplatz; map p.108. Leading light among Berlin's modern German restaurants, serving fresh, light and innovative versions of traditional combinations from a weekly menu that includes the likes of boiled veal with radish, beetroot, potato and leeks, or rump steak with green beans and rosemary potatoes. Prices are fair (mains €15.60–27.50), the interior blandly cool and the service excellent. It's as much a place for Berlin's beautiful people to be seen as it is a place to eat. Daily 6pm–3am (kitchen until midnight).

★**Glass** Uhlandstr. 195 ☎030 54 71 08 61, ⓦglassberlin.de; Ⓤ Uhlandstrasse; map p.108. Run by talented young Israeli chef Gal Ben-Moshe, this restaurant blends a relaxed, low-key interior with high-end cuisine in the shape of five- or seven-course menus (€75/95 respectively). Vegan versions are available and, whatever you do, save some room for the fabulous deconstructed dessert. Tues–Sat 6–11pm.

Good Friends Kantstr. 30 ☎030 313 26 59, ⓦgoodfriends-berlin.de; Ⓢ Savignyplatz; map p.108. One of Berlin's few really authentic Cantonese restaurants, with plain decor and a full range of classics (mains €11–19.70). It's always busy; evening bookings recommended. Daily noon–2am.

Jules Verne Restaurant Schlüterstr. 61 ☎030 31 80 94 10, ⓦjules-verne-berlin.de; Ⓢ Savignyplatz; map p.108. The interior feels classically French but the menu is quite broad, ranging from *Flammkuchen* and schnitzel to couscous and satay. Lunchtime deals (€7.50–10.50)

THE IMBISS

The German term **Imbiss** was originally coined for little food stalls at medieval markets, and Berliners are certainly past masters in serving inexpensive food for eating on the hoof. The city's immigrant population has built on the tradition, adapting recipes to produce quick portable meals. Today virtually every Berlin street has an *Imbiss*, with major concentrations in commercial areas and at train stations. Some have limited seating, but many only offer a couple of high tables on which to lean. It's pretty much guaranteed that a local *Imbiss* will be more interesting than many of the international fast-food chains that dot the city (though the national fish and seafood specialist chain *Nordsee* is worth a try). All the *Imbisses* reviewed in this chapter are listed under "cheap eats".

The simple sausage has traditionally been the most popular *Imbiss* item and in Berlin it's been transformed into the local speciality **Currywurst** – a chubby smoked pork sausage smothered in curried ketchup – often served with French fries (*pommes frites*). Another local *Imbiss* speciality is the **Boulette**, a hamburger patty made from ground beef, eggs, butter, herbs and onions, which was introduced by the French Huguenots in the late 1600s. These days, however, the most common of all are **Greek**, **Turkish** and **Middle Eastern** *Imbiss* stands selling *döner*, *gyros* or *shawarma* respectively – all essentially meat or chicken kebabs bundled into a pitta, tortilla or ciabatta-style bread sandwich with salad and a sauce – usually hot (*scharf*), herb (*Kräuter*) or garlic (*Knoblauch*). All are likely to be delicious and fill you up for around €3. The standard of *Imbiss* food throughout Berlin is very good since most rely on local business, so in general it's not worth going out of your way to track down a particular place. That said, if you want to make sure you are having as good a *Currywurst* as the city can offer, try **Bier's Kudamm 195** (see p.203), **Konnopke's Imbiss** (see p.211) or **Curry 36** (see p.206).

13

change weekly. Daily 9am–1am (kitchen till 11.45pm).

★**Lubitsch** Bleibtreustr. 47 ☎030 88 62 66 60, ⓦrestaurant-lubitsch.de; Ⓢ Savignyplatz; map p.108. Named after German film director Ernst Lubitsch, this slick bistro has a wonderfully old-school Berlin feel. The food is generous and hearty – dumplings, schnitzel, cucumber salad – and though the ambience is vaguely formal (linen tablecloths) and it's popular with business people, it's also a friendly place. Breakfasts start at €4.50; two-course lunches €9.50; dinner mains from €15.50. Mon–Fri 8.30am–11pm, Sat & Sun 8.30am–1am.

Marjellchen Mommsenstr. 9 ☎030 883 26 76, ⓦmarjellchen-berlin.de; Ⓢ Savignyplatz; map p.108. It's obvious from the window displays – books, photos and other paraphernalia – that this is a time-warped kind of place. Indeed, *Marjellchen* specializes in cuisine from East Prussia, Pomerania and Silesia, all served up in a cosy, traditional atmosphere. Portions are generous and service is friendly. Mains €11.80–20.50. Daily 5pm–midnight.

Ottenthal Kantstr. 153 ☎030 313 31 62, ⓦottenthal .com; Ⓢ Savignyplatz or ⓤ Uhlandstrasse; map p.108. White-clothed tables and relatively sparse white walls lend this place an unfussy, classic feel that ties in well with the Austrian cuisine – simple, yet some of the best in the area. Organic ingredients feature on the menu, which includes fish, risotto and a famed *Wiener Schnitzel*; mains €18–27.50. Good Austrian wine list too. Daily 5pm–1am.

Paris Bar Kantstr. 152 ☎030 313 80 52, ⓦparisbar.net; Ⓢ Savignyplatz or ⓤ Uhlandstrasse; map p.108. Once the city's most famous meeting places for artists, writers and intellectuals, and now (due to its high prices and reputation) the preserve of the moneyed middle classes, B-list local actors and the occasional celebrity. The food – French and Viennese in style – is decent enough, and the service veers between snooty and warm, depending on the night. Mains €21–35. Daily noon–2am.

Zwölf Apostel Bleibtreustr. 49 ☎030 312 14 33, ⓦ12-apostel.de; Ⓢ Savignyplatz; map p.108. Deluxe and very popular pizzeria with a smart, Baroque-style interior and kitsch religious frescoes. The huge, thin crust pizzas (from €9.90) have unusual toppings like fresh salmon and cream cheese; other Italian mains €9–22). The weekday business lunch (11.30am–4pm, €7.50–9.95) is excellent, and the terrific Sunday brunch buffet (€22.50) comes with a glass of sparkling wine and a hot drink. Booking recommended in the evenings. Daily 11am–1am.

SCHÖNEBERG

CHEAP EATS

★**Baharat Falafel** Winterfeldtstr. 37 ☎030 216 83 01; ⓤNollendorfplatz; map p.114. A bare-bones falafel joint, you might think; but these are the best falafels this side of Baghdad. Some seating. Daily noon–2am.

Dolores Bayreuther Str. 36 ☎030 54 82 15 90, ⓦdolores -berlin.de; ⓤWittenbergplatz; map p.114. The more recently opened version of the Mitte Cali-Mex place (see p.199) does the same fine line in burritos, including vegetarian-friendly options. Mon–Sat 11.30am–10pm, Sun 1–10pm.

Ebbes Crellestr. 5 ☎030 70 09 48 13, ⓦebbes-in-berlin .de; Ⓢ Julius-Leber-Brücke; map p.114. This quirky Swabian deli is overflowing with meatloaf and trays of fresh *spätzle* (pasta) from southern Germany. Buy a picnic and wander north to Kleist-Park, or grab a stool outside and try one of the daily specials, including *Maultaschen* in broth (€3.50). Mon–Fri 10am–7.30pm, Sat 9am–4pm.

Garda Pizza Crellestr. 48 ☎030 78 09 79 70; ⓤJulius-Leber-Brücke; map p.114. Locals flock here for thin-crust pizza (€1.80–2.50/slice) particularly the version with fresh aubergine, mushroom, sheep's salami and artichokes. Join the crowd on the pavement, or, with kids, mosey down a few metres to the neighbouring playground. Daily 11.30am–9pm; Dec–Feb closed Sun.

CAFÉS AND BARS

Café BilderBuch Akazienstr. 28 ☎030 78 70 60 57, ⓦcafe-bilderbuch.de; Ⓢ Julius-Leber-Brücke; map p.114. Lovely rambling café in the Viennese tradition. It doesn't look particularly special from outside, but the comfortable back parlour may well hold you captive for hours. Great breakfasts (€5.40–€7.90), lovely cakes, elegant coffees and courtyard seating, too. Mon–Sat 9am–midnight, Sun 10am–midnight.

Café Einstein Kurfürstenstr. 58 ☎030 261 50 96, ⓦwww.cafeeinstein.com; ⓤNollendorfplatz; map p.114. Housed in an elegant nineteenth-century German villa, with parquet floors and leather banquettes, this is about as close as you'll get to the ambience of a prewar Berlin *Kaffeehaus*, complete with international newspapers, breakfast served until 2pm and a classic European menu that's all schnitzels, steak frites and home-made cakes. On sunny afternoons make a beeline for the spacious garden and after dark hit the first-floor *Lebenstern* bar for refined cocktails and cigars. Daily 8am–midnight.

Café M Goltzstr. 33 ☎030 216 70 92, ⓦcafe-m.de; ⓤNollendorfplatz; map p.114. Scattered with tatty plastic chairs and precious little else, *M* is a favoured rendezvous for self-styled creative types and the conventionally unconventional. Usually packed, particularly for its famous breakfasts; cocktails €5.50 during happy hour (8–10pm). Mon–Fri 9.30am–late, Sat & Sun noon–late.

Inka Eis Belziger Str. 44 ☎030 78 09 70 50, ⓦinka-eis .de; ⓤEisenacher Strasse; map p.114. A little taste of Latin America in a quiet corner of Schöneberg, *Inka Eis* serves scrumptious scoops of tamarind ice cream as well as home-made cakes and exotic sandwiches like *bottifarra* and *pan con chorizo* (prices €3–5). Daily 11am–7pm; closed Jan & Feb.

13

TOP 5 TRADITIONAL LOCAL FOOD

Altes Zollhaus See p.208
Marjellchen See p.205
Ratskeller Köpenick See p.215
Zum Schusterjungen See p.214
Zur letzten Instanz See p.199

Möve im Felsenkeller Akazienstr. 2 ☎ 030 781 34 47; ⓢ Julius-Leber-Brücke; map p.114. Perfect for when you're nostalgic for old Berlin. Founded in 1923, this unpretentious old bar is famous for its eight beers on tap drawn the old-fashioned way, so be prepared to wait. Hearty, simple food includes lentil soup and swede stew (€5). No music, but plenty of atmosphere and a hip young crowd. Mon–Fri 4pm–1am, Sat noon–2am.

Oliv Eat Potsdamer Str. 91 ☎ 030 552 338 23, ⓦ oliv-cafe .de; ⓤ Kurfürstenstrasse; map p.114. Second branch of the Mitte original (see p.200), which offers the same selection of home-made and organic sandwiches, cakes and soups in a swanky interior. Mon–Fri 8.30am–7.30pm, Sat & Sun 10am–6pm.

Winterfeldt Schokoladen Goltzstr. 23 ☎ 030 23 62 32 56, ⓦ winterfeldt-schokoladen.de; ⓤ Nollendorfplatz; map p.114. Once an apothecary, this café-chocolate shop now serves a lovely selection of pastries to cure all ills. Scones with clotted cream and jam and warm chocolate fondant cake (both €3) are popular. Mon–Fri 9am–8pm, Sat 9am–6pm, Sun noon–7pm.

RESTAURANTS

Café Aroma Hochkirchstr. 8 ☎ 030 782 58 21, ⓦ cafe -aroma.de; ⓤ/ⓢ Yorckstrasse; map p.114. Rustic Italian gem tucked away on a sleepy residential street and the unofficial headquarters for Berlin's slow food movement. The antipasti spread at Sunday brunch (11am–2pm; €12) is legendary, while dried cod with polenta (€7.50) and squid with baby chard (€15.50) satisfy the dinner crowd. The terrace is a peaceful haven in summer. Mon–Fri 6pm till late, Sat noon till late, Sun 11am till late.

Edd's Thailändisches Lutzowstr. 81 ☎ 030 215 52 94, ⓦ edds-thairestaurant.de; ⓤ Kurfürstenstrasse; map p.114. Huge portions of superbly cooked fresh Thai food make this sumptuous place popular all week. Bearing in mind the quality and authenticity – many family recipes stem from Edd's gran (including the signature banana

blossom salad), who cooked in Bangkok's Royal Palace – the prices are reasonable, with mains around €15–23. Booking essential and credit cards not accepted. Tues–Fri 11.30am–3pm & 6pm–midnight, Sat 5pm–midnight, Sun 2pm–midnight.

Ixthys Pallasstr. 21 ☎ 030 81 47 47 69; ⓤ Nollendorfplatz; map p.114. A tiny café run by two Korean widows who've festooned the walls with biblical slogans, this place is all about great home-style cooking. Guests squeeze in to enjoy home-made noodles with vegetables (€5) or seafood (€7.50) and the fiery, sizzling *bibimbap* (€7.50). Mon–Sat noon–10pm.

Joseph Roth Diele Potsdamer Str. 75 ☎ 030 26 36 98 84, ⓦ joseph-roth-diele.de; ⓤ Kurfürstenstrasse; map p.114. Quirky restaurant that pays homage to the life and work of interwar Jewish writer Joseph Roth and adds a splash of charm and colour to a fairly nondescript corner of central Berlin. Very popular, with very reasonably priced daily specials (€4.95–11.95), though the food is fairly basic. Mon–Fri 10am–midnight, Sat 6pm–midnight.

Maharadscha Fuggerstr. 21 ☎ 030 213 88 26, ⓦ maharadscha2.de; ⓤ Wittenbergplatz; map p.114. This popular Indian restaurant, running since 1984, has around fifty dishes from every part of the subcontinent, including meat, fish and vegetarian options. If you can't find what you like, just ask and they will make it. Mains from €8–12. Daily except Wed 5–11pm.

Petite Europe Langenscheidtstr. 1 ☎ 030 781 29 64; ⓤ Kleistpark; map p.114. Unpretentious Italian place that dishes up filling home-made pastas and stone-oven pizzas (average €10) in an informal, lively atmosphere. Booking advised. Daily 5pm–1am.

Renger-Patzsch Wartburgstr. 54 ☎ 030 784 20 59, ⓦ renger-patzsch.com; ⓤ Eisenacher Strasse; map p.114. Rustic restaurant, with dark wood interiors and white tablecloths covering long communal tables, serving excellent cuisine from the Alsace region – a mix of French and German. In spring, don't miss the dandelion salad with lardons (€8); in winter, try the braised ox cheeks with bacon-wrapped plums, turnips and mashed potatoes (€18). Look out too, for wild boar. Mains €14–18. Booking advised. Mon–Sat 6–11.30pm.

Taverna Ousies Grunewaldstr. 16 ☎ 030 216 79 57, ⓦ taverna-ousies.de; ⓤ Eisenacher Strasse; map p.114. This kitschy, raucous Greek taverna is a perennial favourite. There are no real duds, so go wild with the meze menu (€4.70–8) and be entertained by the jolly staff. Reservations essential at weekends. Daily 5pm–midnight.

WESTERN KREUZBERG

CHEAP EATS

Curry 36 Mehringdamm 36 ☎ 030 251 73 68, ⓦ curry36.de; ⓤ Mehringdamm; map p.118. Everyone in Berlin has a favourite place to eat *Currywurst* but *Curry 36*

(along with *Konnopke's*; see p.211) is cited more often than most. It's a buzzy place to grab a snack (around €2–4) and even has its own merch in the shape of hoodies and Curry 36 ketchup. Daily 9am–5pm.

FROM TOP ANNA BLUME (P.212); MUSTAFAS (P.208) >

13

TOP 5 RAINY-DAY HANGOUTS

Al Hamra See p.212
Café BilderBuch See p.205
Macondo Café See p.211
Spielwiese See p.211
Wohnzimmer See p.212

Knofi Bergmannstr. 11 & 98 ☎030 69 56 43 59, ⓦknofi.de; ⓤGneisenaustrasse; map p.118. There are two *Knofis* opposite each other. At no. 11 you'll find a small *Imbiss* serving tasty Turkish food – stuffed vine leaves, hummus and more (mixed vegetarian platter €8.20). Over the road is a Turkish deli. Daily 9am–midnight.

Mustafas Mehringdamm 32 ⓦmustafas.de; ⓤMehringdamm; map p.118. People will wait in line for an hour at any time of day at this cult *Imbiss* kiosk; all the fuss is about the delicious kebabs (around €3.50–4) made with lots of fried vegetables (some cooked within the meat itself), feta cheese and plenty of garlic and coriander. Daily 10.30am–2am.

Pagode Bergmannstr. 88 ☎030 619 26 40, ⓦpagode -thaifood.de; ⓤGneisenaustrasse; map p.118. Crowded, noisy and steamy place where the Thai meals enjoy a high reputation among Berlin's *Imbiss* aficionados. Dishes span delicious soups, rice and noodle dishes, including *pad Thai*; mains €6.70–9.20. Mon–Thurs noon–11pm, Fri & Sat noon – midnight.

CAFÉS AND BARS

Barcomi's Bergmannstr. 21 ☎030 694 81 38, ⓦbarcomis.de; ⓤGneisenaustrasse; map p.118. American-style coffee house with thirteen exotic blends accompanied by bagels, brownies and other oversized American baked goods – great cheesecake and carrot cake. Scattered copies of *The New Yorker* too. Mon–Sat 8am–9pm, Sun 9am–9pm.

Café Atlantic Bergmannstr. 100 ☎030 691 92 92, ⓦcafeatlantic.de; ⓤGneisenaustrasse; map p.118. Large, classic café, with colourful paintings in the back and bar stools in the front, serving an abundant weekend breakfast (eleven ways to scramble your eggs, from €7.50) till 5pm, and daily lunch specials and dinner options too. Daily 9am–1am.

Molinari & Ko Riemannstr. 13 ☎030 691 39 03, ⓦmolinari-ko.de; ⓤGneisenaustrasse; map p.118. Welcoming Italian café/bar/restaurant hidden away on a residential street. With a wooden interior and friendly staff it offers a menu of breakfasts, snacks, pasta and pizza, with a decent wine and beer selection that makes it good for evenings too. Mon–Fri 8am–midnight, Sat & Sun 9am–midnight.

Sale e Tabacci Rudi-Dutschke-Str. 23 ☎030 252 11 55, ⓦsale-e-tabacchi.de; ⓤKochstrasse; map p.118.

Authentic and beautiful Italian café near Checkpoint Charlie where journalists and architects linger over espresso. It's a little overpriced, with mains around €25, but the daily changing menu uses top-notch ingredients, and it does serve some great seafood, impressive Italian wines and there's garden seating out back. Daily 11am till late.

RESTAURANTS

Altes Zollhaus Carl-Herz-Ufer 30 ☎030 692 33 00, ⓦaltes-zollhaus-berlin.de; ⓤPrinzenstrasse or Hallesches Tor; map p.118. Very classy place in an old half-timbered building overlooking the Landwehrkanal, serving modern German food such as duck from Brandenburg with potato dumplings, and home-made *crema catalana* with blueberries. Three-course set menus €39. Tues–Sat 6pm–1am.

Austria Bergmannstr. 30 ☎030 694 44 40, ⓦaustria -berlin.de; ⓤGneisenaustrasse; map p.118. Generous portions of excellent Austrian food – particularly the huge *Wiener Schnitzel* – served on solid wood tables in dark, rustic surrounds where the mounted antlers evoke the feel of a hunting lodge. Mains €16.80–19.50. Mon 6–11pm, Tues–Sun noon–11pm.

Bar Centrale Yorckstr. 82 ☎030 786 29 89, ⓦbar -centrale.net; ⓤMehringdamm; map p.118. Chic Italian locale, popular with affluent young people and exiled Italians. The daily changing menu always features good, fresh antipasti, pasta, fish and meat dishes (mains €13–27) and there's an international wine list. Daily 4pm–1am.

E.T.A. Hoffmann Yorckstr. 83 ☎030 78 09 88 09, ⓦrestaurant-e-t-a-hoffmann.de; ⓤMehringdamm; map p.118. Upmarket bistro overseen by Thomas Kurt, who serves rich European dishes such as terrine of duck foie gras (€22), Fine de Claire oysters (€21 for six, served with a shallot sauce) or a set menu of two, three or four courses (€45, €55 and €65 respectively). The interior is classic and comfortable, and there's a lovely courtyard. Daily except Tues 5pm–late.

Nobelhart & Schmutzig Friedrichstr. 218 ☎030 25 94 06 10, ⓦnobelhartundschmutzig.com; ⓤKochstrasse; map p.118. No restaurant quite emphasizes the locavore – local sourcing – trend in Berlin than this chic joint venture between sommelier Billy Wagner (formerly of *Weinbar Rutz*; see p.201) and young, dynamic chef Micha Schäfer. Using ingredients sourced exclusively in Berlin and Brandenburg, the menu consists of ten seasonally themed courses (€95) that can be paired, at extra cost, with local wines as well as

---

TOP 5 GOURMET DINING

E.T.A. Hoffmann See above
Fischers Fritz See p.198
Glass See p.204
Hugos Restaurant See p.202
Nobelhart & Schmutzig See above

13

craft beers and ciders. The interior is rustic-luxe, seats are limited to 27, and everyone get to watch the chefs at work in the open kitchen. Tues–Sat 6.30pm till late.

Tomasa Kreuzbergstr. 62 ☎ 030 81 00 98 85, ⓦ tomasa .de; ⓜ Mehringdamm; map p.118. This old-school villa, on the edge of Viktoriapark, is a particularly pleasant place for a relaxed breakfast or lunch. The classic interior, good, seasonal menu (from tapas to pasta) and friendly service attract a mixed clientele, families included. Business lunches are available daily (noon–3pm) from €6, otherwise most dishes cost around double that. Mon–Thurs & Sun 9am–1am, Fri & Sat 9am–2am.

EASTERN KREUZBERG

CHEAP EATS

★ **Burgermeister** Oberbaumstr. 8; ⓜ Schlesisches Tor; Skalitzer Str. 136; ⓜ Kottbusser Tor; ⓦ burger-meister .de; map pp.128–129. Cult burger joint in a converted old Prussian public toilet by the elevated underground station at Schlesisches Tor, serving fresh and delicious burgers (€3–5) that could hold their own in far classier surroundings. There are a couple of places to sit, but mostly it's standing room only and often packed; the newer Kottbusser Tor branch has inside seating. Mon–Thurs & Sun 11am–3am, Fri & Sat 11am–4am (Kottbusser Tor branch from noon Sat & Sun).

Maroush Adalbertstr. 93 ☎ 030 69 53 61 71, ⓦ maroush-berlin.de; ⓜ Kottbusser Tor; map pp.128–129. Cosy Lebanese café with authentically Middle Eastern decor and above-average sandwiches, kebabs, falafels and fresh salads for around €8–10. Daily 11am–2am.

Nachtigall Imbiss Ohlauer Str. 10 ☎ 030 611 71 15; ⓜ Görlitzer Bahnhof; map pp.128–129. Middle Eastern specialities, including the delicious *shawarma* kebab – lamb and hummus in pitta bread. Good vegetarian salads as well. Daily 11am–2am.

Yellow Sunshine Wiener Str. 19 ☎ 0157 81 23 12 54, ⓦ yellow-sunshine.de; ⓜ Görlitzer Bahnhof; map pp.128–129. Vegetarian and organic self service burger bar, with set meals including fries and a drink for €9. Mon–Thurs & Sun noon–11pm, Fri & Sat noon–midnight.

CAFÉS AND BARS

Café V Lausitzer Platz 12 ☎ 030 612 45 05; ⓜ Görlitzer Bahnhof; map pp.128–129. Cosy, dimly lit, bohemian place beside a leafy Kreuzberg park and as good a hangout as it is a place to eat. With a fully vegetarian (and mostly vegan) ethos – think plenty of tofu and seitan (wheat gluten) – the menu ranges from gluten-free pizzas to delicious salads. Mains €8–12. Menus change weekly. Daily 10am–2am.

Kvartira Nr. 62 Lübbener Str. 18 ☎ 030 62 90 15 47; ⓜ Schlesisches Tor; map pp.128–129. Atmospheric Russian café with 1920s-era dark red and gold decor, serving Russian classics such as *borscht* (€4.70), delicious *pelmeni* (dumplings; €6.50) and tea flavoured with jam – as well as some great chocolate cake. Occasional live music and readings, plus Tatort screenings too. Daily 5pm–late.

Ron Telesky Dieffenbachstr. 62 ⓦ 030 61 62 11 11, ⓦ rontelesky.de; ⓜ Schönleinstrasse; map pp.128–129. Canadian pizza served from a canoe – how could you refuse? Especially when toppings include sweet potato, mango, feta and maple syrup. The interior also features national emblems like a moose head. Vegan options available. Slices from €2.90. Mon–Fri 12.30–10pm, Sat & Sun 1.30–10pm.

Tiki Heart Wiener Str. 20 ☎ 030 61 07 47 03, ⓦ tikiheart.de; ⓜ Görlitzer Bahnhof; map pp.128–129. Hawaiian-rockabilly-themed joint with an unapologetically kitsch interior and innovative menu. The breakfasts, served until 5pm, feature items like the "Oi-Fast" – a heady mix of scrambled eggs and chorizo (€7). There are veggie burgers and – one for the serious rockers – a Lemmy burger grilled in whisky. Strong cocktails, too. Mon–Fri 11am–late, Sat & Sun 10am–late.

RESTAURANTS

Amrit Oranienstr. 202 ☎ 030 612 55 50, ⓦ amrit.de; ⓜ Görlitzer Bahnhof; map pp.128–129. The seating is always a bit of a squeeze at this busy Indian restaurant, where the huge portions are inexpensive (mains €8–15) and delicious. Not the sort of place to linger after a meal; reservations are recommended in the week and essential at weekends. Daily noon–midnight.

Baraka Lausitzer Platz 6 ☎ 030 612 63 30, ⓦ baraka -berlin.de; ⓜ Görlitzer Bahnhof; map pp.128–129. One for North African food fans with tasteful authentic decor and food – tagines, chicken skewers, *shawarma* – that's some of the best in town, and at decent prices (mains €7–13). The mixed plate for two is immense. Mon–Thurs & Sun 11am–midnight, Fri & Sat 11am–1am.

Defne Planufer 92 ☎ 030 81 79 71 11, ⓦ defne-restaurant.de; ⓜ Kottbusser Tor or Schönleinstrasse; map pp.128–129. A great menu of Turkish/Mediterranean food using fresh ingredients. Classics include "Imam Fainted" (aubergines with pine nuts, peppers and tomato-herb sauce; €9.90) and lamb cutlets (€15). The interior is simple and spacious; the terrace, overlooking the Landwehrkanal, is lovely in summer. Daily: April–Sept

---

TOP 5 FOOD WITH A VIEW

Café am Neuen See See p.202
Hugos Restaurant See p.202
Käfer Dachgarten See p.198
Schlosscafe Köpenick See p.214
Sphere See p.199

13

4pm–1am; Oct–March 5pm–1am (kitchen till midnight all year).

★**Henne** Leuschnerdamm 25 ☎030 614 77 30, ⓦ henne-berlin.de; ⓣ Moritzplatz; map pp.128–129. Pub-style restaurant serving the best fried chicken (€8.60) in Berlin, served with cabbage and potato salad sides (€3.70). The interior hasn't been changed, the owners claim, since 1905. Reservations essential. Tues–Sat 6pm until late, Sun 5pm until late.

Long March Canteen Wrangelstr. 20 ☎0178 88 49 899, ⓦ longmarchcanteen.com; ⓣ Görlitzer Bahnhof; map pp.128–129. The dim sum here (€6.50–11.50) is celebrated citywide, and the buzzy atmosphere pulls in the Berlin's hip and famous. The broad selection includes pak choi salad and marinated chicken skewers with water chestnuts. Daily 6pm–midnight.

★**Morgenland** Skalitzer Str. 35 ☎030 611 32 91, ⓦ morgenland-berlin.de; ⓣ Görlitzer Bahnhof; map pp.128–129. Relaxed café with a welcoming vibe, which serves a mix of European snacks. The amazing brunch

buffet (Sat & Sun 10am–4pm; €9.50) seems to attract most of the neighbourhood. Mon–Fri 9am until late, Sat & Sun 10am until late.

RosaCaleta Muskauer Str. 9 ☎030 69 53 78 59, ⓦ rosacaleta.com; ⓣ Görlitzer Bahnhof; map pp.128–129. Jamaican/European fusion restaurant that's created quite a buzz in a city hopelessly devoid of Caribbean cuisine. There's plenty of Jerk-style food on the menu, but also dishes like oven-roast pork fillet, mango-ginger lentil salad and tofu and vegetable stew (mains from €9.50). It also functions as an art space and hosts DJs. Tues–Fri 11am–1am, Sat 6pm–1am, Sun 2pm–1am.

Weltrestaurant Markthalle Pücklerstr. 34 ☎030 617 55 02, ⓦ weltrestaurant-markthalle.de; ⓣ Görlitzer Bahnhof; map pp.128–129. Spacious restaurant that attracts a young crowd with its long communal tables and hearty portions of German food. Look out for the €8.50 daily special and leave space for the phenomenal cakes. Daily noon–midnight.

NEUKÖLLN

CAFÉS AND BARS

Ankerklause Kottbusser Damm 104 ☎030 693 56 49, ⓦ ankerklause.de; ⓣ Kottbusser Tor or Schönleinstrasse; map pp.128–129. This nautically themed café-bar overlooking the bucolic Landwehrkanal has been transformed into a hip bar playing a mixture of techno and easy listening. Great breakfast choices (served until 4pm) include first-class French toast and a Mexican breakfast that will tide you over until dinner. Usually packed by 11pm. Tues–Sun 10am–4am, Mon 4pm–4am (kitchen open until 11pm).

Cabslam Innstr. 47 ☎030 68 69 624, ⓦ cabslam.com; ⓣ Rathaus Neukölln; map p.130. Created by a Californian musician longing for an escape from the typical German breakfast of cold cuts and *Brötchen* (rolls), this Neukölln hipster haven is big on portions as well as flavour, with fluffy pancakes and dozens of different egg dishes, such as spicy *huevos rancheros*, all prepared from scratch with fresh ingredients. Breakfast (dishes €4.50–7.50) served till 4pm. Daily 10am–midnight.

Café Rix Karl-Marx-Str. 141 ☎030 686 90 20, ⓦ caferix .de; ⓣ Karl-Marx-Strasse; map p.130. This Neukölln institution is chiefly famous for its pleasant outdoor courtyard area, which is tucked away off a busy street. But the interior, a former ballroom, is elegant too and the food is a perfectly reasonable spread of German classics and excellent cakes. The Sunday brunch (10am–2.30pm; €10.50) is good too. Daily 10am–midnight.

Pêle-Mêle Innstr. 26 ☎030 36 46 75 23, ⓦ pele-mele-berlin.de; ⓣ Karl-Marx-Strasse; map p.130. One of the most reliable vegan cafés in the city, *Pêle-Mêle* offers simple but delicious breakfasts, lunches and snacks that

range from soups and bagels to healthy smoothies. Sunday brunch 10am–3pm; €13.50. Daily 10am–7pm.

RESTAURANTS

Café Jacques Maybachufer 8 ☎030 694 10 48; ⓣ Schönleinstrasse; map pp.128–129. Traditional French cuisine is the mainstay here on the leafy banks of the Landwehrkanal, but other foods like pasta and couscous also make an appearance, as do seasonal ingredients including asparagus and globe artichokes. Mains around €12–21. Daily 6pm–late.

Chutnify Pflügerstr. 25 ☎030 25 89 31 00, ⓦ chutnify .com; ⓣ Hermannplatz; map p.130. The sister restaurant of the Prenzlauer Berg original (see p.213) is just as colourful and serves the same delicious array of south Indian cuisine. Tues–Sun noon–11pm.

Industry Standard Sonnenallee 83 ☎030 62 72 77 32, ⓦ industry-standard.de; ⓣ Rathaus Neukölln; map p.130. Small, trendy restaurant that delivers on the hype with a creative spin on rustic French and Mediterranean cuisine – think red peppers and sardines with pecorino and pistachios for €11. Great natural wine list to match. Wed–Sun 7pm–midnight.

Lavanderia Vecchia Flughafenstr. 46 ☎030 627 22 152, ⓦ lavanderiavecchia.wordpress.com; ⓣ Boddinstrasse; map p.130. This Italian spot reached cult status pretty quickly after opening in 2013 – chiefly for its evening set menus, which consist of antipasti, *primi*, *secondi* and *dolci* (€58 per person). The delicious and abundant food is worth every penny, though the lighter lunch deals are much cheaper (three courses from €10). Evening reservations essential. Small courtyard garden at the back. Mon–Sat noon–2.30pm & 7.30–11pm.

Musashi Kottbusser Damm 102 ☎030 693 20 42; ⊕ Schönleinstrasse; map pp.128–129. Tiny spot with just a few bar tables serving decent sushi in a refreshingly designer-free space, decorated with posters of sumo wrestlers. The Japanese chefs prepare fresh, tasty and well-priced *makis* and inside-out rolls. Sushi platters from €10. Mon–Fri & Sun noon–10.30pm, Sat 2–10pm.

FRIEDRICHSHAIN

CAFÉS AND BARS

Aunt Benny Oderstr. 7 ☎030 66 40 53 00, ⊛ auntbenny.com; ⊕ Frankfurter Allee; map pp.128–129. Welcoming modern café run by an all-Canadian team. The range of teas and coffees (€2–3) is good, there are bagels, daily soups and other breakfast and lunch options available (most around €5), and home-made baked treats. Tues–Fri 9am–8pm, Sat & Sun 10am–8pm.

Café Datscha Gabriel-Max-Str. 1 ☎030 70 08 67 35, ⊛ cafe-datscha.de; ⊕/⑤ Warschauer Strasse; map pp.128–129. Built in the style of a smart traditional Russian home – wooden furniture, tall ceilings – with a rich spread of Russian and Ukrainian dishes like *borscht*, *blini* and *solyanka* (a spicy, sour soup). There's a daily changing lunch menu (€8) and Sunday brunch (10am–3pm; €12.90). Daily 10am–late.

Café Sybille Karl-Marx-Allee 72 ☎030 29 35 22 03, ⊛ cafe-sibylle.de; ⊕ Strausberger Platz; map pp.128–129. Airy café with a *fin-de-siècle* feel – it's been here more than a century – and a diverting exhibition about the socialist origins of the Karl-Marx-Allee in the back. Worth a visit for the cakes (€2–3) and ice creams alone. Mon 11am–7pm, Tues–Sun 10am–7pm.

Cupcake Berlin Krossener Str. 12 ☎030 25 76 86 87, ⊛ cupcakeberlin.de; ⊕ Samariterstrasse; map pp.128–129. The goodies at Berlin's first cupcake shop and café are home-made and baked fresh daily. They include vegan cupcakes, brownies, banana bread, fantastic New York cheesecake and pecan pie (all around €2.80). Daily 10am–8pm.

Goodies Berlin Warschauer Str. 69 ☎0151 53 76 38 01, ⊛ goodies-berlin.de; ⊕ Frankfurter Tor; map pp.128–129. Tiny café – with other branches in Prenzlauer Berg and Kreuzberg – that serves wholesome home-made baked goods, sandwiches and bagels (€3–5.50). The organic soup changes daily and there's a small but varied selection of salads and vegan options. Children's area. Cash only. Mon–Fri 7am–8pm, Sat & Sun 9am–8pm.

Macondo Café Gärtnerstr. 14 ☎030 54 73 59 43, ⊛ www.macondo-berlin.de; ⊕ Samariterstrasse; map pp.128–129. Kitted out with fraying vintage furniture, this local chill-out spot offers a good selection of books and board games and a great atmosphere for lounging. A simple Sunday brunch is served 10am–3pm (around €7) and breakfast the rest of the week; snacks are €3–6 and served all day. Daily 10am–late.

Spielwiese Kopernikusstr. 24 ☎030 28 03 40 88, ⊛ spielwiese-berlin.de; ⊕/⑤ Warschauer Strasse; map pp.128–129. Advertising itself as a "game library", this café stocks more than 2000 games, from chess to Risk. For a small fee, you can either play them in the café (€0.50–1/ hr) or rent them (€1–3/day) to take home. Food and drink here is nothing special – such as waffles from packet mixes – but it's inexpensive (snacks €2–5). A great place to lose yourself for a couple of hours. Mon & Thurs–Sat 5pm–midnight, Sun 3–8pm.

RESTAURANTS

Fliegender Tisch Mainzer Str. 10 ☎030 29 77 64 89, ⊛ fliegender-tisch.de; ⊕ Samariterstrasse; map pp.128–129. "The flying table" is a small, cosy place with just a few wooden tables. It's justly popular thanks to its tasty Italian staples like thin-crust pizza and risotto at decent prices (€6–8). Daily 5pm–late.

Pizza Meyman Warschauer Str. 80 ☎030 64 49 68 80, ⊛ pizzeria-meyman.de; ⊕ Frankfurter Tor; map pp.128–129. This unassuming restaurant is great for late-night cravings or for a break between bar hops. Aside from pizza they also specialize in tasty Moroccan and Arabic dishes. Ingredients are fresh, prices are reasonable (€5.50–7.90 for a main), and there's usually a table free. Mon–Thurs & Sun noon–2am, Fri & Sat noon–3am.

Schneeweiss Simplonstr. 16 ☎030 29 04 97 04, ⊛ schneeweiss-berlin.de; ⊕/⑤ Warschauer Strasse; map pp.128–129. One of Friedrichshain's few upmarket restaurants, "Snow White" is an understated and minimalist place offering what it calls an "Alpine" menu: Italian, Austrian and south German dishes such as schnitzel and *Käsespätzle*. There's also a decent weekend brunch (€14.90), a fireplace lounge and a low-key bar vibe in the evening. Mon–Fri 6pm–1am, Sat & Sun 10am–1am.

PRENZLAUER BERG

CHEAP EATS

★ **Konnopke's Imbiss** Schönhauser Allee 44a ☎030 442 77 65, ⊛ konnopke-imbiss.de; beneath ⊕ Eberswalder Strasse; map p.136. *Pommes* and *Wurst* served from a pre-fab cabin beneath the U2 viaduct since 1930 – it's survived fascism, communism and World War II. Incredibly it's been run by the same family all that time, and remains one of the best places in the area for a quick bite. Mon–Fri 9am–8pm, Sat 11.30am–8pm.

13

CAFÉS AND BARS

Al Hamra Raumerstr. 16 ☎030 42 85 00 95, ⓦalhamra .de; ⓤ Eberswalder Strasse; map p.136. Comfortable Middle Eastern café with shabby decor but decent Mediterranean food (dishes €4–14), beer, water pipes, backgammon and chess. Daily 10am–3am.

Anna Blume Kollwitzstr. 83 ☎030 44 04 87 49, ⓦcafe- anna-blume.de; ⓤ Eberswalder Strasse; map p.136. Part flower shop, part café, part bakery, this Art Deco classic – named after a Kurt Schwitters poem, whose lines are elegantly inscribed on the walls inside – is one of the area's best-known cafés. Slide into one of the red leather banquettes and sample one of their superb cakes (€4) or a daily special (€7.50). Daily 8am–11pm.

Bonanza Coffee Heroes Oderberger Str. 35 ☎0178 14 41 123, ⓦbonanzacoffee.de; ⓤ Eberswalder Strasse; map p.136. Coffee connoisseurs flock to tiny *Bonanza* to sample the creations of their famed baristas: perfect lattes and flat whites knocked up on a fancy Slayer machine. The cool staff are friendly. Mon–Fri 8.30am–6.30pm, Sat & Sun 10am–7pm.

Café Hilde Metzer Str. 22 ☎030 040 50 41 72, ⓦhilde -berlin.com; ⓤ Senefelderplatz; map p.136. This sizeable café on the corner of busy Prenzlauer Allee is a lovely spot to unwind, with books and magazines to read during the day, home-made cakes and lunches (€4–9), plus occasional book readings in the evenings. They also serve up a hearty Irish breakfast every day, as well as salads, soups, quiches and more. Mon–Fri 9am–11pm, Sat & Sun 9.30am–11pm.

Café November Husemannstr. 15 ☎030 442 84 25, ⓦ cafe-november.de; ⓤ Senefelderplatz; map p.136. Uncluttered, exposed-wood place, just north of Kollwitzplatz, with imaginative German daily specials (€9– 21), a reasonable weekend breakfast (10am–4pm) and outdoor seating in a pleasantly quiet residential street. Mon–Fri 6pm–1am, Sat & Sun 10am–1am.

Kauf Dich Glücklich Oderberger Str. 44 ☎030 44 35 21 82, ⓦkaufdichgluecklich.de; ⓤ Eberswalder Strasse; map p.136. Come here for waffles with ice cream (around €4) – and a spot of cutely kitsch capitalism. "Buy yourself happy" is an irrepressibly cheerful place where you can not only get great coffee and sweet treats, but also buy any of the secondhand furniture – tables, chairs, lamps, sunglasses – you see around you. Mon–Fri noon–1am, Sat & Sun 10am–1am.

★**Morgenrot** Kastanienallee 85 ☎030 44 31 78 44, ⓦ cafe-morgenrot.de; ⓤ Eberswalder Strasse; map p.136. This collective-run café which offers organic and vegetarian dishes, including a buffet breakfast (until 3pm) is excellent (€6–12: pay according to how wealthy you consider yourself). Tues–Thurs noon–1am, Fri & Sat 11am–3am, Sun 11am–midnight.

Sgaminegg Seelower Str. 2 ☎030 44 73 15 25, ⓦsgaminegg.de; ⓤ/Ⓢ Schönhauser Allee; map p.145. There is a dearth of decent cafés north of Stargarderstr., but *Sgaminegg* is an absolute treasure thanks to its delicious coffees, home-made lunches – couscous, lentil and south German dishes (two *Munich Weisswürste* – sausages served with a pretzel – cost €5.80) and a little shop that sells local produce. Tues–Fri 8.30am–6pm, Sat 9.30am–6pm.

Suicide Sue Dunckerstr. 2. ☎030 64 83 47 45, ⓦsuicidesue.com; ⓤ Eberswalder Strasse; map p.136. This local favourite features crumpled leather armchairs, chunky wooden tables and a street-facing espresso bar. The food is tasty, including fresh croissants and cakes, scrambled eggs and beans served in a tiny frying pan, and *Stullen* – thick slices of home-made bread with toppings you mix and match yourself. Mon–Fri 8am–6pm, Sat 9am–7pm, Sun 10am–7pm.

Wohnzimmer Lettestr. 6 ☎030 445 54 58, ⓦwohnzimmer-bar.de; ⓤ Eberswalder Strasse; map p.136. The rumpled and ramshackle living room atmosphere helps make this a relaxed and sociable hangout at any time – and the comfy sofas make it difficult to leave. At weekends a cocktail bar pops up between its two rooms. Breakfast served until 4pm; a simple coffee and croissant or roll costs only €3.50. Daily 10am till late.

Zuckerfee Greifenhagener Str. 15 ☎030 52 68 61 44, ⓦ zuckerfee-berlin.de; ⓤ/Ⓢ Schönhauser Allee; map p.136. Gastronomic concept based on Tchaikovsky's *The Nutcracker* and named after the Sugar Plum fairy. The immaculate interior – all Victorian dolls and tasteful ornamentation – reflects the menu, which features delicious waffles and uniquely presented breakfasts (€4.90–9.50; book ahead at weekends), snacks and cakes. Tues–Sun 10am–6pm.

Zula Hummus Café Husemannstr. 10 ☎030 41 71 51 00, ⓦzulaberlin.com; ⓤ Senefelderplatz; map p.136. One of the best hummus spots in town, *Zula* is slightly more upmarket than most. The traditional hummus plate is delicious, but you can also get it served with minced beef or chicken, or try the delicious falafels. There's a leafy terrace and decent wines, too. Mains from €6.90. Daily 11am–11pm.

RESTAURANTS

AKEMI Rykestr. 39 ☎030 44 01 31 88, ⓦakemi-berlin .squarespace.com, ⓤ Senefelderplatz; map 136. This chic Vietnamese-run spot has a dapper interior and a stellar menu of pan-Asian tapas (€3–4 each) that spans beef bowls and salmon teriyaki, spring rolls and sushi. Salads and mains from €8.50; lunch menus €6.50–7.90. Daily noon–midnight.

The Bird Am Falkplatz 5 ☎030 51 05 32 83, ⓦthebirdinberlin.com; ⓤ Schönhauser Allee; map p.136. Hugely popular New York-style steakhouse with punk-rock attitude, international staff and gigantic tasty burgers, spicy chicken wings, steaks, hand-cut fries and so on. Mains €10–20, other dishes around half that. Finish with a sumptuous cheesecake, if you can manage it. Mon–Thurs 6–11pm, Fri 4pm–midnight, Sat & Sun noon–midnight.

Chez Maurice Botzowstr. 39 📞 030 425 05 06, 🌐 chez-maurice.com; ⓢ Greifswalder Strasse; map p.136. Finer dining spot that's a little out of the way but worth it for the authentic food and theatrics of the energetic French chef Maurice. Service can be slow, so count on spending the better part of an evening here, enjoying the huge wine list (with more than 200 varieties from France alone). The *plat du jour* specials (noon–3.30pm) are good value (two courses €11, three courses €16) or you can go wild with the ten-course *dégustation* offering (€95). Reservations recommended. Daily 6–11pm.

Chutnify Sredzkistr. 43 📞 030 44 01 07 95, 🌐 chutnify.com; ⓘ Eberswalder Strasse; map p.136. Single-handedly challenging Berlin's dire reputation for mediocre, spice-avoiding Indian cooking, *Chutnify* specializes in south Indian street food with an emphasis on delicious dosas and spicy chai teas. Designed by owner Aparna Aurora, it looks good too, with colourful furnishings and outside seating in summer. A newer branch exists in Neukölln (see p.210). Tues–Sun noon–11pm.

Gugelhof Knaackstr. 37 📞 030 442 92 29, 🌐 gugelhof.de; ⓘ Senefelderplatz; map p.136. Lively Alsatian restaurant put on the map by Bill Clinton's surprise visit in 2000, and successful ever since. It serves inventive and beautifully presented German, French and Alsatian food (mains €8–18) – the *Flammkuchen* is particularly worth trying. Mon–Fri 5pm–midnight, Sat & Sun noon–1am.

Lucky Leek Kollwitzstr. 54 📞 030 66 40 87 10, 🌐 lucky-leek.com; ⓘ Senefelderplatz; map p.136. This high-end vegan spot occupies a smart space inside an old building on one of Prenzlauer Berg's loveliest streets. The menu is inventive and service excellent, but you'll certainly pay above average for the experience. Mains around €18; three-course menu €33. Wed–Sun 6–10pm.

MaoThai Wörther Str. 30 📞 030 441 92 61, 🌐 maothai.de; ⓘ Senefelderplatz; map p.136. Perhaps a bit overpriced, but the Thai food, garnished with delightful little sculpted vegetables, is generally excellent – tasty classics include *tom ka gai*, spring rolls and glass-noodle salads. Staff, in traditional garb, are unfailingly polite. Mains €11–20. Daily noon–11.30pm.

Maria Bonita Danziger Str. 33 📞 0176 70 17 94 61, 🌐 maria-bonita.com; ⓘ Eberswalder Strasse; map p.136. Tucked away amid the slew of *Imbisses* and kebab shops hereabouts, *Maria Bonita* stands out for above average Mexican street food. You couldn't swing an enchilada inside, but the burritos, tacos and quesadillas – and the guacamole for that matter – are all winners. Daily noon–11pm.

Marien Burger Marienburger Str. 47 📞 030 30 34 05 15, 🌐 marienburger-berlin.de; ⓘ Senefelderplatz; map p.136. This diminutive but buzzy burger hangout lures locals back again and again with huge, delicious beef, chicken, fish or vegetarian burgers (the €6 Marienburger is almost too big to eat in one sitting). Organic options available. Daily 11am–10pm.

Osseria Langhansstr. 103 📞 030 92 90 04 36, 🌐 osseria.de; tram #M2 to Prenzlauer Allee/Ostseestrasse; map p.136. This "living shrine" to GDR cuisine and culture is located just north of Prenzlauer Berg in the district of Weissensee. As well as a menu of East German classics (*Eisbein*, jacket potatoes with quark) and an interior decorated with all kinds of relevant paraphernalia (photos of Trabants, political cartoons, radios), the venue also hosts quiz nights and other GDR-themed events. Mon–Fri 9am till late, Sat & Sun 10am till late.

Pappa e Ciccia Schwedter Str. 18 📞 030 61 62 08 01, 🌐 pappaeciccia.de; ⓘ Senefelderplatz; map p.136. This smart-casual Italian restaurant has long been serving up good-quality Italian dishes, and is particularly strong for vegetarians. It's great for weekend brunch (Sat & Sun 10am–4pm), with a menu spanning Bircher muesli (€4) and spinach Benedict (€10) – or go for the veggie brunch platter (€16) – while the evening menu includes meat or veggie tagliatelle, risotto and pasta dishes (mains €10–18). In summer, diners gather at the long communal tables outside. Tues–Fri 6pm–midnight, Sat & Sun 10am–midnight.

Pasternak Knaackstr. 22–24 📞 030 441 33 99, 🌐 restaurant-pasternak.de; ⓘ Senefelderplatz; map p.136. Long-standing Jewish-Russian restaurant, named after the author of *Doctor Zhivago*, and best known for its incredible Sunday brunch (9am–3pm; €13.90): a regal spread of blinis, caviar, fish and much more; it's so popular you'll need to wake up early to find a seat (no reservations). Fixed-price menus also available. Daily 9am–1am.

★ **Restauration 1900** Husemannstr. 1 📞 030 442 24 94, 🌐 restauration-1900.de; ⓘ Eberswalder Strasse; map p.136. A Kollwitzplatz culinary highlight, serving traditional German dishes that spring a few surprises, as well as some pasta and vegetarian options (€12–21). It's also another excellent choice for a Sunday buffet brunch (10am–4pm; €13.90). Check out the photographs of the neighbourhood before and after reunification. Daily 10am until late.

Sasaya Lychener Str. 50 📞 030 44 71 77 21, 🌐 sasaya-berlin.de; ⓘ/ⓢ Schönhauser Allee; map p.136. Delicious, traditional and innovative Japanese food using fresh, high-quality ingredients. Swift service ensures this a serious contender for best sushi spot in the city. Mon & Thurs–Sun noon–3pm & 6–11.30pm.

Weinstein Lychener Str. 33 📞 030 441 18 42, 🌐 weinstein.eu; ⓘ Eberswalder Strasse; map p.136. This intimate wine bar and restaurant, all sturdy wooden

13

tables and wine barrel decoration, is a bit of a local secret. It serves up food as traditional as the interior, but has a strong emphasis on local produce and German wines and cheeses, as well as imported high-quality products like Iberian ham. Mains start at €10.50, and from Mon to Thurs you can get eight small courses for €48. Mon–Sat 5pm–2am, Sun 6pm–2am; kitchen 6–11.30pm.

Zum Schusterjungen Danziger Str. 9 ☎ 030 442 76 54, ⓦ zumschusterjungen.com; ⓤ Eberswalder Strasse; map p.136. Large portions of no-nonsense German food served in the back room of a locals' *Kneipe*. The plastic-and-formica decor has echoes of the GDR and, at around €9–11 per dish, the prices are almost as cheap as back then, too. Daily noon–midnight.

PANKOW

CAFÉS AND BARS

Café Schönhausen Florastr. 27 ☎ 030 42 00 45 36, ⓦ schoen-hausen.de; ⓤ/Ⓢ Pankow; map p.145. This charming *Kindercafé* (café for families) is an ideal stopoff whether you're exploring the district with kids or not. The menu ranges from bio-breakfasts and home-made cakes to waffles, soups and a selection of coffees. Dishes €5–8. They also sell artisanal children's toys and products. Daily 10am–6pm.

Milchmanns Berliner Str. 119 ☎ 030 91 42 32 82, ⓦ milchmanns.de; ⓤ/Ⓢ Pankow; map p.145. This smart and spacious corner café, with its large windows and cheery interior design, is a welcoming spot to enjoy breakfast (everything from croissants to eggs), lunch (soups and sandwiches) or just a decent coffee and delicious home-made cake. Dishes €6–9. Mon–Fri 9am–6pm, Sat & Sun 10am–6pm.

WEDDING AND GESUNDBRUNNEN

CAFÉS AND BARS

Café Dujardin Uferstr. 12 ☎ 030 52 66 68 05, ⓦ cafedujardin.de; ⓤ Nauener Platz; map p.146. This pleasant spot for Francophiles, a former cinema, enjoys a leafy location opposite the banks of the Panke River. During the day it offers light lunches like quiches and soup (plus the obligatory range of delicious home-made cakes), and by night draws a low-key local crowd. The pavement terrace is great for people-watching. Mon–Fri 10am till late, Sat & Sun 11am till late.

RESTAURANTS

Café Pförtner Uferstr. 8–11 ☎ 030 50 36 98 54, ⓦ pfoertner.co; ⓤ Pankstrasse; map p.146. Located opposite the Uferhallen complex (to which it's officially connected) close to the Panke and marked by an old bus

outside the front door, this slightly ramshackle bar and restaurant has local cult status due to its intimate setting, decent pasta dishes and salads and home-made cakes. Mains from €10. Mon–Sat 9am–11pm.

El Pepe Prinzenallee 25 ☎ 030 55 27 42 18, ⓤ Pankstrasse; map p.146. Small but *gemütlich* joint serving delicious tapas (from €4), coffee and cakes, as well as sangria and a very good selection of Spanish wines. Cash only. Daily 6.30pm–midnight.

Volta Brunnenstr. 73 im Pavillon ☎ 0176 77 55 64 22, ⓦ dasvolta.com; ⓤ Voltastrasse; map p.136. A symbol of the subtle but increasing hipsterization of the area, this burger joint has an industrial interior, a wooden bar and a menu that extends beyond the boutique bun-fest to salads and pork belly blinis, plus decent cocktails and beer from the local Eschenbräu brewery. Mains from €8. Tues–Sat 6–11pm.

THE EASTERN SUBURBS

CAFÉS AND BARS

China Teehaus Eisenacher Str. 99, Marzahn ☎ 0179 394 55 64, ⓦ china-teehaus.de; ⓤ Cottbusser Platz then bus #195 to "Gärten der Welt" stop; map p.150. Chinese Garden teahouse in the Gärten der Welt (see p.153; where you can take part in a traditional tea ceremony (reservations necessary and six-person minimum; €8). April–Oct daily 10.30am–6pm; Nov–March Sat & Sun 10.30am–6pm in fine weather.

Mütter Lustig Müggelheimer Str. 1, Köpenick ☎ 030 64 09 48 84, ⓦ mutter-lustig.berlin; Ⓢ Spindlersfeld; map p.156. This daytime café is situated by the bay close to Schloss Köpenick. The large terrace has great views (and a tiny Christmas market in December), the menu spans paninis and salads up to pasta and fish dishes (€8.90–14.50), and there's also a small but

pleasant garden. Mon–Fri 11am–10pm, Sat 10am till late, Sun 10am–9pm.

Schlosscafé Köpenick Schlossinsel, Köpenick ☎ 030 65 01 85 85, ⓦ schlosscafe-koepenick.de; Ⓢ Spindlersfeld; map p.156. Elegant café beside Schloss Köpenick with lake views and excellent fresh daily dishes (mains €9–19), good cakes and a wonderful Sunday brunch (10am–2pm; €16.50). Mid-April to early Oct Wed–Sat 11am–6pm, Sun 10am–6pm; early Oct to mid-April Fri & Sat 11am–6pm, Sun 10am–6pm.

RESTAURANTS

Bräustübl Restauration Müggelseedamm 164, Friedrichshagen ☎ 030 37 44 67 69, ⓦ braeustuebl -mueggelsee.de; Ⓢ Friedrichshagen and then a 15min walk, or tram #M50/51 to Müggelseedamm/Bölschestr.;

map p.156. Waterside restaurant serving meat-heavy German and well-priced international dishes (*Currywurst*, *Eisbein*, spare ribs, stews; mains €7–10) and a Sunday brunch (11am–3pm; €11.95). Mon–Sat 8am–midnight, Sun 11am–midnight.

Ratskeller Köpenick Alt Köpenick 21, Köpenick ☎030 655 51 78, ⓦratskeller-koepenick.de; Ⓢ Spindlersfeld; map p.156. Authentic *Ratskeller* full of locals and serving decent, good-value German food from €12.50. Regular live jazz on Fri and Sat. Mon–Sat 11am–midnight, Sun 11am–10pm.

Windflüchter Josef-Nawrocki-Str. 25, Friedrichshagen ☎0159 03175876, ⓦwindfluechter.berlin; Ⓢ Friedrichshagen; map p.156. Former passenger ship that's been transformed into a lovely floating restaurant. It's set right at the entrance to the Müggelsee, and you can enjoy excellent lake views as well as a diverse menu of breakfasts (€3.90–10.90), salads (€7.90–10.90) and *Flammkuchen* (€7.30–10.80). Mon–Fri noon till late, Sat & Sun 10am till late.

THE WESTERN SUBURBS

CHEAP EATS

Thai Park Konstanzer Str., Wilmersdorf; Ⓤ Fehrbelliner Platz; map p.108. Every sunny weekend in summer, Wilmersdorf's Preussenpark is taken over by a semi-legal ensemble of mobile Thai kitchens that serve up a wide range of delicious home cooking featuring all the curries, satays, spring rolls and noodle soups you could want. Prices are cheap (soups from €4) and the vibe is friendly. April–Oct Sat & Sun noon–6pm.

CAFÉS AND BARS

Barfly Brüderstr. 47, Spandau ☎030 331 55 55, ⓦcafe-barfly.de; Ⓤ Rathaus Spandau/Ⓢ Spandau; map p.162. Laidback, living-room-style café with a good, ever-changing selection of food. All meats are organic and the weekend brunch buffet (9am–2pm; €11.10) a winner. Daily 8am–midnight (Fri & Sat till 1am).

Florida Eiscafé Klosterstr. 15, Spandau ☎030 331 56 66, ⓦflorida-eiscafe.de; Ⓤ Rathaus Spandau/Ⓢ Spandau; map p.162. Spacious ice-cream parlour with a Berlin-wide reputation; you'll need to wait in line to see what the fuss is all about, but that gives you time to choose from the 41 flavours. Pleasant terrace for warm weather too. Daily noon–10pm.

RESTAURANTS

Engelbecken Witzlebenstr. 31, Charlottenburg ☎030 615 28 10, ⓦengelbecken.de; Ⓤ Sophie-Charlotte-Platz; map p.162. A quality restaurant that serves Bavarian and Alpine cuisine – schnitzel, goulash – with an emphasis on organic products and home-made sauces (mains €12–23). The park-facing terrace is nice in the summer. Mon–Fri 5pm–1am, Sat 4pm–1am, Sun noon–1am; kitchen till 11pm.

Fischerhütte am Schlachtensee Fischerhuttenstr. 136, Zehlendorf ☎030 80 49 83 10, ⓦfischerhuette -berlin.de; Ⓤ Krumme Lanke; map p.170. While the main restaurant serves fairly high-end German-Austrian cuisine like *Wiener Schnitzel* and beef goulash in a sophisticated interior (mains €16–28), the umbrella-covered terrace offers great views across the lake and a cheaper menu that includes grilled chicken, salads and pasta dishes (€5–10.50). There's also a private beach and children's playground. Restaurant daily 10am–11pm, beer garden April–Oct daily 9am–11pm.

La Bottega Da Franco Breite Str. 56–58, Spandau ☎030 36 75 01 71; Ⓤ Altstadt Spandau; map p.162. Unpretentious Italian trattoria with exceptional food and prices for every budget: mains €8–18. Great home-made pasta. Mon–Sat 9am–midnight, Sun 9am–10pm.

Drinking and nightlife

Since the days of the Weimar Republic, Berlin's nightlife has had the reputation for being some of the best – and occasionally steamiest – in Europe, an image fuelled by the savage caricatures of George Grosz and films like *Cabaret*. Even during the lean postwar years, West Berlin maintained a respectable ensemble of hangouts – the era during which the city's famous late-night opening hours were established in order to keep the economy going. After the *Wende* the inner city was again transformed into something of an adult playground as abandoned spaces and homes were transformed into impromptu and informal cafés, bars, and clubs, often without official licences. And while Berlin's nightlife has moved on since the 1990s, the legacy of these places lives on in a slew of shabby-chic cafés, semi-dilapidated drinking dens and techno clubs that often continue until the next morning – sometimes longer.

One of the most distinctive aspects of the city's **drinking** culture is how the division between different types of establishments is notoriously fluid, with considerable overlap between each, which means that that some cafés, bars, clubs and even arts and concert venues may well double as venues of some sort into the small hours. The city's traditional **Kneipen** (pubs) are supplemented by a smattering of **beer gardens** that emerge from hibernation around the end of March and serve as convivial outdoor gathering points. Some of the best are in the suburbs, particularly on lakeshores in Köpenick and Zehlendorf, but there are several stellar ones in the centre; all serve food and some are covered in the "Eating" chapter (see p.199 & p.202). Berlin's taste for artfully mixed **cocktails** continues unabated, but its slew of fancy cocktail establishments has been joined in recent years by more and more bars specializing in **craft beer**. At the time of writing there is at least one dedicated craft beer pub or **microbrewery** (*Hausbrauerie*) in most neighbourhoods; the majority are in Wedding, a result of the relatively cheaper rents there.

Of course a speciality of the Berlin scene is its enviable **live and electronic music** scenes. Venues for the former, ranging from slick hangouts to raucous punky dives, are varied and inexpensive, and bolstered by the city's unpretentious grittiness. In addition to the music venues, all but the most committed techno **clubs** will often have live performances too. Clubs often open for days on end, and are famously tolerant of most things – except taking photos. Note that **LGBT bars and clubs** – the vast majority in Schöneberg – are covered in "LGBT Berlin" (see p.254).

There are several distinct **nightlife districts,** making it easy to spend an evening trawling the bars of a particular area before ending up in a late-night club nearby. That said, with the U- and S-Bahn running nonstop on Friday and Saturday nights – and restarting from about 4am on other nights – jumping between areas of town could hardly be easier. Most of the edgier places are to be found scattered throughout **Friedrichshain, eastern Kreuzberg** and **Neukölln** – and increasingly in **Treptow** – with **Spandauer Vorstadt, Prenzlauer Berg** and **City West** having succumbed to gentrification and offering mostly cocktail bars and commercial clubs rather than raves. As in most major cities, Berlin's nightspots change rapidly: although we've included reviews of both well-established and newer places, the scene changes rapidly, so be prepared for some places to have changed by the time you arrive.

ESSENTIALS

Listings There are several English-language websites and blogs in the city that list events and venues, the best of which include ⓦiheartberlin.de, ⓦstilinberlin.de, ⓦslowtravelberlin.com and ⓦspottedbylocals.com. In addition you might want to check listings magazines, *Tip* (ⓦtip-berlin.de) and *Zitty* (ⓦzitty.de), available at any newsstand, and the free magazine *030* (ⓦberlin030.de), mainly distributed in bars and cafés.

Opening times Opening times are very relaxed and "last orders" doesn't really exist. Some places have fixed times but typically bars will close between 1am and 5am, usually depending on how busy they are and the mood of the staff – and may well reopen a couple of hours later. Club hours are also open-ended – it's rare for any to get going before

midnight and some stay open beyond 6am and even well into the daytime.

Admission policies Berlin's clubs are smaller, cheaper and less exclusive than their counterparts in London or New York. And don't worry too much about a dress code – the city's prevalent shabby-chic aesthetic means you can get into most (though not all) places without making much of an effort.

Costs Bars are usually free or charge a minimal entry fee (sometimes "for the DJ") while club cover charges tend to run from €5 for the smaller venues up to €18 for the bigger clubs (usually at weekends). Prices can be higher for live shows and special events. Where there is no admission fee listed, entry is free.

BARS AND BEER GARDENS

UNTER DEN LINDEN AND AROUND

Newton Bar Charlottenstr. 57 ☎030 20 29 54 21, ⓦnewton-bar.de; ⓤStadtmitte; map p.36. Helmut Newton's life-size shots of nude Amazons stare out across

the leather and marble interior of this chic bar, popular with a mature, well-heeled crowd. Watch Berlin's sharp dressers puff on cigars and sip well-made cocktails. Daily 11am till late.

14

BEER IN BERLIN

Germany's noble tradition of brewing is mostly associated with Bavaria and the south, but Berlin's own significant beer history stretches back several centuries. In the early eighteenth century there were some four hundred breweries dotted around the city – mostly drawing on Bavarian techniques – and Frederick the Great ordered his soldiers to drink home-brew rather than coffee. The number of breweries declined through the latter half of the eighteenth and early nineteenth centuries, which culminated in the rise of mega-companies such as Kindl and Schultheiss. War and division decimated the brewing landscape somewhat, but **Schultheiss** (w schultheiss.de) remains, nowadays brewing Berliner Kindl brands, and has been joined in recent years by a growing number of smaller breweries.

The standard beers found throughout the c are cloudy wheat beers (*Weissen*), Pilsners and dark beers (*Dunkels*), though this comparatively narrow range is being increasingly challenged and supplemented by brews from the city's slew of **microbreweries and craft beer** spots. Many of these are either fighting or creatively interpreting the traditional **Reinheitsgebot**, the German purity law that states that the only ingredients that could be used in the production of beer are water, barley and hops, and brewing a broader range of ales including American-style IPAs, porters and seasonal beers. One local quirk to look out for is the **Berliner Weisse** – a brew that is only just fermented and still quite watery and sour, and is traditionally drunk with a shot of fruity syrup, or *Schuss*. Ask for it *mit grün* and you get a dash of woodruff, creating a green beverage with a herby taste; *mit rot* secures a raspberry-flavoured drink that works wonders on a breakfast-time hangover.

TOP 5: MICROS AND CRAFT BREWERS
Brauhaus Lemke am Schloss See p.224
Brauhaus Südstern See p.220

Eschenbräu See p.223
Hops & Barley See p.222
Vagabund Brauerei See p.224

Windhorst Dorotheenstr. 65 ☏ 030 20 45 00 70; ⓤ/ⓢ Friedrichstrasse; map p.36. This little cocktail haven is tucked away, and though it's not in a residential area, feels like a neighbourhood spot. It's a smart, fairly simple place, but the cocktails are above average and go well with the jazz (on vinyl) that they love to play. Mon–Fri 6pm till late, Sat 9pm till late.

ALEXANDERPLATZ AND AROUND
Brauhaus Georgbräu Spreeufer 4 ☏ 030 242 42 44, w brauhaus-georgbraeu.de; ⓤ Klosterstrasse; map p.60. This microbrewery attracts a merry, touristy crowd, and is also popular among locals for its excellent beer and traditional German food. Daily noon–midnight.

Zum Nussbaum Am Nussbaum 3 ☏ 030 242 30 95; ⓤ Klosterstrasse; map p.60. In the heart of the Nikolaiviertel, "The Nut Tree" is a convincing copy of a prewar bar – destroyed in an air raid – that stood on the Fischerinsel and was favoured by the artists Heinrich Zille and Otto Nagel (see p.66). This replica verges on the expensive, but the traditional beer and food is good quality, and it's a good place to soak up a bit of (ersatz) old Berlin ambience. Daily noon–midnight.

THE SPANDAUER VORSTADT
am to pm Am Zwirngraben 2 ☏ 030 24 08 53 01, w amtopm.de; ⓢ Hackescher Markt; map pp.70–71.

Though it's nothing special, this nonstop café-cum-bar-cum-club under the S-Bahn tracks is a good people-watching spot during the day, and a handy spot to start, or finish, a night out. Daily 24hr.

Amano Rooftop Bar Auguststr. 43 ☏ 030 80 94 150, w amanogroup.de; ⓤ Rosenthaler Platz; map pp.70–71. Located on the roof of the *Amano* hotel (see p.189), this rooftop bar has become a firm summer favourite, not only for its see-and-be-seen ambience and views across the Mitte rooftops but also an excellent array of summery wines and cocktails – the Amano Mule, made with 42 Below vodka and wheat beer, is a keeper. May–Sept Mon–Fri 4pm till late, Sat & Sun 2pm till late.

Brauhaus Mitte Karl-Liebknecht-Str. 13 ☏ 030 24 78 38 31 11, w brauhaus-mitte.de; ⓤ/ⓢ Alexanderplatz; map pp.70–71. All the trappings of a Bavarian beer hall, including excellent beers – try the delicious *Weissen* – re-created in this city-centre microbrewery in the heart of Berlin. Good for basic pub food, with well-priced lunch specials for around €6. Mon–Sat 10am–midnight, Sun 11am–midnight.

Hackbarth's Auguststr. 49a ☏ 030 282 77 04; ⓤ Rosenthaler Platz; map pp.70–71. Dominated by a huge triangular bar, *Hackbarth's* attracts a very mixed crowd. The good choice of food includes tasty breakfasts and excellent tapas (from €2). Daily 10am till late.

Kim Bar Brunnenstr. 10 w kim-bar.com; ⓤ Rosenthaler

Platz; map pp.70–71. This small, fairly unprepossessing space with minimal furnishings is big on atmosphere on the right night. Mostly though it's a low-key hangout with a well-curated and eclectic soundtrack and a fairly loyal local crowd. Tues–Sat 8pm till late.

Mein Haus Am See Brunnenstr. 197–198 ☎030 23 88 35 61, ☻mein-haus-am-see.blogspot.com; ☻Rosenthaler Platz; map pp.70–71. Spacious café-bar, a stumbling distance from Rosenthaler Platz. Filled with comfy flea-market furnishings, it's a great spot for reading or chatting during the day, and for a more upbeat drink late at night when DJs play anything from disco to Latin. The weekend-only club space down in the cellar kicks off around midnight on Fri and Sat. Daily 24hr.

Oscar Wilde Irish Pub Friedrichstr. 112a ☎030 282 81 66, ☻oscar-wilde-irish-pub.de; ☻Oranienburger Tor; map pp.70–71. Perennially popular and sociable Irish bar with all the usual ingredients: Guinness, Kilkenny and Strongbow on draught (German beers too), various whiskies, Irish breakfasts and Sky Sports on the big screen. All this makes it a hub for Berlin's English-speaking expats, especially at weekends when there are quiz nights, karaoke and live music. Mon–Thurs 4pm–2am, Fri & Sat noon–3am, Sun noon–midnight.

Reingold Novalisstr. 11 ☎030 28 38 76 76, ☻reingold .de; ☻Oranienburger Tor; map pp.70–71. A sophisticated Art Deco cocktail lounge with a 20- and 30-something clientele lounging on the leather and velvet seating. The soundtrack is jazz, trip-hop, house and the like. Tues–Sat 9pm–4am.

Verkehrsberuhigte Ost-Zone Kleine Präsidentenstr. 4a, Am Monbijoupark ☎030 24 62 87 81, ☻veboz.de; ☻Hackescher Markt; map pp.70–71. Great little bar if you are looking for a dose of *Ostalgie* (see box, p.65) with your beer – there's an abundance of GDR memorabilia. It's hidden away in the arches of the S-Bahn overlooking the Spree, which might be what keeps it from being touristy. Daily 8pm–3am.

★ **Weinerei Forum/Perlin** Fehrbelliner Str. 57 ☎030 440 69 83, ☻weinerei.com; ☻Rosenthaler Platz; map pp.70–71. This members' club-style bar and wine shop (Veteranenstr. 14; Mon Fri 1 8pm, Sat 11am–8pm) operates on an honesty-box system after 8pm: pay what

TOP 5 PLACES TO START A NIGHT OUT
Das Hotel See p.220
Hops & Barley See p.222
Kim Bar See opposite
Oscar Wilde Irish Pub See above
Zu mir oder zu dir See p.223

14

you feel is fair for your drinks when you leave. This makes it popular with a mix of leftie sympathizers, students and freeloaders. The wine is decidedly average but the atmosphere friendly. The owners run another wine bar, *Perlin*, nearby (Griebenowstr. 5; Wed–Sat from 6.30pm – late). Daily 10am–midnight.

CITY WEST

F37 Fasanenstr. 37 ☎030 88 92 92 03, ☻f-37.de; ☻Spichernstrasse; map p.108. Pricey cocktail bar and art gallery (Wed, Fri & Sat 2–6pm) that hails from the 1950s. A meeting point for lounge lizards, actors and artists. Tues–Sat 8pm until late.

Gainsbourg Jeanne-Mammen-Bogen 576–577 ☎030 313 74 64, ☻gainsbourg.de; ☻Savignyplatz; map p.108. The name may pay homage to the master of risqué *chanson*, but the cocktails (€8–10) and food are more mainstream. Nevertheless, the drinks are some of the best in the neighbourhood. Daily 5pm until late.

Monkey Bar Budapesterstr. 40 ☎030 12 02 21 210, ☻25hours-hotels.com; ☻/☻Zoologischer Garten; map p.108. Located on the top floor of the *25hours Hotel Bikini Berlin* (see p.190), this slick cocktail spot has stellar views across City West and the adjacent zoo through floor-to-ceiling windows, a very good drinks list and a bubbly crowd of locals and tourists. Mon–Thurs & Sun noon–1am, Fri & Sat noon–2am.

SCHÖNEBERG

E&M Leydicke Mansteinstr. 4 ☎030 216 29 73, ☻leydicke.com; ☻/☻Yorckstrasse; map p.114. Claiming to be the oldest *Kneipe* in western Berlin – though some of the decor looks suspiciously modern – this place is famed for its fruit wines and theme nights, from

---

PUB CRAWLS

If the idea of venturing into Berlin's legendary nightlife seems daunting, or you fancy the company of young visitors, consider a **pub crawl tour**. For around €12–14 (cover charges included) you'll be taken to half-a-dozen or so watering holes and a club. You'll be given free shots on the street along the way, so it's not the most dignified way to spend an evening, but it can be good fun if the crowd's right. Pub crawls trawl Berlin every night and companies include: New Berlin Tours (☻newberlintours.com), Insider Tours (☻insiderberlintours.com) and Alternative Berlin (☻alternativeberlin.com). The last offers something a bit different, hitting more unusual nightspots than the competition and with smaller group sizes.

14

TOP 10 BEER GARDENS

Brachvogel See below
Brauhaus Spandau See p.224
Café am Neuen See See p.202
Emil's Biergarten See p.223
Fischerhütte am Schlachtensee
 See p.215
Golgatha See below
Pavillon See p.223
Pfefferbräu See p.223
Prater See p.223
Schleusenkrug See p.202

---

rockabilly to belly-dancing. Daily 6pm until late.

Green Door Winterfeldtstr. 50 ☎030 215 25 15, ⓦgreendoor.de; ⓤNollendorfplatz; map p.114. Somewhat snobby, dimly lit cocktail bar, attracting a well-dressed crowd of young professionals and local party-goers. Press the buzzer to get in: the place can be fun, and the bar staff can mix a really good cocktail. Mon–Thurs & Sun 6pm–3am, Fri & Sat 6pm–4am.

Mister Hu Goltzstr. 39 ☎030 217 21 11, ⓦmisterhu .de; ⓤEisenacher Strasse; map p.114. Warm red cocktail bar with a relaxed atmosphere and great range of drinks (€6–11) mixed by some of the city's best bartenders. Fri & Sat 6pm–4am, Sun–Thurs 6pm–3am.

Pinguin Club Wartburgstr. 54 ☎030 781 30 05; ⓤEisenacher Strasse; map p.114. Tiny and friendly bar, connected to *Renger-Patzsch* (see p.206), with Fifties and Sixties Americana decor and a local rather than trendy clientele. Doesn't really get going until after midnight. Daily 7pm–3am.

★Victoria Bar Potsdamer Str. 102 ☎030 25 75 99 77, ⓦvictoriabar.de; ⓤKurfürstenstrasse; map p.114. Much-loved cocktail bar with a long bar that's great for a low-key and decently mixed drink in the week or a livelier weekend night. Subdued lighting and discreet but upbeat music. Mon–Thurs & Sun 6.30pm–3am, Fri & Sat 6.30pm–4am.

Zoulou Bar Hauptstr. 4 ☎030 70 09 47 37, ⓦzouloubar .de; ⓤKleistpark; map p.114. Wonderfully low-key bar, packed after 11pm with sociable Schönebergers, quaffing draught Kölsch (Cologne's famous beer) and several good cocktails. Mon–Thurs & Sun 8pm–5am, Fri & Sat 8pm–6am.

WESTERN KREUZBERG

Brachvogel Carl-Herz-Ufer 34 (an der Brachvogelstr.) ☎030 69 30 432, ⓦbrachvogel-berlin.de; ⓤHallesches Tor or Prinzenstrasse; map p.118. Situated along the Landwehrkanal, *Brachvogel* offers not only a pleasant beer garden and decent drinks and (German and Mediterranean)

food but also live music, minigolf and a playground. Daily 9am till late (beer garden April–Oct only).

Golgatha Dudenstr. 48–64 ☎030 785 24 53, ⓦgolgatha-berlin.de; ⓤPlatz der Luftbrücke; map p.118. Enormous and hugely popular summer-only beer garden perched in the Viktoriapark near the top of Kreuzberg's hill. Mixed-grill platter €6.50; half-litre beer €3; breakfast served until 3pm. Hosts an alfresco disco on summer weekends (and sometimes during the week) from 10pm – good fun on warm evenings. April–Sept daily 9am until late.

Zyankali Bar Gneisenaustr. 17 ☎030 68 83 01 70, ⓦzyankali.de; ⓤGneisenaustrasse; map p.118. Laboratory-themed bar brimming with its own weird science. Furniture includes hospital beds and a vertical indoor garden, and the speciality drinks span bootlegged cocktails, home-made absinthe and some interesting molecular/mixology food and drink pairings. There's also a dancefloor in the basement and a beer garden outside. Daily 4pm until late.

EASTERN KREUZBERG AND TREPTOW

Brauhaus Südstern Hasenheide 69 ☎030 69 00 16 24, ⓦbrauhaus-suedstern.de; ⓤSüdstern; map pp.128–129. This Kreuzberg/Neukölln brewery and beer garden backs onto the Volkspark Hasenheide. It offers a local, low-key ambience during the day and occasional live music (jazz, funk) at night. They also run tours and brewing workshops, and have roasts on Sundays. Mon–Sat 2pm till late; Sun noon till late.

Das Hotel Mariannenstr. 26a ☎030 84 11 84 33, ⓦdashotelclassic.blogspot.co.uk; ⓤKottbusser Tor; map pp.128–129. Split-level spot where crowds gather to drink, chat and watch the occasional film. Divided into three areas, it features a main bar, with occasional DJs playing Latin and 1960s music, and a rustic bar with a more relaxed vibe with wooden tables and candlelight. Daily 2pm until whenever.

Haus Zenner Alt-Treptow 14–17, Treptow ☎030 533 73 70, ⓦhauszenner.de; Ⓢ Treptower Park; map pp.128–129. A large and popular beer garden by the Spree River. Don't be thrown off by the *Burger King* on the ground floor. April–Sept daily noon till late.

Konrad Tönz Falckensteinstr. 30 ☎030 612 32 52, ⓦkonradtoenzbar.de; ⓤSchlesisches Tor; map pp.128–129. Cheesy bar with 1970s trappings; sip cocktails (€7.50–10) while grooving to retro sounds and easy listening. Daily 8.15pm until late.

Luzia Oranienstr. 34 ☎030 81 79 99 58, ⓦluzia.tc; ⓤKottbusser Tor; map pp.128–129. Though it has lost its edge in the last couple of years, this hipster hangout – with its exposed brickwork, velvet armchairs and bizarre upstairs space that you have to climb a ladder to get to – is

still a fairly funky pre-club bar. Decent drinks and cocktails are slightly undermined by nonchalant service. Daily midnight–5am.

★**Möbel-Olfe** Reichenberger Str. 177 ☎030 23 27 46 90, ⓦmoebel-olfe.de; ⓤKottbusser Tor; map pp.128–129. Sandwiched between a string of Turkish snack bars in a run-down building behind Kottbusser Tor, this unusual, smoky, local bar attracts gays, hipsters, ageing drunks and more. There are regular DJ nights but it's more about experiencing the diversity of the Kreuzberg crowds. Tues–Sun 6pm until late.

Schwarze Traube Wrangelstr. 24 ☎030 23 13 55 69; ⓤGörlitzer Bahnhof; map pp.128–129. Like many of Berlin's best drinking spots, this cocktail bar looks fairly nondescript from the outside. Knock on the door and – if it's not full – you'll be ushered into a cosy, dimly lit bar with rickety furnishings and award-winning drinks. Daily 7pm till late.

White Trash Fast Food Am Flutgraben 2, Treptow ☎030 551 50 65 87, ⓦwhitetrashfastfood.com; ⓢTreptower Park; map pp.128–129. With a Wild West saloon meets Chinese restaurant theme, this perennially popular den of kitsch acts as restaurant, bar and club/live venue. The food – mostly burgers, nachos and barbecue – is decent enough (weekday lunches available) and matches the informal nature of the crowd, who come to chill in the beer garden and check out the regular DJs and bands (mostly country, punk and 50s- and 60s-era tunes). Daily noon until late.

Wiener Blut Wiener Str. 14 ⓦwienerblut.org; ⓤGörlitzer Bahnhof; map pp.128–129. Former student bar that now draws a mixed crowd but still has table football and a buoyant, spirited atmosphere and occasional dancefloor action. Daily 6pm until late.

Würgeengel Dresdener Str. 122 ☎030 615 55 60, ⓦwuergeengel.de; ⓤKottbusser Tor; map pp.128–129. One of the best bars in Kreuzberg, "the exterminating angel" has red walls, great tapas, decadent decor and an extensive cocktail and wine list. The feel is timeless, though with a trendy clientele. Daily 7pm till late.

NEUKÖLLN

Ä Wirtschaft Weserstr. 40 ☎030 30 64 87 51, ⓦae-neukoelln.de; ⓤRathaus Neukölln; map p.130. This popular Neukölln hangout bar has a classic ramshackle vibe, complete with low lighting, flea-market furnishings and table football. There's usually a good soundtrack of indie and electro plus occasional concerts and other midweek events. Daily 5pm until late.

Das Gift Donaustr. 19 ⓦdasgift.tumblr.com; ⓤRathaus Neukölln; map p.130. Funded by Barry Burns, of Scottish post-rock band Mogwai fame, this trendy spot combines a traditional wooden pub interior with a bespoke drinks menu that includes Scottish ales, German craft beers

and cocktails. There's also decent British-themed food and a separate room that occasionally hosts late-night parties and pop-up events. Daily 5pm till late.

★**Klunkerkranich** Karl-Marx-Str. 66 ⓦklunkerkranich .org; ⓤRathaus Neukölln; map p.130. This shabby-chic rooftop hangout is hidden on top of a distinctly unglamorous shopping centre. The urban bar vibe is complemented by a sandy floor, great views over the city and occasional concerts and film screenings. Mon–Sat 10am–1.30pm, Sun noon–1.30am.

FRIEDRICHSHAIN

Babette Karl-Marx-Allee 36 ☎0176 38 38 89 43, ⓦbarbabette.com; ⓤSchillingstrasse; map pp.128–129. Cool and sparsely furnished bar in the glass box building of a former cosmetics shop. At night, its only identifying feature is the warm glow of the interior lights. The upstairs former treatment rooms occasionally have live music but mostly art exhibitions behind the bar area are the cultural focus of interest. Daily 6pm until late.

Dachkammer Simon-Dach-Str. 39 ☎030 29 04 90 54, ⓦdachkammer.com; ⓤ/ⓢWarschauer Strasse; map pp.128–129. The largest and possibly most sociable place on the strip – the combination of rustic bar downstairs and retro bar upstairs has made this a local classic. Daily 1pm until late.

★**Hops & Barley** Wühlischstr. 22/23 ☎030 29 36 75 34, ⓦhopsandbarley-berlin.de; ⓤSamariterstrasse or ⓤ/ⓢWarschauerstrasse; map pp.128–129. This unassuming wood-and-tiles pub combines the trend for brewpubs with a diverse crowd that ranges from international hipsters to elderly locals. The friendly staff serve up five draft beers (three standards and two experimental ones) that are produced on site, supplemented by rotating guest beers and simple snacks such as sausages and brewer's grain bread. Mon–Fri 5pm till late, Sat & Sun 3pm till late.

Kptn. A. Müller Simon-Dach-Str. 32 ☎030 54 73 22 57; ⓤ/ⓢWarschauer Strasse; map pp.128–129. Ramshackle, sociable and very popular budget bar on the Simon-Dach-Strasse strip, with free table football – though you'd better be good to challenge the locals. Daily 6pm until late.

PRENZLAUER BERG

August Fengler Lychener Str. 11 ☎030 44 35 66 40, ⓦaugustfengler.de; ⓤEberswalder Strasse; map p.136. One of the few bars in the neighbourhood whose history predates the *Wende*, it offers a low-key local vibe with a mix of characters and usually decent music. Daily 7pm until late.

Bar3 Weydingerstr. 20 ☎030 97 00 51 06; ⓤRosa -Luxemburg-Platz; map p.136. Just across the street from the Volksbühne, this low-key, in-the-know hangout pulls in a creative crowd, who get intimate around the horseshoe-shaped bar. It can get quite buzzy at weekends, but never clubby. Thurs–Sat 9pm till late.

Becketts Kopf Pappelallee 64 ☎030 44 03 58 80, ⓦbecketts-kopf.de; Ⓤ/Ⓢ Schönhauser Allee; map p.136. It would be easy to walk straight past this clandestine cocktail bar – but you'd be missing out. Look out for the glowering head of Mr Beckett staring at you from the darkness, and enter to find a sophisticated and intimate space with one of the best cocktail lists in town. Daily 8pm until late.

Dr Pong Eberswalder Str. 21 ⓦdrpong.net; Ⓤ Eberswalder Strasse; map p.136. The action here revolves – literally – around the ping-pong table in the middle of the main room. Rent a bat (or bring your own) and join the crowd as they move slowly around the table, bats in one hand, beer bottles in the other, playing a communal game. DJs grace the sound system from time to time, though be warned the bar is on the tourist beer crawl route and can get packed. Mon–Sat 8pm until late, Sun 7pm until late.

★**Emil's Biergarten** Berliner Str. 80 ⓦwbb-pankow. de/biergarten/; Ⓤ Vinetastrasse; map p.145. Set within a partly revived but still semi-dilapidated nineteenth-century brewery right next to a bustling main road between Prenzlauer Berg and Pankow, this beer garden has a somewhat unique ambience. It offers a decent selection of beers and wines, a ramshackle assortment of deckchairs, benches and garden chairs, and decent pizza, too. April–Oct daily 3–10pm (from 5pm on rainy days).

Herman Schönhauser Allee 173 ☎030 44 31 28 54; Ⓤ Senefelderplatz; map p.136. Located along the busy section of Schönhauser Allee that links Mitte with Prenzlauer Berg, this Belgian-themed bar – run by welcoming and knowledgeable owner Bart Neirynck – has an incredibly broad selection of beers. It's a great place to start the night, but chances are you'll end up staying for longer than planned. Daily 6pm–3am.

Pavillon Friedenstr. in Volkspark ☎0172 750 47 24, ⓦpavillon-berlin.de; Ⓤ Strausberger Platz; map p.136. This atmospheric beer garden, surrounded by the laidback greenery of Volkspark Friedrichshain, is at its best in summer. Occasional public events and parties (Halloween, New Year's Eve, football screenings) take place in the main hall. March–Oct Mon–Fri 11am until late, Sat & Sun 10am until late.

Pfefferbräu Schönhauser Allee 176 ☎030 44 35 48 53, ⓦpfefferbraeu.de; Ⓤ Senefelderplatz; map p.136. Popular outdoor beer garden, in the courtyard of an 1841 brewery that was resurrected in 2013 to create its own range of draught beers. Also has a good (year-round) restaurant with a strong emphasis on seasonal produce (mains €14–18). Beer garden April–Sept Tues & Wed 6pm–midnight, Thurs & Fri 4pm–midnight, Sat & Sun

2pm–midnight; restaurant Tues–Thurs 5.30pm–midnight, Fri 4pm–midnight, Sat 1pm–midnight, Sun 1–11pm.

★**Prater** Kastanienallee 7–9 ☎030 44 48 56 88, ⓦpratergarten.de; Ⓤ Eberswalder Strasse; map p.136. In summer you can swig beer, feast on Bratwurst and other native food, and listen to 1970s German rock in the traditional beer garden, which dates back to 1837; the beer hall offers a similarly authentic experience. Beer garden April–Sept daily noon–midnight; restaurant Mon–Sat 6pm–midnight, Sun noon–midnight.

Scotch & Sofa Kollwitzstr. 18 ☎030 44 04 23 71; Ⓢ Senefelderplatz; map p.136. This highly agreeable, quietly hip neighbourhood bar is a fine spot for sinking into an old sofa, sipping on a decently made cocktail and having a tête-à-tête. They always play interesting music – everything from Elvis to rap – and smokers and ping-pong fans can indulge their passions downstairs. Mon–Thurs & Sun 6pm–1am, Sat 6pm–4am.

Zu mir oder zu dir Lychener Str. 15 ☎0176 24 42 29 40, ⓦzumiroderzudir.com; Ⓤ Eberswalder Strasse; map p.136. Groovy, very Seventies lounge-bar with a sociable vibe and lots of sofas to crash out on. A good place to start a night out, even if the cheeky name – translating as "your place or mine?" – suggests you might end it here. Daily 8pm until late.

WEDDING AND GESUNDBRUNNEN

★**The Castle Pub** Hochstr. 2 ☎015 16 76 76 757, ⓦcastlepub.de; Ⓤ/Ⓢ Gesundbrunnen; map p.146. This former Irish pub has been transformed into one of the city's largest craft beer spots. The interior maintains a classic pub feel, complete with a back room for karaoke and sports screenings, but the menu features a vast array of craft beers as well as sustenance like burgers and fish and chips. Mon–Fri 3pm until late, Sat & Sun noon until late.

Eschenbräu Triftstr. 67 ☎030 462 68 37, ⓦeschenbraeu.de; Ⓤ/Ⓢ Wedding; map p.146. One of Wedding's original microbreweries, *Eschenbräu*'s allure lies in its excellent home-brewed and seasonal beers and its quirky location in the basement of a residential apartment. The courtyard opens in summer and simple snacks are also served. Daily 3pm till late.

Fos Bar Grüntaler Str. 9 ☎0176 668 45984; Ⓤ Pankstrasse; map p.146. Usually referred to as the "F-Bar", this grungy-looking spot has local artworks on the walls, flea-market furniture to lounge in, and a surprisingly impressive range of beers and gins. Occasional live bands or DJs. Daily 5pm until late.

Kugelbahn Grüntaler Str. 51 ⓦkugelbahn-wedding .com; Ⓢ Bornholmerstrasse; map p.145. It would be easy to walk by this place and disregard it as an irrelevant old-timer *Kneipe*. But in fact it's as hipster as they come – from the two-lane, nine-pin bowling alley in the basement

14

14

that's given over to regular concerts, to the main room's art exhibitions and pop-up community meals. The selection of tequila and mezcal is second to none. Daily 6pm–1am.

★**Vagabund Brauerei** Antwerpener Str. 3 ☎030 52 66 76 68, ⊛vagabundbrauerei.com; ⊕Amrumer Strasse; maps p.146 & pp.308–309. This crowd-sourced brewery is run by three American friends with a highly infectious passion for craft beer. As well as their own excellent brews, they sell classic Belgian ales and lager from family breweries in southern Germany, all in a welcoming, unpretentious atmosphere that draws locals and expats alike. Mon–Fri 5pm till late, Sat & Sun 1pm till late.

THE EASTERN SUBURBS

Gestrandet Am Müggelsee 216, Friedrichshagen ☎0159 031 75876, ⊛gestrandet-am-mueggelsee.de; Ⓢ Friedrichshagen; map p.156. A central Berlin beach bar that's landed on the shores of the Müggelsee. Deck-chairs, beer and cocktails in a pleasant spot not far from the Spreetunnel, ideally placed for before or after a wander along the lakeshore. May–Sept Mon–Fri noon till late, Sat & Sun 10am till late.

THE WESTERN SUBURBS

Alter Krug König-Luise-Str. 52, Dahlem ☎030 83 27 000, ⊛alter-krug-berlin.de; ⊕Dahlem-Dorf; map p.170. Rustic pub opposite Domäne Dahlem and close to

the U-Bahn. The large beer garden is an ideal stop after the nearby museums, or you could prepare yourself for your culture fix with a breakfast or Sunday brunch buffet (10am–2pm; €16.50). There's lots of traditional German cuisine as well as burgers on the regular menu; mains around €12. Daily 10am–11pm (beer garden April–Oct only).

Brauhaus Lemke am Schloss Luisenplatz 1, Charlottenburg ☎030 30 87 89 79, ⊛brauhaus-lemke .com; ⊕Richard-Wagner-Platz; map p.162. Large microbrewery offering a menu of reasonably priced traditional staples (most mains around €13) – sausage salad, pepper steak, pork chops – until 11pm. Daily 11am–midnight.

Brauhaus Spandau Neuendorfer Str. 1, Spandau ☎030 353 90 70, ⊛brauhaus-spandau.de; ⊕Altstadt Spandau; map p.162. Brewery with a beer garden, various beer halls and lots of shiny brewing equipment; reliable for schnitzels and the like. April–Oct Mon–Thurs & Sun 10am–midnight, Fri & Sat 10am–1am; Nov–March Mon 4pm–midnight, Tues–Thurs 11am–midnight, Fri & Sat 11am–1am, Sun 10am–midnight.

Loretta am Wannsee Kronprinzessinweg 260 ☎030 803 51 56, ⊛loretta-berlin.de; Ⓢ Wannsee; map p.170. Inviting tree-lined beer garden with Wannsee views enjoyed by a mixed crowd digging into snacks and beer. Daily noon until late.

CLUBS AND LIVE VENUES

UNTER DEN LINDEN AND AROUND

Tausend Schiffbauerdamm 11 ☎030 27 58 20 70, ⊛tausendberlin.com; ⊕/Ⓢ Friedrichstrasse; map p.36. Signposted by an enormous eye emitting a golden glow over its tunnel-shaped space, this upmarket club attracts a decidedly dapper crowd – so be sure to look the part. Inside you'll find a mix of upbeat disco and 1980s nights, as well as the *Cantina* tapas restaurant (last order 11pm). Entry €10. Tues–Sat 7.30pm until late (mid-July to Aug Fri & Sat only).

ALEXANDERPLATZ AND AROUND

2BE Club Klosterstr. 44 ☎030 60 93 96 23, ⊛2be-club .de; ⊕Klosterstrasse; map p.60. One of the city's main hip-hop clubs, spread over two big dancefloors, with a playlist that encompasses reggae, ragga and r'n'b. Attracts occasional big-name DJs and artists. Entry €10. Sat 11pm until late.

Golden Gate Dircksenstr. 77–78 ☎030 577 04 278, ⊛goldengate-berlin.de; ⊕/Ⓢ Jannowitzbrücke; map p.60. Lurking beneath the S-Bahn tracks, this club consists of two wilfully shabby rooms kitted out in secondhand furniture and is dedicated to two- or three-day-long free-for-alls. The crowds here tend to be a dressed-down, unpretentious lot who arrive well after midnight to try

their luck with the difficult bouncers. Music is mostly house and techno with some surprises. Entry €8–10. Thurs–Sat from 11.55pm.

House of Weekend Alexanderplatz 7 ☎030 24 63 16 76, ⊛week-end-berlin.de; ⊕/Ⓢ Alexanderplatz; map p.60. Occupying the former GDR state travel agency, this club is typical of Berlin's creative transformations. The fifteenth-floor views over central Berlin are spectacular and the roof terrace wonderful. All this makes up for the coolly offhand manner of many of its patrons as they groove to house and techno. Entry €10–12. June–Sept daily 11pm until late.

THE SPANDAUER VORSTADT

★**b-flat** Dircksenstr. 40 ☎030 283 31 23, ⊛b-flat -berlin.de; Ⓢ Hackescher Markt; map pp.70–71. Founded in 1995, this cosy jazz bar offers a mix of local musicians and the occasional international act. Popular at weekends, and there's also a busy free jam session on Wed. Entry €12. Mon–Thurs & Sun 8pm till late, Fri & Sat 9pm until late.

★**Clärchens Ballhaus** Auguststr. 24 ☎030 282 92 95, ⊛ballhaus.de; Ⓢ Oranienburger Strasse; map pp.70–71. Opened in 1913, providing a hedonistic venue throughout the 1920s and just about surviving fascism and communism, this dancehall is back in style, hosting a range of dance nights, from swing to tango and waltz, with instruction provided (times on website). Sunday afternoons see the upstairs mirror room – unused during GDR days for being too glitzy – acting as a concert venue. Great pizza, too. Entry free up to €12, depending on event. Daily 10am until late.

Grüner Salon Rosa-Luxemburg-Platz 2 ☎ 030 24 59 89 36, ⊛ gruener-salon.de; ⊕ Rosa-Luxemburg-Platz; map pp.70–71. Club beside the *Roter Salon* (see below) that preserves something of the 1920s in its chandeliers and velvet decor. Renowned for its varied programme of live music, comedy and cabaret. Entry €5–20. Opening times vary.

Kaffee Burger Torstr. 60 ☎ 030 28 04 64 95, ⊛ kaffeeburger.de; ⊕ Rosa-Luxemburg-Platz; map pp.70 71. Smoky 1970s retro-bar legendary for its Russian-themed disco nights. These still happen occasionally but otherwise there's a slightly unpredictable mix of genres from Balkan to surf rock, hip-hop and pop, with regular live concerts. Be warned: at weekends it can have a bit of a desperate, meat-market atmosphere. Entry €1–5. Open daily 9pm till late.

King Size Bar Friedrichstr. 112b ⊕ Oranienburger Tor; map pp.70–71. This ironically titled bar might have a tiny interior but it's big on atmosphere and fun – especially at weekends when local scenesters rub shoulders with well-heeled tourists to a soundtrack of r'n'b, hip-hop and the occasional house/techno set. Most punters dress to impress. Wed–Sun 10pm–6am.

Kitty Cheng Torstr. 99 ☎ 030 92 36 89 75, ⊛ kittycheng .de; ⊕ Rosanthaler Platz; map pp.70–71. With its vague Renaissance theme – red-and-white-striped walls, regal furnishings – and lengthy drinks list, this slightly under-the-radar spot manages to attract the attention of Mitte's buzzy party crowd. The best parties are at the weekend and the music is refreshingly diverse. Tues & Wed 9pm–2am, Thurs–Sat 9pm–5am.

Kunsthaus ACUD Veteranenstr. 21 ☎ 030 98 35 26 13, ⊛ acud.de; ⊕ Rosenthaler Platz; map pp.70–71. One of the few remaining cultural spaces left from the immediate post-Wall era, ACUD contains a theatre, cinema, club, bar and studio, and puts on regular concerts. Entry and opening times vary.

Roter Salon Rosa-Luxemburg-Platz 1 ☎ 030 24 06 55, ⊛ volksbuehne-berlin.de; ⊕ Rosa-Luxemburg-Platz; map pp.70–71. Tatty club within the Volksbühne theatre, with lurid red decor and chintzy furniture giving it the feel of a 1950s brothel. Readings, concerts and talks are held here. Wed is tango night. Entry €6–7. Mon & Wed–Sat 11pm–4am.

★Schokoladen Ackerstr. 169 ☎ 030 282 65 27, ⊛ schokoladen-mitte.de; ⊕ Rosenthaler Platz; map pp.70–71. The spartan, bare-brick interior of this former

TOP 5 LIVE INDIE MUSIC CLUBS

Kunsthaus ACUD See abvoe
Lido See p.227
Schokoladen See above
SO36 See p.227
Wild at Heart See p.227

chocolate factory is a hangover from its time as a squat in the early post-*Wende* days. Now a venue for theatrical and art events, live indie-pop and up-and-coming singer/songwriters. Entry up to €12, depending on event. Mon–Thurs 8pm until late, Fri & Sat 9pm until late, Sun 7pm until late.

Zosch Tucholskystr. 30 ☎ 030 280 76 64, ⊛ zosch -berlin.de, ⊕ Oranienburger Strasse, map pp.70–71. Alternative place that started as a squat when the Wall came down, and has retained much of that feel. A good place for gigs and club nights in the cellar, where a fun-loving local Creole jazz band often plays amid the smoky ambience and constant chatter. Daily 4pm till late.

POTSDAMER PLATZ AND TIERGARTEN

40seconds Potsdamer Str. 58 ☎ 030 890 64 20, ⊛ 40seconds.de; ⊕/Ⓢ Potsdamer Platz; map pp.90–91. Named after the amount of time it takes the elevator to get to its top-floor location, this part futurist, part 1980s throwback bar has great views over Potsdamer Platz. There are three lounge areas, lit by Verner Panton lamps, and balconies for summer. The mood is glamorous, the music is standard r'n'b, house and electronica, and the dress code is smart-casual or sporty-elegant. Entry €10. Fri & Sat 11pm till late.

Haus der Kulturen der Welt John-Foster-Dulles-Allee 10 ☎ 030 39 78 70, ⊛ hkw.de; ⊕ Bundestag; map pp.90–91. The city's number-one venue for world music (see p.103) is always worth checking out though concerts are irregular. Entry and opening times vary.

CITY WEST

A-Trane Bleibtreustr. 1/Pestalozzistr. ☎ 030 313 25 50, ⊛ a-trane.de; Ⓢ Savignyplatz; map p.108. Small and smoky jazz den – a good place for both up-and-coming and well-known jazz artists. Best during Saturday-night jams, when musicians arrive from other venues and join in at will throughout the evening. Around the corner, a new restaurant, *Jazzcafé Grolman* (Grolmanstr. 53; ☎ 030 31 80 37 80, ⊛ jazzcafeberlin.de), is a great spot for dinner and drinks before a show. Entry €10 21. Daily 9pm until late.

Puro Sky Lounge Tauentzienstr. 11 ☎ 030 26 36 78 75, ⊛ puroberlin.de; ⊕ Kurfürstendamm; map p.108. Probably Berlin's snazziest club with a twentieth-storey location in the Europa Center and great views of the City

14

14

TOP 5 JAZZ AND BLUES VENUES
A-Trane See p.225
Badenscher Hof See p.229
b-flat See p.224
Quasimodo See below
Yorckschlösschen See below

West nightscape as its main selling point. But it's an elitist place and one of the few clubs in Berlin with any kind of dress code: if it's not designer, you won't get in – and if it's not a 1980s classic it probably won't be played. Entry free up to €10, depending on event. Bar Thurs–Sat 8pm until late; club Thurs 10pm till late, Fri & Sat from 11pm till late.

Quasimodo Kantstr. 12a ☎030 318 045 60, ⓦ quasimodo.de; Ⓤ/Ⓢ Zoologischer Garten; map p.108. This casual cellar bar is one of Berlin's best jazz spots, with black-and-white photos, low ceilings and intimate tables. The nightly programme involves a high-quality mix of international, usually American, stars and up-and-coming names. Also funk, blues and Latin and a neighbouring restaurant (noon till midnight). Entry €7–30. Daily 8pm–2am.

SCHÖNEBERG

Havanna Hauptstr. 30 ☎030 784 85 65, ⓦ havanna-berlin.de; Ⓢ Julius-Leber-Brücke; map p.114. Upbeat Latin social club, with seven bars and four dancefloors: one for salsa and merengue, and the others to groove to funk, reggaeton, hip-hop, disco and r'n'b. Dance classes available; entry €8. Wed 9pm–4am, Fri & Sat 10pm–4am.

★**Kumpelnest 3000** Lützowstr. 23 ☎030 261 69 18, ⓦ kumpelnest3000.com; Ⓤ Kurfürstenstrasse; map p.114. Carpeted walls and a mock-Baroque effect attract a rough-and-ready crew of 30- and 40-somethings to this erstwhile brothel, which gets going around 2am, when there's standing room only. The best place in the area, it's good fun and infamous as a hook-up bar for people of all sexual orientations. Daily 7pm till late.

WESTERN KREUZBERG

★**Gretchen** Obentrautstr. 19–21 ☎030 25 92 27 02, ⓦ gretchen-club.de; Ⓤ Mehringdamm; map p.118. A bit off the beaten track, but few clubs can boast that they occupy the 1854 stables of Queen Victoria's Prussian First Guards. This mid-sized club has a pedigree too, as it rose from the ashes of the legendary *Icon*, a late-1990s club-scene pioneer. Drum'n'bass is big here, but all species of innovative electronic music thrive, as do live shows. Entry €5–12. Hours vary, usually Thurs–Sat 11.30pm till late.

Junction Bar Gneisenaustr. 18 ☎030 694 66 02,

ⓦ junction-bar.de; Ⓤ Gneisenaustrasse; map p.118. Nightly live music covering the full spectrum of sounds, played to a very mixed crowd in a basement club. Always busy, and DJs keep the night going after the bands finish. Entry €3–6. Wed–Thurs 8.30pm–3am, Fri & Sat 10pm–4am.

Solar Stresemannstr. 76 ☎0163 765 27 00, ⓦ solarberlin.com; Ⓢ Anhalter Bahnhof; map p.118. Swanky lounge bar whose seventeenth-floor location provides exceptional views over the city. There's also a pricey restaurant, but the place to be is among the beautiful people (celebs like Hugh Grant and Michel Gondry have been spotted here) grooving to ambient techno in the bar above. The entrance is slightly hidden at the back of a small car park opposite Anhalter Bahnhof and the door policy can be stringent and unpredictable: there's no need to dress up, but don't dress down either. Mon–Thurs & Sun 6pm–2am, Fri & Sat 6pm–3am.

Yorckschlösschen Yorckstr. 15 ☎030 215 80 70, ⓦ www.yorckschloesschen.de; Ⓤ Mehringdamm; map p.118. Century-old local institution that's preserved a 1970s feel and is still famous as an artists' drinking den and a place to enjoy free live jazz, swing, blues and country. Basic food served. Summer daily 10am–3am; rest of year Mon–Sat 5pm–3am, Sun 10am–3am.

EASTERN KREUZBERG AND TREPTOW

★**Arena Berlin** Eichenstr. 4, Treptow ☎030 533 20 30, ⓦ arena-berlin.de; Ⓢ Treptower Park; map pp.128–129. This huge area next to the Spree – built as a bus repair yard in the nineteenth century – hosts several notable daytime and nightlife venues, including the *Arena Club*, *Glashaus* and the Badeschiff (see p.250), all well known for their electronic music parties, as well as the quirky *Hoppetosse* (ⓦ hoppetosse.berlin), a café and bar on a boat that puts on rock and metal shows. *Club der Visionaere* is right next door, too. Admission usually €4–14. Opening times vary.

Club der Visionaere Am Flutgraben 1, Treptow ☎030 69 51 89 42, ⓦ clubdervisionaere.com; Ⓤ Schlesisches Tor; map pp.128–129. Legendary summer-only techno bar enjoying a unique setting on the intersection of the Spree and Flutgraben canal. The bar and DJ booth is in an old ceramic-tiled boathouse, and punters stand (and dance) on the floating docks outside. It's minimal techno all the way

TOP 5 PLACES TO END A NIGHT OUT
Berghain See p.228
Golden Gate See p.224
Kumpelnest 3000 See above
Möbel-Olfe See p.222
Rosi's See p.228

and a fantastically upbeat place. Entry €1–5. May–Sept Mon–Fri 3pm till late, Sat & Sun noon till late.

Insel Alt-Treptow 6, Treptow ☎030 20 91 49 90, ⓦinselberlin.de; ⓢPlänterwald; map pp.128–129. Reliable venue for thrash/punk gigs and club nights, on a Spree island that's part of Treptower Park. Occasional outdoor raves on the large terrace in summer. Tues–Fri noon till late, Sat & Sun 3pm till late.

Kit-Kat Club Köpenicker Str. 76 (entrance on Brückenstr.) ⓦkitkatclub.org; ⓤHeinrich-Heine-Strasse; map pp.128–129. Famously debauched club, sharing premises with the *Sage Club* (see below), for people looking for casual and public liaisons – voyeurs are not welcome. The door policy is strict: wear something revealing or fetishistic. Check the website for guidelines, and for details of theme evenings. Entry up to €15, depending on party. Daily 11pm till late.

Lido Cuvrystr. 7 ☎030 69 56 68 40, ⓦlido-berlin.de; ⓤSchlesisches Tor; map pp.128–129. Old-school club in a former theatre that's been championing new indie music – with the occasional techno or house event – for more than a decade. Attracts a younger crowd. Entry €8–20. Opening times vary.

Madame Claude Lübbener Str. 19 ☎030 84 11 08 61, ⓦmadameclaude.de; ⓤSchlesisches Tor; map pp.128–129. This buzzy international hangout has shows six days a week, ranging from indie-rock and experimental to folk. Be prepared to feel slightly unsettled by the decor, much of which hangs upside down from the ceiling. Pay what you want to enter. Daily 7pm till late.

Monarch Skalitzer Str. 134 ☎030 61 65 60 03, ⓦkottimonarch.de; ⓤKottbusser Tor; map pp.128–129. Unpretentious and slightly ragged place that attracts a hip crowd who groove to a wide range of tunes – swing, rockabilly, folk, punk, indie (no techno) – and enjoy views over Kottbusser Tor from huge windows. Entrance is via an unmarked door and stairwell opposite the *Misir Casisi* kebab shop. Entry varies but often as low as €3. Tues–Sat 9pm till late.

Prince Charles Prinzenstr. 85f ⓦprincecharlesberlin .com; ⓤMoritzplatz; map pp.128–129. This chic nightspot, located in a former swimming baths (the bar is in what used to be the pool), draws in a fairly underground yet mixed crowd with a music programme that ranges from hip-hop to house. Entry up to €10. Mon–Thurs 7pm till late, Fri & Sat 11pm till late.

Privatclub Skalitzer Str. 85–86 ☎030 616 759 62, ⓦprivatclub-berlin.de; ⓤSchlesisches Tor; map pp.128–129. Set inside a former post office, *Privatclub* hosts international and local indie and retro bands, with regular parties like Kiss All Hipsters and the Northern Soul All-Nighter. Entry €5–10. Fri & Sat 11pm until late.

Ritter Butzke Ritter Str. 24 ⓦclub.ritterbutzke.de; ⓤMoritzplatz; map pp.128–129. This former factory

now comprises two main club rooms and an outside space, usually only used in summer. The music is usually electronic (house, electro, techno) and the crowd a considered but dedicated bunch. Admission €8–15. Fri & Sat 11.59pm till late.

Sage Club Köpenicker Str. 76 ☎030 278 98 30, ⓦsage -club.de; ⓤHeinrich-Heine-Strasse; map pp.128–129. One of Berlin's premier rock clubs, with multiple dance-floors and a good range of rock'n'roll and live bands. Always a good vibe and popular with a younger set. Entry up to €8. Thurs 11pm–5am.

★S036 Oranienstr. 190 ☎030 61 40 13 06, ⓦso36 .de; ⓤGörlitzer Bahnhof; map pp.128 129. Legendary club, named after the district's old postcode, which has its roots in punk, post-punk and alternative music – a string of musical heroes have played here, including Iggy, Bowie and Einstürzende Neubauten. Nowadays it hosts alternative and electronic shows, including monthly parties like Gayhane, a Turkish "homoriental" party, where you can catch an exquisite array of Berlin-based artists playing everything from garage to synth-pop. Entry €3–10 (more for some concerts). Opening times vary.

Tresor Köpenicker Str. 70 ☎030 695 37 70, ⓦtresorberlin.de; ⓤHeinrich-Heine-Strasse; map pp.128–129. A key player in Berlin's electronic music scene, this convoluted bunker-style club attracts clubbers from all over Europe with thumping techno booming in every nook. The volume, intensity and light show all have to be experienced to be believed. Entry Mon €8, Wed €7, Fri & Sat €12–15. Mon–Wed, Fri & Sat midnight until late.

Watergate Falckensteinstr. 49 ☎030 61 28 03 96, ⓦwater-gate.de; ⓤSchlesisches Tor; map pp.128–129. A top Berlin nightspot, with a glorious riverside location by the Oberbaumbrücke. The futuristic club has impressive light installations and sprawls over two levels with a large main floor and another with a lounge; music is varied but mostly electronic. Some big-name DJs. Entry €10–18. Wed, Fri & Sat midnight till late, occasional Tues & Thurs events.

Wild at Heart Wiener Str. 20 ☎030 611 70 10, ⓦwildatheartberlin.de; ⓤGörlitzer Bahnhof; map pp.128–129. Cornerstone live music venue for rock 'n' roll, indie and punk, with something always going on well into the small hours. Daily 8pm until late.

TOP 5 TECHNO CLUBS
Berghain See p.228
Kater Blau See p.228
Sisyphos See p.229
Tresor See above
Watergate See above

14

14

NEUKÖLLN

Loophole Berlin Boddinstr. 60 ⓦ loophole-berlin .com; ⓤ Rathaus-Neukölln; map p.130. Expect everything from experimental concerts and films to sculpture installations at this small but edgy space. Tues– Sat 9pm–late.

FRIEDRICHSHAIN

://about blank Markgrafendamm 24c ⓦ aboutparty .net; ⓤ Ostkreuz; map pp.128–129. Set inside a nondescript concrete block a short walk from Ostrkeuz S-Bahnhof, this is one of the city's better underground clubs. With two main dancefloors, lots of nooks and crannies, and a garden where DJs spin in the summer, the dominant music policy is house and techno with occasional forays into related electronic genres plus live concerts. Entry €10–14. Club Thurs–Sun midnight till late; from 7pm for midweek live shows.

★**Berghain** Am Wriezener Bahnhof ☎ 030 29 36 02 10, ⓦ berghain.de; Ⓢ Ostbahnhof; map pp.128–129. This vast, artfully scuzzy old power plant is considered by many people to be the best club in the world. Minimal techno and house – on a fantastic sound system – cannonball around the two dancefloors, which are peppered with a unique combination of shirtless gay guys and fashion-conscious hipsters; other desires are catered for with an array of laidback bars and darkened backrooms. The club ensures and abuses its legendary status with a picky, indefinable door policy: try to avoid looking like a tourist or arriving in any kind of group. And remember headline acts often start at noon on Sunday – so there's no rush to get here early; about 5am or even after lunch is ideal, when the wait to get in generally drops below an hour. Entry €14–18. Fri & Sat midnight until late (usually late afternoon the next day).

Kantine am Berghain Rüdersdorfer Str. 70 ☎ 030 29 36 02 10, ⓦ berghain.de; Ⓢ Ostbahnhof; map pp.128– 129. A friendly atmosphere and tiny but jolly summer beer garden mean that this venue is far more than simply a haven for people rejected by the neighbouring *Berghain* – to which its music often compares but also diverges from.

Entry €5–10. Opening times vary.

★**Kater Blau** Holzmarktstr. 25 ☎ 30 510 521 34, ⓦ katerblau.de; ⓤ/Ⓢ Jannowitzbrücke; map pp.128– 129. The latest incarnation of previous legendary clubs *Bar 25* and *Kater Holzig*, the "Blue Cat" is a continuation of the same ethic: hedonistic partying in a DIY environment. If you're patient enough for the long queues and brave enough to face the picky door staff, you'll find the party nights reliably good. The club is slated to become part of a broader public cultural complex complete with hotel and accessible family areas. Cultural events and concerts midweek, entry up to €14. Mon–Thurs 7pm til late; Fri & Sat midnight till late.

★**RAW Gelände** Revaler Str. 99 ⓦ raw-tempel.de; ⓤ/Ⓢ Warschauer Strasse; map pp.128–129. Sprawling, heavily graffitied ensemble of former train yard buildings that now hosts one of the city's most alternative clubbing and cultural complexes. There are several shabby-chic bars and clubs, including the laidback *Crack Bellmer* (ⓦ crackbellmer.de) and the more upbeat electro and techno clubs *Cassieopeia* (ⓦ cassiopeia-berlin.de) and *Suicide Circus* (ⓦ suicide-berlin.com). *Urban Spree* (ⓦ urbanspree.com), a beer garden that often has DJs and live music into the night, is at the Warschauer Strasse side. Entry prices and opening times vary.

Rosi's Revaler Str. 29 ⓦ rosis-berlin.de; Ⓢ Ostkreuz; map pp.128–129. Oddball, upbeat club that sports Berlin's classic unfinished and improvised feel in a mix of semi-derelict buildings. There's a definite sense of crashing a house party here, with even a small kitchen and living room to hang out in between bouts on the dancefloors – where indie or techno pounds. In the beer garden, the table tennis is a big attraction. Entry up to €20. Thurs–Sat 6pm till late, Sun 2pm till late.

Salon zur Wilde Renate Alt Stralau 70 ☎ 030 25 04 14 26, ⓦ renate.cc; Ⓢ Ostkreuz; map pp.128–129. Set inside a former squat across the river from Treptower Park, this idiosyncratic, multi-roomed, artist-run venue offers good local DJs, a disco and house-oriented music policy, plus a garden area for fresh air. The same owners run *Else*, an open-air venue just across the other side of the Spree

---

OUTDOOR VENUES

International **big-name acts** visiting town regularly play at one of several stadiums and larger venues around town and generally the act rather than the venue will be the big draw. The exceptions to this are those performing in the Olympic Stadium (see p.166) and at the two other suburban venues below.

Kindl-Bühne Wuhlheide ☎ 030 53 07 953, ⓦ wuhlheide.de; Ⓢ Wuhlheide; map p.150. Small outdoor venue, tucked away in the forest near Köpenick, and a favourite for summertime festivals.

Waldbühne Berlin Glockenturmstr./Passenheimer Str. ☎ 01806 57 00 70 (tickets), ⓦ waldbuehne-berlin.de; Ⓢ Pichelsberg; map p.162. Near the Olympic Stadium, this open-air natural amphitheatre regularly attracts big-name acts in the summer and is great fun on a warm evening.

(ⓦ else.tv). Entry €10–14. Tues–Sat 2pm till late, Sun noon till late.

Sisyphos Hauptstr. 15, Rummelsburg ⓦ Sisyphos -berlin.net; ⓢ Berlin-Rummelsburg Betriebsbahnhof; map p.150. Even further along the Spree than *Renate*, this industrial space – a former dog-food factory - has a few different dancefloors and a spacious outdoor area that backs onto the river, plus a pizza place on site. Great parties that sometimes go on all weekend. Entry €10–14. Check website for times and events.

PRENZLAUER BERG

★8MM Schönhauser Allee 177 ☎ 030 40 50 06 24, ⓦ 8mmbar.com; ⓤ Senefelderplatz; map p.136. This small, blacked-out room is a superb place for low-key, late-night hedonism, with a little bar, a DJ spinning anything from rock to northern soul and 8mm films projected onto one wall. Entry €3–5. Daily 9pm till late.

Ausland Lychener Str. 60 ☎ 030 447 70 08, ⓦ ausland -berlin.de; ⓢ Prenzlauer Allee; map p.136. Non-profit experimental club in an undecorated bunker in front of an apartment block. It's committed to promoting performances and events that struggle to find a home anywhere else, so the range is huge, from free jazz and sound art gigs to movies and installations. Door fees go directly to the artists. Tickets around €5–9. Check website for times.

Badfish Stargarder Str. 14 ☎ 030 547 147 88, ⓦ badfishbarberlin.com; ⓤ/ⓢ Schönhauser Allee; map p.136. This New York-style neighbourhood bar has become a popular in-spot for expats and natives alike. Smoky and

boisterous (especially at weekends), and with a hip selection of sounds on the jukebox, friendly staff and an excellent array of craft beers, whiskies and shots, it makes for an almost guaranteed fun night out. "Angry hour" 5–7pm and free popcorn at all times. Daily 5pm till late.

Duncker Dunckerstr. 64 ☎ 030 445 95 09, ⓦ dunckerclub.de; ⓢ Prenzlauer Allee; map p.136. Indie, industrial and unashamedly Goth refuge from the mainstream and techno scenes. Aptly enough it's located in a striking neo-Gothic church. Entry €3–5 (free concerts every Thursday). Mon & Thurs 10pm till late, Tues, Fri & Sat 11pm till late.

WEDDING AND GESUNDBRUNNEN

Panke Gericht Str. 23 ☎ 0163 831 47 55, ⓦ pankeculture. com; ⓢ Humboldthain; map p.146. This alternative cultural hub, run by a group of Lithuanian friends, is hidden away in a network of run-down industrial courtyards. Expect underground DJ nights, which veer from hip-hop and soul to world and funk (never techno). Decent bar and café. Admission varies. Wed–Sat from 6pm till late.

THE WESTERN SUBURBS

Badenscher Hof Badensche Str. 29, Wilmersdorf ☎ 030 861 00 80, ⓦ badenscher-hof.de; ⓤ Berliner Strasse; map p.108. Lively café-restaurant and long-standing jazz venue that draws in a loyal and local crowd for its frequent concerts. Expect any type of jazz – from mainstream to modern – or blues. Mon–Fri 4pm until late, Sat 6pm until late.

14

HAMBURGER BAHNHOF

The arts

Berlin is justifiably renowned for its art and cultural scene – so much so that many expats continue to move to the city to work as musicians or artists, open independent galleries, or simply to get inspired by its artsy milieu. As with most European cities, the scene can be divided into two separate but overlapping categories: mainstream institutions such as opera houses, big classical music venues and fine arts museums, many of which are officially funded and maintained; and a constellation of independent galleries and venues that range from small, edgy and obscure to substantial and internationally renowned. Many of the former establishments can trace their history as far back as the nineteenth or even eighteenth centuries while the latter often owe their indie spirit to the early post-Wall era.

ESSENTIALS

Information The main English-language publication, *Exberliner* (ⓦexberliner.com), is good for what's on information, supported by a number of local English-language websites and German-language listings magazines *Zitty* and *Tip* (see p.33). On a more commercial level, the city's tourist information website (ⓦvisitberlin.de), is useful too. For art shows, check the English/German bi-monthly magazine *artery Berlin* (€3; ⓦartery-berlin.de), found in most galleries, where you can also usually pick up the free *Galerien Berlin* listings brochure (ⓦberliner-galerien.de). Look out too for a similar leaflet produced by Index (ⓦindexberlin.de) whose website has a useful browsable city map of all the galleries with all the latest exhibition details. Other useful online resources include ⓦberlinartlink.com and ⓦartconnect.com, which helps connect incoming and local artists to venues and events.

Booking and tickets You can book for most events through ⓦvisitberlin.de. Otherwise ticket offices (*Theaterkassen*) are usually the easiest way of buying tickets for all major arts events, though they often charge a hefty commission; try Koka 36, Oranienstr. 29, Kreuzberg (ⓣ030 61 10 13 13, ⓦkoka36.de; ⓤKottbusser Tor). The first place to try, however, for just about anything, is Hekticket (ⓣ030 230 99 30, ⓦhekticket.de); which sells half-price tickets from 2pm. Offices include Hekticket am Zoo (Hardenberg Str. 29a; Charlottenburg, ⓤ/Ⓢ Zoologischer Garten) and Hekticket am Alex (Alexanderstr. 1, Mitte; ⓤ/Ⓢ Alexanderplatz).

15

CONTEMPORARY ART

Complementing the superb, state-owned **Hamburger Bahnhof** (see p.105), Berlin's local art scene is astoundingly good, with an estimated 440 galleries spread around town. Today, you can find art shows in any neighbourhood, though the city's less commercial and more rough-and-ready scene operates outside the mainstream galleries and moves from one improvised space to the next. You'll stumble upon smaller, independent places – including many pop-up spaces – in less polished neighbourhoods, such as **Kreuzberg**, **Neukölln** and **Wedding**, though as these tend to move and change quite quickly it's best to check online (see above) for specific exhibitions and openings.

GALLERIES

★**Camera Work** Kantstr. 149, Charlottenburg ⓣ030 310 07 73, ⓦcamerawork.de; ⓤUhlandstrasse; map pp.90–91. Hidden in a courtyard and blessed with huge north-facing windows and wonderfully even light, this relaxed photography gallery spreads over two floors. Exhibitions often focus on big figures like Man Ray, Irving Penn, Horst P. Horst, Peter Lindbergh and Helmut Newton but the occasional up-and-coming name also gets a look-in. A second space, CWC Gallery can found be found in the former Jewish girls' school in Mitte (Auguststr. 11–13; ⓣ030 24 04 86 14; Tues–Fri 10am–6pm, Sat 11am–6pm, Ⓢ Oranienburger Strasse). Tues–Sat 11am–6pm.

Capitain Petzel Karl-Marx-Allee 45, Friedrichshain ⓣ030 24 08 81 30, ⓦcapitainpetzel.de; ⓤStrausberger Platz; map pp.128–129. Joint venture between two art dealers from Cologne and New York. Housed inside an eye-catching, Soviet-era modernist glass cube that once housed the former Kunst im Heim gallery of the GDR, it's now a cornerstone of the contemporary Berlin art scene. Tues–Sat 11am–6pm.

Carlier Gebauer Markgrafenstr. 67, Kreuzberg ⓣ030 24 00 86 30, ⓦcarliergebauer.com; ⓤKochstrasse; map p.118. Superb art gallery where you never quite know if you'll find home-grown or international art; either way, it's sure to be cutting-edge. Tues–Sat 11am–6pm.

★**C/O Berlin** One of the city's leading photography spaces now occupies the Amerika Haus in City West. Expect a mix of local and global exhibitions as well as lectures, contests and more. See p.110.

Contemporary Fine Arts Am Kupfergraben 10, Mitte ⓣ030 288 78 70, ⓤ/Ⓢ Friedrichstrasse, map p.36; Grolmanstr. 32/33, Charlottenburg ⓣ030 88 77 71 67, ⓤUhlandstrasse, map p.108; ⓦcfa-berlin.com. Specializing in international and local, established and up-and-coming artists, these two galleries – one in the east and one in the west – are great places to feel the pulse of the Berlin art scene. Names on show rotate but include locals like Anselm Reyle as well as international big names like Cecily Brown, Dana Schutz and Georg Baselitz. Tues–Fri 10am–6pm, Sat 11am–4pm (Grolmanstrasse gallery also open Mon 10am–6pm).

daadgalerie Oranienstr. 161, Kreuzberg ⓣ030 261 36 40, ⓦdaadgalerie.de; ⓤMoritzplatz; map pp.128–129. Exhibitions, concerts, readings and film screenings by big-name artists working in the city on fellowships. Mon–Sat 11am–6pm.

EIGEN+ART Auguststr. 26, Mitte ⓣ030 280 66 05, ⓦeigen-art.com; Ⓢ Oranienburger Strasse; map pp.70–71. Run by Gerd Harry Lybke, who opened his first private gallery in Leipzig back in 1983, this is one of the most important Auguststrasse galleries. Originally a showcase for East German talent, the programme now covers sculpture, painting, installations, conceptual art and photography by established and emerging international artists. A second gallery, EIGEN+ART Lab, opened nearby at Torstr. 22 in 2015 (ⓣ030 30 87 79 40, ⓦeigen-art-lab.com; ⓤOranienburger Tor; map pp.70–71). Tues–Sat 11am–6pm.

15

Galerie Anselm Dreher Pfalzburger Str. 80, Wilmersdorf ☎030 883 52 49, ⓦgalerie-anselm-dreher.com; ⓤHohenzollernplatz; map p.108. Long-standing city gallery, showing international avant-garde artists and particularly keen on sound installations. Tues–Fri 3–6pm, Sat 11am–2pm.

Galerie Barbara Thumm Markgrafenstr. 68, Kreuzberg ☎030 28 39 03 47, ⓦbthumm.de; ⓤKochstrasse; map p.118. Gallery showcasing art by local and international artists working in all media; one of several on or around this city block. Tues–Fri 11am–6pm, Sat noon–6pm.

Galerie Thomas Schulte Charlottenstr. 24, Mitte ☎030 20 60 89 90, ⓦgaleriethomasschulte.de; ⓤStadtmitte; map p.36. Well-presented conceptual art, photography and sculpture; frequently featuring established artists from America. Tues–Sat noon–6pm.

Hamburger Bahnhof/Museum für Gegenwart The state-owned Hamburger Bahnhof, the flagship venue for contemporary art in Berlin, has an exciting, heavyweight post-1950s collection that includes the likes of Andy Warhol, Marcel Duchamp and Joseph Beuys. See p.105.

König Galerie St.-Agnes-Kirche, Alexandrinenstr. 118–121, Kreuzberg ☎030 26 10 30 80, ⓦkoeniggalerie.com; ⓤPrinzenstrasse; map p.118. Set inside the revived Brutalist church of St Agnes, this high profile gallery – set up by Johann König – showcases engaging contemporary art of all kinds (sculpture,

paintings, installations), usually by acclaimed international and local artists. Tues–Sun 11am–6pm.

★ **Kunstraum Kreuzberg/Bethanien** Mariannenplatz 2, Kreuzberg ☎030 902 98 14 55, ⓦkunstraumkreuzberg.de; ⓤGörlitzer Bahnhof; map pp.128–129. Group and themed exhibits of contemporary art often relating to social issues, in a wing of the Künstlerhaus Bethanien, a giant old hospital turned arts venue in a Kreuzberg park. There's space for graffiti art, local fashion and artists from developing countries who'd struggle to get space elsewhere. Daily noon–7pm.

★ **KW Institute for Contemporary Art** Independent gallery set in a former factory building, where exhibits often include astute reflections on contemporary Berlin. Organizer of the Berlin Biennale (ⓦberlinbiennale.de). See p.82.

Loock Galerie Potsdamer Str. 63, Mitte ☎030 394 09 68 50, ⓦloock.info; ⓤKurfürstenstrasse; map p.114. Owner Friedrich Loock opened his first gallery in his Mitte flat in 1988, and now specializes in promoting important East German photographers like Sibylle Bergemann and Ulrich Wüst as well as international contemporary art with a focus on Japan. Tues–Sat 11am–6pm.

me Collectors Room Quirky and diverse museum that houses a personal collection of fascinating objects from the sixteenth century to the present day. See p.82.

Raab Galerie Goethestr. 81, Charlottenburg ☎030 261 92 18, ⓦraab-galerie.de; ⓢSavignyplatz; map p.108. Avant-garde and contemporary art at this popular meeting

---

BERLIN'S ART AND FASHION EVENTS

Berlin's big art and fashion events, often on the cutting edge, draw in hundreds of international curators and designers. One of the biggest events is the **Berlin Biennale** (ⓦberlinbiennale.de), which showcases a global spread of cutting-edge art in the city's major and independent gallery spaces in even-numbered years. The first major fixed date on Berlin's contemporary art calendar is **Gallery Weekend Berlin** (ⓦgallery-weekend-berlin.de) in late April/early May, when over fifty galleries co-ordinate their efforts to startle and impress. The biggest dates, however, fall close together in mid- to late September: **Berlin Art Week** (ⓦberlinartweek.de), involves all of Berlin's large contemporary art museums; **Art Berlin Contemporary** (ABC; ⓦartberlincontemporary.com), gathers collectors from around the world at Station Berlin in northwest Kreuzberg (Luckenwalder Str. 4–6; ⓤGleisdreieck; map p.118); and the artist-led and more offbeat **Berliner Liste** (ⓦberliner-liste.org) focuses on showcasing new local talent in a different venue each year.

July is the key month for **fashion shows**; the headliner tends to be **Mercedes-Benz Fashion Week Berlin** (ⓦberlin.mbfashionweek.com), a glitzy spectacular dominated by big-name international designers and their sycophantic retinue, but also with slots for new names. Held in tandem, the **Premium** (ⓦpremiumexhibitions.com) trade fair also showcases many fashionable brands. The smallest, least predictable, but often most interesting event, also in June/early July, is **Projekt Galerie** (ⓦprojektgalerie.net), which sees many city art galleries open their doors to fashion designers of all stripes. More offbeat still and arguably more in step with Berlin is the **Bread & Butter** (ⓦbreadandbutter.com) fashion festival in September, which takes over Arena Berlin (see p.226) to showcase streetwear of the sort that you'll probably see in the city's subway the following month.

Another spate of fashion excitement takes place in Berlin in **mid-January**, with Bread & Butter, Berlin Fashion Week and Projekt Galerie all reappearing in smaller form and with different seasonal collections.

place for the art in-crowd. Mon–Fri 10am–7pm, Sat 10am–4pm.

Sammlung Boros Reinhardtstr. 20, Mitte ☎ 030 24 08 33 300, ⓦ sammlung-boros.de; ⓤ/Ⓢ Friedrichstrasse; map pp.70–71. One of Berlin's most unique art spaces, Boros Sammlung inhabits a hulking, five-floor World War II concrete bunker, whose 2m-thick walls contain a wealth of contemporary installations and internationally acclaimed works by the likes of Ai Weiwei, Olafur Eliasson, Alicja Kwade, Wolfgang Tillmans and more, all owned and curated by collector Christian Boros, who lives in a penthouse suite on top of the building. Access is by pre-booked guided tour only, €12. Thurs–Sun 9am–6pm.

Sammlung Hoffman Private collection of top-notch contemporary art by a mix of local luminaries and international big hitters. See p.75.

Soy Capitan Prinzessinnenstr. 29, Kreuzberg ☎ 030 80 92 19 77, ⓦ soycapitan.de; ⓤ Moritzplatz; map pp.128–129. Run by well-known art aficionado Heike Tosun, this relatively new space (2012) primarily showcases contemporary work from Berlin-based artists like Benja Sachau and Matthias Dornfeld. Wed–Sat noon–6pm and by appointment.

Zwinger Galerie Mansteinstr. 5, Schöneberg ☎ 030 28 59 89 07, ⓦ zwinger-galerie.de; ⓤ Yorckstrasse or Ⓢ Yorckstrasse (Grossgörschenstrasse); map p.114. One of the city's most important galleries, presenting a mixture of avant-garde and conventional art. Tues–Sat noon–6pm.

CLASSICAL MUSIC AND OPERA

15

For years classical music in Berlin meant one man and one orchestra: Herbert von Karajan and the Berlin Philharmonic. Since his death in 1989, the **Philharmonie** has had its former supremacy questioned by the rise of the excellent **Deutsches Symphonie Orchester**. Yet the Philharmonic still remains arguably the world's best orchestra (see p.94). In addition, many smaller orchestras play at sites in and around the city, and museums and historic buildings often host chamber concerts and recitals. A major annual music festival is the **Festtage** in early April, which is organized by the Staatsoper, but staged both there and at the Berliner Philharmonie. Also popular is the **Musikfest Berlin** (ⓦ berlinerfestspiele.de), an acclaimed international music festival during the first half of September, when guest orchestras arrive from around the world to take part in a programme that features innovative modern works.

ORCHESTRAS AND VENUES

Berliner Symphoniker ⓦ berliner-symphoniker.de. Founded in 1966, the Berliner Symphoniker used to be East Berlin's main symphony orchestra. Today, it's based in the west of the city, playing at the Philharmonie, and is conducted by Lior Shambadal. Tickets €10–44.

Deutsche Oper Bismarckstr. 35, Charlottenburg ☎ 030 34 38 43 43, ⓦ deutscheoperberlin.de; ⓤ Deutsche Oper; map p.162. This postwar iteration of Berlin's biggest opera house, founded in 1912 and reflecting the ethos of a "democratic" theatre devoid of pomp and plush, was built by Fritz Bornemann in 1961. Excellent visibility and acoustics provide a framework for superb musical and theatrical performances. Tickets €18–170.

Deutsches Symphonie Orchester Berlin ⓦ dso-berlin.de. Under music director Robin Ticciati, the DSO Berlin performs mainly at the Philharmonie but has no permanent base. Tickets €15–61.

Komische Oper Behrenstr. 55–57, Mitte ☎ 030 202 600, ⓦ komische-oper-berlin.de; ⓤ Französische Strasse; map p.36. Less traditional than the Staatsoper, but a reliable venue for well-staged operatic and dance productions. The building doesn't look like much from the outside, but the interior is a wonderful 1890s frenzy of red plush, gilt and statuary and a great place to enjoy cutting-edge interpretations of modern works alongside more traditional shows. Tickets €10–149.

Konzerthaus Berlin Gendarmenmarkt, Mitte ☎ 030 20 30 90, ⓦ konzerthaus.de; ⓤ Stadtmitte; map p.36.

Regarded to be among the best classical concert venues in the world, this super venue often serves visiting musicians, orchestras and ensembles but is also the home of the Konzerthausorchester Berlin. Two concert spaces occupy the Schinkel-designed building (see p.48): the Grosser Konzertsaal for orchestras and its Kammermusiksaal for smaller groups and chamber music. Look out for performances on the famed organ. Tickets €10–99.

★ **Philharmonie** Herbert-von-Karajan-Str. 1, Mitte ☎ 030 25 48 80, ⓦ berlin-philharmonic.de; ⓤ/Ⓢ Potsdamer Platz; map pp.90–91. Home to the world-famous Berlin Philharmonic, Hans Scharoun's distinctive building (see p.94) is acoustically near-perfect. Current conductor Sir Simon Rattle has created his own distinctive sound with the orchestra, broadening the repertoire from its traditional Germanic comfort zone of Brahms and Beethoven with more contemporary music; Kirill Petrenko will take over in 2019. The Philharmonic also contains the smaller, more intimate Kammermusiksaal (Chamber Music Hall). Your best chance of getting a ticket is when guest orchestras are playing, or console yourself watching a live stream on ⓦ digitalconcerthall.com. Tickets €34–138.

Rundfunk Symphonieorchester Berlin ⓦ rsb-online.de. Dating back to 1923, the RSB is the second-oldest orchestra in Berlin after the Philharmonic, and a little more daring than its older sister. The orchestra appears at both the Philharmonie and the Konzerthaus, and, starting in the 2017–2018 season, will be led by

Russian conductor, Vladimir Jurowksi. Tickets €20–59.

Staatsoper Unter den Linden 5–7, Mitte ☎ 030 20 35 45 55, ⓦ staatsoper-berlin.de; ⓤ Französische Strasse; map p.36. The city's oldest and grandest music venue, built for Frederick the Great in 1742 to a design by Knobelsdorff (see p.44). During the GDR years, political isolation meant that performers didn't match the glamour of the venue, but the appointment of Daniel Barenboim in 1992 as musical director gradually helped bring the Staatsoper to the forefront of the international opera scene. The Staatsoper has been performing at the Schiller Theater in west Berlin while the building has been undergoing renovation, due to be completed in 2017. Each summer the venue hosts Staatsoper für Alle, a free open-air classical concert led by Barenboim. Tickets €18–160.

THEATRE

Alongside the mainstream **civic and private theatres**, whose offerings can be too unadventurous and expensive for some tastes (though last-minute tickets can cut costs), is a dynamic **fringe** scene. The thousands of eager young Germans that flock to the city every year, rent a space, and stage their productions, make Berlin a major venue for **experimental work**, and if your German is up to it, a number of such groups are worth the ticket price. The scene is active, though it's worth remembering that many theatre companies take a break in August; check the theatre sections of magazines like *Exberliner*, *Top* or *Zitty* (see p.33) for up-to-the-minute listings. Groups that have the word *Freie* in their name are not dependent on city or state subsidies, and thus are not subject to official regulation or creative constraints.

CIVIC AND PRIVATE THEATRES

Admiralspalast Friedrichstr. 101, Mitte ☎ 01805 20 01, ⓦ mehr.de; ⓤ/Ⓢ Friedrichstrasse; map pp.70–71. The Admiralspalast (see p.83) provides much the same round-the-clock entertainment as it did in its 1920s heyday – though without the brothel it incorporated then. These days it's the eclectic events programme, including comedy, live music, burlesque and operas, plus a casino, that draws in the punters. Tickets €25–78.

Berliner Ensemble Bertolt-Brecht-Platz 1, Mitte ☎ 030 28 40 81 55, ⓦ berliner-ensemble.de; ⓤ/Ⓢ Friedrichstrasse; map pp.70–71. Brecht's old theatre (see p.82) still features a lot of his work (see box, p.86), though thankfully the productions are a little livelier than in GDR days and much of the rest of the programme is given over to a range of reliable pieces by Ibsen, Schiller and the like. There are also occasional experimental productions on the Probebühne (rehearsal stage). Tickets €5–30.

Deutsches Theater Schumannstr. 13, Mitte ☎ 030 28 44 12 25, ⓦ deutschestheater.de; ⓤ Oranienburger Tor; map pp.70–71. Good, solid productions taking in everything from Schiller to Mamet make this one of Berlin's best theatres and frequently sold out. Also includes a second theatre, the Kammerspiele. Tickets €4–48.

Maxim-Gorki-Theater Am Festungsgraben 2, Mitte ☎ 030 20 22 11 15, ⓦ gorki.de; ⓤ/Ⓢ Friedrichstrasse; map p.36. Established in 1952 as a contemporary theatre, the Gorki continues to maintain a critical perspective. Plays – contemporary and new adaptations are the rule – usually revolve around stories of modern-day society and feature multilingual casts. The smaller stage shows even more experimental works. Tickets €10–34.

Renaissance-Theater Knesebeckstr. 100, Charlottenburg ☎ 030 312 42 02, ⓦ renaissance-theater.de; ⓤ Ernst-Reuter-Platz; map pp.90–91. Contemporary international theatre, mainly productions with strong social or emotional themes. Also readings and musical revues. Tickets €10–48.

Schaubühne am Lehniner Platz Kurfürstendamm 153, Wilmersdorf ☎ 030 89 00 23, ⓦ schaubuehne.de; ⓤ Adenauerplatz; map p.162. State-of-the-art theatre that hosts performances of the classics and some experimental pieces, with plenty of young energy and an accent on dance. Advance booking advisable. Tickets €7–48.

Theater des Westens Kantstr. 12, Charlottenburg ☎ 01805 44 44; ⓤ/Ⓢ Zoologischer Garten; map p.108. Musicals and light opera, and the occasional Broadway-style show, sometimes in English. Housed in a beautiful *fin-de-siècle* building. Tickets €40–120.

Theater im Palais Am Festungsgraben, Mitte ☎ 030 201 06 93, ⓦ theater-im-palais.de; ⓤ/Ⓢ Friedrichstrasse; map p.36. Traditional pieces performed with a contemporary spin – conversational delivery, music, storytelling – while preserving theatrical simplicity. Expect pieces by the likes of Fontane, Heine or E.T.A. Hoffmann. Tickets €5–25.

★**Volksbühne am Rosa-Luxemburg-Platz** Linienstr. 227, Mitte ☎ 030 24 06 55, ⓦ volksbuehne-berlin.de; ⓤ Rosa-Luxemburg-Platz; map pp.70–71. Originally founded in 1914, the Volksbühne has since 1992 experienced something of a rebirth under director Frank Castorff (whose tenure finishes in 2017) and is now a leading venue for experimental and political art, pushing far beyond the boundaries of mainstream classic theatre. Tickets €10–36.

EXPERIMENTAL AND FREE THEATRE

BAT Studiotheater Belforter Str. 15, Prenzlauer Berg ☎ 030 755 41 77 77, ⓦ bat-berlin.de; ⓤ Senefelder Platz; map p.136. Originally founded in 1975 for workers and students, this can usually be relied on to come up with challenging experimental offerings. Tickets €10.

FROM TOP A PERFORMANCE OF *PARSIFAL*, STAATSOPER; CHAMÄLEON (P.236) >

15

English Theatre Berlin Fidicinstr. 40, Kreuzberg ☎ 030 691 12 11, ⊛ etberlin.de; Ⓤ Platz der Luftbrücke; map p.118. Theatre, performance, comedy, music and more, all using English as the dominant language. Tickets €8–15.

HAU Hebbel am Ufer Stresemanstr. 29 Kreuzberg ☎ 030 25 90 04 27, ⊛ hebbel-am-ufer.de; Ⓤ Hallesches Tor/Ⓤ Möckenbrücke; map p.118. Spread across three neighbouring locations spanning the Landwehrkanal, this is the place for short runs of varied theatre, performance and dance productions, sometimes in English, often interesting, modern and experimental. The theatre also features a major annual contemporary dance festival in August (see p.27). Tickets €5–30.

★**Schaubude Berlin** Greifswalder Str. 81–84, Prenzlauer Berg ☎ 030 423 43 14, ⊛ schaubude-berlin .de; Ⓢ Greifswalder Strasse or tram #M4; map p.136. Former GDR puppet theatre now presenting weekly changing shows for adults and children – from *Hansel and Gretel* to *Faust* to performances on atomic physics. The kids' programme starts aged 4 and their tickets are €5. Tickets €9.50–12.50.

CABARET

In the 1920s and 1930s, Berlin had a rich and intense **cabaret scene**: hundreds of small clubs presented acts that were often deeply satirical and political. When the Nazis came to power these quickly disappeared, to be replaced by anodyne entertainments in line with Party views. Sadly, the cabaret scene never recovered: most of what's on show today is drag or semi-clad titillation for tourists. However, a few places are worth trying, notably the Friedrichstadt-Palast for mainstream shows and the Chamäleon for more eclectic acts. Be warned, though, that most cabaret venues make their money by charging very high prices at the bar.

CABARET VENUES

Bar Jeder Vernunft Scharperstr. 24, Wilmersdorf ☎ 030 883 15 82, ⊛ bar-jeder-vernunft.de; Ⓤ Spichernstrasse; map p.108. Hip young venue for all manner of modern cabaret and comedy with the occasional chanson act too; a good bet, though a good knowledge of German is often needed. Tickets €12.50–39.

★**Chamäleon** Hackesche Höfe, Rosenthaler Str. 40–41, Mitte ☎ 030 400 05 90, ⊛ chamaeleonberlin .de; Ⓢ Hackescher Markt; map pp.70–71. Lively, innovative cabaret and vaudeville shows with jugglers, acrobats and the like. Seating is around tables and there's a bar, so there's no harm in turning up early. Tickets €36–69.

Friedrichstadt-Palast Friedrichstr. 107, Mitte ☎ 030 23 26 23 26, ⊛ palast.berlin; Ⓤ Oranienburger Tor; map pp.70–71. Big, flashy revue shows with leggy chorus girls and fantastical costumes. Tickets €17–105.

Grüner Salon/Roter Salon Volksbühne, Mitte. Lots of interesting and varied goings on, with occasional performances in English (see p.225).

Kleine Nachtrevue Kurfürstenstr. 116, Schöneberg ☎ 030 218 89 50, ⊛ kleine-nachtrevue.de; Ⓤ Witten bergplatz; map p.114. Berlin burlesque, intimate and dimly lit, going for that 1920s feel; much titillation but pretty hit-or-miss in terms of quality. Tickets €30–35.

La Vie en Rose Flughafen Tempelhof ☎ 030 663 83 88, ⊛ lavieenrose-berlin.de; Ⓤ Platz der Luftbrücke; map p.118. A drag variety revue with lots of glitter and lots of skin, magic and comedy in one of the old Tempelhof airport buildings. There's also a piano bar. Tickets €25–32.

Scheinbar Varieté Monumentenstr. 9, Schöneberg ☎ 030 784 55 39, ⊛ scheinbar.de; Ⓤ Yorckstrasse or Ⓢ Yorckstrasse (Grossgörschenstrasse); map p.114. Experimental and fun; open stage on many nights. Tickets €8.50–10.

Tipi am Kanzleramt Grosse Querallee, Tiergarten ☎ 030 39 06 65 50, ⊛ tipi-am-kanzleramt.de; Ⓤ Bundestag; map pp.90–91. Mixed cabaret performances in a huge permanent tent. The more expensive shows start with gourmet food and then progress to lightweight, but often entertaining galas. Tickets €15–55. Shows Mon–Fri 8pm, Sun 7pm.

Wintergarten Potsdamer Str. 96, Mitte ☎ 030 588 433, ⊛ wintergarten-variete.de; Ⓤ Kurfürstenstrasse; map p.114. Glitzy attempt to re-create the Berlin of the 1920s, with live acts from all over the world – cabaret, musicians, dance, mime, magicians. Meals served while you watch. Tickets €28–65.

DANCE

Apart from those regular venues listed below, expect dance performances to pop up at various theatres, particularly the more experimental ones. You can also see modern ballet and experimental works at the **Komische Oper** (see p.233). HAU Hebbel am Ufer (see above) puts on a major dance festival, **Tanz im August** (⊛ tanzimaugust.de) in summer.

DANCE COMPANIES AND VENUES

★**Sophiensaele** Sophienstr. 18, Mitte ☎ 030 283 52 66, ⊛ sophiensaele.com; Ⓤ Weinmeisterstrasse; map pp.70–71. Experimental and avant-garde dance stronghold in a refurbished 1905 craftsmen's association centre – its programme also incorporates unconventional fringe theatre, music and performance art. Many plays are either in English or non-spoken word. Tickets around €15.

Staatsballett ⊛ staatsballett-berlin.de. Berlin's premier ballet company performs at the Staatsoper,

15

BERLIN FILM FESTIVALS

Every February, the **Berlinale** film festival (⊕ berlinale.de) dominates the city's cultural life. Second only to Cannes among European film festivals, it offers a staggering number of movies from around the world and is much more accessible to the public than the French festival. The programme includes many premieres, usually shown in their original versions with German (sometimes English) subtitles. Action is concentrated around the Potsdamer Platz multiplexes (see below), though many screenings are repeated across the city.

Although the Berlinale dominates the annual calendar, there are several other smaller events worth checking out. These include the **Berlin Independent Film Festival** (BIFF; ⊕ berlinfest .com), also in February; the **Jewish Film Festival** (⊕ jffb.de), held in spring or early summer, and **Berlin Short Film Festival** (⊕ berlinshort.com) in June/July.

Deutsche Oper and Komische Oper Berlin (see p.233). Tickets €12–128.

Tanzfabrik Berlin Möckernstr. 68, Kreuzberg ☎ 030 786 58 61, ⊕ tanzfabrik-berlin.de; ⑤ Yorckstrasse; map p.118. Experimental and contemporary works, usually fresh and exciting. This is also Berlin's biggest contemporary dance school. Tickets up to €13 (sometimes free).

Uferstudios Uferhallen, Uferstr. 8, Gesundbrunnen ☎ 030 46 06 08 87, ⊕ uferstudios.com; ⊕ Pankstrasse; map p.146. Set inside a sprawling complex of spaces that formerly belonged to BVG, Uferstudios is a collaboration between the Hochschulübergreifendes Zentrum Tanz (HZT), an inter-university dance collective, and Tanzfabrik Berlin. It serves as a vibrant local hub for contemporary dance – including events and courses – as well as other artistic disciplines. Tickets free to €25.

FILM

When the all-night drinking starts to get too much, it's always possible to wind down in front of the silver screen. The independent film scene is thriving in Berlin, and art-house cinemas abound. If a film is listed as **OF** or **OV** (*Originalfassung*) it's in its original language; **OmU** (*Originalfassung mit Untertiteln*) indicates that it has German subtitles. Otherwise, the film will have been dubbed into German. Occasionally films are listed as **OmE** – original with English subtitles. The small selection of cinemas below are either particularly strong on screening English-language versions of films or just particularly atmospheric. **Ticket prices** range from €9 to €15, but there are always reductions for children and sometimes for students, too. Also, one day a week, designated *Kinotag* ("KT"), normally a Mon, Tues or Wed, the price is discounted, sometimes halved.

CINEMAS

Babylon Dresdener Str. 126, Kreuzberg ☎ 030 61 60 96 93, ⊕ yorck.de; ⊕ Kottbusser Tor; map pp.128–129. Nestled in East Kreuzberg's lively bar district, Babylon – part of a group of twelve independent and traditional cinemas – shows new indie films in English. Discounts on Mon.

★ **Babylon Mitte** Rosa-Luxemburg-Str. 30, Mitte ☎ 030 242 59 69, ⊕ babylonberlin.de; ⊕ Rosa-Luxemburg-Platz; map pp.70–71. Central Berlin's best rep cinema, housed in a landmark theatre, shows a mix of indie, trash and cult movies and hosts concerts, readings and workshops; films regularly have English subtitles. Every Saturday at midnight you can catch a silent film accompanied by the famed (reconstructed original) in-house organ, free of charge.

CineStar Sony Center Potsdamer Str. 4, Tiergarten ⊕ cinestar.de; ⊕/⑤ Potsdamer Platz; map pp.90–91. Eight-screen cinema in the bowels of the Sony Center, with almost every screening – mostly Hollywood blockbusters – in the original (usually English) language.

Hackesche Höfe Kino Hackesche Höfe, Rosenthalerstr. 40–41, Mitte ☎ 030 283 46 03, ⊕ hoefekino.de; ⑤ Hackescher Markt; map pp.70–71. Five-screen multiplex, on the top floor of the busy Hackesche Höfe, showing upscale independent foreign films and documentaries, some in English, most with subtitles. *Kinotag* Mon & Tues.

Kino Central Hackesche Höfe, Rosenthaler Str. 39, Mitte ☎ 030 28 59 99 73, ⊕ kino-central.de; ⑤ Hackescher Markt; map pp.70–71. A main programme mostly in the OV – usually English with German subtitles – and an English language open-air cinema in the courtyard in summer. *Kinotag* Mon.

Kino International Karl-Marx-Allee 33, Mitte ⊕ kino-international.com; ⊕ Schillingstrasse; map pp.128–129. Big, comfortable GDR cinema showing new releases – of interest in part because of its status as a landmark. *Kinotag* Mon, smaller discounts Tues & Wed.

Odeon Hauptstr. 116, Schöneberg ☎ 030 78 70 40 19, ⊕ yorck.de; ⊕/⑤ Innsbrucker Platz; map p.114. If you're after the more intelligent English-language releases, the Odeon – another in the Yorck group – will often have them first. *Kinotag* Mon, smaller discounts Tues & Wed.

★ **Zeughauskino** Unter den Linden 2, Mitte ☎ 030 20 30 44 21, ⊕ zeughauskino.de; ⑤ Hackescher Markt; map p.36. Cinema in the Zeughaus (see p.45), which often unearths fascinating films from the pre- and postwar years.

15

Shopping

In addition to the usual malls and department stores that you can find all around Europe, Berlin has many small, interesting shops that are perfect for browsing. A remarkable number of quirky specialist stores are thriving; we've reviewed some of the more interesting and distinctive places. As a rule the level of customer service is excellent – and if a shop can't supply you with what you need the assistants will not hesitate to suggest alternatives. The city is also an excellent place for secondhand shopping: if you like foraging you'll love the Berlin's many flea markets and its interesting vintage clothes shops. Note that shops are closed on Sundays, with the exception of a handful of "special" shopping days each year; dates can be found on ⓦvisitberlin.de.

Glitz and dazzle have traditionally been the preserves of **City West**, with its 3km of large chain stores on or around the **Kurfürstendamm**, while **Friedrichstrasse** is more modest in size but also lined with plenty of opulent stores. The largest and best central **malls** are the new Mall of Berlin on Leipziger Platz and Bikini Berlin mall in City West, alongside the Alexa Centre, just southeast of Alexanderplatz. Meanwhile, many of the city's funkiest speciality shops and expensive boutiques are concentrated in **Charlottenburg**, **Mitte** and **Prenzlauer Berg**, and more independent stores can be found around **Kreuzberg**, **Friedrichshain** and **Neukölln**.

BOOKS AND MAGAZINES

Berlin boasts a great variety of new and secondhand bookstores – several of them either entirely or partly specializing in English-language tomes – and it's an ideal city for leisurely browsing. Children's bookshops are covered under "Kids" (see p.246).

ENGLISH-LANGUAGE AND GENERAL

Another Country Riemannstr. 7, Kreuzberg ☎ 030 69 40 11 60, ⓦanothercountry.de; ⓤGneisenaustrasse; map p.118. English-language secondhand books sold in an intimate living-room-like space, where you can borrow any book for €1.50. Mon 2–8pm, Tues–Fri 11am–8pm, Sat & Sun noon–6pm.

★**Dussmann** Friedrichstr. 90, Mitte ☎ 030 20 25 11 11, ⓦkulturkaufhaus.de; ⓤ/ⓢFriedrichstrasse; map p.36. Giant emporium with five levels of books, CDs (see p.247) and … more books. A small shop at the back also features sheet music. Mon–Fri 9am–midnight, Sat 9am–11.30pm.

Marga Schoeller Knesebeckstr. 33, City West ☎ 030 881 11 12, ⓦmargaschoeller.de; ⓢSavignyplatz; map p.108. Opened in 1929 by Frau Schoeller, this bookshop is one of the longest running in Europe, and was once a focal point for West Berlin's postwar literary scene. The shop continues to sell a fantastic range of German- and English-language books on the arts as well as fiction, history and biographies, with lots on Berlin. Mon–Wed 9.30am–7pm, Thurs & Fri 9.30am–8pm, Sat 9.30am–6pm.

Saint George's Bookshop Wörther Str. 27, Prenzlauer Berg ☎ 030 81 79 83 33, ⓦsaintgeorgesbookshop.com; ⓤEberswalder Strasse; map p.136. One of the most popular British-run bookstore in the city, Saint George's sells a fine selection of new and used English-language books. There's a sofa to chill on and free wi-fi; they also buy used books. Mon–Fri 11am–8pm, Sat 11am–7pm.

Shakespeare & Sons Warschauer Str. 74, Friedrichshain ⓦshakesbooks.de; ⓤFrankfurter Tor; map pp.128–129. This bright, open space is one of the city's biggest English-language bookshops, offering around 15,000 titles (including many French volumes) on all topics, with free wi-fi and an associated bagel shop. Conveniently located close to Warschauer Strasse station. Mon–Sat 9am–8pm, Sun 10am–8pm.

LOCAL INTEREST

Berlin Story Unter den Linden 40, Mitte ☎ 030 20 45 38 42, ⓦberlinstory.de; ⓤ/ⓢFriedrichstrasse; map p.36.

The city's most extensive bookshop on Berlin itself, with everything from travel guides to specialist histories, and offered in a range of languages. Daily 10am–6pm.

THE ARTS

Bücherbogen Stadtbahnbogen 593, City West ☎ 030 31 86 95 11, ⓦbuecherbogen.com; ⓢSavignyplatz; map p.108. Airy and spacious spot under the S-arches where you can spend hours browsing books on art, architecture, film and photography. Plenty of English-language books – all non-fiction. Mon–Fri 10am–8pm, Sat 10am–7pm.

★**Gestalten Space** Budapester Str. 38–50, City West ☎ 030 26 55 88 23, ⓦgestalten.com; ⓤ/ⓢZoologischer Garten; map p.108. This slick wood-and-concrete publisher-run bookshop can be found on the rooftop of the Bikini Berlin mall (see p.242). Its designer shelves and tables are full of beautifully crafted tomes on art, design, architecture, food and more, and there's an equally smart café on site too. Mon–Sat 10am–8pm.

Onkel & Onkel Oranienstr. 195, Kreuzberg ☎ 030 61 07 39 57, ⓦonkelundonkel.com; ⓤKottbusser Tor; map pp.128–129. This magazine shop specializes in graphic design, photography and street art, and also publishes its own titles. Tues–Sat noon–7pm.

★**Overkillshop** Köpenicker Str. 195a, Kreuzberg ☎ 030 61 07 66 33, ⓦoverkillshop.com; ⓤSchlesisches Tor; map pp.128–129. An essential spot for sneaker and streetwear fans – as well as street art aficionados – with a huge variety of graffiti-related books and magazines along with all the paraphernalia you need to make your mark. A second shop next door (no. 194) sells sneakers and urban accessories specifically for women and kids. Both shops Mon–Sat 11am–8pm.

Pro QM Almstadtstr. 48, Mitte ☎ 030 24 72 85 20, ⓦpro-qm.de; ⓤRosa-Luxemburg-Strasse; map pp.70–71. Run by an artist and an architecture professor couple, this smart and surprisingly spacious store specializes in books and magazines dedicated to these subjects, as well as design and craft, and spans lifestyle as well as academic publications. Mon–Sat 11am–8pm.

16

MAGAZINES AND COMICS

★do you read me?! Auguststr. 28, Mitte ☎ 030 69 54 96 95, ⓦdoyoureadme.de; ⓢRosenthaler Platz; map pp.70–71. A magazine lover's paradise, this multilingual store offers a vast assortment of reading material from around the world, covering fashion, art, culture, literature, photography and architecture. Check the website for regular news updates and occasional events. Mon–Sat 10am–7.30pm.

Grober Unfug Torstr. 75, Mitte ☎ 030 28 17 331, ⓦgroberunfug.de; ⓤRosa-Luxemburg-Platz; map pp.70–71. Large display of international comics, plus T-shirts and cards on sale. Mon–Fri 11am–7pm, Sat 11am–6pm.

TRAVEL

Chatwins Goltzstr. 40, Schöneberg ☎ 030 21 75 69 04, ⓦchatwins.de; ⓤEisenacher Strasse; map p.114. Friendly bookshop run for and by travellers, with a vast array of guidebooks and travel writing. Mon–Fri 10am–7pm, Sat 10am–4pm.

Schropp Hardenbergstr. 9a, City West ☎ 030 23 55 73 20, ⓦlandkartenschropp.de; ⓤ/ⓢZoologischer Garten; map p.108. Specialist store – in operation since 1742 – with a large, well-chosen selection of travel books and maps, including detailed cycling maps of Berlin and Germany. Mon–Fri 10am–8pm, Sat 10am–6pm.

CLOTHING AND ACCESSORIES

Although they like to think of themselves as such, Berliners aren't exactly trendsetters, and despite the many innovative designers in the city their work is mostly small-scale and tends to lack international impact. Still, it's possible to pick up bargains at the many **secondhand** clothes stores: you'll find unusual (and stylish) pieces here at low prices. Ku'damm and Friedrichstrasse boast **designer** clothes shops targeting the rich and conservative, as well as several leather outlets with cheap but good-quality jackets, and some excellent shoe shops. For the most cutting-edge boutiques head to the Alte Schönhauser Strasse and its offshoot streets, where **urban and haute-couture** styles dominate.

16

ACCESSORIES AND UNDERWEAR

Fiona Bennett Potsdamer Str. 81–83, Schöneberg ☎ 030 28 09 63 30, ⓦfionabennett.com; ⓤKurfürstenstrasse; map p.114. Avant-garde designer hats for men and women. Mon–Wed 10am–6pm, Thurs & Fri noon–8pm, Sat noon–6pm.

Freitag Store Berlin Max-Beer-Str. 3, Mitte ☎ 030 24 63 69 61, ⓦfreitag.ch; ⓤWeinmeisterstrasse; map pp.70–71. Swiss merchant of bags and accessories all made from old truck tarps. Each is unique and their fatigued, reused look feels very at home in Berlin. Also stocks clothing made of flax and hemp fibres. Mon–Fri 11am–8pm, Sat 11am–7pm.

ic! Berlin Max-Beer-Str. 17, Mitte ☎ 030 247 27 200, ⓦic-berlin.de; ⓤWeinmeisterstrasse; map pp.70–71. Internationally famous spectacles thanks to the wonderful designs of the handmade screwless frames, worn by a wide range of celebs from Tom Cruise to Shakira. Vintage styles also available. Pricey. Mon–Thurs 11am–3.30pm & 4–8pm, Fri & Sat 11am–8pm.

Körpernah Uhlandstr. 39, City West ☎ 030 21 00 50 90, ⓦkoerpernah-berlin.de; ⓤUhlandstrasse; map p.108. Fashionable underwear and lingerie for both sexes spread over two floors. A range of sizes and styles available here and in their other stores in Schöneberg (Maassenstr. 8) and Zehlendorf (Teltower Damm 43–45). City West store: Mon–Fri 10am–7pm. Sat 10am–4pm.

Michaela Binder Gipsstr. 13, Mitte ☎ 030 28 38 48 69, ⓦmichaelabinder.de; ⓤWeinmeisterstrasse; map pp.70–71. Smart shop stocking Binder's stylish rings, bracelets, ear studs and necklaces in clean, basic shapes, from silver and gold. There's also a line of (cheaper) steel

and stone vases. Tues–Fri noon–7pm, Sat noon–4pm.

Mykita Rosa-Luxemburg-Str. 6, Mitte ☎ 030 67 30 87 15, ⓦmykita.com; ⓤ/ⓢAlexanderplatz; map pp.70–71. Berlin-based company that has achieved international fame due to the stylish twists of its sunglasses and spectacles. Mon–Fri 11am–8pm, Sat 11am–6pm.

Rio Bleibtreustr. 52, City West ☎ 030 313 31 52, ⓦrio-modeschmuck-berlin.de; ⓢSavignyplatz; map p.108. Decorative costume jewellery, with lots of unusual offerings from Paris, as well as their own line, named "after 5pm" for its natural eveningwear flamboyance and glamour. Also specializes in affordable earrings. Mon–Wed & Fri 11am–6.30pm, Thurs 11am–7pm, Sat 11am–6pm.

FASHION

Allet Rund Dresdener Str. 16, Kreuzberg ☎ 030 27 01 48 36, ⓦalletrund.de; ⓤKottbusser Tor; map pp.128–129. Women's fashion for larger sizes (42–60). Everything is fair trade; the fabrics are European and the clothes are made in Kreuzberg. Mon–Fri noon–7pm, Sat noon–5pm.

Andreas Murkudis Potsdamer Str. 81e, Schöneberg ☎ 030 68 07 98 305, ⓦandreasmurkudis.com; ⓤKurfürstenstrasse, map p.114. Vast designer store with an idiosyncratic array of high-end design and fashion items curated by fashion designer Murkudis. Alongside his own creations you can find everything from Valextra briefcases to clothing by Dries van Noten plus contemporary furniture, accessories and homeware. Mon–Sat 10am–8pm.

Apartment Memhardstr. 8, Mitte ☎ 030 28 04 22 51, ⓦapartmentberlin.de; ⓤ/ⓢAlexanderplatz; map pp.70–71. You'll have to be careful not to walk right past what looks like an all-white art space: the goods lie downstairs (follow the spiral staircase), where you'll find jeans, jackets, shoes and accessories with a distinctly Berlin twist. Mon–Fri 2–7pm, Sat 2–6pm.

Claudia Skoda Mulackstr. 8, Mitte ☏ 030 40 04 18 84, ⓦ claudiaskoda.com; ⓞ Weinmeisterstrasse; map pp.70–71. Berlin's knit-master and most famous designer, whose shop is filled with her renowned and instantly recognizable knitwear. Chic and expensive and geared mostly towards women. Mon, Tues, Fri & Sat 12.30–6.30pm; Wed by appointment.

Core Tex Selector Oranienstr. 195, Kreuzberg ☏ 030 37 44 88 72, ⓦ coretexrecords.com; ⓞ Görlitzer Bahnhof; map pp.128–129. New store a few doors down from Core Tex Records (see p.247), which is dedicated to British clothing labels like Dr. Martens, Fred Perry and Brixton. Mon–Fri noon–7pm, Sat noon–6pm.

Das Neue Schwarz Mulackstr. 38, Mitte ☏ 030 27 87 44 67, ⓦ www.dasneueschwarz.de; ⓞ Weinmeisterstrasse; map pp.70–71. "The New Black" is a handsome boutique store that stocks innovative garments for men and women, often from previous seasons to keep the prices down. Stock is always changing but expect handbags and shoes, suits and jackets from top designer brands. Mon–Sat noon–8pm.

Eisdieler Kastanienallee 12, Prenzlauer Berg ☏ 030 28 38 12 91, ⓦ eisdieler.de; ⓞ Eberswalder Strasse; map p.136. Urban fashion design for men – clothing and accessories – including brands like Qwstion, Onitsuka Tiger, Spring Court and Schmoove. A nice selection of vintage sunglasses from the likes of Le Specs too. Mon–Fri noon–8pm, Sat 11am–7pm.

Esther Perbandt Almstadtstr. 3, Mitte ☏ 030 88 53 67 91, ⓦ estherperbandt.com; ⓞ Weinmeisterstrasse; map pp.70–71. The Berlin fashion scene veteran specializes in pricey avant-garde and androgynous clothing, complemented by bags, belts, jewellery and more. Mon–Fri 10am–7pm, Sat noon–6pm.

★Flagshipstore Oderberger Str. 53, Prenzlauer Berg ☏ 030 43 73 53 27, ⓦ flagshipstore-berlin.de; ⓞ Eberswalder Strasse; map p.136. Great one-stop shop to explore the urban collections of some thirty local designers with a vast range of clothing and accessories (for women and men), all with an ethical emphasis. Mon–Sat noon–8pm.

God Bless You Kastanienallee 31, Prenzlauer Berg ☏ 030 29 66 68 80, ⓦ god-bless-you.be; ⓞ Eberswalder Strasse; map p.136. Quirky dressers will adore this store, which stocks unusual street designs for men and women as well as iron-on patches (guitars, grenades) so you can customize your own clothing. Mon–Sat 11am–8pm.

Herz + Stöhr Winterfeldtstr. 52, Schöneberg ☏ 030 216 44 25, ⓦ herz-stoehr.de; ⓞ Nollendorfplatz; map p.114. Intelligent, elegant designs from this German fashion duo – the dresses and suits are grown-up but not dowdy, and everything can be altered to fit. Mon–Fri 11am–7pm, Sat 11am–4pm.

Mientus Wilmersdorfer Str. 73, Charlottenburg ⓞ Adenauer Platz, map p.162; Kurfürstendamm 52, City West ⓢ Savignyplatz, map p.108; ☏ 030 323 90 77, ⓦ mientus.com. Casual and formal up-to-the-minute mens- and womenswear, ranging in price from reasonable to outrageously expensive. Wilmersdorfer Strasse is the flagship store; Kurfürstendamm only stocks menswear. Mon–Sat 10am–7pm.

Nix Oranienburger Str. 32, Mitte ☏ 030 281 11 80 44, ⓦ nix.de; ⓢ Oranienburger Strasse; map pp.70–71. Urban, feminine, functional and sustainable designs for women. Mon–Sat 11am–8pm.

Respectmen Neue Schönhauser Str. 14, Mitte ☏ 030 283 50 10, ⓦ respectmen.de; ⓞ Weinmeisterstrasse; map pp.70–71. Good tailoring and nice design mark out the suits and casual wear of this men's store. Mon–Fri noon–8pm, Sat noon–7pm.

Soma Alte Schönhauser Str. 27, Mitte ☏ 030 281 93 80, ⓦ soma-berlin.de; ⓞ Weinmeisterstrasse; map pp.70–71. Cool labels like numph and King Louie, plus an impressive range of accessories. Mon–Sat noon–8pm.

Thatchers Kastanienallee 21, Prenzlauer Berg ☏ 030 24 62 77 51, ⓦ thatchers.de; ⓞ Eberswalder Strasse; map p.136. Upmarket fashion store for women who like their clothes classy and sexy but not over the top. Perfect place for sensual evening dresses, sophisticated club wear and nowadays also a few refined gifts. Mon–Sat 11am–7pm.

Trüffelschwein Rosa-Luxemburg-Str. 21, Mitte ☏ 030 70 22 12 25, ⓦ trueffelschweinberlin.com; ⓞ Rosa-Luxemburg-Platz; map pp.70–71. This mid- to high-end men's shop has a wide range of dapper clothing, including smart-casual jumpers and tees to more formal – but always slick – shirts and suits. Labels include Universal Works, Folk, Howlin' and Superga. Mon–Fri noon–6pm, Sat noon–7pm.

Voo Store Oranienstr. 24, Kreuzberg ☏ 030 69 57 97 27 10, ⓦ vooberlin.com; ⓞ Kottbusser Tor; map pp.128–129. Another of the city's key concept stores, Voo is tucked away in a Kreuzberg courtyard. Mixing up clothing and goods from both local and international designers, all set out within an industrial interior, it's the place to find boutique labels like Acne Studios and Kenzo, upscale Berlin-themed knick-knacks and – in the connected café – top-notch third-wave coffee. Mon–Sat 10am–8pm.

SHOES

Luccico Bergmannstr. 8, Kreuzberg ☏ 030 69 13 257, ⓦ luccico.de; ⓞ Mehringdamm; map p.118. Wild and wacky Italian shoes, plus plainer varieties. Four other Berlin locations, including Oranienburger Str. 23. All stores: Mon–Sat noon–8pm.

16

★**Trippen** Hackeschen Höfe IV & VI, Rosenthaler Str. 40–41, Mitte ☎030 28 39 13 37, ⓦtrippen.com; ⓈHackescher Markt; map pp.70–71. Hot Berlin design company specializing in wooden-soled shoes with a rounded toe, but selling men's and women's shoes for every occasion in a range of materials. This is the flagship store, with several other branches in the city. Footwear can be made to order. Mon–Fri 11am–8pm, Sat 10am–8pm.

VINTAGE
Colours Bergmannstr. 102, Kreuzberg ☎030 694 33 48, ⓦkleidermarkt.de; ⓤMehringdamm; map p.118. A retro fan's paradise with secondhand clothes spanning the 1960s to 1980s, but particularly good on the 1970s, as well as new designs. Mon–Fri 11am–8pm, Sat 10am–4pm.
Garage Ahornstr. 2, Schöneberg ☎030 211 27 60, ⓦkleidermarkt.de; ⓤNollendorfplatz; map p.114. The largest secondhand clothes store in Europe – good for jackets, coats and jeans. You pay according to weight (the clothes', not yours), with a 30 percent discount offered Wed 11am–1pm. Mon–Fri 11am–7pm, Sat 11am–6pm.
Humana Frankfurter Tor 3, Friedrichshain ☎030 422 20 18, ⓦhumana-second-hand.de; ⓤFrankfurter Tor; map pp.128–129. Gigantic branch of a local secondhand chain that has a dozen stores in Berlin, offers great bargains on items that are (back) in style. Mon–Sat 10am–8pm.

Jumbo Second Hand Wiener Str. 63, Kreuzberg ☎030 218 96 60; ⓤGörlitzer Bahnhof; map pp.128–129. A bewildering amount of clothes, from dresses to bags, sunglasses and more. Can be a little overpriced and it's worth trying to bargain. Mon–Sat 10am–8pm.
Made in Berlin Neue Schönhauser Str. 19, Mitte ☎030 21 23 06 01, ⓦkleidermarkt.de; ⓤWeinmeisterstrasse; map pp.70–71. One of four shops in the city that sell cutting-edge, mostly vintage clothes for girls and boys. You'll find everything from hats and shoes to blouses and faintly bizarre appendages. Tues noon till 3pm is happy hour (20 percent off all vintage). Mon–Sat noon–8pm.
★**ReSales** Potsdamer Str. 105, Schöneberg ⓦresales-shop.de; ⓤKurfürstenstrasse; map p.114. This north German chain of secondhand stores has half a dozen branches in central Berlin, each with a vast array of garments that range from hip streetwear to glamorous, silky evening dresses. All tend to be fairly priced, too. Mon–Fri 9.30am–7pm, Sat 9.30am–4pm.
Secondo Mommsenstr. 61, City West ☎030 881 22 91, ⓦsecondoberlin.de; ⓈSavignyplatz; map p.108. Exclusively designer clothes at massively knocked down prices: most items are in top condition, though of course many designs are a bit dated – which is half the fun for vintage nuts. You'll find a number of similar shops further up and down the street. Mon–Fri noon–6.30pm, Sat noon–3.30pm.

DEPARTMENT STORES AND MALLS

Several glossy new **malls** have opened up in recent years; Bikini Berlin and Mall of Berlin have the trendiest selection of stores, while the longer-established Stilwerk is a classy place for interior furnishings. There are few surprises inside most of Berlin's **department stores**; KaDeWe, Quartier 206 and Galeries Lafayette are the best for luxury items, or even just for a browse.

DEPARTMENT STORES
Galeries Lafayette Friedrichstr. 76, Mitte ☎030 20 94 80, ⓦlafayette-berlin.de; ⓤFranzösische Strasse; map p.36. Branch of the upscale Paris-based department store. Surprisingly small, but packed with beautiful and expensive things and including a food department with French imports. Mon–Sat 10am–8pm.
★**KaDeWe** Tauentzienstr. 21, Schöneberg ☎030 212 10, ⓦkadewe.de; ⓤWittenbergplatz; map p.108. Content rather than flashy interior decor rules the day here. From surprisingly well-priced designer labels to the extraordinary displays at the international delicatessen, where you can nibble on exotica, there's everything the consumer's heart desires at this, the largest department store on the continent. Mon–Thurs & Sat 10am–8pm, Fri 10am–9pm.
Karstadt Kurfürstendamm 231, City West ☎030 88 00 30, ⓦkarstadt.de; ⓤKurfürstendamm; map p.108. A smaller and cheaper version of KaDeWe. Everything is nicely laid out, and there's a good menswear department. Other branches dotted around Berlin. Mon–Sat 10am–8pm.

MALLS
Alexa Centre Grunerstr. 20, Mitte ☎030 269 34 01 21, ⓦalexacentre.com; ⓤ/ⓈAlexanderplatz; map p.60. Opened in 2007, this five-floor fuschia mall might often be regarded as one of central Berlin's ugliest modern buildings, but its 180 shops (boutiques to books, electronics to toys) and diverse food court remain perennially popular. There's also a Kindercity play area for kids and the Loxx Berlin Miniature World is on the fourth floor (see p.60). Mon–Sat 10am–9pm.
Bikini Berlin Budapester Str. 44, City West ☎030 55 49 64 54, ⓦbikiniberlin.de; ⓤ/ⓈZoologischer Garten; map p.108. One of the biggest recent retail developments to hit West Berlin, this good-looking concept mall – which occupies the original 1950s Bikini building – has a slew of stores and flagships, from local designers like hip Berlin glasswear company Mykita to bigger brands like Kusmi Tea. There are also pop-ups and a few neat spaces to enjoy coffee and snacks. Mon–Sat 10am–8pm.
Mall of Berlin Leipziger Platz 12, Mitte ☎030 20 62 17 70, ⓦmallofberlin.de; ⓤMohrenstrasse; map

pp.90–91. Opened in 2014, this sprawling design mall has 270 outlets that range from stylish stores like Karl Lagerfeld and Peek & Cloppenburg to high-street retailers like H&M and Zara. As well as fashion you can find an abundant choice of food, electronics, toys and household goods. Mon–Sat 10am–9pm.

Potsdamer Platz Arkaden Alte Potsdamer Str. 7, Tiergarten ☎030 255 92 70, ⊕potsdamerplatz.de; ⊕/ ⊕ Potsdamer Platz; map pp.90–91. This modern, glass-roofed shopping arcade – part of the Sony Center – was one of the first modern malls to open in Berlin, back in 1998. It's as popular as ever, with over 130 shops that offer a broad range of goods from high street to niche fashion, as well as a number of fast-food outlets, the Cinemaxx complex and a casino. Mon–Sat 10am–9pm.

Quartier 206 Friedrichstr. 71, Mitte ☎030 20 94 65 00, ⊕q206berlin.de; ⊕Stadtmitte; map p.36. Unapologetically posh department store with flagships for the likes of Etro, Bally and Moschino, all set in a lavish, Art Deco-inspired interior. Mon–Fri 10.30am–7.30pm, Sat 10am–6pm.

Stilwerk Kantstr. 17, City West ☎030 31 51 50, ⊕stilwerk.de; ⊕Savignyplatz; map p.108. Swanky designer mall, located near Zoologischer Garten, featuring shops dedicated to home decoration, including top-quality furniture, and jewellery. Expect high-end stores like Bang & Olufsen, with one or two cheaper options as well. There's a café and even a babysitting service on Sat. Mon–Sat 10am–7pm.

ELECTRONICS, RADIOS AND RECORD PLAYERS

Media Markt Grunerstr. 20, Mitte ☎030 263 99 70, ⊕mediamarkt.de; ⊕/⊕Alexanderplatz; map p.60. Located inside the Alexa shopping mall, this electrical superstore has phones, cameras, iPads, computers and the like. This is the most central of sixteen Berlin branches. Mon–Sat 10am–9pm.

Radio Art Zossener Str. 2, Kreuzberg ☎030 693 94 35, ⊕radio-art.de; ⊕Gneisenaustrasse; map p.118. Fantastic and visually satisfying shop for radio fans, musos and lovers of nostalgia, with shelves brimming with vintage (and some modern) radio sets and record players. Thurs & Fri noon–6pm, Sat 10am–1pm.

FOOD AND DRINK

COFFEE, TEA AND CHOCOLATE

Barcomi's Bergmannstr. 21, Kreuzberg ☎030 28 59 83 63, ⊕barcomis.de; ⊕Gneisenaustrasse; map p.118. Good selection of top-notch, house-roasted coffee, including organic and caffeine-free varieties. Mon–Sat 8am–9pm, Sun 9am–9pm.

Leysieffer Kurfürstendamm 218, City West ☎030 885 74 80, ⊕leysieffer.de; ⊕Uhlandstrasse; map p.108. This Ku'damm branch of the famed German chocolaterie does a brisk trade. Aside from the usual sweet goodies, there's also a small coffee bar. Mon–Fri 9am–7pm, Sat 10am–5pm.

Paper & Tea (P & T) Bleibtreustr. 4, City West ☎030 55 57 98 080, ⊕paperandtea.com; ⊕Savignyplatz; map p.108. A Zen-style breath of fresh air in a city obsessed with coffee, this minimal and chic teahouse feels as much like a museum as a shop, with its gorgeously curated goods laid out on trays with detailed notes. Related accessories and gifts also available. Mon–Sat 11am–8pm.

Tchibo Alexanderhaus, Alexanderplatz 2, Mitte ☎030 24 72 06 96, ⊕tchibo.de; ⊕Alexanderplatz; map p.60. The city's most popular stand-up coffee place with good-quality beans and the chance to mix your own blend from a small choice at the counter. Many other branches. Mon–Sat 9am–8pm.

DELIS

Alimentari e Vini Skalitzer Str. 23, Kreuzberg ☎030 611 49 81, ⊕alimentari.de; ⊕Kottbusser Tor; map pp.128–129. A slick shop in scruffy Kreuzberg offering wines, pastas and other Italian deli items. A second branch is in the Marheineke Markthalle (see below). Mon–Fri 9am–8pm, Sat 9am–4pm.

Goldhahn und Sampson Dunckerstr. 9, Prenzlauer Berg ⊕goldhahnundsampson.de; ⊕Eberswalder Strasse; map p.136. Foodies' paradise selling herbs, spices and other tasty delicacies from all over the world, plus cookbooks and kitchen utensils. Regular wine tasting and cooking courses. Mon–Fri 8am–8pm, Sat 9am–8pm.

FOOD MARKETS

Marheineke Markthalle Marheinekeplatz 15, Kreuzberg ☎030 398 96 10, ⊕meine-markthalle.de; ⊕Gneisenaustrasse; map p.118. While not as famous as the trendy Markthalle Neun (see below), this covered market hall is still an excellent – and very popular – place for grocery shopping, as well as breakfast and lunch. Many of the meat, fish and veg stalls have an emphasis on regional products, but you'll also find crêpes, tapas and Italian coffee, as well as much organic produce. Regular art exhibitions and events. Mon–Fri 8am–8pm, Sat 8am–6pm.

Markthalle Neun Eisenbahnstr. 42–43, Kreuzberg ☎030 61 07 34 73, ⊕markthalleneun.de; ⊕Görlitzer Bahnhof; map pp.128–129. One of the city's most popular revitalized covered market halls, this Kreuzberg institution offers a comprehensive farmers' market on Fridays and Saturdays (smaller Tues–Thurs), a buzzy street

16

food market on Thursdays (5–10pm) and other regular and one-off food-related events from breakfast to sweet markets. There are also several permanent coffee and eating spots so it's worth dropping by at any time (except Sun). Main market Tues–Fri noon–6pm, Sat 10am–6pm.

Ökomarkt am Kollwitzplatz Kollwitzplatz, Prenzlauer Berg ☎030 44 33 91 37; map p.136. In keeping with Prenzlberg's middle-class leanings, this atmospheric Saturday market has an emphasis on all things organic and *bio*. As well as the usual meat, fish and vegetable traders from nearby farms, there are also lots of local sellers hawking everything from freshly made pasta to cured meats and several food stalls offering juices, *gözleme* (Turkish flatbread), *falafel* and *Fischbrötchen*. A smaller version of the market takes place on Thursdays. Thurs noon–7pm, Sat 9am–4pm.

Türkischer Markt Kottbusser Damm/Maybachufer, Neukölln; ⓤ Kottbusser Tor; map pp.128–129. Definitely worth a visit, especially on Fri. Handy for all things Turkish, especially cheese, bread, olives and dried fruits, all at rock-bottom prices. Tues & Fri noon–6pm.

Wochenmarkt Boxhagener Platz Boxhagener Platz, Friedrichshain ☎01784 762242, ⓦ boxhagenerplatz .org; ⓤ Frankfurter Tor; map pp.128–128. This buzzy Saturday food market has abundant fruit and veg stalls supplemented with boutique stalls selling everything from fresh, delicious bruschetta to home-made sauces and jams. There's plenty of takeaway food too, including Turkish delicacies, freshly grilled fish and more. Sat 9am–3.30pm.

Wochenmarkt Winterfeldtplatz Winterfeldtplatz, Schöneberg; ⓤ Nollendorfplatz; map p.114. Operating every Saturday since 1990, this much-loved weekly market offers scores of stalls selling not only meat, fish, fruit and veg, but also clothes and flowers. Sat 8am–4pm.

HEALTH FOOD

Einhorn Mommsenstr. 2, City West ☎030 88 14 241, ⓦ einhornonline.de; ⓤ Uhlandstrasse; map p.108. Excellent wholegrain breads and cakes, baked in-house, at this popular veggie caff (see p.203). Mon–Fri 10am–5pm.

LPG BioMarkt Kollwitzstr. 17, Prenzlauer Berg ☎030 322 97 14 00, ⓦ lpg-naturkost.de; ⓤ Senefelderplatz; map p.136. Europe's largest organic supermarket with a staggering 18,000 products, many from the countryside around Berlin, plus a great in-house bakery. There are another five branches in central Berlin. Mon–Sat 9am–9pm.

WINES AND SPIRITS

Absinth Depot Weinmeisterstr. 4, Mitte ☎030 281 67 89, ⓦ erstesabsinthdepotberlin.de; ⓤ Weinmeisterstrasse; map pp.70–71. All kinds of "Green Fairy" liquor but also a wide variety of props for the true absinthe experience. You can even have a little taste. Mon–Fri 2pm–midnight, Sat 1pm–midnight.

Weinkeller Blücherstr. 22, Kreuzberg ☎030 693 46 61, ⓦ weinkeller-berlin.de; ⓤ Gneisenaustrasse; map p.118. A good selection of Spanish, French, Italian and German wines, plus sherries and whiskies from the cask. Tues–Fri 2–8pm, Sat 11am–4pm.

16

BERLIN FOR FOODIES

Berliners love their **food**. Not only is the variety on offer extremely good: the quality is high and prices reasonable. The key player at the top end is the food court on the sixth floor of the luxurious **KaDeWe** department store (see p.242) where a mind-boggling array of gourmet delights arrive daily from around the world. You can choose from 400 types of bread, 1200 cheeses and 1400 meats, never mind the bewildering number of cakes and confectionery. But probably its best feature is its many counters where you can sample freshly prepared goodies. **Galeries Lafayette** (see p.242) also has a good gourmet food section with delectables from around the world

One of the city's greatest passions is locally sourced **organic** food, as evidenced by the success here of Europe's largest organic supermarket, the **LPG BioMarkt** (see above), along with the health-food shops (*Naturkostläden*) with their vegetarian goodies, that thrive in almost every neighbourhood. In some ways the success of these places is surprising given Berlin's terrific covered and open-air **food markets** (see opposite), some of which have been selling well-priced, good-quality fruit, veg and local produce for decades.

Also not to be missed are the small neighbourhood **bakeries** scattered throughout the city: wholemeal bread, multigrain rolls and simple cakes fresh from the oven are real foodie delights. Of the city's **supermarkets** Pennymarkt, Netto, Lidl, Aldi and Plus are by far the cheapest, although they offer limited choice; Kaiser's and REWE are more expensive but better quality and more comprehensive (many have in-store fish and meat counters). **Ullrich**, on Hardenbergstrasse, underneath the railway bridge by Zoo Station, has an excellent selection of foods, wines and spirits, keeps long hours and is cheap despite its central location. **Speciality food shops** are spread throughout the city, with an extra emphasis on Vietnamese stores in Prenzlauer Berg and Turkish and Middle Eastern foods most readily available in Kreuzberg and Neukölln.

HOMEWARE

Hallesches Haus Tempelhofer Ufer 1, Kreuzberg ⓦhallescheshaus.com; ⓤHallesches Tor; map p.118. Set in an attractive red-brick post office, this chic, multi-faceted space combines a smart café, flower shop and a design and furniture store. A great spot for home decor (lamps, tables) as well as quirky and interesting gifts, often made by local companies. Mon–Fri 9am–7pm, Sat 11am–4pm.

KIDS

There's a fair but not overwhelming selection of **children's shops** in Berlin, with an emphasis on wooden toys, ecological themes and multicultural education.

Anagramm Mehringdamm 50, Kreuzberg ☎030 785 95 10, ⓦanagramm-buch.de; ⓤMehringdamm; map p.118. Neighbourhood bookshop with an excellent children's section and a reading corner. Mon–Fri 9am–7pm, Sat 10am–4pm.

Flying Colors Eisenacher Str. 81, Schöneberg ☎030 78 70 36 36, ⓦflying-colors.de; ⓤEisenacher Strasse; map p.114. Suberb kite shop – the place to come before heading off to the Tempelhofer Park. Mon–Fri 11am–7pm, Sat 11am–5pm.

Levy's Contor Hackesche Höfe VII, Rosenthaler Str. 40–41, Mitte ☎030 280 82 03, ⓦlevyscontor.de; ⓢHackescher Markt; map pp.70–71. Although most of this store is dedicated to Judaica, it also stocks wooden toys, sophisticated puzzles and children's books. Mon–Sat 11am–7pm.

Mundo Azul Choriner Str. 49, Prenzlauer Berg ☎030 49 85 38 34, ⓦmundoazul.de; ⓤSenefelderplatz; map p.136. "Blue World" stocks beautiful books for kids in a broad range of languages, and also runs events and illustration exhibitions. A must for visiting parents and book fans. Mon 10am–6pm, Tues–Fri 10am–7pm, Sat 10am–4pm.

★**Onkel Philipp's Speilzeugwerkstatt** Choriner Str. 35, Prenzlauer Berg ☎030 44 90 491, ⓦonkel-philipp.de; ⓤEberswalder Strasse; map p.136. You won't find any PlayStations or iPads here: rather, the shelves of this charming, time-warped toy store are chock-a-block with classic toys like kites and teddy bears, bikes and musical instruments – many of them secondhand and repaired in the on-site workshop, which can fix your broken toys too. Ask to see the special exhibition of GDR toys in a secret room. Tues, Wed & Fri 9.30am–6.30pm, Thurs 11am–8pm, Sat 11am–4pm.

Spielbrett Körtestr. 27, Kreuzberg ☎030 692 42 50, ⓤSüdstern, map pp.128–129; Berliner Str. 132, Wilmersdorf ☎030 873 15 35, ⓤBlissestrasse, map p.108; ⓦspielbrett-berlin.de. Massive selection of games and puzzles with some picture books too. Kreuzberg branch Mon–Fri 10am–6.30pm, Sat 10am–4pm; Wilmersdorf branch Mon–Fri 9.30am–7pm, Sat 10am–4pm.

Zauberkönig Hermannstr. 84, Neukölln ☎030 49 20 57 51, ⓦzauberkoenig-berlin.de; ⓤLeinestrasse; map p.130. Illusions and tricks for magicians and their apprentices. Tues–Sat 11am–7pm.

MARKETS, JUNK SHOPS AND ANTIQUES

If you're looking for antiques, hunting around Berlin's flea markets can be fruitful but hard work. A good bet for junk shops and antiques is **Suarezstrasse** in Charlottenburg (map p.162): get off at ⓤSophie-Charlotte-Platz and work your way along the street. Goltzstrasse in Schöneberg (map p.114) and Bergmannstrasse in Kreuzberg (map p.118) are also good bets.

ANTIQUES

Bleibtreu-Antik Detmolder Str. 62a, Wilmersdorf ☎030 883 52 12, ⓦbleibtreu-antik.com; ⓢBundesplatz; map p.160. Well-established shop with a great selection of antiques from 1900 to the 1960s, plus stylish 1960s and 1970s jewellery. Thurs noon–6pm and by appointment.

Berliner Antik und Flohmarkt Bahnhof Friedrichstrasse (under the railway arches), Georgenstr. 190–203, Mitte ☎030 208 26 55, ⓦwww.antikmarkt-berlin.de; ⓤ/ⓢFriedrichstrasse; map p.36. Tending more toward the antique end of things, with several shops selling everything from books to jewellery. Not particularly cheap. Daily except Tues 11am–6pm.

FLEA MARKETS

Berliner Kunstmarket Am Zeughaus, Mitte ☎0173 366 2312, ⓦkunstmarkt-berlin.com; ⓢHackescher Markt; map p.36. A good mix of real antiques, schlocky souvenirs, used books and bootleg CDs. Sat & Sun 11am–5pm.

Berliner Trödelmarkt Str. des 17 Juni, Charlottenburg ☎030 26 55 00 97, ⓦberlinertroedelmarkt.com; ⓢTiergarten; map pp.90–91. Pleasant enough for a Sun morning stroll, but it's the most expensive of the flea markets, and geared toward tourists. Good for embroidery and lace, though. Sat & Sun 10am–5pm.

Flohmarkt am Boxhagener Platz Boxhagener Platz, Friedrichshain; ⓤ/ⓢWarschauer Strasse; map pp.128–129. Small flea market catering to the needs of the student quarter, with vinyl, vintage fashion and more. Good Eastern Bloc memorabilia. Sun 9am–4pm.

Flohmarkt am Mauerpark Bernauer Str. 63–64,

16

Prenzlauer Berg ☎030 29 77 24 86, ⓦflohmarkt immauerpark.de; ⓤBernauer Strasse; map p.136. Huge flea market on the edge of Prenzlauer Berg with a bit of everything that's cheap, including a legion of freshly stolen and spray painted bikes. Few real antiques, but a good place to make a day of it, with good ethnic food stalls and a fun open-air karaoke at 3pm. Sun 8am–6pm.

Flohmarkt am Rathaus Schöneberg John-F.-Kennedy-Platz 1, Schöneberg; ⓤRathaus Schöneberg; map p.114. Some professionals selling books and collectables, but also amateur vendors who have cleared out the garage or attic and are selling the motley results. Sat & Sun 8am–4pm.

Hallentrödelmarkt Treptow Eichenstr. 4, Treptow ☎0172 30 35 775, ⓦhallentrödelmarkt-berlin-treptow .de; Ⓢ Treptower Park; map pp.128–129. Ideal rainy-day option: there's something of everything in this huge indoor flea market. The stalls are all permanent fixtures and thoroughly chaotic. Sat & Sun 10am–4pm.

★**Kunst- & Trödelmarkt am Fehrbelliner Platz** Fehrbelliner Platz 1, Wilmersdorf ⓦfehrbi.info; ⓤFehrbelliner Platz; map p.108. Small but very good flea market for reasonably priced antiques and collectables with a local flavour. There's a pleasant café too, but the large number of Thai families selling fantastic street food in the adjacent park are a bigger attraction. Sat & Sun 10am–4pm.

Trödelmarkt am Arkonaplatz Arkonaplatz, Mitte ☎0171 710 16 62, ⓦtroedelmarkt-arkonaplatz.de; ⓤBernauer Strasse; map pp.70–71. Popular flea market in the city's yuppie district, thick with 1960s and 70s junk and cult objects in equal measure. Sun 10am–4pm.

MUSIC

Berlin has plenty of small **record shops**, generally dedicated to just one style of music, and many of which are thriving alongside the city's dynamic clubbing scene.

Core Tex Records Oranienstr. 3, Kreuzberg ☎030 61 28 00 50, ⓦcoretexrecords.com; ⓤGörlitzer Bahnhof; map pp.128–129. The best place in the city to stock up on punk or hardcore music, as well as related T-shirts, accessories and books. Mon–Fri 11am–7pm, Sat 11am–4pm.

DaCapo Kastanienallee 96, Prenzlauer Berg ☎030 448 17 71, ⓦda-capo-vinyl.de; ⓤEberswalder Strasse; map p.136. New and used vinyl shop with a wide selection of jazz, 1960s–80s rock and releases on East German label Amiga. Tues–Fri noon–7pm, Sat noon–6pm.

Dussmann Friedrichstr. 90, Mitte ☎030 20 25 11 11, ⓦkulturkaufhaus.de; ⓤ/Ⓢ Friedrichstrasse; map p.36. Good selection of rock, jazz, dance, world and international vocalists. You can spend a whole afternoon listening to CDs without being interrupted by a salesperson. Mon–Fri 9am–midnight, Sat 9am–11.30pm.

Hard Wax Paul-Lincke-Ufer 44a, Kreuzberg ☎030 61 13 01 11, ⓦhardwax.com; ⓤKotbusser Tor; map pp.128–129. Premier specialist for underground house and techno, as well as a great reggae and dub selection. Mon–Sat noon–8pm.

L&P Classics Welserstr. 28, Schöneberg ☎030 88 04 30 43, ⓦlpclassics.de; ⓤWittenbergplatz; map p.114. Store devoted entirely to classical music with extremely knowledgeable and helpful staff. Mon–Sat 10am–7pm.

Melting Point Kastanienallee 55, Mitte ☎030 44 04 71 31; ⓤRosenthaler Platz; map pp.70–71. A techno and house stalwart since the 1990s; there's also disco, soul, funk, jazz, hip-hop, rock and more. Masses of vinyl and some CDs. Mon–Sat noon–8pm.

Mr Dead & Mrs Free Bülowstr. 5, Schöneberg ☎030 215 14 49, ⓦdeadandfree.com; ⓤNollendorfplatz; map p.114. Lovely, dusty little music shop crammed full of everything from the latest imports to rare vintage albums; primarily pop, folk, indie and country vinyl on independent labels. Mon–Fri noon–7pm, Sat 11am–4pm.

Oye Oderberger Str. 4, Prenzlauer Berg ☎030 66 64 78 21, ⓦoye-records.com; ⓤEberswalder Strasse; map p.136. Originally devoted to Latin, soul and funk vinyl, but now covering an impressive range of styles, from Afrobeat and hip-hop to Berlin house and techno. Mon–Fri 1–8pm, Sat noon–8pm.

Soultrade Sanderstr. 29, Neukölln ☎030 694 52 57, ⓦsoultrade.de; ⓤSchönleinstrasse; map pp.128–129. Specialists in soul, hip-hop, funk, house and jazz. Mon–Fri 1–8pm, Sat 1–6pm.

★**Space Hall** Zossener Str. 33 & 35, Kreuzberg ☎030 53 08 87 18, ⓦspacehall.de; ⓤGneisenaustrasse; map p.118. This two-store, multi-roomed record shop is one of the best stocked in the city, with a large CD collection (rock, pop, electronic, rap) and DJ-friendly vinyl at no. 35, and hardware (record players, speakers, drum machines) at no. 33. No. 33 Tues–Fri noon–6pm; no. 35 Mon–Wed & Sat 11am–8pm, Thurs & Fri 11am–10pm.

SOUVENIRS AND GIFTS

Ampelmann Galerie Hackescher Höfe V, Mitte ☎030 44 72 64 38, ⓦampelmann.de; Ⓢ Hackescher Markt; map pp.70–71. Joyous celebration of the traffic-light man (Ampelmann) that reigns supreme on the eastern side of the city. After being threatened with replacement by his svelte West Berlin counterpart he became the subject of protests and a cult figure. Pick up T-shirts, mugs, lights and the like at the original shop here; seven other branches in

16

central Berlin. Mon–Sat 9.30am–9pm, Sun 1–8pm.

Ararat Bergmannstr. 9, Kreuzberg ☎ 030 694 95 32, ⓦ ararat-berlin.de; ⓤ Gneisenaustrasse; map p.118. Postcards, cards and a wealth of gimmicky gifts. It's easy to lose yourself here; when you've finished you can head over the road to where another branch sells picture frames and artworks. Mon–Fri 10am–6.30pm, Sat 10am–4pm.

★ **Heimspiel** Niederbarnimstr. 18, Friedrichshain ☎ 030 20 68 78 70, ⓦ heimspiel.design; ⓤ Samariterstrasse; map pp.128–129. This cute little store is always worth stopping by, offering a fresh assortment of trendy women's clothing, kitsch Berlin-themed postcards and games plus locally produced artworks. Mon–Fri 11am–8pm, Sat 11am–6pm.

Supalife Kiosk Raumerstr. 40, Prenzlauer Berg ☎ 030 44 67 88 26, ⓦ supalife.de; ⓤ Eberswalder Strasse; map p.136. This funky little boutique sells the wares of Berlin urban artists, from comics and fanzines to silkscreen prints and paintings. They're well connected to some of the city's best-known artists, so expect one-offs too. Mon–Sat noon–7pm.

TRAVEL EQUIPMENT

Globetrotter Schlossstr. 78–82, Steglitz-Zehlendorf ☎ 030 850 89 20, ⓦ globetrotter.de; ⓤ/ⓢ Rathaus Steglitz; map p.160. Massive, well-stocked outdoor shop with gimmicks including a -25°C freezer to try out jackets and sleeping bags and a special section for kids (Kinderland). A bit of a trek from the centre, but directly above the station. Mon–Fri 10am–8pm, Sat 9am–8pm.

16

BADESCHIFF

Sports and outdoor activities

While Berliners go in for healthy eating in a big way, they're not famous for being fitness fanatics – they need all their energy for the frenetic nightlife. Nonetheless there is a surprising variety of participatory sports available in the city. Municipal facilities for many sports are excellent, and the city is also cycle-friendly (see p.24). Meanwhile, despite a shortage of top-flight teams, the spectator sports scene is vibrant, with some fanatical support for virtually every team. Major and some minor sporting events are listed in *Tip* and *Zitty* (see p.33), but the best index of facilities and events is at the German-only site ⓦcitysports.de.

17

PARTICIPATORY SPORTS

POOLS, SAUNAS AND SPAS

Most city districts have both indoor and outdoor swimming pools, the majority of which are municipal (ⓦ berlinerbaederbetriebe.de), charge around €5 for a swim and have complicated opening hours – from as early as 7am to as late as 10pm on some days, with some closing in the summer and some offering men- and women-only times and family times. Some pools also have saunas which typically cost around €16–18 for three hours, and require you to leave any Anglo-Saxon prudishness at home for they are inevitably naked and mixed-sex. Women uncomfortable with this arrangement should look out for women-only sessions offered regularly at most facilities, while men should be aware that men-only sessions, where offered, are frequently cruisey – anywhere advertising itself as a men's sauna is an out-and-out gay venue. If you're looking for a waterpark, you could head outside the city to Tropical Islands, a luxurious indoor complex with a constant temperature of 26°C (see box, p.183). Note that towels and dressing gowns can usually be rented from spas, though not from municipal pools and saunas.

Hamam Mariannenstr. 6, Kreuzberg ☎ 030 615 14 64, ⓦ hamamberlin.de; ⓤ Kottbusser Tor; map pp.128–129. Women-only, Turkish-style bathhouse in women's centre Schokofabrik (see p.253). Various beauty treatments available. Mon 3–11pm, Tues–Sun noon–11pm.

Haubentaucher Revaler Str. 99, Friedrichshain ☎ 030 29 71 66 70, ⓦ haubentaucher.berlin; ⓤ/Ⓢ Warschauer Strasse; map pp.128–129. The newest opening inside the sprawling RAW Gelände complex (see p.134), Haubentaucher ("Great Crested Grebe") has quickly become one of the city's trendiest pools, drawing a crowd of hip young things as well as the occasional family. As well as a sizeable (28 x 10m) pool, there are designer sun-loungers, a beer garden, food kiosks and even a large concert and club space. Daily noon till late.

★ **Liquidrom** Möckernstr. 10, Kreuzberg ☎ 030 258 00 78 20, ⓦ liquidrom-berlin.de; Ⓢ Anhalter Bahnhof; map p.118. Cutting-edge health spa, whose claim to fame is its atmospheric saltwater pool into which ambient music is piped. The unique underwater sound experience is complemented by mildly psychedelic projections on the ceiling and floors. There are also a couple of hot tubs – one outdoor – three saunas, a steam room and a bar. Mon–

Thurs & Sun 9am–midnight, Fri & Sat 9am–1am.

Olivin Wellness Lounge Schönhauser Allee 177, Prenzlauer Berg ☎ 030 44 04 25 00, ⓦ olivin-berlin.com; ⓤ Senefelderplatz; map p.136. With its exposed brick walls, saunas and an excellent bamboo garden, this Finnish sauna is a great way to unwind whatever the season. Special offers are available in winter and massages start at €18 for 20min. No access to men on Thursdays. Cash only. Daily: autumn/ winter noon–midnight; summer 5pm–midnight.

Sommerbad Olympiastadion Olympischer Platz (Osttor), Charlottenburg ☎ 030 22 19 00 11, ⓦ berlin erbaederbetriebe.de; ⓤ Olympia Stadion; map p.162. Outdoor 50m pool with several diving boards that's part of the impressive 1930s-era Olympic Stadium complex (see p.166). Mid-May to mid-Sept daily; check website for times.

Stadtbad Charlottenburg – Alte Halle Krumme Str. 10, Charlottenburg ☎ 030 22 19 00 11, ⓦ berlinerbaederbetriebe.de; ⓤ Bismarckstrasse; map p.162. A delightful, old-fashioned tiled pool, seldom crowded, with three saunas and a steam room. Hours vary wildly by day and season.

Stadtbad Neukölln Ganghoferstr. 3, Neukölln ☎ 030 22 19 00 11, ⓦ berlinerbaederbetriebe.de; ⓤ Karl-Marx-Strasse; map p.130. Swim and relax in a setting that resembles a Hungarian spa. Two pools (one heated, one cool) decorated with fountains and mosaic tiles, encased in a maze of archways and colonnades. Sauna and steam room available. Check website for times.

Strandbad Wannsee Wannseebadweg 25, Zehlendorf ☎ 030 22 19 00 11, ⓦ berlinerbaederbetriebe.de; Ⓢ Nikolassee; map p.170. Berlin's famed beach, with lots of activities in summer – volleyball, table tennis, basketball, boat rental – when it is usually packed. There are *Strandkörbe* (stylish beach cabanas that seat two; €8) for rent. April–Sept daily 10am–6pm, usually till 8 or 9pm June–Aug.

Thermen am Europa-Center Nürnberger Str. 7, Charlottenburg ☎ 030 257 57 60, ⓦ thermen-berlin .de; ⓤ Wittenbergplatz; map p.108. Big complex with no fewer than nine saunas, as well as indoor and outdoor saltwater pools, fitness rooms and beauty treatments. Mon–Sat 10am–midnight, Sun 10am–9pm.

Wellenbad am Spreewaldplatz Wiener Str. 59h, Kreuzberg ☎ 030 22 19 00 11, ⓦ berlinerbaederbetriebe

---

BADESCHIFF

A dip in the River Spree might not sound like such a good idea until you visit **Badeschiff** (May–Sept daily 8am–midnight; pool €5; ☎ 030 533 20 30, ⓤ Schlesiches Tor; map pp.128–129), an old industrial barge converted into a clear blue, 20m-long swimming pool that bobs in the river. A wooden jetty that's perfect for sunbathing connects the pool to a beach – complete with a happening beach bar, *Escobar* (Thurs–Sun from 6pm)– that's been constructed on the bank. The entrance is hidden behind a maze of old tram sheds beside the Arena complex.

.de; ⊙ Görlitzer Bahnhof; map pp.128–129. Popular 25m indoor pool complete with wave machine that makes it popular with families. Also a good sauna. Daily: check website for times.

JOGGING

With so many parks it's easy to find a good place to jog in Berlin. Best are the Tiergarten, Volkspark Friedrichshain, Treptower Park and the immense grounds of Tempelhofer Feld. The lakes around the city are also popular with joggers: try the Schlachtensee, Krumme Lanke or Grunewaldsee. If you're into long-distance running there's always the Berlin Marathon (see p.27) on the last weekend in September.

GYMS

Berlin's private gyms are usually members-only and you'll normally need to be a guest of a member to qualify for a day pass, which is likely to be around €15. However, if you are in Berlin for a few weeks it should be fairly easy to get a short-term membership at your nearest gym. One chain with several branches in Berlin is Fit Sportstudio (ⓦ fit-sportstudios.de).

IN-LINE SKATING

Skate by Night ⓦ berlin.skatebynight.de. In-line skating is extremely popular in Berlin, as evidenced by Skate by Night, when thousands take to cordoned-off streets in the city centre: a magnificent opportunity to see some of Berlin from an unusual viewpoint. Setting off at 8pm on selected summer

Sundays (June–Sept), with skaters returning in a loop back to the starting point, the event costs €2. If you need to rent skates, arrive early – they have a limited number of free rentals – or visit Ski Shop Charlottenburg, Schustehrusstr. 1 (ⓣ 030 341 48 70, ⓦ ski-shop-charlottenburg.de; ⓤ Richard-Wagner-Platz), who rent out skates for €10/day.

SKATEBOARDING

The most obvious place for skateboarders to head is the Skatehalle Berlin, but other skate-parks, ramps and pipes are scattered around the city's parks, with some of the best at the old Radrennbahn (velodrome) in Weissensee and Grazer Platz in Schöneberg. A full overview is given at ⓦ skate-spots.de.

Skatehalle Berlin Revaler Str. 99, Friedrichshain ⓦ skatehalle-berlin.de; map pp.128–129. The city's main skate-park, within the RAW Gelände complex (see p.134) is well equipped for both skateboarders and BMX-riders. €6 entry. Opening times vary; check website.

ICE-SKATING

Small open-air rinks sprout near Christmas markets in the centre of town, but the proper rinks are all a little way out. These usually have several 3hr sessions per day which cost around €4 and the same again to rent skates.

Horst-Dohm-Eisstadion Fritz-Wildung-Str. 9, Wilmersdorf ⓣ 030 89 73 27 34, ⓦ eissport-service.de; ⓤ/ⓢ Heidelberger Platz; map p.162. The city's largest rink is an outdoor facility, with a track surrounding the central rink.

SPECTATOR SPORTS

Though no Berlin sports team is world-class, all play in competitive leagues and have a loyal and entertaining fan base. The most high-profile is Hertha BSC, the city's major **football team**, though most other Berlin teams tend to do better in their respective leagues. The biggest sporting spectacles, however, are the city's annual events, including the **Sechstagerennen** (six-day nonstop cycle race; see p.26) in late January and the late-September **Berlin Marathon** (see p.27).

TEAMS AND VENUES

Alba Berlin ⓣ 030 300 90 50, tickets ⓣ 01805 57 00 11, ⓦ albaberlin.de. Berlin's premier basketball team, and one of the top dozen in Europe, competes in the German League and at European level, and plays in the Mercedes-Benz Arena in Friedrichshain (map pp.128–129). Tickets €9.50–65. Season Sept–June.

EHC Eisbären ⓣ 030 97 18 40 40, ⓦ eisbaeren.de. Fanatically supported eastern Berlin ice hockey team, which has been competing at the very top of the premier German division for years. The razzmatazz surrounding the teams and players brings it close to the likes of an NHL, and the game quality is not too far off either. The Eisbären, or polar bears, play in the Mercedes-Benz Arena (map pp.128–129). Tickets €16–40. Season Aug–April.

FC Union Berlin ⓣ 030 656 68 80, tickets ⓣ 030 65 66 88 93, ⓦ fc-union-berlin.de. Eastern Berlin's football team, with a fiercely loyal working-class following, plays in

the second division. Despite some shock success in German cup matches and even in Europe, the day-to-day picture is less exciting. Matches are played in the Stadion An der Alten Försterei in Köpenick (map p.150). Tickets €11–40. Aug–May.

Hertha BSC ⓣ 01805 18 92 00, ⓦ herthabsc.de. Berlin's Bundesliga also-rans, who have never quite achieved real glory, despite lots of promise and the occasional successful European outing. But the Olympic Stadium (see p.166) is glorious whatever the team or result. Tickets are generally easy to come by, either online or via the Hertha fan shop in the Europa Center (see p.112). Tickets €15–89. Aug–May.

Trabrennbahn Karlshorst Treskowallee 129, Lichtenberg ⓣ 030 740 12 12, ⓦ pferdesportpark-berlin-karlshorst .de; ⓢ Karlshorst, map p.150. Enjoy a day at the races Berlin-style, watching harness racing. The racetrack, at the Pferdesportpark, is to the east of Treskow allee, just south of the S-bridge. Free entry. Year-round.

LGBT Berlin

Berlin's LGBT scene is world-class – certainly on a par with those of San Francisco or New York – and the city is a huge magnet for gay men and women from all over Germany, Europe and beyond. This has been the case since the 1920s, when Christopher Isherwood and W.H. Auden both came here, drawn to a city where, in sharp contrast to oppressive London, the gay community did not live in fear of harassment and legal persecution – although that changed with the arrival of the Nazis and then the GDR in former east Berlin. Today the city is more than tolerant enough to support and absorb the LGBT community and it's not uncommon to see LGBT folk mingling in all kinds of cafés, bars and clubs – and not just *Berghain*. The best time to arrive and plunge yourself into the hurly-burly is Gay Pride Week, centred on the Christopher Street Day parade (ⓦcsd-berlin.de; see box, p.254) in late June.

GUIDES AND LISTINGS

Magazines and guides Siegessäule (Ⓦ siegessaeule. de), an online magazine, has listings of events and an encyclopedic directory of gay and lesbian contacts and groups, and also puts out a city map you can find in information centres and most gay bars. Other useful online city guides in both German and English are Ⓦ out-in -berlin.de, Ⓦ iheartberlin.de and Ⓦ travelsofadam.com. The German/English-language *Spartacus Berlin Gay Guide* (previously *Berlin von Hinten* or "Berlin from behind") is the city's most useful gay print guide.

INFORMATION CENTRES

Aha-Berlin Monumentenstr. 13, Schöneberg ☎ 030 89 62 79 48, Ⓦ aha-berlin.de; Ⓢ Yorckstrasse; map p.114. Non-profit cooperative that organizes workshops and events for gay and lesbian groups.

Begine Potsdamer Str. 139, Schöneberg ☎ 030 215 14 14, Ⓦ begine.de; Ⓤ Bülowstrasse; map p.114. Women's centre with a mixed programme ranging from earnest lectures and films, through excellent performances by women musicians and dancers to televised women's soccer and disco evenings. Mon–Fri 5pm–late, Sat 7pm–late.

EWA Prenzlauer Allee 6, Prenzlauer Berg ☎ 030 442 55 42, Ⓦ ewa-frauenzentrum.de; Ⓤ Rosa-Luxemburg-Platz; map p.136. EWA offers courses and counselling, as well as various cultural events, and has an airy women-only café-gallery with a children's play area. Good for events information and flyers. Mon–Thurs 11am–10pm.

Frauenzentrum Schokofabrik Mariannenstr. 6, Kreuzberg ☎ 030 615 29 99, Ⓦ schokofabrik.de; Ⓤ Kottbusser Tor; map pp.128–129. One of Europe's largest women's centres, with a drop-in meeting place for women and girls from Turkey and other countries, a café/gallery, a furniture workshop and sports facilities, including a women-only Turkish bath (see p.250) and diverse events. Mon–Thurs 10am–2pm, Fri noon–4pm.

Mann-O-Meter Bülowstr. 106, Schöneberg ☎ 030 216 80 08, Ⓦ mann-o-meter.de; Ⓤ Nollendorfplatz; map p.114. One of the city's main gay information centres and meeting points. Mon 5–7.30pm, Tues–Fri 5–10pm, Sat & Sun 4–8pm.

GALLERIES AND MUSEUMS

Das Verborgene Museum Schlüterstr. 70, Charlottenburg ☎ 030 313 36 56, Ⓦ dasverborgenemuseum.de; Ⓢ Savignyplatz; map p.108. A gallery founded by women artists for the research, documentation and exhibition of women's art. Entry varies with what's on show but normally free or around €2. Thurs & Fri 3–7pm, Sat & Sun noon–4pm.

Schwules Museum Lützowstr. 73, Schöneberg ☎ 030 69 59 90 50, Ⓦ schwulesmuseum.de; Ⓤ Kurfürstenstrasse; map p.114. Interesting queer museum with changing exhibitions on local and international gay history and culture, and a huge archive and library to browse through. Entry €7.50. Museum Mon, Wed, Fri & Sun 2–6pm, Thurs 2–8pm, Sat 2–7pm; archive Mon, Wed, Thurs 2–8pm.

Spinnboden Anklamer Str. 38, Mitte ☎ 030 448 58 48, Ⓦ spinnboden.de; Ⓤ Bernauer Strasse; map pp.70–71. A comprehensive archive of every aspect of lesbian experience, with a beautifully housed collection of books, videos, posters and magazines. Wed & Fri 2–7pm.

ACCOMMODATION

Most **accommodation** in Berlin is gay-friendly, and there are some places, listed below, that are run for and by the gay community.

Art Hotel Charlottenburger Hof Stuttgarter Platz 14, Charlottenburg ☎ 030 32 90 70, Ⓦ charlottenburger -hof.de; Ⓢ Charlottenburg; map p.162. Bright contemporary hotel, replete with modern art, Bauhaus design and multicoloured furniture. Perks include an on-site café-restaurant with terrace and courtyard. Rates can often be slashed by booking specials online. Breakfast extra. **€63**

Art Hotel Connection Fuggerstr. 33, Schöneberg ☎ 030 210 21 88 00, Ⓦ arthotel-connection.de; Ⓤ Wittenbergplatz; map p.114. Hetero-friendly gay hotel located near KaDeWe in the gay village. Most rooms are large and en suite, bright, pleasant and ordinary; the "playroom", however, comes with chains and slings. **€89**

Tom's Hotel Motzstr. 19, Schöneberg ☎ 030 219 66 04, Ⓦ toms-hotel.de; Ⓤ Nollendorfplatz; map p.114. One of the largest gay hotels in town, with a great location in Berlin's gay village and its own vibrant café and bar. Bright simple rooms, with a bowl of fruit provided along with a pass for discounts at a number of local businesses. **€140**

CAFÉS

You'll find the majority of gay and lesbian **hangouts** in Schöneberg, Kreuzberg and Prenzlauer Berg. In addition to the cafés there are several very active and convivial mixed-use venues, popular within the lesbian scene. Gay women might also want to check out any possible happenings at the Begine women's centre (see above).

18

Café Berio Maassenstr. 7, Schöneberg ☎030 216 19 46, ⓦcafeberio.de; ⓤNollendorfplatz; map p.114. This round-the-clock gay café and bar is an ideal spot for *Kaffee und Kuchen* in the Viennese tradition during the day; later on the drinks specials (7–9pm) are the main draw. Occasional exhibitions, too. Open 24hr.

Café Seidenfaden Dircksenstr. 47, Mitte ☎030 283 27 83, ⓦfrausuchtzukunft.de; ⓤWeinmeisterstrasse; map pp.70–71. Women-only café with inexpensive lunch specials (€3–5) and a no alcohol policy. Mon–Fri 8am–4pm, Sat noon–6pm.

Melitta Sundström Mehringdamm 61, Kreuzberg ☎030 692 44 14, ⓦmelitta-sundstroem.de; ⓤMehringdamm; map p.118. Legendary but small, low-key and comfortable mixed café – often a warm-up for the legendary *SchwuZ* club (see opposite). Occasional exhibitions and unplugged concerts with young musicians in the first-floor Bel Etage room. Daily 2pm–4am.

Sorgenfrei Goltzstr. 18, Schöneberg ☎030 30 10 40 71, ⓦsorgenfrei-in-berlin.de; ⓤNollendorfplatz; map p.114. This gay-friendly café will take you straight back to the 1950s, with Hawaiian-style toast on the menu and Bing Crosby on the speakers. The Bakelite radios and kidney-shaped tables aren't just for decoration – most items are for sale. Tues–Fri noon–7pm, Sat 10am–6pm, Sun 1–6pm.

BARS AND CLUBS

The longest-standing and most concentrated area of **gay bars** is in Schöneberg around and between Wittenbergplatz and Nollendorfplatz. Many mainly straight clubs have gay nights – see *Tip*, *Zitty* or Siegessäule for details. Berghain (see p.228), Kit-Kat Club (see p.227) and Kumpelnest 3000 (see p.226) are all mixed venues with a strong gay presence that have become legendary. Other nights not to miss are the **GMF** events (ⓦgmf-berlin.de), which pop up at different venues around town (including *2BE Club*; see p.224), and have over the years become a stalwart of the Berlin scene – think stripped-to-the-waist revellers dancing to pounding house music; other favourites are Homopatik *at ://about blank* (see p.228) and the less regular – and more arty – Pornceptual parties (ⓦpornceptual.com).

CITY WEST

Vagabund Bar Knesebeckstr. 77 ☎030 881 15 06, ⓦvagabund-berlin.com; ⓤUhlandstrasse; map p.108. This popular mixed gay bar, opened in 1968, gets crowded after 3am and has an anything goes, trashy aesthetic – very flirty, very fun, and not only for men. Daily midnight till late.

SCHÖNEBERG

Connection Fuggerstr. 33 ☎030 23 62 74 44, ⓦconnectionclub.de; ⓤWittenbergplatz; map p.114. Long-running gay entertainment complex with regular DJ club nights. It's seen better days but can still be a fun place at weekends. Daily 3pm till late.

Hafen Motzstr. 19 ☎030 211 41 18, ⓦhafen-berlin.de; ⓤNollendorfplatz; map p.114. Long-established cruisey mixed bar for all ages, with everything from techno and Schlager nights to pub quizzes. Always packed and a great place to start a night out. Daily 8pm until late.

★**Heile Welt** Motzstr. 5 ☎030 21 91 75 07; ⓤNollendorfplatz; map p.114. A convivial second living room for many local gay men and the women who love them. During the week, it's all about lounging on the sofas, drinking famously strong cocktails; at weekends the action picks up and it gets crowded, with music running the gamut from soul and dance to house and home-grown "Schlager", a folksy German pop genre. Daily: May–Sept 8pm–late; Oct–April 7pm–late.

Neues Ufer Hauptstr. 157 ☎030 78 95 97 00, ⓦneuesufer.de; ⓤKleistpark; map p.114. Lovely neighbourhood gay bar. Bowie used to drink here in the 1970s, when it was *Anderes Ufer*. Daily 2pm–2am.

Prinzknecht Fuggerstr. 33 ☎030 23 62 74 44, ⓦprinzknecht.de; ⓤWittenbergplatz; map p.114. A refined version of an American sports bar, all bare brick and gleaming chrome, attracting a broad range of middle-aged gay men and some women. The men-only cellar darkroom is underused. Mon–Thurs & Sun 3pm–2am, Fri & Sat 3pm–3am.

CHRISTOPHER STREET DAY

Berlin's **Christopher Street Day** (CSD; ⓦcsd-berlin.de) – otherwise known as **Berlin Pride** – is a gay pride parade and festival, usually in June, that was originally held as a tribute to the 1969 Stonewall Riots in New York. An annual fixture since 1979 – and with a different LGBT theme each year – the march traditionally draws around 700,000 people for the main parade (known as the CSD Demo), which starts on Ku'damm at noon and winds its way to the Brandenburger Tor for the final rally (CSD Finale) at around 5pm. The parade usually anchors a series of events and parties around it (some on the same evening), such as the Gay and Lesbian Street Party in Schöneberg, CSD on the Spree, Kreuzberg Pride, Gay Night At The Zoo (ⓦgay-night-at-the-zoo.de) and the CSD Gala. Dates and events vary from year to year so check the website for more information.

Scheune Motzstr. 25 ☎030 213 85 80, ⓦscheune -berlin.de; ⓤNollendorfplatz; map p.114. Very popular leather club with regular theme parties for devotees of rubber, uniforms or stark nakedness. Darkroom, baths and other accoutrements. Mon–Sat 9pm–7am, Sun 9pm–midnight.

★ **Tom's Bar** Motzstr. 19 ☎030 213 45 70, ⓦtomsbar .de; ⓤNollendorfplatz; map p.114. Dark, sweaty and debauched men-only cruising establishment with a large darkroom. Among Berlin's most popular gay bars, and a great place to finish off a night out. Drinks are two for the price of one on Mon. Daily 10pm–6am.

EASTERN KREUZBERG

Barbie Deinhoff Schlesische Str. 16 ⓦbarbiedeinhoff .de; ⓤSchlesisches Tor; map pp.128–129. Colourful and fun-loving dive bar that attracts a heady mix of transvestites, gay men and curious onlookers. The decor runs from deliberately kitsch to colourfully futuristic and there are regular DJs and events. Popular happy hour on Tues until midnight. Daily 7pm–late.

Facciola Forster Str. 5 ☎0176 303 689 03, ⓦfacciola -berlin.de; ⓤGörlitzer Bahnhof; map pp.128–129. Lesbian-owned wine bar with a friendly atmosphere and regular queer cultural events. The wines, mostly Italian, are top-notch, and there are tasty bar snacks on offer too. Tues–Sat 6pm till late.

★ **Roses** Oranienstr. 187 ☎030 615 65 70; ⓤKottbusser Tor; map pp.128–129. Legendary kitsch gay club with a strong lesbian presence. The fun vibe makes it one of the venues of choice for a solo night out for either sex. Sun is the main day – and the "gayest" – but women are welcome anytime. Daily 10pm–5am.

CINEMAS

Kino International Karl-Marx-Allee 33, Friedrichshain ☎030 24 75 60 11, ⓦyorck.de; ⓤSchillingstrasse; map pp.128–129. The "Mongay" event every Mon involves a screening of a cult gay or lesbian film – the bar opens at 9pm, the film is at 10pm and the party really starts afterwards.

BOOKSHOPS

Anakoluth Schönhauser Allee 124, Prenzlauer Berg ☎030 87 33 69 80, ⓦanakoluth.de; ⓤSchönhauser Allee; map p.136. Well-stocked lesbian bookstore, which also puts on exhibitions and readings. Mon–Fri 10am–8pm, Sat 10am–6pm.

SPORT

Vorspiel SSL Berlin Martin-Luther-Str. 56, Schöneberg ☎030 44 05 77 40, ⓦvorspiel-berlin.de; ⓤEisenacher Strasse; map p.114. Berlin's gay and lesbian sports club,

NEUKÖLLN

★ **SchwuZ** Rollbergstr. 26 ☎030 57 70 22 70, ⓦschwuz .de; ⓤRathaus-Neukölln; map p.130. Dance club much loved by all stripes of the gay community, and always crowded and convivial. Music varies from pop and retro tunes to house and techno mixes from local DJs. Fri & Sat 11pm–late.

FRIEDRISCHSHAIN

Die Busche Warschauer Platz 18 ☎030 29 60 800, ⓦdiebusche.de; ⓤ/Ⓢ Warschauer Strasse; map pp.128–129. Long-standing club for gays and lesbians in the city as well as from surrounding Brandenburg. There are two a/c floors playing oldies and newies, as well as karaoke and other fun stuff. Entry usually around €5. Fri & Sat 10pm–late.

Himmelreich Simon-Dach-Str. 36 ☎030 293 69 292, ⓦhimmelreich-berlin.de; ⓤFrankfurter Tor or ⓤ/Ⓢ Warschauer Strasse; map pp.128–129. Relaxed queer, gay and lesbian bar close to Boxhagener Platz that draws a friendly crowd and serves decent cocktails. Tuesday is queer night. Mon–Sat 6pm–late, Sun 4pm–late.

PRENZLAUER BERG

Greifbar Wichertstr. 10 ☎030 89 75 14 98, ⓦgreifbar .com; ⓤ/Ⓢ Schönhauser Allee; map p.136. This wicked cruising den is the cornerstone of gay debauchery in Prenzlauer Berg. Attracts the full range of the gay community, gets them in the mood with videos and provides an area around the back to release mutual tension. Daily 10pm–6am.

Schall und Rauch Gleimstr. 23 ☎030 443 39 70, ⓦschall-und-rauch.de; ⓤ/Ⓢ Schönhauser Allee; map p.136. Tasteful, designer elegance in this hip young mixed bar. A place to see and be seen – and eat, thanks to an imaginative and ever-changing menu. Daily 9am–2am.

Xenon Kino Berlin Kolonnenstr. 5, Schöneberg ☎030 78 00 15 30, ⓦwww.xenon-kino.de; ⓤJulius-Leber-Brücke; map p.114. Gay cinema that often screens English-language independent films. Tickets €7.50.

Prinz Eisenherz Motzstr. 23, Schöneberg ☎030 313 99 36, ⓦprinz-eisenherz.com; ⓤNollendorfplatz; map p.114. Friendly and informative queer bookstore with helpful assistants. Excellent for relaxed browsing, free magazines and information about current LGBT happenings. Mon–Sat 10am–8pm.

offering a variety of activities for every level of fitness and ability. Mon 1–3pm, Tues 5–7pm, Thurs 10am–1pm.

Kids' Berlin

Attitudes to young children in Berlin are, on the whole, very positive. The city has a large number of single-parent families and excellent social services provisions, and Berliners are generally quite tolerant of kids in "adult" places, especially restaurants or bars. As for keeping kids entertained, though the city boasts a higher proportion of lakes, parks and woodland than any other European capital, there are few official attractions in those places directly geared towards entertaining children. Be prepared to do Berlin versions of the obvious things – zoos, museums, shops (covered in Chapter 16; see p.246) – rather than much overly unique. In addition to browsing the selections that we have covered here, you should also check the "Familie" listings of *Tip* and *Zitty* (see p.33), as well as dedicated family magazine *Himbeer* (ⓦhimbeer-magazin.de), for details of what's on.

SIGHTSEEING

Tours Depending on your children's level of interest, some sightseeing might be enjoyable. A ride on the #100 or #200 bus doesn't cost much, and will take in all the main sights between Alexanderplatz and Bahnhof Zoo, connecting several key places and offering superb views of Berlin from on high. Most other bus tours will end up being a bit too much for younger kids, but boat tours are a possibility (see box, pp.24–25).

Cycling With its many cycle paths, Berlin is a bike-friendly city for kids – those who can be relied on to stop at junctions, at least. However, few bike rental places offer children's bikes – among the few that do is Yaambike, An der Schillingbrücke (April–Oct; ☎ 0178 804 97 54, ⓦ rent-a-bike-berlin.net; ⓢ Ostbahnhof; map pp.128–129) at the start of the East Side Gallery.

THE GREAT OUTDOORS

With more than a third of Berlin being forest or parkland, often with playgrounds dotted around, there's no shortage of spaces for children to let off steam. The most central and obvious choice is the **Tiergarten**, northeast of Bahnhof Zoo, though this is rather tame compared to the rambling expanses of the **Grunewald**. In both parks, paddle and rowing boats can be rented. The Grunewald borders the **Wannsee** beach (see p.172), and it's fun to take the ferry over to the **Pfaueninsel**, or Peacock Island, where there's a castle and strutting peacocks. Alternatively, **Freizeitpark Tegel** (ⓤ Alt-Tegel; walk to the lake, then turn right) has playgrounds, trampolines, table tennis and paddle boats, while the **Teufelsberg** (see p.166), a large hill to the west of the city, is a good place to go kite-flying at weekends. A little more central, the immense **Tempelhofer Feld** (see p.125), site of the former Nazi airport, is also a popular place for cycling, kite-flying, roller-blading and more. On the southeastern edge of the city, the woods around the **Grosser Müggelsee** (see p.157) offer lakeside walking trails, and, just to the south, there's also a good nature trail around the **Teufelssee** (see p.158).

MUSEUMS AND ATTRACTIONS

Almost all the city's museums give discounts for children; those listed here are particularly recommended for kids, mainly thanks to fun interactive exhibits.

Anne Frank Center Kids can explore the life and experiences of the famous teenager in this informative and interactive permanent exhibition. See p.74.

Berlin Dungeon A genuinely scary experience, more suited to older kids. See p.64.

Deutsches Spionagemuseum Covering the fascinating history of espionage, including James Bond film paraphernalia, this slick museum is a great place for curious-minded little ones. See p.94.

Deutsches Technikmuseum Berlin The German Technology Museum has a great collection of old steam trains and carriages, fascinating exhibits on everything from musical instruments to planes, plus the experimental displays of the adjacent Science Center Spectrum. See p.124.

Filmpark Babelsberg These legendary film studios in Potsdam now offer a guided tour, stunt shows and a 4D

cinema experience. See p.182.

Labyrinth Kindermuseum Berlin Osloer Str. 12, Gesundbrunnen ☎ 030 800 93 11 50, ⓦ labyrinth -kindermuseum.de; ⓤ Pankstrasse; map p.146. This huge children's museum is set inside a former matchstick factory. Set up for kids between 3 and 11 years old, it offers a wealth of interactive play areas as well as regular exhibitions, usually very inventive and thoughtful, on themes from world cultures to children's rights, and regular art and craft workshops. There's a basic café inside but bringing your own food and drinks is allowed. Admission (adults and kids) €5.50. Outside school hols Fri 1–6pm, Sat & Sun 11am–6pm; in school hols Mon–Fri 9am–6pm, Sat & Sun 11am–6pm.

Legoland Discovery Centre Berlin Let the kids loose on thousands of different Lego blocks, as well as ride the dragon train and enjoy a 4D cinema experience. See p.93.

19

BABYSITTING AND CHILD CARE

Berlin has several reliable agencies for English-speaking **babysitters**, but one that stands out for professionalism and convenience is Kinderinsel, Eichendorffstr. 17 (☎ 030 41 71 69 28, ⓦ kinderinsel.de; ⓢ Nordbahnhof). Here parents can leave their children (aged up to 14 years) in good hands, for anything from a couple of hours to several days. The programme of outings and activities offered by the friendly and dynamic centre ensures the kids won't get bored; rates are €15/hr, €75 for an overnight stay. Not only can they provide a pick-up and drop-off service, but they can also supply babysitters if you'd rather keep the kids at your place.

TOP 5 VIEWS FOR KIDS

Fernsehturm The viewing area has mind-blowing dimensions and an otherworldly feel. See p.61

Panoramapunkt The most exciting views, though it does require a head for heights. See p.93

Reichstag dome This unusual structure with its many mirrors is always entertaining for kids. See p.37

Siegessäule Lots of steps make this slightly hard work for little legs but great for energetic youngsters. See p.103

Viktoriapark Climb up to the top of Berlin's biggest hill and admire the views over Kreuzberg and beyond. See p.125

Loxx am Alex – Miniatur Welten Berlin This impressively detailed miniature Berlin will keep adults and kids alike entertained for a morning or afternoon. See p.60.

Madame Tussauds Berlin The local iteration of the famous waxworks franchise features a host of German and international celebrities, including Angela Merkel. See p.41.

Museumsdorf Düppel Reconstruction of a medieval country village, with demonstrations of traditional handicrafts and farming methods. Better for older children. See p.171.

Museum für Kommunikation Robots career around the main lobby in the hands-on Communications Museum,

which offers older kids devices to play with. See p.122.

Museum für Naturkunde The Natural History Museum has a gigantic Brachiosaurus skeleton as well as one of Tristan the T. rex, plus plenty more to keep animal-crazy kids happy for an hour or so. See p.86.

Puppentheater-Museum This fascinating museum showcases all kinds of puppets from across the globe and also hosts exhibitions, workshops and performances. See p.131.

The Story of Berlin Easily the most captivating of the city's history museums, with lots of multimedia gimmicks to bring the experience alive for kids. See p.113.

ZOOS AND AQUARIUMS

As a hangover from the old East–West days, Berlin has two full-sized **zoos**. The **aquariums**, meanwhile, are very good wet-weather options.

Sea Life Berlin A much smaller variety of species than at the Berlin Aquarium, but with some flashy tanks and good activities for kids, including quiz questions (in English) and the chance to touch manta rays and starfish in a tank. See p.64.

Tierpark Berlin The old eastern zoo is a slightly longer trek from the centre than its western counterpoint, but its more open-air approach and updated areas and facilities

make a visit more than worthwhile. See p.152.

Zoologischer Garten Berlin/Berlin Aquarium City West's zoo is the longer established of the two city zoos, and offers an underground nocturnal area (where varieties of gerbil-like creatures, and bats, do their thing), a good playground and a new petting area. It also boasts a very good aquarium featuring all sorts of fish plus interesting creatures from crocodiles to bees to snakes. See p.110.

PLAYGROUNDS, LEISURE COMPLEXES AND CHILDREN'S FARMS

Berlin has a number of ragtag **adventure playgrounds** featuring creative wooden structures that are perfect to charge around and explore – many of them are supervised, too. Information on these along with the location of the city's **children's farms** are at the German-only website ⓦ akib.de.

Domäne Dahlem Working farm and craft museum with plenty to entertain kids besides farmyard animals, especially during weekend craft fairs when there are games and shows especially for children. See p.169.

FEZ-Berlin An der Wuhlheide 197, Köpenick ☎ 030 53 07 10, ⓦ fez-berlin.de; ⓢ Wuhlheide; map p.150. A large GDR-era recreation park, packed with play and activity areas for kids of all ages and unusual features such as a BMX track (rentals available) and a popular narrow-gauge railway, the 7km-long Berliner *Parkeisenbahn*

(ⓦ parkeisenbahn.de). Hours vary according to school terms, but core times: Tues–Fri & Sun 9am–10pm, Sat & Sun noon–6pm.

Kinderbauernhof auf dem Görlitzer Görlitzer Park, Wiener Str. 59, Kreuzberg ⓦ kinderbauernhofberlin.de; ⓤ Görlitzer Bahnhof; map pp.128–129. The most central of several of Berlin's educationally oriented children's farms, which can still be fun even if you don't know the language. Mon, Tues, Thurs & Fri 10am–7pm (5pm in winter), Sat & Sun 11am–6pm (5pm in winter).

19

CIRCUSES

Cabuwazi Zirkus Wiener Str. 59h, Kreuzberg ☎ 030 29 04 78 40, ⓦ cabuwazi.de; ⓤ Görlitzer Bahnhof; map pp.128–129. Resident circus, and one in which youngsters perform. Also a popular venue for visiting circuses. Another four venues in Berlin. Opening hours vary.

ufaFabrik Viktoriastr. 10, Tempelhof ☎ 030 75 50 30, ⓦ ufafabrik.de; ⓤ Ullsteinstrasse; map p.160. Various programmes from theatre, world music, cabaret, to dance, plus a children's circus. Show times vary, usually Wed–Sat 8pm with an open-air programme in the summer.

THEATRES AND CINEMAS

Most cinemas show **children's films** during the school holidays but these are likely to be German-language only. The one time you're likely to catch English-language kids' films is during the Berlinale in February (see box, p.237), as part of its children's programme. Berlin supports a remarkable number of **puppet theatres**, most of which put on worthwhile performances that kids don't need a knowledge of German to enjoy. For details of children's films and theatre performances, check the listings websites (see p.33).

GRIPS Theater Altonaer Str. 22, Tiergarten ☎ 030 39 74 74 77, ⓦ grips-theater.de; ⓤ Hansaplatz; map pp.90–91. Very good children's and young people's theatre that's been going since the 1960s to become a world leader in the art. Shows are often improvised.

Schaubude Berlin Long-standing top-quality puppet theatre that presents a range of sophisticated pieces for kids aged 2 and up. See p.236.

19

THE REICHSTAG IN RUINS AFTER WORLD WAR II

Contexts

History

As the heart of the Prussian kingdom, cultural centre of the Weimar Republic, headquarters of Hitler's Third Reich and a key Cold War flashpoint, Berlin has long been a weather vane of European and even world history. But World War II left the city devastated, with bombs razing 92 percent of all its shops, houses and industry, so it's the latter half of the twentieth century that shaped much of what's visible today. This was a period when the world's two most powerful military systems stood, glaring face to face, over that most tangible object of the Iron Curtain, the Berlin Wall. As the Wall fell in November 1989, Berlin was again at the forefront of world events, ushering in a period of change as frantic, confused and significant as any in the city's history.

All this historic turmoil provides a troubling fascination, and understanding it unlocks the secrets of a cityscape that is only just beginning to settle down from the slew of post-unification building work that once again made Berlin Germany's capital. In its wake, the city has successfully cultivated a fashionable and cosmopolitan outlook, and is now firmly established as a hothouse of contemporary trends and dilemmas, where the hopes and challenges of not only eastern and western Europe, but also increasingly the world, collide as Berlin again becomes a world city to be reckoned with.

Beginnings

Archeologists believe people have lived in the vicinity of modern-day Berlin for about 60,000 years. Traces of hunter-gatherer activity dating from about 8000 BC and more substantial remains of Stone Age farming settlements from 4000 BC onwards have been discovered. The Romans regarded this as barbarian territory and left no mark. Although **Germanic tribes** first appeared during the fifth and sixth centuries AD, many left during the great migrations of later centuries, and the vacated territories were occupied by **Slavs**. Germanic ascendancy only began in the twelfth and thirteenth centuries, when Saxon feudal barons of the Mark (border territory) of Brandenburg expelled the Slavs. The **Saxons** also granted municipal charters to two humble riverside towns – where the Berlin story really begins.

The twin towns

Sited on marshlands around an island (today's Spreeinsel) at the narrowest point on the River Spree, **Berlin** and **Cölln** were on a major trade route to the east and began to prosper as municipalities. Despite many links (including a joint town hall built in 1307), they retained separate identities throughout the fourteenth century.

The Black Death struck the twin towns in 1348 – the first of many major devastations – killing ten percent of the population and unleashing anti-Jewish

720	948	983
The region known today as Berlin is settled by Slavic and Germanic tribes.	Germans take control over the area of present-day Berlin.	The Slavs rebel (successfully) against German rule.

pogroms as part of a search for a scapegoat. Things looked up twenty years later with the admission of Berlin and Cölln to the powerful **Hanseatic League** of city-states in 1369, confirming their economic and political importance. Powerful trade guilds and prosperous burghers ran the towns and, by 1391, made them virtually autonomous from the Mark of Brandenburg, which grew ever more chaotic in the early fifteenth century. Order was eventually restored by **Friedrich Hohenzollern**, burgrave of Nürnberg, when in 1411 the Holy Roman Emperor invited him to take over – the start of a dynasty that would rule Berlin for half a millennium. Friedrich's subjugation of the province was initially welcomed by the burghers of Berlin and Cölln. However, when his son Johann attempted to follow suit, they forced him to withdraw to Spandau. It was only divisions in their ranks that enabled **Friedrich II**, "Irontooth" Johann's brother, to take over the two cities. Some guilds offered him the keys to the gates in return for backing them against the Berlin-Cölln magistrates. Friedrich obliged, then built the **Berliner Schloss** (see box, p.52) and instituted his own harsh rule, forbidding any further union between Berlin and Cölln.

After swiftly crushing a 1448 **rebellion**, Friedrich imposed new restrictions. To symbolize the **consolidation of Hohenzollern power**, a chain was placed around the neck of Berlin's heraldic symbol, the bear, which remained on the city's coat of arms until 1875. After the Hohenzollerns moved their residence and court here, Berlin-Cölln assumed the character of a *Residenzstadt* (royal residence city) and rapidly expanded, its old wattle-and-daub dwellings replaced with substantial stone buildings – culminating in a Renaissance Schloss finished in 1540. Yet life remained hard; despite being involved in the Reformation, Berlin-Cölln lagged behind the great cities of western and southern Germany, and in 1576 was ravaged by plague.

The **Thirty Years' War** (1618–48) marked another low point: Europe was riven by Protestant–Catholic conflicts and national rivalries, and leaders who could ill afford to pay their mercenary armies promised them loot instead. Both Catholic Imperial troops and Protestant Swedes occupied and ransacked the twin towns who lost half their population and one third of their buildings by the end of the war.

The Great Elector

The monumental task of postwar reconstruction fell to the Mark's new ruler, Elector **Friedrich Wilhelm of Brandenburg** (1620–88), who was barely out of his teens. Massive fortifications were constructed, besides the residences and public buildings necessary to make Berlin-Cölln a worthy capital for an Elector. (Seven Electors – three archbishops, a margrave, duke, count and king – were entitled to elect the Holy Roman Emperor.) In recognition of his achievements, Friedrich Wilhelm came to be known as the **Great Elector**. After defeating the Swedes at the Battle of Fehrbellin in 1675, the Mark of Brandenburg was acknowledged as a force to be reckoned with, and its capital grew accordingly. Recognizing the value of a cosmopolitan population, the Elector permitted Jews and South German Catholics to move here and enjoy protection as citizens.

A later wave of immigrants affected Berlin-Cölln even more profoundly. Persecuted in France, thousands of **Protestant Huguenots** sought new homes in England and Germany. The arrival of five thousand immigrants – mostly skilled craftsmen or traders – revitalized Berlin-Cölln, whose own population was just twenty thousand. French

1100s	1244	1247
Germans take over the land again.	Berlin is first mentioned in written records.	The city of Cölln is founded right next to Berlin.

became an almost obligatory second language, indispensable for anyone looking for social and career success. Another fillip to the city's development was the completion of the **Friedrich Wilhelm Canal**, linking the Spree and the Oder, which boosted it as an east–west trade centre.

Carrying on from where his father had left off, Friedrich III succeeded in becoming king of Prussia to boot (thus also gaining the title Friedrich I), while Berlin continued to expand. The **Friedrichstadt** and **Charlottenburg** quarters and the **Zeughaus** (now the Deutsches Historisches Museum) were created during this period, and Andreas Schlüter revamped the Elector's palace. In 1709, Berlin-Cölln finally became a single city named **Berlin**. None of this came cheap, however. Both Berlin and the Mark of Brandenburg were heavily in debt by the end of Friedrich's reign, to the point where he even resorted to alchemists in the hope of refilling his treasury.

Berlin under the Soldier King

The next chapter in the city's history belongs to Friedrich I's son, **Friedrich Wilhelm I** (1688–1740). Known as the **Soldier King** and generally reckoned to be the father of the Prussian state, he dealt with the financial chaos by enforcing spartan conditions on his subjects and firing most court servants. As much as eighty percent of state revenues were then directed to building up his army, and culture took a back seat to parades (eventually he even banned the theatre). While the army marched and drilled, the populace had a draconian work ethic drubbed into them – Friedrich took to walking about Berlin and personally beating anyone he caught loafing.

Friedrich tried to introduce conscription but had to make an exception of Berlin when the city's able-bodied young men fled en masse to escape the army. Despite this, Berlin became a **garrison town** geared to maintaining the army: the Lustgarten park of the royal palace was transformed into a parade ground, and every house was expected to have space available for billeting troops. Much of modern Berlin's shape and character can be traced back to Friedrich – squares like **Pariser Platz** (the area in front of the Brandenburg Gate) began as parade grounds, and **Friedrichstrasse** was built to link the centre with the Tempelhof parade ground. When Friedrich died after watching rehearsals for his own funeral (and thrashing a groom who made a mistake), few Berliners mourned.

Frederick the Great and the rise of Prussia

His son, Friedrich II – known to historians as **Frederick the Great** (1712–86) and to his subjects as "Der alte Fritz" – enjoyed a brief honeymoon as a liberalizer, before reverting to his father's ways. Soon Prussia was drawn into a series of wars that sent Berlin taxes through the roof, while the king withdrew to Sanssouci Palace in Potsdam, where only French was spoken, leaving the Berliners to pay for his military adventurism. Friedrich's saving grace was that he liked to think of himself as a philosopher king, and Berlin's **cultural life** consequently flourished. This was thanks in part to the work of the leading German Enlightenment figures, like playwright Gotthold Ephraim Lessing and philosopher Moses Mendelssohn, both of whom enjoyed royal patronage.

1451

Berlin becomes the royal residence of the Brandenburg Electors and has to give up its status as a free Hanseatic city.

1539

The city becomes officially Lutheran.

It was the **rise of Prussia** – particularly the invasion and subsequent annexation of Silesia in 1740 – that alarmed Austria, Saxony, France and Russia into starting the **Seven Years' War** in 1756. Four years later they occupied Berlin and demanded a tribute of four million thalers, causing city president Kirchstein to faint on the spot. This was later reduced to 1.5 million when it was discovered that the city coffers were empty. Berlin was eventually relieved by Frederick, who, with British aid, went on to win the war (if only by default) after Russia and France fell out. A general peace was concluded in 1763 and victory confirmed Prussia's power in Central Europe, but keeping the peace meant maintaining a huge standing army.

Besides direct taxation, Frederick raised money by establishing **state monopolies** in the trade of coffee, salt and tobacco. Citizens were actually required to buy set quantities of these commodities whether they wanted them or not. Thus were born some of Berlin's most celebrated dishes: sauerkraut, *Kassler Rippchen* (salted pork ribs) and pickled gherkins were all invented by people desperate to use up their accumulated salt. Popular discontent was muffled by Frederick's **secret police** and **press censorship**.

Unter den Linden came into its own during Frederick's reign, as grandiose new edifices like the **Alte Bibliothek** sprang up. Just off the great boulevard, the **Französischer Dom** was built to serve the needs of the Huguenot population, while the construction of Schloss Bellevue in the Tiergarten sparked off a new building boom, as the wealthy flocked into this newly fashionable area.

Decline and occupation

After Frederick's death Prussia went into a **decline**, culminating in the defeat of its once-invincible army by French revolutionaries at the Battle of Valmy in 1792. The decline went unchecked under **Friedrich Wilhelm II** (1744–97), continuing into the Napoleonic era. As Bonaparte's empire spread across Europe, the Prussian court dithered, appeasing the French and trying to delay the inevitable invasion. Life in Berlin continued more or less as normal, but by August 1806 citizens were watching Prussian soldiers set off on the march west to engage Napoleonic forces. On September 19, the king and queen left the city, followed a month later by Count von der Schulenburg, the city governor, who had assured Berliners that all was going well right up until he learned of Prussia's defeat at Jena and Auerstadt.

Five days later French troops marched through the **Brandenburg Gate** and Berlin was occupied. On October 27, 1806, Napoleon himself arrived to head a parade down Unter den Linden – greeted as a liberator by the Berliners, according to some accounts. **French occupation** forced state reform: ministries were streamlined, nobles could engage in trade and guild membership became more accessible. And during this time Berlin embraced the **Romantic movement** – a rebellious celebration of German spirit and tradition in opposition to the cold rationality of the French Enlightenment. From the movement sprouted notions of what it meant to be German and the idea that all Germans should be unified in a single state – though this wouldn't happen until 1871.

The rebirth of Prussia

After his defeats in Russia and at the 1813 Battle of Leipzig, Napoleon's empire began to collapse, allowing Prussia to pull out of their forced alliance and resume self-rule. Symbolically, the **Quadriga** (the Goddess of Victory in her chariot) was restored to the

1576	**1618**
Nearly five thousand inhabitants of Berlin are wiped out by the bubonic plague.	The Thirty Years' War begins. It has a devastating impact on Berlin with a third of houses damaged and half of the population left dead.

Brandenburg Gate, but despite high hopes for reform the people of Berlin gained only the promise of a constitution for Prussia, which never materialized. Otherwise the pre-Napoleonic status quo was restored, and the real victor was the **Prussian state**, which acquired tracts of land along the Rhine, including the Ruhr, that contained the iron and coal deposits on which its military might would be rebuilt.

The war was followed by an era of reaction and oppression, which did so much to stifle intellectual and cultural life in Berlin that the philosopher Wilhelm von Humboldt resigned from the university in protest at the new authoritarianism. Gradually this mellowed out into the **Biedermeier years**, characterized by the retreat into private and family life, tranquil art and Neoclassical architecture. Meanwhile, Prussia's industrial fortunes began to rise, laying the foundation of its Great Power status. Berlin continued to grow: factories and railways and the first of the city's *Mietskaserne*, or **tenement buildings**, were constructed – foreshadowing what was to come with full industrialization.

Revolution and reaction

Berlin enjoyed more than thirty years of peace and stability after 1815, but shared the revolutionary mood that swept Europe in **1848**. Influenced by events in France and the writings of Karl Marx (who lived here from 1837 to 1841), Berliners demanded a say in the running of their own affairs. **King Friedrich Wilhelm IV** (1795–1861) refused to agree. On March 18, citizens gathered outside his palace to present their demands. The soldiers who dispersed them accidentally fired two shots and the demonstration became a **revolution**. Barricades went up and a fourteen-hour battle raged, with rich and poor alike joining in. During the fighting 183 Berliners and eighteen soldiers died.

Aghast at his subjects' anger, Friedrich Wilhelm IV ordered his troops to withdraw to Spandau, leaving the city in the hands of the revolutionaries, who established a parliament and citizens' militia, but lacked direction: rather than assaulting Spandau, declaring a republic or seizing public buildings, the new assembly concerned itself with law and order. On March 21, the king appeared in public wearing the tricolour black, red and gold emblem of the revolution. Having failed to suppress it, he now proposed to join it. He spoke, promising nothing much but paying lip service to the idea of German unity, which impressed the assembled liberals. Order was fully restored, then in October, a Prussian army under General Wrangel entered Berlin and forced the **dissolution of parliament**. Berliners either gave up or followed millions of fellow Germans into exile.

Suppression followed. Friedrich gave up the tricolour and persecuted liberals, before going insane shortly afterwards. His brother Prince Wilhelm – who had led the troops against the barricades – became king. **Otto von Bismarck** was appointed chancellor (1862), despite the almost universal loathing he inspired among Berliners. Meanwhile, Berlin continued to grow apace, turning into a cosmopolitan, modern industrial city. Its free press and revolutionary past exerted a liberal influence on Prussia's emasculated parliament, the **Reichstag**, to the irritation of Bismarck and the king (who was soon to proclaim himself emperor, or Kaiser). However, Bismarck became a national hero after Prussian victory at the **Battle of Königgrätz** (1866) smashed Austrian military power, clearing the way for Prussia to unite – and dominate – Germany. Although militaristic nationalism caused liberalism to wither elsewhere, Berlin continued to elect liberal

1685

Friedrich Wilhelm offers asylum to the Huguenots. More than 15,000 come to Brandenburg and six thousand settle in Berlin.

1699

Inauguration of Schloss Charlottenburg, commissioned by Sophie Charlotte, wife of Friedrich I.

Reichstag deputies, which became the parliament of the whole nation after **German unification** in 1871.

Berlin remained a maverick city. It was here that three attempts were made to kill Kaiser Wilhelm I; the final one on Unter den Linden (1878) left him with thirty pieces of shrapnel in his body. While the Kaiser recovered, Bismarck used the event to justify a **crackdown on socialists**, closing newspapers and persecuting trade unionists. The growth of unionism was a direct result of relentless urbanization. Between 1890 and 1900, Berlin's population doubled to two million and thousands of tenement buildings sprang up in working-class districts like **Prenzlauer Berg** and **Wedding**. The poor conditions here meant its residents were solidly behind the Social Democratic Party (**SPD**), whose deputies were the chief dissenters within the Reichstag. By 1890 Wilhelm II had become Kaiser and dropped Bismarck, but the country continued to be militaristic and authoritarian. While Berlin remained defiantly liberal, it steadily acquired the attributes of a modern capital. Now an established centre for commerce and diplomacy, it boasted electric trams, an underground railway, and other technical innovations of the age. In the arts Berlin also moved forward, developing its own form of Modernism, in the **Berlin Secession** movement, which rejected the art establishment and included artists Max Liebermann, Edvard Munch and Walter Leistikow.

World War I and its aftermath

The arms race and alliances that polarized Europe during the 1890s and the first decade of the twentieth century led inexorably towards **World War I**. Its 1914 outbreak was greeted with enthusiasm by most German civilians – only pacifists and communists resisted the heady intoxication of patriotism. In Berlin, Kaiser Wilhelm II spoke "to all Germans" from the balcony of his palace, and shop windows across the city were festooned with national colours. Military bands played *Heil dir im Siegerkranz* ("Hail to you in the Victor's Laurel") and *Die Wacht am Rhein* ("The Watch on the Rhine") in cafés, while Berliners threw flowers to the Imperial German army, or Reichswehr, as it marched off to war. The political parties agreed to a truce, and even the Social Democrats voted for war credits.

The General Staff's calculation that France could be knocked out before Russia fully mobilized soon proved hopelessly optimistic, and Germany found itself facing a war on two fronts – the very thing Bismarck had dreaded. As casualties mounted on the stalemated western front, 350,000 German men perished in the war. Rationing and food shortages began to hit poorer civilians and **disillusionment** set in. By the summer of 1915 housewives were demonstrating in front of the Reichstag, a portent of more serious popular unrest to come. Ordinary people were beginning to see the war as an exercise staged for the rich at the expense of the poor.

In December 1917, nineteen members of the SPD announced that they could no longer support the war and formed an independent socialist party known as the USPD. This party joined the "International Group" of **Karl Liebknecht** and **Rosa Luxemburg** – later known as the Spartacists – which had opposed SPD support for the war since 1915. This grouping later formed the nucleus of the postwar Kommunistische Partei Deutschlands, or **KPD**. Meanwhile, fuel, food and even beer shortages added to growing hardships on the home front.

1701	1709
Berlin becomes the capital of Prussia.	Cölln and Berlin become known simply as "Berlin", the larger of the two cities.

Defeat and revolution

With their last great offensive spent, and America joining the Allied war effort, even Germany's supreme warlord, Erich von Ludendorff, recognized that **defeat** was inevitable by the autumn of 1918. Knowing the Allies would refuse to negotiate with the old absolutist system, he declared (on September 9) a democratic, **constitutional monarchy**, whose chancellor would be responsible to the Reichstag and not the Kaiser. A government was formed under Prince Max von Baden, and extensive reforms agreed. But it was too little, too late for the bitter sailors and soldiers on the home front, where the contrast between privilege and poverty was most obvious. At the beginning of November the Kiel Garrison led a **naval mutiny** and revolutionary **Workers' and Soldiers' Soviets** mushroomed across Germany. Elements of this revolutionary unrest were mirrored in the Dada art movement, which put down firm roots in the city in 1919, while the fresh, functional **Bauhaus** design movement (see box, p.101) began to tidy some of the chaos.

Caught up in this wave of unrest, Berliners took to the streets on November 8–9, where they were joined by soldiers stationed in the capital. Realizing that the game was up, **Kaiser Wilhelm II abdicated**, producing a situation of dual power: almost at the same time as Philipp Scheidemann of the SPD declared a "**German Republic**" from the Reichstag's balcony, Karl Liebknecht was proclaiming a "Free Socialist Republic" from a balcony of the royal palace just 2km away. In the face of increasing confusion, SPD leader Friedrich Ebert took over as head of the government. A deal was struck with the army, which promised to protect the republic if Ebert forestalled a full-blooded socialist revolution by the Spartacists. Ebert ruled Berlin for nearly three months but many of the revolutionary soldiers, sailors and workers who controlled the streets favoured a Soviet-style government and refused to obey his orders. Things came to a head with the **Spartacist uprising** in Berlin during the first half of January 1919. This inspired lasting dread among the bourgeoisie, who applauded when the Spartacists were eventually crushed by the militarily superior **Freikorps**: armed bands of right-wing officers and NCOs from the old Imperial army, dedicated to protecting Germany from "Bolshevism". The torture and **murder of Liebknecht and Luxemburg** by Freikorps officers (who threw their bodies in the Landwehrkanal) remained unpunished once the fighting was over. This hardly augured well for the future of the **new republic**, whose National Assembly elections were held on January 19.

The Weimar Republic

The elections gave the SPD 38 percent of the vote and confirmed them the new political leaders of the country. Ebert was made president, Scheidemann chancellor. **Weimar**, the small country town that had seen the most glorious flowering of the German Enlightenment, was chosen in preference to Berlin as the place to draft a national constitution, which was tinged by monarchic and military associations.

The **constitution** drawn up was hailed as the most liberal, democratic and progressive in the world. While it incorporated a highly complex system of checks and balances to prevent power becoming too concentrated in either particular parts of government or regions, it crucially lacked clauses outlawing parties hostile to the system. This opened the way for savage attacks on the republic by extremists at both ends of the political spectrum. With public opinion divided between a plethora of parties promoting

1740

1745–47

Friedrich II – known as Frederick the Great – comes to power and rules until 1786. He turns Berlin into a centre of Enlightenment.

Schloss Sanssouci is built as the summer palace of Frederick the Great.

sectional interests, all Weimar-era governments became unwieldy coalitions that often pursued contradictory policies in different ministries and had an average life of only about eight months, providing a weak framework that later readily allowed the Nazis to take control.

1920s Berlin

Much of Germany's **1920s** history was dictated by the Allies and the harsh terms of the **Treaty of Versailles:** Alsace-Lorraine was handed back to France. In the east, Germany lost a large chunk of Prussia to Poland, giving the latter access to the Baltic, but cutting off the German province of East Prussia from the rest of the country. The overseas empire was dismantled; the Rhineland occupied. But what aggrieved Germans most was the treaty's war guilt clause that held Germany responsible "for causing all the loss and damage" suffered by the Allies in the war. This was seen as a cynical victors' justice, yet provided the validation for a gigantic bill of reparation payments: a total of 132 billion gold marks.

The early 1920s was a bad time for Berlin. As the mark began to plunge in value, the government was shocked by the **assassination of Walter Rathenau.** As foreign minister, he had just signed the Treaty of Rapallo, aimed at promoting closer economic ties with the Soviet Union, since the western powers remained intransigent. Rathenau was killed at his own Grunewald house by Freikorps officers. When France and Belgium occupied the Ruhr in response to alleged defaults in the reparations payments, a **general strike** was called across Germany in January 1923.

The combination of reparations and strikes sent the mark plummeting, causing the worst **inflation** ever known. As their savings were wiped out and literally barrowloads of paper money weren't enough to support a family, Berliners experienced the terrors of hyperinflation. In working-class districts, street fighting between right and left flared up. Foreigners flocked in to pay bargain prices for carpets and furs that even rich Germans could no longer afford, and fortunes were made and lost by speculators. In the midst of all this, on November 8, Berliners' attention was briefly diverted to Munich, where a motley crew of right-wing ex-army officers including General Ludendorff attempted to mount a putsch. It failed, but Berliners were to hear of one of the ringleaders again – **Adolf Hitler.**

The mark was finally stabilized under the supremely able foreign minister, **Gustav Stresemann**, who believed relief from reparation payments was more likely to come from cooperation than stubborn resistance. The Allies too moderated their stance, realizing Germany needed to be economically stable in order to pay. So, under the **1924 Dawes Plan**, loans poured into Germany, particularly from America, leading to an economic upsurge.

Nightlife and the arts

Economic recovery transformed the social life of Berlin. For many people the centre of the city had shifted from Friedrichstrasse and Unter den Linden to the cafés and bars of the Kurfürstendamm. Jazz hit the **nightclubs** in a big way, along with drug abuse (mainly cocaine) and all kinds of sex. There were clubs for transvestites, clubs where you could watch nude dancing, or dance naked yourself – and usually the police didn't

1788–91	1806	1810
The Brandenburg Gate is built.	Napoleon conquers Berlin but grants self-government to the city.	Humboldt University is founded by Prussian educational reformer and linguist Wilhelm von Humboldt.

give a damn. This was the legendary era later to be celebrated by writer **Christopher Isherwood** and others, when Berlin was briefly the most open, tolerant city in Europe, a spiritual home for anyone who rejected conventions and traditions.

The 1920s was also a boom time for the arts, as the Dada shockwave rippled through the decade. **George Grosz** satirized the times in savage caricatures, while **John Heartfield** used photomontage to produce biting political statements. Equally striking, if less didactic, was the work of artists like **Otto Dix** and **Christian Schad**. Producer **Max Reinhardt** continued to dominate Berlin theatre, as he'd done since taking over at the Deutsches Theater in 1905. **Erwin Piscator** moved from propaganda into mainstream theatre at the Theater am Nollendorfplatz, without losing his innovative edge, and in 1928 **Bertolt Brecht**'s *Dreigroschenoper* (*Threepenny Opera*) was staged for the first time. Appropriately, Berlin also became a centre for the very newest of the arts. Between the wars the **UFA film studios** (see p.182) at Babelsberg was the biggest in Europe, producing legendary films like **Fritz Lang**'s *Metropolis*, *The Cabinet of Doctor Caligari* and *The Blue Angel* (starring Berlin-born **Marlene Dietrich**).

Middle- and lowbrow tastes were catered for by endless all-singing, all-dancing **musicals**, featuring platoons of women in various states of undress. This was also the heyday of the Berlin **cabaret** scene, when some of its most acidic exponents were at work.

Political extremism and the Nazis

With inflation under control, Germany returned to relative **political stability**. The 1924 elections demonstrated increased support for centre-right and republican parties. When President Ebert died (February 28, 1925) and was succeeded by the former commander of the Imperial army, **General Field Marshal von Hindenburg**, monarchists and conservatives rejoiced. Nevertheless, it was now that the extreme right, particularly the **National Socialist German Workers' Party** (NSDAP), or Nazis, began gradually gaining ground, starting in Bavaria.

Germany's late-1920s economic upsurge would last only until the **Wall Street Crash** in October 1929. That suddenly ended all American credit and wiped out Germany's economic stability. The poverty of the immediate postwar period returned with a vengeance. Everyone suffered: hyperinflation wiped out middle-class savings, and by 1932 there were six million unemployed. Increasingly people sought radical solutions in political extremism, and started supporting two parties that bitterly opposed one another but shared a desire to end democracy: the **Communists** and the National Socialist German Workers' Party. While red flags and swastika banners hung from neighbouring tenements, gangs from the left and right fought in the streets in ever-greater numbers, with the brown-shirted Nazi **SA** (*Sturmabteilung*) Stormtroopers, fighting endless pitched battles against the communist **Rote Frontkämpferbund** (Red Fighters' Front). The threat of a return to the anarchy of the postwar years increased Nazi support among the middle classes and captains of industry (who provided heavy financial support) who feared for their lives and property under communist rule. Fear of the reds also helped the Nazis ensure little or nothing was done to curb their violence against them. Growing Nazi popularity was also attributable to Hitler's record as a war veteran, his identification of Jews as scapegoats and a charisma that promised

1841	**1861**	**1871**
Berlin's Museum Island is dedicated to "art and science" by Friedrich Wilhelm IV of Prussia.	Wedding, Moabit and several other suburbs are incorporated into Berlin.	Berlin becomes the capital of a unified German Empire, under Otto von Bismarck's chancellorship.

to restore national pride. Meanwhile, the Communists found it difficult to find support beyond the German working classes.

By September 1930, the Communists and Nazis together gained nearly one of every three votes cast and in the July 1932 **parliamentary elections** the Nazis took 37 percent of the vote – their biggest total in any free election – making them the largest party in the Reichstag; the Communists took fifteen percent. Very soon, Nazi thugs began attacking Jewish shops and businesses throughout Germany and intimidating liberals into muted criticism or silence. But what eventually brought the Nazis to power in 1933 was in-fighting among conservatives, who persuaded the virtually senile Hindenburg to make Hitler chancellor. This move was based on a gamble that the Nazis would usefully crush the left but fail to form an effective government – so that within a few months Hitler could be nudged aside. Hitler became chancellor on January 4, 1933 and Berlin thronged with Nazi supporters bearing torches. For the vast majority of Berliners it was a nightmare come true: three-quarters of the city had voted against the Nazis at the last elections.

Nazi takeover

The pretext for an all-out **Nazi takeover** was provided by the **Reichstag fire** (February 28, 1933), which was likely started by them, rather than the simple-minded Dutch communist Marius van der Lubbe on whom it was blamed. An **emergency decree** the following day effectively legalized a permanent state of emergency, which the Nazis quickly used to start crushing the communists and manipulate the 1933 **elections** in which the Nazis won 43.9 percent of the vote. Though short of a majority, this need was quickly rendered unnecessary by the arrest of communist deputies and SPD leaders to pass an **Enabling Act** that gave the Nazis dictatorial powers. Hitler was only just short of the two-thirds majority he needed to legally abolish the Weimar Republic. The SPD salvaged some self-respect by refusing to agree, but Catholic centrists meekly supported the Bill in return for minor concessions. It was passed by 441 votes to 84, hammering the final nails into the coffin of German parliamentary democracy. With Hindenburg's death in the summer of 1934, Hitler merged the offices of president and chancellor declaring himself **Führer** of the German Reich and producing an absolute dictatorship.

Nazi terror begins

Once in absolute power Hitler quickly consolidated his control by removing opposition and tightening the Nazi grip on all areas of society. Rival political parties were effectively banned, unions quickly disbanded, and leaders of both arrested and sent to **concentration camps**. Then the persecution of Nazi opponents was extended to embrace "active church members, freemasons, politically dissatisfied people … abortionists and homosexuals". On May 11, 1934, they shocked the world by **burning thousands of books** that conflicted with Nazi ideology on Opernplatz (now Bebelplatz) in central Berlin. The **exodus from Berlin** of known anti-Nazis and those with reasons to fear them began in earnest. Well-known names including Bertolt Brecht, Kurt Weill, Lotte Lenya and Wassily Kandinsky all left the city, joining the likes of Albert Einstein and George Grosz in exile.

Nazi ruthlessness extended to their own, and in 1934 the party was purged during a night later called the "**Night of the Long Knives**". Under **Ernst Röhm**, the SA had grown

1894	**1901**
The Reichstag is completed after ten years of building work.	Actress and singer Marlene Dietrich is born in Schöneberg.

JEWISH BERLIN

Though commonly remembered in the context of their persecution under the Third Reich, **Jews** had had a far longer and happier history in Berlin, which, as one of the most progressive cities in Europe, had fostered a large Jewish population between the late seventeenth century and the 1930s (see box, pp.78-79).

---

to 500,000 men and their power worried big business, the regular army and rival Nazis like Himmler and Göring. United in their hostility towards the SA they persuaded Hitler that Röhm and his allies were conspiring against him with the result that on the night of June 30, the SA leaders were taken to Stadelheim Prison and shot in the courtyard by SS troopers; it came as such a surprise that some believed it was an army coup, and died shouting "Heil Hitler!" In Berlin alone, 150 SA leaders were executed. Other victims included conservative politicians such as General Schleicher and several of von Papen's assistants, while local police and Gestapo chiefs added personal enemies to death lists. Meanwhile, the Nazis put their own men into vital posts throughout local governments – in Berlin and the rest of Germany. This was the first stage of *Gleichschaltung* ("coordination"), whereby the machinery of state, and then society itself, would be Nazified.

The other big night of Nazi savagery in the prewar period was **Kristallnacht** (November 9, 1938) when the **boycott of Jewish** businesses, medical and legal practices in Berlin – enforced by the SA since April 1, 1934 – turned into bare-faced **attacks on Jewish shops and institutions**. Just as the Reichstag fire was used as an excuse to consolidate power, the Nazis used the assassination of Ernst vom Rath, a German official in Paris, by Herschel Grynszpan, a young German-Jewish refugee, as an excuse to unleash a general pogrom on German Jews. Grynszpan was protesting his parents' forced deportation to Poland with ten thousand other Jews. (Ironically, vom Rath was an anti-Nazi whom Grynszpan had mistaken for his intended target, the German ambassador.) In retaliation the Nazis organized "spontaneous" anti-Jewish demonstrations – directing the police to ensure that attacks on the Jewish community, mainly by SA men in civilian clothes, were not hindered. After *Kristallnacht* the Nazi government enacted anti-Semitic laws confiscating property and making life difficult and dangerous for German Jews, paving the way for the greater horrors to come.

Daily life and the Olympics

Given the suppression, fear, exodus and the tightening grip of Nazi control on all areas of life, the atmosphere in Berlin changed irrevocably. The unemployed were drafted into labour battalions, set to work on the land or building autobahns; the press and radio were orchestrated by Goebbels; children joined Nazi youth organizations; and every tenement building had Nazi-appointed wardens who doubled as Gestapo spies. It was even decreed that women should eschew make-up as an "un-German" artifice – one of the few edicts that wasn't taken seriously. Anti-Nazi criticism – even of the mildest kind – invited a visit from the Gestapo. Although Germans might avoid joining the NSDAP itself, it was difficult to escape the plethora of related organizations covering every aspect of life, from riding clubs and dog breeders to the "Reich Church"

1918	**1920**
Berlin witnesses the end of World War I and the proclamation of the Republic.	Berlin is established as a separate administrative zone under the Greater Berlin Act. A dozen villages and estates are incorporated into the city to expand it.

or "German League of Maidens". This was the second stage of *Gleichschaltung* – drawing the entire population into the Nazi net.

As the capital of the Reich, Berlin became a showcase city of banners, uniforms and parades. An image of order and dynamism, of a "new Germany" on the march, was what the Nazis tried to convey. This reached its zenith during the **1936 Olympics**, held at a vast purpose-built stadium in suburban Berlin, which helped raise Germany's international standing and temporarily glossed over the realities of Nazi brutality.

World War II

Throughout the 1930s the Nazis made **preparations for war**, expanding the army and gearing the economy for war readiness by 1940, to dovetail with Hitler's foreign policy of obtaining *Lebensraum* ("living space") from neighbouring countries by intimidation. From 1936 onwards Hitler even spent much time with his favourite architect, **Albert Speer**, drawing up extensive plans for a remodelled and grandiose Berlin, to be called "Germania", that would reflect a postwar role as world capital of the "Thousand Year Reich". His megalomania inspired hours of brooding on how future generations might be awed by Germania's monumental ruins, in the way that contemporaries venerated the ruins of ancient Roman and Middle Eastern civilizations – hence the need to build with the finest materials on a gigantic scale.

The road to war was swift. In 1936 the German army occupied the Rhineland (demilitarized under the terms of the Treaty of Versailles) to token protests from the League of Nations. The **Anschluss** ("annexation") of Austria in 1938 was likewise carried off with impunity, and a few months later Britain and France agreed to dismember Czechoslovakia. Encouraged by their appeasement, Hitler made new demands on Polish territory in 1939, probably hoping for a similar collapse of will by the western powers, the more so since he had pulled off the spectacular coup of signing a nonaggression pact with his ultimate enemy, the Soviet Union, thus ensuring that Germany could avoid a war on two fronts. But two days after the German invasion of Poland began on September 1, Britain and France declared war in defence of their treaty obligations.

Outbreak and early success

The outbreak of **World War II** was greeted without enthusiasm by Berliners, despite German victories in Poland. There were few signs of patriotic fervour as the troops marched off to war through the streets, and Hitler cancelled further parades out of pique. Only the spectacle of the military parade to mark the fall of France (July 18, 1940), when German troops marched through the Brandenburg Gate for the first time since 1871, really attracted the crowds.

Initially, Berlin suffered little from the war. Although citizens were already complaining of meagre rations, delicacies and luxury goods from occupied Europe gravitated towards the Reich capital. What remained of the diplomatic and foreign press community and all the Nazi bigwigs continued to maintain chic lifestyles. Open dissent seemed impossible, with Gestapo informers believed to lurk everywhere, while much wartime misery was softened by Nazi welfare organizations and a blanket of propaganda.

1928	**1933**
British novelist Christopher Isherwood arrives in Berlin.	Adolf Hitler comes to power shortly after a fire devastates the Reichstag.

THE WANNSEE CONFERENCE

The conference at the **Wannsee villa** on January 20, 1942, was held at the instigation of Reinhard Heydrich, Chief of Reich Security Head Office, who had been ordered by Göring to submit plans for rounding up, deporting and destroying all Jews in Reich territory. Heydrich summoned SS and government officials, including Adolf Eichmann and Roland Freisler, who later gained infamy as the judge at the Volksgerichthof (see box, pp.98–99). Eichmann kept a complete set of minutes of the meeting, and these documents, discovered after the war – despite the fact that all recipients had been requested to destroy their copies – played an important part in the Nürnberg trials of war criminals.

The problem Heydrich delineated was that Europe contained eleven million Jews: the "Final Solution" to the "Jewish Question" was that these people should be taken to camps and worked to death, if they were able-bodied, or murdered on arrival if not. Those who survived would eventually be executed, since, under Nazi principles of natural selection, they would be the toughest, and in Heydrich's words could be "the germ cell of a new Jewish development". In these early stages systematic killing machines like Auschwitz and Treblinka were not yet fully operational. More discussion was spent on how the Jews should be rounded up: deception would prevent panic and revolt, so the pretence that Jews were being moved for "resettlement" extremely important. Heydrich charged Eichmann with this task, which eventually cost him his life when he was sentenced to death for war crimes in Israel in 1960.

At no time during the conference were the words "murder" or "killing" written down; careful euphemisms shielded the enormity of what was being planned. Reading the minutes, it's difficult not to be shocked by the matter-of-fact manner in which the business was discussed, and the way in which politeness and efficiency absorb and absolve all concerned. When sterilization was suggested as one "solution" it was rejected as "unethical" by a doctor present, and there was much self-congratulation as various officials described their areas as "Judenfrei" (free of Jews).

Heydrich died following an assassination attempt in Prague a few months later; some of the others present did not survive the war either, but, in contrast to the millions who were destroyed by their organizational ability, many of the Wannsee delegation lived on to gain a pension from the postwar German state.

Air raids

Göring had publicly boasted that Germans could call him "Meyer" (a Jewish surname) if a single bomb fell on Berlin. Notwithstanding, the British RAF dropped some for the first time on August 23, 1940, and a further night raid on August 28–29 killed ten people – the first German civilian casualties. These raids had a marked demoralizing effect on Berliners, who had counted on a swift end to the war, and Hitler had to reassure the populace in a speech at the Sportpalast. Holding up a Baedeker travel guide to Britain, he thundered that the Luftwaffe would raze Britain's cities to the ground one by one.

However, these early **bombing raids** on Berlin caused little real damage and it wasn't until March 1, 1943 – when defeat in the Western Desert and difficulties on the eastern front had already brought home the fact that Germany was not invincible – that Berlin suffered its first heavy raids. The British bombed by night, the Americans by day, establishing a pattern that would relentlessly reduce Berlin to ruins. "We can wreck Berlin from end to end if the USAAF will come in on it. It will cost us between 400 and 500 aircraft. It will cost Germany the war", the head of Bomber Command,

1936

The Olympic Games are held in Berlin.

1938

Jewish shop windows are smashed and businesses attacked throughout Germany on *Kristallnacht*, also called the Night of Broken Glass.

Sir Arthur "Bomber" Harris, had written to Churchill in 1943. The first buildings to go were the Staatsoper and Alte Bibliothek on Unter den Linden. On December 22, the Kaiser-Wilhelm-Gedächtniskirche was reduced to a shell. By the year's end, daily and nightly bombardments were a feature of everyday life.

During the 363 air raids until the end of the war, 75,000 tons of high-explosive or incendiary bombs killed between 35,000 and 50,000 people and rendered 1,500,000 Berliners homeless. Yet despite the colossal destruction that filled the streets with 100 million tons of rubble, at the war's end seventy percent of the city's industrial capacity was still functioning.

Apart from chipping away at Nazi power, the destruction also intensified **underground resistance**. Despite the Gestapo stranglehold some groups managed minor successes and several failed attempts on Hitler's life were made, most notably the **July Bomb Plot** (see box, pp.98–99). But resistance was piecemeal and included assistance given to **Jews** to help them evade being rounded up onto trains bound for concentration camps, as part of the Nazi "**Final Solution**" to the Jewish question as decided in a villa beside Berlin's Wannsee (see box, p.273).

The fall of Berlin

Enjoy the war while you can! The peace is going to be terrible…

Berlin joke shortly before the fall of the city.

By autumn 1944, it was obvious to all but the most fanatical Nazis that the end was approaching fast. Even so, Hitler would hear no talk of surrender or negotiation. But by January 1945, distance between the Allied forces was narrowing inexorably and on January 27, Soviet forces crossed the Oder 160km from Berlin. Only Hitler now really believed there was any hope for Germany. The Nazis threw all they could at the eastern front and mobilized the Volkssturm, an ill-equipped home guard of old men, boys and cripples. Thirteen- and fourteen-year-old members of the **Hitler Youth** were briefly trained in the art of using the Panzerfaust bazooka, then sent into the fray against tanks and battle-hardened infantrymen. As thousands died at the front to buy a little time for the doomed Nazi regime, life in Berlin became a nightmare. The city was choked with refugees and terrified of the approaching Russians; it was bombed day and night, and the flash of Soviet artillery could be seen on the horizon.

Behind the lines, **flying court martials** picked up soldiers and executed anyone suspected of "desertion" or "cowardice in the face of the enemy". On February 1, 1945, Berlin was declared *Vertedigungsbereich* (a "zone of defence") – to be defended to the last man and the last bullet. The civilian population – women, children and forced labourers – were set to work building tank traps and barricades; stretches of the U- and S-Bahn formed part of the fortifications. Goebbels trumpeted a "**fortress Berlin**", while Hitler planned the deployment of phantom armies, which existed on battle charts, but hardly at all in reality.

As Berlin frantically prepared to defend itself, the Russians consolidated their strength. On April 16, at 5am Moscow time, the **Soviet offensive** began with a massive bombardment lasting 25 minutes. When the artillery fell silent, 143 searchlights spaced 200m apart along the entire front were switched on to dazzle the enemy as the Russians began their advance. Three army groups totalling over 1.5 million men moved forward

1938–45	1939
Thousands of Jews (and other minorities) living in Berlin are sent to death camps.	World War II begins.

under marshals Zhukov, Konev and Rokossovsky – and there was little the vastly outnumbered Germans could do to halt them. By April 20 – Hitler's 56th birthday (celebrated with tea and cakes in the *Führerbunker*) – the Red Army was on the edge of Berlin. The next day the city centre came within range of their guns, and several people queuing outside the Karstadt department store on Hermannplatz were killed by shells. On April 23, Soviet troops were in the Weissensee district, just a few kilometres east of the centre.

Hitler's birthday party was the last time the Nazi hierarchy assembled before going – or staying – to meet their respective fates. The dictator and his partner Eva Braun chose to remain in Berlin, and Goebbels elected to join them in the **Führerbunker** with his family. It was a dank, stuffy complex of reinforced concrete cells beneath the garden of the Reich Chancellery. Here Hitler brooded over Speer's architectural models of unbuilt victory memorials, subsisting on salads, herbal tisanes and regular injections of dubious substances by one Dr Morell. To hapless generals and faithful acolytes, he ranted about traitors and the unworthiness of the German *Volk*, and after learning that General Steiner's army had failed to stop Zhukov's advance declared that the war was lost and that he would stay in the bunker to the end.

The final days

By April 25, Berlin was completely **encircled by Soviet troops**, which met up with US forces advancing from the west. Over the next two days, the suburbs of Dahlem, Spandau, Neukölln and Gatow fell to the Russians, and the city's telephone system failed. On April 27, the Third Panzer Army was completely smashed; survivors fled west, leaving Berlin's northern flank virtually undefended. The obvious hopelessness of the situation didn't sway the top Nazis' fanatical **refusal to surrender**. As the Red Army closed in, Goebbels called hysterically for "rücksichtslose Bekämpfung" – fight without quarter – and SS execution squads worked around the clock, killing soldiers, Volkssturm guards or Hitler Youth who tried to stop fighting.

In the city the horrors mounted. The **civilian population** lived underground in cellars and air-raid shelters, scavenging for food wherever and whenever there was a momentary lull in the fighting. Engineers blasted canal locks, flooding the U-Bahn to prevent the Russians from advancing along it and drowning scores of sheltering civilians in the process. On April 27, the Ninth Army was destroyed attempting to break out of the Russian encirclement to the south, and unoccupied Berlin had been reduced to a strip 15km long from east to west, and 5km wide from north to south, constantly under bombardment. Next the Russians captured the Tiergarten, reducing the **last pocket of resistance** to the Regierungsviertel, where fighting focused on the Reichstag and Hitler's Chancellery, and on Potsdamer Platz, only a few hundred metres from the *Führerbunker*, by now under constant shellfire.

Hitler still hoped one of his phantom armies would relieve Berlin, but on April 28 his optimism evaporated when he heard that Himmler had been suing for unconditional surrender with the western Allies. In the early hours of the following day, he married Eva Braun, held a small champagne reception, and dictated his will. As the day wore on, savage fighting continued around the Nazi-held enclave. At a final conference the commandant of Berlin, General Weidling, announced that the Russians were in the nearby *Adlon Hotel*, and that there was no hope of relief.

1943–45	**1945**
Over ninety percent of Berlin is destroyed in air raids.	The Allies take Berlin, and divide it into Russian, American, French and British zones.

A breakout attempt was proposed, but Hitler declared that he was staying put. On the afternoon of April 30, after testing the cyanide on his pet German shepherd dog, **Hitler and Eva Braun committed suicide**: he with a revolver, she by poison. The bodies were taken to the Chancellery courtyard and doused with two hundred litres of petrol; Hitler's followers gave the Nazi salute as the corpses burned to ashes. Meanwhile, Soviet troops battled for the Reichstag, and at 11pm two Russian sergeants raised the red flag on its rooftop.

After Hitler's death, chief of staff Krebs was sent out to parley with the Russians. After hasty consultation with Stalin, General Chuikov replied that only unconditional surrender was acceptable. When Krebs returned to the bunker, Goebbels rejected this and ordered the fighting to continue. That night he and his wife killed themselves, having first poisoned their six children. Almost all the rest of the eight hundred or so bunker occupants decided to try and break out. Weidling agreed not to surrender until the following dawn in order to give the fugitives time to **escape** through the railway tunnels towards northern Berlin; about a hundred made it – the rest were either killed or captured.

Capitulation and surrender

At 5am, Weidling offered the **capitulation of Berlin** to General Chuikov, who broadcast his surrender proclamation from loudspeaker vans around the city. At 3pm, firing in the city centre stopped, although sporadic, sometimes fierce, fighting continued on the outskirts, where German troops tried to break out to the west to surrender to the more merciful British or Americans rather than the vengeful Russians. The **official surrender of German forces** occurred at a Wehrmacht engineers' school in the Berlin suburb of Karlshorst on May 8, 1945. By then Berliners had already emerged from their shelters and started to clear the dead and the rubble from the streets.

With the final act of surrender complete, it was time to count the **cost** of the Battle of Berlin. It had taken the lives of 125,000 Berliners (including 6400 suicides and 22,000 heart attacks), and innumerable German soldiers from the 93 divisions destroyed by the Red Army. The Soviets themselves had suffered some 305,000 casualties in the battle, while the city was left in ruins, without even basic services. But for those civilians who remained in the city, this was just the start of the worst as the Soviets unleashed an **orgy of rape and looting** on the capital.

Occupation

During the immediate postwar months, civilian rations of food, fuel and medicine, if forthcoming at all, were cut to the bone to support the two-million-strong **Soviet occupation forces**. Civilians had to use all their wits to stay alive. The Soviet Union had taken steps towards establishing a civilian, communist-dominated administration even before the war was over. On April 30, a group of exiled German communists were brought to Berlin to establish a temporary headquarters in Lichtenberg. Directed by **Walter Ulbricht**, the future leader of the GDR's communist party, they set about tracking down old Berlin party members and setting up a new **municipal administration**.

The **western occupation sectors** had been demarcated by the Allies as far back as 1943, but the troops didn't move in until July 1–4, 1945, when fifty thousand British,

June 1948	1949
The Russians cut off all overland routes between West Germany and West Berlin, so the Berlin airlift begins, with Allied planes delivering essential supplies around the clock.	The Federal Republic of Germany is founded in West Berlin and the German Democratic Republic in East Berlin.

American and French soldiers replaced the Red Army in western Berlin. Here, the food situation improved marginally once American supplies began to find their way through, but public health remained a huge problem. Dysentery and TB were endemic, and there were outbreaks of typhoid and paratyphoid, all exacerbated by an acute shortage of hospital beds. British and American soldiers had endless opportunities to profit from the burgeoning **black market**: trading cigarettes, alcohol, gas, NAAFI and PX supplies for antiques, jewellery or sexual favours. Huge black-market centres sprang up around the Brandenburg Gate and Alexanderplatz.

From July 17 to August 3 the **Potsdam Conference** took place at Cecilienhof Palace. It was to be the last great meeting of the leaders of the Big Three wartime alliance. Churchill took the opportunity to visit the ruins of the Reich's Chancellery, followed by a mob of fascinated Germans and Russians. Mid-conference he returned to Britain to hear the results of the first postwar election – and was replaced by the newly elected Labour prime minister, Clement Attlee, who could do little but watch as Truman and Stalin settled the fate of postwar Europe and Berlin.

Starvation and unrest

For Berliners, things stayed miserable. German agriculture and industry had virtually collapsed, threatening acute **shortages of food and fuel** just as winter approached. Mass graves were dug and coffins stockpiled for the expected wave of deaths, and thousands of children were evacuated to the British occupation zone in the west, where conditions were less severe. To everyone's surprise the winter turned out to be uncommonly mild. Christmas 1945 was celebrated after a fashion, and mothers took their children to the first postwar *Weihnachtsmarkt* (Christmas fair) in the Lustgarten.

Unfortunately the respite was only temporary, for despite the good weather, food supplies remained overstretched. In March rations were reduced drastically, and the weakened civilian population fell prey to typhus, TB and other **hunger-related diseases**; the lucky ones merely suffered enteric or skin diseases. The Allies did what they could, sending government and private relief, but even by the spring of 1947 rations remained at malnutrition levels. **Crime and prostitution** soared. In Berlin alone, two thousand people were arrested every month, many from the juvenile gangs that roamed the ruins murdering, robbing and raping. Trains were attacked at the Berlin stations, and in the countryside bandits ambushed supply convoys heading for the city. The winter of 1946–47 was one of the coldest since records began. Wolves appeared in Berlin and people froze to death aboard trains. There were rumours of cannibalism and Berlin hospitals treated 55,000 people for frostbite.

Allied tensions

Meanwhile, **political developments** that were to have a lasting impact on Berlin were occurring. In March 1946, parts of the SPD were forced into a shotgun merger with the KPD, to form the **SED** (Sozialistische Einheitspartei Deutschlands – "Socialist Unity Party of Germany"), or future **communist party** of East Germany, underlining the political division of the city as the wartime alliance between the western powers (France had also been allotted an occupation zone) and the Soviet Union fell apart, ushering in a new era of conflict that would all too often focus on Berlin. The Allied Control Council met for the last time on March 20, when Marshal Sokolovsky, the

June 1953	1961
An uprising of industrial workers against the Communist regime in the East is brutally put down; at least 200 people die.	Germany signs an agreement that grants Turks temporary work visas; many start to settle in Berlin.

Soviet military governor, protested British and American attempts to introduce economic reform in their zones.

Tension mounted over the next few months as the Allies went ahead with economic reform, while the Russians demanded the right to board Berlin-bound Allied trains, and on June 16 walked out of the four-power *Kommandantura* that had ultimate control over Berlin. Things came to a head with the **introduction of the D-Mark** in the western zone (June 23, 1948). On that day, the Soviets demanded from Berlin's mayor that he accept their Ostmark as currency for the whole city. But the city's parliament voted overwhelmingly against it. Everyone knew that this was asking for trouble, and trouble wasn't long in coming. On the night of June 23–24, power stations in the Soviet zone cut off electricity supplies to the western half of Berlin, and road and rail links between the western part of Germany and Berlin were severed. This was the beginning of the **Berlin Blockade**, the USSR's first attempt to force the western Allies out of the city. SPD politician Ernst Reuter, soon to be mayor of West Berlin, addressed a crowd at the Gesundbrunnen football field, promising that Berlin would "fight with everything we have". In the end the greatest weapon proved to be American and British support when on June 26, 1948, they began the **Berlin airlift**, flying supplies into the city to keep it alive against the odds for almost a year (see box, p.126).

The 1950s: the birth of two Germanys

Within six months, the political division of Germany was formalized by the creation of two rival states. First, the British, French and American zones of occupation were amalgamated to form the **Federal Republic of Germany** (May 1949); the Soviets followed suit by launching the **German Democratic Republic** on October 7. As Berlin lay deep within GDR territory, its Eastern sector naturally became the official GDR capital. However, much to the disappointment of many Berliners, the Federal Republic chose Bonn as their capital. West Berlin remained under the overall control of the Allied military commandants, although it was eventually to assume the status of a *Land* (state) of the Federal Republic.

Political tension remained a fact of life in a city that had become an arena for superpower confrontations. The Soviets and GDR communists had not abandoned the idea of driving the Allies out of Berlin, and mounted diverse operations against them, just as the Allies ran spying and sabotage operations in East Berlin. In this cradle of **Cold War espionage**, the recruitment of former Gestapo, SD or Abwehr operatives seemed quite justifiable to all the agencies concerned. On one side were Britain's SIS (based at the Olympic Stadium) and the American CIA, which fostered the Federal Republic's own intelligence service, the Gehlen Bureau, run by a former Abwehr colonel. Opposing them were the Soviet KGB and GRU (based at Karlshorst), and the GDR's own foreign espionage service and internal security police. The public side of this rumbling underground war was a number of **incidents** in 1952. An Air France plane approaching West Berlin was fired upon by a Russian MiG; and East German authorities blocked streets leading from West to East Berlin and expropriated property owned by West Berliners on the outskirts of the Eastern sector.

August 1961	**June 1963**
The tension between East and West culminates in the building of the Berlin Wall.	US President John F. Kennedy visits West Berlin, delivering his famous "Ich bin ein Berliner" speech.

The economic miracle and the Berlin Wall

Throughout the 1950s important events took place in **West Germany** under Chancellor Konrad Adenauer. Foremost among them was the so-called **"economic miracle"**, which saw West Germany recover from the ravages of war astonishingly quickly and go on to become Europe's largest economy. Although West Berlin's **economic recovery** was by no means as dramatic as that of West Germany, the city did prosper, particularly in comparison to East Berlin. **Marshall Plan aid** and West German capital were transforming West Berlin into a capitalist showcase, whereas the GDR and East Berlin seemed to languish, partly the result of the Soviets' ruthless **asset-stripping** – removing factories, rolling stock and generators to replace losses in the war-ravaged USSR. The **death of Stalin** on March 5, 1953 raised hopes that the situation in Berlin could be eased, but these were soon dashed. In the Eastern sector, the communists unwittingly fuelled smouldering resentment by announcing a ten percent **rise in work norms** on June 16, leading to a widespread uprising that was brutally suppressed (see box, p.121).

So, as the economic disparity between East and West Germany (and their respective halves of Berlin) worsened throughout the 1950s, West Berlin became an increasingly attractive destination for East Germans and East Berliners, who were able to cross the **zonal border** more or less freely at this time. Many moved over and found work in the western half of the city, benefiting from the purchasing power of the D-Mark – others at the very least went over at night to enjoy entertainment and culture lacking in the more spartan East. This steady **population drain** undermined the GDR, as young and highly skilled workers headed west for higher living standards and greater political freedom. Roughly 2.5 million people quit the GDR during the 1950s, mostly via the open border with West Berlin, which an average of nineteen thousand East Germans crossed every month.

Both the GDR and Soviet governments saw this as a threat to East Germany's existence, and on November 10, 1958, Soviet leader Nikita Khrushchev demanded that the western Allies relinquish their role in Berlin to "normalize" the GDR. Two weeks later, he suggested the Allies should withdraw and make Berlin a free city – coupled with a broad hint that if no agreement was reached within six months, a blockade would be reimposed. The Allies rejected the ultimatum, and the Kremlin allowed the deadline to pass without incident.

By 1961, Ulbricht's regime was getting desperate, and rumours that the border might be sealed began to circulate. In mid-June Ulbricht assured the world that no one had "the intention of building a wall". Simultaneously, however, border controls were tightened, while the flood of people voting with their feet continued to rise. It was obvious that something was about to happen. Shortly after midnight on August 13, 1961, East Germany sealed the border, dividing the city with the **Berlin Wall** (see pp.84–85).

Reaction in the West

Despite public outrage throughout West Germany and formal **diplomatic protests** from the Allies, everyone knew that a firmer line risked nuclear war. The West had to fall back on symbolic gestures: the Americans sent over General Lucius Clay, organizer of the Berlin airlift, and Vice-President Lyndon Johnson on August 18. The **separation of families** plunged morale in East Berlin to new depths and **economic problems** hit West Berlin, which was suddenly deprived of sixty thousand skilled workers who formerly

1971	**1976**
Access is guaranteed across East Germany to West Berlin with the Four Powers agreement.	David Bowie moves to Schöneberg and starts work on his Berlin trilogy.

commuted in from the GDR. They could only be replaced by creating special tax advantages to attract workers and businesses from the Federal Republic. American support for West Berlin was reaffirmed in August 1963 by President **John F. Kennedy**'s "Berliner" speech (see p.116), but for all its rhetoric and rapturous reception, the West essentially had to accept the new status quo.

The 1960s

The **gradual reduction of political tension** that occurred after the Wall had been standing a couple of years was partly due to improved relations between the superpowers, but mostly to local efforts. Under SPD mayor **Willy Brandt**, talks were opened up between the West Berlin Senate and the GDR government, resulting in the "**Pass Agreement**" of December 1963, whereby 730,000 West Berliners were able to pay brief visits to the East at the end of the year. Three more agreements were concluded over the next couple of years until the GDR decided to use border controls as a lever for winning **diplomatic recognition** (which the Federal Republic and its Western allies refused to give). Access to West Berlin via routes through GDR territory was subject to official hindrance; on one occasion, deputies were prevented from attending a plenary session of the Bundestag, held in West Berlin in 1965. New and more stringent **passport and visa controls** were levied on all travellers from June 1968 onwards.

As the direct threat to its existence receded, West Berlin society began to fragment along generational lines. Partly because Berlin residents could legally evade West German conscription, young people formed an unusually high proportion of the population – many gravitating towards squats and cheap digs in Kreuzberg. The immediate catalyst was the 1967–68 wave of **student unrest**, when grievances over unreformed, badly run universities soon spread to embrace wider disaffection with West Germany's materialistic culture. As in West Germany, the APO, or **extra-parliamentary opposition**, emerged as a strong and vocal force in West Berlin, criticizing what many people saw as a failed attempt to build a true democracy on the ruins of Nazi Germany. Another powerful strand was anti-Americanism, fuelled by US policy in Southeast Asia, Latin America and the Middle East. Both these viewpoints tended to bewilder and enrage older Germans.

The police reacted to street demonstrations in Berlin with a ferocity that shocked even conservatives. On June 2, 1967, a student was shot by police during a protest against a state visit by the Shah of Iran. When someone tried to kill student leader **Rudi Dutschke** (April 11, 1968), there were huge and violent demonstrations. Although the mass-protest movement fizzled out towards the end of the 1960s, a new and deadlier opposition would emerge in the 1970s – partly born from the West German establishment's violent response to what was initially a peaceful protest movement.

Ostpolitik and détente

The international scene and Berlin's place in it changed considerably around the turn of the decade. Both superpowers now hoped to thaw the Cold War and agree to a détente, while elections in the Federal Republic brought to power Willy Brandt, a chancellor committed to rapprochement with the GDR. On February 27, 1969, US President

1982	**1987**
US President Ronald Reagan visits Berlin for the first time.	During his second Berlin visit, Reagan makes a speech in front of the Brandenburg Gate, demanding Mr Gorbachev "tear down this Wall!"

BERLIN ON BERLIN

Remarkably, Berlin doesn't really have one single great **museum** all about its own history. But maybe this isn't even desirable, since the process of exploring its scattered single-perspective museums is so rewarding and revealing.

With little or no background knowledge of the city, the obvious place to start is the flashy but relatively superficial **Story of Berlin** (see p.113). Another good starting point is the more formal, less Berlin-centric approach of the **Deutsches Historisches Museum** (see p.45).

Undoubtedly Berlin's most fascinating epoch began with the Industrial Revolution and the best places to get a feel for this are three nineteenth-century apartments: **Museumswohnung Zimmermeister Brunzel** (see p.139) and the Prenzlauer Allee (see p.142) and Heynstrasse 8 (see p.144) branches of the **Museum Pankow**. For a more art-centric perspective, the **Zille Museum** (see p.67) shows industrial Berlin portrayed by its most famous cartoonist, and the **Berlinische Galerie – Museum für Moderne Kunst** (see p.120) gathers together local art for a revealing insight into the early twentieth-century city. The **Deutsche Kinemathek – Museum für Film und Fernsehen** (see p.92) is most fascinating for its coverage of German cinema in the same era.

The Nazi era effectively destroyed much of all this, and several collections provide insights into the regime. Foremost among them is the **Gedenkstätte Sachsenhausen**, at the former concentration camp (see p.184), and the **Haus der Wannsee Konferenze** (see p.171), where the Jewish Holocaust was planned; both lie on the edge of Berlin. In the centre you can complete the picture with the **Topographie des Terrors** exhibition on Nazi terror apparatus (see p.122), the **Gedenkstätte Deutscher Widerstand** (Memorial to German Resistance; see p.100), the **Holocaust memorials** (see p.38 & p.95), and the **Museum Blindenwerkstatt Otto Weidt** (see p.73), a brushmaker's workshop where a Jewish family went into hiding. The best insights into the war in Berlin itself are provided by the **bunker tours** of Berliner Unterwelten (see p.147).

Essential to Berlin's Cold War chapter is the last remaining complete section of the Berlin Wall at the **Gedenkstätte Berliner Mauer** (see p.86); the **Wall Museum at the East Side Gallery** (see p.134); the **Tränenpalast** (see p.83), the city's main former border crossing; the **Stasi Museum Berlin** (see p.151); and the eerily well-preserved Stasi prison **Hohenschönhausen** (see p.149). Also worth visiting are the cluster of museums around **Checkpoint Charlie** – Mauermuseum, BlackBox, Asisi Panorama – as well as the outdoor exhibition there (see pp.120–122). For an overview of all this and reminders of the GDR's better sides, visit the **DDR Museum** (see p.65), while to see it all from the West's point of view visit the **Alliierten-Museum** (see p.170) or the **Museum The Kennedys** (see p.80).

As Berlin busies itself with closing previous chapters of its history, it still awaits a single museum to properly record the post-reunification era. Until such a place exists, the story is all around; taking a **walking tour** (see box, pp.24–25) should reveal much.

Richard Nixon called for an easing of international tension during his visit to Berlin. Soon afterwards, **Four Power Talks** were held in the former Allied Control Council building in the American sector. Participants decided to set aside broader issues in an effort to fashion a workable agreement on the status of the divided city resulting in the **Quadripartite Agreement** (September 3, 1971), followed in December by inter-German agreements regarding transit routes to West Berlin and travel and traffic regulations for West Berliners. In 1972, the Federal Republic and the GDR signed a **Basic Treaty**, which bound both states to respect each other's frontiers and de facto sovereignty. In return for diplomatic recognition, the GDR allowed West Germans access to friends

1989

The first Love Parade is organized in Berlin; just 150 people take part.

November 9, 1989

Following a series of mass demonstrations across East Berlin, and a confused government press conference, border crossings in the Wall finally open.

and family across the border, which had effectively been denied to them (barring limited visits in the mid-1960s). However, the freedom to move from East to West was restricted to disabled people and senior citizens.

The 1970s

During the 1970s Berlin assumed a new identity, breaking with the images and myths of the past. Thanks to the easing of Cold War tensions, West Berlin was no longer a frontline city, and East Berlin lost much of its intimidating atmosphere. Throughout the decade, **West Berlin** had similar problems to those of West Germany: economic upsets triggered by the quadrupling of oil prices in 1974, and a wave of terrorism directed against the establishment. In addition, West Berlin suffered from a deteriorating stock of housing and rising unemployment – both alleviated to some extent by financial help from West Germany. **East Berlin** remained relatively quiet. A new East German leader, **Erich Honecker**, who was regarded as a "liberal", succeeded Ulbricht in 1971. Living standards improved and there was some relaxation of the tight controls of the Ulbricht days. However, most people regarded the changes as essentially trivial, and escapes continued to be attempted, although by now the Wall was formidably deadly. In 1977, a rock concert in Alexanderplatz turned into an explosion of street unrest, which the authorities suppressed with deliberate brutality.

The 1980s

Throughout the 1970s and early 1980s, the Quadripartite Agreement and the inter-German treaties formed the backdrop to relations between West and East Berlin. The main irritant was the **compulsory exchange** of D-Marks for Ostmarks, which the GDR raised in value from DM6.50 to DM25 in 1980, deterring significant numbers of visitors. But on the whole, a degree of stability and normality had been achieved, enabling both cities to run relatively smoothly. Even after the partial resumption of the Cold War following the Soviet invasion of Afghanistan in 1979, Berlin remained relatively calm. The only notable event was the shooting of an American officer on an alleged spying mission in Potsdam in the spring of 1985.

As elsewhere in West Germany, Berlin witnessed a crystallization of issues and attitudes and the flowering of new radical movements. Concern about the arms race and the environment was widespread; feminism and gay rights commanded increasing support. Left-wing and Green groups formed an **Alternative Liste** to fight elections, and a left-liberal newspaper, *Tageszeitung*, was founded. Organized squatting was the radical solution to Berlin's **housing crisis**. In 1981, the new Christian Democrat administration (elected after a financial scandal forced the SPD to step down) tried to evict the squatters from about 170 apartment buildings, and police violence sparked rioting in Schöneberg. The administration compromised by allowing some of the squatters to become legitimate tenants, which had a big effect on life in West Berlin. For the first time since the late 1960s, the social divisions that had opened up showed signs of narrowing. Alternative Liste delegates were elected to the Berlin Senate for the first time in May 1981, and the same year witnessed a boom in **cultural life**, as the arts exploded into new vitality.

October 3, 1990	1997
The two parts of Berlin are unified within the Federal Republic of Germany.	Peter Eisenman's controversial design for a Memorial to the Murdered Jews of Europe is chosen.

The **early 1980s** saw a resumption of frostiness in US–Soviet relations, which heightened concern about **nuclear weapons**. Anti-nuclear activists protested during the Berlin visit of President Ronald Reagan in June 1981. But the tension and sabre-rattling of the 1950s and 1960s Cold War didn't return to Berlin even though ideological hostility prevented the two halves of the city from jointly celebrating Berlin's 750th **anniversary** in 1987. In East Berlin anniversary celebrations were preceded by a massive **urban renewal project**, in both the city centre and the inner suburbs; the reconstructed Nikolaiviertel (see p.66) stems from this time. In West Berlin, the elections of spring 1989 swept the CDU administration from power, and an **SPD/Alternative Liste coalition** took over, with Walter Momper as mayor. In Kreuzberg, demonstrations against what many regarded as an Alternative Liste sellout were put down with unwarranted force, sparking running street battles.

When, in 1985, **Mikhail Gorbachev** became the new Soviet leader and began campaigns for *glasnost* and *perestroika*, their initial impact on East Germany was slight. The SED regarded them with deep suspicion, so while Poland and Hungary embarked on the road to democracy, Erich Honecker declared that the Berlin Wall would stand for another fifty or one hundred years if necessary.

Die Wende

The year 1989 ranks as both one of the most significant years in German history and one of the most unforeseeable. Within twelve months **die Wende** ("the turning") transformed Germany completely. With little warning East Germany suddenly collapsed in the wake of the general easing of communism in the Eastern Bloc of the late 1980s. The Berlin Wall was breached on **November 9, 1989**, symbolizing an end to the Cold War, making a lifetime's dream come true for most Germans – above all, for those living in the East. Several events then fairly logically and briskly followed: the union of the two Germanys; the reassertion of Berlin as capital; and the start of the lengthy process of putting those responsible for the GDR's crimes on trial.

The first holes in the Iron Curtain

Despite the unyielding position of the GDR government, as the 1980s wore on things started to happen. The **Protestant Church** provided a haven for **environmental and peace organizations**, whose members unfurled protest banners calling for greater freedom at an official ceremony in East Berlin in January 1988. They were immediately arrested, imprisoned, and later expelled from the GDR. The end of the regime didn't seem nigh – so when Chris Gueffroy was shot dead trying to cross the Berlin border at Neukölln on February 6, 1989, no one fathomed that he would be the last person killed in such an attempt. However, the impetus for East German collapse came from other Eastern European countries: in 1988 Hungary began taking down the barbed-wire fence along their Austrian border, creating a **hole in the Iron Curtain**, across which many East Germans fled. A similar pattern emerged in Czechoslovakia.

The October revolution

The East German government's disarrayed response to these goings-on galvanized into action thousands who had previously been content to make the best of things.

1999	2005
Berlin becomes capital of a reunified Germany.	Openly gay mayor Klaus Wowereit dubs Berlin "poor but sexy", which becomes a slogan for the city.

Fledgling **opposition groups** like the **Neues Forum** emerged, and unrest begun in Leipzig and Dresden soon spread to Berlin. Then, at the beginning of October, at the pompous official celebration of the GDR's **fortieth anniversary**, Gorbachev stressed the need for new ideas and stunningly announced that the USSR would not interfere in the affairs of fellow socialist states. Protests and scuffles along the cavalcade route escalated into a huge demonstration as the day wore on, which the police and Stasi (the East German secret police) brutally suppressed. Thousands of arrests were made, and prisoners were subjected to the usual degrading treatment. The following week, **nationwide demonstrations** came close to bloodshed in **Leipzig**, where seventy thousand people marched through the city, forcing the sudden replacement of Erich Honecker with **Egon Krenz** as party secretary, who immediately announced that the regime was ready for dialogue.

The final week of October saw a growing exodus of GDR citizens via other Eastern Bloc countries, while pressure on the streets kept rising. Then on November 4, East Berlin saw more than one million citizens demonstrate, forcing authorities to make hasty **concessions**, including dropping the requirement for GDR citizens to get visas to visit Czechoslovakia – in effect, permitting emigration. People swarmed across the Czech border, and within two days fifteen thousand had reached Bavaria – bringing the number of East Germans who had fled the country in 1989 to 200,000.

The Wall opens

The **opening of the Berlin Wall** was announced almost casually, on the evening of Thursday November 9, when East Berlin party boss Günter Schabowski told a televised press conference that East German citizens were free to leave the GDR with valid exit visas, which would henceforth be issued without delay. Hardly daring to believe the announcement, Berliners on both sides of the Wall started heading for border crossings.

Huge crowds converged on the **Brandenburg Gate**, where the Volkspolizei gave up checking documents and simply let thousands of East Germans walk into West Berlin. An impromptu **street party** broke out, with West Berliners popping champagne corks and Germans from both sides of the Wall embracing. The scenes of joy and disbelief flashed around a world taken by surprise. West German Chancellor **Helmut Kohl** interrupted a state visit in Warsaw to rush to West Berlin, where the international press was arriving in droves. Inside the GDR, disbelief turned to joy as people realized that the unimaginable had happened. On the first weekend of the opening of the Wall – November 11 and 12 – 2.7 million exit visas were issued to East Germans, who formed kilometre-long queues at checkpoints. West Germans – and TV-viewers around the world – gawped at streams of Trabant cars pouring into West Berlin, where shops enjoyed a bonanza as East Germans spent their DM100 "welcome money", given to each of them by the Federal Republic. By the following weekend, **ten million visas** had been issued since November 9 – an incredible number considering the entire population of the GDR was just sixteen million.

The road to Reunification

Despite the opening of the border East German demonstrations continued and anti-government feelings still ran high, forcing the immediate dismantling of the

2006	2006
Demolition begins on the former East German parliament, the Palast der Republik.	The new Hauptbahnhof is opened.

formidable Stasi security service and an agreement to have free elections, for which the **SED** hastily repackaged itself as a new, supposedly voter-friendly **PDS** – Partei des Demokratischen Sozialismus (Democratic Socialist Party), partly by firing the old guard. But the next initiative came from the West when **Chancellor Kohl** visited Dresden on December 19, addressing a huge, enthusiastic crowd as "dear countrymen", and declaring a **united Germany** his ultimate goal. East Germans began to agree as they discovered that West Germany's standard of living eclipsed anything in the GDR, and found out exactly how corrupt their government had been – with the result that the GDR's first free elections on March 18, 1990 returned a victory for a right-wing alliance dominated by the CDU and Kohl.

The **economic union** was hammered out almost immediately and the GDR began rapidly to fade away. Eastern produce vanished from shops to be replaced by western consumer goods, and superficially it seemed as though a second "economic miracle" had begun. Yet for many East Germans, the excitement was tempered by fears of rent increases and factory closures during the transformation to a market economy. Already the first legal claims by former owners of apartment buildings in East Berlin were being lodged.

With confirmation that a united Germany would respect its post-World War II boundaries, the wartime allies agreed to reunification. After an all-night Volkskammer session on August 23 it was announced that the GDR would become part of the Federal Republic on **October 3, 1990**.

Street-level changes

The two Berlins, meanwhile, were already drawing together as the border withered away during the course of the year. Passport and customs controls for German citizens had ceased early in 1990 and, by the time of currency union, nationals of other countries, although nominally still subject to control, could cross the border unhindered. During the course of the year most of the central sections of **the Wall** were demolished and numerous cross-border streets linked up once again.

As border controls in Berlin and elsewhere throughout the former Soviet bloc eased, Berlin became a magnet for the restless peoples of eastern Europe. The first arrivals had been the **Poles**, who set up a gigantic impromptu street market on a patch of wasteland near the Wall, much to the chagrin of Berliners, who felt the order of their city threatened by the influx of thousands of weekend street traders selling junk out of suitcases. They were followed by **Roma**, fleeing alleged persecution at home and hoping, by taking advantage of visa-free access to what was still the GDR, to secure a place for themselves in the new Germany. Post-unification visa regulations were to put a stop to the commuting activities of the Poles, but as asylum-seekers the Romanians had the right to remain, and the sight of Roma begging on the streets of Berlin became commonplace.

Reunification and the 1990s

On **October 3, 1990**, the day of **reunification**, Chancellor Kohl spoke to assembled dignitaries and massive crowds in front of the Reichstag. A conscious effort was made to rekindle the spontaneous joy and fervour that had gripped the city on the night the

2006	**2009**
The football World Cup is held in Germany, with the final played in Berlin's Olympic Stadium.	Celebrations mark the twentieth anniversary of the fall of the Wall. Work begins on a major restoration of original paintings at the Berlin Wall's East Side Gallery.

Wall was opened and during Berlin's first post-*Wende* new year, but for many ordinary people already experiencing the economic side effects of the collapse of the GDR the celebrations left a bitter taste. On the sidelines anti-unification demonstrators marched through the streets, precipitating minor **clashes with the police**.

Just over a month later, on the night of November 13, the reunited Berlin experienced its first **major upheaval** when SPD mayor Walter Momper ordered the police to evict **West Berlin squatters** who had occupied a number of tenement blocks in the eastern Berlin district of Friedrichshain. The violent tactics of the police, coupled with the uncompromising stance of the radical Autonome squatters, who responded with petrol bombs and a hail of missiles from the rooftops, resulted in the fiercest **rioting** seen in the city since 1981, with dozens of police injured and more than three hundred squatters arrested. Politically, the unrest resulted in the **collapse** of the fragile Red-Green SPD/Alternative Liste coalition that had governed West Berlin for the previous twenty months.

December 2, 1990 saw Germany's first nationwide elections since 1933. Nationally the CDU, in coalition with the FDP (Free Democrats), triumphed easily. One surprise was that the PDS secured 25 percent of the vote in East Berlin on an anti-unemployment and anti-social inequality ticket. At the start of 1991, with the celebrations of the first united Christmas and New Year over, it was time for the accounting to begin in earnest. The new year brought vastly unpopular tax increases in western Germany to pay for the spiralling cost of unification. As the year wore on, and unemployment continued to rise, Kohl's honeymoon with the East ended. He became reluctant to show himself there, and when he finally did, in April, he was greeted by catcalls and egg-hurlers.

Ill-feeling between easterners and westerners also became apparent and increased throughout the decade. West Germans resented the tax increases and caricatured easterners as naive and lazy. East Germans resented patronizing western attitudes and economic inequalities that made them second-class citizens, so mocked westerners for their arrogance and materialism. Feelings got worse as it became apparent that the ever-increasing cost of reunification had pushed the German economy into recession. As the instability of the transitional period began to ebb, witch-hunts for those responsible for the crimes of the GDR's repressive regime began in earnest, many resulting from an increasing access to old Stasi files. **Trials** throughout the 1990s brought Politbüro members, border guards, and even sports coaches who had doped players without their knowledge, before the courts. On June 20, 1991, a Bundestag decision to relocate the national government to Berlin ushered in a new era: a tremendous task, and one undertaken in the late 1990s with the usual German thoroughness.

Berlin today

Since the start of the twenty-first century Berlin has been a city on the move, with plenty of building sites still dotted around. This era of **transition**, however, is finally reaching its conclusion, with the reconstruction work that began in the aftermath of World War II and the Cold War almost complete. Magically this has almost wound back the clock to the 1920s, before Nazism struck, with Berlin once again one of

2010	2011
The original date for the opening of Berlin-Brandenburg airport comes and goes; years later its launch date remains anyone's guess.	Six thousand people march on Neukölln's streets to protest rent increases; a large anti-capitalist festival in Lunapark protests Berlin's growing internationalization.

Europe's most **cosmopolitan and upbeat** cities. But also like the 1920s, Berlin is plagued by economic and social problems to which there are no easy solutions. Its underperforming **economy** is perhaps the hardest nut to crack; despite signs of improvement (there was a 1.7 percent increase in GDP in 2016, for example), it's still effectively a financial drain on the rest of Germany, with the second highest unemployment rates of any German federal state, while **housing shortages** and **declining public services** are eroding the quality of life for many. A worrying trend for this city of immigrants has been the successful **rise of populist right-wing parties** such as AfD (Alternative für Deutschland), who entered the state parliament for the first time following the 2016 Berlin state elections with a historic 14 percent of the local vote.

Party capital
As host of the 2006 football World Cup finals, Berlin was able to project its friendly and youthful dynamism to the world, hosting several games, including the final, in the fine old Olympic Stadium. Visiting fans quickly realized that the city deserved its reputation for partying hard – earned in part as a consequence of the (now defunct) annual Love Parade – and since then barely a week has passed without a big event. Twenty-somethings from all over Europe continually jet in for the **all-night club scene** that continues to be as wild and cutting-edge as it ever was. The **LGBT scene** is thriving too, thanks in no small part to its support from its sociable, gay former mayor Klaus Wowereit ("Wowi"), who held the post for thirteen years until he quit (partly over the Berlin-Brandenburg Airport debacle) in 2014.

The economy
Greatly weakened by the costs of pulling the two Germanys together, and heavy investment in construction projects like the new airport and the Stadtschloss (Royal Palace), the city has long been economically compromised – hence its famous "poor but sexy"maxim, coined by Wowi. Berlin's **unemployment** rate stood at 10.5 percent in 2015 (around 191,000), and many Berliners live on benefits, despite the rich political elite at the city's heart that controls Europe's mightiest economy. Part of the problem has been the **death of manufacturing** which in 2014 accounted for just 4.4 percent of the local economy. Other pressures include the ongoing **euro crisis**, the huge influx of **refugees** since 2015 and **Brexit** – though the latter two present opportunities as well as challenges (see p.288).

On the positive side, Berlin is helped by its central location at the **heart of the European Union** and by its increasingly hip image, which has helped firms to lure skilled workers here so that both can benefit from the city's relatively **cheap real estate**. A clutch of small **fashion designers** moved first into the city centre and more recently into surrounding neighbourhoods, and the banks of the River Spree have become the base for Universal Music, MTV and other media firms. The biggest phenomenon in recent years, though, has been the rise of the local **start-up scene**, which in 2016 spanned around 2500 companies, collected €2.4 billion in venture capital in the previous year (as well as subsidies from the Federal Ministry of Finance) and has spawned social hubs such as Factory Berlin, which houses seven hundred mostly millennial tech workers in a former nineteenth-century brewery, and events such as Tech Open Air (see p.27). Despite its fast and impressive growth, though, the scene

2013	2014
Reconstruction of the Berliner Schloss, dubbed the Berlin Palace–Humboldt Forum, begins, with an estimated completion date of 2019 and cost of €670 million.	A city referendum vote on Tempelhofer Feld rejects large-scale property planning on the site; over 250,000 fans flock to the Fanmeile in Tiergarten to watch Germany beat Argentina 1–0 in the World Cup Final.

remains comparatively small, and major successes have been few and far between.

Meanwhile information technology parks in the southern suburbs continue to grow, as has the research and development sector, thanks largely to the presence of three universities in the city. **Tourism** also continues to be a major growth area, with Berlin receiving 29 million visitors annually at the latest count – a sixfold increase since the early 1990s – making it third in Europe after London and Paris.

International Berlin

Berlin's economic green shoots and the ever-increasing numbers coming to the city continue to keep the property market buoyant, with many Berliners bemoaning the **gentrification** of blue-collar districts like Kreuzberg and Neukölln – thanks in part to the influx of hip young types from elsewhere in Europe – with the consequent rent increases and change in atmosphere.

These growing pains seem part of the general process of Berlin turning itself back into a key world city, but they have also stimulated older frictions. Among them are complaints from the disadvantaged in the former east who blame foreigners for their plight and are attracted to **right-wing extremism** and neo-Nazi ideals, although just as disadvantaged and angry are many descendants of Turkish "guest workers" who arrived in Berlin in the 1960s and preferred to settle rather than return home. These racial tensions have been exacerbated by Angela Merkel's decision in 2015 to accept over a million **refugees** from war-torn states such as Iraq, Syria, Afghanistan and Eritrea, feeding further the rise of the far right – not just AfD but others even more extremist and pointedly anti-immigration such as Pegida, or Patriotic Europeans Against the Islamisation of the West (Occident). However, the refugees have for the most part been accepted positively by Berlin on a municipal and local level, and an impressive number of open-minded and creative responses from individuals, community groups and start-ups have helped ease the messy bureaucratic pressure somewhat. With most refugees still placed in interim shelters outside of the city centre, the national impact of this demographic change still remains to be seen, however.

Another major but as yet invisible change has been the 2016 vote by the **United Kingdom to leave the European Union**, which seems certain to have an impact on economies across Europe – not least due to the interim uncertainty – and financial forecasts in Germany have been downsized accordingly. On the other hand, Germany will likely benefit from the relocation of UK investments and businesses, which are already eyeing up the country – and Berlin specifically due to its international climate. Soon after the referendum, the senator for economics, technology and research, Cornelia Yzer, proactively sent hundreds of letters to British businesses encouraging them to make the move, and a mobile billboard bearing the message "Dear start ups, keep calm and move to Berlin" was spotted on a truck in London.

2015	2016
Berlin takes in 80,000 refugees from war-torn countries.	Around 5000 left-wing activists in Friedrichshain protest the violent eviction of a squat; 123 policemen are injured.

Books

Huge numbers of books have been written about Berlin. The collection below shows a bias towards unravelling the evil mysteries of the Third Reich, the double-dealing of the Cold War and getting to grips with the *Wende*. But Berlin has also attracted dozens of specialist guides, the most useful of which are books on its architecture, new and old. Books marked with a ★ are particularly recommended.

HISTORY

GENERAL HISTORY AND PRE-THIRD REICH

Otto Friedrich *Before the Deluge: A Portrait of Berlin in the 1920s*. An engaging social history, full of tales and anecdotes, of the city when Dada and decadence reigned. An excellent history of Berlin's most engaging period.

Anton Gill *A Dance Between Flames*. Gill's dense but readable account of Berlin in the 1920s and 1930s has lots of colour, quotation and detail but leans so heavily on a single source – the diaries of Harry Kessler (see below) – that you feel he should be sharing the royalties. Even so, one of the best books on the period.

Mark Girouard *Cities and People*. A well-illustrated social and architectural history of European urban development that contains knowledgeable entries on Berlin, particularly the eighteenth- and nineteenth-century periods.

Alex de Jong *The Weimar Chronicle*. While not the most comprehensive of accounts of the Weimar Republic, this is by far the liveliest. A couple of chapters focus on Berlin, and the book is spiced with eyewitness memoirs and a mass of engaging detail, particularly about the arts in the city.

Count Harry Kessler *Berlin in Lights*. The later diaries of art collector, diplomat and aristocrat Harry Graf Kessler span the end of World War I through to his death in 1937, and offer astute historical and political analysis of the Weimar era.

Giles MacDonogh *Berlin*. The book's thematic rather than chronological organization can initially be a bit baffling – and doesn't really work in uncovering themes from the city's past as it intends – but there's a wealth of fascinating anecdotes on aspects of daily life here that's ignored by traditional histories.

Andreas Nachama et al *Jews in Berlin*. Packed with source material of every kind, this well-illustrated book charts the troubled history of Berlin's Jewish community between 1244 and 2000.

Alexandra Richie *Faust's Metropolis*. A thick and thorough general history of Berlin, beginning with the very first settlers and ending in the 1990s. Richie debunks a number of myths about the city – such as its supposed

anti-Nazism – but her conservatism too often intrudes on the narrative.

Ronald Taylor *Berlin and Its Culture*. Profusely illustrated survey of the cultural movements and personalities that constituted the artistic life of the city; especially good on Weimar writing and cinematography.

THIRD REICH

Allied Intelligence Map of Key Buildings. This large, detailed map published by After The Battle is an excellent resource for anyone searching for Nazi and prewar remains in the city.

★**Anonymous** *A Woman in Berlin*. Remarkable war diary kept by a female journalist who vividly describes the pathetic lot of Berlin's vanquished in the closing days of the war, when looting and gang rape were part of daily life. The honesty of the book caused such an uproar when it was first published in 1950s Germany – when society was unprepared to face its recent trauma – that it wasn't reprinted again during the author's lifetime; she died in 2001.

Antony Beevor *Berlin the Downfall 1945*. Berlin doesn't actually start to fall until the middle of the book, but once there a synthesis of many sources provides a riveting account of how the city's defences crumbled and its civilians suffered, with few harrowing details spared. Beevor was congratulated by many female victims of brutal rapes by Soviet troops for at last telling their story as in *A Woman in Berlin* (see above).

Christabel Bielenberg *The Past is Myself*. Bielenberg, the niece of Lord Northcliffe, married German lawyer Peter Bielenberg in 1934 and was living with her family in Berlin at the outbreak of the war. Her autobiography details her struggle to survive the Nazi period and Allied raids on the city, and to save her husband, imprisoned in Ravensbrück as a result of his friendship with members of the Kreisau resistance group.

George Clare *Berlin Days 1946–1947*. "The most harrowing and yet most fascinating place on earth" is how Clare begins this account of his time spent as a British army translator. This is Berlin at what the Germans called the *Nullpunkt* – the zero point – when the city, its economy, buildings and society began to rebuild almost from scratch. Packed with characters and observation, it's a captivating – if at times depressing – read.

D. Fisher and A. Read *The Fall of Berlin.* Superb and essential account of the city's *Götterdämmerung*, carefully researched with a mass of anecdotal material you won't find elsewhere.

Bella Fromm *Blood and Banquets.* Fromm, a Jewish aristocrat living in Berlin, kept a diary from 1930 until 1938. Her job as society reporter for the *Vossische Zeitung* gave her inside knowledge on the top figures of Berlin society, and the diaries are a chilling account of the rise of the Nazis and their persecution of Berlin's Jews.

Tony Le Tissier *The Battle of Berlin.* Soldierly (the author is a retired lieutenant-colonel) shot-by-shot account of Berlin's final days. Authoritative, if a little dry. The same author's *Berlin Then and Now* is a collection of photographs of sites in the city during the war years, contrasted with the same places today. This extraordinary book is the best way to find what's left of Berlin's Nazi buildings – a startling number have barely changed.

Martin Middlebrook *The Berlin Raids.* Superbly researched account of the RAF's campaign to destroy the capital of the Third Reich by mass bombing. Based on interviews with bomber crews, Luftwaffe fighter pilots and civilians who survived the raids – a moving, compassionate and exciting read.

★**William Shirer** *The Rise and Fall of the Third Reich.* Shirer was an American journalist stationed in Berlin during the Nazi period, and his history of the German state before and during the war has long been recognized as a classic. Notwithstanding its length and occasionally outdated perceptions, this book is full of insights and is ideal for dipping into, with the help of its exhaustive index.

Marie Jalowicz Simon *Gone to Ground.* The latest in a long line of powerful memoirs by Jewish residents who survived the Holocaust by going underground. Simon's story, published in 2015 (seventeen years after her death), is a powerful and poignant tale of courage and audacity – her own but also of the Berliners that helped her.

Hugh Trevor-Roper *The Last Days of Hitler.* A brilliant reconstruction of the closing chapter of the Third Reich, set in the Bunker of the Reich's Chancellery on Potsdamer Platz.

Marie Vassiltchikov *The Berlin Diaries.* These diaries, written by the daughter of a Russian émigré family, provide a vivid portrait of wartime Berlin and the July 1944 bomb-plot conspirators – whose members numbered among her friends.

Peter Wyden *Stella.* Stella Goldschlag was a young, very "Aryan"-looking Jew who avoided deportation and death by working for the SS as a "catcher", hunting down Jews hiding in wartime Berlin – including former friends and even relatives. The author, who knew the young Stella, traces her life story and tries to find some explanation for the motives behind what seem incalculably evil actions. A gripping, terrifying story.

POSTWAR HISTORY AND SOCIAL STUDIES

★**Anna Funder** *Stasiland: True Stories From Behind the Berlin Wall.* Engrossing account of the experiences of those East Germans who found themselves tangled in the web of the State Security Service (Stasi) in the GDR.

★**Timothy Garton Ash** *The File: A Personal History.* Garton Ash lived and worked as a journalist in East Berlin in 1980, making him the subject of surveillance and a Stasi file. In this book he tracks down the file and interviews informers using an informal style to weave everything together and marvellously evoke the era. His book *We the People* (US title: *The Magic Lantern*) is an equally enjoyable first-hand account of the fall of the Wall.

Norman Gelb *The Berlin Wall.* The definitive account of the building of the Wall and its social and political aftermath up until 1986. Includes a wealth of information and anecdotes that you won't find in other books.

Anne McElvoy *The Saddled Cow.* Thorough and witty analysis of the GDR by Berlin's *Times* correspondent who witnessed the fall of the Wall. The book also draws on the author's time in East Germany before and after the *Wende*: its title is a quote from Stalin, who once said that "Communism fits Germany as a saddle fits a cow".

David E. Murphy, Serfei A. Kondrashev and George Bailey *Battleground Berlin: CIA vs KGB in the Cold War.* A detailed account by participants of the tense skirmishes in Berlin between the spies of the two superpowers.

Hermann Waldenburg *The Berlin Wall Book.* A collection of photographs of the art and graffiti the Wall inspired, with a rather self-important introduction by the photographer.

ART AND ARCHITECTURE

Peter Adam *The Art of the Third Reich.* Engrossing and well-written account of the officially approved state art of Nazi Germany – a subject that for many years was ignored or deliberately made inaccessible. Includes more than three hundred illustrations.

★**Karl Baedeker** *Berlin and its Environs.* First published in 1903, the learned old Baedeker is an utterly absorbing read, describing a grand imperial city now long vanished. There's advice on medicinal brine-baths, where to buy "mourning clothes", the location of the Estonian embassy, and beautiful fold-out maps that enable you to trace the former course of long-gone streets. An armchair treat.

★**Duane Philips and Alexandra Geyer** *Berlin: A Guide to Recent Architecture.* Ideal pocket guide to many key Berlin buildings, with good photographs and an interesting commentary, even if it's occasionally mired in opaque architectural snobbery.

Michael Z. Wise *Capital Dilemma: Germany's Search for a New Architecture of Democracy.* Engaging discussion of the historical, political and architectural considerations in the rebuilding of Berlin.

GUIDES AND TRAVEL WRITING

Stephen Barber *Fragments of the European City.* Written as a series of interlocking poetic fragments, this book explores the visual transformation of the contemporary European city, focusing on Berlin. An exhilarating evocation of the intricacies and ever-changing identity of the city.

Rory Maclean *Berlin: Imagine a City.* Part history, part fiction, Maclean's intriguing book tells the story of the city from the Middle Ages until today through profiles of some of its major personalities.

★**Heather Reyes, Katy Derbyshire (eds)** *City Lit Series Berlin.* Superb anthology that provides an intellectual tour of Berlin in some hundred pieces written by various historians, journalists and writers; among them Christopher Isherwood, Ian McEwan and David Bowie. Great for a quick sense of the city's historical context, its ongoing cultural and architectural evolution and its countercultural vibe.

Peter Schneider *Berlin Now: The Rise of the City and the Fall of the Wall.* Acclaimed journalist and author Peter Schneider (see p.292) here turns his attention to capturing the contemporary thrust of his adopted city.

Paul Sullivan and Marcel Krueger *Berlin: A Literary Guide for Travellers.* A look at the city through the many writers who have called it home over the centuries, from E.T.A. Hoffmann and Joseph Roth to Christa Wolf and Chloe Aridjis.

Uwe Seidel *Berlin & Potsdam.* Illustrated guide to the city, with much detail on places that you can't see anymore. Useful if you're after knowledge of the what-stood-where kind.

Ian Walker *Zoo Station.* A personal recollection of time spent in Berlin in the mid-1980s. Perceptive, engaging and well informed, it's the most enjoyable account of pre-*Wende* life in the city.

FICTION

Len Deighton *Winter: A Berlin Family 1899–1945.* Fictional saga tracing the fortunes of a Berlin family through World War I, the rise of Nazism and the collapse of the Third Reich: a convincing account of how a typical upper-middle-class family fared. Better known is *Funeral in Berlin*, a spy-thriller set in the middle of Cold War Berlin and based around the defection of an Eastern chemist, aided by hard-bitten agent Harry Palmer (as the character came to be known in the film starring Michael Caine). *Berlin Game* pits British SIS agent Bernard Samson (whose father appears in *Winter*) against an arch manipulator of the East Berlin secret service, and leaves you hanging for the sequels *Mexico Set* and *London Match*.

Alfred Döblin *Berlin-Alexanderplatz.* A prominent socialist intellectual during the Weimar period, Döblin went into exile shortly after the banning (and burning) of his books in 1933. This is his weightiest and most durable achievement, an unrelenting stream-of-consciousness epic of the city's proletariat.

Hans Fallada *Alone in Berlin.* This story of one couple's brave and cunning resistance to the Nazis is poignant and gripping. Also now a major film.

Theodor Fontane *Effi Briest.* This story of a woman's adultery in the second half of the nineteenth century offers a vivid picture of Prussian mores, with the sort of terrible and absurd climax that's virtually unique to Fontane and to German literature. One of the few classics to come out of Berlin.

Hugo Hamilton *Surrogate City* is a love story between an Irish woman and a Berliner and strongly evocative of pre-*Wende* Berlin. *The Love Test*, the tale of a journalist researching the history of a woman's involvement with the Stasi, gives a realistic account of 1990s Berlin.

Robert Harris *Fatherland.* A Cold War novel with a difference: Germany has conquered Europe and the Soviet Union, and the Cold War is being fought between the Third Reich and the USA. Against this background, Berlin detective Xavier March is drawn into an intrigue involving murder and Nazi officials. All this owes much to Philip Kerr (see p.297) but Harris's picture of Nazi Berlin in 1964 is chillingly believable.

Lillian Hellman *Pentimento.* The first volume of Hellman's memoirs contains "Julia", supposedly (it was later accused of being heavily fictionalized) the story of one of her friends caught up in the Berlin resistance. This was later made into a finely acted, if rather thinly emotional, film of the same name.

★**Christopher Isherwood** *Goodbye to Berlin.* Set in the decadent atmosphere of the Weimar Republic as the Nazis steadily gain power, this collection of stories brilliantly evokes the period and brings to life some classic Berlin characters. It subsequently formed the basis of the films *I Am a Camera* and the later remake *Cabaret*. See also Isherwood's *Mr Norris Changes Trains*, the adventures of the eponymous overweight hero in pre-Hitler Berlin and Germany.

★**Wladimir Kaminer** *Russian Disco: Tales of Everyday Lunacy on the Streets of Berlin*. Unusual, entertaining and well-written collection of snapshots of Berlin through the eyes of a Russian immigrant from Moscow. Kaminer has since become a local celebrity, DJing *Russendisko* nights at *Kaffee Burger* (see p.225).

Philip Kerr *Berlin Noir: March Violets, The Pale Criminal* and *A German Requiem*. Three great novels on Berlin in one omnibus edition. The first is a well-received detective thriller set in the early years of Nazi Berlin. Keen on period detail – nightclubs, the Olympic Stadium, building sites for the new autobahn – and with a terrific sense of atmosphere, the book rips along to a gripping denouement. Bernie Gunther, its detective hero, also features in the second title – a wartime Berlin crime novel. But the best, *A German Requiem*, has Gunther travelling from ravaged postwar Berlin to run into ex-Nazis in Vienna.

Ian McEwan *The Innocent*. McEwan's novel brilliantly evokes 1950s Berlin as seen through the eyes of a post office worker caught up in early Cold War espionage – and his first sexual encounters. Flounders in its obligatory McEwan nasty final twist, but laden with a superbly researched atmosphere.

Ulrich Plenzdorf *The New Sufferings of Young W.* A satirical reworking of Goethe's *Die Leiden des jungen Werthers* set in 1970s East Berlin. It tells the story of Edgar Wibeau, a young rebel without a cause adrift in the antiseptic GDR, and when first published it pushed the borders of literary acceptability under the old regime with its portrayal of alienated, disaffected youth.

Holly-Jane Rahlens *Becky Bernstein Goes Berlin*. A young Jewish girl from Queens falls in love with a German, emigrates to Berlin and discovers a new love for the city. A bouncy and funny novel full of New York wit.

Sven Regener *Berlin Blues*. The story of barman and local drifter Herr Lehmann and his friends is regarded as a classic for its insights into Kreuzberg life during the 1980s.

Peter Schneider *The Wall Jumper*. A fantastic insight into life into the divided city, told by the West Berlin-based narrator who crosses the border regularly to visit friends and have clandestine conversations about politics and more.

Film

Berlin's cinema history goes back to some of the very first experiments in the medium. It rapidly became the cornerstone of Germany's film industry, a position consolidated in the 1920s and then throughout the Nazi era, despite the mass exodus of many of the country's key stars and directors. After World War II East Germany quickly made the most of all the equipment that had fallen into their hands in the Soviet-controlled suburbs of Berlin to produce a programme of tightly controlled film-making. Meanwhile, generous subsidies lured many of Germany's most cutting-edge film-makers to West Berlin. But it's since the *Wende* that the city's film industry has really begun to blossom again.

The beginnings: showmen and inventors

Berlin first whirred into cinema history on November 1, 1895 when former fairground showman Max Skladanowsky and his brother Emil put on a show with their home-made film projector – which they called a *Bioskop* – at the city's Wintergarten music hall. It was quickly replaced by better methods and techniques in Paris later that year, but Berlin continued to play a crucial role, with locals like Oskar Messter pioneering and setting standards for many production techniques.

Once established, Germany's early twentieth-century film industry grew steadily. The outbreak of World War I and subsequent boycott of French films stimulated growth, and Berlin consolidated its role in 1917 with the founding of the giant and partially nationalized **Universum Film AG** (UFA) studio – which was established largely to imitate the very effective Allied propaganda films.

Boom in Weimar Germany

After the war, movies became a popular form of escapism in the hard times of **Weimar Germany**, with new genres emerging to portray forbidden love, myths, and other populist themes. The film industry boomed, churning out vast quantities of celluloid – six hundred feature films a year in the 1920s – thanks partly to hyperinflation, which allowed film-makers to borrow money that would vastly devalue before repayment. Even so, studio bankruptcies were common and film budgets relatively tight, forcing directors to work with less and so helping to prompt the rise of **German Expressionist cinema**. The genre relied on symbolism and artistic imagery, as evidenced in the era's most famous film, *Das Kabinett des Doktor Caligari* (*The Cabinet of Dr Caligari*; 1920), shot in Berlin. Here, the wild, non-naturalistic and exaggeratedly geometric sets, with images painted on floors and walls evoking objects, light and shadow, complemented the highly stylized performances to create affecting psychological yarns. The era's other great film-making landmark was Fritz Lang's futuristic **Metropolis** (1927), a gigantic project for which UFA was massively expanded and which included 750 extras, becoming Weimar Germany's most expensive film and a commercial flop. The film's exploration and critique of social power structures and hierarchies was common to many of the overwhelmingly left-wing films made at the time, which the Nazis would quickly quash. The arrival of sound at the end of the 1920s produced a final artistic flourish for German film before the collapse of the Weimar Republic. **Der Blaue Engel** (*The Blue Angel*; 1930), directed by Josef von Sternberg, was Germany's first talking film and, shot simultaneously in German and English, made an international star of Marlene Dietrich, a local girl discovered at a Berlin variety show.

Film in Nazi Germany

Marlene Dietrich was one of many performers to leave the country after the Nazi seizure of power in 1933. The uncertain economics and politics of Weimar Germany had already prompted many to leave the country, primarily for the USA, but after 1933 this turned into a flood. Around 1500 directors, producers, actors and other film professionals fled the Third Reich, among them Fritz Lang. All those in exile were either excluded from or rejected the *Reichskulturkammer*, the Nazi cultural organization that excluded Jews and anyone politically questionable and defined who could work in the media, effectively bringing to an end the glory days of German cinema. Nevertheless, even the Nazi period produced a few cinematic masterpieces, particularly by **Leni Riefenstahl**: *Triumph des Willens* (*The Triumph of the Will*; 1935), which documented the 1934 Nuremberg Rally, and *Olympia* (1938), an awe-inspiring tribute to Berlin's 1936 Summer Olympics, both of which obviously remain controversial for propagandizing Nazi ideals.

Evolution in a divided Germany

After the war **East Germany** was quick to capitalize on the fact that much of Germany's film infrastructure, notably the former UFA studios, lay in the Soviet occupation zone. Film production quickly got off the ground with Soviet encouragement and Berlin's cinemas were reopened in May 1945, within three weeks of German capitulation. However, strict controls limited topics to those directly contributing to the communist state project. A particular strength turned out to be **children's films**, notably fairytale adaptations such as *Drei Haselnüsse für Aschenbrödel* (*Three Nuts for Cinderella*; 1973), but also genre works, such as *Der schweigende Stern* (*The Silent Star*; 1960), an adaptation of a Stanislaw Lem sci-fi novel, and "red westerns" such as *The Sons of the Great Mother Bear* (1966) in which the heroes tended to be Native American.

Meanwhile the **West German** film industry of the 1950s could no longer measure up to those of France, Italy or Japan. German films were perceived as provincial and only rarely distributed internationally. Cinema attendance began to stagnate and drop in the 1950s, and plummeted in the 1960s. One reaction to this, and a perceived artistic stagnation, was the 1962 **Oberhausen Manifesto** in which a group of young film-makers proclaimed "Der alte Film ist tot. Wir glauben an den neuen" ("The old cinema is dead. We believe in the new"), rejecting the commercial dictates of the German film industry and resolving to build a new industry based on artistic excellence and experimentation. Many up-and-coming film-makers allied themselves with this group, among them Volker Schlöndorff, Werner Herzog, Wim Wenders, Hans-Jürgen Syberberg and Rainer Werner Fassbinder. The lure of new subsidies quickly brought many to Berlin, where the **New German Cinema** movement returned the country's film industry to international acclaim: *The Tin Drum* (1979), by Schlöndorff, became the first German film to win the Academy Award for Best Foreign Language Film, and *Das Boot* (1981) still holds the record for most Academy Award nominations for a German film (six).

A post-Wende renaissance

During the 1980s the vitality of the New German Cinema movement ebbed and the country's film industry struggled against a glut of private TV channels, videos and DVDs. Not until almost ten years after the *Wende* did it really begin to find its feet again. Unlike the more sober and artistic films of the 1970s, this time success was based on an ability to marry arthouse sensibilities with a more commercial outlook, yet still addressing difficult topics from Germany's history and the country's contemporary issues. Three films set in Berlin – *Good Bye Lenin!* (2003) and *The Lives of Others* (2005), dealing respectively with the lighter and darker sides of the GDR (see box, p.65), along with *Downfall* (2004), depicting Hitler's final days (and now immortalized in a thousand YouTube parodies) – were the standout examples of the mid-2000s. *Good Bye Lenin!* was a particularly important landmark in relaunching German cinema abroad, grossing $80m, most of it from overseas. Appropriately the film was first screened at the internationally recognized **Berlinale film festival** (see box, p.237), where it won a coveted Golden Bear award as the best European film of 2003. The Berlinale itself has also become a symbol of the city's cinematic prowess, steadily growing and attracting international talent, critics and filmgoers in increasing numbers. *The Lives of Others*, meanwhile, followed with even greater international success, scooping the Oscar for Best Foreign Language Film in 2006.

The last decade

Despite the founding of the **German Film Academy** in Berlin in 2003, specifically to promote German cinema abroad – and the associated Deutscher Filmpreis (aka the Lolas), which offers a cash prize of €3 million – major successes since the mid-2000s have been few and far between, though *The White Ribbon* (2010), *Oh Boy* (released in English as *A Coffee in Berlin*; 2013) and *Victoria* (2015) have all created an international buzz and deservedly won various awards and acclaim. On the other hand, the city has become the star of **international blockbusters**: in the footsteps of *The Bourne Supremacy* came *Inglourious Basterds*, *The Monuments Men*, *The Fifth Element* and *Bridge of Spies*, all of which were filmed at least partly here.

The **local cinema scene**, in keeping with its creative reputation, tends to lean towards the independent and avant-garde. There are almost a hundred cinemas – not counting the dozens of venues where a projector is often set up for the occasional screening of avant-garde local works – as well as a growing number of small but popular festivals that showcase everything from world cinema (often country-specific, from Australia to Israel) to locally produced films, international shorts and feminist movies.

A BERLIN FILMOGRAPHY

Over the years Berlin has provided the inspiration and setting for a great many films, which now offer a valuable glimpse of a city that vanished in the mayhem of its twentieth century. The following filmography is laid out in chronological order; films marked with a ★ are particularly recommended.

Berlin: Sinfonie einer Grosstadt (*Berlin: Symphony of a Great City*; Walter Ruttmann; 1927). Expressionist silent documentary that magnificently captures a day in the life of 1920s Berlin.

★ **Metropolis** (Fritz Lang; 1927). Futuristic classic and masterpiece of film architecture that was both inspired by and filmed in Berlin.

Mutter Krausens Fahrt ins Glück (*Mother Krause's Journey to Happiness*; Phil Jutzi; 1929). Film version of the working-class Berlin portrayed and caricatured by Heinrich Zille (see p.66). Set in Wedding, where most of the actors came from.

M (Fritz Lang; 1931). Dark Berlin thriller and one of the forerunners of *film noir*.

Olympia (Leni Riefenstahl; 1938). Olympic majesty as never captured on film before or since, based on literally hundreds of kilometres of footage taken during the 1936 Berlin Olympics.

The Big Lift (George Seaton; 1950). Dramatized version of the Berlin Air Lift, starring Montgomery Clift. Of middling quality, but filmed on location.

Funeral in Berlin (Guy Hamilton; 1966). Spy film in which Michael Caine stars as a British agent sent to Berlin. Much cloak and dagger action, but a little slow.

Cabaret (Bob Fosse; 1972). Weimar Berlin as glimpsed through the peepholes of the famed *Kit Kat Klub*, described by Christopher Isherwood, then reinterpreted by Bob Fosse and made iconic by Liza Minnelli.

Die Legende von Paul und Paula (*The Legend of Paul and Paula*; Heiner Carow; 1973). Love story set in East Berlin and filmed in Marzahn. Good for a dose of genuine *Ostalgie*.

★ **Berlin Alexanderplatz** (Rainer Werner Fassbinder; 1980). Epic portrayal – all 931 minutes of it– of 1920s Berlin, based on the Alfred Döblin novel of the same name. It follows a small-time criminal on his journey into Berlin's underworld.

Christiane F. – Wir Kinder vom Bahnhof Zoo (Christiane F.; Uli Edel; 1981). Gritty, dark and disturbing fictionalized film about heroin addiction in the underbelly of 1970s West Berlin. It pulls no punches.

Berlin Tunnel 21 (Richard Michaels; 1981). Reasonable made-for-TV-movie about a former American officer who leads an attempt to build a tunnel underneath the Wall in 1961; not bad at providing a feel of early-1960s Berlin.

Taxi zum Klo (Frank Ripploh; 1981). Groundbreaking film documenting gay culture in West Berlin directed by the lead, who possibly plays himself: an oversexed shaggy-haired teacher who has an interest in film-making.

Octopussy (John Glen; 1983). Probably Roger Moore's best outing as James Bond – who arrives in Berlin to investigate 009's death.

Der Himmel über Berlin (*Wings of Desire*; Wim Wenders; 1987). Iconic classic – which inspired the imaginations of countless film-makers – about love in a divided city, where angels swoop in on postwar Berlin.

Linie 1 (Reinhard Hauff; 1988). Musical based on a girl from the country arriving in the big city, meeting various oddball and low-life characters and travelling extensively up and down U-Bahn Line 1; based on a play created by the GRIPS Theater (see p.259).

★ **Lola Rennt** (*Run Lola Run*; Tom Tykwer; 1998). Fast-paced film set to a pounding techno soundtrack, evoking a real sense of city life and speckled with wry examples of Berlin humour.

Sonnenallee (Leander Haussmann; 1999). Well-received teen comedy set in 1970s East Berlin, and one of the earliest examples of *Ostalgie*.

★ **Berlin Babylon** (Hubertus Siegert; 2001). Fascinating documentary on the rebuilding projects after the fall of the Wall, based on four years of footage.

Invincible (Werner Herzog; 2001). True story of a Jewish strongman in Weimar Berlin who becomes convinced he's been chosen by God to warn his people of imminent danger.

Berlin is in Germany (Hannes Stöhr; 2001). A look back at the GDR era through the eyes of a convict released after the *Wende* and struggling to come to terms with the new Germany he faces.

Was Tun, Wenn's Brennt? (Gregor Schnitzler; 2002). A tale of anarchists squatting in 1980s Berlin, going their separate ways and then being reunited a dozen years later when charged with a crime. Neat insights into the time and Berlin's grittier aspects.

★ **Good Bye Lenin!** (Wolfgang Becker; 2003). Arguably the finest *Ostalgie* film, with dozens of humorous moments and a melancholy look at the *Wende* and its influence on daily lives.

Der Untergang (*Downfall*; Oliver Hirschbiegel; 2004). Much-debated film portraying the last days of Hitler (played by Bruno Ganz) in his bunker, it also believably depicts scenes from the Battle of Berlin.

Die Fetten Jahre sind vorbei (*The Edukators*; Hans Weingartner; 2004). *Good Bye Lenin!*'s Daniel Brühl plays one of three activists who kidnap a businessman in one of Berlin's affluent suburbs. The film at times takes itself a bit too seriously but delivers some fun snatches of life in Noughties Berlin, and the plot has several interesting twists.

Gestpenster (*Ghosts*; Christian Petzold; 2005). Modern urban alienation in Mitte, focusing on the life of a late-teenage orphan with mental problems.

★ **Das Leben der Anderen** (*The Lives of Others*; Florian Henckel von Donnersmarck; 2005). Highly evocative Stasi drama set in an East Berlin that's riddled by agents, informers and bugging devices. The film became an international success, potently informing the world about Stasi crimes.

Ich bin ein Berliner (Franziska Meyer Price; 2005). Fluffy but watchable comedy by one of Germany's foremost female directors.

Valkyrie (Bryan Singer; 2008). American dramatization of the July Bomb Plot (see box, pp.98–99) in which Tom Cruise stars as Klaus Schenk von Stauffenberg.

Berlin Calling (Hannes Stöhr; 2008). A German electronic artist known as DJ Ickarus (played by real life DJ and artist Paul Kalkbrenner) has his career ruined by taking too many drugs and winding up in a psychiatric unit. More entertaining than it sounds.

Russendisko (Oliver Ziegenbalg; 2012). Film version of Wladimir Kaminer's book (p.292); panned by critics but watchable nonetheless.

Oh Boy (*A Coffee in Berlin*; Jan-Ole Gerster; 2012). Classily shot in black and white, this tragicomedy follows a university dropout (Tom Schilling) as he aimlessly wanders the streets of Berlin and ponders the meaning of life.

Victoria (Sebastian Schipper; 2015). Famously shot in one seamless take, this gripping thriller offers hyper-realistic insights into Berlin life and a big plot twist at the end.

Bridge of Spies (Steven Spielberg; 2015). Based on the true story of a 1960s spy exchange between the USA and East Germany, this blockbuster conjures up the noir-ish Cold War atmosphere of the city and stars Tom Hanks and Mark Rylance.

Architecture

"Berlin is a new city; the newest I have ever seen," remarked Mark Twain in 1891. A curious thing for an American to say, but the statement still rings true. Certainly, by European standards the city is relatively young – founded in the thirteenth century and only blossoming from the late sixteenth – but it's the obliterating destruction of World War II that has made it so new. Few buildings hark back to before this time (those that appear to are mostly replicas), and the city has become a haven for modern architecture and experimentation.

Prussia's imperial capital

A chronological tour of Berlin's architecture kicks off in the Nikolaiviertel, with the medieval **Nikolaikirche** (see p.66). This is followed by the ornate Baroque buildings of the seventeenth century – the best examples are the grand **Schloss Charlottenburg** (see p.161) and the **Brandenbuger Tor** (see p.35). South of here, magnificent churches with splendid domes stand on the **Gendarmenmarkt** (see p.47). These and many other buildings – such as the **Neue Wache** (see p.47) and the **Altes Museum** (see p.55) – were later adorned by Karl Friedrich Schinkel (1781–1841; see box, p.46), with his unmistakable Neoclassical touch. As all these grand edifices were assembled, the Industrial Revolution in Berlin's suburbs was leading to an explosion in the population: to combat the need for housing a system of tenements around a series of courtyards was developed – the **Hackesche Höfe** (see p.72) are a good example of this design.

The founding of the German empire in 1871 ushered in *Gründerzeit* architecture, whose premise was largely to recycle earlier styles, and then to add ostentatious flourishes – the **Reichstag** (see p.37) and the **Berliner Dom** (see p.53) are models of the style.

Modernism to Third Reich

As a backlash against all this nostalgia, **Modernism** arrived in Berlin in the early twentieth century. Foremost among the Modernist architects was Peter Behrens (1868–1940), who removed ornamentation and favoured glass, concrete and steel building materials. One of the finest buildings from the period is Emil Fahrenkamp's **Shell-Haus** (see p.100). The Nazis brought any Modernist enterprises to an end, preferring powerful-looking Neoclassical buildings for their **Third Reich**. An imposing remodelling of Berlin was envisaged but defeat in the war scuppered the plans – however, a few Nazi buildings remain, including the magnificent **Tempelhof airport** (see p.125) and the **Olympiastadion** (Olympic Stadium; see p.166).

The divided city

Postwar town planners and architects on both sides of the divided city were presented with a relatively blank canvas. East Berlin continued monumentalist traditions with its enormous **Karl-Marx-Allee** (see p.134) housing schemes built in Stalin's favourite *Zuckerbäckstil* (wedding-cake style), while its top project was the **Fernsehturm** (see p.61), focal point of the showpiece GDR square, Alexanderplatz. Long threatened with demolition in favour of modern skyscrapers, several of the late 1960s architectural slabs around the square have recently been listed – suggesting an acceptance of their importance to Berlin's messy but compelling architectural whole.

Meanwhile, planners in West Berlin strived to project a modern yet more sensitive image: the use of greenery around buildings was as important as the architecture itself, as at the **Kongresshalle** (now the Haus der Kulturen der Welt; see p.103), and Scharoun's **Philharmonie** (see p.94). Prestige projects aside, both Berlins needed affordable housing and both approached this in similarly dismal ways, illustrated by the high-rises of Marzahn (see p.153). More sensitive **regeneration projects** followed in areas like Prenzlauer Berg in the east and Kreuzberg in the west.

Reunification and the twenty-first century

After the *Wende*, attention shifted to the building projects in areas where the Berlin Wall once stood. The Sony Center and skyscrapers of **Potsdamer Platz** (see p.89) were the most striking, but impressive too were the developments on **Pariser Platz** (see p.36), in the **Regierungsviertel** (Government quarter; see p.104), and those that fringe the Tiergarten, such as the Nordic and Mexican **embassies** (see p.101) and the immense **Hauptbahnhof** (see p.105).

There followed several monuments and museums designed to help Berlin address its past, including Daniel Libeskind's **Jüdisches Museum** (see p.119), the **Memorial to the Murdered Jews of Europe**, since joined by three further monuments to Nazi crimes nearby (see p.38 & p.95) and the stark **Topographie des Terrors** (see p.122). The biggest commercial construction projects of the last decade or so – generally a mix of residential, office and retail – have focused on **Europaplatz**, the huge space to the north of the Hauptbahnhof, and in City West, where swanky new hotels and malls like **Bikini Berlin** (see p.242) have helped regenerate the area. More creative and cultural overhauls have taken place at the **RAW Gelände** complex (see p.134) and the **Holzmarkt** site, where the *Kater Blau* nightclub (see p.228) is gradually morphing into a sustainable urban village area; both are in Friedrichshain.

Though the pace of building work in Berlin is slowing, there is still much underway. The two biggest projects are the catastrophically bungled **Berlin-Brandenburg Airport**, originally due to have opened in 2010 and still embarrassing the city authorities, and the ambitious and controversial reconstruction of the **Berlin Palace** (see p.51), which, like the airport, is expected to be delayed well beyond its 2019 target date.

Language

English speakers approaching German for the first time have one real initial advantage, which is that German – as a close linguistic relative of English – shares with it a lot of basic vocabulary. It doesn't take long to work out that the *Milch* for your breakfast *Kaffee* comes from a *Kuh* that spends its life eating *Gras* in a *Feld*, or that *Brot* is nicer when spread with *Butter*.

Two things conspire to give German a fearsome reputation among non-native speakers, however. The first is the **grammar**: it *is* complex – many Germans never really master it properly – but for the purposes of a short stay you shouldn't need to wade too deeply into its intricacies. The second is the **compound noun** – the German habit of creating enormously long words to define something quite specific. These aren't as difficult as they first appear, since they're composed from building blocks of basic vocabulary, so that, if you break them down into their component parts, you can often puzzle out the meaning without a dictionary. (All nouns in German are written with a capital letter, by the way.) German uses the same **alphabet** as English, with the exception of the letter ß ("scharfes S"), pronounced like "ss", with which it is phonetically interchangeble and so has been replaced by ss in this guide. The vowels o, a and u can be modified by using the Umlaut to ö, ä and ü, changing the pronunciation.

Pronunciation and grammar

Unlike English, German is written more or less **phonetically**, so that once you understand how the vowels and consonants are pronounced there's rarely any ambiguity. Exceptions include foreign words that have been incorporated into German – including, in recent years, a great many from English (see box below). The equivalent sounds detailed below are in British English.

Vowels and umlauts

a long "a" as in farther (eg sagen); short "a" as in hat (eg Hand)

e long "e" as in lay (eg wenig); short "e" as in ten (eg gelb)

i "i" as in meek (eg Tiger); short "i" as in pin (eg Tipp)

o long "o" as in open (eg oben); short "o" as in hop (eg offen)

u long "u" as in in loot (eg Kuh); short "u" as in foot

(eg und)

ä is a combination of "a" and "e", sometimes pronounced like "e" in set (eg Hände) and sometimes like "ai" in laid (eg Gerät)

ö roughly like a long or short version of the vowel in sir (eg möchte)

ü no exact equivalent; roughly a long or short version of the vowel sound in few (eg über)

ENGLISH IN BERLIN

With tourism on the up, it's got to the point where in central Berlin you're as likely to hear **English** as German spoken, and most Berlin businesses now even maintain English-language-only websites. But the roots of the language in Berlin mainly go back to the start of the Cold War, when British and American military personnel settled here in numbers. English became a compulsory subject in West Berlin's schools and, since reunification, the trend has been for all German kids to learn English from an increasingly early age – even in Kindergarten. So most West Berliners, and all Berliners under the age of about 35, will have a good grounding – good enough that English words are often and increasingly used in spoken and written German, and particularly in magazine headlines. All this is good news for English speakers trying to get by – but it does make it harder to practise your German.

Vowel combinations

au as in mouse (eg Haus)
ie as in tree (eg Bier)
ei as in pie (eg mein)

eu as in boil (eg Freude)
ai as in pie (eg Kaiser)

Consonants and consonant combinations

ch is pronounced like Scottish "loch" (eg ich)
g is always a hard "g" sound, as in "go" (eg Gang), except in words ending with -ig (eg Leipzig), when it is like a very soft German "ch"
j is pronounced like an English "y" (eg ja)
s is pronounced similar to English "z" at the end of a word like "s" in glass (eg Glas), and like "sh" before a consonant (eg Sport)

sch is like English "sh"
th is pronounced like English "t"
v is roughly "f" (eg von)
w is pronounced like English "v" (eg wann), except at the end of the word, as in the Berlin place names Kladow and Gatow, which rhyme with "pillow"
z is pronounced "ts"

Gender and adjective endings

German nouns can be one of three **genders**: masculine, feminine or neuter (the = der, die or das). Sometimes the gender is obvious – it's der Mann (the man) and die Frau (the woman) – but sometimes it seems baffling: a girl is das Mädchen, because Mädchen – "little maiden" – is a diminutive, and diminutives are neutral. There are some hard and fast rules to help you know which is which: nouns ending in -er (der Böcker, der Sportler) are masculine; the female form ends in -in (die Böckerin, die Sportlerin). Words ending in -ung, -heit, -keit or -schaft are feminine (die Zeitung, die Freiheit, die Fröhlichkeit, die Mannschaft). Definite (der; "the") and indefinite (ein; "a") **articles** and **adjective endings** can change according to the precise grammatical role in the sentence of the noun, which is where things start to get complex. If in doubt, stick to "der" or "das" for single items: once there is more than one of anything, it becomes "die" anyway.

Politeness

You can address children, animals and, nowadays, young people (but only in relaxed social situations, and really only if you're the same age) with the familiar "**du**" to mean "you". For anyone else – and particularly for older people or officials – stick to the polite "**Sie**"; if they want to be on familiar terms with you, they'll invite you to be so – "Duzen wir?". Incidentally, unmarried German women should be addressed as "**Frau**", the word "**Fräulein**" to describe a young, single woman now considered old-fashioned and rather sexist.

WORDS AND PHRASES

GREETINGS AND BASIC PHRASES

Good morning	Guten Morgen	**Do you speak English?**	Sprechen Sie Englisch?
Good evening	Guten Abend	**I don't speak German**	Ich spreche kein Deutsch
Good day	Guten Tag	**Please speak more slowly**	Könnten Sie bitte langsamer sprechen?
Hello (informal)	Hallo		
Goodbye (formal)	Auf Wiedersehen	**I understand**	Ich verstehe
Goodbye (informal)	Tschüss (but also Servus)	**I don't understand**	Ich verstehe nicht
		I'd like ...	Ich möchte ...
Goodbye (on the telephone)	Auf Wiederhören	**I'm sorry**	Es tut mir leid
How are you? (polite)	Wie geht es Ihnen?	**Where?**	Wo?
How are you? (informal)	Wie geht es dir?	**When?**	Wann?
Yes	Ja	**How much?**	Wieviel?
No	Nein	**Here**	Hier
Please/ You're welcome	Bitte/Bitte schön	**There**	Da
Thank you/Thank you very much	Danke/Danke schön	**Open**	Geöffnet/offen/auf
		Closed	Geschlossen/zu
		Over there	Drüben

This one	Dieses
That one	Jenes
Large	Gross
Small	Klein
More	Mehr
Less	Weniger
A bit	Ein bisschen
A little	Ein wenig
A lot	Viel
Cheap	Billig
Expensive	Teuer
Good	Gut
Where is …?	Wo ist …?
How much does that cost?	Wieviel kostet das?
What time is it?	Wieviel Uhr ist es?/
	Wie spät ist es?
The bill, please	Die Rechnung, bitte!
	(or Zahlen, bitte!)
Separately or together?	Getrennt oder zusammen?
Receipt	Quittung
Where is the toilet?	Wo ist die Toilette, bitte?
Women's toilets	Damen/Frauen
Men's toilets	Herren/Männer

NUMBERS

1	eins
2	zwei
3	drei
4	vier
5	fünf
6	sechs
7	sieben
8	acht
9	neun
10	zehn
11	elf
12	zwölf
13	dreizehn
14	vierzehn
15	fünfzehn
16	sechszehn
17	siebzehn
18	achtzehn
19	neunzehn
20	zwanzig
21	einundzwanzig
22	zweiundzwanzig
30	dreissig
40	vierzig
50	fünfzig
60	sechzig
70	siebzig
80	achtzig
90	neunzig

100	hundert
1000	tausend

DAYS, MONTHS, TIME AND SEASONS

Today	Heute
Yesterday	Gestern
Tomorrow	Morgen
The day before yesterday	Vorgestern
The day after tomorrow	Übermorgen
Day	Tag
Night	Nacht
Week	Woche
Month	Monat
Year	Jahr
Weekend	Wochenende
In the morning	Am Vormittag/Vormittags
Tomorrow morning	Morgen früh
In the afternoon	Am Nachmittag/
	Nachmittags
In the evening	Am Abend
Seven thirty	Halb acht (ie half before
	eight)
Quarter past seven	Viertel nach sieben
Quarter to eight	Viertel vor acht
Now	jetzt
Later	später
Earlier	früher
At what time?	Um wieviel Uhr?
Monday	Montag
Tuesday	Dienstag
Wednesday	Mittwoch
Thursday	Donnerstag
Friday	Freitag
Saturday	Samstag/Sonnabend
	(northern Germany)
Sunday	Sonntag
January	Januar
February	Februar
March	März
April	April
May	Mai
June	Juni
July	Juli
August	August
September	September
October	Oktober
November	November
December	Dezember
Spring	Frühling
Summer	Sommer
Autumn	Herbst
Winter	Winter
Holidays	Ferien
Bank holiday	Feiertag

TRANSPORT AND SIGNS

Abflug	Departure (airport)
Abreise/Abfahrt	Departure (more generally)
Ankunft	Arrivals
Ausfahrt	Motorway exit
Ausgang	Exit
Ausgang freihalten	Keep clear/no parking in front of exit
Autobahn	Motorway
Baustelle	Roadworks (on Autobahn etc)
Einbahnstraße	one-way street
Eingang	Entrance
Fähre	Ferry
Führerschein	Driver's licence
Kein Eingang	No entrance
Nicht rauchen/ Rauchen verboten	No smoking
Notausgang	Emergency exit
Plakette	Colour-coded sticker for cars, needed if travelling in the city centre (see p.23).
Reisepass/Pass	Passport
Tankstelle	Petrol station
Umleitung	Diversion
Unfall	Accident
Verboten	Prohibited
Vorsicht!	Attention!/Take care!
Zoll	Customs

A FOOD AND DRINK GLOSSARY

BASIC TERMS

Breakfast	Frühstück
Lunch	Mittagessen
Coffee and cakes	Kaffee und Kuchen – a mid-afternoon ritual
Supper, dinner	Abendessen/Abendbrot (bread with cold toppings)
Knife	Messer
Fork	Gabel
Spoon	Löffel
Plate	Teller
Cup	Tasse
Mug	Becher
Bowl	Schüssel
Glass	Glas
Menu	Speisekarte
Wine list	Weinkarte
Set menu	Menü
Course	Gang
Starter	Vorspeise
Main course	Hauptgericht
Dessert	Nachspeise
Restaurant bill	Rechnung
Tip	Trinkgeld
Vegetarian	vegetarisch

COOKING TERMS

blau	boiled
eingelegt	pickled
frisch	fresh
gebacken	baked
gebraten	fried, roasted
gedämpft	steamed
gefüllt	stuffed
gegrillt	grilled
gekocht	boiled (also more generally means "cooked")
geräuchert	smoked
geschmort	braised, slow-cooked
gutbürgerlich	traditional German
hausgemacht	home-made
heiss	hot
lauwarm	lukewarm
kalt	cold
roh	raw
am Spiess	skewered
Topf, Eintopf	stew, casserole
überbacken	with a hot topping (especially cheese)
zart	tender (eg of meat)

BASICS

Belegtes Brot	sandwich
Bio	organic
Brot	bread, loaf
Brötchen	bread roll
Butter	butter
Ei	egg
Essig	vinegar
Fisch	fish
Fleisch	meat
Gemüse	vegetables
Honig	honey
Joghurt	yoghurt
Kaffee	coffee
Käse	cheese
Marmelade	jam
Milch	milk
Obst	fruit
Öl	oil
Pfeffer	pepper

Sahne	cream
Salatsoße	salad dressing
Salz	salt
scharf	spicy
Schrippe	bread roll (in Berlin)
Senf	mustard
Soße	sauce
Süßstoff	artificial sweetener
Tee	tea
Wasser	water
Zucker	sugar

SOUPS AND STARTERS

Blattsalat	green salad/salad leaves
Bohnensuppe	bean soup
Bunter Salat	mixed salad
Erbsensuppe	pea soup
Flädlesuppe/	clear soup with pancake
Pfannkuchensuppe/	strips
Frittatensuppe	
Fleischsuppe	meat soup
Gulaschsuppe	spicy thick meat soup with paprika
Gurkensalat	cucumber salad
Hühnersuppe	chicken soup
Kartoffelsalat	potato salad
Leberknödelsuppe	clear soup with liver dumplings
Linsensuppe	lentil soup
Sülze	brawn
Suppe	soup
Wurstsalat	sausage salad

MEAT AND POULTRY

Backhähnchen	roast chicken
Bockwurst	chunky boiled sausage
Bratwurst	grilled sausage
Cordon Bleu	a Schnitzel stuffed with ham and cheese
Currywurst	sausage served with tomato ketchup and curry powder
Eisbein	boiled pigs' hock
Ente	duck
Frikadelle/Bulette	German burger
Gans	goose
Geschnetzeltes	shredded meat
Gyros/Dönerkebap	kebab
Hackfleisch	minced meat
Hirsch, Reh	venison
Huhn/Hähnchen	chicken
Jägerschnitzel	cutlet in wine and mushroom sauce
Kassler Rippen	smoked and pickled pork

	chops
Kohlroulade	cabbage leaves stuffed with mincemeat
Kotelett	cutlet, chop
Lamm	lamb
Leber	liver
Leberkäse	baked meatloaf
Lunge	lungs
Rindfleisch	beef
Sauerbraten	braised pickled beef (or horse, in which case the menu description will specify "vom Pferd")
Schaschlik	diced meat with piquant sauce
Schinken	ham
Schweinebraten	roast pork
Schweinefleisch	pork
Schweinshaxe	roast pig's hock (knuckle)
Speck	bacon
Truthahn/Puter	turkey
Weisswurst	Veal sausage seasoned with lemon zest and parsley
Wiener Schnitzel	thin cutlet in breadcumbs: either veal (vom Kalb) or pork (vom Schwein)
Wienerwurst	boiled pork sausage
Wild	wild game
Wildschwein	wild boar
Wurst	sausage
Zigeunerschnitzel	cutlet in paprika sauce

FISH

Aal	eel
Forelle	trout
Garnelen	prawns
Hecht	pike
Hering/Matjes	herring
Hummer	lobster
Kabeljau	cod
Karpfen	carp
Krabben	shrimps
Lachs	salmon
Muscheln	mussels
Rotbarsch	rosefish
Saibling	char
Scholle	plaice
Schwertfisch	swordfish
Seezunge	sole
Thunfisch	tuna
Tintenfisch	squid
Zander	pike-perch

PASTA, DUMPLINGS AND NOODLES

Kloß/Knödel	potato dumpling
Maultaschen	a form of ravioli
Reis	rice
Semmelknödel	bread dumpling
Spätzle	German pasta

VEGETABLES

Blumenkohl	cauliflower
Bohnen	beans
Bratkartoffeln	fried potatoes
Champignons	button mushrooms
Dicke Bohnen	broad beans
Erbsen	peas
Grüne Bohnen	green beans
Gurke	cucumber or gherkin
Karotten/Möhren	carrots
Kartoffelbrei	mashed potatoes
Kartoffelpüree	creamed potatoes
Kartoffelsalat	potato salad
Knoblauch	garlic
Kopfsalat	lettuce
Lauch/Porree	leek
Maiskolben	corn on the cob
Paprika	green or red peppers
Pfifferling/Eierschwamm	chanterelle mushroom
Pellkartoffeln	jacket potatoes
Pilze	mushrooms
Pommes frites	chips/French fries
Reibekuchen/ Kartoffelpuffer	fried potato cake
Rosenkohl	Brussels sprouts
Rote Rübe	beetroot
Rotkohl	red cabbage
Rübensalat	turnip salad
Salzkartoffeln (Petersilienkartoffeln)	boiled potatoes (with parsley)
Sauerkraut	pickled cabbage
Spargel	asparagus
Weisskohl	white cabbage
Wok-Gemüse	stir-fried vegetables
Zwiebeln	onions

FRUIT

Ananas	pineapple
Apfel	apple
Aprikose	apricot
Birne	pear
Brombeeren	blackberries
Datteln	dates
Erdbeeren	strawberries
Feigen	figs
Himbeeren	raspberries
Johannisbeeren	redcurrants
Kirschen	cherries
Kompott	stewed fruit
Melone	melon
Obstsalat	fruit salad
Pampelmuse	grapefruit
Pfirsich	peach
Pflaumen	plums
Rosinen	raisins
Schwarze Johannisbeeren	blackcurrants
Trauben	grapes
Zitrone	lemon

CHEESES

Käseplatte	cheese board
Quark	low-fat soft cheese
Schafskäse	sheep's cheese
Weichkäse	cream cheese
Ziegenkäse	goat's cheese

DESSERTS AND BAKED GOODS

Apfelstrudel (mit Sahne)	apple strudel (with cream)
Pfannkuchen	jam doughnut
Dampfnudeln	yeast dumplings served hot with vanilla sauce
Eierkuchen	pancake
Eis	ice cream
Gebäck	pastries
Käsekuchen	cheesecake
Keks	biscuit
Kuchen	cake
Lebkuchen/Printen	spiced gingerbread
Nüsse	nuts
Nusskuchen	nut cake
Obstkuchen	fruitcake
Schlagsahne	whipped cream
Schokolade	chocolate
Schwarzwälder Kirschtorte	Black Forest gateau
Torte	gateau, tart

Glossary of German terms

Altstadt Old part of a city.

Auskunft Information.

Ausländer Literally "foreigner", the word has come to be a pejorative term for any non-white non-German.

Ausstellung Exhibition.

Bäckerei Bakery.

Bahnhof Station.

Bau Building.

Berg Mountain or hill.
Berliner Schnauze Sharp and coarse Berlin wit.
Bezirk City district.
Brücke Bridge.
Burg Mountain or hill.
Bushaltestelle Bus stop.
Denkmal Memorial.
Dom Cathedral.
Dorf Village.
Einbahnstrasse One-way street.
Feiertag Holiday.
Flughafen Airport.
Fluss River.
Fremdenzimmer Room for short-term let.
Gasse Alley.
Gastarbeiter "Guest worker": a foreigner who comes to Germany to do menial work.
Gasthaus, Gasthof Guesthouse, inn.
Gaststätte Traditional bar that also serves food.
Gedenkstätte Memorial.
Gemälde Painting.
Grünen, die The Greens: political party.
Haupteingang Main entrance.
Hof Court, courtyard, mansion.
Insel Island.
Jugendherberge Youth hostel.
Jugendstil German version of Art Nouveau.
Junker Prussian landowning class.
Kaiser Emperor.
Kammer Room, chamber.
Kapelle Chapel.
Kaufhaus Department store.
Kino Cinema.
Kirche Church.
Kneipe Bar.
Konditorei Cake shop.
Krankenhaus Hospital.
Kunst Art.
Markt Market, market square.
Motorrad Motorbike.
Not Emergency.

Platz Square.
Quittung Official receipt.
Rathaus Town hall.
Reich Empire.
Reisebüro Travel agency.
Rundgang Way round.
S-Bahn Suburban train network.
Sammlung Collection.
Schicki Abbreviation of "Schicki-Micki": yuppie.
Schloss Castle, palace.
See Lake.
Staatssicherheitsdienst (STASI) The "State Security Service" or secret police of the GDR.
Stadt Town, city.
Stammtisch Table in a pub or restaurant reserved for regular customers.
Stiftung Foundation.
Strand Beach.
Strassenbahn Tram.
Tankstelle Petrol station.
Tor Gate, gateway.
Trabi The Trabant, East Germany's two-cylinder, two-stroke people's car.
Turm Tower.
U-Bahn Network of underground trains.
Verkehrsamt/Verkehrsverein Tourist office.
Viertel Quarter, district.
Volk People, folk; given mystical associations by Hitler.
Vopo Slang for Volkspolizei, a member of the East German police force.
Wald Forest.
Weimar Republic Parliamentary democracy, established in 1918, which collapsed with Hitler's assumption of power in 1933.
Wende Literally, "turning point" – the term used to describe the events of November 1989 and after.
Zeitschrift Magazine.
Zeitung Newspaper.
Zeughaus Arsenal.
Zimmer Room.

Acronyms

BRD (Bundesrepublik Deutschland) Official name of former West Germany.
CDU (Christlich Demokratische Union) Christian Democratic (Conservative) Party.
DDR (Deutsche Demokratische Republik) Official name of former East Germany.
GDR (German Democratic Republic) English equivalent of DDR.
NSDAP (Nationalsozialistische Deutsche Arbeiterpartei) "National Socialist German Workers'
Party", the official name for the Nazis.
PDS (Partei des Demokratischen Sozializmus) The revamped SED after the collapse of the Wall.
SED (Sozialistische Einheitspartei Deutschlands) "Socialist Unity Party of Germany", the official name of the East German communist party before December 1989.
SPD (Sozialdemokratische Partei Deutschlands) Social Democratic (Labour) Party.

Map index

Listings key

■ Accommodation

● Eating

■ Drinking and nightlife

● Shopping

City plan

The **city plan** on the pages that follow is divided as shown:

N

0   250
metres

Map symbols

Railway	Ⓤ U-Bahn station	✈ Airport	⛪ Church
Path	Ⓢ S-Bahn station	▲ Hill	⬭ Stadium
River	★ Bicycle/scooter station	🏛 Monument	Christian cemetery
Wall	⊞ Hospital	Museum	Jewish cemetery
Bridge	⊙ Statue	Synagogue	Muslim cemetery
Place of interest	E Embassy	Garden	Park
Post office	🐘 Zoo	Building	Beach
ⓘ Tourist office			

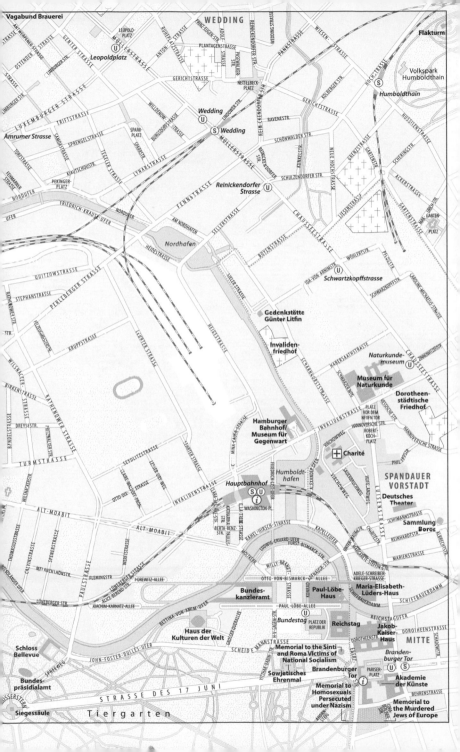

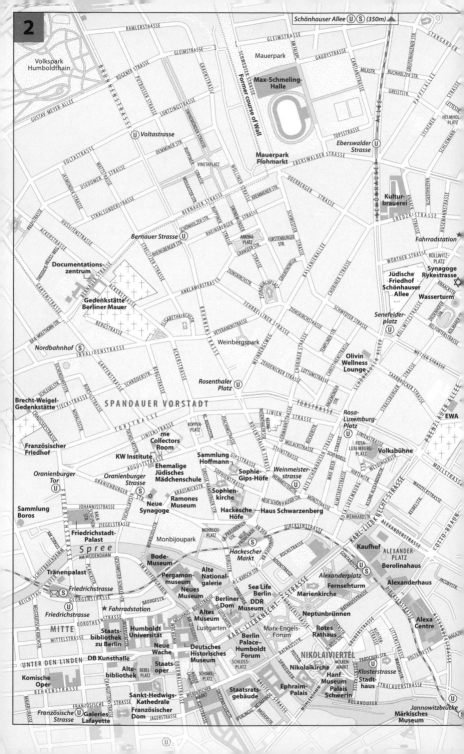

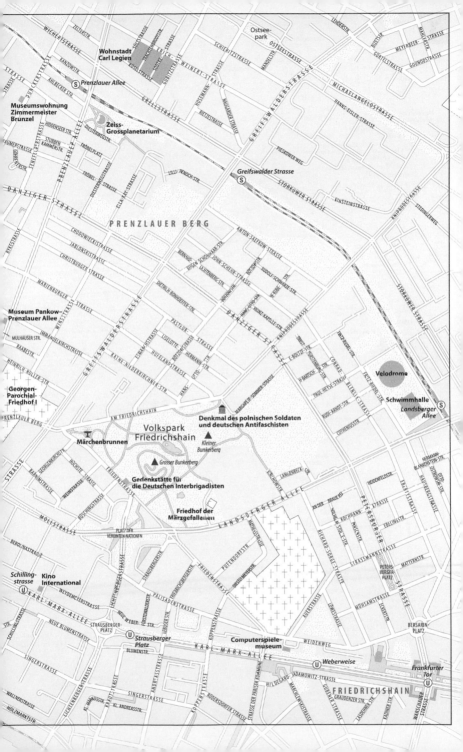

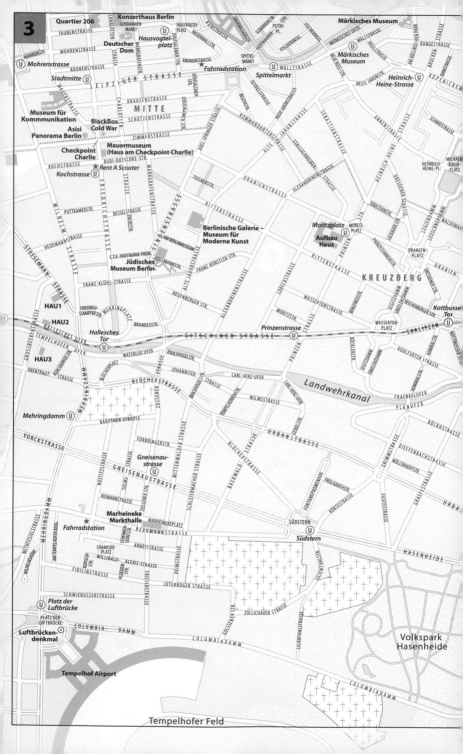

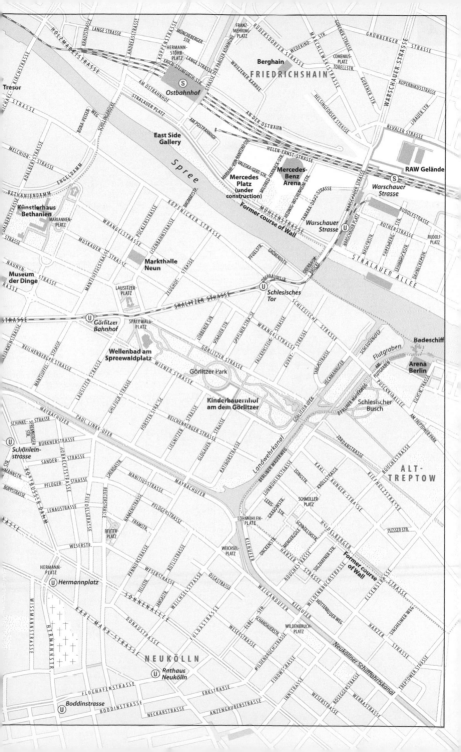

4

OTTO-SUHR-ALLEE

M-E-LÜDERS HAUS

BISMARCKSTRASSE

ERNST-REUTER-PLATZ

STRASSE DES 17 JUNI

MÜLLER-BRESLAU-STRASSE

TIERGARTENUFER

GARTENUFER

Neuer See

S Ernst-Reuter-Platz

HARDENBERGSTRASSE

FASANENSTRASSE

HERTZALLEE

Zoologischer Garten Berlin

T-DEHLER

LICHTENSTEINALLEE

DRAKESTR

SCHILLERSTRASSE

HERDERSTR

GOETHESTRASSE

KNESEBECKSTRASSE

STEIN-PLATZ

GROLMANSTRASSE

CARMERSTRASSE

Museum für Fotografie

Zoologischer Garten

S

HARDENBERGPLATZ

KATHARINA-HEINROTH-UFER

KANTSTRASSE

PESTALOZZISTRASSE

SAVIGNY-PLATZ

C/O Berlin (Amerika Haus) Theater des Westens

Camera Work

KANTSTRASSE

U

BUDAPESTER STRASSE

Bikini Berlin

Aquarium Berlin

BREITSCHEID-PLATZ

BUDAPESTER STRASSE

WICHMANNSTR

S Savignyplatz

WIELANDSTRASSE

NIEBUHRSTRASSE

GROLMANSTRASSE

KNESEBECKSTRASSE

BLEIBTREUSTRASSE

Kaiser-Wilhelm-Gedächtniskirche

Europa-Center

Hotel Palace

KURFÜRSTENSTRASSE

MOMMSENSTRASSE

FASANENSTRASSE

TAUENTZIENSTR

i

Kurfürstendamm

ANSBACHER STR

BAYREUTHER STR

U Uhlandstrasse

JOACHIMSTHALER STR

LOS-ANGELES-PLATZ

Augsburger Str

MARBURGER STR

NÜRNBERGER STR

KaDeWe

U Wittenbergplatz

WITTENBERG-PLATZ

KLEISTSTRASSE

DÄ

KURFÜRSTENDAMM

Käthe-Kollwitz-Museum

RANKESTRASSE

Augsburger Strasse

PASSAUER STR

BAMBERGER STR

The Story of Berlin

SCHLÜTERSTRASSE

KNESEBECKSTRASSE

UHLAND

MEINEKESTR

EISLEBENER STR

WÜRZBURGER STR

BAYREUTHER STR

Ku'damm Karree

LIETZENBURGER STRASSE

FÜRTHER STR

FUGGERSTRASSE

OLIVAER PLATZ

SCHAPERSTRASSE

MOTZSTR

WELSER STR

PARISER STR

LUDWIGKIRCH-STRASSE

FASANEN-PLATZ

MEIEROTTOSTRASSE

BUNDESALLEE

SPICHERNSTR

PRAGER STR

BRANDENBURG

HEILBRONNER STR

ANSBACHER STRASSE

GEISBERGSTRASSE

Viktoria-Luise-Platz

DARMSTÄDTER STR

SÄCHSISCHE STR

EMSER STR

PFALZBURGER STR

DÜSSELDORFER STRASSE

UHLANDSTRASSE

FASANEN STRASSE

Spichernstrasse U

REGENSBERGER STRASSE

RUMMISBURGER STR

VIKTORIA-LUISE-PLATZ

LUITPOLDSTRASSE

NACHODSTRASSE

HOHENSTAUFENSTRASSE

HOHENZOLLERNDAMM

STRASSE

MOTZSTRASSE

MÜNCHENER STRASSE

LANDSHUTER

U Hohenzollernplatz

NIKOLSBURGER PLATZ

TRAUTENAUSTRASSE

Prager PLATZ

ASCHAFFENBURGER STR

BAMBERGER STR

SPEYERER STR

SCHWÄBISCHE STR

TRAUTENAUSTR

BERCHTESGADENER STRASSE

Preussen-park

POMMERSCHE STRASSE

EMSER PLATZ

BARBAROSSA STRASSE

U Fehrbelliner Platz

WEGENERSTR

WIESBADENER STR

NASSAUISCHE STR

Güntzelstrasse U

GÜNTZELSTRASSE

HELMSTEDTER STRASSE

PRINZ-REGENTEN-STRASSE

MECKLENBURGISCHE STR

GÜNTZELSTRASSE

ROSENHEIMER STRASSE

Eisenacher Strasse

BRANDENBURGISCHE STR

MANNHEIMER STR

GASTEINER STRASSE

W I L M E R S D O R F

THARANDTER-STR

LANDHAUSSTRASSE

BADENSCHE STRASSE

BAYERISCHER PLATZ

VIKTORIA-LUISE-PLATZ

BOZENER STR

APOSTEL-PAULUS-STR

WARTBURGSTR

GRUNEWALDSTRASSE

Bayerischer Platz U

WARTBURG-PLATZ

Blissestrasse U

BERLINER STRASSE

Berliner Strasse U

MEHLITZSTR

WILHELMSAUE

WILHELMSAUE

BERLINER STRASSE

BUNDESALLEE

KUFSTEINER STR

WERNER STR

MARTIN-LUTHER-STRASSE

MEININGER STR

BELZIGER

Heidelberger Platz

S

U

STRASSE AM SCHOELERPARK

AM VOLKSPARK

HILDEGARDSTRASSE

MAINZER STRASSE

DUBLICHER STRASSE

Rathaus Schöneberg

Rathaus Schöneberg U

Rudolph-Wilde-Park

JOHN-F-KENNEDY-PLATZ

FRITZ-ELSAS-STR

HAUPTSTRASSE

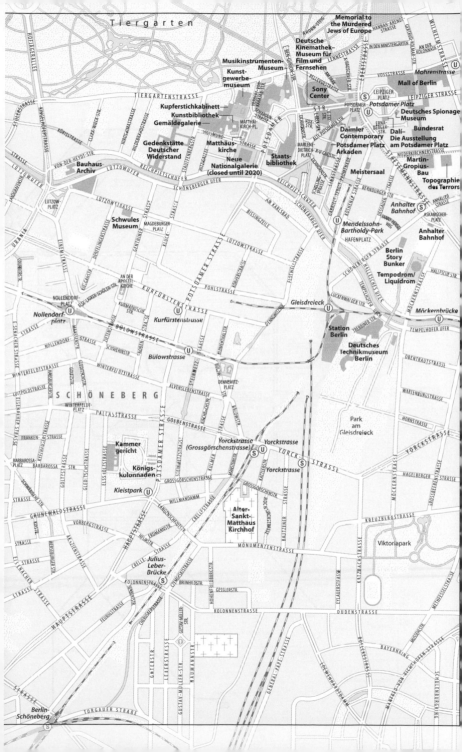

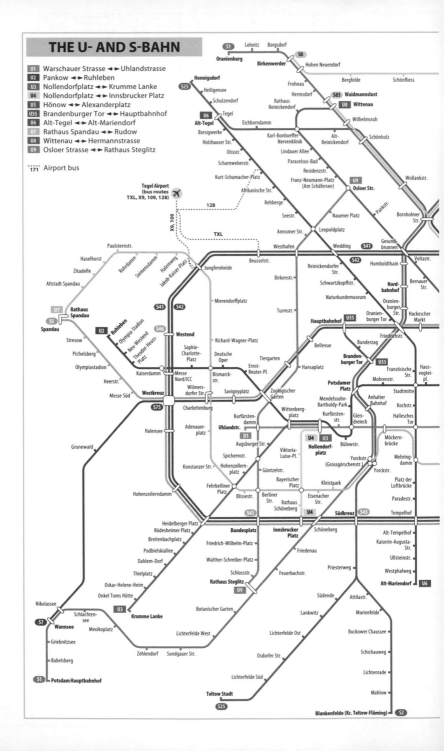

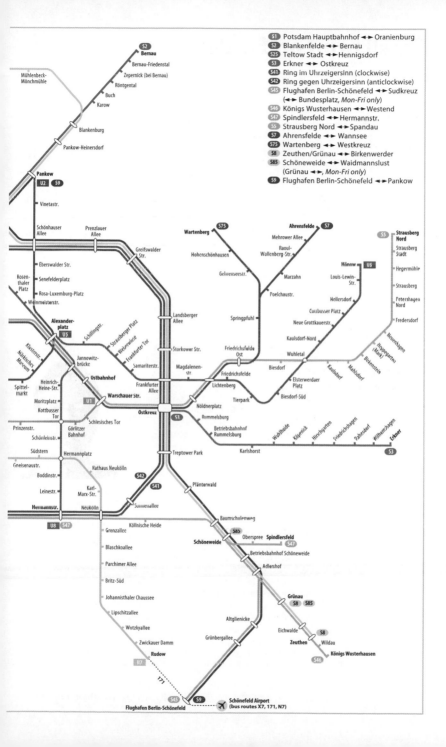

Small print and index

ABOUT THE AUTHOR

Paul Sullivan made Berlin his home in 2008 and still considers it one of the best cities in the world. He has written and contributed to almost 25 books on travel, music and culture, and his words and images appear regularly in *The Guardian, The Sunday Times, The Telegraph* and others. He also runs local travel website ⓦslowtravelberlin.com, through which he organizes cultural-historical tours of the city.

A ROUGH GUIDE TO ROUGH GUIDES

Published in 1982, the first Rough Guide – to Greece – was a student scheme that became a publishing phenomenon. Mark Ellingham, a recent graduate in English from Bristol University, had been travelling in Greece the previous summer and couldn't find the right guidebook. With a small group of friends he wrote his own guide, combining a contemporary, journalistic style with a thoroughly practical approach to travellers' needs.

The immediate success of the book spawned a series that rapidly covered dozens of destinations. And, in addition to impecunious backpackers, Rough Guides soon acquired a much broader readership that relished the guides' wit and inquisitiveness as much as their enthusiastic, critical approach and value-for-money ethos. These days, Rough Guides include recommendations from budget to luxury and cover more than 120 destinations around the globe, from Amsterdam to Zanzibar, all regularly updated by our team of roaming writers.

Browse all our latest guides, read inspirational features and book your trip at **roughguides.com**.

Rough Guide credits

Editor: Edward Aves
Layout: Pradeep Thapliyal and Nikhil Agarwal
Cartography: Ed Wright
Picture editor: Phoebe Lowndes
Proofreader: Karen Parker
Managing editor: Monica Woods
Assistant editor: Divya Grace Mathew

Production: Jimmy Lao
Cover photo research: Sarah Stewart-Richardson
Editorial assistant: Aimee White
Senior DTP coordinator: Dan May
Programme manager: Gareth Lowe
Publishing director: Georgina Dee

Publishing information

This eleventh edition published March 2017 by
Rough Guides Ltd,
80 Strand, London WC2R 0RL
11, Community Centre, Panchsheel Park,
New Delhi 110017, India
Distributed by Penguin Random House
Penguin Books Ltd, 80 Strand, London WC2R 0RL
Penguin Group (USA), 345 Hudson Street, NY 10014, USA
Penguin Group (Australia), 250 Camberwell Road,
Camberwell, Victoria 3124, Australia
Penguin Group (NZ), 67 Apollo Drive, Mairangi Bay,
Auckland 1310, New Zealand
Penguin Group (South Africa), Block D, Rosebank Office
Park, 181 Jan Smuts Avenue, Parktown North, Gauteng,
South Africa 2193
Rough Guides is represented in Canada by DK Canada, 320
Front Street West, Suite 1400, Toronto, Ontario M5V 3B6
Printed in Singapore
© Rough Guides, 2017
Maps © Rough Guides

328pp includes index
A catalogue record for this book is available from the
British Library
ISBN: 978 0 24127 034 9
The publishers and authors have done their best to
ensure the accuracy and currency of all the information
in **The Rough Guide to Berlin**, however, they can accept
no responsibility for any loss, injury, or inconvenience
sustained by any traveller as a result of information or
advice contained in the guide.
1 3 5 7 9 8 6 4 2

Help us update

We've gone to a lot of effort to ensure that the eleventh
edition of **The Rough Guide to Berlin** is accurate
and up-to-date. However, things change – places get
"discovered", opening hours are notoriously fickle,
restaurants and rooms raise prices or lower standards.
If you feel we've got it wrong or left something out,
we'd like to know, and if you can remember the

address, the price, the hours, the phone number, so
much the better.

Please send your comments with the subject line
"Rough Guide Berlin Update" to mail@uk.roughguides.
com. We'll credit all contributions and send a copy of the
next edition (or any other Rough Guide if you prefer) for
the very best emails.

Acknowledgements

Paul Sullivan: Paul Sullivan would like to thank all the
local businesses and individuals who cooperated on this
update. Special thanks go to ⓦ visitberlin.com for their

ever-useful statistics and insights, and Edward Aves for his
patience and expert guiding hand throughout the entire
project.

Readers' updates

Thanks to all the readers who have taken the time to write in with comments and suggestions (and apologies if we've
inadvertently omitted or misspelt anyone's name):

Helen Booth; Michael and Jane Dunn; Amelia Hill; Gareth
Logue; Rachel Michaelides; Gareth Mitchell; Colin Steward;

Peter Vezeridis; Adrienne Wallman

Photo credits

All photos © Rough Guides, except the following:
(Key: t-top; c-centre; b-bottom; l-left; r-right)

Index

Maps are marked in grey